Sierra Leone

the Bradt Travel Guide

Katrina Manson & James Knight

Updated by
Sean Connolly

www.bradtguides.com

Bradt Travel Guides Ltd, UK
The Globe Pequot Press Inc, USA

edition
3

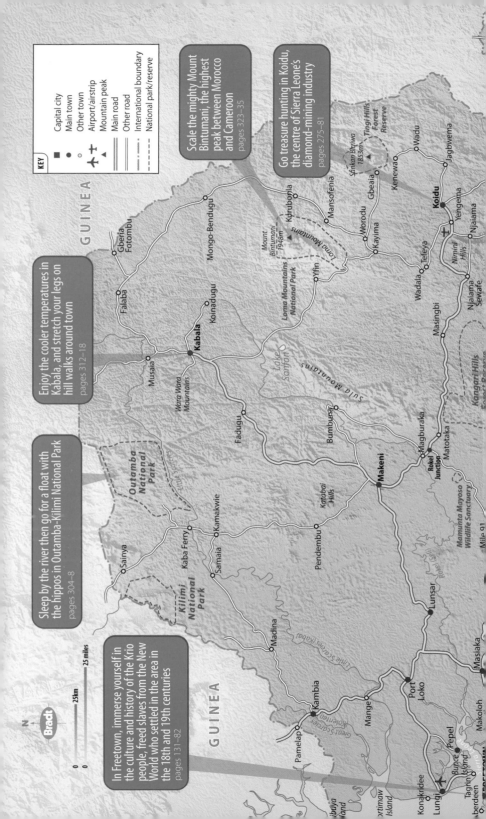

KEY

■ Capital city
● Main town
○ Other town
✈ Airport/airstrip
▲ Mountain peak
══ Main road
── Other road
─·─ International boundary
---- National park/reserve

GUINEA

Scale the mighty Mount Bintumani, the highest peak between Morocco and Cameroon
pages 323–35

Go treasure hunting in Koidu, the centre of Sierra Leone's diamond-mining industry
pages 275–81

Enjoy the cooler temperatures in Kabala, and stretch your legs on hill walks around town
pages 312–18

Sleep by the river then go for a float with the hippos in Outamba-Kilimi National Park
pages 304–8

In Freetown, immerse yourself in the culture and history of the Krio people, freed slaves from the New World who settled in the area in the 18th and 19th centuries
pages 131–82

Bradt

N

0   25km
0   25 miles

GUINEA

Gberia Fotombu
Falaba
Musaia
Koinadugu
Kabala
Wara Wara Mountains
Faeba
Mongo-Bendugu

Mount Bintumani 1948m ▲
Sankan Biriwa 1853m ▲
Tingi Hills Forest Reserve
Loma Mountains
Loma Mountains National Park
Kiruboyila
Mansofenia
Worodu
Gbeaia
Kenewa
Wadu
Jagbwema
Koidu
Yengema
Njaiama
Kayima
Teteya
Wadala

Lake Sonfon
Suila Mountains

Faola Fadugu
Bumbuna
Magburaka
Masingbi
Nimini Hills
Njaiama Sewafe

Outamba National Park
Little Scarcies
Sainya
Kaba Ferry
Samaia
Kamakwie
Katabai Hills
Pendembu
Makeni
Rokel Junction
Matotaka
Mamuinta Mayoso Wildlife Sanctuary
Mile 91
Kangari Hills Forest Reserve

Kilimi National Park
Madina
Lunsar
Rokel (Seli)
Little Scarcies (Kaba)

Masiaka

Pamelap
Kambia
Mange
Great Scarcies (Kolenten)
Port Loko
Makoloh

Konakridee
Pepel
Bunce Island
Tagrin Island
Lungi
Aberdeen
ortimaw Island

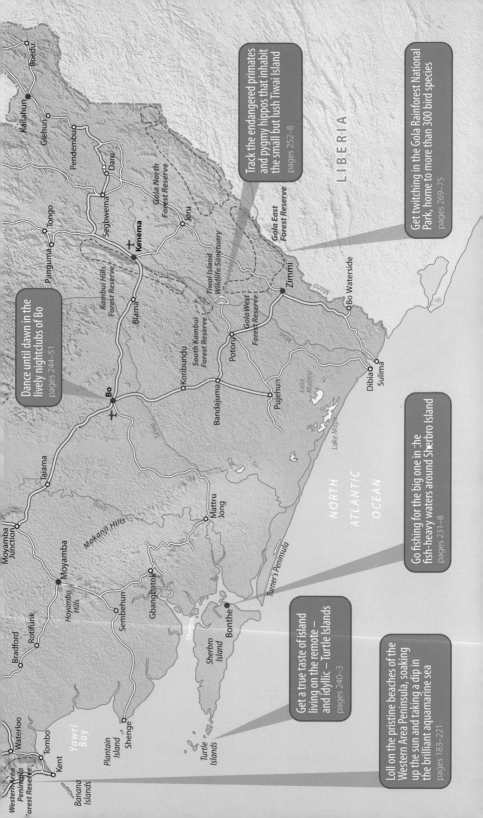

Track the endangered primates and pygmy hippos that inhabit the small but lush Tiwai Island
pages 252–8

Get twitching in the Gola Rainforest National Park, home to more than 300 bird species
pages 269–75

Dance until dawn in the lively nightclubs of Bo
pages 244–51

Go fishing for the big one in the fish-heavy waters around Sherbro Island
pages 231–8

Get a true taste of island living on the remote — and idyllic — Turtle Islands
pages 240–3

Loll on the pristine beaches of the Western Area Peninsula, soaking up the sun and taking a dip in the brilliant aquamarine sea
pages 183–221

LIBERIA

NORTH
ATLANTIC
OCEAN

Yawri Bay

Western Area
Peninsula
Forest Reserve

Banana
Islands

Plantain
Island

Turtle
Islands

Sherbro
Island

Turner's Peninsula

Lake
Mabesi

Lake Mape

Mano

Moa

Sewa

Gbangbatok

Shenge

Kent

Tombo

Waterloo

Bradford

Rotifunk

Moyamba
Junction

Moyamba

Sembehun

Kwamebai Hills

Mokanji Hills

Mattru
Jong

Bonthe

Taiama

Bo

Koribundu

Bandajuma

Pujehun

Dibia

Sulima

Bo Waterside

Zimmi

Potoru

Tiwai Island
Wildlife Sanctuary

Gola West
Forest Reserve

Gola East
Forest Reserve

Gola North
Forest Reserve

South Kambui
Forest Reserve

Kambui Hills
Forest Reserve

Joru

Kenema

Blama

Panguma

Tongo

Segbwema

Daru

Pendembu

Giehun

Kailahun

Buedu

Sierra Leone

Don't miss...

Diverse wildlife

Widely varied habitats support a wealth of flora and fauna, including some 15 primate species. Get close to chimpanzees at the Tacugama Chimpanzee Sanctuary
(IH/TCS) pages 187–90

Cultural celebrations

Whether bewitched by the National Dance Troupe or joining in the raucous Ma Dengn beach party, the lively Freetown festival scene will keep you partying well into the small hours (KM)
pages 162 & 166

Climbing the mist-shrouded peak of Mount Bintumani
The highest peak between Morocco and Cameroon, the mountain is known as 'Loma Mansa' (King of Mountains) in Kuranko (KM) pages 323–35

Pristine beaches along the Peninsula
Whatever your idea of seaside bliss, there is a beach here to match. Spend the day lounging on the perfect crescent of sand at Mama Beach (KM) pages 217–20

Slave history
Sierra Leone suffered greatly during the slave trade and icons of the past, such as the ruins of Bunce Island's fort, serve as a reminder of this dark time (NTBSL) pages 194–9

Sierra Leone in colour

left   Fixing a pose at a fashion shoot in Freetown. With its stylish prints and bright textiles, Sierra Leonean fashion is in demand (KM) page 168

below   If you're searching for tree bark to brew some antimalarial tea, browse the traditional medicine street stalls in Freetown; traders sell everything from flip-flops to pigs' feet in the busy downtown market (both KM) pages 166–9

bottom   The rainy season from May to December regularly floods the streets of Lumley — don't forget your umbrella (KM) page 4

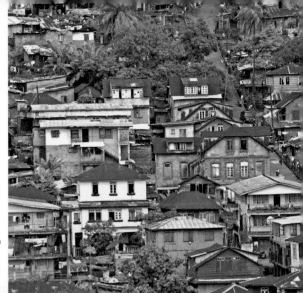

right The capital's hotch-potch selection of architecture — these colourful Krio houses with their distinctive wooden-board construction were built by the descendants of freed slaves (KM) page 180

below Arguably the grandest building in Freetown, the Courts of Justice have been restored to their former glory (KM) page 176

bottom At St John's Maroon Church in Freetown, history is literally built into the walls: parts of the interior roof and two pews are built from salvaged slave ships (KM) pages 181–2

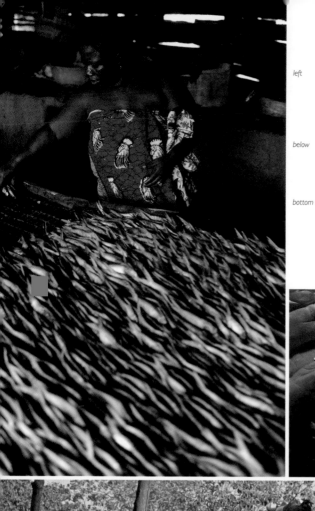

left Fish provides the bulk of the animal protein consumed by Sierra Leoneans, and is often smoked before being transported around the country (JB) page 221

below Sierra Leone's markets are always colourful affairs, where even the pigs' trotters are bright pink (KM)

bottom On the move — street food stand at a *poda poda* stop. These mobile canteens serve local dishes to travellers, such as cassava leaf, *krane krane* and grilled corn (KM) page 104

AUTHORS

Katrina Manson is an award-winning journalist who covered Africa for 12 years. She is US foreign policy and defence correspondent for the *Financial Times*, based in Washington DC, and is also writing a book about money, power and influence networks in Africa. Previously, she was the FT's East Africa correspondent, covering 13 territories including Somalia, and before that a Reuters correspondent in DR Congo, Tanzania, Sierra Leone and Burkina Faso.

James Knight has more than ten years' experience working on emerging market countries as a journalist, writer and consultant. He now works at the Foreign and Commonwealth Office, having previously been a Senior Associate at a London-based communications agency, and freelanced for Reuters, ITV and *The Sunday Times*. He has lived across Africa, in Buenos Aires and Brussels, and draws on West Ham United FC and Afrobeat for inspiration.

UPDATER

Sean Connolly first visited West Africa as a student in 2008, and since then has been returning to the continent regularly to research, teach English or simply to soak up the ambiance in Africa's countless little-visited corners. When he's not discussing verb tenses, diplomatic recognition or the merits of camel meat, you may find him riding in the back of a grain truck, sampling questionable local delicacies or seeking out a country's funkiest records. Raised in Chicago, Sean has updated or contributed to the Bradt guides to Somaliland, Malawi, Mozambique, Rwanda, Ghana and Uruguay, and is the author of the first Bradt guide to Senegal. He stays on the move whenever possible, though lately you'll find him most often in Berlin.

AUTHORS' STORY

It all started in a bar in Ouagadougou, Burkina Faso's capital. The music was raging, but we could just make out the words: 'It's the most beautiful place in the world.' That had us hooked. The fact that this total stranger was talking about Sierra Leone – not exactly top of everyone's 'must-visit' wish list – made the comment even more astounding. A little more than a year later we were there. The raw beauty of the place is overwhelming. You can track monkeys and rare hippos; dine on an unspoilt, empty beach with only the moon for company; step onto a former slave island drenched in history; clamber to the top of mist-shrouded mountains; swim around a tiny island poking out of the Atlantic; and camp in a treasured patch of rainforest.

Such a feast of picture-perfect moments is miles from what people might expect from a 'war-torn' country. A few years ago the only place you could find Sierra Leone on a book spine was in sections far more grisly than travel. Things have long since changed, and Sierra Leone offers a chance to explore beautiful wilderness, stunning beaches and extraordinary culture. Even so, when we first told people about writing a travel guide to Sierra Leone, many snorted with derision. Except Bradt. And anyone who had actually been there.

PUBLISHER'S FOREWORD *Adrian Phillips*

Bradt has built its reputation on publishing the first guides to emerging destinations – often countries recovering from the effects of civil war. We brought out the first dedicated guides to Rwanda and Mozambique, for example. We were thrilled to add Sierra Leone to that list, and proud to see the names of Katrina Manson and James Knight – authors of our wonderful guide to Burkina Faso – on the cover. It wasn't so long ago that Sierra Leone was war-torn, a place of dark acts and despair. However, it is now a safe and peaceful country of brilliant beauty and fascinating wildlife; we hope that the third edition of this book continues to help spearhead its deserved rebirth as a tourist destination.

Third edition published January 2018
First published May 2009
Bradt Travel Guides Ltd
IDC House, The Vale, Chalfont St Peter, Bucks SL9 9RZ, England
w bradtguides.com
Print edition published in the USA by The Globe Pequot Press Inc,
PO Box 480, Guilford, Connecticut 06437-0480

Text copyright © 2018 Katrina Manson & James Knight
Maps copyright © 2018 Bradt Travel Guides Ltd Includes map data © OpenStreetMap contributors
Photographs copyright © 2018 Individual photographers (see below)
Project Manager: Laura Pidgley
Cover research: Pepi Bluck, Perfect Picture

ISBN: 978 1 78477 063 1 (print)
e-ISBN: 978 1 78477 526 1 (e-pub)
e-ISBN: 978 1 78477 427 1 (mobi)

British Library Cataloguing in Publication Data
A catalogue record for this book is available from the British Library

Photographs Alamy: Tommy E Trenchard (TET/A); FLPA: Ignacio Yufera (IY/FLPA); James Knight (JK); Joerg Boethling (JB); Katrina Manson (KM); National Tourism Board of Sierra Leone (NTBSL); Sean Connolly (SC); Shutterstock: feathercollector (f/S), Luca Nichetti (LN/S), Michael Fitzsimmons (MF/S), MartinMaritz (MM/S), robertonencini (r/S), Vladimir Wrangel (VW/S); Tacugama Chimpanzee Sanctuary: Izzy Hirji (IH/TCS)

Front cover Surfer on Bureh Beach (TET/A)
Back cover Baby chimp at Tacugama Chimpanzee Sanctuary (IH/TCS); Bureh Beach (KM)
Title page Turtle Islands (KM); Women at Freetown's market (KM); Mount Bintumani (KM)

Maps David McCutcheon FBCart.S; colour map base by Nick Rowland FRGS
Illustrations Carole Vincer

Typeset by Ian Spick, Bradt Travel Guides Ltd
Production managed by Jellyfish Print Solutions; printed in the UK
Digital conversion by **w** dataworks.co.in

Acknowledgements

KATRINA MANSON AND JAMES KNIGHT All these people and institutions have provided invaluable help, advice and support in the course of writing this book. All errors are of course our own. We also apologise in advance for any omissions from this list.

Aaron Kortenhoven; Abdulai Barrie; Abu-Bakarr Jalloh (ABJ); Adam Jackson; Ade Daramy; Adnan; Ajay Patel; Alan Duncan; Alfred; Ali Molina; Allison George; Amadu Massally; Amy Lemar; Andre Radloff; Andrej Machacek; Anne Bennett; Aongus O'Keeffe; Aubrey Wade; Bala Amarasekaran; Balanta Dance Academy; Bambay Sawaneh; Beatrice Chaytor; Bernd Eckhardt; Bimbola Carrol; Bonthe Holiday Village; Cath Harris; Cecil Williams; Charly Cox and Etai Presenti; Chin Chin; Chloe Poynton; Chris Charly; Chris Herwig; Christopher and Merrill Knight; Conor Doyle; Conservation International; Conservation Society of Sierra Leone; Daniel Gbondo; Daniel Shimmin; Danny Glenwright; Danny Yarker; David Keen; David and Ebu Shears; DD Saffa; DJ Boxx; Dr Joe Alie; Drucil Taylor; Eddy Aruna; Eduardo Celades; Edward Sawyer; Elinor David; Elizabeth Knight; Emad Khoury; Emmerson; Environmental Foundation for Africa; Erika Boak; Finda from Celtel; Florence Katta from CTN; Gabriel Madiye; Gary Walker; Gianni Brusati; Gladys and Mike Carrol; Government of Sierra Leone; Grant Wilson; Greg Crompton; Grigorios Delichristos; Gums; Hannah Tappis; Iain Commander IMATT; Ian and Esther Walker; Ian Sinclair; Idriss Kpange; Ione and Ziad; Isatu Thorlu-Bangura; Isha Tejan-Cole and Arne Johansen; ITMB; Ivo; James Lynch; James Roscoe; James Sandford; James Scott; Jan Joubert; Jane Hobson; Jared Kneitel; Jeffrey Bowlay-Williams; Jeremy Shapiro; Jeremy Waiser; Jessica Lincoln; Joanna Reid and Geert Cappelaere; John S Koroma; John Sisay; Jon Foray; Joy Samake; Juan Luis López Frechilla; Julian Donald; Julius Spencer; Kate Press; Kelvin Lewis; Kenneth Gbengba; Kevin Burgess; King Milan; Kofie Macauley; Krystle Lai; Lans Juana; Lawrence Spencer-Coker; Lisa Curtis; Lotta Teale; Lucy Balmer; Lucy Goodman; Mackay Taggart; Maeve Gill; Major Jonny Bristow; Marisa Zawacki; Mary; Matan Sofer; Meghan Roecklein; Michael Venn; Michel Sho-Sawyer; Michelle Delaney; Modou; Mohamed; Mohamed from Comium; Mohamed Kallon; Naomi Jefferies; National Tourist Board of Sierra Leone; Nazia Parvez; Neil Tobin; Niall O'Cathasaigh; Nicholas Luyckx; Nick Demeter; Nikki Spencer-Coker; Oliver Grange; Oluniyi Robin-Coker; Oscar Mateos; Osman Bah; Osman Gbla; Paige McClanahan; Paps (Saidu Kallon); Paul Fish; Paul Munro; Pentax; Peter Andersen; Peter Donelan; Peter Ryan; Pietro Toigo; President Ernest Bai Koroma; Professor Joseph Opala; Prince Williams; Quentin Ranson and Suraiya Rampuri Ranson; Rachel Blake; Ransford Wright; Rebecca Stringer; Richard Hogg; Rob Hughes and Paddy Howlett; Rob Mckee; Robert Collett; Roland Ulreich; RSPB; Rugiatu Turay; Ryann Manning; Sandra; Sarah Fox; Sarah Mackintosh; Saramba; Sareta Ashraph; Sean Brady; Sean

Connolly; Sebastien; Sexy Bob; Sheka Tarawallie; Shin; Simon Charters; Sister Joyce; Stafi; Stanley; Star Zero; Suleyman of Balanta; Tigie; Tim Ohlenburg; Tom and Bee Yan Walsh; Tom Cairnes; Tommy Garnett; Toufic; Trash and Janet Manson; Tristan Reed; Uncle Ben; Valnora Edwin; Vickie Remoe-Doherty; Victor Angelo; Victor Barnett and Patrick Kamara; Wahid and Zubairu Wai.

Thanks also to the many kind, dedicated and very close-reading people; you gave us invaluable feedback on drafts.

A lot of the pictures in this book are taken with Pentax digital cameras, whether the *istD, the K10D or the K20D. We are very grateful for the company's sponsorship, and chuffed with the performance of the K20D, the macros and wide-aperture lenses in particular.

SEAN CONNOLLY Thanks are first and foremost due to Katrina Manson and James Knight for entrusting me with their exemplary guide, and to Laura Pidgley for all of her careful editing and invaluable input, as well as Rachel Fielding and all of the team at Bradt.

Even more thanks go out to Imke Rueben for sharing her wellspring of laughter, support, advice and companionship with me; to the late Simon Fenton for his friendship, and for accompanying me on part of this journey; and to all my friends, family and flatmates for their patience with me as this book was written.

Otherwise, I owe a great debt to all *mi padi dem* (my friends) in Sierra Leone, Guinea, Guinea-Bissau & Senegal who hosted me, hung out and shared their invaluable expertise, including Jill Gavin, Julio De Souza, Kathrine Roldsgaard Nielsen, Chloé Michaudel, Karel Van Roey, Erin Polich, Katherine Zachara, Anna Fraenzel, Mirco Keller, Fenella Beynon, Mita Sahu, Carlos Costa, David Sommers, Jinnah Nyallay, Tamba Johnny and Amin Sahad Bin Mahaz.

In researching this guide, I was graciously received by dozens of dedicated professionals in Sierra Leone who are working to preserve, promote and share the beauty of this most enchanting country with the world. In no particular order, my thanks are also very much due to Bimbola Carrol & Ayodele Awuna (VSL), Osman Koroma, Mr Bah, Bema Dao (The Hub), Jenovive, Paul and Emile (New Brookfields), Muhammed Lumen and Francis Massaquoi (Gola), Mustafa Mansaray (Outamba-Kilimi), Samuel (Sierra Paradise), American Woodie, Bala Amarasekaran and Mariska (Tacugama), Saleh and JJ Yahya (Doha's), Yassin Kargbo and Lucinda Kargbo (National Tourist Board), Kolleh Bangura and Kate Garnet (NPAA), Wissam and Emily Stanger Sfeile (Bafa), Greg Delichristos (Dalton's), Alusine Bangura (Hotel Mariam), Ayo and Beth (Ategbeh Garden), Felix and Alpha (Kabala Hill View), Mariama Boima and Emmanuel Metzger (Luawa), Andrew James Lloyd, Katherine Laursen, Britt Mann, Andrew McFarlane, Mark Maughan (The Place), Nathan Johnson (Cockle Point), Edward Shallop (Country Lodge) and Daniel Sekoni (Radisson Blu).

DEDICATION

For Edward Sawyer

Contents

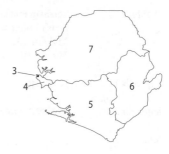

Introduction

From the wingflash of an emerald starling, to the shouts of the star-fruit seller in the market, to the salty fur of the ocean, Sierra Leone gleams with life, brilliance and pain.

Salone, as it is affectionately known (and Sweet Salone for extra affection), is not always an easy country, or a happy one. Plenty of things don't work, and won't work for a good while yet. Energy, water, roads, education and healthcare – these basics are erratic, if present at all. Travelling across the capital is tough, let alone going a few miles down the coast or trekking upcountry.

But Sierra Leone's love of life, the determination to make something of itself, even while it shuffles near the bottom of the UN's human development index, shows a spirit the world should gasp at. Young rappers sing of their love of peace, nature-lovers strive to protect rare species, fashion designers pioneer proud African looks, campaigners agitate for justice and health workers, now and during the recent Ebola epidemic, bravely care for their communities, often in the direst of circumstances.

In short, Salone keeps trying: after all, this is the place with a rousing history so full of fortitude that it took three waves of former slaves to found the capital in their search for freedom.

It is not yet a 'destination' in the travel industry sense of the word. Once a playground for the French jetset, and adventurous couples in search of an untrammelled paradise, today only 10,000 of 54,000 annual visitors a year call themselves tourists. While this book is for that growing number of intrepid spirits, it is also for the other 44,000: primarily those in the Sierra Leone diaspora visiting friends and relatives, perhaps thinking they might just come home for good this time; and for the business people, development workers and diplomats who come to stay for a while.

More than any outstanding vista, perhaps the greatest pleasure, and privilege, lies with some of the extraordinary people you may meet. We try to tell a fraction of their stories, but thousands more exist far beyond these pages. This guidebook is a jumping-off point: it is not exhaustive, and Sierra Leone never stands still long enough for all of what we have said here to apply in six months, let alone two years. Ask questions, and listen to the people around you.

'We need people to know that Sierra Leone is a destination that is safe, in spite of the fact that we have come out of war. There's no mayhem in the streets,' Cecil Williams, former manager of the National Tourist Board, told us on one of our trips.

His favourite story revolves around five travel journalists who were meant to visit. Prior to arriving, two backed out because they were too scared to come. 'The first night I took them out and by one o'clock I went home,' he said, with the beginnings of a smile. 'The next day I found out they had stayed out until four in the morning and they had never felt so safe. They did it every day until they left.'

HOW TO USE THIS GUIDE

AUTHORS' FAVOURITES Finding genuinely characterful accommodation or that unmissable off-the-beaten-track café can be difficult, so the author has chosen a few of his favourite places throughout the country to point you in the right direction. These 'authors' favourites' are marked with a ✳.

MAPS

Keys and symbols Maps include alphabetical keys covering the locations of those places to stay, eat or drink that are featured in the book. Note that regional maps may not show all hotels and restaurants in the area: other establishments may be located in towns shown on the map.

Grids and grid references Several maps use gridlines to allow easy location of sites. Map grid references are listed in square brackets after the name of the place or site of interest in the text, with page number followed by grid number, eg: [103 C3].

KEY TO MAP SYMBOLS

—·—	International boundary	♀	Bar
-----	State boundary	☆	Nightclub/casino
✈ ✛	Airport/airstrip	@	Internet café
🚢 ⛴	Vehicle ferry/small ferry	✝	Church/cathedral
🚐	Bus station, taxi rank	⊊	Mosque
⛽	Petrol station	⬜	Cemetery
🄸	Tourist information	🗼	Lighthouse
🄴	Embassy	⚑	Golf course
🏺	Museum/art gallery	⟶	Border crossing
🎭	Theatre/cinema	▲	Mountain peak
⌗	Historic building	●	Other attraction
⚱	Statue/monument	🏃	Sporting facility
$	Bank		Swamp/marsh
✉	Post office		Beach
✚	Hospital		Urban market
✚	Pharmacy		Urban park
🏠	Hotel/guesthouse		National park
✕	Restaurant		

Part One

GENERAL INFORMATION

SIERRA LEONE AT A GLANCE

Location North Atlantic coast of West Africa
Neighbouring countries Guinea, Liberia
Size 71,740km^2
Climate Tropical, with hot, humid, rainy season May–December and dry season December–April
Political status Republic with democratically elected president and unicameral parliament. Peaceful elections held 2007 and 2012.
Population 7 million (2016 estimate)
Life expectancy 58.2 years
Capital Freetown (1.07 million, 2015 estimate)
Other main towns Bo, Kenema, Makeni
Economy Agriculture (rice, palm, cocoa, coffee, sugarcane, rubber), fishing, trade, transport, communications, mining (rutile, diamonds, bauxite, iron ore, gold)
GDP US$10.64 billion (US$1,700 per capita according to purchasing power parity)
Languages English is the official language. Also Krio, Mende, Temne and several other local languages.
Religion Muslim (c60%), Christian (c30%), animist (c10%)
Currency Leone (abbreviated to Le)
Exchange rate £1 = approx Le10,100; US$1 = approx Le7,600; €1 = approx Le9,000 (October 2017)
National airport Lungi International Airport
International telephone code +232
Time zone GMT
Electrical voltage 220–240V AC; 50Hz in Freetown
Weights and measures Metric
Flag Horizontal tricolour of (from top) green, white and blue
National anthem High We Exalt Thee
National motto Unity, Freedom and Justice
Public holidays 1 January; Maulid-un-Nabi; Good Friday; Easter Monday; 27 April; 1 May; 15 August; Eid al-Fitr; 1 November, Eid al-Adha; 25 December; 26 December (see also page 107)

1

Background Information

GEOGRAPHY

About the size of South Carolina or Ireland, Sierra Leone manages to squeeze beaches, rainforests, mountains, savannah grasslands, marshes, mangrove swamps and rivers into its relatively small 71,740km². It sits on the southwest corner of the West African bulge, at a latitude of 8° 30'N, and a longitude of 11° 30'W.

The country is, appropriately, shaped like a cut diamond, tapering to a point in the south where coastal and inland borders meet. It runs about 332km north–south and about 304km west–east, bordered to the north and northeast by Guinea, and to the east and southeast by Liberia, with the Mano River forming a natural barrier between the two countries. The beaches and mangrove swamps of the southwest form a coastline of 403km along the north Atlantic coast.

The Freetown Peninsula is one of the few parts of coastal Africa – and indeed the only part of West Africa – where mountains rise from the sea, giving the capital and surrounds its magical landscape. Highest points include Sugar Loaf Mountain (760m) and Picket Hill (888m). The Peninsula is also home to the deepest harbour in West Africa, free of sandbanks, which has long made it an important trading and refuelling stop-off. Along the rest of Sierra Leone's coastline runs the swampy mangrove landscape common to sub-Saharan Africa from Senegal southwards.

The southeast area consists mainly of tropical evergreen forest, traditionally the home of cash crops such as coffee, cocoa, kola and oil palm. Potential arable land makes up 30% of the country's land area, but only 8% is cultivated – upcountry the rainfall, soil and plateau are conducive to rice, although currently for subsistence rather than export. To the northeast, where the rains are shorter and the *harmattan* winds (page 4) more pronounced, lies savannah woodland, at an altitude of 400–600m. The savannah is home to cattle-rearing and groundnut plantations.

The southwest portion of the country is a lowland plain, generally below 75m, with occasional inselbergs – small isolated mountains that rise abruptly from the plains. An escarpment runs northwest–southeast, topped by the eastern plateau, generally 300–600m above sea level, which rises to the Niger watershed in the northeast frontier. Ranges on this plateau include the Tingi Hills, Wara Wara Mountains and Loma Mountains, and they are home to two notable peaks: Sankan Biriwa (1,709m) in Tingi and Mount Bintumani (1,948m) in Loma, the latter being the highest point in West Africa until you hit Mount Cameroon thousands of kilometres further east. Seven large river systems flow southwest towards the sea, very roughly parallel, passing from the northern uplands to the mangrove swamps of the coast.

Areas of tropical rainforest have a canopy of about 30m and are found where rainfall exceeds 50mm for nine or more months of the year. Where this level of rainfall decreases to fewer than four months of the year, semi-evergreen forest is evident; below that woodland savannah is dominant.

CLIMATE

For a country that basically has two seasons – wet (May to October) and baking (November to April), it's extraordinary that Sierra Leone rivals the UK as far as conversations about the weather go. Perhaps that's because the tiniest deviation from this binary seasonal experience is such a shock to the system, and can so easily affect agriculture for its many farmers, that every nuance counts.

Umbrellas can be seen year-round – acting as a shield first from the unyielding sun, and then the thrashing rain, but both elements are so extreme that they don't do much good. Hot and dusty months come during the stretch between November and February (worst during December and January), when the harmattan winds arrive full of Saharan sand, blotting the sky, and carpeting the land with dust. Coughs and sore throats increase, and people can usually only manage a whisper of 'harmattan', by way of explanation. The sizzling months come in March and April, when temperatures can reach 38°C. Most of the time the temperature deviates little from 27°C to 30°C, although in some inland areas such as Kabala, temperatures can drop at night.

Despite the lack of rain in these six months, it's a bit of a cheek to call it the 'dry' season. Sweaty season is more like it: do nothing but breathe, and you can expect to be drenched. In Graham Greene's *Heart of the Matter,* which is set in Sierra Leone, characters are forever writing with blotting paper under their hands to prevent the ink from smudging. While air temperatures only hug the 30°C mark, humidity upwards of 75% (ranging from 69% in January to 82% in August) makes the going pretty excruciating. If you're on the coast, the sea breeze does provide some respite, particularly in the evenings, but you have to be on the beach to derive much benefit.

Come the rainy season, with its August peak, it's as if the sky itself might fall. 'In the wet season, rain batters down, as if spite elementalised, on to iron roofs; then the torrid air streams, insects breed in millions and malaria rages,' wrote Elspeth Huxley of Sierra Leone's rainy season in 1954.

Not much has changed. Furious pelting beats an incessant tattoo on iron roofs; soaked pedestrians caught outside wade knee-deep through sudden torrents, cadge piggy-back rides and generally forget there was ever a time they were dry. Roads turn into fast-flowing orange rivers as even the deepest of gutters overspill and cars submerge. Lightning flashes described by Governor John Clarkson in 1792 as 'cataracts of fire' are just as head-turning today.

May deceives, with spurts of crashing, crackling thunder and lightning that never quite breaks into rain. July and August redefine your notion of wet, when more than half the year's rain drives down. By the end of September the skies are pretty much all washed out, but the occasional downpour can arrive as late as November.

Rainfall at the coast can reach 5,000mm; inland rainfall tends to average 3,000mm, while drier northern areas receive 2,000mm, with up to 7,000mm falling on some of the peaks.

No waterproof can keep the rain out. Take the best you have, but there's no doubt the region's wettest country will have its way with you. Damp takes hold, as leather bags, shoes, clothes, belts and more turn white with mildew.

NATURAL HISTORY AND CONSERVATION

With a range of habitats that takes in coastal areas, mangrove swamps, savannah, and the biodiversity of primary and secondary forest, Sierra Leone's wildlife is enormously varied. It is also difficult to spot, often well hidden because of a lack of adequately equipped nature areas that can maintain forest paths or construct hideouts and watering holes that will attract animals with predictable regularity. A thriving bushmeat trade does little either for animal numbers or their ease around human beings, and unfortunately often the most likely place to see some wildlife up close is still the stalls of a local village market, including severed monkey hands. The biggest draw is probably primate life, especially in Tiwai Island and the Gola Forest. The remote montane forest of the Loma Mountains, and the forest-savannah of Outamba-Kilimi, offer opportunities to view both primates and antelope and larger mammals. Brief notes on recognition and behaviour are included on pages 6–9, although for fuller details we recommend several field guides (pages 361–2).

Diligence, dedication and infectious enthusiasm at the Conservation Society of Sierra Leone (CSSL) are an inspiration. If you are at all interested in wildlife, drop into their Freetown office (call in advance as the team is incredibly busy). Staff can advise on trips to areas of interest, and you may even be able to tag along with one of their frequent research or monitoring trips: a chance to see not only wildlife but also conservation in action.

For all encounters, a pencil and notebook are handy companions, greatly enhanced by a pair of binoculars (8x40 binoculars provide a good balance between fair magnification power and a good field of view, helpful for tracking animals – especially birds – in the thick vegetation; for open seas, however, greater magnification such as 10x50, or even a telescope, is more useful), a camera and a recording device. Wherever you are, but especially in forest areas, try to move as slowly and as quietly as possible: the deceptive calm of the floor often hides a din of activity, much of which takes place far above head height in the canopy, so your ears are arguably as important as your eyes. Thick undergrowth can be unforgiving, so long trousers, with pockets for equipment, are a better bet than shorts. And as with all hikes in the bush, take a wide-brimmed hat, suncream and plenty of water.

FLORA While Sierra Leone strikes the observer as green and well wooded, the impact of subsistence agriculture and commercial logging had reduced the area of primary forest from more than 70% to 4% by 2010. That drastic fall underlines how important it is to preserve the country's last remaining patch of genuine rainforest at Gola (pages 269–75). You don't have to go that far afield to see the devastating effects of deforestation: the once-thickly wooded peaks above Freetown are now almost totally bare to make way for a glut of new residences. See pages 361–2 for suggested tree field guides; below are some of the most common species.

The **red mangrove** (*Rhizophora racemosa*) is impossible to miss in swamp areas. Growing up to 30m, dense forests are most visible around Sherbro and other areas of the western coast. Most striking are the knarled prop-roots that branch off from the mangrove's ramrod-straight trunk just above the water line.

The **oil palm** (*Elaeis guineensis*) is tremendously important for Sierra Leoneans as both a source of income – via the extraction of palm oil that is used domestically and commercially – and of palm wine, which is why you see men and boys shinning up the tall thin trunks with such enthusiasm. **Hooker's wine palm** (*Raphia hookeri*) has a much thicker trunk, and, despite the name, its leaves are used to make roofing for huts and the strong piassava fibre that for a while was widely exported for broom and brush heads.

The centre of Freetown has perhaps the best-known example of the towering **cotton tree** (*Ceiba pentandra*), also known locally as the *kapok*. It is found more commonly in semi-deciduous forest, and often associated with magical properties. If surrounded by other trees near a village, it is often an indicator of the meeting place of the secret *poro* society.

1

Rainforest areas are known for the towering, wavy-leaved **red ironwood tree** (*Lophira alata*). As the name suggests, it is highly resistant to fire. Fibrous young twigs are used as bush toothbrushes by local people. The **African piptadenia-like tree** (*Piptadeniastrum africanum*) is almost impossible to miss, because of its enormous trunk buttresses that snake out across the forest floor. Its wood is a popular logging target, and the bark used heavily in local medicine. A third widely occurring forest tree is the **uapaca** (*Uapaca guineensis*), often found alongside streams and rivers. It has stilt roots, a rich, dense crown and grey-pink bark.

In open country, the most common trees include the **red-flowered locust bean,** (*Parkia biglobosa*), beloved of baboons and small children for the sweet pulp of its seed pods. Its bark is used in tanning, dyeing and pottery decoration. Meanwhile the seeds go into a cooking flavouring known as *kenda*. Watch out for the smell though, which has given rise to the proverb *Ogiri de laf kenda fo smel* ('Ogiri laughs at *kenda* for smelling' – essentially a variation on the pot calling the kettle black, since both spices smell pungent before cooking).

The **cowfoot**, or **monkey bread** (*Piliostigma thonningii*), is thought to have antibacterial properties, and its reddish-brown pods are eaten by elephants. A foreign introduction, large, leafy **mango trees** (*Mangifera indica*) are a focal point of many villages, prized for their shade as much as their fruit. The **rose apple** (*Eugenia jambos*), **papaya** (*Carica papaya*), and shrubby **guava** (*Psidium guajava*), are other common fruit trees.

Once the rains begin, in savannah areas **elephant grass** (*Pennisetum purpurewn*) shoots up to well above head height, obscuring even the tops of the giant, deserted termite hills that dot the landscape.

Rare and exotic **orchids** in Sierra Leone have long attracted the lusts of explorers. Frederick Boyle's 1841 work lists a man named Schroeder as among 'the martyrs of orchidology' who met his end in Sierra Leone. Legend has it (as repeated in the opening lines of the Kaufman brothers' 2002 film *Adaptation*) that this seasoned collector fell to his death from Tingi Hills just as he reached the orchid he'd set about searching out. The variety 'Baron Schroeder', with its hopeful pink flowers, is named after him. Among the species still going in the country today is the *Angrawcum leonis*, with its 7in tails. The nervous excitement at any orchid sighting is clear in Boyle's fondness for the *Bulbo barbigerum*: 'This tiny but amazing plant comes from Sierra Leone. The long yellow lip is attached to the column by the slenderest possible joint, so that it rocks without an instant's pause. At the tip is set a brush of silky hairs, which wave backwards and forwards with the precision of machinery. No wonder that the natives believe it a living thing ... The lip, so delicately balanced, quivers at every breath,' quivered Boyle himself. Today, Tingi Hills, Bumbuna and other hard-to-reach high spots are likely breeding grounds for the plant.

FAUNA

Primates There are thought to be 15 species of primate in the country, of which six are threatened: the western chimpanzee, the Diana monkey, the black-and-white colobus monkey, red colobus, and olive colobus. Tiwai Island, Gola Forest, the slopes of Mount Bintumani and Outamba-Kilimi National Park are good places to start.

Chimpanzee

The **western chimpanzee** (*Pan troglodytes verus*) known in Krio as *babu*, is probably the closest thing Sierra Leone has to a national animal. It is the country's largest primate, and its only member of the great ape family.

Much respected, it wins plaudits from the Krios for its cunning; as the phrase goes: *monki wok, babu it* – 'the monkey works; the chimpanzee eats'. It also manages to infuriate farmers – regularly raiding fields and crops; despite being illegal to kill it (and because it's illegal to carry firearms since the war) some young men have even developed a way of training dogs to wrestle chimps to the ground and then attack them with machetes. Highly adaptable and sociable, chimpanzees are comfortable either on the ground or in the treetops, usually walking on four legs but capable of bipedalism. A fruit-heavy diet is supplemented by insects, birds and their eggs, honey, soil, and even small duiker and warthog. Males can even turn to hunting other smaller monkeys, particularly red colobus, working in highly co-operative teams to do so. Unlike monkeys, the presence of an opposable thumb enables the use of tools, whether stripping sticks to poke after ants or extract honey, using leaves as sponges for water, or (and this has been observed in Sierra Leone) using stones to crack open nuts. Chimps can live for 40 to 45 years in the wild (up to 60 in captivity), and their variety of calls and expressive facial gestures seem to convey a peculiarly human-like range of emotion. Estimates of wild population are vague, between 1,500 and 2,500, but the Gola Rainforest National Park, Loma Mountains and Tiwai Island are three of their last habitats, while, for those visitors shackled to Freetown, the Tacugama Sanctuary (page 187) guarantees a glimpse of chimp behaviour up close.

The **colobid** family of monkeys are generally distinguished by their large bodies, small heads and gibbon-like faces. The name comes from the Greek *colobe*, meaning 'cripple' – a reference to their stunted thumbs. A rustling in the canopy is often the first sign of the agile **black-and-white** or **pied colobus** (*Colobus polykomos*). Its all-white tail is a giveaway, as is the strange horseshoe-shaped loop of white fur that starts on the shoulder and rings the face. Highly territorial, they tend to live in groups of seven to 11, combining one male, several females and their young. The best time to track them down is dusk, when a chorus of low, croaky roars overhead draws attention to where they are.

Black-and-white colobus

Easier to spot because of its bulkier body, tiny head and rust-brown coat, the **red colobus** (*Piliocolobus badius*) is a powerful jumper, tends to follow routine patterns of movement, and is found only near permanent water. Diet is highly localised, and in Sierra Leone consists mostly of older leaves, rather than the young leaves and seeds they prefer, because of increased primate competition. Large territorial groups of up to 100 compose numerous males, while females tend to circulate between troops. A khaki-brown colour and fondness for the dense undergrowth of the lower canopy makes the smallest colobid, the **olive colobus** (*Procolobus verus*) particularly elusive. Nevertheless, you should be able to spy it on Tiwai Island.

Unlike its tree-swinging colobid cousins, the **Sooty mangabey** (*Cercocebus atys*) spends up to 75% of its time on the floor, and the rest of its time in the lower reaches of the forest canopy. Named after its distinctive smoky colour, which lightens on the belly, it has a pinkish face and black muzzle and ears. Found near swamps and palm forests, it is still a difficult spot, but its distinctive staccato bark and whooping are a telltale sign. The pretty **Diana monkey** (*Cercopithecus diana*) is so named because of the browband of white across its forehead that looks like the bow of Diana, Roman goddess of the hunt. It also has a white throat, ruff, beard, underarms, and a white stripe on its thighs, and a long, thin, hanging tail. Its chatter is a regular presence in primary forest, particularly on a walk around

Many Sierra Leoneans have a profound association not only with the land itself but with the animals that live on it. One way this is expressed among the Temne people is through *tana*, or animal totems that are specific to individual family clans; other groups, including the Kuranko and Susu, do something similar. The *tana* acts as an emblem similar to a coat of arms among European houses, but family folklore will often cite the founder of the clan as that animal, or associate the animal with the establishment of a dynasty. For family members, these animals then have to be avoided at all costs – even catching sight of one can provoke a powerful, usually negative, physical reaction.

CLAN

Bangura	leopard, guineafowl
Kamara	fire finch, python
Kanu	viper, weaver bird
Koroma	viper, monitor lizard
Sesay	crocodile, soldier bird
Turay	electric fish

Tiwai Island, and research has shown that animals can vary their warning calls for different types of predator. This however makes it an easy target for hunters, which is why the species is classed as endangered.

The **Campbell's monkey** (*Cercopithecus (mona) campbelli*) is another fairly well-dispersed tree dweller, with a high concentration found around the Bumbuna Dam area. Feeding habits tend to alternate between fruits and insects throughout the day, and animals are recognised by their long tails and transition from dark grey hindquarters to flecked brown backs. In Sierra Leone, its call of 'Kahoo kahoo' is interpreted as 'A lie! A lie!'. The **lesser spot-nosed monkey** (*Cercopithecus (cephus) petaurista*) is widespread throughout lowland forest and riverine gallery forest, and easily identified by its small size and white nose and underparts. The **green** or **vervet monkey** (*Cercopithecus (aethiops) pygerythrus*) is found in more arid northern savannah areas. Gregarious, it has no fear about raiding crops and approaching human habitation, while another often-seen savannah

Vervet monkey

native is the distinctive, long-limbed **patas** or **red monkey** (*Cercopithecus (Erythrocebus) patas*).

Patas monkey

Although in Krio *babu* means any kind of monkey or chimp, Sierra Leone is home both to the **Guinea baboon** (*Papio papio*) and the **Anubis** or **olive baboon** (*Papio anubis*). The baboon is easily distinguished from other primates by a dog-like face, and a curved tail that looks like a bull-whip. Omnivorous, baboons roam in troops of up to 200, often walking over long distances in search of food, and show little fear of other animals, including humans. Their highly sociable, organised societies rely on matriarchal lineages, although between two and four dominant males have charge over each group, and will readily fight any challengers to their authority.

Cute, nocturnal bush babies, the **Senegal galago** (*Galago senegalensis*) and **Demidoff's galago** (*Galagoides demidoff*), Africa's smallest primate, show up easily at night on account of the reflection of their giant eyes; along with the slow-climbing **potto** (*Perodicticus potto*), which resembles an African tree sloth and is widespread in Tiwai, Bumbuna, Loma, Gola and many other areas.

Antelope At home in forest or bush, **duiker** are small antelopes found across Sierra Leone's various ecosystems – the odd name derives from the Dutch word for 'diver' due to its habit of rushing into undergrowth when disturbed. Despite wide variations in size, the distinctive low-slung body on thin, shapely legs, a wedge-shaped head beneath a plume of long hair and large wide eyes generally makes them easy to recognise. Learning to imitate their bleating call can summon them from the forest.

Maxwell's duiker (*Cephalophus maxwelli*) is the most commonly seen, and called *fritambo* in Krio for its fruit-eating habits. However, the similar, slate-grey **black duiker** (*Cephalophus niger*) is seriously endangered through overhunting: the fondness for its meat has prompted the local name 'bush goat'. Both the **zebra duiker** (*Cephalophus zebra*), with its distinctive back pattern of black stripes, and the equally striking, much larger **Jentink's duiker** (*Cephalophus jentinki*), with a distinctive black colouring on its front half, are also fast disappearing. The **yellow-backed duiker** (*Cephalophus silvicultor*) has been seen in the secondary forest around Tiwai, while the **red-flanked duiker** (*Cephalophus rufilatus*) is found in the northern savannah along with the **bay duiker** (*Cephalophus dorsalis*).

Bushbuck

Even smaller, the white-spotted, hornless **water chevrotain** looks like it has walked off the set of *Bambi*, and the tiny **royal antelope** (*Neotragus pygmaeus*) is known for its jumping skills. Both the large, shaggy **waterbuck** (*Kobus ellipsiprymus*) and smaller, reddish-brown **bushbuck** (*Tragelaphus scriptus*) are a common sight in Outamba-Kilimi; the forest-dwelling **bongo** is rarely seen, but its russet colour, white stripes and dramatically swept-back horns make it a highly attractive spot in the Loma Mountains.

Large mammals The quality of Sierra Leone ivory work was first mentioned by the Portuguese, indicating the presence of the world's largest land mammal. 'In Serra Lyoa the men are very clever and inventive, and make really marvellous objects out of ivory of anything you ask them to do, for instance they make spoons, or salt-cellars, or dagger-handles, or other subtle work,' wrote Alvaro Velho, who spent the years 1499–1507 in West Africa. Traditionally, paramount chiefs' walking sticks were carved from ivory, and an ivory trumpet was used to announce his arrival, while there are records of an 'ugly clay idol with elephant's teeth'. The civil war all but wiped out the country's remaining elephant population, and even before it there were only 200–300, but there is encouraging evidence that the **forest elephant** (*Loxodonta Africana cyclotis*) is starting to return to northern areas in small numbers from Guinea, in search of better grazing and to avoid a growing poaching problem there. Outamba-Kilimi National Park offers the best chance of seeing them, or at least

African elephant

evidence of their presence. The forest elephant is considerably smaller than the **bush elephant** more traditionally associated with African savannah, of which there are none remaining in Sierra Leone. Reaching about 8ft in height (compared with 10–13ft), it has a narrower trunk, rounder ears and less-curved tusks, and if you really get up close and personal, an extra toenail on the front and hind feet. Females with young calves are fiercely protective of their young and easily spooked.

Extremely sedentary, the **common hippopotamus** (*Hippopotamus amphibius*) is readily located, although during the day the visitor is unlikely to see much more than a pair of nostrils, ears and the occasional yawn. Hippos tend only to come on to land at sunset to search for food and sleep overnight before returning to the water the following early morning. The best place for a sighting is at Outamba-Kilimi, where one pod congregates at a number of watering pools in the Little Scarcies River. Despite their enormous bulk (up to three tons) they are capable of charging at 45km/h over short distances, and are also good swimmers. Society is organised around dominant males who are ready to defend their harems of females to the death, and mothers are particularly protective of young calves. Extremely easily agitated, particularly if its route to water is barred, the hippo is responsible for more deaths than any other animal in Africa.

The **pygmy hippopotamus** (*Hexaprotodon liberiensis*) is considerably lighter and smaller, standing half as tall at the shoulder (about 80cm). An extremely limited distribution means it is found only in Sierra Leone, Liberia and, possibly, Nigeria. The distinctive forward slope of the spine and less pronounced nostrils and orbits makes it slightly resemble a grumpy seal. Eschewing large pods, the pygmy hippo leads a solitary life, spending most days underwater before coming ashore at night to roam forest paths in search of ferns and fruits: its elusiveness means that little is known about breeding habits in the wild. A sighting is extremely unlikely, but if you are prepared to dig in and wait, quite possibly through the night, Tiwai Island is the place to go (pages 252–8).

The **African manatee** (*Trichechus senegalensis*) looks like an enormous sea cow, with front flippers and a tail, and is considered one of the most endangered species in Africa. Incapable of moving on earth it spends all day resting on the water's surface, feeding at night on plants, particularly water hyacinth. Once plentiful in virtually every river in Sierra Leone, particularly around Bonthe, an extremely sedentary nature makes it vulnerable to hunting. The meat is prized locally, and the ear bones are used in fetish-making.

The **dwarf** or **red buffalo** (*Syncerus caffer brachyceros*) is smaller than its cousin of the East African savannah, and more reddish-brown in colour, resembling a fearsomely well-built, short-legged cow with sharply curling horns. Occasionally seen in groups of three to 20 under the shade of trees during the hottest hours, the best time for a sighting is at the beginning or end of the day as they make their way to water. When hurt or angered, buffalos charge readily, and can occasionally become spontaneously bad-tempered at dusk. Herds have been seen emerging from the mist on the slopes of Mount Bintumani.

The **red river hog**, or **bush pig** (*Potamocherus porcus*) is the most common of the wild pigs, although it has suffered from overhunting. A russet coat, topped with white along the spine, and a white jaw, brow and cheeks, make it distinguishable from other hogs. At home near rivers and streams, a forest walk will often reveal evidence of its digging for roots and tubers along the banks. It is disliked by farmers for its raids on cassava and groundnut plantations. The **common warthog** (*Phacochoerus africanus*) is

Warthog

more likely to be seen in the open montane grassland of the Loma Mountains. The reclusive, and threatened, **giant hog** (*Hylochoerus meinertzhageni*) is thought to exist still, although hunting, and its fondness for deep forest cover, make a sighting highly unlikely.

Big cats The largest cat in Sierra Leone, the **leopard** (*Panthera pardus*) is a master hunter. With its excellent sense of smell and hearing the leopard prefers to hunt at night; during the day it retires to the shade and shelter of treetops or rocks to rest or eat. It is not a fussy eater, most likely hunting primates or bush pig, small antelope or carnivores, birds and their eggs, and reptiles, but is highly prized by the Mende, who use the leopard skin for the devil masquerades of the men's poro society, and for the costumes of society high-ups. Back in the early 16th century, Portuguese traveller Alvaro Velho recorded that should a local kill a leopard, he must 'give the king the skin and the teeth as a sign of subjugation' – the teeth would be turned into highly valued collars (valued at four or more slaves), while the spotted skin would be draped behind him like a robe. The leopard's stocky, heavy build is well disguised by its distinctive camouflage patterning of broken black circles enclosing smaller yellow ones. The leopard is now rare in Sierra Leone – back in 1980 there were thought to be only 50 to 100 – but most likely to be seen around watering holes, as it drinks frequently.

Leopard

Fairly widespread, although still best seen at night, the **serval** (*Leptailurus serval*) is occasionally glimpsed foraging in the daytime. The **golden cat** (*Felis aurata*), marked by its spotted underbelly, prefers forests to savannah areas, and is more exclusively nocturnal; its heavier jaw suggests it preys on stronger animals.

Smaller carnivores The low-slung, attractively marked **African civet** (*Civettictis civetta*) thrives in Sierra Leone's secondary forest but again is almost exclusively nocturnal. There is a record of a son of the King of Bullom ransoming a friend from a French frigate with two civet cats in 1667, and secretions from its perineal glands were used in the perfume industry. The **African palm civet** (*Nandinia binotata*) is much smaller and more feline-looking, and exclusively a forest dweller. Accustomed to the treetops, the **blotched genet** (*Genetta tigrina*) which looks like a cross between a leopard and a rat, has the same soft fur, semi-retractable claws, and solitary habits as the civets.

African civet

Of the mongoose varieties in Sierra Leone, only the rat-like **cusimanse** (*Crossarchus obscurus*) is a forest-dweller, often found in small hunting parties of four to 12. The short-legged **slender mongoose** (*Herpestes sanguinea*) is found throughout the country (and often wrongly called the dwarf mongoose, *Helogale parvula*) while the **Egyptian** or **large grey mongoose** (*Herpestes ichneumon*) occupies savannah areas, occasionally raiding poultry, along with the **marsh mongoose** (*Atilax paludinosus*). The former is more easily spotted due to its diurnal habits, the latter often seen in tree branches.

The **ratel** or **honey badger** (*Mellivora capensis*) is another little-known nocturnal predator. Powerfully built and low to the ground, it has developed a partnership

1

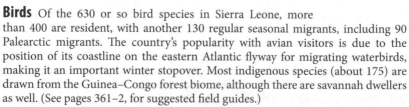

Honey badger

with the aptly named indicator bird (*Indicator indicator*), which will direct it to honey with its calls and attitude. The ratel is a good climber and can destroy a bees' nest with its sharp claws, protected from the fury of their stings by its thick skin and coat.

Sierra Leone is home to two **otter** species: the large, thick-necked **Cape** or **African clawless otter** (*Aonyx capensis*) and the **spot-necked otter** (*Lutra maculicollis*), which prefers clear water and rocky, calm areas.

Smaller mammals The **tree** or **white-bellied pangolin** (*Phataginus tricuspis*) is the most widespread of Sierra Leone's anteaters, occasionally heard dropping out of trees on to the forest floor. Also found are the **long-tailed pangolin** (*Uromanis tetradactyla*) and the **giant pangolin** (*Smutsia gigantea*), respected for its strength in Mende culture (where it is called *Pangolin* *kimbo*) by the proverb 'He who strives can pull out a kimbo'. All have tough armour plating covering a powerful tail and a long snout, and rely on the defence mechanism of rolling up tightly into an impregnable ball; they are also all listed as vulnerable by the International Union for the Conservation of Nature (IUCN).

With its distinctive long snout and ears, the **aardvark** (*Orycteropus afer*) is easily recognised but rarely seen due to its night-time habits. Grand engineers of the bush, aardvark tunnel construction is second to none, with *Aardvark* warrens 3m deep containing up to 30 separate entrances, which are clearly visible at ground level. Abandoned tunnels are used by other inhabitants, hence the Salone proverb: 'The aardvark works for the warthog'. The animal is associated with magical properties: it can act as a lethal weapon if pointed at someone, and can bring rain if pointed at the sky.

Two types of porcupine, the **brush-tailed porcupine** (*Atherurus africanus*) and the **crested porcupine** (*Hystrix cristata*) are present. Various rodents include a number of squirrels, the most common being the **ground squirrel** (*Xerus erythropus*). The **marsh cane-rat** (*Thryonomys* *Ground squirrel* *swinderianus*) is more commonly known as **grasscutter** (and, locally, as 'cutting grass'), and most likely your first encounter with it will be via the cooking pot rather than the safari. Large colonies of **straw-coloured fruit bat** (*Eidolon helvum*) occur in Freetown – one in the boughs of the giant cotton tree in the centre of town, where a cacophony of squeaking competes with the traffic honking past – and on Yele Island off Sherbro Island.

Birds Of the 630 or so bird species in Sierra Leone, more than 400 are resident, with another 130 regular seasonal migrants, including 90 Palearctic migrants. The country's popularity with avian visitors is due to the position of its coastline on the eastern Atlantic flyway for migrating waterbirds, making it an important winter stopover. Most indigenous species (about 175) are drawn from the Guinea–Congo forest biome, although there are savannah dwellers as well. (See pages 361–2, for suggested field guides.)

The forests of eastern Sierra Leone form the western part of the Upper Guinea Forest's Endemic Bird Area (EBA), and 14 of its 15 range-restricted species occur

Expert ornithologist, Professor Peter Ryan, co-author of Birds of Africa South of the Sahara, *was among the first birders to visit Sierra Leone after the war, in search of some of its winged wonders. With the white-necked picathartes firmly in his sights, his party was not disappointed. He reveals some highlights from his trip, escorted by local guide Kenneth Gbengba of Fact Finding Tours (pages 70–1).*

Eager to get to green pastures, we head east to where range-restricted specials await. At dawn on Tiwai Island, the harsh calls of olive and spot-breasted **ibises** ring out as they fly over the camp site.

As the light improves, a dazzling array of birds and mammals vies for our attention. Among the Upper Guinea endemics, **white-tailed alethes** are abundant and easily seen once we cue into their mournful peeoo whistle. **Green-tailed bristlebills** are less common, but even more responsive to playback. By comparison, **western wattled cuckoo-shrikes** are easily overlooked as they move through the canopy in bird parties, which include a rich diversity of Guinea–Congo forest species. Come nightfall we fail to find any **rufous fishing-owls** on the rain-swollen river, but are consoled by an obliging **potto** (*Perodicticus potto*).

From Tiwai we head north to Kenema, where we visit a **picathartes** colony on a giant boulder overhanging a forest stream. The somewhat arduous 1-hour hike to the site is forgotten in an instant, as the first picathartes materialises next to the rock. They have to be one of the most thrilling birds to see in Africa, and one of the greatest passerines of the gigantic order Passeriformes, often known as 'perching birds' world-wide. During the next hour at least five of these truly bizarre birds bound around us continuously, sometimes passing within a few metres as we sit opposite their colony.

The Nimini Hills, south of the Loma Mountains, give some of the best forest birding of our time in Sierra Leone, with numerous sightings of the normally scarce **fiery-breasted bush-shrike**, brilliant views of a displaying **rufous-sided broadbill**, and one of the more stunning birds of the trip, the **red-cheeked wattle-eye**.

Back on the Peninsula, probably the highlight of the trail to the Tacugama Chimpanzee Sanctuary above Regent is watching an unlikely mix of birds feeding at a termite emergence. In addition to the more usual **bulbuls** and **weavers** enjoying the alates (termites that can reproduce), a **blue malkoha** bounds up to the top of adjacent trees, then glides down, grabbing alates in flight. And a stunning male **crimson seedcracker** looks distinctly out of place hawking alates from more than 30m up a large cottonwood tree. The party comes to an abrupt end, however, when a very pale **Ayre's eagle** stoops through, narrowly missing the seedcracker.

We leave Sierra Leone with an enviable list of birds seen, and several good reasons to return: for the **Sierra Leone prinia**, the elusive **Gola malimbe**, the **black-headed rufous warbler** and another juicy attraction – the rumour of a reliable **Shelley's eagle-owl** near Pujehun in the far southeast.

Background Information   NATURAL HISTORY AND CONSERVATION

1

in the country. There are also 14 species of global conservation concern, including the **white-breasted guineafowl** (*Agelastes meleagrides*), considered one of the most threatened birds in continental Africa; the **Sierra Leone** or **white-eyed prinia**

(*Schistolais leontica*); the **western wattled cuckoo shrike** (*Lobotos lobatus*); and the celebrated **white-necked picathartes** (*Picathartes gymnocephalus*), of which there are fewer than 2,500 pairs left in the world. To date, ten sites in Sierra Leone have been surveyed and identified as Important Bird Areas (IBAs), covering a total of 5,776km^2, or 8% of the land area. The coastal areas of interest are the Sierra Leone River estuary and, further south, Yawri Bay; forest areas include Lake Sonfon, the Loma Mountains, Tingi Hills, Kangari Hills, Kambui Hills, Gola Forest, Outamba-Kilimi and the Western Area Peninsula. Highlights of specific bird species in each of these areas are included in the relevant chapters, and full species lists for each are available from the Conservation Society of Sierra Leone.

Reptiles, fish, amphibians and insects Crocodiles are often misnamed 'alligators' in Krio, and there are three species in Sierra Leone: the largest is the **Nile crocodile** (*Crocodylus niloticus*); the **slender-snouted crocodile** (*Crocodylus cataphractus*), is found near forest streams; while the smaller **dwarf crocodile** (*Osteolaemus tetraspis*) prefers mangrove swamps and damp forest. Highly prized for their skins, hunters used to have to bring their kills before the chief for removal of the gall bladder, which is thought to contain a powerful poison.

Eddie Aruna, a turtle specialist of the Conservation Society of Sierra Leone (CSSL), has established that all five species of sea turtle – the giant **leatherback** (*Dermochelys coriacea*); the most commonly seen **green** (*Chelonia mydas*); the **loggerhead** (*Caretta caretta*); **hawksbill** (*Eretmochelys imbricata*); and the tiny **olive ridley** (*Lepidochelys olivacea*) – are present in Sierra Leone's waters. Of these, green and leatherback turtles can be found nesting on Sherbro Island and the appropriately named Turtle Islands. Fishermen along Freetown's Lumley Beach even catch and tag them sometimes, in concert with the CSSL. Known locally as *kong*, leatherback meat is highly prized, and all species of turtles are subject to heavy poaching, particularly of eggs at their nesting sites.

The **Nile monitor lizard** (*Varanus niloticus*), often wrongly referred to as an iguana, can grow up to 7ft in length. More arboreal than the crocodile, it is frequently found sunning itself on tree branches overhanging a river, although it ventures further from water in the rainy season, feeding on fish, clams, mussels, birds and reptiles. Meanwhile, in towns and compounds the **agama lizard** (*Agama agama*) is seen virtually everywhere, males easily distinguished by their red heads, blue bodies and orange tails; the shy, web-toed **Brook's gecko** (*Hemidactylus brookii angulatus*) is often found inside houses picking off insect life. The well-camouflaged, bug-eyed **Senegal chameleon** (*Chamaeleo senegalensis*) is also present.

There are 130 species of freshwater fish in Sierra Leone, including the **Nile perch**, which can reach up to 200lb and likes the water around fallen trees and submerged logs, the leaping **tiger fish**, the frequently occurring **catfish**, and the ubiquitous **tilapia**, much beloved of local cuisine. (For more on sport fishing in Sierra Leone, see pages 164–5 and 237–8.)

An endemic **frog** (*Bufo cristiglands*) is found in the Tingi Hills, and an endemic **toadfrog** (*Cardioglosa aureoli*) in the Western Area Peninsula Forest.

The forest is also home to the **black cobra** (*Naja melanoleuca*) while the **spitting cobra** (*Naja nigricollis*) is found near coastal towns (including Freetown), in grassland and forest; the tree-dwelling **green mamba** (*Dendroaopsis viridis*) can be found in forest clearings. While the vipers have less powerful venom, they are less likely to move away at the approach of humans. The bulky but largely docile **Gabon viper** (*Bitis gabonica*) can grow up to 6ft and is slow moving; the **rhinocerous viper**, sometimes called the river jack (*Bitis nasicornis*), prefers moister surroundings, while the aggressive, easily provoked **carpet viper** (*Echis carinatus*), often mistaken for a puff adder, is found in the drier parts of northern Sierra Leone. Look out too for the much smaller **night adder** (*Causus rhombeatus*) easily trodden on around human habitations due to its nocturnal habits, although its venom is not generally life-threatening.

Relatively few endemic invertebrates are known to exist (besides the butterfly family; see below), but these include two **dragonfly** species, *Argiagrion leoninum* and *Allohizucha campioni*. For the micro-minded, the forest floor is a teeming source of life, from **beetles** to **worms** to **spiders** to **snails**, and the ever-present industry of various **ants** and **termites**. The same is true of any campsite in the forest, and if you are sleeping in a pre-existing tent that has been pitched for some time, it might be worth a quick sweep to see whether you are bedding down next to any unexpected guests. In towns, the insects you are most likely to see are usually most unwelcome: the **American cockroach** (*Periplanata americana*); and the slender brown malaria-carrying **Anopheles** mosquito, and black, silver-flecked, dengue and yellow fever-carrying **Aedes** mosquito. The hairy brown **Huntsman spider** (*Sparassidae* spp) is likely to spook non-African visitors due to its large size, scary appearance, and fondness for dwelling in cupboards. It's unlikely to bite unless threatened, and in any case is not poisonous.

Butterflies Of the 750 species of butterfly found in Sierra Leone, 12% are endemic to Africa west of the Dahomey Gap; a further 17 species carry names referring to the country or localities within it. This is explained partly by Freetown's importance as a colonial outpost: the expatriate traders, sailors and young civil servants who passed through sought to supplement their income by supplying the display cases of Victorian England with plenty of decent specimens, making Sierra Leone the site of many firsts for butterfly discoveries.

The Wesleyan Mission station at Moyamba appears to have conducted a steady trade, building on the work of the naturalist (and abolitionist) Henry Smeathman (page 132), who spent time growing plants and collecting fauna on the Banana Islands in the 18th century. In 1782, he sent what is thought to be one of the earliest descriptions of an African butterfly species, *Antanartia delius*, to the famous collector Dru Drury. In the same year a specimen of the rare **African giant swallowtail** (*Papilio antimachus*), with a wingspan of 25cm, was found in Sierra Leone, and not seen again for almost another 100 years.

A more recent and highly detailed survey of the fauna of Bumbuna Dam has turned up some rare and exquisite butterfly finds. Two sites in particular, 'Rashida's Forest' and 'Radio Hill' proved home to high densities of endemic butterflies, which could make Bumbuna a centre for butterfly study in the region, and certainly a focus for keen lepidopterists. Endemic species found include *Pentila cf condamini*, *Iolaus moyambina*, *Charaxes northcotti*, and the extremely rare *Neurellipes staudingeri* and *Acraea vesperalis* (pages 310–12).

HISTORY

It could have been the leonine lie of the land; perhaps it was the thundery roar from above the seas; maybe great cats even prowled the hills in jaw-clenching numbers. Whatever the explanation, Lion Mountains – the translation of the Portuguese *Serra Lyoa* – has stuck, without anyone ever quite being able to put their finger on why Pedro da Cintra, as he sailed past a mountainous West African shore in 1462 – identified humpbacked Banana Islands with the shape of a big cat.

even confirmed that they fully planned for the West African colonies to one day be given up, and the Africans to take over their own government.

But, amid depressed world commodity prices – undermining the value of palm, coffee and cocoa exports – the Colony of Freetown, which was meant to pay for itself, had begun to struggle, and in the wake of a flawed decision to hike customs duties to claw back revenue, coastal areas increasingly found they did a roaring trade without ever bothering to pass by Freetown and pay its inflated taxes. That put the colony even more out of pocket, and ever more envious of the local chiefs making a mint from duty-free trade. As wars flourished throughout the lands, over trade, succession or the odd falling-out, British merchants were among those who thought British annexation would quell the lawlessness and let them get back to the business of profit.

A further impetus to take the hinterland was provided by wealthy Krios (the descendants of freed slaves) in Freetown, including prominent lawyer Sir Samuel Lewis, nervous at losing out to traders in the interior. 'I must candidly confess that the future welfare of Sierra Leone depends, in the main, on the annexation of the adjacent countries,' said William Grant, another Krio man, in 1874.

The Brits slowly dipped their nervous toes ever further into colonial waters, agreeing to more 'treaties of friendship' as a means of bringing prosperous areas outside Freetown under customs control, but refusing to spend money on policing, developing or governing them. This two-tier approach led to difficulties that persist to this day – land rights, traditional rule and customs are worlds apart in the former colony and the former protectorate. More than 100 years later, the Truth and Reconciliation Commission, reporting on the causes of the 1991–2002 civil war in 2004, would deem that 'the colonial government effectively created two nations in the same land'. When finally the British introduced law enforcement in 1890 – the Frontier Police – their members soon grew a reputation for dispensing casual [in] justice, imprisoning chiefs, beating people up, raping women and making chiefs of their mistresses.

Missionaries and other zealous colonisers would put the expansion debate in more lofty terms, talking of 'civilising' the hinterland. Krio barrister Alfred Sawyerr, son of a Freetown printmaker, bookseller and member of the Legislative Council, was having none of that, throwing scorn on the sort of 'rum and gin civilisation' the British could offer. Time and again, the British made treaties of friendship with local rulers by giving them casks of booze and an annual payment. Such influence led to some improbable airs and graces – one local queen in the 1890s went to meetings carried in a hammock and wearing a black top hat. More often than not, the small print was less about a treaty and more about ceding sovereignty, something few chiefs realised until it was too late. 'Civilised nations annex to benefit themselves, not to civilise,' concluded Sawyerr.

More than any other factor, growing French interest in the region sealed its fate. By then, Britain was mighty glad of its deep-sea port at Freetown, the only one on the coast of West Africa and a perfect depot for restocking coal for its steamships, and wasn't about to let it go. Politely termed 'spheres of influence' had started growing somewhat earlier. The French secured their supply of groundnuts – wanted as a cheaper alternative to olive oil – to the north of Freetown, which was fine with the lardy Brits, who were perfectly satisfied with butter. The French then started busily promoting their own treaties of friendship with the same people the British had already signed up. 'Efforts should be made ... to prevent the French from further surrounding and hemming in the colony,' wrote the Colonial Office in 1890, demanding that 'the sphere of British influence should be extended as far as possible'. Sometimes groups even asked the British to take over their land, such as the Sherbro, who were much more fearful of the French after a ship anchored offshore and bombarded their town of Bendu.

A Mandingo, Muslim, horseriding warlord, Samori Toure, along with his battle-hardened Sofa warriors, did a fine job of putting the wind up both imperial powers, fighting first the French and later the British, happily torching and terrorising local villages. Initially the British supplied Samori with arms from Freetown, since he seemed to do a good job of keeping French incursions at bay. As his forces weakened, he asked the Brits to take over his patch in preference to the French, who had humiliated him in battle elsewhere in the region. The French chased Samori east and the British also asked him to back off, but as the French clocked up a run of victories against the feared warrior, the British also began to worry quite how close to their beloved Freetown and its port they would get. Samori was their only buffer, and an increasingly weak one. So the British did a deal with the French and breathed a sigh of relief.

In a brazen about-turn, British influence was extended to the hinterland beyond Freetown, and justified as 'best for the interests of the people in the territories adjacent to the colony of Sierra Leone'.

But those people had never been asked what they thought best served their interests. The prompt imposition of a five-shilling tax on every home in the protectorate caused outrage, prompting northern warrior Bai Bureh (see box, page 332) to lead a ferocious nine-month revolt, joined by the Mende rulers of the south, and known as the Hut Tax War of 1898 (and to revisionists keen to avoid clichés of African living, as the House Tax War). Relying on guerrilla tactics and secret societies, it was Sierra Leone's first large-scale bush war. British traveller Mary Kingsley at the time called the hut tax 'a piece of rotten bad law', but the government didn't budge: 'What a fatal lesson to the west native coast – you have only to rebel and the English government will never dare impose on you that direct taxation it imposes on everyone else,' argued one British parliamentarian in 1899. The British sent 1,000 troops marching through the protectorate, hanged 96 people, and Joseph Chamberlain, then secretary for state, decided to keep the tax.

The Hut Tax War was lost, but resentment against the British went nowhere. By 1912, the *Sierra Leone Weekly News* was in no doubt as to their influence. The white man had turned from an angel sounding a note of peace to an avenger bringing a 'war-whoop': 'Force is the enthroned deity,' said the fuming editorial. 'Nothing seems to give pleasure like the scampering of bewildered blacks over hill and dale before masters who whack and kick.'

The hypocrisy of attempting to take over the land for the people's own interests was well illustrated by the fact that domestic slavery continued unabated. Proclaiming the land a protectorate meant English law applied, and that slavery was banned. But there was a more pressing ban in place – the Frontier Police were specifically banned from interfering in cultural matters, which were deemed to include slavery. While the British continued to pat themselves on the back for founding Freetown, they were quite happy to play Pilate when it came to picking and choosing the law in the protectorate. The people had to pay rent, and their traditional rulers had to change their titles from king and queen to paramount chief, to show that now they all worked under one true queen, Victoria. When a paramount chief wasn't to British liking, they replaced him or her. The British also undertook mineral exploration in wastelands that were sometimes home to the sacred bush of secret societies: to ease the way they made sure the chief won a portion of the mining ground rents. Following the 1898 rebellion, they made chiefdom units even smaller so they'd be easier to control, and people would be less likely to band together. They sated the chiefs by offering them 5% of the hut tax takings – making colonial civil servants of them – and honouring them with gifts as sweeteners, thus ingraining and nurturing corruption in a system they willingly created. Slavery was abolished in the protectorate only in 1928, a full decade after the end of World War I had shamed the colonial power for putting blacks to work as soldiers who died for a country that wouldn't let them go free, almost 150 years after Freetown had been founded.

GROWING INEQUALITY Krio dominance began to wane in the new, post-protectorate set-up. Traders from Europe and what is now Lebanon squeezed their position in Freetown, becoming retailers as well as wholesalers. Upcountry, many other groups began to exploit their own positions, mining and farming to the exclusion of Krio interests. Government positions were increasingly filled by Europeans, and Britain seemed to lose sight of its 1865 commitment to ready Africa for self-government. Whereas in 1892 about half of senior government posts were held by Africans (and Sierra Leone had black governors), by 1912 it was about a tenth. Black doctors trained in London were no longer allowed into the West African medical service.

Palm oil exports boomed, reliant on the railway, and favoured as an ingredient in margarine, a cheap butter substitute. Run by European marketeers, the railway helped them grow rich from the country's produce. Sierra Leone's economy muddled along. Post-war, a railway strike in 1919 signified dissatisfaction with low wages and rising food prices. Jobs at the naval base that had been so important in defeating the Germans (based in Cameroon) were slashed, and many blamed Lebanese settlers and traders for their misfortunes, attacking and looting their shops.

As dissent against the British-run system grew, two new constitutions, in 1924 and again in 1947 – after 17,000 Sierra Leoneans fought for Britain in World War II – began to make advances towards self-government. To the dismay of the Krios, who had always thought of themselves as the ruling class, ultimate power followed the numbers, and for them this was an unwinnable game: while the colony could muster 60,000 people, the protectorate by this stage was home to about two million. Colony seats in the new Legislative Council were outnumbered two to one by those in the protectorate. Many Krios considered upcountry Africans as illiterate peasants whose interests they feared would overwhelm them. As early as the 1870s, Krio newspaper editor J A Fitzjohn had bewailed the influx of people from the hinterland, considering the 'increasing number of these Aborigines in the city as a matter to be deplored'.

The situation was uneven. While the protectorate had a system of indirect rule through British-created chieftancies, the colony had headmen. While land in the protectorate was held for the people in perpetuity by the chiefs, land in the colony could be bought and sold privately. Some hoped something of a nation might emerge from this country of two unequal halves, and some optimistic, pan-African Krios even changed their names to signal their Salone solidarity, such as the Reverend E N Jones, who re-emerged as Laminah Sankoh in 1924.

Political parties formed, and the Sierra Leone People's Party (SLPP), formed by southern Mendes as well as northern trade unionist (and future president) Siaka Stevens, started up in the 1950s, with a notable pro-protectorate bent. Another new constitution in 1951 provided the framework for decolonisation, and the SLPP swept the board in elections. The Krio party was marginalised, and the British chose only SLPP members to serve on the Executive Council. Local ministerial responsibility was introduced in 1953, when SLPP leader Milton Margai was appointed chief minister. An elderly, patrician, pipe-smoking medical doctor, Margai was a conservative leader who sympathised with the chiefs, many of whom abused their power, extracted forced labour, oppressed their people and triggered violent riots nationwide in the mid 1950s. Milton's brother Albert, along with Siaka Stevens, led a breakaway party, and in 1960 Stevens formed the radical All People's Congress (APC). Stevens desperately wanted an election before independence to show that there was an alternative to the cosy patronage of the past. But the popular APC never got to challenge the SLPP protectorate elite: fearful of the outcome of a free and fair election, Milton Margai instead declared a state of emergency and locked up all 43 APC leaders for a month. On the eve of independence, in April 1961 (the day before the anniversary of the Hut Tax War), Prime Minister Margai promised to make the country 'a land worth living in, a land worth serving', to 'stand for the freedom and prosperity of men everywhere' and to 'lay traditions of which you will proud'. Representation – let alone democracy – was already way off track.

INDEPENDENCE In 1958, Margai had said in parliament: 'I have often pointed out here in this House, that we on this side can never run smoothly without my friends on the other side.' Twenty years later, Sierra Leone had become a one-party state, with all the attendant horrors that political persecution and execution bring on a nation and its way of thinking and being.

Milton's lawyer brother Albert, who took over the reins of power for three years from 1964, tried to consolidate his power by banning other parties, but failed in 1966 in the face of opposition from the APC, backed by a groundswell of popular support.

It was not until APC leader Siaka Stevens – who picked his way through three military coups pretty much within his first year of being elected in 1967, a fourth in 1971, and a suspected fifth in 1974 – was fully established that he slowly ground the nation beneath his boot. At first there was euphoria at the victory: the party was packed with idealistic, Western-educated, young trade unionists and intellectuals. But the excitement quickly wore off. 'Paranoia flourished and the nerves of the nation were stretched taut as a dancer's hamstring. All that bound the men ruling our country together was a fondness for power and an eye for an opportunity,' wrote Aminata Forna, in her memoir *The Devil that Danced on the Water*. Her father and one-time finance minister Mohamed Forna was hanged in 1974 with seven others for his alleged role in the alleged coup plot, four years after he had left the party in protest against APC corruption and Stevens's fondness for dictatorship. 'The country was crawling with spies, who reported every conversation, every whisper to the president.' In the 1973 election every opposition candidate was withdrawn, fearful of violence. A 1978 referendum on a new constitution made the APC the only legal political party in the country.

Freed of opposition, internal and external, and perhaps conscious of how short-lived its time might be, a spirit of wantonness infected the administration. This is the period many people blame for the coming of the war – full of corruption, rampant borrowing on vanity projects (such as the hosting of the Organisation of African Union Conference in 1980, which virtually bankrupted the country), the ruthless silencing of political dissent, the deliberate withering of the army in case it attempted a coup; all were accompanied by a slow slide into appalling poverty that steadily eroded the education, growth and enterprise that had previously marked the country out. Siaka Stevens dug up the railway in 1970, thinking it too much of an SLPP–Mende axis for extracting stones from the east, instead linking the diamond fields with the northern APC capital at Makeni before heading down to Freetown. Taking control of the US$300 million-a-year industry personally, and promoting Lebanese cronies to run them rather than potential Sierra Leonean rivals, his personal fortune after this 'seventeen-year plague of locusts' is thought to have reached US$500 million. While two million carats were exported in 1970, by 1988 official exports had dropped to 48,000.

When the 80-year-old Stevens – self-styled 'father of the nation' – peacefully handed over to his hand-picked successor Major-General Joseph Saidu Momoh – commander of the armed forces and, like Stevens, a Limba – in 1985, the new man was full of promises. 'The malpractice of smuggling, tax evasion, profiteering, hoarding of vital commodities and black-market activities will be challenged with the greatest speed and most effective methods,' Momoh blustered at his inauguration. Labelled *dandogo* by his Limba brethren – 'fool' – nothing changed at all. In 1989, six men were hanged for their parts in a coup plot. Although Momoh went on to preside over a 1991 report that recommended re-establishing the multiparty system, the idea went nowhere.

CIVIL WAR Images of Sierra Leone's 1991–2002 civil war remain ingrained: amputated limbs, men wielding machetes, child soldiers wildly firing Kalashnikovs, their minds lost to drugs. The violence goes beyond extremes, beyond the power of words like 'horror' or 'atrocity' that try to describe it.

The country is still recovering. It is still difficult to explain what the war was about, what started it, who it was between and why it went on so long. Conflict provided each of the factions with dividends at times, and the quest was often less for outright victory than its continuation. As dynamics changed, new grievances, plots and power struggles rose up. Each time a near-peace was brokered, one group or another was left out, creating renewed resentments and dashing hopes for calm.

In addition to the 400-odd members of the Revolutionary United Front (RUF) who first invaded the country in 1991 and later claimed their 'armed uprising of the people' was 'guided by a liberation theology' in the attempt to 'remove a rotten system', other players included the Sierra Leone Army (SLA), whose job it was to protect the government of the day and defeat the rebels. But a series of splits in the SLA was responsible for two coups – first by the junior officers of the National Provisional Ruling Council (NPRC) in 1992, and second by the rank and file soldiers of the Armed Forces Revolutionary Council (AFRC) in 1997. This first coup also contributed in part to the notion of the 'sobel' – soldier by day; rebel by night – and the army also went on to spawn the West Side Boys faction that gained notoriety for taking 11 British soldiers hostage in 2000. Local militias formed from secret hunting societies grew up – most notably the Kamajors after 1995, under the umbrella of the Civil Defence Forces, and allied to what was left of the state army (CDF; see box, page 32).

Allegiances shifted throughout. Sometimes the RUF fought the AFRC; sometimes they fought together. The Kamajors sometimes fought not only the RUF but also the soldiers with whom they were supposed to be allied, later fought the AFRC, and later still fought with some AFRC remnants against the RUF.

Despite the complexities, the war had two constants: the similarity of the fighters – many of them young, poor men made angry and desperate through poverty, a sense of injustice, psychological and physical abuse, and drugs; and the fact that civilians, rather than other combatants, were overwhelmingly their targets.

This doesn't explain why the violence was so bad, or how it took hold. Some suggest that the torture techniques used during training of forced recruits, and the horrors they saw in the attempts to sever ties to family, village and self, alongside hard drug-taking, made them into potential abusers. Others have suggested that the extreme violence was a kind of rage aimed at the eradication of shame. Most of the worst atrocities happened when sides were losing – outraged that the local population wouldn't support their supposedly populist cause.

Atrocities Methods of killing were so crude, sometimes in the absence of ammunition, and numbers of killers so slight, that terror became a greater weapon. When the fighting got tougher, opponents were brought pretty much to a standstill, such as at the end of 1993 with a better organised Sierra Leone Army; when mercenaries arrived in 1995; and when the British sent in reinforcements in May 2000. But in the absence of one decisive campaign to stop them, fighters from all sides relied on the tactics that came to characterise the war.

Perhaps 4,000 people, maybe many more, had limbs amputated – an arm, sometimes two, an ear, their nose, their cheek, their leg. An estimated 1,600 survived in 2004 when the Truth and Reconciliation Commission concluded their work. An estimated one in three women and girls were raped. Girls as young as seven were taken as 'bush wives' – cooks and sex slaves. Entire villages were forced to strip, identify their relatives and have sex with them. A girl was made to sing and dance as attackers cut open her aunt's stomach in front of her to find the gender of her baby in a Le10,000 bet. The alternative was to be beaten to death, like her mother, who had refused to perform. Young boys were forced to watch men gang-rape their mothers and then abducted to be trained as soldiers who would one day do the same. Decapitated chief's heads were paraded through shocked villages. Disembowelled guts were strung up across roads as checkpoints. Men were forced to eat their own ears; one wife was forced to provide seasoning to cook her husband's severed head. Women were sexually violated with long sticks so violently they emerged from their mouths.

An estimated 10,000 child soldiers – some as young as five – were abducted and forced to fight. The same number again was taken for sexual slavery and forced labour. Those whose legs buckled under the weight of carrying loads of looted coffee, cocoa, weapons or tools were killed. Commanders took names such as Adama Cut-Hand, First Blood, Rambo, Superman, Dead Man No Count and Junior Daddy (the last two both child soldiers). No-one quite has the numbers, but people suppose more than 50,000 were killed, and well over a million displaced, perhaps more than twice that. Only at the end of 2005, nearly four years after the war ended, did the UN peacekeepers pull out. At their peak of 17,500, they had numbered the largest peacekeeping force in the world.

Search for understanding The causes and course of the war have become a topic of international debate in political, academic and development circles, to determine why such atrocities took place, how to punish those involved and prevent it happening again, and what the conflict reveals about Western attitudes towards Africa.

'Much of Africa is set to go over the edge,' wrote Robert Kaplan, a political advisor and journalist whose words were faxed to every US embassy the world over in 1994. According to him, Sierra Leone was 'widely regarded as beyond salvage'. The controversial fatalism about war in West Africa, borne out of what Kaplan saw as a volatile cocktail of tribal hatred, overpopulation, resource scarcity and looming environmental disaster, underpinned his article *The Coming Anarchy*, in which he predicted 'a rundown, crowded planet of skinhead Cossacks and juju warriors, influenced by the worst refuse of Western pop culture and ancient tribal hatreds' that would 'find liberation in violence'.

The only thing that matches the horror of the war is the tales of hope, determination and daily bravery that have come out of it. Bambay Sawaneh's story is one of them. Amid the devastation that persists and the accounts of unfathomable violence, it's easy to hear, and even easier to believe, that Sierra Leoneans are a peaceful people.

When the 22-year-old farmer came face to face with the man who had ordered rebel fighters to cut off both his forearms three years earlier, he asked a baying crowd not to lynch his attacker.

'I told the people if they kill him it will not make my hands come back,' says Sawaneh, who recognised the man during a physiotherapy session to help him use prosthetic limbs in Freetown.

The rebels arrived at his village when he was 15 years old. First they tried to cut off his arms with an axe. But the blade was too blunt to cut through the flesh and bone, so they resorted to using cutlasses – local parlance for machetes.

'I have forgiven him,' he says of the man he once swore to kill, wiping sweat from his brow with his left stump after a Bible class in Freetown.

Yet his forgiveness has not come without a price. Sawaneh and hundreds like him still have to live with the stigma of being amputees, a reminder of a past most would prefer to forget.

'People fear you. Children run from you crying; people start winding the car window up when they see you. You can get discouraged. I was always crying … thinking that I'm nothing.'

He contemplated suicide, but his determination to carry on has seen him master his prosthetic limbs. He can now use a hoe, and he has enough mobility in his right stump to open text messages on his mobile phone. He wanted so badly to become a farmer that on attaching wooden sticks to his arms and working on his land for the first time, he was so happy he didn't even notice the blood pouring from his chafed stumps.

Helped by foreign funding, he started farming chickens in Freetown, selling about 40 eggs a day for Le25,000 (US$3.50). He bought a small plot of land inland at Makeni, where he hopes to keep more chickens and grow crops.

'I'm excited. It is the one thing that I have achieved,' he says. 'When this thing happened to me I didn't want to mingle with people. Now I have courage. Now I'm actually happy. I know I'm a person and not a nothing.'

Other academics have challenged the view that the war was inevitable, or the product of a natural inclination to savagery, by variously highlighting a combination of factors specific to Sierra Leone – its ethnic soup; an angry rump of urban youth; a long history of social resistance; the cumulative collapse of the corrupt state; a worn-down, under-resourced military swollen with criminal recruits; grinding poverty; crippling external debt and social exclusion; the interference of a neighbouring state; the lust for diamonds to feed unscrupulous Western interests; the drug-fuelled, enervating reliance on cruelty; the copycat nature of the combat; a regional dimension that included turf wars going back decades; international terrorism, including al-Qaeda; and the use of mercenaries to provide firepower and security. All these make a straightforward analysis of cause and effect exceptionally difficult.

Journalists tended to focus on the horrors without understanding who was committing them, simplifying the conflict to give the public a view of 'good'

Africans versus 'bad' Africans. Many unwittingly hid the role of the AFRC, assessed to be responsible for the horrors of the January 1999 Freetown invasion, and instead clung only to observations about the RUF, which was easier to describe. Journalists too are blamed in part for the rising spate of amputations, because of their eagerness to report atrocities, which meant publicity for whomever was carrying them out: 'When we started cutting hands, hardly a day BBC would not talk about us,' said one fighter, while an ex-combatant of the SLA thought that 'for any war there must be an atrocity for the outside world to know there is something wrong in the place'.

It's hard to know where to look for the accurate narrative and interpretation. Trial documents from the Special Court for Sierra Leone (see box, pages 36–7) establish parts of history that hadn't yet come out, but the witnesses, and even the judges, are occasionally challenged. The thousands of pages of the Truth and Reconciliation Commission (TRC) – set up in 2000 to chart the war and published in 2004 – comes closest to a complete account.

The brief account on pages 26–8 provides a timeline to cling on to, and a discussion of some of the turning points. It doesn't claim to be comprehensive. It is perhaps easier to start with what the war wasn't: it didn't happen because of diamonds, or because of ethnic or religious hatred. Although, by 1997, smuggled diamonds fuelled the war to the tune of perhaps as much as US$25–125 million a year – making mules of villagers, funding arms, turning gems into blood stones – they didn't start it (see box, pages 284–5). Despite the fact there have long been tensions between the north and south of the country, ethnic differences didn't start the conflict, although they did mark out some areas and some people for attack at certain points.

The deep-seated crisis that eroded the nation for more than 20 years in the 1970s and 1980s institutionalised smuggling, embezzlement, and theft of the country's potential, breeding ever-growing despair and anger. Perhaps the TRC comes closest to explaining why. 'Years of bad governance, endemic corruption and the denial of basic human rights … created the deplorable conditions that made conflict inevitable.' But, thousands of witnesses later, that still doesn't do enough for the TRC to explain the litany of cruelty meted out to human beings by other human beings: 'it is difficult to answer the question why the combatants fought the war,' it says.

What did the RUF want? When Foday Sankoh – a one-time travelling photographer and 50-something army corporal who had spent four years in prison from 1971–75 – gave President Momoh a 90-day warning to get out of power on 1 March 1991, few took it seriously. Fewer still took seriously a bunch of former student radicals who had trained as commandos, including many of the student radicals themselves. Back in the 1980s, as Siaka Stevens choked the country, a secretive group of pot-smoking undergraduates had convinced themselves they were revolutionaries. A handful attended commando training in 1987 in Libya, including an expelled university student president, Alie Kabbah; Rashid Mansaray, who would one day become the RUF First Battalion Commander; and Foday Sankoh, who would go on to lead the RUF. When the budding revolutionaries fell out, Sankoh was diverted towards neighbouring Liberia. There, the National Patriotic Front of Liberia (NPFL), involved in its own guerrilla war, was under the stewardship of Charles Taylor. Liberian president from 1997 to 2003, Taylor was indicted for crimes against humanity by the Special Court at The Hague. On 26 April 2012, the Special Court ruled that Taylor was guilty on all 11 counts of aiding and abetting war crimes and crimes against humanity; his 50-year sentence was upheld on appeal in 2013 and he remains incarcerated in County Durham, England, after the UK answered a call from the United Nations seeking a country who would hold Taylor after his conviction.

23 March 1991 First shots fired at Bomaru, in the east, in an apparent attempt by the Liberian NPFL to claim a Sierra Leone Army vehicle they had 'paid' for with smuggled goods, which the SLA had not released to them.

27 March 1991 1,600 members of the NPFL and 400 of the RUF 'vanguard' cross the border from Liberia on two fronts – into Kailahun in the east and Pujehun to the south.

29 April 1992 Military coup deposes President Momoh and sees Captain Valentine Strasser, at 26, form the NPRC and become the world's youngest head of state.

19 December 1992 Twenty-six 'coup plotters' executed a day after their arrest; Strasser said their trials were conducted posthumously by the NPRC.

13 November 1993 The RUF on the verge of total defeat in Kailahun; leader Foday Sankoh circulates new jungle warfare strategy of 'guerrilla tactics' to the waning RUF in order to survive.

27 April 1995 On the anniversary of independence, Valentine Strasser reintroduces party politics and promises a consultative conference ahead of handover to civilian rule.

16 January 1996 'Palace coup' within the NPRC replaces Valentine Strasser with Julius Maada Bio, apparently because Strasser was planning to stand as president in forthcoming elections, breaking the 1991 constitution rule of a minimum age of 40. Bio sets about transition to democracy.

15 March 1996 The SLPP's leader Ahmed Tejan Kabbah elected president with 59.4% of the second-round poll; the SLPP also wins 51 of the 80-seat legislature. Kabbah appoints Chief Sam Hinga Norman, leader of the CDF, deputy minister of defence and agrees to keep on foreign security companies. Hinga Norman's close relationship with the Kamajors angers the army.

30 November 1996 Peace agreement signed in Abidjan between Kabbah and the RUF, with the stipulation that Executive Outcomes leaves the country by January 1997; cut-off date for crimes tried by the Special Court (nothing before this date counts).

January 1997 Executive Outcomes formally withdraws from Sierra Leone and the Kabbah government establishes a power-sharing multi-party cabinet, with Sankoh made Chairman of the Commission for the Management of Strategic Resources, National Reconstruction and Development, with the status of vice president.

February 1997 Kabbah announces that a Nigerian-led security investigation has pinpointed members of the previous Maada Bio government as coup plotters.

2 March 1997 Most RUF bases overthrown, including headquarters Camp Zogoda. The RUF's second-in-command, Mohamed Tarawallie, thought killed in Zogoda siege. RUF leader Foday Sankoh flies to Nigeria, apparently on an official mission, but is arrested soon after his arrival. RUF morale drops further.

25 May 1997 Government coup by the Armed Forces Revolutionary Council (AFRC), an army breakaway group of junior soldiers who protest against corrupt seniors and attempts to reduce the size of the army; Kabbah flees to Guinea to mobilise international support; Major Johnny Paul Koroma becomes head of state and suspends the constitution, bans demonstrations, and abolishes political parties. Koroma calls for the formation of the People's Army, linking the RUF and AFRC.

July 1997 Commonwealth suspends Sierra Leone.

September 1997 The CDF launches Operation Black December in Bo and Kenema.

8 October 1997 The United Nations Security Council adopts Resolution 1132, which Britain helps to draft, introducing sanctions against the regime in Sierra Leone, barring the supply of arms and petroleum products. A British company, Sandline, nonetheless supplies 'logistical support', including 35 tons of weapons, to Kabbah allies. Sandline says the understanding was that the embargo only applied to the military junta, not the deposed regime of Kabbah.

23 October 1997 The Conakry Peace Plan attempts to ensure the AFRC will hand over to civilian power by a given deadline.

2 February 1998 The Nigerian-led West African intervention force, ECOMOG, storms Freetown in an attempt to take back the capital and depose the AFRC. Facing landmines and AFRC-hired Ukrainian mercenaries, ECOMOG wins Freetown by 13 February.

10 March 1998 President Kabbah is restored; declares state of emergency.

May–end 1998 The AFRC attacks the north and begins to make its way south; the RUF attacks focus on the east and in August it announces that unless leader Foday Sankoh is released from prison, it will launch Operation Spare No Soul.

19 October 1998 Twenty-four officers associated with the AFRC executed for treason by the Kabbah government.

18 December 1998 The RUF wins back diamond-rich Koidu.

6 January 1999 Invasion of Freetown by the AFRC, killing thousands and committing widespread atrocities.

February 1999 Inquiry in the UK into the supply of weapons to Kabbah supporters by Sandline – at the time of a UN embargo – is highly critical of British civil servants and ministers.

18 May 1999 A ceasefire is greeted with cautious optimism in Freetown.

17 July 1999 Kabbah and Foday Sankoh sign the Lomé Peace Accord following six weeks of talks in the Togo capital; a power-sharing agreement in which the RUF wins government posts. The RUF are given assurances that it will not be prosecuted for war crimes.

October 1999 A cabinet reshuffle finally accommodates the Lomé agreements, making Foday Sankoh equivalent to vice president and in charge of mineral resources; the West Side Boys militia formed from strands of the SLA in the Western Area.

December 1999 UN troops arrive to police the peace agreement – but one rebel leader, Sam 'Mosquito' Bockarie, says they are not welcome. Meanwhile, ECOMOG troops are attacked outside Freetown; Mosquito announces he is leaving the country because of differences with Sankoh.

January 2000 The UN sends in more United Nations Mission in Sierra Leone (UNAMSIL) peacekeeping forces to Sierra Leone to oversee implementation of the Lomé Peace Accord.

May 2000 ECOMOG forces withdraw; the RUF take hundreds of under-resourced and inexperienced UN peacekeepers hostage; Britain sends in 1,000 troops to

Sierra Leone and Liberia had fallen out after Sierra Leone's President Momoh let West African peacekeeping forces launch attacks on Taylor's NPFL in Liberia from Sierra Leone's airport in 1990. In retaliation, Liberia rounded up Sierra Leoneans living in the country and jailed them, whether urchins, criminals, teachers or doctors; in 1990, Taylor threatened that his neighbour would 'taste the bitterness of war'. Foday Sankoh, by now without his student radical friends to slow him down, and close to Taylor, went about forcibly recruiting hundreds of these jailed Sierra Leoneans. He thought of them as a vanguard of ideological revolutionaries. But while some joined of their own accord, most were co-opted, and then trained under such extreme violence at Camp Namma in Liberia that they were eventually ready to inflict it on others. Much like the 'red water' option of old (page 17), joining the Revolutionary United Front (RUF) seemed the only ticket to escaping Liberia and staying alive, just as slavery had been 'an option' to avoid lethal poison back in the 18th century.

When the 385-strong RUF re-entered Sierra Leone in March 1991, they were preceded by about 1,600 fighters from Liberia's NPFL, as well as the odd mercenary from Burkina Faso. The NPFL fighters, who had declared Sierra Leoneans the enemy, attacked with abandon. They looted, displaced, raped, killed, cannibalised, committed atrocities and spread unrelenting fear. According to the TRC, the majority role played by the NPFL, along with Charles Taylor's support, 'marked the abortion of the revolution even before it had started'.

The first amputation, in Kono in November 1992, was thought to have been performed by a Liberian bored with not having a line of villagers of his own to decapitate. NPFL and RUF fighters fought among themselves and several high-level

evacuate British citizens, secure Freetown and the airport; later reduced to 200 military training troops by September.

8 May 2000 So-called peace march of armed AFRC, West Side Boys and Kamajors takes RUF strongholds throughout the capital; Foday Sankoh is captured a week later in Freetown.

June–July 2000 British military task force sent to help restore order departs, leaving behind a training force and UN troops surrounded by rebels.

August 2000 The UN agrees to pursue rebels through an international tribunal; the West Side Boys capture 11 British troops, who are later rescued by British paratroopers in September.

10 November 2000 The Abuja peace process begins, resulting in the Abuja Cease-Fire Agreement – Abuja I.

2 May 2001 Second peace meeting in Abuja – Abuja II.

14 May 2001 Cessation of Hostilities signed at Mammy Yoko Hotel, the UNAMSIL headquarters.

January 2002 Peace ceremony at Lungi.

plots to assassinate top brass were repeatedly hatched throughout 1992. Even after Charles Taylor recalled his NPFL fighters, most nonetheless stayed until they ran out of ammunition. In contrast to the marauding NPFL, the Sierra Leonean RUF were returning to their homeland, the eastern and southern Mende heartlands of Kailahun and Pujehun that opposed the corrupt APC more than any other area. At first many villagers lent support, 'giving their sons' to the self-cast liberator Sankoh and his 'freedom fighters', who promised to rid the country of its long-rotten ruling class.

But while the RUF is sometimes painted as an ideological force, and the blame for the atrocities laid at the door of new recruits gone crazy or members of the AFRC military junta, the more you look, the harder it becomes to find the space for RUF ideology. Any villager with a hint of authority was condemned as an APC supporter. Sankoh imprisoned his ideological pal from his Libyan training days – Rashid Mansaray – because Mansaray didn't want to work with the NPFL. The RUF also started forcibly recruiting people from their homes to further swell its ranks, and by late 1992 numbered 10,000 fighters. Sankoh was clearly charismatic and rousing, attracting people of the southern SLPP heartlands to his cause within the first few weeks of his invasion with rallying cries against the APC regime. But the tract that attempted to define and justify the RUF political philosophy, *Footpaths to Democracy*, only came out four years later, retrospectively couching much of the action in the usual ragtag rhetoric of lofty Afro-Marxist aims.

'Sometimes we have the presence of mind to indulge our young ones with sweets and toys,' says *Footpaths*, neglecting to mention the potent mixture of cocaine and gunpowder, known as *brown brown*, that was ingested, or rubbed into deliberate cuts in new recruits' skin. 'I was later given a tablet, which made me see people like birds. I then became perfect in using the gun and killed a lot of people in every attack,' said one forcibly recruited child soldier later. Claiming itself 'a democratic revolution' with the mass support of the people, the RUF didn't mention village after village and life after life it destroyed.

It also didn't mention that despite the high-minded rhetoric, plenty of RUF recruits despaired of education – *noto buk wo dis* ('this is not a book war') said some – or that some RUF said 'civilians don't have blood', or that the group's 'stringent discipline' saw mass rape, amputation and more.

While his recruits were taught with torture, fired on during training, high on drugs and with commanders to look up to in place of dead or lost family, Foday Sankoh would occasionally apologise to the people; while the RUF had an internal investigations unit, some fighters who tried to stem the violence were killed, and while Liberian fighters were mostly gone by the end of 1992, the TRC found that the RUF and NPFL combined committed more than 60% of the atrocities during the war, although some dispute the accuracy of this figure.

Forgotten soldiers One often-overlooked precursor to the war was the long-term depletion of the army. Siaka Stevens deliberately ran down its wherewithal to fight lest it attempted a coup, and instead built up his own personal guard. So when only 2,000 combined RUF and NPFL fighters invaded in 1991, there were barely 1,000 decent soldiers to stand in their way, most in the wrong place and with no decent vehicles, communications, rations or combat-readiness, divided by age, ethnicity and rank.

After poorly equipped and unpaid soldiers started dying in the effort to turn the rebels back, junior officers – painfully aware of sinking army morale – lost little time in mounting a coup against Momoh's government and installing their own military rule with a view to civilian handover. The world's youngest head of state at just 26, Captain Valentine Strasser vowed to handle the war better. His National Provisional Ruling Council (NPRC) is remembered affectionately by some – meetings would start on time, latecomers would be barred, the future president Kabbah was brought on board as an advisor; and Strasser promised the first multi-party elections since 1967. It is remembered with bitterness by others – as the 'haves' were targeted by the 'have-nots' in spates of farm-burning and discrimination. When the soldiers of the NPRC overthrew the APC regime in 1992, no-one seemed to notice that both the RUF and NPRC, in theory, shared the same vision to rid the country of the corrupt APC regime and create a better life for its people. Instead, they kept fighting each other.

Hoping to prosecute the war with more might than the desultory APC, the NPRC embarked on a mass recruitment drive that invited a large number of decidedly unsavoury elements into the ranks, including most of Freetown's underworld – drug-takers, petty criminals and unemployed hoodlums, collectively termed later by one commentator the 'lumpenproletariat'. Some joined only to grab themselves a gun and desert to the RUF. 'The wrong people were recruited,' admitted one colonel. Between 1991 and 1994, the army is thought to have swelled from 3,000 to 16,000.

As the RUF began 'false flag' raids dressed in army uniforms, confidence in the army fell further; they were declared unwelcome in many eastern and southern regions. Anyone thought to have harboured the RUF was victimised by the army; in the face of RUF tactics often soldiers couldn't recognise whether villagers were civilians or RUF and targeted them just in case. It began to make sense for some fighters to change affiliation according to their best chances of survival. The NPRC also began to lose its nerve, and its focus – it arrested, tortured and executed 26 'coup plotters' and Momoh supporters on Lumley Beach in December 1992. Their trials were held after they'd been killed; their fates sealed once Strasser's deputy S A J Musa reportedly cut off their ears as he interrogated them.

Despite its ineptitude, the army, alongside the only air firepower in the country, and considerable troop backup from Nigeria and Guinea, gave the NPRC the upper hand in the warzone. NPFL soldiers were recalled to Liberia by Charles Taylor and fighters ran short of ammunition. By February 1993, the Sierra Leone Army (SLA) had ousted the RUF from Kono, then Kailahun, and by November had squeezed it to the eastern border with Liberia at Koindu. Had Strasser the presence of mind to press home his advantage, the war might have ended there. Instead, calling a ceasefire gave the RUF a chance to regroup and come up with a new mode of fighting – launching raids and ambushes for food and arms from the jungle in a prolonged phase of guerrilla warfare.

By then the RUF ideology was long gone. Rebels staked out sites for a week or more, attacked SLA convoys for arms, lay in wait along village escape routes, stole children from villages, raped girls and set up training camps in which new recruits would be fed drugs to 'boost their morale' or else be shot for failing to run fast enough.

RUF bases had been nearly obliterated at the end of 1993, but by the start of 1995 they had spread far beyond the Zogoda headquarters in the Kambui Hills of Kenema, to the Kangari Hills of the north, to Mattru Jong in the south and to the western jungle in the Western Area, 20 miles from Freetown. RUF units took over the rutile and bauxite mines in the south, the country's big money-spinners. With fewer and fewer places to turn, and the SLA imploding, Strasser opted for mercenaries to do the job his own army couldn't manage. Executive Outcomes (EO), a UK-registered South African private security outfit, was enlisted in March 1995.

'I knew the military was not going to save us and I was in charge of the military. I thought EO was the only chance to save our country,' said Julius Maada Bio, NPRC strongman and later head of state. Within two months, thanks to US$1.8 million a month, helicopters, good communications, night-vision and only 250 men, EO's operation had the RUF quaking. Having secured Freetown by May, EO later moved out towards the RUF's rural strongholds, co-operating with and training the local Kamajors (see box, page 32), and taking back the rutile mine in 1996. EO-associated companies allegedly began mining diamonds in the east as part-payment for their services.

Defeats again brought the RUF to the negotiating table, attending peace talks to slow the pace of the war while continuing to fight on the sly. The months preceding elections in February 1996 were marked by the first widespread spate of mass amputations, mostly of arms, fingers and thumbs as part of Operation Stop Elections; a way either of preventing people from, or punishing them for, voting. 'After they cut off my hand,' said one amputee, Morlai Conteh, 'they gave it to me and told me to take it to the government.'

Strasser, overthrown in 1996 by his vice chairman Julius Maada Bio, went off to Warwick University in the UK to study, but soon dropped out when people found out about his past. Maada Bio, who would reappear on the political scene 16 years later with a run for the presidency, set about making a return to civilian rule more viable. The election in 1996 returned NPRC advisor and 20-year UN stalwart Ahmed Tejan Kabbah to power in the second round of voting. Under the new president, EO continued to train up the Kamajors, as Kabbah planned to reduce the size of the inflated, unreliable army. But as defeat after defeat forced concessions from the RUF, it cannily made one condition for peace: the withdrawal of EO by January 1997.

As villagers realised not only the army's ineffectiveness but its potential treachery – both real and created by the RUF's raids in army uniforms – communities began to take up arms to defend themselves. The Kamajors – formed from secret hunting societies of the southern Mende – emerged in early 1995. At times armed by ECOMOG (Economic Community of West African States Monitoring Group) and trained by mercenary outfit Executive Outcomes (EO), they were moved around the country to take on their targets. The Kamajors were joined by other similar forces – in the north Gbethes, Kapras and Tamaboros, and in the east Donsos – and these groups became known and vaguely organised as the Civil Defence Forces (CDF). The TRC says they 'played a vital role in defending the nation'. But as they took on an ever-growing role in the defence of the state they also critically eroded any vestiges of faith that people held in the military and, worse, undermined and angered the ranks of the army itself.

They also sent many recruits to their death. Highly superstitious, with a strong belief in magic, Kamajors were taught that their initiation ceremonies rendered them immune to bullets; and senior commanders were credited with control over where mortar shells hit. The TRC notes that amateur herbalist, roving magician and almost constant drunk Allieu Kondewa, self-styled Kamajor High Priest and 'King Dr', would regularly initiate members by firing at them with shotguns – the cartridges and casings had been removed, although the weapons still made an impressive bang. For this, he also charged a fee, and recruit after recruit paid to be initiated at 'Base Zero' in the southern swamplands of Bonthe district. Cannibalism was practised as a Kamajor ritual; some new recruits trained under torturous conditions ate human organs cooked in communal meals, sometimes without knowing; some enemies were forced to eat their own ears.

The CDF determination to defend its own turf, without the SLA, was resolute. Although the Kamajor commander, Sandhurst-trained Chief Samuel Hinga Norman, was made deputy defence minister in 1996, as national co-ordinator of the CDF he promoted his own militia above the army. Kamajors refused to work with the SLA, even if they were attached to ECOMOG, turning the south into a no-go area for the country's regular army. Trust haemorrhaged, and even President Kabbah tried to hatch a plan to replace Hinga Norman when relations soured. Although that attempt failed, Kabbah went on to appoint a Limba CDF commander for the north without informing Hinga Norman, and the two commanders failed to co-ordinate. Hinga Norman refused to supply the northern CDF with arms, leaving it to fall prey to the AFRC and its atrocities. With Kabbah in exile throughout 1997, Hinga Norman had free rein, raising funds for a renewed attack on the AFRC military junta through diamond mining in Tongo Fields in the east.

The TRC found the CDF responsible for 6% of all violations during the war, and in May 2008 the Special Court convicted Allieu Kondewa and Moinina Fofana, another senior Kamajor leader, on several counts of human rights violations, handing down sentences of 20 and 15 years respectively. In 2015, Fofana became the first person convicted in the Special Court of crimes against humanity to be released; he remains on conditional release in Bo and is scheduled to complete his sentence entirely in May 2018.

Another coup in May 1997 put an end to all thoughts of negotiated peace, however, as the dysfunctional army broke ranks for good. Angered that rice rations were cut from 25,000 bags a month to 8,000 bags a month, with no reduction for the officers, and undermined by the increasing support government lent to traditional hunters, low-ranking soldiers took matters into their own hands. At one point, soldiers even attacked Kamajors in a raid and nearly killed Hinga Norman. Not keen on civilian handover, and not keen on their own generals, this bottom-up putsch, started by a group that called itself the Armed Forces Revolutionary Council (AFRC), had less to do with the war and more to do with opportunistic soldiers' grievances with the system for which they fought. Unlike the NPRC coup of 1992, it was not greeted with popular support.

President Kabbah was having his early-morning shave when he heard about the coup in progress and soon escaped by chopper to Guinea. The 17 coup plotters – mostly the army's footballers – took over the army headquarters and were soon joined by thousands of disgruntled soldiers, many of whom were ex-criminals. They set prisoners free, including the poorly educated, British-trained, 33-year-old Major Johnny Paul Koroma. He was in jail awaiting trial for treason at the time, on suspicion of another army coup plot; he had also been among the first government troops who went to Bomaru to put a stop to the RUF invasion in 1991. Now installed as head of state, he quickly made the call to AFRC and RUF sympathisers to come to Freetown and join the united 'People's Army', whose name cloaked the widespread attacks on the people they professed to defend.

As the RUF poured into the city, vengeful atrocities mounted. The government-in-exile worked for months towards its own restoration, securing economic sanctions, supporting and arming the Civil Defence Forces where it could (whose own atrocities were increasing), and hoping Nigerian-led West African troops (ECOMOG) could put a stop to the AFRC and its newly adopted Ukrainian mercenaries. Nine months later, ECOMOG, backed by logistical and intelligence support from the British private security company Sandline International – which shared a London office in Chelsea with Branch Energy, a diamond company associated with EO – and the Kamajors stormed Freetown, toppling the short-lived AFRC/RUF junta.

Restoration of the Kabbah government eventually came in March 1998, after which mob justice saw revenge attacks, including torchings on the streets of Freetown for anyone even thought to be associated with the AFRC. The radio station 98.1FM, set up with British money to be the mouthpiece of the government-in-exile, read out names of supposed 'collaborators' and ECOMOG did nothing to stop the lynch mobs – in some cases they may have joined in the atrocities. More than 3,000 'collaborators' were rounded up and imprisoned at Pademba Road Prison, meant for 300 people. After sustained detention in appalling conditions, 24 officers – only two of whom were among the 17 AFRC coup plotters – were found guilty of treason and executed by firing squad at Goderich. Hundreds more waited to hear if their fate was the same, including prominent family members of the expelled AFRC junta. The retreating AFRC forces were seething – they officially had until 22 April 1998 to hand over peace. While it was doubtful they would have done so, the deadline was utterly ignored by the Kabbah-allied forces. As a result, they went on a campaign of violence after fleeing to the east and north of the country that lasted throughout 1998. Operation No Living Thing was followed by a final AFRC assault on Freetown – buoyed by thousands of villagers captured upcountry and deployed as human shields – in January 1999. The ensuing carnage killed 6,000; leaving amputations, charred remains, and utter terror in its wake.

Only at Congo Cross Bridge – today named Peace Bridge – was ECOMOG able to turn the furious force back, when they retreated, according to the TRC, in 'an orgy of looting, destruction, abduction, rapes and killings' and fled north again to Makeni. This was the vengeful last-gasp of fighters who had spent so long in the bush they knew nothing else, and now had nothing to show for their crimes. Raging at a democratically elected government from which they were excluded, civilians were the only target they had left.

Tense resolution In May 1999, the Lomé Peace Accord established a ceasefire, granting amnesty for a backlog of atrocities. The RUF wanted Foday Sankoh – held in Nigeria since March 1997 – released as a result, but he soon lost universal command, and many splinter groups, such as the one headed by Sam 'Mosquito' Bockarie – a one-time hairdresser and disco dancer – went on fighting, until at the end of 1999 he left the country for Liberia due to differences with Sankoh. The continuation was partly insurance – given the state-sponsored executions of 1998, many RUF members feared the government was not sincere in its talk of peace and resolution. The AFRC also felt excluded after it was given no representation at Lomé, bar commander 'Leather Boot' (Idrissa Hamid Kamara) whom they regarded as pro-RUF. As a sop, President Kabbah appointed Johnny Paul Koroma head of the commission for the consolidation of peace, a role to which he was entirely unsuited. In an October 1999 cabinet reshuffle, Sankoh was given a role equivalent to vice president, but not respected as such, and both these roles in the so-called power-sharing government served to undermine peace from the outset. A further four ministers and four deputy ministerial posts were awarded to the RUFP (the added P stood for Party), but the most senior was the trade portfolio, and other plum jobs never materialised. For the fighters on the ground, those few who were co-opted into the RUFP stood to gain status and a role from the peace; the rest realised the bullet was still their only source of power, and the faction split open even wider.

Freetown became a city of enclaves, but the ceasefire held, just. Sankoh lived in a house guarded by, ironically, AFRC soldiers, most of whom had at one time fought against the RUF. Koroma was guarded by fighters from the largely AFRC People's Army, including some rag-tag RUF as well as the West Side Boys, a splinter group of the Sierra Leone Army – many of whom had been part of the AFRC attack on Freetown in 1999 and now demanded reintegration into the army. By then the RUF and AFRC had fallen out – Koroma had apparently been caught trying to smuggle out diamonds; and RUF commander Superman and AFRC commander S A J Musa had refused to co-operate on joint operations.

As combatants began to fear for their futures, the RUF began kidnapping UN peacekeepers, thousands of whom arrived in December 1999. It's not quite clear whether Sankoh initiated or approved this, or whether he was having such a hard time keeping the RUF together that he couldn't dare tell them to release the hostages. In one week at the beginning of May 2000, the RUF took 550 peacekeepers. Civil society, appalled at the potential of this hostage-taking to derail the fragile peace process, planned a huge march on Sankoh's Spur Road house in Freetown for 8 May. Keen to manipulate the situation, Koroma bussed in his AFRC gorillas and West Side Boys, armed them with guns and an anti-aircraft missile and called them his 'Peace Task Force'; the Kamajors were also deployed, with the assent of the president, and marched on Sankoh's house, ostensibly on the pretext that Sankoh was plotting a coup. The firefight that ensued killed dozens of people from all sides, including civilians, revealing the power-sharing agreement for the sham it was.

RUFP ministers were arrested; the RUFP deputy minister Susan Lahai was abducted and gang-raped to death. Sankoh escaped into the bush, only to return to Freetown nine days later, where he was arrested and transferred to British custody – he later died pending war crimes charges in July 2003.

Only then, a decade into the war, did the British intervene in their former colony, touting an 'ethical foreign policy'. The Truth and Reconciliation Commission (TRC) saw it differently, claiming the Brits offered minimal support, turned up late and were tangled up in the Sandline arms-to-Africa scandal: 'Sierra Leoneans are justified in their view that they were abandoned by the United Kingdom in their hour of need', the report said.

British troops arrived in Freetown to provide support for the UN forces, guard the airport and evacuate their own. Commander Brigadier David Richards, who later became head of the British army, extended the official UK role substantially. In a more successful example of mission creep, he says he turned an evacuation plan into an operation to push back the rebels. In the days that followed, fierce fighting saw the RUF defeated and pushed out of Masiaka, while Superman was also killed. In July 2000 the West Side Boys, from their base in the Okra Hills, abducted 11 soldiers of the Irish Guards who were training West African peacekeepers. A September raid freed the hostages and raised the profile of the British military, which also fought off attacks on Lungi Airport.

Two meetings in Abuja – in 2000 and 2001 – began to seal a more lasting peace, and a final peace ceremony was held in January 2002. By 2004, the disarmament process was complete. Also in 2004, a UN-backed war crimes court, the Special Court of Sierra Leone, began holding trials of senior leaders from the RUF, AFRC and CDF, as well as, later, ex-Liberia president Charles Taylor. RUF leaders Issa Sesay and Morris Kallon were convicted of 16 of the 18 charges against them and Augustine Gbao was found guilty on one of the counts. They were sentenced to 52 years, 40 years and 25 years apiece and are serving out their prison time in Rwanda. Taylor's trial was moved to The Hague for security reasons. In December 2005, UN peacekeeping forces pulled out of Sierra Leone. About 72,000 combatants were given money and training as part of a disarmament, demobilisation and reintegration programme. More than 13 years after the close of the TRC and the publication of its report underlining the need for civilian reparations, only a fraction of the war's many victims have received any form of compensation, and at this stage that seems most unlikely to change.

TOWARDS PEACE AND DEVELOPMENT Recent history has so overwhelmed this small country that the great strides made since the end of the war are sometimes forgotten. For a long time people felt politicians too easily blamed the lack of economic and social progress on the war, without ever getting to grips with the underlying mess that pre-dated it, or attempting to inject much urgency to the effort to rebuild and get on.

In October 2008, the UN peacebuilding office – the unit charged with helping the country get back on its feet post-war – scaled down from about 300 to a team of fewer than 70; by 2014 it had closed entirely. Both the army and police have undergone huge transformations in discipline, training and ethos, and although there's much further to go, the country is making its uneven first steps towards development (pages 43–4). Sierra Leone's army now contributes to international peacekeeping missions elsewhere in Africa.

A year earlier, in September 2007, Sierra Leone elected an ever-smiling president who vowed he would have his own family members go to prison should they be

The Special Court for Sierra Leone, set up in 2001 at the behest of then-president Kabbah, was given a mandate to prosecute those 'who bear the greatest responsibility' for crimes against humanity, war crimes and other serious violations of international law during Sierra Leone's armed conflict. Backed by the national government and the UN, the prosecutor at the hybrid court (able to draw upon both domestic and international law) eventually deemed that responsibility lay only with 13 individuals, indicted them and set about bringing them to justice. It has taken a lot longer than hoped, and cost much more as well – a staggering US$300 million at the end of the day. By contrast, the Truth and Reconciliation Commission (TRC) struggled with less than £25,000 a year from the government, besides other donor funding. 'The guns may be silent, but the trauma of the war lingers on,' said Sierra Leone's president when the TRC started work in 2002. A TRC-linked US$3 million War Victims Fund to pay out reparations was launched years late, in mid 2008. The Court was late too: expected to wrap up in 2005, it wasn't officially dissolved until December 2013. Of the 14 indictees, three critical figures died before being tried (RUF leader Foday Sankoh, CDF leader Chief Sam Hinga Norman and RUF commander Sam 'Mosquito' Bockarie, who prosecutors say was killed by Taylor before he could have a chance to testify against him) and one remains at large, presumed dead after 2003 (AFRC leader Johnny Paul Koroma). Only nine, including ex-Liberia president Charles Taylor, eventually made it to trial. The court decided to try the accused only for events that occurred after 30 November 1996.

Critics point out that many Sierra Leoneans remain deeply ambivalent about the activities of the Special Court, not least because of its colossal expense. While justice may have no price, many victims feel their suffering has gone un-noted, and certainly uncompensated. In contrast, those remanded by the court eat well, enjoy 24-hour electricity, satellite TV and a ping-pong table, and witnesses in The Hague

found guilty of corruption – not that that's happened just yet. Ernest Bai Koroma, a former insurance executive, was elected following tense polls. Despite some rioting, the hiring of ex-combatants as 'bodyguards' by all parties, and ballot-stuffing to the extent that 477 of 6,171 polling stations were invalidated, the elections went off relatively peacefully and were greeted as among Africa's best to date. That's partly because it's rare in Africa for an opposition party to sweep to power at the ballot box; certainly it was the first time it had ever happened in Sierra Leone. The result, and the conduct of the campaign is a credit to the country – in particular to the organisation and dedication of the independent National Electoral Commission headed by ex-nun Christiana Thorpe, international donors and the UN.

Amid a desire for decent roads, electricity, reliable water supply and jobs, the All People's Congress – responsible for decades of corruption in the 1980s – was elected on the promise of delivering the change for which people were still clamouring. Popular disillusion was enough to edge out the incumbent party's candidate, Vice President Solomon Berewa. Koroma won in a second round of voting, with 54.6%, and 59 of 112 elected seats in parliament went to the APC too.

2012 brought another round of elections, pitting Koroma the incumbent against SLPP candidate Julius Maada Bio, best known for leading the country for three months in 1996 as head of the National Provisional Ruling Council, aged 31. These elections, declared 'remarkably transparent and well-managed' by the Carter

– where Charles Taylor was tried – have cooks and cleaners. Each judge receives 'an honorarium' of US$170,000 a year, before allowances. One lawyer said the only people benefiting from the court were the lawyers and employees themselves.

Supporters point out several 'firsts'. Recruiting child soldiers has, for the first time under international law, been made a crime as a result of proceedings at the Court, creating an important precedent. Likewise forced marriage. And it is cheaper than Rwanda's International Criminal Tribunal (although far fewer people are on trial). It's also only the second time an ex-president has been indicted: when Nigeria eventually gave Taylor up, the world, and dictators everywhere, paid attention.

Convictions have been handed down for three leaders of the Armed Forces Revolutionary Council (AFRC) military junta (Alex Tamba Brima, Brima Bazzy Kamara and Santigie Borbor Kanu), who were found guilty on 11 counts of war crimes and crimes against humanity, including terrorism, rape and enslavement. Brima and Kanu were each sentenced to 50 years, and Kamara to 45 years. The two surviving CDF defendants, Alieu Kondewa and Moinina Fofana, were also convicted of a host of criminal acts, including murder, cruel treatment and collective punishments, for which Kondewa received 20 years and Fofana 15 years. Fofana is now on conditional release in Bo and will complete his sentence in 2018. The three RUF defendants – Issa Sesay, Morris Kallon and Augustine Gbao – are now serving out their sentences in Rwanda. On 26 April 2012, the Special Court ruled that Taylor was guilty on all 11 counts of aiding and abetting war crimes and crimes against humanity. Taylor subsequently appealed, but the court's last major act was to uphold his 50-year sentence in 2013, and he remains behind bars in the UK as part of a UN-brokered agreement.

Members of civil society who watched proceedings from behind a glass screen and in the villages were generally pleased that 'big men' are pursued, and that the international community cared enough to go after them.

Center, saw the APC consolidate their position as Sierra Leone's dominant political party, with Koroma defeating Maada Bio outright in the first round of voting, 59% to 37%, and an extraordinary 87% of voters participating. The APC also increased its parliamentary majority, picking up a further eight seats, mostly at the expense of Charles Margai's People's Movement for Democratic Change (PMDC), which lost all ten of the seats it carried in 2007.

Koroma's cabinet mixes plenty of old faces among the new, and he's been remarkably successful in delivering at least one tangible result – electricity. During his first term, Koroma promised 'light' to a capital city that, until recently, ran on nothing but gas-guzzling private generators, when it had power at all. By Christmas 2007, a new city generator and plenty of diesel churned out power to parts of the city most of the time. A hydro-electric dam in the north of the country at Bumbuna, 30 years in the making, finally came online in late 2009, with the capacity to deliver 50MW, thereby reducing the need for expensive short-term fuel delivery; in 2017, new or rehabilitated micro-hydro-electric dams were scheduled to come online at Charlotte, Bankasoka and Makali, each providing 2.2MW, and plans are in the works for a new 10MW dam near Moyamba. Koroma pledged to run the country like a business, drawing up 'contracts' with all of his ministers, but many Sierra Leoneans complain that his promised crackdown on graft has not been as thorough or as severe as they would have hoped. That impression was driven home in late 2011, when the Arabic news channel Al-Jazeera revealed that Koroma's vice president, Sam Sumana, had accepted a bribe to allow a particular timber concession to go ahead. His eventual sacking didn't take place until March 2015, and for unrelated reasons at that; he was replaced by APC stalwart Victor Bockarie Foh.

Koroma has also been working to stimulate foreign investment in agriculture, fisheries, mining and tourism, and though his administration has made good progress on this front, some of it has proven frustratingly fleeting. A slew of new deals have flowed through the pipeline during his decade in office, but many of these big-budget contracts have failed to deliver as promised: the formerly London-listed African Minerals promised to pour US$1.4 billion into iron ore mining but declared bankruptcy in the face of low ore prices in March 2015; London Mining and its US$2 billion investment suffered the same fate in October 2014; Hainan Natural Rubber Industry Group, a Chinese company, is still in the game with a US$1.2 billion investment in rubber and rice plantations; India's Siva Group has an ongoing US$1.2 billion investment in oil palm plantations; and the Swiss firm Addax Bioenergy sold its US$340 million investment in sugarcane plantations for ethanol production to Sunbird Bioenergy in 2016. The shifting fortunes of these companies have made an outsized impact on the country's economy. Sierra Leone's GDP, which averaged steady but unremarkable single-digit growth rates for much of the 2000s, expanded by more than 20% in 2013, largely due to iron ore production, but a cruel double whammy of unexpectedly low commodity prices and the Ebola crisis sent the economy into a tailspin, recording a 20% contraction in 2015.

Koroma has thrown his weight behind big, vote-winning infrastructure projects, which was a major factor in his decisive victory in the 2012 elections. Unsatisfied with the steady but still-insufficient trickle of electricity from the new dam at Bumbuna, the administration kicked off an even more ambitious hydro-power project to build a second major dam 30km away at Yiben. Dubbed Bumbuna II, it's been almost as delay-plagued as its namesake, but it will quadruple the country's electricity supply once it's finally complete. Hang on to your generator for now though – it's not scheduled to come online until 2021 at the earliest.

More immediately, Koroma has also started an impressive spurt of road building, in Freetown and around the country. The highway leading off the Peninsula is being expanded into a dual carriageway all the way to the main junction at Masiaka, and roads to Bo, Kabala, Koidu, Kambia and elsewhere in the country have all been resurfaced since he took office, along with the mountain road to Freetown and the nearly complete beachside route via River Number Two. Meanwhile, the streets of Freetown, Makeni, Kabala, Lunsar, Port Loko, Kambia and other cities upcountry are getting serious facelifts, with road-building crews installing gutters and pavements and laying asphalt – in many places, for the first time.

It is all part of Koroma's Agenda for Change, a 179-page manifesto that outlines his vision for the country. When he first took office in 2007, he promised to turn the country around within an ambitious three years; a decade later, it wasn't clear that fuzzy objective had been achieved, but there was little doubt that the country was moving, if slowly, in the right direction. Then came Ebola.

EBOLA The cruel reversal of fortune that would soon bring life to a standstill in the Mano River countries began just over the border in Guinea's Nzérékoré Region, with the December 2013 death of two-year-old Emile Ouamouno in the pinprick village of Meliandou, less than 25km from the border. While it's now generally believed that Emile contracted the disease from contact with free-tailed bats (*Mops condylurus*) in the village, Ebola wasn't previously thought to be endemic to the region, and as such it would take several months of mysterious deaths, most thought to be Lassa fever or cholera, before the alarm was raised that something unusual was going on.

The first cases of Ebola arrived in Sierra Leone in May 2014, but the funeral of a traditional healer who claimed to have a cure for the disease saw it spread explosively across the country. Traditional funerary rites in the region call for the washing, touching and holding of the deceased – precisely the moment at which the body is most contagious – and this one funeral alone is now thought to have led to as many as 365 Ebola-related deaths.

Despite closing its borders with Guinea and Liberia, Sierra Leone could not control the spread of the virus. The summer months saw the number of cases begin to spiral out of control and the health service teetered on the brink of collapse, with critical shortages of beds, ambulances, protective gear and trained staff – more than 40 doctors died during the epidemic, nearly 30% of only 136 in the country before Ebola arrived.

On 6 August, President Koroma declared a nationwide state of emergency, introducing a two-year prison sentence for anyone found hiding an infected person and enforcing strict quarantines on the hardest-hit districts. Cinemas, shops and markets were all shuttered and a curfew was imposed; children wouldn't get back to their classrooms until April 2015. The World Health Organisation (WHO) finally declared the outbreak to be a Public Health Emergency of International Concern in August, but it wasn't until November that international aid began to arrive, by which time the situation had become desperate with 20 deaths per day, unclaimed bodies on the streets and public riots. However, in January 2015 the rate of transmission began to slow, thanks to the creation of new medical centres and the heroic efforts of local and international doctors and aid workers. It took until 7 November, 42 days (two incubation cycles) after the last reported case, for Sierra Leone to be declared Ebola-free – a night of jubilation and remembrance across the country. A minor re-emergence in January meant the 42-day clock had to be run out once more, but the outbreak finally ended on 17 March 2016.

The final WHO reports on the outbreak indicate 28,616 confirmed, probable and suspected cases in the three countries, with 11,310 deaths. Of these cases, 14,124 occurred in Sierra Leone, along with 3,956 deaths.

Today, Ebola is, for most Sierra Leoneans, a distressing but fading memory, and though its legacy seems unlikely to prove as crippling or long-lasting as that of the war, it's nonetheless left deep and irreparable scars for many, not least on the more than 12,000 orphans who've lost their primary caregiver (see the full report at w street-child.co.uk/ebola-orphan-report). Although the 'Ebola is real', 'ambulances are safe', and 'na mi go don Ebola' (Ebola stops with me) billboards have long since faded, many have been replaced with ones warning off yet another pernicious scourge – stigma. These signs, many featuring President Koroma posing with survivors, brandish slogans like 'do not push away children Ebola survivors', reflecting the ongoing problems faced by survivors attempting to reintegrate in to society. Survivors' unions have even been formed, such as Fatou Wourie's Survivor Dream Project (see box, pages 40–1).

PICKING UP THE PIECES Thus, after Ebola brought the country to its knees for some 18 months, Salone's people and politicians have spent the months since doing their best to get back on the path they were diverted from in 2014. The -20.6% economic contraction posted in 2015 is poised to give way to an encouraging 5.4% growth rate for 2017, and another set of presidential and parliamentary elections

Women were worst affected by the West African Ebola epidemic, and yet in the aftermath of the crisis, there was no gender-based strategy for female survivors. Fatou Wurie decided to change that. This article first appeared on Pulse Ghana.

When Ebola struck Sierra Leone, Magdalene, a nurse in Freetown, found herself on the front lines, battling a disease spread through contact with infected bodily fluids. When colleagues fled, Magdalene stayed. And then she contracted the disease herself. But Magdalene did what almost 4,000 of her country people did not: she survived Ebola. President Koroma honoured Magdalene for her efforts during the crisis, but the nurse, who has returned to work at Freetown's Connaught Hospital, is among those who still face stigma, rejection and segregation as a result of their survivor status.

The outbreak of Ebola in West Africa in 2014 was the first in the region, and the worst in history. There were more than 15,000 laboratory-confirmed cases, and more than 11,000 deaths. The majority of the dead were women: in Sierra Leone, that figure was reportedly 59%, while in neighbouring Liberia, women comprised 75% of the death toll.

Fatou Wurie was working as a gender consultant and communications specialist for the United Nations Mission for Ebola Emergency Response when it became clear that despite the number of women affected, the Sierra Leonean government and international NGOs grappling with the crisis were ignoring their needs. As primary caretakers of the young, elderly and ill, performers of traditional rites for the dead, as well as occupying the majority of nursing positions, women were perhaps doomed to fare worst in the Ebola crisis. Wurie had seen firsthand the crisis' catastrophic effect on mothers-to-be. An article published in *The Lancet* in March 2015 said: 'without emergency maternity care or family planning services available and immunisation programmes halted, the Ebola crisis could quickly erase the gains Sierra Leone, Liberia, and Guinea had made in maternal healthcare.' The countries, the article stated, were already 'among the worst places to be a mother'.

Six months into the crisis, Wurie's friends and colleagues in the diaspora requested her help. Where public hospitals were overrun or shutting down, Wurie referred the women to private hospitals, paying for their care.

As the crisis wore on, groups of survivors began attending conferences held at fancy hotels, where they received a free meal, a new mattress and a few hundred dollars. Then, they were sent back into the world. The prevalence of illiteracy in the population, traditional mindsets and ill-founded rumours about how Ebola spread meant communities were reluctant to accept survivors back. Wurie says faces at these conferences soon became familiar; the women did not know where else to turn for support.

Her assessment of the situation was stark. 'As a UN response, we failed Sierra Leonean women.' Wurie attributed the failure to the 'scattered' approach to reintegration, resulting from poor data collection. Two years on from the crisis' inception, the numbers of men, women, children and health workers who died in the epidemic had not been made public.

Wurie gathered 20 of these survivors – the familiar faces – who ranged in age from 14 to 52. They were students, orphans, traders, widows, nurses, heroes. Together, they became sisters in the Survivor Dream Project (**w** *thesdp.info*), an organisation Wurie founded in the wake of the epidemic – the only one to have provided 'holistic, consistent psycho-social and entrepreneurial survivor reintegration in the country'.

The women, from both rural and urban communities in the Western Area, began meeting in safe spaces established to discuss their experiences. Soon, a picture of their lives as Ebola survivors emerged. One of the girls had failed the exams she was required to pass to stay in her prestigious government school. She'd taken the test a month after being cleared of the disease. Another woman's husband had been a health worker during the crisis and unknowingly contracted the virus. The woman survived the disease that killed her husband, but was left homeless, ostracised by a community that threatens to kill her if she returned. Another survivor, a healthcare worker, became suicidal after a patient refused her touch. She had returned to work four days after discharge from an Ebola Treatment Unit.

Wurie says despite efforts of community groups, government and international NGOs, the stigma surrounding survivors was inevitable. 'The term itself is complicated', she says. 'You've gone through something horrible, yes you've survived, but what does that really mean? For me, the project is being able to look at what surviving looks like, and dream about superseding that.' One of the first meetings involved a makeover and photo shoot. The explanation given was simple. 'Today we're going to remind you that you're beautiful', Wurie told the survivors.

'Your pictures are going to show you at your best, because you have been dealing at your lowest for a long time. It was almost like, you're not allowed to be happy again because you're diseased, you're othered, you don't deserve this.' Wurie says before the makeover that, some of the women hadn't been touched in more than a year. 'Some people didn't even know what lipstick was anymore because they didn't feel the need to be beautiful.'

Since then, Wurie and her team have been brokering tension in schools, workplaces and communities where survivors have been made to feel unwelcome to return. In addition to sharing their stories with each other, Wurie encouraged the women to share them with the world. A collection of photos, curated by the survivors, was exhibited at a swanky Freetown restaurant in May 2016. Attendees, who included the WHO country director for Sierra Leone, were asked to wear white, symbolising a blank slate.

Still, unease lingered. Among the expatriates and Sierra Leoneans in attendance, some had never seen an Ebola survivor. 'Can you imagine?' Wurie says. 'They had lived in Sierra Leone throughout the epidemic and had never seen a survivor. And they would come to me and say, "can I sit near them?" and I'm like, "Are you kidding me?"'

The women in the programme continue to receive ongoing support. Traders graduating from business training will be given access to a seed fund. The programme's school-age girls will be supported until college.

Since the project's founding, Wurie has expanded its ambit to include both men and women who've survived traumatic events. Its mandate remains: giving them the opportunity to dream.

Follow the Survivor Dream Project on w *thesdp.info and* f *@TheSDP.*

is scheduled for March 2018. President Koroma is widely expected to step down as it will be the end of his second term, but as of October 2017 it remained unclear who will be representing either the APC or SLPP in the upcoming polls. There have also been persistent – though now supposedly quashed – rumours of a 'more time' campaign in the APC seeking to extend or renew Koroma's term, on the unconventional basis that the months lost to Ebola was time the president could have been furthering his development agenda for the country, and he should be given a chance to do so. It doesn't seem to have any legs, but it's spawned a snappy new way to order beer at any rate (page 105).

Another cruel twist of fate hit Sierra Leone just as this book was going to print. After days of intense rainfall, a side of the 760m Sugar Loaf Mountain calved in the early morning hours of 14 August 2017, sending uncountable tons of earth on to the village of Regent below, crushing an entire neighbourhood. Given the rampant development and deforestation on hillsides in the area, the disaster is unfortunately surprising only in scale. The destruction of the peninsula forest and its repercussions have been known for years, but intense population pressures, limited available land and little-to-no building code enforcement means planning guidelines are routinely ignored. The mudslide buried colonnaded mansions as much as it did corrugated zinc shacks.

As of September 2017, more than 500 bodies had been unearthed, but another 600 people remained missing, many of them presumably dead, making for a heartbreaking death toll of over 1,000 souls lost in a single day. Morgues in Freetown were overwhelmed and the Ebola cemetery in Waterloo was once again pressed in to service for emergency burials. The mudslide also sent a surge of earth and debris barrelling along Lumley Creek in to the densely populated neighbourhoods of Kamayama and Kaningo below. Bodies were still being recovered at the time of writing; some 20 people were pushed out to sea and found washed up as far away as Conakry.

GOVERNMENT AND POLITICS

Sierra Leone lives its politics. Musicians pen overnight hits about corrupt practices, cab drivers insult their customers over their ideologies, and boys in ghettoes, light-headed on palm wine, wear their council tax receipts dangling from string around their necks with pride.

They might like to talk a good game; far fewer actually like to get involved: 'Most of the enlightened people don't want to get involved because politics is seen as a dangerous game, a dirty game,' said one businessman and former high-ranking civil servant.

Regional loyalties have dominated since the creation of the Northern, Southern and Eastern provinces in 1946, and political parties in Sierra Leone have rarely had a national agenda. One survey undertaken by PhD student Oscar Mateos found that youth in Freetown more readily identified themselves via their football team than as Sierra Leoneans.

The bloated, 10,500-strong army is due to 'downsize', while a Human Rights Commission established at the end of 2006 is charged with implementing the recommendations of the Truth and Reconciliation Commission on issues such as reparations and women's and children's rights. A review of the 1991 constitution also made various recommendations, including additions on citizenship, human rights, a 44-member Senate (in addition to the elected House of Representatives), and the establishment of an Extractive Industries Transparency Commission to ensure due process and transparency in mining payments. Although it stopped short of abolishing the death penalty, it promised to review it every two years.

WOMEN The constitutional review also stopped short of recommending, unlike Liberia, Rwanda and Uganda, a 30% quota for women in parliament and decision-making bodies – against the wishes of various women's groups. Following elections in 2012, there were only 15 women in parliament, four female cabinet ministers and 88 female local councillors (of 435). Nevertheless, the government has begun to take steps to heed calls to bolster the position of women in Sierra Leone, partly as a result of donor emphasis on improving the lot of women and boosting the justice sector in general. In June 2007, three significant bills were passed: the Domestic Violence Act, which criminalises violence in the family; the Registration of Customary Marriage and Divorce Act, which gives women more rights in marriage; and the Devolution of Estates Act, which gives women greater access to property. The Child Rights Act also makes marriage illegal for under-18s.

But while laws mark a step forward, sustained and successful implementation will be key. Many think little is changing and campaigners believe women's lack of political representation reflects widespread and deeply engrained social discrimination. 'Attitudes are constantly surprising,' says Lotta Teale, Legal Programme Officer at International Rescue Committee, an NGO working in the sector. 'Some people, even at the forefront of the women's activist movement, want to make it a criminal offence to wear a short skirt, while rape of non-virgins is felt by many to be a contradiction in terms.'

Women and girls face constant attacks on their welfare and safety, making survival a challenge on a daily basis. Husbands beat wives as a matter of course – indeed many men say they beat their wives to prove they love them, and a 2005 UNICEF report found that 73.4% of women felt their partners were justified in beating them if they went out without telling them. Many women in customary marriages – often married as young girls – cannot afford to return the 'bride price' to allow them to leave their husband, and if they do, it is thought to curse their children. Women whose husbands die must marry the husbands' brothers if they are to maintain a link to the marital property. Sexual and physical abuse is generally blamed on the victim and carries such shame it tends to go unreported. Only 38% of women are literate compared with 59% of men, further increasing their reliance on them. There are still some signs of encouragement, however, and women in civil society are increasingly making their voices heard, with prominent members often going on to become prominent politicians. Former health and foreign minister Zainab Bangura, for example, was co-founder of a local NGO, the Campaign for Good Governance, and Rugiatu Turay, now Deputy Minister for Social Affairs, Gender and Children, founded the anti-FGM Amazonian Initiative Movement (AIM; see box, page 293).

ECONOMY

Potential is a bittersweet word in Sierra Leone. The country has it in spades – vast mineral resources, verdant land, stunning beaches, fertile seas. But so many barriers exist that at times realising that potential seems a futile hope.

More than 50% of people don't even make US$1.90 a day. One in 17 mothers dies as a result of childbirth, and nearly one in five children will never reach the age of five. The last two figures are the highest of any country in the world.

Languishing in the bottom 5% of the UN's ranking of 187 countries according to their human development, the average gross domestic product (GDP) per person is US$693. Even if you take into account how much further dollars go in Sierra Leone, the figure adjusted for 'purchasing power parity' is US$1,700. At roughly US$4.29 billion, the economy is about 617 times smaller than that of the UK.

Not even that figure is all its own doing – donors continue to contribute about a third of the government's budget every year.

DONOR MONEY Fifteen years after the end of the civil war, Sierra Leone still remains highly aid-dependent. About half of the country's economic growth in the late 2000s was driven by donor money, according to the ex-governor of the Central Bank; by 2014 foreign funds (in the form of grants and loans) accounted for 41% of expenditure, and this rose to 51% in 2015, due in part to crisis responses to the Ebola epidemic.

According to figures from the OECD, official development financing stood at US$1.09 billion in 2016, the most recent year for which numbers are available, and among donor countries the UK remains the biggest single foreign supporter of Sierra Leone; its 2014–15 average was more than twice the next closest donor, at US$365.8m. It was followed by the World Bank and IMF, each providing about US$100 million. The EU spent US$76 million and the US US$64 million. As the fleets of white 4x4s attest, there are also still plenty of international non-governmental organisations working on the ground, including Oxfam, Save the Children, Médecins Sans Frontières and ActionAid.

While the country is perhaps surprisingly stable just over a decade after the war, despite all this money and activity little sustained recovery or development has taken place: progress, in the words of one development specialist, has been 'excruciatingly slow'. According to the World Bank, the poverty headcount is estimated to have fallen by as much as 6% between 2004 and 2007 owing to a sustained high growth rate. However, attempts to develop tourism potential, properly manage and exploit the minerals and fisheries sector, and encourage better farming techniques and improvements in rural livelihoods are in their infancy.

The Ebola crisis was not only a humanitarian challenge; its effects on longer-term development were felt in the deaths of a large proportion of healthcare professionals and in the thousands of missed days of school for Sierra Leone's children. A drop in iron prices further reduced economic output in 2015–16, leading to a reconfiguration of Sierra Leone's development priorities in conjunction with donors to try and ensure both a recovery from the immediate shocks and concrete progress for the future.

Health and education services remain dysfunctional, and Sierra Leone failed to meet the Millennium Development Goals (MDGs), the lofty set of UN-designed measures to halve poverty between 1990 and 2015. These have been replaced by the Sustainable Development Goals (SDGs) through to 2030, although it is too early to judge how realistic achieving them will be.

On the macroeconomic front, some hard-won progress has been made. In 2006, the government secured substantial debt relief from the World Bank and other creditors; its debts were slashed from US$1.6 billion to US$300 million, saving the country about US$35 million in annual repayments. An IMF report in 2017 still judged Sierra Leone at 'moderate' risk of debt distress.

Debilitating food and fuel price hikes in 2007, 2008 and again in 2011 nudged inflation to more than 17%, when it had stood at single digits in the early 2000s.

It had retreated to a fairly steady year-on-year rate of around 10% between 2013 and 2016, before spiking to 20% at the start of 2017. However, this figure is nothing compared with a 1980s level of 50%, rising to 115% at the start of the war in 1991.

SECTORS Today's fastest-growing sectors are mining and agribusiness, but the bulwark remains small-scale agriculture, fisheries and forestry, which together make up nearly half the economy and support the livelihoods of 75% of the population. Wholesale and retail trade represents almost 10%, while transport, storage and communications manage 7.6%. Manufacturing registers a paltry 2% contribution.

The mining industry has recovered strongly since the war, and now accounts for more than 90% of exports, and this may even increase as new deposits come online in the years ahead.

Almost half the government's budget comes from the Goods and Services Tax (18%) and from international donors (c30%). Once-encouraging progress towards budgetary independence was largely lost in 2015, thanks to depressed commodity prices and the Ebola crisis. Mining-related royalties and licences make up 10% of revenues, while personal income tax contributes 14% and corporate income tax another 6%. Loud-hailers mounted on pick-up trucks in the streets might encourage folk to pay their taxes, but few do; the majority of employment is still informal, especially among women and young people.

The main challenges to economic growth include limited energy and transport infrastructure, a poorly skilled and trained labour force, and a regulatory environment for business and the private sector that ranks among the worst in the world. According to the World Bank's 2016 index for ease of doing business, Sierra Leone ranks 148th out of 190 countries – not stellar, but at least an improvement from the 168th ranking it earned in 2006.

Extractive industries Diamonds, gold, rutile, iron ore, zircon, uranium, top-notch timber, offshore oil and more. You name it, Sierra Leone might just have it. Not that the country has managed to profit from its riches in the past.

As early as 1499, Sierra Leone was luring visitors with its riches: 'And in this country there is **gold**, and it is the finest gold in all the land of Guynee,' said Portuguese traveller Alvaro Velho, who spent eight years in West Africa. Today experts suspect much of Sierra Leone's gold – which tends to occur with great reliability in the country's diamond areas – is smuggled out of the country as dust into neighbouring Guinea. In time, legitimate exports are likely to increase; industrial-scale gold mining remains largely exploratory, but several international mining concerns have been issued development licences, and there are plans for an underground (as opposed to an open pit) mine at Nimini in the Kono district.

In the 1920s came discoveries of platinum – most of which has now been mined from the Peninsula – chromium and iron ore, and a decade later **diamonds** first sparkled. In 1931, minerals made up less than 5% of exports; by 1961 this had grown to 87%.

Diamonds have gone on to cause many more problems than they have solved. While resumption of production after the war was a fillip for the economy, the industry provides only US$3–4 million a year in revenues to the government. Smuggling is still a problem, as dealers tend not to declare the larger, exponentially more valuable stones – with a few notable exceptions (page 280). Nevertheless, efforts to improve the management of the trade have met with some success, and official exports have risen substantially since the war, from US$26 million in 2001 to US$159 million in 2016, although they fell off in 2015 thanks to the Ebola crisis. When revenues began to pick back up after the war, the government raised its tax on diamonds valued at more than half a million dollars from 6.5% to 15%, in an effort to recoup some more fiscal benefit.

The UN-approved Kimberley Certification Scheme for exporting diamonds has led to a dramatic increase in legal exports the world over. It's not perfect: countries with no diamond resources are permitted to be members, and there are still plenty of ways of hiding a diamond, or several; there's also no way to trace where a cut diamond came from. Sierra Leone has also set export duties on stones mined by the country's 200,000–300,000 artisanal miners at just 3%, in the hope of dissuading smuggling. Small-scale mechanised mining companies, which use bulldozers and water pumps to sort through diamond-rich earth, must pay a 6% royalty. Some complain these low taxes mean the country doesn't see enough benefit from what lies beneath its soil. Some geologists estimate that diamonds have a limited future in the country, however, and that due to massive over-mining during the war some fields will be exhausted in the next 20 to 25 years. At one point, the country also sat on one of the largest reserves of **rutile** in the world (page 230), and mining the titanium ore provides hundreds of jobs in the south. Nearby, another mine exports a million tonnes of **bauxite** a year.

The country also has vast reserves of **iron ore**, the primary ingredient in steel production. In the 1950s, 40% of Britain's iron came from the Marampa Mines at Lunsar, but production tapered off in the 1970s and stopped completely in the run-up to the war. Recent investments mean the mineral is once again a major part of Sierra Leone's economy, though a collapse in global prices means that iron ore hasn't proven quite the economic lifebuoy it was expected to be in the early 2010s.

The amount of investment in the sector has been impressive, however – one company alone, African Minerals, built a 200km railway and refurbished the deepwater port at Pepel as part of its plans to exploit a 13-billion-tonne deposit – one of the biggest proven reserves in the world – at Tonkolili, east of Makeni. When the first exports left the port at Pepel in 2011, iron ore was selling at US$171 per tonne – it was US$58 per tonne in 2017. In the face of this price collapse, African Minerals sold off the whole kit and caboodle to the Chinese-owned Shandong Steel after just a few years. London Mining also began exports in 2011 from the Marampa mine site near Lunsar (smaller at 2.2 billion tonnes), and is also now defunct, but in a high-stakes game of musical mines, the former African Minerals CEO, Romanian-born Frank Timis, bought out the collapsing London Mining with his personal corporation, Timis Corp. As of 2016, with Shandong Steel operating the Tonkolili mine, and Timis Corporation at Marampa, the two companies were embroiled in a dispute over rights to use the port at Pepel, with the ex-management of African Minerals now locked out of using the port infrastructure they themselves developed just a few years prior.

All of this investment is making its mark on Sierra Leone's economy. Even if the ore boom hasn't turned out to be as much of a cash cow as was hoped, at the end of 2011, the former African Minerals had already raised US$1.4 billion to invest in Tonkolili, while Sierra Leone's total GDP amounted to just US$2.9 billion that same year. In 2016, GDP stood at a healthier US$3.7 billion, even after 2013's 20% growth (the IMF was at one stage predicting over 50% growth) went crashing right back down – also by 20% – in 2015, thanks largely to unexpectedly low commodity prices and the Ebola crisis.

In 2009, with a host of new mining projects in the pipeline, parliament passed a new Mines and Minerals Act, overhauling legislation that had governed the sector since 1994. The new law substantially strengthens the government's hand in regulation, giving the Director of Mines the right to temporarily halt activity at any site in order 'to prevent danger to life, property, or the environment'. The law also grants the Minister of Mines the right to cancel any agreement if a company is found to be employing child labour, grossly violating health and safety regulations, or lying to the ministry. He can also yank any permits if a company fails to submit any required reports – including an Environmental Impact Assessment (EIA).

London Mining's former operations near Lunsar were suspended briefly in November 2010 when the government discovered that the company had failed to submit an EIA for its operation. The company hastily promised to get its documents in order, and operations were allowed to restart after just a one-day halt. But the experience showed, at least for now, that the government is not afraid to flex its regulatory muscle.

With jungle and mangrove carpeting the land, European traders were quickly attracted to **timber** and exports started back in 1816, taking off once the slave trade was banned in 1807. By 1826, 80,560 tons of tropical wood had been loaded up from Rokel and Port Loko, floated down in rafts to Tombo on the Peninsula, and two other depots at Tasso and Bunce Island, and exported for shipbuilding and cabinet-making. After elections in 2007, the new government banned all timber exports pending a review, following 'indiscriminate destruction' by unlicensed loggers. Again, much timber was smuggled out via Guinea, deals were agreed locally with paramount chiefs without heed to central government and there was widespread fear that Chinese companies were snaffling huge amounts of rosewood and more for export.

Sierra Leone may also soon join the swelling ranks of West African **oil** exporters: Texas-based company Anadarko struck oil during two separate deepwater explorations off the country's southern coast in 2010. Two years later, both Anadarko and London-listed African Petroleum announced that they had discovered oilfields offshore, though production still remained a way off at the time of writing in 2017.

Agriculture Minerals might get most of the press, but agriculture is the mainstay of the economy. More than 60% of the workforce is involved in farming, forestry and fishing, and in 2016, agriculture accounted for 71% of the country's economy.

'The future of the country is in agriculture, because even minerals will pass away,' said the president, who has made agribusiness, along with fisheries, tourism and mining, one of his key sectors. But Sierra Leone still has a long way to go, with most Sierra Leoneans living on small, scattered farms, following a scheme of bush-fallow rotation, slash-and-burn field preparation, and limited use of fertiliser. The war had a huge impact on agriculture, as displacement left swathes of land uncultivated. Many never returned to their villages to take up farming again. Even after a post-war drive to increase agricultural productivity, Sierra Leone, with its extremely fertile soils, is home to a population where 50% of households were considered food insecure in 2016. To reduce these numbers, the scope of activities needs to widen into agro-processing; and fisheries and production of major agricultural commodities needs to return to pre-war levels.

1

THE PROMISE OF MANGO JUICE

At a shiny new factory in Newton, about 50km outside of Freetown, workers in bright yellow shirts busy themselves sorting fruit and turning dials. Thick clouds of steam rise from the chugging machinery in front of them, lacing the air with the sweet, tropical scent of fresh-picked mangoes.

Welcome to the home of Africa Felix Juice (AFJ), a little company that's playing an important role in Sierra Leone's economy. The workers here are busy making mango juice concentrate, the country's first significant value-added export since the civil war broke out in 1991.

Sierra Leone may have abundant minerals, fertile soil and fish-heavy seas, but many businesses still hesitate to set up shop in-country, thanks to bad roads, low power supply and a reputation for corruption and violence. So for the past 25 years, Sierra Leone has exported only raw materials, all of which are processed in other countries.

But then Africa Felix Juice came along, with Claudio Scotto, an Italian, at the helm. Scotto got a helping hand from First Step, a commercial subsidiary of the US-based NGO World Hope International. First Step bought a 20ha plot in Newton and lobbied parliament to turn it into a special economic zone (SEZ) where companies could operate tax free, and where critical infrastructure like roads and sewage systems would be taken care of. The company, which began production in May 2011, was the first business to set up shop inside the SEZ.

Africa Felix Juice collects its mangoes from co-operatives set up among villages north and east of Makeni, where the fruit litters the ground from February to April, the height of the dry season. AFJ employees travel among the villages to collect the mangoes, paying the fruit pickers as much as eight times what they would earn selling the same product at the local markets.

The resulting purée is shipped to industrial buyers in Europe. You can't find the stuff anywhere in Freetown unfortunately – Africa Felix Juice doesn't do any bottling – but at least the rest of the world finally has the chance to taste the country's sweetest fruit.

'I think it is quite a great achievement,' Sierra Leone's president, Ernest Koroma, said as he walked out of the mango juice factory after a tour on the day of its launch. 'It will have knock-on effects for the whole economy.'

Find out more about Africa Felix Juice at **w** www.africafelix.com.

Agricultural exports in 2010 amounted to nearly US$31.4 million, up from US$7.5 million in 2001, and consisted of cocoa, coffee, palm kernels, palm oil, tapioca of cassava, kola nuts, and sugar. **Rice**, grown by 80% of farmers, is the staple crop, along with plenty of cassava, millet and yams. Sweet potato, potato, maize, black beans, plantain and sugar beet are also grown, as well as groundnuts, coconuts, tomatoes and peppers. Fruits include the sweetest pineapples, mangoes, star fruit, papaya and bananas. Planting usually takes place just before the rains, from April to June, while harvesting usually takes place after September, when the rains stop. It's all done by women, sometimes aided by their children in the fields.

Upon taking office in 2007, President Koroma said he wanted the country to be rice sufficient within three years, an ambitious goal given that the average Sierra Leonean eats more than 100kg of the stuff every year – one of the highest consumption rates in sub-Saharan Africa. The president's deadline was not met, but his goal remains.

Until the diamond rush in 1952, Sierra Leone was a net rice exporter. It has been an importer ever since, after overeager farmers downed tools in the frenzied dream of quick and easy wealth. One bright spot is The Rokupr Rice Research Institute, located in the Northern Province, which breeds high-yielding varieties for seed. Another is Sierra Leonean scientist Monty Jones, who helped develop a new form of rice, known as Nerica – New Rice for Africa – which increases yields by up to 50% by combining the hardiness of traditional African strains with the productivity of Asian varieties. He was voted one of *Time* magazine's most influential people in 2007 for his efforts.

PEOPLE

For such a small country Sierra Leone has rich ethnic diversity, with at least 16 different groups recognised. While there are strong cultural identities and plenty of rivalries between them, which occasionally spill over into resentments, Sierra Leone is not prey to the kinds of ethnic hatreds that have consumed other West African states. Historically, the land has been subjected to waves of invasion from outsiders, but this has usually resulted in assimilation to varying degrees, and a high level of intermarriage (many men take several wives – the richer they are, the more they can afford) and exchange, rather than pogroms and purges. Traditionally tribes have been open to the idea of outsiders: the Loko invited a Mandinka ruler from Kankan to be their chief after he had helped them in war; a Fula ruled Yoni country south of the Rokel; and the Limba have often taken non-Limba chiefs.

KRIOS Also known as Creoles, pre-independence they enjoyed great influence, and were responsible for building one of the most forward-thinking cities in Africa. Their origins grew out of the original groups of black settlers returning to Africa in the late 18th century: a disparate grouping of black poor from Great Britain (who arrived in 1787), freed slaves from Nova Scotia who had fought for the British in the War of Independence and set sail for Africa in 1792, and Maroons from Jamaica who arrived in 1800. Their ranks were swelled by recaptive slaves from Cameroon to Senegal who were repatriated to Freetown by the British navy. The slightly strange, lofty concept of Freetown as both grand social experiment and moral imperative, and the more pragmatic concerns of how the settlement would actually work, played their part in forming Krio consciousness – education, language and religion were prioritised, on top of a sense that Freetown was a promised land.

The Krios adopted English manners, clothes, tastes and institutions. 'The successful do not pine for wives and cattle, they want to be called to the Bar,' wrote Elspeth Huxley in 1954. Top hats, suits on Sundays and balls were all par for the course.

They also saw it as their duty to travel upcountry either to save souls, administrate on behalf of the empire, or simply to make money. Many Krio recaptives went even further afield, returning to the African lands of their childhood to continue their work, such as Bishop Samuel Adjai Crowther, who returned to Nigeria to found an Anglican mission there in 1843.

Education was a cornerstone of Krio society. James Africanus Beale Horton, son of an Ibo recaptive from Gloucester village and William Broughton Davies, son of an Aku recaptive from Wellington, were the first Krios to qualify in Britain as doctors, retiring with the rank of Surgeon-Major after joining the army in 1859. Sub-Saharan Africa's first university, Fourah Bay College, was started originally as a training place for the priesthood and by 1876, an affiliation with Durham University meant that students effectively graduated with UK degrees if they passed.

Yet the Krios were not British stooges, and their education meant that they were vocal and articulate agitators for a greater level of self-autonomy. The 1898 rising, in which groups in the south and north revolted against the imposition of a British hut tax, was a turning point, and the position of the Krios suffered. The British extended educational opportunities in the hinterland, but packed administrative positions with Europeans, not Krios. With the new constitution of 1947, the protectorate was allowed to return twice as many members to the Legislative Council as the colony. Their position in trade and business was also displaced by Lebanese and Syrian immigrants. Today Krios still dominate professions such as the judiciary, finance, medicine and civil service, although as a group they do not have the collective clout to challenge for high political office – they number some 100,000 of a population of seven million. Many adopt African names, and now distinctions between Krio and non-Krio matter much less, although it's not uncommon to meet Krios who have never been upcountry.

MENDE Accounting for about a third of the population, the Mende are the largest of Sierra Leone's groups, perhaps due to their ability to assimilate so well with other communities, such as the Vai, the Krim and the Kisi. 'It will some day play a great part in the future of West Africa,' wrote the historian T J Alldridge in 1901 of Mende society. Since independence, they have tended to enjoy political dominance, with a succession of early patrician Mende leaders establishing the group as a *de facto* ruling class, strengthening their sense of manifest destiny within Sierra Leone but fostering resentment among other groups. Their spiritual homeland is the area around Bo and Kenema.

The Mende are thought to descend from hunters and raiders who forayed south and west from Guinea and Liberia in search of prey. Certainly this is supported by language: much of Mende vocabulary is Mande in origin, although the grammar is different. The pursuit of large game, such as elephants, demanded more permanent settlements, and gradually they became more sedentary. Although not originally coastal, they then migrated from inland areas, often trading their country cloth for salt to take back to their farms and settlements.

Traditionally, society consisted of household units known as *mawe*, often three generations deep and containing various members. Each is headed by a *koloku* whose job it is to keep the household in order. The Mende also traditionally believe in a supreme being, known as *ngewo* or *leve*, a sky-god. Ancestral spirits are a powerful force, as are nature spirits known as *dyinyinga*, which can be beneficial, playful or downright harmful depending on whether they have been paid proper respects, usually in the form of gifts or sacrifices.

The Mende elect their kings – now paramount chiefs – by an electoral college of elders, based on merit rather than divine right. This leads to patrilineal and matrilineal forms of succession, and female paramount chiefs: the legendary Mammy Yoko was the first, in 1906.

In traditional Mende family life, the mother's brother, known as the *kenya*, plays a special role. He helps with the marriage payment, and marriage to the *kenya*'s daughter is favoured – she is known as the 'goat's head' as a reference to the tradition of sharing the head of any animal he kills with his nephew.

Closely associated with today's Sierra Leone People's Party, the first head of state and first president were Mende brothers.

TEMNE Predominantly located in the north of the country, the Temne had some of the earliest contact with Europeans through their control of the Freetown Peninsula.

It was a Temne, King Tom, who ceded the land to the first settlers (and whose English-educated son, also King Tom, would go on to wage war on the fledgling colony). The Temne, who today account for about 30% of the population, are thought to have arrived from Guinea, supported by their own belief that dead chiefs return to Futa Jalon. In the early 16th century, they swept on to the Freetown Peninsula in a fierce campaign led by the general Farama Tami, dislodging the indigenous tribe, the Sherbro (known to the Portuguese as the *Capez*; see page 52). This area they held for the next 300 years in the face of pressure from the Susu to the north and Mende to the south.

Temne warrior kings united large tracts of the Sierra Leone hinterland; elders recall that Farama 'taught people the art of war' and regard the town of Robaga – where he settled in Koya chiefdom by the Rokel River – as a sacred place. All Temne paramount chiefs must make a pilgrimage to this town and his shrine. After Farama Tami, Borea the Great (1630–64), who died fighting for the British against the Dutch, enjoys quasi-mythic status, and Naimbanna the Great (1720–93) doubled the size of the Temne kingdom. Finally, the great chief Bai Bureh led a guerrilla war in 1898 against the British hut tax.

Traditionally kings (*o'bai*) go through a series of training and tests (*kantha*) to prepare them for leadership. While this may improve their mettle, it also makes them sacred – which means, in contrast to the relatively more democratic selection mechanisms of the Mende and Limba, they cannot be deposed and thus rule for life. The Temne are divided into 25 patrilineal clans (*bona*), each represented by an animal totem, and the *poro* tradition is strong, possibly assimilated from the Sherbro. They believe in a sky-god known as *kuru*, or *kurumasaba*, and a lesser deity more closely related to the earth known as *kumba*; then various spirits called *krifi*, good and bad, which require propitiation in order to ensure they are not offended.

The Temne have a saying about the Mende: *a buk ong'an o Meni* – literally 'A snake bites a Mende …': the rest of the proverb, not usually expressed, is equivalent to 'and he makes soup of it'. Half-suspicion, half-compliment at Mende ingenuity, it perfectly expresses the relationship between the two groups. In the opposite direction, the Mende word for the Temne, *Teilaleimui*, translates as 'one who opens the town' – generally understood to mean warrior.

LIMBA The Limba may be the oldest inhabitants of Sierra Leone. Certainly, early Europeans distinguished between the Limba and other groups, whom they believed had arrived in the territory more recently. This is borne out by the lack of a myth in Limba folklore explaining how they came to arrive in the land, and because of significant linguistic differences between Limba and other tongues.

They are based in the north of the country across seven provinces, alongside the Temne, Kuranko and Susu and comprise about 8% of the national population. Towns are usually recognisable by the prefix 'ka-', rather than the more common Temne prefixes 'ma-' or 'ro-'. In another difference, the Limba historically specialised in building from stone – extremely rare among rural peoples in Africa at the start of the 20th century. Another highly prized skill is the Limba expertise in tapping palm trees for *poyo* – fresh palm wine.

The Limba consider themselves to be a mountain people, and have at points in their history found themselves pushed further into the hills, particularly during periods of Susu expansionism. They have also had to fight off incursions from the Fula and Mandingo. Their spiritual home is at Kakoia, and they believe all Limbas return to the mountain above the town, through a 'door' in the rock (influenced perhaps by the door-shaped patch of discolouration on the rockface itself). Belief in spirits known as *krifi* is also strong.

Affairs of state in Limba country tend to be slightly less hierarchical than other cultures; there are fewer intermediaries and courtiers ranged between kings and their people, and any subject can approach his chief directly.

SHERBRO The Sherbro are also thought to be among the country's earliest inhabitants, as they share with the Limba no mythology of how they arrived in the country. Also known as the Bullom – the coastline stretching south of the Freetown Peninsula is sometimes still referred to as the Bullom Coast – they were one of the first groups to have contact with European traders: the 'Buloes' are one of only two tribes (the other was the Temne) mentioned by Portuguese explorer Valentim Fernandes in his description of the West African coast, written between 1506 and 1510 – one of the earliest surviving accounts of Sierra Leone. They were later referred to, along with other coastal people such as the Krim and Vai, simply as *Capez* or *Sapes* (logged extensively by another Portuguese explorer, Alvares d'Almada, in his *Tratado Breve dos Rios de Guiné do Cabo Verde*, published in 1594). The Bullom were subjected to conquest in the mid 16th century by an inland people, known as the Manes, who have not survived. It is thought the name 'Sherbro' came from a Mane leader, Sherabola, who ruled over the Bullom in the late 16th century. Their grip on the coast north of Freetown was also squeezed by the Temne, and waves of Mende migration from the hinterland have impacted on their homogeneity. Nowadays their homeland is around Shenge and Bonthe, as well as the coastal villages of the Peninsula.

Political organisation has similarities to the Mende, and may have influenced it: an elected ruler (*Bei Sherbro*) presides over a system of sub-chiefs and village chiefs, and the ruling class is closely intertwined with the poro.

The Sherbro are considered to be master fishermen, and folklore dwells on the seamanship of their heroes. Women are known for mat-making and pottery, and the quality of Sherbro ivory work was highly esteemed by Portuguese traders, although it died out in the 16th century.

FULA The Fula, distributed throughout West and Central Africa and known elsewhere as Fulani, Fulbe or Peul, might be less nomadic than they once were, but their cattle-rearing and commercial prowess keeps them well stocked with money and pride. As pastoralists, the Fula are generally well travelled, but their presence in Sierra Leone is principally the result of their 18th-century seizure of Futa Jalon, in what is now Guinea. Once Futa Jalon was established as an Islamic state, Fulas themselves went forth in search of grazing land for their cows, and more ready converts for Allah. They are still known as Islamic scholars as well as traders, often flush with economic and educational success.

The frequent contact between the commercially savvy Fula and indigenous, more sedentary people has not been without its problems. As traders, Fulas were associated with slavery – so were the local chiefs and raiding parties they did business with, but with the Fula that stigma still persists. To this day you may hear a Fula tease a Kuranko, Limba or Yalunka friend about being a slave; the comeback seems to be to label the Fula as thieves. Healthy banter, or racism? You can decide if and when you come across it.

In a country as poor as Sierra Leone, where subsistence agriculture is the main occupation and every harvest is a matter of life and death, tensions still exist between farmers and Fula herders. In the 1970s and 1980s, Siaka Stevens tried to drive out the Fula, and on a much smaller scale trouble flared in Kabala in early 2007 when Limba farmers started killing cows that had encroached on their rice and cassava plantations. Human violence quickly followed, and local trade ground to a halt – revenues from the sale of beef provide a steady stream of start-up capital for small Fula businesses, and in protest at the attacks they closed their shops and petrol stations. The Fula and Yalunka also clashed in a brutish war 25 years previously, and as desertification and deforestation encroach further, limiting pasture and arable land, the likelihood of more trouble could increase.

OTHER GROUPS Another Mande-speaking group, the **Kuranko** originally arrived from Guinea. Their number, which makes up about 3% of the population, is centred on Koinadugu and Kono districts, particularly around Kabala and Mount Bintumani.

Kuranko tradition holds that their first ruler in Sierra Leone was Mansa Kama (1650–c1720); the name means 'elephant leader', after his hunting skill. Temne in the area with a strong Kuranko strain call their traditional rule *Masakma* after him. He is credited with leading the first wave of migration from what is now Mali into northeast Sierra Leone, via Guinea. Said to have travelled with an Islamic scholar, charm-maker and teacher (known as an *alfa*), they stopped near the Rokel River and founded Kamadugu, a town named in tribute after him (*dugu* means town). Later, following an incursion along the coast, they returned north to found a new base at Rowala.

The hunting tradition is still strong, with a rigid hierarchy about any bushmeat that is caught: if big game is killed the right thigh goes to the chief and the left goes to the hunter's wife. The Kuranko are also lovers of the *balanji* – a kind of xylophone, with calabashes under the keys to vary the pitch. Every chief has his own call.

The **Susu** in Sierra Leone are small in number and live primarily in Kambia district, with most of the group found across the border in Guinea. Many arrived in Sierra Leone after the fall of their former kingdom Futa Jalon to the Fula in the 18th century. While first welcomed by Limba and Temne kings, they ended up taking power from them; they forced the Limba into more remote and secure mountainous territory to the east; others were allowed to set up at Sendugu opposite Port Loko. While most are Muslim, there is a belief too in animal totems. Known for their skills as blacksmiths and for their metal and leatherwork; musical instruments include the *bolonyi*, a three-stringed instrument played like a cello. The **Yalunka** were initially more welcoming of Islam in Futa Jalon than the Susu, and stayed there much longer, but after becoming increasingly subjugated under a stricter Fula state, they moved south to found a new capital at Falaba, in northeast Sierra Leone, and merged with surrounding Kuranko, Kisi and Limba communities.

Originally pastoral like the Fula, the **Mandingos** (often called Malinkas) of Sierra Leone are now chiefly associated with trade, often because of well-established networks with neighbouring Guinea. Traders were originally drawn to Sierra Leone in search of salt, but in the early part of the 20th century were pivotal in the diamond trade. Travelling as holy men, scholars, preachers and charm-sellers in the 18th and 19th centuries, they played an important role in spreading Islam throughout the country.

Linguistically and ethnically close to the Mende, the **Loko** are thought to be descendants of a Mane raiding party sent south in the 1550s. They settled, and were then separated by a Temne incursion; subsequent culture has been enormously influenced and practically assimilated by the Temne. The settlement of Port Loko derives not from their spiritual homeland but because it became a trading centre for Loko slaves captured by Temne raiders, who were sold to Portuguese traders.

The **Kono** – found mostly in the eastern diamond district of the same name, making up about 5% of the population – are thought to be a Mandingo offshoot, from a group that stayed put in mountainous areas following a wave of southern migration (oral myths suggest that a salt shortage in what is now Guinea prompted a massive exodus towards the coast). They eventually switched from agriculture to pastoralism, and are respected now for their prowess as hunters and athletes. The name derives from those who continued the trek southwards after their compatriots decided to stay put – *kono* means 'those who wait behind' in Vai.

The **Vai** were originally called *gallinas* by the Portuguese traders who first encountered them, due to the trade they did in poultry (*gallina* is Portuguese for chicken). Closely related to the Kono, they are centred on the Pujehun district, around the estuaries of the Mano and Moa rivers, with a population that extends into Liberia. They have created their own 160-character syllabic alphabet, one of a small handful of indigenous African scripts.

Although they have been largely assimilated by the Mende, the **Kisi** remain a distinct ethnic group in the east of the country. *Kisi* is the Kono word for 'blessed', given when the tribe fought alongside them to defeat the Mende, and their warrior Kai Lundu founded the town of Kailahun. The **Krim** are another Mende- and Sherbro-speaking people located southeast of Sherbroland. The Sherbro call them *akima* – 'those who ran away'. The **Gola** are found mostly in Liberia, but a small population has spilled over into the forested areas on the border.

There are also an estimated 4,000 **Lebanese** in the country. They first arrived in the 19th century, on boats heading for South America that stopped off on the way, and then worked as petty traders hawking fake coral beads (they were even known as 'The Corals'), and traded up again and again. By 1966, 73% of all shops were Lebanese-owned. Today they are heavily involved in import–export activity and run a disproportionate number of businesses in the country across the service and hospitality sector. They also control much of the diamond trade. While they have been in Sierra Leone many years, their economic foothold comes from their ability to access finance from outside the country, through established diaspora networks. Many are Muslim (both Sunni and Shia); some are Christian. There are several hundred **Indians** and also a growing clutch of **Chinese**, **Koreans** and **Filipinos**. There are also several thousand **expatriates**. An increasing number of Sierra Leoneans are slowly returning to the country from the diaspora, spurred on in part by a recent law that allows dual nationality. More than 50,000 have returned since the end of the war, and a further 270,000 Sierra Leoneans still live outside the country, sending home remittances worth US$48 million a year.

TRADITIONAL RULERS Sierra Leone's traditional rulers are known as chiefs. Their role is much more than symbolic, covering everything from upholding customs and punishing adultery to extracting labour, collecting taxes, determining land rights, settling disputes and administering customary law – no straightforward task given these laws are unwritten and vary from chiefdom to chiefdom. Each of Sierra Leone's 190 chiefdoms has a single paramount chief at the top, with many more section chiefs (between five and 15 for every chiefdom) and town chiefs as part of the hierarchy below. Twelve paramount chiefs – one from each district in the former protectorate (excluding Freetown and the Western Area, which formed the former colony) – are even elected by elders to sit in parliament, bringing the total in the house to 124. Only in 1896 did the system begin to resemble its current form, when the British invented and bestowed the term 'paramount chief' on those rulers whom they wanted to report directly to their own district commissioner. It was their way of ensuring British administrative tentacles could reach out to the smallest settlement in the cheapest way possible. Apart from their private residences, which are important centres of local homage – as a stranger you should always call on the local village or town chief if you arrive somewhere unannounced – the centre of any paramount chief's power is the *barrie*; a central, shaded area, often close to his or her compound and quarters, where other chiefs, speakers and village headmen congregate to consider local matters and dispense justice. It's a place for *palavers* – an elegant, evocative word to describe not so much outright fights as advice-giving, derived from the Portuguese, *palabra*, meaning talk.

The Mende pioneered the system of election for paramount chiefs – it is not open to all citizens, but rather to members of certain clans who can show a legitimate ancestral claim to past chieftaincy; often this means that in certain areas one or two families tend to alternate. Chiefs can be deposed, but usually only death triggers an election, and often posts can remain unfilled for years if the elders cannot find suitable candidates to stand.

Becoming a paramount chief requires wit, campaign skills, promises, charm and determination. As one paramount chief explained, not only do you have to be eligible, but you have to convince the tribal elders why you should lay hands on the 'staff'; the now-ubiquitous ceremonial symbol of office given out to each chief by Queen Elizabeth II at the country's independence.

Several chiefs-in-waiting live abroad, hoping for the day they can return à la prodigal son. One was a truck driver in the US before he came back to bid for (and win) the honoured post. Another trained in Russia.

'It's a thing of war to be a paramount chief,' commented one, who won election after a fierce battle that went to a second round. 'The person that is popular is always the target. My strategy was to speak to everyone individually so my opposition underrated me.'

At worst, traditional rule can abuse and exclude, serving only the interests of a tiny elite. Legal judgements can be arbitrary or deliberately unfair; polygamy, regarded as the right of 'big men', can become a form of sexual control, along with customary forced marriages at ages of 15 and below; and while tax, which the paramount chiefs are supposed to collect for the government, is usually set at about Le10,000 a year per person, it's more easily talked about than collected: 'Trying to take money from the paramount chiefs is like trying to uproot a tooth from a live snake,' one local commentator told the World Bank. At its best, however, the system can keep the peace, provide a forum for local decision-making and, in an environment where government-run courts and magistrates are few and far between and tainted in many people's eyes, it can also try to arrive at a decent administration of justice.

Since 2004, after a long hiatus of more than 30 years, there has also been a somewhat confused parallel system of local government, with councillors and wards. An attempt is underway to work out how elected councillors, whose job it is also to collect taxes and administer local social services, can manage to work alongside a tier of traditional rulers who want their own income from revenues, and to hold sway over the administration of local justice. The government's drive towards devolution and local government, strongly backed by donors (including the British, who created the paramount chieftancy in the first place), led to only the second set of local elections since 1972, which were held in 394 wards in July 2008, and again – this time right on schedule – in 2012, with another round scheduled to coincide with the March 2018 presidential election. These conflicting mandates have left many paramount chiefs frustrated at the circumscription of their powers, however, particularly in the key areas of domestic law and community taxation.

This curtailment might not be such a bad thing, however. 'The chieftaincy is not as it used to be,' moaned one paramount chief, whose office doubled as the local office of the Sierra Leone People's Party, complete with party political wall-hanging calendar. 'Everything should be free – fish, palm oil, everything. They [the people] used to pay tax or do community labour for us, such as bush fires, or giving their children to the paramount chief as a wife. They give us their daughters and we give them ours. But people now feel they have no right to come and feed the chief. You have to convince people to come to you.'

LANGUAGE

The country has 23 living languages. Of the African languages, two dominate in rural areas: Mende in the south and Temne in the north. Many more are still in use, including Bassa, Bom, Bullom, Fullah, Gola, Kisi, Klao, Kono, Krim, Kuranko, Limba, Loko, Maninka, Sherbro, Susu, Vai and Yalunka. If that seems like a recipe for getting tongue-tied, bear in mind that with its origins as a home for about 60,000 freed slaves from all over Africa, there were as many as 200 languages spoken in Freetown in the 1850s.

Today the official language is English, although regular use is limited to a literate minority, mostly based in the capital Freetown. Krio is the *lingua franca* that connects the majority of the population. Pages 344–5 have beginners' guides, some history and vocabulary for Krio, Mende and Temne. Elsewhere throughout this book are snippets of other languages, referenced near the places you might encounter them. Sierra Leone has a relatively large amount of literature relating to it (and not only its recent history), by both indigenous and foreign writers. This is dealt with on pages 357–62.

EDUCATION

So impressive was learning in the early days of the colony that Freetown won itself a much-respected title as the 'Athens of West Africa'. The 1860 census showed that 22% of the colony was educated, better than in Prussia (16%) and England (13%), a result of the zeal of missionary societies, combined with the enthusiasm shown by Krio families anxious to take advantage of new opportunities for their children. Even today, alongside ethnic grouping and religion, education is among key social markers. The clutch of elite high schools are the meeting grounds for the country's rulers of tomorrow. 'Our school mates became our brothers, and that relationship became more durable than blood or tribe,' said President Ernest Bai Koroma at a visit to his old school in Magburaka.

The intellectual cornerstone of Sierra Leone is Fourah Bay College (renamed the University of Sierra Leone in 1967), the first and only European-style university in West Africa for 100 years, which has since turned out most of the country's notables, including the current president, and the first post-independence president, Milton Margai. Founded in 1827 as the Fourah Bay Institution by the Church Missionary Society, it became a fully fledged university in 1848. The original shell of the building still just about stands in Cline Town, while a new campus sits on the crest of Mount Aureol, with a magnificent view down to Freetown (page 178). Ex-UK prime minister Tony Blair's father lectured on law here during the 1960s. Njala Training College, near Bo, became a university in 1964, and in 1972 became (along with Fourah Bay) part of the newly formed University of Sierra Leone.

The colony could not maintain its early educational success. By the end of the 1890s, the number of schools and schoolchildren was on the wane, despite a growing population. The colony was too poor to enforce universal compulsory education, many rural parents could not afford to send their children to school, and teaching standards started to decline.

At 48%, Sierra Leone's current adult literacy rate is among the lowest in the world, and the gender divide is marked – only 38% of women over 15 can read and write in either English, Mende, Temne or Arabic. Education is officially free for primary school children and approximately 79% attend school. This has resulted in massive enrolment increases, and an active schools' building programme. However, completion rates pale in comparison, and the system lacks teachers. Those who already have jobs are chronically underpaid, and increasingly thinly stretched, particularly in urban areas.

The schooling might be free, but numerous additional costs exist, and act as a disincentive for many parents: these range from legitimate expenses for uniforms, books and stationery; to 'taxes' that in some cases are arbitrarily generated by teachers to generate additional income – these include charges for school cleaners, the marking of pupils' homework, or even the right to sit exams. Stories of teachers selling sweets to children, taking donated textbooks and selling them in markets, and demanding sex for grades are alarmingly common.

Despite progress in primary enrolment, only 25% of children carry on to secondary school, and not all chiefdoms have junior secondary schools to meet the needs of children desiring to continue at that level. In rural areas, only 13% of boys and 9% of girls attend senior secondary school. Again, it was not always like this: in 1906, the government established Bo School – the first notable school upcountry that aimed to prepare the sons of chiefs for Western education (and therefore perhaps well placed to uphold indirect rule). Freetown's Prince of Wales School, opened in 1925, was more progressive, non-denominational, with an accent on scientific education. Nowadays, a dearth of properly qualified science teachers and a lack of technology limit what secondary schools can achieve, and continuing high poverty levels mean that girls are often removed from school early so that they can contribute to income-generating activities within the home. An estimated 48% of girls marry before they are 18 (61% in rural areas), although a new law makes this illegal. Only 17% of girls go to secondary school.

University life and connections remain a hidden but powerful force among the Sierra Leone elite, in a similar way to the arcane societies of many North American institutions. Like a modern-day poro, initiation rituals are intense and details of them are kept secret. Groups are referred to as 'black' and 'white' depending on

1

their ideologies and outlook – which itself is generally kept under wraps. Among the societies, the Future Shock and Radical societies are both considered 'black', and associated with the SLPP, for example; while Status Quo and Gardeners are in the 'white' camp, associated with the APC. Most are little more than talking shops providing politically active students with a ready audience of like-minded firebrands, but that has not always been the case. College students emerged as the only real post-independence opposition during years of one-party APC dominance. Even today, authorities occasionally ban all club activities and 'rusticate' students on the grounds of 'cultish' behaviour, and student strikes remain powerful tools of expression. At its birth, the Gardeners was one of the student groups responsible for organising opposition to the APC government in the late 1970s and 1980s. It was joined by groups such as the Green Book study club, the Juche Idea group, the Socialist Club and the Pan African Union, as the student body became increasing radicalised through the 1980s. A 1984 demonstration that coincided with the APC party congress in Freetown led to rioting on the streets, and the university was closed for eight weeks. Student union President Alie Kabba, before he was expelled in 1985, developed close ties with Libya, through which he came into contact with future RUF leader Foday Sankoh, for whose movement he became the ideological mouthpiece.

For the tiny proportion of Sierra Leoneans who go to university, their affiliations can have a significant bearing on their path up the ladder: the odd cigarette burn on the back of a hand, or a scar on a behind, indicates – should it be seen – membership of a certain society that can land a plum job, or a flat rejection.

RELIGION AND CULTURAL BELIEFS

About 60% of Sierra Leone is Muslim (some surveys suggest as high as 78%), 20–30% Christian, and 5–10% indigenous and other religious beliefs. Traditionally the Muslim population was concentrated in the north of the country, with a more Christian south and coastal belt, but the war brought such population upheaval that Freetown has large populations of both, who live together without any problems. Foreign, often American, Christian missionary organisations are still on the ground, as are numerous examples of mosques built with alms from the Arab world. While Christians sent missionaries to Sierra Leone, and had enormous success, Muslim conquest was sometimes, but not exclusively, the result of *jihad* (holy war). Northern towns such as Falaba opposed Islam for many years, until finally they capitulated to Samori Toure in 1884. For many years Fulas and Yalunkas were fighting: nowadays northern groups such as the Mandingo, Fula, Susu and Yalunka all tend to be exclusively Muslim. Historically, a strong mixing of Islam and traditional beliefs has explained the use of *gris gris* – magical fetishes – by some Islamic teachers.

Homegrown and high profile, evangelical Christianity also has many followers. The most energetic movement is probably the 'Flaming Bible' church, whose Sunday services pack out pews with dancing, singing converts. Freetown is often plastered with posters advertising the most up-to-date religious campaigns. One recent one was labelled 'Operation PUSH' – Pray Until Something Happens.

Alongside the two main religions is a strong flavour of indigenous beliefs, although many more people practise animist rituals than own up to them. Often important family decisions will be accompanied by a visit to a priest or *imam* and also a traditional healer.

Most indigenous beliefs attribute authorship of the universe to a supreme creator (*ndewo* in Mende; *kuku* in Temne) who is not immanent in the world. The world is populated however by a host of other entities, including the *ngafe* (in Mende; *krifi*

HIGH SOCIETY

When the president was inaugurated for his first term at the national stadium in November 2007, it was an occasion for packed stands, brass bands, military salutes, judicial wigs, traditional dance troupes, anthems, speeches, and, of course, magic, devils and secret societies. As the following extract from w *dispatchessierraleone. blogspot.com describes, alongside formal state trappings there were 'fiery demonstrations of traditional beliefs'.*

Among the thousands of people that now filled the field were at least four or five 'devils': spiritual beings associated with Sierra Leone's secret societies, clad in elaborate masks and long raffia skirts to erase any notion of a human being underneath. Each was surrounded by a crowd of society members: chanting, singing, dancing, drumming. From time to time the crowd around one of the devils would crouch to the ground, accompanied by most of the people in the neighbouring stands. A man next to us explained that anyone who didn't fall to the ground when told to do so by the devil would be shot by a 'witch gun', a magical weapon that strikes you down with sorcery without making a sound.

One of the societies was carrying a stretcher, covered with a pile of green palm fronds. We later noticed that below the fronds lay what seemed to be a motionless human body, draped in a white sheet. Blood soaked the sheet near where the person's neck would be, and several of those dancing around were also smeared with blood (or what looked like blood). The man next to us explained that the person under the sheet had been sacrificed in honour of the celebrations, but would come back to life later. 'What if he doesn't come back to life?' we asked. 'Well, then he's dead,' he answered matter-of-factly. Staring in horror, I convinced myself that the body must be either fake or actually alive, just as I've generally chalked up stories of ritual murder to overwrought rumour. Surely the society, even if it had sacrificed someone, wouldn't carry the body so boldly into the stadium, past police and soldiers and tens of thousands of people. Eventually the stretcher disappeared into the crowd. I never saw the body arise.

in Temne) – ancestral spirits that are forces either for good or evil, and often the subject of rituals to honour or appease them. There are also genii, or nature spirits (*dyinganga* in Mende), more unpredictable than ancestral spirits, who may impart important knowledge or fortune if they receive something in return. To stay on the good side of all devils, human likenesses are often placed beneath trees, covered by leaves, surrounded by offerings of bits of cloth, broken pieces of ceramics or glass, brass rings, and beads.

Among all members of society, the belief in magic is strong. Hunters' belief in the power of amulets and charms to ward off harm is a feature of their attire – often they will have a piece of mirror dangling from their clothes, and small pouches in bands wrapped around their arms and necks will contain secret concoctions that have been specially prepared to safeguard them. Many of your most erudite Sierra Leonean friends may think nothing of consulting a witch doctor on a really vitally important matter: politicians might consult a *juju* man in the countdown to elections. Likewise, witch investigators will often arrive in a town where an unexplained death, particularly of a child, has taken place (page 228).

Background Information   **RELIGION AND CULTURAL BELIEFS**

1

SECRET SOCIETIES 'Nothing of very great importance ever takes place in the country until a "Porroh" has been sent down […] in the utmost privacy, and under terrible fetich oaths,' wrote T J Alldridge in *Sherbro and its Hinterland*, in 1901.

Many Sierra Leoneans are initiated into secret societies, which they belong to for the duration of their lives. They not only bind members to each other, but also to their ancestors. Tantalising because they are so readily namedropped, these societies are still shrouded in secrecy to outsiders. The poro is the best known (and most exclusive), drawing membership from the Mende, Temne, Sherbro, Vai and Loko.

These groups are powerful, active social networks, often working outside, and above, more conventional Western-based political or business hierarchies through distinct 'lodges' throughout the country, in a similar way to the operation of masonic lodges in the UK. In the past, societies have been used to mobilise resistance to the British, or for intriguing against outside rivals. Members, gathering places and meeting times are all known: but what actually goes on is forbidden, on pain of death, to be revealed to any non-initiate.

Often senior society members may not themselves be paramount chiefs. The otherworldly authority they claim from their ancestors counterbalances the secular power of the chiefs: indeed, chiefs could be dismissed by the poro, and inter-clan disputes were mediated by them.

Initiation often takes place at adolescence, and lasts for life, and the ordeals that prospective members must pass through provide them with a powerful sense of attachment to their chosen society. The young initiates receive a new name, depending on the order that they enter the bush, and their birth names are no longer used; in some societies they may receive cuts on their neck, back and breasts – these both act as a mark of initiation that may be recognised by other initiates. Females undergo excision (see below).

Members can throughout their lives return to the bush-camps where initiation takes place for further 'levels' of training, thus improving their standing within the society. Apart from the *poro*, societies include the *ragbenie*, *wunde* or, for the Limba, *gbangbani*; the *sande* and *bundu* for women; or the *humoi* for both sexes.

The best introduction to the public face of the societies is on public holidays, when many societies bring out their own 'devils' to dance through the streets and fields. They are heralded by whistles, drums and flutes. Look out for them on Christian festival days such as Boxing Day, New Year's Day, and Easter Monday.

As an example of its efficiency, the poro co-ordinated the Hut Tax Revolt of 1898. The poro war sign was a burnt palm leaf, dispatched to all parts of the country from Bumpe chiefdom, as a sign to the young warriors to prepare for the coming conflict. It also acted as a countdown; local organisers then knew they had to start removing a set number of stones from a pile until no more were left – that was the sign to act.

More recently, many members of secret societies combined to fight the RUF under the banner of the Civil Defence Forces (CDF), although the murky nature of society rituals resurfaced when three of its senior members were put on trial by the UN Special Court for crimes against humanity.

Excision The initiation rites of women's secret societies in Sierra Leone involve the removal of part of the clitoris. Detractors refer to it as female genital mutilation (FGM), while those keener on the practice are likely to call it female circumcision. Locally, it tends to be called 'cutting'. For its adherents, it is considered the central element in a rite of passage that binds communities to each other, and to their ancestors, and governs standards of behaviour throughout later life.

Dutch trader Olfert Dapper wrote of his observations of the poro *in 1688, based on his travels to the estuaries of the Moa and Mano rivers in Gallinas country.*

They say it is a death, a resurrection, and incorporation in the assembly of spirits or souls, with whom the members appear in the bush and help to eat the sacrifice which has been prepared for the spirits. But this is secret from the women and from unknown men, for they pretend that the spirits eat this food, and that they themselves eat nothing; also that those who out of inquisitiveness or presumption want to know too much, or to reveal to others something they have guessed, will be fetched away by the spirits when they get to hear of it and killed.

And they tell amazing things about it. Namely, that they are killed, cooked and completely transformed; that they die out from their old life and ways, and receive a new understanding and knowledge. The [poro] marks are several rows of cuts which go from the neck over both shoulder blades and have the appearance of having been pressed in with nails. Those who have this sign regard themselves as enlightened, and when they are old they may appear in any gathering or political discussion, and also when anyone is condemned to death they may appear and give their verdict.

After the resurrected man is brought among the people and in the village, he may swear by the Belli-Paaro, that is as much as to say by the law or the wrath of God … Whoever goes against this oath incurs a penalty according to the serious of the case. Whoever breaks the prohibition is put in a basket full of thorns, which tear the skin and flesh, and is carried up and down through the village. At the same time also Buasille, that is pepper mixed with water, is poured into his mouth, eyes and ears, indeed over his whole body.

The incidence of excision in Sierra Leone is among the highest in West Africa. It is performed by all indigenous groups, except Christian Krios – some Muslim Krios perform excision as a religious rite. Secret society membership is the driving factor. An estimated 95% of women belong either to the bundu or sande societies, and, while there are no exact figures, the World Health Organization (WHO) estimates that 88% of women in Sierra Leone have been cut.

Desire among young girls to join a secret society tends to be extremely strong. The purpose of these initiation ceremonies is to prepare girls for womanhood by passing on the secrets of social grace, good health, domestic skills, fertility, and successful childbirth, and therefore membership is seen as a lifelong advantage. Often uninformed about the realities of excision, they tend only to see the respect and material gifts showered on the smiling, singing, painted girls newly arrived back in their villages from the bush. They are also aware of the social exclusion and stigmatisation that accompanies the decision not to join a society.

Most people are extremely reluctant to talk about the subject, because of the secrecy that shrouds initiation rites, and growing controversy. There is a belief that they will suffer physical pain or even death if they reveal any details of the bundu. This loyalty means that the pain of the process goes unreported. Not only does the crudely performed operation, often carried out with an unsterilised knife, take place without any anaesthesia, painful after-effects can include haemorrhaging, urinary and pelvic infection, septicaemia and tetanus, lifelong painful intercourse, and prolonged and obstructed childbirth due to scarring and/or infection.

In addition, the women practitioners of excision (called *digba, sowei* or *majo* in local languages) carry a powerful status in their communities, and are both feared and revered. They are considered particularly powerful in magic, often being consulted by paramount chiefs. They also receive payment for their cutting services, so have a deep vested interest in fiercely opposing any changes to the practice.

Publicly most politicians try and ignore the issue, while there is widespread anecdotal evidence that support for cutting, particularly because of the financial burden it imposes on poor families, is an effective and practised form of political leverage. The practice was officially banned for the first time in 2014 in an effort to curtail the spread of Ebola and was punishable with a fine of Le500,000. Though the ban was at least partially respected and has yet to be officially lifted, enforcement dropped off as the crisis came to an end, and it's thought that excision levels have now returned to pre-Ebola levels. Aside from this unenforced injunction, Sierra Leone remains among the last countries in the region without legislation restricting or banning the practice.

Campaign work in this area can also be dangerous (see box, page 293). An early activist, Dr Olayinka Koso-Thomas, received death threats and crowds gathered to express their outrage against her position; in 1996, after a newspaper article discussed the pros and cons of initiation rites the paper's offices were vandalised. Today it's less controversial to find bundu discussed in the press, but the debate remains just as heated. The 2016 death of a 19-year-old bundu initiate in Makeni and subsequent arrest of the practitioners touched off a nationwide debate over the practice. Some reformist agendas suggest cutting should take place in hospitals, others suggest an age limit of 18 (an idea that several chiefdoms have begun to take on board), or that ending excision need not detract from bundu beliefs, traditions and rites.

If there is to be a shift, it will have to come from local women – or fathers – who are prepared to publicly disavow the practice for their own children and engender a shift in opinion, working with secret societies and practitioners to outline the health risks to young girls; and successfully convincing them that trying to limit excision is not an attack per se on traditional culture, or on the initiation process.

CULTURE

MUSIC After the first set of post-war elections in 2002, people everywhere sang Celine Dion's 'New Day' as an anthem of hope for a brighter future. Thankfully, since then Sierra Leone has regained something of its own musical heritage, and the resurgent local industry is lively, opinionated, creative and fun. Whereas 90% of the music played before 2001 was foreign, an estimated 70% of all tunes are now homegrown, mostly produced almost exclusively with keyboards and digital mixers in the absence of reliable recording or performing facilities for live instruments.

The barrage of beats is inescapable, blending varying degrees of hiphop, calypso, dancehall and merengue. On the radio, DJs relentlessly promote up-and-coming street artists; on the dancefloor cult classics are quickly adopted. Established musicians fill the national football stadium in all-night concerts, while in *poda poda* minibus taxis, respectable, besuited men make their way to work to the sounds of hit club tracks such as *Your Pussy Clean*. But it's not all about bump'n'grind: often artists have an eye for social commentary and political satire that would shame the bling-obsessed rap stars of the West.

LET'S FACE THE MUSIC, AND DANCE

When Sierra Leonean Zubairu Wai returned to his home country after three years, he was bowled over by how spirited the local music scene had become, as this extract from w *sierraconnection.com shows.*

I stood there trying to absorb the shock and conceal my excitement at what I was hearing and seeing. At Paddy's Beach Bar (now Quincy's) that fateful Friday evening, the night scene was amazing like usual, but unlike previously when it was dominated by mostly foreign music, the music played this time round was predominantly Sierra Leonean. The depth of the artistic quality of the songs, their hypnotic rhythms, crisp and professional production, and beauty of their lyrics were astoundingly admirable and made me stop in my tracks. Soon, I found myself reluctantly sliding into spasmodic gyration of my body, responding to the rhythm even as I tried very hard to resist doing so. The music was just too good. I could hear 'Cam Inside' blasting, then 'Girl U Know', then 'Sugar Mammy', then 'Che Che' and then 'Turn to Me'; by the time the DJ toasted 'More Fire' and 'Tutu Party', the crowd had gone crazy, ecstatic and wildly raunchy. I was excited too, gradually increasing my tempo until the full-blown frenzy of dance consumed me, sweating profusely in the process.

Artists are more likely to rail against the lack of water or light than to sing about their love of women, fast cars and drugs. They often work for free, and even the starriest act carries himself with humility.

More traditional music – along with some remarkable instruments – is less easy to come across, but nevertheless exists. Probably the best-known traditional artist whose work is available outside Sierra Leone is Ansumana Bangura, a German-based artist who was formerly a percussionist with the legendary Miriam Makeba. Among instruments to look out for, the *kondi* is a rectangular or square 'pluck box' popular with the Limba and Loko. The *marimba* equates to the *balafon* of Guinea, and is referred to as the 'talking drum', while the *balangi* is a Limba wooden-keyed instrument like a xylophone bound with rope. The banjo-like *siraman*, and the Foulah guitar and violin are also popular, as is the *shegureh*: a Mende calabash shaker surrounded by cowries. Drums include the large *dun-dun*, and the double-ended *sangba* played with a stick. The Fula also have a flute (*hordu*) and the *lala* shaker or rattle.

In a country that has traditionally valued the unique position of the singer and musician in the chief's entourage to criticise and debunk, Sierra Leone's modern music artists don't shirk from pointing out the shortcomings of their political system. Emmerson, the country's most beloved artist, labelled all politicians *2 Fut Arata* – Krio for 'two-legged rats' – ahead of the 2007 election. The release of his album *Borbor Bele* (literally 'boy's belly') had several politicians running to the gym in an effort to rid themselves of their swollen stomachs, grown fat, according to his song, on the proceeds of their illicitly earned wealth. To prove he's not all earnest, Emmerson's anthemic, irrepressibly catchy 'Tutu Party' packs dancefloors in any part of the country.

Ahead of the 2007 elections, Jungle Leaders sang that they wanted the government to 'Pak n Go', while a chirpy anthem 'Gi dem Notice' from Innocent urged the same. That prompted speedy retaliation from artists loyal to the then-ruling party, which released 'We Na De Landlord'. It included the line '*you nor go gi notice to landlord*' ('you can't give notice to your landlord'), meaning that the SLPP had no intention of leaving office.

The lead-up to 2012's polls saw more serious-minded political sparring over cheery reggae-pop beats, with Emmerson's 'Yesterday Better Pass Tiday' questioning the APC administration's achievements quickly receiving a snappy, pro-government rejoinder in the form of Innocent's 'Una Gi Dem Chance'. Partisans were quick to call Emmerson a traitor for questioning his earlier support of the APC, with other branding Innocent an APC stooge for his unflinching allegiance.

But the most respected artists don't nail their colours to a party political mast. Daddy Saj (now known as Diamond Saj), a one-time boy chorister, nursing student, and now chart-topper who has previously been imprisoned for his lyrical barbs, believes allegiance makes no difference: 'The politicians are all the same. We see Sierra Leone like a paradise. But we need a good leader. We need to find a way to build the country. It will happen.' Saj remains best known for his controversial 2003 hit 'Corruption E Do So', but has already telegraphed his intention to weigh in with a new slate of tracks in time for the 2018 election.

This positive approach is epitomised by the Refugee All Stars. Formed during the civil war in a refugee camp in Guinea, the band and its gentle, undemanding brand of reggae was catapulted to worldwide acclaim following the release of a documentary, *Sierra Leone's Refugee All Stars*, that followed the band's tribulations over three years. Today Sierra Leone's most successful musical export, the band breaks the mould for most Salone acts because they perform live with instruments, rather than lip-synching to a backing track. They most recently appeared on *The Long Road*, a 2016 benefit album organised by the British Red Cross to raise funds and encourage understanding of what it means to be a refugee.

'I want to encourage people to maintain the peace,' says lead singer and founder Reuben Koroma. 'We are just coming from war and the best music is talking about peace, harmony and love. If we talk about positive things we can help to bring a positive change, to forgive and forget. I sing "Big Lesson" about the war – to help bring a positive change and let us forgive and forget.'

Today's musicians are trying peacefully to shape this future, to a backdrop of gyrating beats and *tumba*-shaking tunes. During the 2007 election season, worries ran high that violence could reignite following the departure of UN peacekeepers. Music provided the most direct way to connect with legions of unemployed youth who in the past had been stoked to cause trouble. Dry Yai Crew's Pupa Bajah and Baw-Waw Society – among the few Salone acts to tour the US, and who, as early as 1991, sang 'Youth Mans Want for Wok' at the start of the war – released 'Ease di Tension' in an effort to secure calm on polling day. Eleven musicians formed Artists for Peace, taking their election song 'Go Vote No Violence' nationwide and performing in deluging rains in the far east of the country, where rebels first invaded in 1991. 'Music is our weapon against violence,' said Wahid, one of the singers with the group.

The country may have re-elected President Koroma in 2012, but the watchful eyes and switched-on mics of Sierra Leone's cutting lyricists are as tuned in as ever and ready to cry foul when they see it. As Pupa Bajah sings: 'We need a leader with a very good intention. Not a selfish one, not a greedy one. One with a good plan for the nation. That will take us out of sufferation.'

Among female artists, Star Zero (aka Star Zee, or Lina Samai) sings 'Girl Pikin Wahala' ('girl child trouble') about the problems women have to face, such as bosses who install beds in their offices to sleep with their mistresses or to entice secretaries. She was embroiled in controversy and briefly arrested in 2013, when a musical rivalry with songstress Willie Jay saw Jay take her to court for defamation thanks to the allegedly slanderous lyrics aimed at Jay on Zero's 'Bang 2 Zero' track. Look out too for the more established, supercool reggae queen Kadi Black.

You won't find many kids listening to them today, but if you're on the hunt for golden-age Salone sounds, there are a handful of bands to look out for whose eminently funky and irresistibly danceable 30s recordings are warmly remembered by all Sierra Leoneans of a certain age. Foremost among them is the legendary Afro National (whose hits include 'Elef Pan You' and 'Money Palava'), followed by bands like Super Combo (aka Super Combo Kings), Sabanoh 75 and Muyei Power, all of whom recorded a handful of 7" singles and/or LPs in the 1970s, all of which are now hopelessly rare and fetch astronomical sums from record collectors on the internet. To get a taste without breaking the bank, many of these hard-to-find songs are now available on YouTube, and Soundway Records released a compilation of Muyei Power tracks in 2014. If you're really lucky, you'll be in town for the 'Oldies But Goodies' concert and competition, put on annually by Universal Radio in Freetown.

Today, every other Sierra Leonean kid wants to be a rapper or a singer, but artists face an incredibly tough path to secure even moderate success. Opportunities are few, and the distribution side of the industry is stacked against them. One company, Super Sound, produces nearly all the new releases in Sierra Leone; these are then sold by the (delightfully retro) Cassette Sellers Association, which theoretically has a monopoly on distribution, but nearly all music in Sierra Leone today is sent around on WhatsApp, transferred between phones using Bluetooth, or passed from hand to hand on USB sticks chock-a-block with pirated mp3s. Thus, legitimate music sales are few and far between, and even then, an artist would be lucky to receive Le1,000 on a Le10,000 CD that is sold legitimately. Getting music on-air is hard work too, and many managers and artists resort to a little pecuniary offering along with their album requests.

Record labels include Kallboxx Records (co-founded by footballer Mohamed Kallon and DJ Boxx), Studio J, DeeCee Records, Forensic Studio, Supreme, and King Fisher's Bodyguard Studios (which produced *2 Fut Arata*). The godfather of Sierra Leone production is Jimmy B, New Jersey-bred but now Freetown-based, who founded Paradise Records in 2000 when shells were still landing in the city. His arrival was a much-needed shot in the arm for the failing industry, and the label's first release, *Paradise Family: Best of Sierra Leone Volume 1* remains a seminal document of a scene working hard to re-establish itself after the war, and served to jumpstart the careers of a whole host of musicians still on the scene today, including Daddy Diamond Saj, Fisher, Don Kay, Janka Nabay, Attila and Jimmy B himself.

Today's artists are as web-savvy as any Western act, and many have Facebook pages you can follow. Several radio stations now also live-stream their broadcasts online – try w capitalradio.sl, w starradiosl.com and w radiodemocracy.sl, or see what the (very nifty) map-based radio station aggregator at w radio.garden is picking up out of Freetown. YouTube is also a good source of 'live' music footage.

To properly track down this cocktail of sounds though, there's no substitute for the streets. 'I'm an underground artist trying to rise up,' says Saidu Kallon, who goes by his artist's name of Paps, and whose track 'Let We Clean Salone' talks of improving the country, the lack of roads and electricity. 'The street is the heart and soul of Salone.'

The latest act, album of the day, track of the minute, will have long-since changed by the time this book comes out. Look, ask, and most of all, listen; get into the taxis and on to the dancefloors of Freetown.

DEAD MEN DON'T SMOKE MARIJUANA

Just when you thought the various uses of the ubiquitous palm tree had been exhausted – oil, booze, roofing, baskets, party political symbol – it even has a genre of music named after it. Palm wine music, known in Sierra Leone as *maringa*, is known for its acoustic-guitar-led, wistful style; as light and sweet as the breeze wandering over an empty beach, as comforting as the first draught of *poyo*.

Guitars arrived in Sierra Leone with the Portuguese, but it wasn't until the early part of the 20th century that Saloneans forged their own popular music genre, blending elements of Trinidadian calypso with a West African sensibility.

The best-known exponent of palm wine music, and the only artist who managed to break through internationally, is S E Rogie. Born Suleiman Rogers, he trained as a tailor but the guitar proved a bigger draw than the needle. His best-known hit, 'My Lovely Elizabeth' – a simple paean of loyalty to his sweetheart – is a standard across West Africa. Having spent extensive time outside Sierra Leone touring and teaching in both the US and UK, he returned to his home country in 1988. His last album, *Dead Men Don't Smoke Marijuana*, was recorded in London shortly before his death in 1994, and the gentle guitar-picking style and simple melodies, sung mostly in Krio, are a joyful, sultry listen. Another famous Sierra Leonean calypso singer, Ali Ganda, composed 'Freedom, Sierra Leone'.

An early pioneer of palm wine music, who also founded an offshoot known as *goombay*, was Ebenezer Calendar, born to a Barbadian soldier father who settled in Sierra Leone. He began his musical career when he qualified as a carpenter and was put to work carving coffins during the day and then singing at the funerals in the evening. His recordings in the 1950s and 1960s blended Western and traditional instruments, and included an elegy to the arrival of London double-decker buses in Sierra Leone. When he died, local Freetown musicians gathered outside his home for an impromptu jam session of his songs that ended up lasting for 24 hours. Goombay was shaped into 'milo-jazz' by Olofemi Israel Cole (aka Doctor Oloh), named after the brand of chocolate powder whose tins, when filled with stones, were used as signature percussive shakers that backed every song, and his Milo-Jazz Band became a legendary feature of Freetown streets. In the 1970s, bands such as Sabanoh 75 blended the call and response style of palm wine music with Jamaican reggae.

Sadly, much of this music is difficult to track down today, unless you are a denizen of a reliable world music record shop. S E Rogie's music and the odd Sabanoh 75 track is available for purchase on iTunes and Amazon (or simply streaming on YouTube), while the London-based African music specialist Stern's (w *sternsmusic.com*) is worth a look – it has records by, for example, the London-based Sierra Leonean guitarist Abdul Tee-Jay.

FILM You might not hear many people talking about the latest 'Sierrawood' hit just yet, but that could change soon if Ahmed Mansaray, the founding director of Sierra Leone's first-ever film school, has anything to do with it. Opened in 2011 under the auspices (and inside the offices) of the local Institut de Français on Rawdon Street in Freetown, the school aims to teach Sierra Leoneans how to script, cast, shoot and edit their own films. No major productions had been produced at time of writing, but keep your eyes peeled. Someday soon, *Blood Diamond* might not be the first – or at least the only – film that outsiders associate with Sierra Leone (see box, page 163).

2

Practical Information

WHEN TO VISIT

Common advice is that November and December are the best months to visit, because of the welcome combination of very little rain and less fearsome heat. The disadvantage towards the end of this period is the haze created by the harmattan – the desert wind that picks up sand and dust as it comes in over the Sahara – in December and January, sometimes until March. The effect is less choking than countries nearer the desert, but you won't see crystal blue skies. February and March are also good months to visit, warm and dry, while April and May see the hottest weather before the rain arrives around June.

During the wettest months of July and August and for some while after, access to more remote rural areas becomes almost impossible, as dirt roads are turned into mud pie by torrents of water. Rains arrive with spectacular force, but not every day is wet or overcast. Between downpours, with the dust bedded down, the water washes the light clear and strong and the skies blue, making the beaches their beautiful best at the end of the season, around September and October.

HIGHLIGHTS AND SUGGESTED ITINERARIES

Whether you want one of the world's most stunning beaches to yourself; to clamber up a mountainside steeped in rare plants, buffalo and monkeys; to step on to a former slave island; to swim with turtles around a distant island; or walk in a dwindling rainforest – it's all there. The following gives some ideas of what's possible in various timeframes, but we don't pin you down to a strict programme. It's best to stay flexible.

FOUR DAYS Yes, some people really have managed a long weekend in Sierra Leone. In a GMT time zone, and 6 hours by plane (if all goes well), European visitors don't really have much to jetlag to adjust to. For a short trip like this, stick to the beaches on the Peninsula and combine them with a trip to the Tacugama Chimpanzee Sanctuary, a tour of Freetown's Krio houses, crafts market and trade stalls downtown, as well as a beer or two by night, and dancing by early morning.

A WEEK
Beach, babe Head for the Peninsula via the mountain road. Have lunch at Charlotte Falls, make the 16.00 visit at Tacugama Chimpanzee Sanctuary and stay the night. Then to the beaches. After lunch at Kent take a boat across to Banana Island for one or two days of fresh-cooked lobster with only the stars for company. Take a tour of the island; go snorkelling. Next up is camping at Bureh or John Obey with food cooked on the shore, followed by a night of luxury at Florence's or The Place. Then

spend a playful day at River Number Two before heading back to the capital. Enjoy a final day of souvenir shopping for bedspreads, leather shoes, hand-woven hammocks and more, followed by a fancy dinner at Country Lodge, Radisson Blu or Lagoonda and some partying in nightclubs, and you're ready for your flight home.

Birdtastic Hook up with local bird experts and plan the ultimate twitcher trip. Head for River Number Two along the Peninsula in search of the white-necked picathartes (and several others) for a few days, and then on to Bumbuna and the Mamunta-Mayosso Wildlife Sanctuary looking for migratory water birds, before diving deep into the rainforest at Gola (home of the Gola malimbe and seven more species in danger of global extinction). Finally make your way back to the wader-rich shores of the Sierra Leone River estuary for a last spree with the binoculars.

Step back into history Head for the rundown slave fort at Bunce Island, which exported more than 50,000 slaves to North America and is therefore a key site for African Americans today. Wander Freetown and take in its brightly painted wooden *bod os* (board house) relics and other key Krio sites; visit the hilltop towns of Regent, and Leicester, where recaptured slaves set up home as free men once again. Career down the coast, from the Peninsula to Plantain Island, Sherbro Island and, weather permitting, Turner's Peninsula for a sense of where the trade once thrived.

TEN DAYS TO TWO WEEKS Ten days is the ideal minimum length for a short visit – enough time to pack in all the fun of the Peninsula, and head out of Freetown to sample the wildlife. The birdlife is good enough to keep twitchers in clover for two or even three weeks.

Jungle fever Rare chimps and monkeys guaranteed. Head first for Outamba-Kilimi National Park to canoe with hippos, then down south for Tiwai Island and its nine primate species. End in the Gola Rainforest National Park for trekking in one of the last remaining patches of rainforest in West Africa. At each destination, camp out surrounded by the calls of the wild. Pack your binoculars and your sense of adventure.

Misty-eyed for mountains Allow a week to climb Mount Bintumani, West Africa's highest peak; then lose yourself in the cool hills of Kabala for some lighter walking to recover. Or (we'll let you off), head straight for the beach.

Coastal colossus Beach, beach and more beach. OK, plus an island or two. Hire a speedboat and travel to Plantain Island and on to Sherbro, for a stay at Bonthe and some fishing. Transfer to the remote Turtle Islands to sleep on the beach under the stars, with bathtub-perfect waters.

THREE WEEKS AND MORE Start combining – pick your favourites from the options above and stitch them together. For a little extra spice, try adding some of the following. They're demanding in terms of time and effort, so enjoy the journey as much as the anticipation of success at the end.

Animal magic Turn night-owl and camp out at Tiwai Island until finally you catch a glimpse of the shy and secretive nocturnal pygmy hippo. Also track Sierra Leone's rare and endangered bird species.

Big fish For fishing enthusiasts, line and spear fishing are both possible, as well as exploring the waters by motor launch. The world's biggest catches of the ever-spirited tarpon happen right here, off Sherbro Island.

BEYOND THE CALL OF DUTY

- Walk 100km of unbroken beach at Turner's Peninsula, the stretch of coast reaching along the mainland from the tip of Sherbro Island all the way south to Sulima, just before the Liberian border.
- Climb and camp in the Tingi Hills, the double-mountain peak in the east.
- Take a peek into the shadowy world of diamond digging, buying and trading in Kono and Kenema districts in the east of the country.
- Head north of the Freetown Peninsula by boat along the coast up towards Guinea, taking in tiny fishing islands such as Yelibuya, before heading upriver to Kambia.
- Stop off at Rogbonko Village Retreat or in other remote villages upcountry, staying in mud huts courtesy of the chief, tasting local food traditionally prepared, and experiencing the best of rural Salone.

TOUR OPERATORS

Sometimes just making it to Sierra Leone demands the same kind of enterprising spirit and flexibility that characterises travel in the country itself, and most visitors will have to piece things together themselves – few tour operators can put together an all-in-one deal covering flights, transfers, hotels and excursions.

However, some brave specialists are starting to offer trips that cater for a distinct interest, be it adventure travel, exploring the country's natural wonders or seeking out the birdlife. For twitchers in particular the niche market is slightly better developed.

In addition to this committed band of international specialists, there is real value attached to travel companies in-country, as their local knowledge and contacts can prove invaluable in trying to book accommodation, generate itineraries and organise knowledgeable guides. The ranks of both groups are growing slowly as Sierra Leone once again re-establishes its tourism industry.

INTERNATIONAL TOUR OPERATORS AND SPECIALISTS Few and far between, tour operators that had been considering Sierra Leone were in many cases scared off by the 2014–16 Ebola crisis, and the tour market remains small, though hopefully once again set to grow. It's well represented on overland tours of the region, however. Tour operators listed below have already established a presence, and you can expect to see others join the market during the lifespan of this edition.

UK

Dragoman Camp Green, Debenham, Suffolk IP14 6LA; ☎ 01728 861133; e info@dragoman. co.uk; w dragoman.com. Venerable UK-based overlanding outfit offering trips between Freetown & Dakar or Accra.

Exodus Grange Mills, Weir Rd, London SW12 0NE; ☎ 020 8772 3936; e sales@exodus.co.uk; w exodus.co.uk. This well-established British operator used to run a 9-day tour a few times a year, hitting highlights like Tiwai, Tacugama & the

Banana Islands. It was suspended at the time of writing; check back to see if it's been reintroduced.

Lupine Travel 23 King St, Wigan, Lancs WN1 1EQ; ☎ 01942 497209; e info@lupinetravel.co.uk; w lupinetravel.co.uk; see ad, inside back cover. Adventure-focused company offering a combined itinerary to both Sierra Leone & Liberia.

Rainbow Tours 2 Waterhouse Sq, 138–140 Holborn, London EC1N 2ST; ☎ 0203 553 0004; e info@rainbowtours.co.uk; w rainbowtours.co.uk. This UK-based tour operator specialises in tailor-made trips to Africa for sensitive adventure-lovers. Helen Kennedy is their Sierra Leone specialist.

Native Eye Olfrea Hse, White Horse Rd, East Bergholt, Suffolk CO7 6TU; ☎ 020 3286 5995; info@nativeeyetravel.com; w nativeeyetravel.com. Well-regarded firm offering a unique itinerary taking in both Sierra Leone & Guinea.

Overlanding West Africa ☎ 01728 862247; e info@overlandingwestafrica.com; w overlandingwestafrica.com. Small & highly personal overland truck operator offering tours between Freetown & Dakar or Accra.

Responsible Travel 1st Fl, Edge Hse, 42 Bond St, Brighton, East Sussex BN1 1RD; ☎ 01273 823700; e rosy@responsibletravel.com; w responsibletravel.com. Brighton-based outfit offering tours of Sierra Leone as well as Liberia.

Undiscovered Destinations PO Box 746, North Tyneside NE29 1EG; ☎ 0191 296 2674; e info@undiscovered-destinations.com; w undiscovered-destinations.com. A super-friendly UK-based company, this small agency caters for the well travelled who are in search of something new – offering places where tourism is still a relatively new concept & encouraging responsible travel to all destinations. Its 8-day tour of the country mixes

culture, nature & history, including a trip to the former slave fort at Bunce Island & to the wildlife at Tiwai Island.

US
Fambul Tik Tours ☎ +1 469 618 8840, +1 230 393 5791; e amadu.massally@fambultik.com or info@fambultik.com; w fambultik.com; see ad, page 221. Ambitious new agency run by US-based Sierra Leonean Amadu Massally with a focus on Bunce Island, but also plans to develop trips to important heritage destinations throughout Africa & the Caribbean. Uniquely, they also organise trips aimed at Sierra Leoneans interested in meeting their long-lost cousins abroad.

Mauritius & South Africa
Rockjumper Birding Tours Unit 12/13, River View Commercial Centre, Les Gorges Road, Black River, 90624, Mauritius; +230 5759 5394 (Mauritius), +27 88 033 394 0225 (South Africa); e info@rockjumperbirding.com; w rockjumperbirding.com. This Mauritius/South Africa-based bird specialist helped to put Sierra Leone on the twitcher map & still organises made-to-order private tours.

LOCAL TOUR OPERATORS In addition to the local firms listed below, you'll see numerous signs for other 'travel agents' all over central and west Freetown: generally they can book air tickets and transfers, and sometimes offer car hire, but can't arrange a full-scale itinerary with hotels and guides.

Africa Travel Centre Delco Hse, 12 Lightfoot Boston St, Freetown & 227 Shepherds Bush Rd, Hammersmith, London W6 7AS, UK; ☎ 020 3372 6442 (UK); m 078 819 911 (Freetown); e info@sierraleonetravel.net; w sierraleonetravel.net. The successor to Kevin McPhillips's long-serving flight agency acts as an agent for Brussels Airlines, Air France & Royal Air Maroc.

Aureol Travel Agency 19 Sander St, Freetown; ☎ 022 225 571. Can book flights & organise car hire.

Conservation Society of Sierra Leone 14A King St, Freetown; m 030 522 579, 076 633 824; e cssl_03@yahoo.com; w conservationsocietysl.org; see ad, 3rd colour section. Not a tourism operator per se, but anyone with an interest in nature & wildlife should get in touch. Staff at this environmental, non-profit NGO are friendly, committed & highly knowledgeable, with infectious natural enthusiasm. Working in difficult

circumstances, they can offer advice & occasionally help organise trips, & they are happy for visitors or volunteers to accompany them on research & survey trips to the most beautiful corners of the country, whether tagging sea turtles on Turtle Island, exploring the coastal wetlands or birdlife in the Gola Rainforest National Park. No payment required, but you'll need to cover your own expenses such as food & fuel; a generous donation to the society would be a worthwhile way of showing appreciation.

Fact Finding Tours c/o National Tourist Board Information & Business Centre, Beach Rd, Lumley; m 076 520 122, 077 689 774; e factsfinding@yahoo.com. Local birding expert Kenneth Gbengba has a proven track record; his team run a series of birdwatching trips, from half a day in & about Freetown to a 3-week safari through the undergrowth. Name a bird & he'll know where & when to find it, even guiding in

French if you like. A special 'Picathartes Week' takes clients off in search of breeding sites of the famed, rare white-necked bird. In addition to twitching expertise, the company can also arrange 4x4 excursions, nature hikes, cultural & ecotourism with visits to villages, hotel reservations & airport transfers.

IPC Travel 22 Siaka Stevens St, Freetown; m 030 541 231, 077 444 453; e info@ipctravel.com; w ipctravel.com; see ad, 3rd colour section. IPC rules the roost when it comes to booking flights with any of the airlines, although it can also arrange upcountry tours & vehicle hire, whether in a minibus or a 4x4. Prices are higher than other outfits, but service is reliable, with good backup for their fleet of vehicles. They've also got a branch at the Radisson Blu (as well as in Accra & Conakry).

Karl Travel Agency 184 Wilkinson Rd, Freetown; m 076 204 040, 088 031 009; e karltravel@outlook.com; w karltravelsl.com. Popular travel agency for flight bookings. Can also do car hire.

Karou Voyage 10 Lamina Sankoh St, Freetown; \ 022 222 297; m 078 914 998, 076 609 974; e kvsl@email.com or karouvoyage_sl@yahoo.com. Flight bookings only.

KTI Travel & Tours Santano Hse, 10 Howe St, Freetown; \ 022 221 344/5; m 076 879 148, 076 610 633, 076 879 148; e ktifna@yahoo.com. This company, run by US diaspora-returnee Patricia Brown, concentrates on in-country tours, hire cars, hotel bookings & the odd

travel itinerary, as well as flight bookings. It is particularly strong on the cultural side of Freetown & its surroundings, & her rates on hire vehicles – a range of jeeps, buses & minibuses – are competitive.

Levuma Beach Garden Tours Levuma Beach, via Russell, York Rural District; m 076 605 894, 077 322 011; e levumagarden@yahoo.com. Specialises in boats & sea excursions along the Peninsula and south to the Turtle Islands.

Lion Travel Agency 11 Siaka Stevens St, Freetown; m 076 888 888, 076 614 888; e liontravelsl@yahoo.com. This company can arrange flights worldwide, but does not handle bookings for domestic tours or accommodation.

VSL Travel 28 Main Motor Rd, Congo Cross, Freetown; m 025 200 978, 076 258 258, 079 258 258; e info@vsltravel.com; w visitsierraleone.org; see ad, 3rd colour section. Bimbola Carrol has single-handedly done more to promote awareness of Sierra Leone as a tourist destination than anyone else. Book via his website & receive a discount on hotel stays & car hire, or contact the company first to brainstorm an itinerary or join one of several planned trip itineraries he launched in 2008. His 'destination management company' can help you sort your visa, handle all bookings (for vehicles, hotels & trips), & ensure things go smoothly. The website & active blog remain the most useful resource around for planning a trip to Sierra Leone or researching information.

CO-ORDINATORS OF VOLUNTEER TRIPS
If you're interested in giving something back during your trip to Sierra Leone, there are a handful of volunteer-co-ordinating outfits to choose from, but very little when compared with more popular destinations like Ghana or Senegal.

Peace Corps 1111 20th St, Washington, DC, USA; \ +1 800 424 8580; w peacecorps.gov. The United States Peace Corps has about 20 volunteers on the ground in Sierra Leone (& 3,755 to date since 1962), most of whom are staying in remote villages & teaching mathematics, science or English to secondary-school students (see box, page 254). It's a 27-month programme & only US citizens can apply.

Street Child 42–44 Bishopsgate, London EC2N 4AH; \ 020 7614 7696; e info@street-child.co.uk. This organisation provides teacher training, livelihood development & child-protection services in some of Sierra Leone's remotest & poorest communities. They accept volunteers for a variety of positions & lengths

of time, & also organise the annual Sierra Leone Marathon in Makeni.

Voluntary Services Overseas 27A Carlton Dr, Putney, London SW15 2BS; \ 020 8780 7500; e enquiry@vso.org.uk; w vso.org.uk. This British programme places volunteers in a handful of cities around the country, including Freetown, Makeni, Bo & Kabala. People with all types of skills are welcome to apply, doctors especially. The programme is open to citizens of all countries, although you may be recruited via an office outside your home country if you're not based in the UK. Stints range from a few months to 2 years or more. Volunteers are typically paid a stipend that's roughly equivalent to a local salary.

RED TAPE

Beside the usual visas, jabs and health certificates, you still officially need to be invited to the country. No casual encounter here; this is a full-on formal date. If you are going to visit a friend or contact in Sierra Leone ask for a short letter from them. If you are going on a genuine holiday, then arrange one through your tour operator or hotel, or see the note on page 171 about the letter-free virtual route to a visa.

VISAS Citizens of the 15 West African Economic Community (ECOWAS) countries (Benin, Burkina Faso, Cape Verde, Gambia, Ghana, Guinea, Guinea-Bissau, Ivory Coast, Liberia, Mali, Niger, Nigeria, Senegal, Sierra Leone and Togo) do not need a visa or entry permit to enter Sierra Leone if staying for 90 days or fewer. Everybody else does. These can usually be issued within a few days, and your application must come with the letter of invitation described above.

Some bodies, such as Visit Sierra Leone and IPC travel agency, offer fast-tracked tourist board-approved services to skip this archaic letter-writing hurdle. Visit w visitsierraleone.org/online-visa for an up-to-date list of visa prices, as well as information on how to secure your visa in advance without visiting your local Sierra Leone high commission or embassy – scan the relevant passport page, provide your name and dates of travel, and let Visit Sierra Leone do the hard work, for an admin fee of US$30. It'll be a single-entry, one-month visa, and you pick up a scan of it via email and carry it with your passport.

OTHER DOCUMENTS A yellow fever certificate is required for entry. Expect to be checked upon arrival at the airport as well as at major border crossings with Liberia and Guinea. If you don't have a valid certificate, you could be in for either a fine or a jab on the spot; best to sort this out before you travel.

Your passport will be date-stamped on entry. If you're staying longer than a month, you need to get this date stamp extended, even if your visa is valid way beyond that date. You can do so at the immigration office in Freetown (page 143).

EMBASSIES

SIERRA LEONE EMBASSIES ABROAD Contact details and listings may change from time to time. To stay up to date, visit w statehouse.gov.sl/index.php/foreign-missions and w visitsierraleone.org/visiting-sierra-leone/before-you-travel/sierra-leone-diplomatic-and-consular-missions-abroad, although their details vary in some cases.

EMBASSIES IN SIERRA LEONE Add the international prefix +232 and remove the initial zero if you are dialling any of the following numbers from outside Sierra Leone. Contact details and listings may change from time to time. For an up-to-date list, visit w visitsierraleone.org/visiting-sierra-leone/before-you-travel/foreign-diplomatic-and-consular-missions-in-sierra-leone. In addition to the embassies below, **Ivory Coast** (*1 Wesley St*; m *076 241 626/666 693*), **Mali** (*40 Wilkinson Rd*; m *076 610 984*), and **Senegal** (*7 Short St, 2nd fl*; m *078 377 192*) have honorary consulates in Freetown, though these are not always necessarily able to issue visas.

China 29 Spur Loop, Wilberforce, Freetown; m 076 601 587; e chinaemb_sl@mfa.gov.cn; w sl.china-embassy.org

Egypt 174c Wilkinson Rd, Freetown; m 076 885 888; e mahmahdy@yahoo.com or mahermahdy1966@gmail.com

e EU Delegation PO Box 1399, Leicester Peak, Freetown; **m** 088 136 000; **e** delegation-sierra-leone@eeas.europa.eu; **w** eeas.europa.eu/delegations/sierra-leone_en

e The Gambia 6 Wilberforce St, Freetown; ☏ 022 225 191/2; **e** gmbmssn_dplmtc@yahoo.com

e Germany 3 Middle Hill Station, Wilberforce, Freetown; **m** 078 732 120; **e** info@freetown.diplo.de; **w** freetown.diplo.de

e Ghana 43 Spur Rd (opp UK high commission), Freetown; **m** 076 100 502/3/4; **e** ghacomsl@sierratel.sl; **w** ghanahighcommissionfreetown.sl

e Guinea 111 Jomo Kenyatta Rd, New England Ville, Freetown; **m** 077 834 154, 077 421 218; **e** ambagui_sl@yahoo.fr

e Ireland 8 St Joseph's Av, off Spur Rd, Freetown; **m** 079 250 623; **w** dfa.ie/irish-embassy/sierra-leone

e Lebanon 22a Spur Rd, Wilberforce, Freetown; **m** 030 911 111, 088 334 455; **e** embleb2013@yahoo.com, freetown.leb@gmail.com

e Liberia 2 Spur Rd (opp UK high commission), Wilberforce; **m** 076 728 647; **e** geraldinelibemb2014@gmail.com

e Nigeria 1 Hill Cot Rd, Freetown; **m** 079 013 604; **e** yonafalujo@gmail.com or nigeria.freetown@foreignaffairs.gov.ng

e UK 6 Spur Rd, Wilberforce, Freetown; **m** 076 541 386, 078 200 190; **e** freetown.general.enquiries@fco.gov.uk; **w** www.gov.uk/world/organisations/british-high-commission-freetown

e US Leicester Sq, Freetown; **m** 099 105 500; **e** consularfreetown@state.gov; **w** sl.usembassy.gov

GETTING THERE AND AWAY

BY AIR Sierra Leone's airport, Lungi International, isn't actually in Freetown, but in fact on the opposite side of the water in Lungi (pages 340–2). Several international airlines pulled their Freetown routes during the Ebola crisis and not all of them had returned at the time of writing. The most notable absence is that of **British Airways**, who suspended their route in 2014 – rumour on the street is it was an unprofitable route to begin with and Ebola provided a convenient pretext to axe the service. A hastily arranged substitute meant to serve the London–Freetown route, **Fly Salone**, both started operations and collapsed within a four-month period in 2015–16, and Sierra Leone remains without a direct air link to the UK. It's not all doom and gloom in the air sector though; **KLM** introduced new direct flights from Amsterdam in March 2017, **Fly Mid Africa** started services to Banjul that May, **Mauritania Airlines** added Freetown to their Dakar–Conakry route in August, and **Turkish Airlines** was in negotiations to start offering connections to Istanbul before the end of the year. According to the Minister of Transport and Aviation, **Emirates** are considering adding Freetown to their network as well.

You can generally pick up a return from the UK for about £700, although deals at certain times of the year can see them drop below that – for example, a month-long return from Freetown at Christmas might go for as little as £500 – while in summer months prices can rocket.

Most international flight tickets already include US$40 departure tax, but local flights tend not to, so be prepared to stump up the extra cash at the airport.

Should they resume, direct flight time between the UK and Sierra Leone is only about 6 hours. Not the most favoured of worldwide destinations, many planes depart Freetown horribly late at night, leading many a confused ticket-holder to arrive a day late for their 02.00 flight. Be prepared too for lengthy delays.

In 2006, the EU banned many African carriers from landing in Europe, although that obviously doesn't stop airlines that don't meet European safety standards from flying within their own region – something to bear in mind when you book your tickets. You can check the updated list at **w** ec.europa.eu/transport/modes/air/safety/air-ban_en.

Airlines

✈ Air Côte d'Ivoire 23 Siaka Stevens St, Freetown; m 076 886 544, 077 777 773; e aircotedivoirefna@aircotedivoire.com; w aircotedivoire.com. Flies to Abidjan most days of the week, some days via Monrovia.

✈ Air France c/o GSA Weasua Air Transport, 13 Lamina Sankoh St, Freetown; ☎ +44 (0)871 663 3777 (UK); e airfrance.freetown@gmail.com; w airfrance.com. Flies to Paris 3-times weekly via Conakry.

✈ Arik Air 13 Howe St, Freetown; m 025 203 949, 078 444 521; e talktous@arikair. com; w arikair.com. A Nigerian airline facing insolvency in 2017 – if operating, they connect to Lagos & Accra a few times a week, & potentially Banjul.

✈ Asky Airlines ☎ +228 223 05 10 (Togo); e headoffice@flyasky.com; w flyasky.com. Still suspended in 2017, if they return to service flights will likely connect to Lomé via Monrovia.

✈ Brussels Airlines 3rd Fl, Access Bank Bldg, 30 Siaka Stevens St, Freetown; m 025 333 777, 076 333 777, 088 333 777; w brusselsairlines.com. 4 flights to Brussels weekly via Monrovia.

✈ Fly Mid Africa Book through Visit Sierra Leone (page 71); ⬛ fb.me/flymidafrica. A new Gambia-based airline offering direct connections to Banjul several times a week.

✈ Kenya Airways First Discount Hse, opposite NASSIT Hse, Freetown; m 077 001 001; e infofnakq@euro-world.in or freetown@kenya-airways.com; w kenya-airways.com. Flies several times weekly from Nairobi via Accra, as well as to/from Accra via Monrovia.

✈ KLM 12 Wilberforce St, Freetown; m 099 998 899; w klm.com. Flights to Amsterdam 3-times weekly via Monrovia.

✈ Mauritania Airlines ☎ (+222) 4525 6747, 4524 0746 (Mauritania); e resa.tarifs@mauritaniaairlines.mr; w mauritaniaairlines.mr. Started flying twice weekly between Dakar & Freetown via Conakry in Aug 2017.

✈ Med-View Airline 13 Pultney St, Freetown; m 077 080 396, 078 020 513; e info@medviewairline.com; w medviewairline.com. A Nigerian airline flying 3-times weekly to Monrovia, Accra & Lagos, which also claims to offer free boat transfers to Lungi in the ticket price.

✈ Royal Air Maroc 19 Charlotte St, Freetown; m 076 221 015; e callcenter@royalairmaroc. com; w royalairmaroc.com. Flies 5 days a week to Casablanca.

Pack your bags Your luggage is rarely only your own. While many might put faith in a small padlock, baggage handlers (who perhaps have understood their job title too literally) will find them a distraction rather than a deterrent. Small, easily pilfered and resaleable items such as beauty products, mobile phones and electronic goods and clothes seem to be the swipes of choice.

Opt for a strong metal padlock and have everything wrapped in cellophane at your departure airport and when flying out of Lungi. Keep an eye on bags heading for the ferry too (see section on airport transfers below).

On arrival or departure, many young men will be keen to carry your baggage or wheel it about on a trolley – they are perfectly legit, and keen for the tips: about US$1 per bag, or Le7,000–8,000 is fine.

Regardless of overall baggage weight restrictions, no single bag may weigh more than 30kg, and you'll be asked to shift items around between bags if you exceed the limit.

At the airport There are now three **ATMs** in the arrivals hall, from UBA, Rokel Commercial Bank and EcoBank, along with a **foreign exchange bureau** (*TAP Foreign Exchange Bureau Ltd*; m *076 736 238*; e *tapbureau@yahoo.co.uk*) and booths to buy local SIM cards and credit if you have brought along an 'unlocked' phone. There are also **restaurants** on both sides of check-in.

Airport transfers If sagas were wanting in Sierra Leone, the sheer madness of arriving in the country would be enough. Freetown's urban planners have to be congratulated for constructing an international airport on the opposite side of a giant river mouth to the capital, with no decent transport links between them. As if this doesn't make arriving fraught enough, most flights coming from Europe arrive in Freetown after dark, adding to the difficulty of the trek.

Lungi has a couple of hotel options if you don't want to travel at night (pages 340–1), but you can't delay forever. Transfers used to be possible by such unlikely means as hovercraft and helicopter, but these were known for sinkings and crashes, some with horrific fatalities, and none is currently in service, leaving you on either the government ferry, government bus, or one of a handful of private water taxis. Leaving Freetown, confer with your travel agency about leaving times – all modes of transport set their timetables according to the flights.

By road It's a (traffic-dependent) 3-hour drive on new tarmac roads via Port Loko. At 185km, it's the least favoured and longest choice for getting to Freetown, on an improbably large loop that seems to take in half the country. However, if you're bypassing the capital and heading straight for Makeni or other points north, leaving Lungi by car is probably your best bet. The **Sierra Leone Road Transport Corporation (SLRTC)** (m *078 524 054/988 822/888 811/888 822*; w *www.slrtc.org*), better known simply as the **government bus**, runs a shuttle to Freetown on this route for Le75,000, or you can of course hire a taxi.

By ferry A pair of rusted old Greek ferries, having long since crossed the river Styx and begun their African afterlife, punt travellers across the Sierra Leone River between Freetown's Kissi Ferry Terminal in the east end and Tagrin, 14km to the south of the airport at Lungi. Life jackets should be provided, and though there have been sinkings in years past, we're not aware of any recent problems.

Tickets cost Le4,000 for the 45-60-minute journey (depending on tides), or Le11,000 for first-class, which consists of a lounge bar that tends to play TV war movies several decibels too high. Many people also enjoy standing on the very top deck – time it right and you'll be handed a perfect sunset moment. As of mid 2017, the ferry departs Freetown at 08.00, 11.00, 14.00, 17.30 and 20.00 daily, returning from Tagrin along the same schedule, though timetables go notoriously unheeded, so if you're heading *to* the airport leave plenty of time. You can confirm the departure schedule with Joseph Kande (m *077 530 487*). Keep not just an eye but your hands on your bags, and your pockets. Petty crime is rife, particularly among crowds as you get on or off the ferry. Some go beyond pickpocketing to mugging.

Once in Tagrin, a charter taxi for the 10-minute drive to the airport is relatively expensive at about Le90,000. For a seat in a shared taxi (or a motorbike taxi ride should you be travelling especially light), expect to pay Le10,000. Alternatively, **Abess Airport Shuttle** (m *076 636 686*) will send a private vehicle and driver to pick you up in Freetown, take you on to the ferry, then deliver you to the airport on the other side (and vice versa as necessary) for a charge of US$100 per vehicle (up to four people). You can also consider hiring a taxi to accompany you on the ferry and drop you to your door. Vehicles on the ferry are charged Le40,000/55,000, and the whole trip should cost in the region of Le230,000–270,000, including ferry charges. **KTI Travel & Tours** (page 71) also has a coach shuttle service to and from the airport to the Aberdeen area of west Freetown, via the ferry.

At the time of writing, all government ferries were serving Tagrin from Kissy Ferry Terminal, *not* Government Wharf in the city centre. For more information, contact the **Sierra Leone Ports Authority** (*Queen Elizabeth II Quay, Cline Town, Freetown;* 022 220 018/9, 022 220 537, 022 226 480, 044 927 678; e *customerservice@slpa.sl;* w *slpa.sl*).

2

By water-taxi The most reliable – and therefore most popular – airport transfer method is via water-taxi. There are now three companies providing this service – **Sea Coach**, **Sea Bird**, and the recently founded **Sovereign Ferries** – each departing from a different part of town. Most frequent travellers in Freetown have a favourite, and singing the praises of one over the other is an easy way to touch off a heated debate. All time their trips to coincide with plane arrivals and departures (so even if your flight is 5 hours late, there should still be a boat to take you across from Lungi). Departing Freetown, you can ring ahead to find out what time the boat is leaving for your flight, or check their Facebook pages, where they sometimes post monthly schedules.

Arriving at Lungi is generally a bit of a scrum, but once you pass through immigration and customs, both Sea Coach and Sea Bird have ticket offices for the ferry ride to Freetown; you can buy your tickets here directly in US dollars without the assistance of any of the would-be fixers you'll encounter, but a tip of US$1–2 is appropriate if you avail yourself of their services. Ticket in hand, head outside and to the right towards the car park (again with no shortage of would-be porters offering their services), where minibuses await to transfer you to the respective ferries. Here your ticket will be checked again and your luggage loaded into another bus, with a corresponding receipt stapled to your ticket. You won't see your luggage again until disembarking in Freetown, so keep anything you want on hand with you. The transfer to the docks takes no more than 5 minutes and the water-taxi ride itself is under half an hour, though there's often a wait before getting on the boat; drinks and seating are available while you wait.

The doyen of the bunch, **Sea Coach Express** (*Aberdeen Bridge, off Sir Samuel Lewis Rd;* m *076 551 155, 077 551 155;* e *info@seacoachferry.com;* w *seacoachferry.com*), is also frequently referred to by its old name of Pelican and charges US$40 each way. Their terminal is on the Freetown side just below the Aberdeen Bridge, where you'll generally find taxis waiting if you need a lift on arrival. You can book tickets in advance, but it's also fine to get them on departure. Boats are also available for private charter.

Departing from their terminal in Murray Town, **Sea Bird Express** (*36 High Broad St, Murray Town, Freetown;* m *099 220 022, 099 330 033, 079 900 909, 079 808 000;* e *seabird-express@hotmail.com;* w *seabird-sl.com;* f *SEA BIRD Express*) operates on much the same model as Sea Coach Express and even charges the same fee, with boats departing Freetown approximately 4 hours before flights take off from Lungi. They've also recently added a 95-seat hovercraft to their fleet.

More convenient for the east side of town, **Sovereign Ferries** (*9th Fl, NIC Bldg, 18–20 Walpole St, downtown Freetown;* m *099 507 906, 079 458 736;* e *info@sovereign-ferries.com*) departs from the city centre at Government Wharf eight–12- times daily. Unlike Sea Bird or Sea Coach, these boats head for Tagrin, directly across the river, rather than up to Lungi itself. Most (though not all) departures are tailored to match flight schedules, and they have a coach to transfer passengers from Tagrin to the airport at Lungi and vice versa. It's slightly cheaper than the competition at US$35 one-way.

By speedboat A posh option is to charter your own speedboat. It's efficient and fun, but from May to October the water is often too rough and the crossing becomes dangerous. Useful as emergency backup or to cut down on the wait at the airport before boarding other services, this 30-minute ride is an on-demand rather than a scheduled service, so will require at least two or three days' warning (*contact Smokey at Cape Shilling;* m *076 814 646*). Make sure someone is waiting at the airport on your arrival to show you where to go. It's not cheap at US$60 per person (for four people), US$75 per person (for two people), or US$160 if you're going solo, but it's a pretty impressive way to greet Freetown. Transfers arrive at the yacht club, under Aberdeen Bridge, and from here it's easy enough to flag down a taxi.

By catamaran Another alternative is a luxury catamaran service, the **Lungi Express** (*again from Cape Shilling; call Smokey on* m *076 814 646*) seating 20 people, taking 25 minutes and arriving to a custom-built jetty at Aberdeen. Taxis are arranged for transfers on the airport side.

BY ROAD Long eschewed by overland travellers thanks to years of turmoil in neighbouring Liberia and Guinea, the newfound political calm in the Mano River neighbourhood means it's now easier than it's been for decades to enter Sierra Leone by land. Whether that means bouncing through the pretty hills and mountains of rural Guinea, or grinding along the steaming swamps and jungle of Liberia, it makes for a pretty spectacular way to arrive.

While the state of the roads and the sheer unpredictability of the environment mean it's no picnic, a road trip to Sierra Leone is certainly not impossible. Make sure you possess Job-like reserves of patience (and charm) to deal with ubiquitous police checkpoints, the only thing south of Tangiers more prominent than Premiership football shirts. Driving down from Europe, hugging the coast via Morocco and Mauritania on tarmac roads to Dakar, takes about three weeks. The Bradt *Africa Overland* guide has some good advice about kit and other essentials.

An entertaining online account of two enterprising Australians who rode on motorbikes from London to Sierra Leone (and then onwards around the world), catalogued at w hardwayhome.blogspot.com, is worth reading.

'We actually had a great experience riding into Sierra Leone and had nothing but praise about our trip and the fact that we are Australians,' says Amy, one of the riders. 'We even got a police escort through some parts of town!'

Border crossings and checkpoints Crossing into Sierra Leone itself is relatively straightforward. The simplest way from the north is via Conakry, the Guinean capital, from where the border is a couple of hours away at Pamelap, on a poorly maintained tarred road that continues to the Sierra Leone town of Kambia. Following the border about 100km northeast, the crossing at Madina Oula is more difficult thanks to the poor state of the roads; it's 65km from the Guinean city of Kindia, which is itself about 3 hours northeast of Conakry. It offers direct access to Outamba-Kilimi National Park once over the border in Salone, but you'll have to take *ocada* transport for at least part of the trip.

There's also a great route into the far northeast of Sierra Leone from near Faranah in Guinea, east of Falaba – good if you're sweeping down south from Mali. Border officials at Gberia Fotombu (also known as Koindu Kura) are courteous and keep the post open 06.00–18.00, with fairly hassle-free paperwork.

Heading into the east of Sierra Leone, the main border crossing from Liberia is at Jendema, linked to the Liberian town of Bo-Waterside by the Mano River Bridge. From here the road to Monrovia is tarred and in a good state of repair, and you can reach the capital in a couple of hours. There's also a pair of decidedly remote crossings in Kailahun district, either at Baidu, near Koindu, or Dawa, near Buedu, from where it's 17km and 25km onwards to the Liberian town of Foya, respectively, on rough roads all the way through.

In general, the main border posts are well signposted, directions are clear, and officials are polite and prompt. While diplomatic plates are likely to be met with a flurry of salutes and smiles, non-diplomatic plates are likely to encounter extreme curiosity and even pride that you are passing through. Resist any requests for bribes with patience.

Both Liberia and Guinea – and to some extent Sierra Leone – have internal police and army checkpoints where bribes are considered the rule rather than the exception. The high-level presence of UN ground troops in Liberia arguably makes it an easier country to travel in than Guinea, where corruption has reached endemic levels. Watch out too for con merchants and petty officials itching to find a ruse to part you from some dollars.

Paperwork Unless you're an ECOWAS citizen, you need visas for both Liberia and Guinea, and neither offered visas on arrival at the time of writing, so it's necessary to arrange these in advance.

A watertight set of papers for a vehicle, if it is your own, includes ownership documents, a record of the vehicle, chassis and engine numbers, up-to-date insurance and a *carnet de passage* – issued by Classic Automotive Relocation Services (*CARS;* w *carseurope.net/carnet-de-passage-en-douanes-cpd*) in the UK. This is essentially a vehicle passport necessary to convince customs officials that you are bringing a vehicle into the country temporarily and will not sell it in their country without paying the necessary import duties. As security, CARS – the only issuer in the UK – needs a bank guarantee, insurance indemnity or full cash deposit, calculated according to the vehicle value and the countries you are visiting. If heading to Guinea, get your *carnet* stamped at the Sierra Leone customs post at Kambia-Gbalamuya; for Liberia it is Zimmi-Jendema.

Plenty of passport photocopies are also helpful to leave with officials to save time and administrative hold-ups. If you are in Sierra Leone and planning to drive back home, CARS can also issue you a *carnet* – do the paperwork by email and fax, and then pay for them to courier deliver it to your door. You don't even have to be British.

To travel through Guinea you will need what is known as a *laissez passer* – 'leave to pass' in French – that needs to be signed by someone in a position of authority that a Guinean policeman would recognise: ideally a police chief at the border or a diplomatic official in Freetown. You should make sure the document gives your name/s, vehicle registration and purpose for being in the country. Even though there's absolutely no official reason for needing one if you already have a carnet, not having it will lead to all kinds of questions and problems at checkpoints – some officials know that it's a way of making life difficult, others genuinely will not believe that you simply want to pass through.

Going through Liberia the experience can be equally painful. In addition to vehicle information, if you are using a local driver you will need proof from both immigration and police that he doesn't have a criminal record. Without a carnet, police may well require that a foreign-registered vehicle should have a 'temporary import permit' to prove you're not intending to sell it in Monrovia. To get one, you will likely need to put up a bond in US dollars that is based on the value of the vehicle. You do get that money back, if you return to the same border crossing before the expiry date on the permit. Negotiate the value of the permit, but demands for additional 'made-up-on-the-spot' fees are not unusual.

For each country you need vehicle insurance. There is nowhere to purchase insurance at the Liberian border, but in Conakry, Guinea, it is possible to buy an ECOWAS policy that is valid in all West African countries. Freetown also has several insurers in the city centre.

Bear in mind that border crossings can be notoriously long-winded, and posts often break for lunch. Leave a full day, and if you arrive late be prepared to spend the night, as most posts close at 18.00. There are several nice guesthouses in Kambia, 10 minutes from the Guinean border, and a couple of rudimentary ones on the Salone side of the Waterside crossing to Liberia. The road from the Guinean border to Freetown is now surfaced, and with roadworks well underway, the same should soon be true for Freetown to the Liberian border, hopefully during the lifespan of this edition.

BY SEA The regular ferry service between Freetown and Conakry has long been out of action, although there are occasionally hopeful rumours of it starting up again. Cargo and passenger ships berth at the Queen Elizabeth II Quay, while some passenger/cargo and private craft can land at Government Wharf in Central Freetown, arriving most often from Conakry and Banjul. Enquires should be made to cargo shipping agencies via the **Sierra Leone Ports Authority** (*Queen Elizabeth II Quay, Cline Town, Freetown;* \022 220 029). Also contact **Sea and Land Services** (*Cline Town, Freetown;* \022 223 453; e *sals@slsa.com.sl*), **Sierra Leone Shipping Agencies** (*Queen Elizabeth II Quay, Cline Town;* \022 229 855) and the **Sierra Leone National Shipping Company** (*45 Cline St, Cline Town;* m *076 721 781, 076 621 978;* e *slnscltd@gmail.com;* w slnsc.org).

AGS (*17 Sir Samuel Lewis Rd;* m *099 907 560;* e *manager-sierraleone@agsmovers. com;* w *agsmovers.com/branches/view/135*) or **Manor River** (w *manorriver.co.uk*) can arrange container freight transport around the world should you buy one souvenir too many.

HEALTH   *with Dr Felicity Nicholson*

PREPARATIONS Sensible preparation will go a long way to ensuring your trip goes smoothly. Particularly for first-time visitors to Africa, this includes a visit to a travel clinic to discuss matters such as vaccinations and malaria prevention. A list of recommended travel clinic websites worldwide is available at w itsm.org, and other useful websites for prospective travellers include w travelhealthpro.org.uk and w netdoctor.co.uk/travel. The Bradt website now carries a health section online (w *bradtguides.com/africahealth*) to help travellers prepare for their African trip, elaborating on most points raised below, but the following summary points are worth emphasising:

- Don't travel without comprehensive medical **travel insurance** that will fly you home in an emergency.
- Make sure all your **immunisations** are up to date. It is wise to be up to date on tetanus, polio and diphtheria (now given as an all-in-one vaccine, Revaxis, that lasts for ten years), and hepatitis A. Proof of vaccination against yellow fever is needed for entry for all travellers in to Sierra Leone regardless of age or where you are flying from. The yellow-fever vaccine is very rarely given before nine months of age as there is an increased risk of severe vaccine reactions before this age. Since July 2016, any yellow-fever certificate is considered to last for life if you are over two years of age and/or you are not immunosuppressed at the time of having the vaccine. If either of those criteria applied then revaccination is recommended at ten years. If the vaccine is not suitable for you then you would be wise not to travel, as West Africa has the highest prevalence of yellow fever and there is up to a 50% mortality rate. If the traveller insists on going then they will need a yellow-fever exemption certificate.
- The biggest health threat is **malaria**. There is no vaccine against this mosquito-borne disease, but a variety of preventative drugs is available, including mefloquine, malarone and the antibiotic doxycycline. The most suitable choice of drug varies depending on the individual and the country they are visiting, so

visit your GP or a travel clinic for medical advice. If you will be spending a long time in Africa, and expect to visit remote areas, be aware that no preventative drug is 100% effective, so carry a cure too. It is also worth noting that no homeopathic prophylactic for malaria exists, nor can any traveller acquire effective resistance to malaria. Those who don't make use of preventative drugs risk their life in a manner that is both foolish and unnecessary.

- Though advised for everyone, a **pre-exposure rabies vaccination**, involving three doses taken over a minimum of 21 days, is particularly important if you intend to have contact with animals, or are likely to be 24 hours away from medical help.
- Anybody travelling away from major centres should carry a **personal first-aid kit**. Contents might include a good drying antiseptic (eg: iodine or potassium permanganate), Band-Aids, suncream, insect repellent, aspirin or paracetamol, antifungal cream (eg: Canesten), ciprofloxacin or norfloxacin (for severe diarrhoea), antibiotic eye drops, tweezers, condoms or femidoms, a digital thermometer and a needle-and-syringe kit with an accompanying letter from a health-care professional.
- Bring any **drugs or devices relating to known medical conditions** with you. That applies both to those who are on medication prior to departure, and those who are, for instance, allergic to bee stings, or are prone to attacks of asthma.
- Prolonged immobility on long-haul flights can result in **deep-vein thrombosis** (DVT), which can be dangerous if the clot travels to the lungs to cause pulmonary embolus. The risk increases with age, and is higher in obese or pregnant travellers, heavy smokers, those taller than 6ft/1.8m or shorter than 5ft/1.5m, and anybody with a history of clots, recent major operation or varicose veins surgery, cancer, a stroke or heart disease. If any of these criteria apply, consult a doctor before you travel.

Protection from the sun Give some thought to packing suncream. The incidence of skin cancer is rocketing as Caucasians are travelling more and spending more time exposing themselves to the sun. Keep out of the sun during the middle of the day and, if you must expose yourself to the sun, build up gradually from 20 minutes per day. Be especially careful of exposure in the middle of the day and of sun reflected off water, and wear a T-shirt and lots of waterproof suncream (at least SPF25 and UVA of four or more stars) when swimming. Sun exposure ages the skin, makes people prematurely wrinkly, and increases the risk of skin cancer. Cover up with long, loose clothes and wear a hat when you can. The glare and the dust can be hard on the eyes, too, so bring UV-protecting sunglasses that carry a label for the British standard BS2724 1987 and, perhaps, a soothing eyebath.

COMMON MEDICAL PROBLEMS

Malaria Along with road accidents, malaria poses one of the biggest serious threats to the health of travellers in most parts of tropical Africa, Sierra Leone included. It is unwise to travel in malarial parts of Africa while pregnant or with children unless there is no other choice and then an in depth consultation with a suitably qualified person is paramount: the risk of malaria in many parts is considerable and these travellers are likely to succumb rapidly to the disease. The risk of malaria at altitudes above 1,800m is low.

Since no malaria prophylactic is 100% effective, it makes sense to take all reasonable precautions against being bitten by the nocturnal *Anopheles* mosquitoes that transmit the disease (see box, page 83). Malaria usually manifests within two weeks of transmission (though it can be as short as seven days), but it can take months, which means that short-stay visitors are most likely to experience symptoms after they return home. These typically include a rapid rise in temperature (over 38°C), and any combination of a headache, flu-like aches and pains, a general sense of disorientation, and possibly even nausea and diarrhoea. The earlier malaria is detected, the better it usually responds to treatment. So if you display possible symptoms, *get to a doctor or clinic immediately*. A simple test, available at even the most rural clinic in Africa, is usually adequate to determine whether you have malaria. And while experts differ on the question of self-diagnosis and self-treatment, the reality is that if you think you have malaria and are not within easy reach of a doctor, it would be wisest to start treatment.

Travellers' diarrhoea Travelling in Sierra Leone carries a fairly high risk of getting a dose of travellers' diarrhoea; perhaps half of all visitors will suffer and the newer you are to exotic travel, the more likely you will be to suffer. Rule one in avoiding diarrhoea and other sanitation-related diseases is arguably to wash your hands regularly, particularly before snacks and meals, and after handling money (one birr notes in particular are often engrained with filth). As for what food you can safely eat, a useful maxim is: PEEL IT, BOIL IT, COOK IT OR FORGET IT. This means that fruit you have washed and peeled yourself should be safe, as should hot cooked foods.

However, raw foods, cold cooked foods, salads, fruit salads prepared by others, ice cream and ice are all risky. It is rarer to get sick from drinking contaminated water but it happens, so stick to bottled water, which is widely available.

TREATING TRAVELLERS' DIARRHOEA   *Dr Jane Wilson-Howarth*

It is dehydration that makes you feel awful during a bout of diarrhoea and the most important part of treatment is drinking lots of clear fluids. Sachets of oral rehydration salts give the perfect biochemical mix to replace all that is pouring out of your bottom but other recipes taste nicer. Any dilute mixture of sugar and salt in water will do you good: try Coke or orange squash with a three-finger pinch of salt added to each glass (if you are salt-depleted you won't taste the salt). Otherwise make a solution of a four-finger scoop of sugar with a three-finger pinch of salt in a 500ml glass. Or add eight level teaspoons of sugar (18g) and one level teaspoon of salt (3g) to one litre (five cups) of safe water. A squeeze of lemon or orange juice improves the taste and adds potassium, which is also lost in diarrhoea. Drink two large glasses after every bowel action, and more if you are thirsty. These solutions are still absorbed well if you are vomiting, but you will need to take sips at a time. If you are not eating you need to drink three litres a day plus whatever is pouring into the toilet. If you feel like eating, take a bland, high carbohydrate diet. Heavy greasy foods will probably give you cramps.

If the diarrhoea is bad, or you are passing blood or slime, or you have a fever, you will probably need antibiotics in addition to fluid replacement. A dose of norfloxacin or ciprofloxacin repeated twice a day until better may be appropriate (if you are planning to take an antibiotic with you, note that both norfloxacin and ciprofloxacin are available only on prescription in the UK). If the diarrhoea is greasy and bulky and is accompanied by sulphurous (eggy) burps, one likely cause is giardia. This is best treated with tinidazole (four x 500mg in one dose, repeated seven days later if symptoms persist).

If you suffer a bout of diarrhoea, it is dehydration that makes you feel awful, so drink lots of water and other clear fluids (see box, page 81). These can be infused with sachets of oral rehydration salts, though any dilute mixture of sugar and salt in water will do you good, for instance a bottled soda with a pinch of salt. If diarrhoea persists beyond a couple of days, it is possible it is a symptom of a more serious sanitation-related illness (typhoid, cholera, hepatitis, dysentery, worms, etc), so get to a doctor. If the diarrhoea is greasy and bulky, and is accompanied by sulphurous (eggy) burps, one likely cause is giardia, which is best treated with tinidazole (four x 500mg in one dose, repeated seven days later if symptoms persist).

Bilharzia Also known as schistosomiasis, bilharzia is an unpleasant parasitic disease transmitted by freshwater snails most often associated with reedy shores where there is lots of water weed. It cannot be caught in hotel swimming pools, but should be assumed to be present in any freshwater river, pond, lake or similar habitat, probably even those advertised as 'bilharzia free'. The riskiest shores will be within 200m of villages or other places where infected people use water, wash clothes, etc. Ideally, however, you should avoid swimming in any fresh water other than an artificial pool. If you do swim, you'll reduce the risk by applying DEET insect repellent first, staying in the water for under 10 minutes, and drying off vigorously with a towel. Bilharzia is often asymptomatic in its early stages, but some people experience an intense immune reaction, including fever, cough, abdominal pain and an itching rash, around four to six weeks after infection. Later symptoms vary but often include a general feeling of tiredness and lethargy. Bilharzia is difficult to diagnose, but it can be tested for at specialist travel clinics, ideally at least six weeks after likely exposure. Fortunately, it is easy to treat at present.

Meningitis This is a particularly nasty disease as it can kill within hours of the first symptoms appearing. The telltale symptoms are a combination of a blinding headache (light sensitivity), a blotchy rash and a high fever. Immunisation protects against the most serious bacterial form of meningitis and the conjugate tetravalent vaccine ACWY (eg: Menveo or Nimenrix) is recommended for Sierra Leone by British travel clinics. If the conjugate form is not available then the polysaccharide form can be used. Although other forms of meningitis exist (usually viral), there are no vaccines for these. Local papers normally report localised outbreaks. A severe headache and fever should make you run to a doctor immediately. There are also other causes of headache and fever; one of which is typhoid, which occurs in travellers to Sierra Leone. Seek medical help if you are ill for more than a few days.

Rabies This deadly disease can be carried by any mammal and is usually transmitted to humans via a bite or a scratch that breaks the skin. In particular, beware of village dogs and monkeys habituated to people, but assume that *any* mammal that bites or scratches you (or even licks intact skin) might be rabid even if it looks healthy. First, scrub the wound with soap under a running tap for a good 10–15 minutes, or while pouring water from a jug, then pour on a strong iodine or alcohol solution, which will guard against infections and might reduce the risk of the rabies virus entering the body. Whether or not you had a pre-exposure vaccination, it is vital to obtain post-exposure prophylaxis as soon as possible after the incident. If you have had three pre-exposure doses of the vaccine then post-exposure treatment is simply two further doses of rabies vaccine given three days apart. However, if you have not had any rabies vaccines before, then you

AVOIDING MOSQUITO AND INSECT BITES

The *Anopheles* mosquitoes that spread malaria are active at dusk and after dark. Most bites can thus be avoided by covering up at night. This means donning a long-sleeved shirt, trousers and socks from around 30 minutes before dusk until you retire to bed, and applying a DEET-based insect repellent (around 50% DEET) to any exposed flesh. It is best to sleep under a net, or in an air-conditioned room, though burning a mosquito coil and/or sleeping under a fan will also reduce (though not entirely eliminate) bites. Travel clinics usually sell a good range of nets and repellents, as well as Permethrin treatment kits, which will render even the tattiest net a lot more protective, and helps prevent mosquitoes from biting through a net when you roll against it. These measures will also do much to reduce exposure to other nocturnal biters. Bear in mind, too, that most flying insects are attracted to light: leaving a lamp standing near a tent opening or a light on in a poorly screened hotel room will greatly increase the insect presence in your sleeping quarters.

It is also advisable to think about avoiding bites when walking in the countryside by day, especially in wetland habitats, which often teem with diurnal mosquitoes. Wear a long loose shirt and trousers, preferably 100% cotton, as well as proper walking or hiking shoes with heavy socks (the ankle is particularly vulnerable to bites), and apply a DEET-based insect repellent to any exposed skin.

---

need to have a full course (four to five doses over a month) and you may also need Rabies Immunoglobulin (RIG), which is unlikely to be available in Sierra Leone. Evacuate as soon as you can. Death from rabies is probably one of the worst ways to go, and once you show symptoms it is too late to do anything – the mortality rate is 100%.

Ebola Ebola is a rare but deadly viral disease caused by the Ebola virus. Both humans and non-human primates are susceptible to the disease. The reservoir is thought to be in bats. People get Ebola via direct contact through broken skin or mucous membranes with blood or other body fluids (eg saliva, vomit, semen, breast milk, etc). It can also be transmitted through contaminated needles and syringes, by eating infected meat or having contact with infected bats or primates. Symptoms of the disease include fever, severe headaches, muscle pain, fatigue, weakness, diarrhoea and vomiting. Unexplained bleeding or bruising, which is characteristic of the infection, occurs only in a proportion of people. Symptoms occur from 2 to 21 days after exposure. The case fatality rate varies from 25 to 90% depending on the outbreak, with an average of about 50%. Recovery from Ebola depends on good supportive clinical care and the strength of the patient's immune response. There is no definitive treatment for Ebola as yet, but some experimental vaccines and treatments are being developed.

Between May 2014 and June 2016, there was an outbreak of the Ebola virus in Sierra Leone, as well as neighbouring Liberia and Guinea. Following the declaration by the World Health Organisation in June 2016 that the countries were Ebola free, all three were put under increased surveillance for 90 days to ensure that any new cases were identified rapidly to prevent spread. The last recorded case of Ebola in Sierra Leone was in January 2016 but, like Guinea and Liberia, Sierra

Leone remains at heightened risk of small localised outbreaks. However, the risk to travellers continues to be extremely low unless there has been contact with blood or other body fluids from infected people. It is still wise to avoid eating bush meat or handling dead animals during your travels. It is wise to check the FCO updates for information on travel restrictions before travel.

Tetanus Tetanus is caught through deep dirty wounds, including animal bites, so ensure that such wounds are thoroughly cleaned. Immunisation protects for ten years, provided you don't have an overwhelming number of tetanus bacteria on board. If you haven't had a tetanus shot in ten years, or you are unsure, get a booster immediately.

HIV/AIDS Rates of HIV/AIDS infection are high in most parts of Africa, and other sexually transmitted diseases are rife. Condoms (or femidoms) greatly reduce the risk of transmission.

Tick bites Ticks in Africa are not the rampant disease transmitters that they are in the Americas, but they may spread tickbite fever along with a few dangerous rarities. They should ideally be removed complete as soon as possible to reduce the chance of infection. The best way to do this is to grasp the tick with your finger nails as close to your body as possible, and pull it away steadily and firmly at a right angle to your skin (do not jerk or twist it). If possible, douse the wound with alcohol (any spirit will do) or iodine. If you are travelling with small children, remember to check their heads, and particularly behind the ears, for ticks. Spreading redness around the bite and/or fever and/or aching joints after a tick bite implies that you have an infection that requires antibiotic treatment, so seek advice.

Skin infections Any mosquito bite or small nick in the skin gives an opportunity for bacteria to foil the body's usually excellent defences; it will surprise many travellers how quickly skin infections start in warm humid climates and it is essential to clean and cover even the slightest wound. Prickly heat, most likely to be contracted at the humid coast, is a fine pimply rash that can be alleviated by cool showers, dabbing (not rubbing) dry and talc, and sleeping naked under a fan or in an air-conditioned room. Fungal infections also get a hold easily in hot moist climates, so wear 100% cotton socks and underwear and shower frequently.

Eye problems Bacterial conjunctivitis (pink eye) is a common infection in Africa; people who wear contact lenses are most open to this irritating problem. The eyes feel sore and gritty and they will often be stuck together in the mornings. They will need treatment with antibiotic drops or ointment. Lesser eye irritation should settle with bathing in salt water and keeping the eyes shaded. If an insect flies into your eye, extract it with great care, ensuring you do not crush or damage it otherwise you may get a nastily inflamed eye from toxins secreted by the creature. Small elongated red-and-black blister beetles carry warning colouration to tell you not to crush them anywhere against your skin.

Sunstroke and dehydration Overexposure to the sun can lead to short-term sunburn or sunstroke, and increases the long-term risk of skin cancer. Wear a T-shirt and waterproof sunscreen when swimming. When visiting outdoor historical sites or walking in the direct sun, cover up with long, loose clothes, wear a hat, and use sunscreen. The glare and the dust can be hard on the eyes, so bring

UV-protecting sunglasses. A less direct effect of the tropical heat is dehydration, so drink more fluids than you would at home.

OTHER MEDICAL PROBLEMS

Snakes and other bites Snakes are very secretive and bites are a genuine rarity, but certain spiders and scorpions can also deliver nasty bites. In all cases, the risk is minimised by wearing closed shoes and trousers when walking in the bush, and watching where you put your hands and feet, especially in rocky areas or when gathering firewood. Only a small fraction of snakebites deliver enough venom to be life-threatening, but it is important to keep the victim calm and inactive, and to seek urgent medical attention.

Other insect-borne diseases Although malaria is the insect-borne disease that attracts the most attention in Africa, and rightly so, there are others, most too uncommon to be a significant concern to short-stay travellers. These include dengue fever and other arboviruses (spread by diurnal mosquitoes), sleeping sickness (tsetse flies), and river blindness (blackflies). Bearing this in mind, however, it is clearly sensible, and makes for a more pleasant trip, to avoid insect bites as far as possible (see box, page 83). Two nasty (though ultimately relatively harmless) flesh-eating insects associated with tropical Africa are *tumbu* or *putsi* flies, which lay eggs, often on drying laundry, that hatch and bury themselves under the skin when they come into contact with humans, and jiggers, which latch on to bare feet and set up home, usually at the side of a toenail, where they cause a painful boil-like swelling. Drying laundry indoors and wearing shoes are the best way to deter this pair of flesh-eaters. Symptoms and treatment of all these afflictions are described in greater detail on Bradt's website (w *bradtguides.com/africahealth*).

OTHER SAFETY CONCERNS

Swimming It's likely you'll want to sample Sierra Leone's beautiful warm waters, but be warned that along the Peninsula coast riptides near the shore can be fierce. A handful of the beaches are installing lifeguard towers, but they are not always manned. If you are not a confident swimmer, go in with someone else and keep them close by, preferably seawards. If you are further from the shore, snorkelling or diving from a boat for example, currents can flow at up to two knots in places – too fast to swim back to a stationary launch. Look out too for large shoals of stinging jellyfish. A couple of antihistamine tabs can be life saving. If you are scuba diving, bear in mind that Sierra Leone does not have a decompression chamber, so if for any reason you surface too quickly there is no treatment available.

Water may be contaminated by other swimmers and from sewage, animal waste and wastewater runoff that can cause diarrhoea, as well as ear, eye and skin infections. Fresh water from lakes and rivers may contain schistosomiasis, and in areas where water is warm potentially fatal primary amoebic meningoencephalitis. Fast-flowing rivers are a better bet than still lakes and pools. Swimming pools are generally safe, as long as you are confident they are adequately chlorinated and maintained. In all cases, try to avoid swallowing water, and open cuts and sores greatly increase the chance of pathogens passing into the body.

Car accidents Dangerous driving is probably the biggest threat to life and limb in most parts of Africa. On a self-drive visit, drive defensively, being especially wary of stray livestock, gaping potholes, and imbecilic or bullying overtaking manoeuvres. Many vehicles lack headlights and most local drivers are reluctant headlight users,

Marie Stopes Sierra Leone, the local branch of the international British charity, runs a network of 12 high-quality clinics scattered around the country. Each clinic is staffed by at least two qualified nurses and undergoes a thorough quality assessment each year. Stop by if you're looking for a medical check-up, contraception, or treatment for a sexually transmitted infection. Where labs are present, the staff can also carry out stool, urine and blood testing – including for malaria and typhoid. All of the clinics have the same opening hours: 08.30–16.30 Monday to Friday and 08.30–12.30 Saturday.

Ahmed Drive Clinic, Labs & Emergency Obstetrics Centre 10 Ahmed Dr, off Aberdeen Rd, Aberdeen, Freetown; m 076 723 143 (obstetrics unit), 076 314 206 (clinic), 076 633 963 (labs)
Kissy Clinic & Labs Low Cost Housing Estate, Old Rd, Kissy, Freetown; m 076 314 157
Waterloo Street Clinic 43 Waterloo St, Freetown; m 076 314 160
Kossoh Town Clinic 39 Main Rd, Kossoh Town, Freetown; m 076 314 158
Mile 91 Clinic & Labs Freetown–Bo Highway, Mile 91; m 076 417 901
Bo Clinic 18B Kissy Town Rd, Bo; m 076 314 159
Pujehun Clinic District Council Rd, Pujehun; m 076 406 704
Kailahun Clinic & Labs Bundeh Compound Mofindor Rd, Kailahun; m 076 406 539
Kenema Clinic & Labs 12 Mission Rd, Kenema; m 076 314 155
Kono Clinic 20 Main Rd, Koidu; m 076 314 207
Makeni Clinic & Labs 7 Ladies Miles, Makeni; m 076 654 876
Kabala Clinic & Labs 16 Gbawuria Rd, Kabala; m 076 699 501

so avoid driving at night and pull over in heavy storms. On a chauffeured tour, don't be afraid to tell the driver to slow or calm down if you think he is driving too fast or being reckless.

SAFETY

Despite the raised eyebrows and occasional grunts of disbelief that greet the news that you are daring to venture into a one-time warzone and epidemic hotspot, Sierra Leone is today among the safest countries in Africa. Honestly.

All arms are now banned from civilian use. United Nations troops left at the end of 2005, and the British-led International Military and Advisory Training Team (IMATT) concluded their mission in 2013.

Today IMATT's successor, the International Security Advisory Team Sierra Leone (ISAT), focuses on advising Sierra Leone's emergency and security services, including the fire brigades, prison service and coast guard. The UN Integrated Peacebuilding Office in Sierra Leone (UNIPSIL) completed its mandate in 2014, and now the UN is active here only as part of the United Nations Development Programme (UNDP), sponsoring poverty eradication and inequality reduction programmes.

CRIME Serious crime is relatively low and most people enjoy their stay with no problems at all. Many houses within compounds are guarded by round-the-clock uniformed guards and perimeter walls are often topped with rolls of barbed wire or broken glass. Very occasional armed attacks on households have occurred, but they tend to be targeted and do not normally involve visitors.

Petty crime, pickpocketing and armed mugging are sadly more common, and while still relatively rare overall they are likely to rise in line with urban poverty. Don't make mistakes you would never dream of making at home, such as leaving room doors unlocked or expensive items on show – things will disappear. Plus, if something goes wrong, don't despair of everyone. A young couple, having had a couple of bags stolen, were approached by the caretaker of the convent they had been staying in. 'There are some really bad people in Sierra Leone,' he said, taking them by the hand as a tear ran down his cheek. 'But don't forget there are some good ones too.'

Among the few potential trouble spots is the Lumley–Aberdeen beach strip in west Freetown after dark. Muggings and car break-ins are common, and smartphones and wallets are regularly stolen. The very southern end near the Golf Club (a regular escape route) is often targeted. Early-morning joggers and anyone on the beach from dusk onwards are at risk, with occasional threats at knifepoint. Save moonlit strolls for the Peninsula. All beach bars, however, are fenced off, with plenty of workers and customers, and are perfectly safe.

Most of the time being on foot in downtown Freetown attracts a lot of attention, from petty traders, moneychangers and beggars. While some can turn thief quickly, it's not generally a dangerous place to be in daylight hours. The national stadium – which can seat 40,000 people – offers a field day for light fingers. Burglary, sometimes armed, and street robbery spike in the lead-up to Christmas.

The only thing worse than being robbed is seeing what happens if some poor unfortunate is caught: mob justice looms large on the streets of Freetown, where suspected thieves can be beaten up, belted or worse by angry bands at a moment's notice. Shout 'thief' (or, in Krio, '*teefman*'), and people are likely to give chase, and land some pretty hard punches too if they can. In rare instances teefmen have been beaten to death. The east end is considered the most dangerous part of Freetown, with higher crime rates, and walking in the area after dark is ill-advised.

Transport Be careful in cars: many thieves, particularly in the Lumley and Regent Road area of west Freetown, are perfectly happy to reach in through an open window and swipe your phone from your ear. Others, working in pairs, may try to distract you; one for example alleging you have knocked into them or their vehicle while another unlocks your door through an open window, and holds you up. Any fumbling by a fellow passenger in the back of a taxi could be a distraction for their accomplice to go for your pockets, or a gaping bag. Most diplomatic missions and donor agencies do not allow their staff to take public transport at all, and some volunteers are not comfortable taking a taxi after dark.

Roads The most dangerous aspect of travel in Sierra Leone is road transport, with many routes erratically paved. Inform people in-country of details of any intended travel, and make arrangements to contact them if necessary at both ends of your journey.

'Serious road accidents occur quite frequently in Sierra Leone owing to the hazardous driving conditions, poor vehicle maintenance and erratic driving,' says the FCO. 'All roads are unlit and pot-holes are common, especially during the rainy season (May to November). The vast majority of roads have no streetlights, signs, painted markings or cat's eyes. The emergency service response to accidents in Freetown is very slow and unreliable. Outside the capital you should assume that there would be no emergency service response to an accident.'

Never drive outside Freetown at night – in addition to the danger of livestock collisions, lorry breakdowns are frequent and many vehicles lack lights. Crews usually sleep under their vehicles, which are often left on one side of the road, with only a tree branch placed a few metres up the road as warning.

HASSLES AND PROTOCOL

Dealing with authority Sierra Leone has a reputation for corruption, and was ranked 123 of 176 countries in 2016 by Transparency International (position number one being least corrupt).

But it's worth bearing in mind that how you are treated may be very much down to you. Some long-standing visitors have never once paid a bribe (although they might have developed a bit of a way with smooth talking); others declare within 72 hours that you can't possibly get anywhere with anyone without passing cash. It just goes to show that corruption is just as much, if not more, down to the 'briber' as the 'bribee'. Generally, it's probably fair to give Sierra Leone better marks than people might expect, and many Sierra Leoneans you are likely to meet will be upstanding, honest and genuinely helpful.

Numerous checkpoints line the entry and exit points to towns upcountry, and there are a handful of police points in Freetown where vehicles are sometimes pulled over. With the presence of so many ex-mercenaries, shady foreign businessmen, the odd cocaine trafficker (a record bust of 700kg in mid 2008 saw several expats arrested) and earnest NGO workers, officers are likely to take an interest in your movements, particularly if you are not travelling on a diplomatic passport, so expect to be asked your business, and your destination.

Police are recognisable by their bright blue uniforms and berets. The armed wing of the police force, the Operational Support Division (OSD), usually wears blue camouflage uniforms with maroon berets and often carry weapons. Traffic policemen usually wear white sleeves over their blue shirts, along with dark trousers and white gloves. You may also find yourself dealing with military police, who wear khaki and red berets, although they, in theory, are not supposed to have any jurisdiction over civilians.

Most dealings with the police go well. News that you might be in Sierra Leone for pleasure will be met with either outright disbelief and suspicion, or joyous incredulity. It can make life tougher, as the unscrupulous might think you are therefore a light touch; but it can also make people go out of their way to help, and feel a sense of pride that you have come to their country.

Should something go wrong, the police are there to help. But often they lack the funds even to fuel a car to reach the scene of a crime and investigate, so too frequently victims have to cough up running expenses. The best port of call is your embassy, high commission or consulate, which can advise on informing the authorities and the next steps.

Checkpoints Despite huge improvements in police and military conduct in the past few years, checkpoints are inevitably a place where officials are likely to try to extort money. This can be done with varying levels of charm and with far more subtlety than in neighbouring Guinea, where the demands are much more blatant. Stay friendly – it's perfectly possible never to pay a bribe and pass unhindered. At no stage lose your cool; ensure your papers are correct; and remain scrupulously polite at all times. And be ready for the strangest of accusations – 'Yes your papers are all correct, but this doesn't apply after 2am,' was one of the best we heard from an enterprising young officer. Another was: 'Do you really think it's appropriate for you to be going to a nightclub at night?' In Freetown the night-time checkpoint on Lumley Beach Road can be particularly trying.

The most important stop in the country is just before the town of Waterloo, on the way on to the Peninsula from upcountry, a kind of gateway to the capital. The worst time to pass is in the late afternoon, when officials know that drivers are in a hurry to get home. Some police officers in the eastern mining districts have tried to extract 'facilitation charges' from travellers simply wanting to get to the town of Koidu.

Local chiefs Outside Freetown, Sierra Leone is an even safer place to be. But upcountry it pays to observe local protocols. As a matter of courtesy, it's always good to check in with the local paramount chief or village headman or headwoman wherever you end up. A small gift, of useful supplies or goods such as sugar, soap or green tea, or a little money, will set the right note of appreciation and respect, and ensure you will be well looked after.

SOLO TRAVELLERS Travelling solo in Sierra Leone is wonderfully doable, whether male or female. Especially upcountry, beyond the towns, politeness and warmth can be found in bucketfuls. It's not without risk, however, and it makes sense to plan your itinerary and let at least three people know about it – one back home, one wherever you're departing from, and one where you're headed (even if it's only a hotel or guesthouse), so someone always keeps tabs on you. Also make sure people back home have details of your travel insurance policy.

WOMEN TRAVELLERS In rural areas, women should find it possible to travel on their own without encountering too much hassle. Although you are likely to be a constant object of attention, which can be wearing, respect tends to be uppermost in people's minds. In towns, however, it's not uncommon for men to accost women out of nowhere with phrases such as 'I like you', 'I want you for friend' and, pushing the boundaries even of Romeo-esque passion, 'I love you'. In all cases this pretty much means they want to get it on or, sometimes just as usefully, get a visa.

Claims of a boyfriend or husband, or a strategically placed ring, marginally decrease interest, although often this isn't seen as at all relevant given your assumed mutual ardour, alongside a rather lax interpretation of fidelity. It's fine to be firm: you won't offend someone by making your 'no' unequivocally clear. As one experienced traveller put it: 'a sense of humour and willingness to chat rubbish helped, as did claiming not to own a mobile or that it was for work.'

Often, when travelling on buses and other transport, it makes sense to try and build rapport with another friendly-looking woman and, if in doubt, follow her lead. While wearing vest tops tends to be fine, exposing knees or excessive cleavage can be seen as uncouth upcountry.

Tampons are available in supermarkets in Freetown, Makeni and Bo but not elsewhere. Sanitary towels are widely available in shops and even market stalls in reasonably sized towns nationwide.

TRAVELLING WITH A DISABILITY There are no facilities for disabled travellers in Sierra Leone. The Sierra Leone Union on Disability Issues (SLUDI) campaigns on behalf of Sierra's Leone's disabled people, and there remain a number of organisations advocating for the interests of war amputees. Nova Afrika in Kent (page 214) is noteworthy as perhaps the country's only fully handicap-accessible hotel.

The UK's **gov.uk** website (**w** *gov.uk/guidance/foreign-travel-for-disabled-people*) provides general advice and practical information for travellers with disabilities preparing for overseas travel. **Accessible Journeys** (**w** *disabilitytravel. com*) is a comprehensive US site written by wheelchair users who have been researching wheelchair-accessible travel full-time since 1985. There are many tips and useful contacts (including lists of travel agents on request) for slow walkers, wheelchair travellers and their families, plus informative articles, including pieces on disabled travelling worldwide. The company also organises group tours. **Global Access News** (**w** *globalaccessnews.com/index.htm*) provides general travel information, reviews and tips for travelling with a disability. The **Society for Accessible Travel and Hospitality** (**w** *sath.org*) also provides some general information.

WHAT TO TAKE

CLOTHES Pack either for hot, wet, or both. Loose cotton clothes are good, as is a sunhat. T-shirts, vests and light shirts will be your stock-in-trade; beachwear is a

LGBTI community in Freetown and now upcountry in Makeni, Bo and Kenema. Working alongside Dignity, there's Pride Equality (m *077 383 761, 078 349 866;* w *prideequality.org*), run by George Freeman. Pride works to protect the rights of LGBTI people in Salone and also works with youth to counter homophobia.

Freeman himself was the victim of a brutal, and as yet unsolved, attack in 2012 after being publicly outed by a local newspaper. Global Rights, an international NGO, works with local activist organisations (like Dignity and Pride) and non-queer groups to help them identify, document and record LGBTI human rights abuses in the country. For more information, go to [w] globalrights.org.

Freetown is the centre of most gay activity and many of its queer secrets are slowly coming out of the closet. The Office nightclub – now closed down – used to be a popular hangout for legitimate Freetown queers. The male gay scene is much more organised and most house parties will be largely male affairs. For women, it is often a question of sharpening your gay-dar and going with your instincts. Like gays and lesbians around the world, many in Freetown's gay community have formed cliques based on class and upbringing. The 'east-end' gays are those from the densely populated east side of Freetown, many of whom are poor and unemployed. The 'west-end' group are those who live in the more affluent western parts of Freetown, as well as those who have lived abroad, in the West. Like the 'A' gays in Armistead Maupin's fictitious tales of San Francisco, this crowd is purposely ostentatious, even giving themselves the nickname 'Royalty'. Although the two groups engage in competition, it is mostly friendly, with the west and east frequently duelling to see who can throw the most extravagant gay party. Freetown gay parties happen frequently throughout the year, often hosting as many as 50 gay men and women from all parts of the city. Check with the groups mentioned above for up-to-date information on parties and events. In the dry season they often move to a private area on Black Johnson Beach – between York and John Obey beaches on the western peninsula – where the Freetown queers come out in all their fabulousness to show off their skimpy swim suits, sip cocktails and hopefully meet a beach buddy.

must, and going out is pretty heavy duty, so there's no need to dress only for the bush. If you hit Sierra Leone during the rainy season, you can buy umbrellas there, but good breathable waterproofs (top and bottom) are worth bringing. Plastic macs or rain jackets from markets will merely increase your sweating. Hotels have towels, but not all guesthouses.

Off the beach, shorts tend to scream 'tourist', and even when trekking they leave you exposed to bites and attacking plants, so full-length trousers are usually a better bet. If you are likely to be in Sierra Leone for a while, bring at least one set of reasonably formal clothes for any functions (certainly if you're working there, but on the off-chance you are invited to a wedding or other 'event'), which can be quite dressy. You can also have clothes tailored in-country. While Sierra Leone is home to a huge Muslim population, many women do not cover their heads.

SHOES Sandals are great most of the time, but running shoes and/or hiking boots are essential if you want to do any exercise or climb any of the hills. There's no reason to leave your high heels at home, as partying is taken pretty seriously. You can buy wellies in Freetown if you are caught in one deluge too many.

KIT If you fancy climbing Mount Bintumani or camping out during your stay (your only option in many areas), ultra-light camping gear is preferable. Some swear by a mosquito hammock (try w mosquitohammock.com for details), doing away with the need for sleeping bag and bulky tent. A mosquito dome, also known as a self-supporting net or bug hut, is great for sleeping out on the beaches. A silk or cotton sleeping-bag liner is just about the best luxury going, whether you are camping or not, as you can feel clean in even the grimiest of guesthouse beds.

Some form of water purifier – iodine, tablets or even a filter – is a good idea, but bear in mind they won't kill giardia.

You can't fly gas canisters into the country and they're nowhere for sale, so a gas camping stove is pretty much useless. Instead buy a big metal pot in the markets (about Le20,000) and cook on a fire out in the wild.

Supermarkets in Freetown are well stocked with shampoo, conditioner, soap, razors, tampons and all the other sundries you might think you should pack but don't need to, although prices can be higher than back home.

Bring plenty of high-factor suncream and mosquito spray with you. Binoculars are a must for birdwatchers (8x40 is better than 10x50 for finding the fast fliers), and a camera. A torch, matches, penknife or utility tool, and a pocket radio are all neat ideas too. A first-aid kit, plus sterile needle set, and travel dental kit, are sensible. Make sure you have a thermometer – normal body temperature is 37°C or 98.6°F.

An 'unlocked' mobile phone is also a good idea (pages 117–19).

ELECTRIC PLUGS Sierra Leone mostly uses UK-style three-pin plugs, with the odd two-pin socket exception. Chances to charge your phone, mp3 player, laptop and camera battery are few and far between owing to power shortages and conservative generator use, so having a rechargeable power bank is eminently useful. Very rarely is any socket or appliance earthed, so wear rubber-soled shoes, just in case. Street shacks offer mobile-phone charging for Le2,000.

MAPS Given that European explorers have been mapping Sierra Leone for centuries, it's ironic how hard it is to get hold of a reliable map. While you're unlikely to have any problems in Freetown, upcountry it's a different matter. No map is accurate, and town and village names are misrendered by cartographers who don't speak the language and rely on aerial photos. It's worryingly easy to find yourself on a road that, according to the map, doesn't exist.

A curious knock-on effect of the Ebola crisis, however, has been a dramatic improvement in mapping nationwide. Because the agencies tasked with tracing and containing the outbreak had to reach even the tiniest communities in the furthest reaches of the country, a drastic improvement in available map cover was required, and thankfully much of that painstakingly gathered data has now been ported over to **Open Street Maps** (w *openstreetmaps.org*), where it's available for all free of charge.

Printed map options include publications from **International Travel Maps** (*12300 Bridgeport Rd, Richmond, BC V6V 1JF, Canada;* +1 604 273 1400; w *itmb.com*), who produces a relatively recent map of the whole country, with a useful inset of the capital. You can order this from the ITMB site or Amazon, or visit a good map store such as **Stanfords** (which also does online ordering) in central London (*12–14 Long Acre, Covent Garden, London WC2E 9LP;* 020 7836 1321; e *sales@stanfords. co.uk;* w *stanfords.co.uk*). However, it doesn't always get place names correct, and some roads are missed.

The National Tourist Board has also produced tourist maps for Sierra Leone, on sale via a number of travel and tour operators. They're available at the **Visit**

Sierra Leone (✆ *022 236 325;* m *076 877 618*) offices at Congo Cross for around Le75,000.

The **Sierra Leone Information Service's (SLIS) Development Assistance Co-ordination Office (DACO)** (*13 Bath St, Brookfields;* ✆ *022 235 348/9*), has an excellent maps department, which has produced a range of district and town maps at a decent scale mostly for government planning purposes, though drawing on data produced back in the 1970s. These can be printed out in colour at good quality for Le45,000 per map.

The maps produced in this guidebook draw heavily on all of the above sources, and we are grateful to ITMB and SLIS for permission to use their copyright where applicable. We have added to these base maps with information we've collected ourselves, and entirely redrawn many maps based on newly available Open Street Maps data for this third edition of the guide. They should all put you on the right track, but be warned they won't win any Ordnance Survey awards.

MONEY

Once upon a time cotton spools were used as currency. Then there was the Kissi penny – a long, thin sliver of metal about the size of a knitting needle, with a 'head' and 'foot' at opposite ends. The money was said to be inhabited by the spirit of the chief, and when a chief died these money sticks were broken and stuck in the ground.

Not any more. Today the currency, named after the country, is the leone, abbreviated to Le. When first introduced in 1964, there were two leones to the pound sterling. Now, decades after it broke from the sterling peg in 1978, it's around ten thousand. The dollar is more acceptable than sterling if you are paying for items in foreign currency. At the time of writing, £1 went for Le10,100, US$1 for Le7,600 and €1 for Le9,000, but this can change significantly from month to month: check before going.

Grubby leone denominations come in a yellowing Le1,000 note; a burnt orange Le2,000; a blue/purple Le5,000 denomination; and a greenish Le10,000. A former Central Bank governor brought in crisper, more plastic paper to help leone banknotes stand a chance of being properly dispensed by an ATM. Meanwhile, local newspaper headlines still regularly castigate market women who stuff their takings down their bras and men who rely on their pants instead. Almost nothing is considered in too bad condition to accept. Banks dispense newer notes but it's pure luck whether you get them or not. Coins range from a big, brassy Le500, down through Le200 and Le100 pieces to a small octagonal Le50 (about one pence sterling). 'One block' refers to Le100.

BANKS There's a small but growing network of international ATMs in the country, with machines in Freetown, Waterloo, Bo, Makeni, Kabala, Koidu and at Lungi airport. That said, the machines frequently break down or run out of bills, but the network was reliable enough that, with a bit of advance planning, we financed our entire 2017 research trip using solely ATMs to draw cash. See the individual chapters for specific banking options in each town. In Freetown, ATMs can be found near Lumley Beach Road (next to Papaya Restaurant), the Lumley Police Station, Bottom Mango roundabout, Congo Cross roundabout, Hill Cot roundabout (outside St Mary's Supermarket), the city centre off Siaka Stevens Street, and inside several of the top-end hotels, including the Radisson Blu, The Hub and Lagoonda.

If the ATMs fail you, another way to withdraw money is via a cash advance on your credit or debit card. You don't need your PIN code but you do need your passport. Rokel Commercial Bank, which has two branches in Freetown and a single branch in several provincial towns, including Makeni, Bo, Kenema and Kono, is the only bank that does this, but allow an hour for the process. If you are taking out a large lump sum to save on banking charges (it costs a minimum Le50,000 for the transaction, or 5% of the total value of the withdrawal) then bring a bag: you'll leave with cash bricks. It can take more than a month for the debit to register in your home bank account, so don't be lulled into a false sense of security. Keep checking your statements even after you leave the country, as fraud using this method has been known.

No matter the currency your home account is held in, the leone amount you leave the bank with is calculated against a dollar conversion, so you lose on the exchange rate twice. Travellers' cheques are only accepted in a few banks, and having them is not convenient.

CASH Cash is by far the easiest option, and most visitors arrive with a well-concealed wedge of greenbacks (see below for further advice). The official exchange rate is very close to the informal, black-market rate. Banks only offer a marginal loss, but with the fillip of receiving freshly minted notes. Moneychangers, known as 'dollar boys', line Siaka Stevens Street in downtown Freetown, and will ask you to change money at every step. Changing money with unlicensed money dealers is illegal, and very public. It's safer to change money at most hotels and official change outlets, with supermarkets being perhaps the most convenient option of all. It's harder to change euros than dollars (super easy) or sterling (reliable), but most times still possible to find someone, even a pharmacist, to help you out in a fix if you're upcountry without a bank nearby.

Dollar peculiarities The greenback is the favoured hard currency, and although not officially a parallel currency you can pay direct in US dollars for many things. In fact, the water-taxi services to and from the airport quote everything in dollars (though they also accept leones), as do pricier hotels.

Almost all supermarkets will accept them for goods, and any that do will usually exchange leones at or close to the going rate, so long as you are changing a fair quantity, say US$50 or more. Hotels, restaurants and bars often give a slightly poorer rate, so check before changing.

The larger the denomination, the better the rate. The golden and inexplicable rule, however, is no 'small heads' (Ulysses S Grant and Benjamin Franklin come in two sizes) or notes from 1996 and before – they won't be accepted, and even older 'big head' bills are likely to be greeted with some scepticism. Generally speaking, newer is always better, and you'd be best equipped with hundreds from 2013 or newer (with the blue strip) and fifties starting from 2004. Most establishments and currency changers – be they dollar boys or forex bureaux – also refuse smaller dollar denominations. There's little point taking one- or ten-dollar bills as tip money either; leones are much better for that. Some may grudgingly accept US$20 bills, but they will penalise you on the exchange rate. While it might feel like they are burning a hole in your pocket, US$50 and US$100 bills are your friends.

TRANSFERS If in dire straits, money transfer works, but the fees eat into the value. Branches of Western Union and MoneyGram dot Freetown and there's usually at least one office in the main towns, and several smaller ones too. MoneyGram has posts in Bo, Freetown, Kailahaun, Kenema, Koidu, Lunsar, Lungi, Magburaka,

Makeni and Moyomba and at branches of Afro International Ltd, GT (Guaranty Trust) Bank Ltd and Sierra Leone Commercial Bank. Western Union has branches in Bo, Freetown, Kambia, Kenema, Kono, Lungi, Lunsar, Makeni, Mattru Jong, Mile 91 and Segbwema.

BUDGETING

Hotels are not as cheap as they should be, largely because paying for electricity involves a private generator and gallons of increasingly expensive fuel. That combines disastrously with an ongoing influx of relatively well-paid, long-term foreign workers, many of whom live in self-catering hotel apartments and villas, which further drives prices up for the traveller. As for commercial property, renting a flat in Freetown is on a par with renting in London.

ON A BUDGET

Stay in a village	Offer Le10,000–20,000 per night
Eat at a street stall or cookery	Le8,000
Drink *poyo*	Le1,000
Travel by taxi or poda poda	Le70,000 should get you from one side of the country to the other; Le2,000 will pay for a one-way ride in town

HALFWAY DECENT

Guesthouse	Le100,000–200,000 per night
Restaurant meal	Le30,000–60,000 a plate
Drink Star beer	Le8,000
Travel by chartered taxi	Le40,000 per hour (in town); plus fuel if going far

AIMING FOR LUXURY

Hotel room	US$75–100
Nice meal out	Le100,000 per main course
Drink imported beer	Le14,000
Travel by hired 4x4 with driver	US$80–300 (Freetown) to US$150–300 (provinces) per day

JET SET

Hotel suite	US$150–200
Dine in style	US$50
Drink European wine	US$40 a bottle
Travel by speedboat	US$400 per day (or chartered plane US$2,000)

GETTING AROUND

Traffic drives on the right, a shift made in 1971 to keep pace with neighbours and fellow right-handers Guinea and Liberia, as well as an attempt to shed the yoke of colonialism. Drivers stuck notes all over their cars to remind themselves, and some radio jingles had people so on-the-ball they switched lanes ahead of time, with disastrous results.

Today you could be forgiven for thinking that many people still aren't quite sure, as cars overtake into oncoming traffic, and hazard lights are switched on by those in a hurry as an apology for doing whatever they like.

2

Accidents are common, and transport is often in a state of ill-repair – think nothing of vehicles with cracked windscreens, missing mirrors and no seatbelts, with so much paraphernalia piled up on the dashboard (family photos, fake flowers, encouraging cards, plastic toys, totems) that it's hard to see out anyway. Roads upcountry are often dire and particularly dangerous during and directly after the end of the rainy season.

BY PODA PODA Poda podas are the backbone of the public transport system. Perhaps it's no surprise then that the phrase is often taken to mean 'slowly slowly'. These wood-slat-seated minibuses travel on numerous fixed routes, and in central Freetown this usually means the most congested roads. They pick up and drop off on request, and are easily hailed. Crammed with people, they are also among the best places to find out the latest music hits.

Give your money in advance to the 'apprentice', the young chap who yells out the destinations, and opens and closes the sliding door, yanking himself back in just as the vehicle gets going again.

BY TAXI For those without transport, taxis are the easiest way to get around. You can spot them by their yellow sides, although there are a few magnificently incongruous black and red London cabs plying routes too. You can hail one whenever you see it, but bear in mind they are shared and tend to keep to fixed routes. Shout out your destination and be prepared to be refused if it's not in the right direction. Learn the key routes and in your head combine them in order to reach your destination.

Taxis are priced by the distance you travel. 'One-way' costs Le2,000 (although this rises in line with petrol price hikes), but is a variable unit of distance (roughly

1–2km). Expect to be overcharged the first few times you use a taxi, and watch how much other passengers pay to get a feel for how far Le2,000 will take you.

Have fun judging the perfect moment to pay: never at the start of the ride; never as you're getting out; but reach over to the driver just as you're coming up to the spot you want to get out, leaving enough time for him to pass back your change in a suitably leisurely fashion. 'No *cha cha*' means you don't want the taxi to yourself, but are prepared to take a ride like a normal passenger.

You can always ask to charter the taxi (in which case, ask for a '*cha cha*'), but expect to pay a premium of Le40,000 an hour. In Freetown, a taxi seats four people (one in the front; three in the back); but for trips upcountry, they seat six (two share the front seat, along with the gear stick; four squeeze up in the back, sometimes with a chicken or bag of charcoal). It's not comfortable. If you want a seat to yourself, pay double.

BY MOTORBIKE Sierra Leone is also home to the motorbike taxi – hop on the back, hold on, and go. Known locally both as Hondas and *ocadas*, they are most popular in the provincial towns of Bo, Makeni and Kenema, but pop up in other towns such as Kabala and Koidu. In Freetown they are a handy way to dodge the traffic in the east of town, and to head out from Lumley to get to the beaches on the Peninsula.

In the provinces, a 'one-way' costs Le2,000, and to charter one for an hour is usually about Le20,000. Negotiation in Freetown is usually a little harder. For longer distances, expect to pay more (sometimes double), and stump up fuel costs too.

WHAT'S IN A NAME?

Among the more original travel games to pass the time in Salone is 'spot the best poda poda name': they tend to have some sort of title, missive or supportive message on offer to passing members of the public, plastered on the outside in bright paint.

Many invoke the religious, from reassuring and sturdy succour such as 'God is great' and 'Allah is supreme' to more inward-looking ideas such as 'I hope to God' and 'Fear Judgement Day'. The collision of modern multi-culturalism is seen in 'God Bless Islam' and 'BigBigGod.com', alongside the joyful but perhaps theologically premature celebrations 'God has done it!' and 'All hail the liberator'.

The other national religion, football, features heavily, in particular the ongoing battle for the ascendancy of either Man United or Arsenal, with the occasional kindly appearance for Liverpool.

While some are more opaque in meaning ('The British man' or 'Black heart', for example), others provide a moral compass – 'Wor nor good' (war's no good), 'No food for lazy man', 'Nor Moless Pikin' (don't molest children), 'Be Patient', 'Fair Play' and 'Be honest' among them. Some stick to the basics ('Hope' and 'Destiny', for example), while others just implore fun: 'Loose you Face' is an entreaty to smile.

If you're really getting keen, feast your eyes on the tax discs and dashboards of taxis across the country. Again there's the same heady mix of religion and moralising, from 'My business is covered with the blood of Jesus' and 'I must eat the fruit of my labour in Jesus's name' on the back of tax discs, to lessons for life such as 'Rumours are created by enemies; spread by ignorants and accepted by fools'. And for the more ontologically minded: 'If anything is something … then everything is nothing.'

ON YOUR BIKE

Medical students Rob Hughes and Paddy Howlett cycled hundreds of miles from Bintumani to Koidu and on to Bonthe Island (with the help of a boat) before heading back to Freetown via stops on the beaches of the Peninsula, over the course of a month. Despite picking the tail-end of the rainy season for their adventure, they found cycling an incredible way to travel, and easy to organise.

As a relatively small country, the distances are very manageable on two wheels, even in the heat! We found cycling was quicker on the average dirt road than poda podas, and there was no more waiting about than we decided we wanted. Plus the scenery is beautiful, and we really could get to places impossible to reach on almost any other form of transport. If we particularly enjoyed a place it was easy to stay the night.

The cycling itself was awesome, challenging and strenuous at times. Neither of us would class ourselves as experienced mountain bikers; more cyclists by necessity around town, with occasional off-road trips. We ambitiously picked the end of the rainy season to go, when some roads become overgrown, rivers swollen and bridges washed out, making them tough terrain impossible to travel in a vehicle. Although the going slowed to walking pace at some points and we had some difficult river crossings, these journeys are possible and very rewarding.

Perhaps the best thing about cycling is that you truly meet people on a different level; most are used to seeing Westerners driving or being driven in the fleets of NGO and UN white Land Cruisers that populate the country. On a bike you can – and do – stop and chat to people every day. Showing your enjoyment of the beauty of Sierra Leone is always appreciated, and the encounters provide you with a fascinating insight into the people of this amazing country.

All the way we were greeted warmly by Saloneans who would shout an inquisitive 'how far?' as we passed, and were always keen to hear where we were going and who we were working for (tourism is unheard of in many areas). We also perfected the art of assimilating often contradictory (yet all confidently given!) directions, and had some great chats cycling side by side.

Once you're deep in rural territory, don't let the lack of hotels and guesthouses put you off; we never had a problem finding a place to stay thanks to the seemingly unending friendliness of the people we met along the way. Arrival at dusk was always greeted with generous offers of a bed for the night and something to eat.

Drivers are supposed to wear helmets and carry a spare for their passenger. Many do, although certainly not all. The number of bikes with three people on one seat (look out for the odd child and chicken too) has dropped since a government crackdown, but you're still likely to see some overloaded ocadas zipping through Freetown.

The rider associations of various towns – Bo in particular – are renowned for bringing together ex-combatants and creating a chance for them to earn a little income (see box, page 249).

BY CAR For travel within Freetown or between regional capitals, a car is fine, but for most anywhere beyond a 4x4 is a prerequisite. That means either having your own, cadging lifts or hiring – a super expensive option. (See Freetown listings for vehicle-hire options – pages 135–6.) Fuel is available in most towns, but often

In fact a highlight for us was a fascinating night spent discussing British and Salonean politics with a young chief (well-informed courtesy of the BBC World Service) who also put us up and gave us some great chop. We spent a couple of nights with different chiefs and while a gift and/or a few leones will be appreciated, in our experience it was not always expected and certainly not demanded.

ROB AND PADDY'S TOP TEN TIPS

- Have a full service for your bike before leaving, and replace any part on the way out. Take the number of a friendly bike workshop for expert telephone advice should anything go wrong.
- Good heavy-duty (ideally waterproof) panniers are almost essential, if only to act as airbags through the big puddles! But travel as light as you can; it's a hilly country.
- When asking directions: distances are a rough estimate, some can be correct to the nearest metre, while others can be missing a zero on the end, so don't be afraid to check and re-check your first response.
- Tighten as you go: the 'bouncy' roads have a habit of loosening nuts and bolts, especially after your first long journey.
- Although water is generally not a problem, always be aware of how much you have left; carry capacity for at least four litres each, and purifying tablets.
- Avoid cycling in the heat of the day; an early start and long lunch break can make the temperatures bearable.
- Carry emergency food supplies, especially when off the beaten track.
- Regarding safety: try not to cycle on the tarmac roads, there is no shame in having a rest and putting your bike on the roof of an obliging poda poda – being passed at speed by overloaded trucks is no fun; wear a helmet at all times; take a decent first-aid kit that you know how to use. Check your travel insurance covers cycling, but remember you are likely to be a fair distance from medical assistance.
- Try to find a good map before you get to Salone.
- Three toolkit essentials: a good multi-tool, spare inner tubes and patches, and small bike pump. Bungees can also be useful for keeping panniers from rattling, and strapping on purchases along the way. Only take spares/tools you know how to use.

from old pumps, and can be full of impurities. Try to fill up in Freetown and provincial capitals where possible.

BY BOAT With 400km of coastline and at least a dozen navigable rivers, travelling on the water is sometimes the only way to reach remote areas. Most long wooden passenger boats are unreliable, time-consuming and prone to capsizing. Many leave from the east end of Freetown and Tombo, at the southern end of the Peninsula. Speedboats are much quicker, and many more times more expensive. Enquire at the **Aqua Club** in Aberdeen, Freetown or with **Cape Shilling** (*54 Cape Rd, Aberdeen;* m *076 814 646*).

ON FOOT Watch women walking for hours with baskets of bananas or rice on their heads, and babies tied to their backs, and you'll soon be shamed into giving it a go.

With thanks to Lucy Goodman for excellent tips

There's barefoot luxury and then there's just barefoot: staying in a village is among the best cultural experiences you can have in Sierra Leone. A night with the stars and fireflies for company, drums and shouts from around the village rising in the background, the smell of bushfire smoke in your blankets and the warm, bitter taste of poyo on your lips is difficult to beat, and the hospitality, care and interest shown towards you can be overwhelmingly warm.

The best thing to do as soon as you reach a village you might like to stay in is ask to speak to the chief. It's best to arrive after 17.00, while it's still light but the chief is likely to be back from the bush or other village duties. Depending on the size and significance of the settlement, the headman might be a town chief, section chief or paramount chief. Some places have all three. Your appointment should really be with the town chief, since you are asking about local matters, but depending on the level of interest you generate, and the size of the village, you might meet its whole population. Unannounced visitors are sometimes duly introduced with the repetitive low beating of a drum – which can at first seem a little alarming – ensuring that everyone comes to the chief's house to see what on earth is going on, and so that you can explain yourself.

You may also hear from the 'speaker', the chief's deputy, of the village. Depending on the size of the village there will also be a village secretary who will read, write and speak enough English to translate for you. Hold your left palm to your right elbow when shaking hands with dignitaries.

Politely asking for a spot to spend the night is simple and usually quickly understood. You could end up anywhere, from a head teacher's house with flushing loo, shower and people running around to make your stay comfortable,

Going on foot in towns is a great way to get the measure of a place, meet people and to enjoy the markets, browsing bright pink pigs' trotters, pungent smoked fish and more. If you're keen to explore villages, go walking in the cooler hills of the north and east, or pick a spot on the map and wander from village to village to see just how remote each can be. In downtown Freetown, it's the best way to immerse yourself in the busy, colourful commercial district, although the swelter will soon soak you through.

BY BICYCLE If some tough off-road cycling and the chance to reach truly remote areas attracts, then perhaps you should get on your bike (see box, pages 98–9). You don't need to be an expert – biking is an achievable option for anyone planning a trip, although unforgiving conditions do require a basic level of fitness.

Some pre-planning is essential, and your local bike shop will probably be able to give plenty of sound advice (see the practical tips in the box). Check with your airline the fee for putting a bike in with your hold luggage, ideally prior to booking your ticket. Heavy-duty panniers and other cycling gear are difficult to obtain locally.

The roads take their toll, so come prepared for mechanical breakdown. You'll have to rely on your own ingenuity, combined with the help of willing and experienced bike-repair shacks dotted around; although beware, they may have limited experience of sophisticated bikes. A phone call to your friendly bike workshop back home and a bike-repair manual can also be a help. If all else fails, it

to a boy's room plastered in faded football posters over the mud-brick walls, to a bed of straw with scuttling rats and crowing cocks for company, and only the shield of a dark night for washing out back in the open with a bucket. If you don't want to kick someone out of their room bring a hammock/tent and you can sling it in the compound in the rainy season, or between two trees in the dry season. In the wet season, an extra tarpaulin can protect against near-horizontal rain.

If the village is near a road, there is a chance there will be a loo block, for which the chief will normally own a key. If there are no facilities, head for the familiar patch of grass and banana trees behind the village (not to be confused with the sacred bush), preferably at night. Women can shower in the raffia enclosures behind people's houses – just ask for a bucket and string your *lappa* – a length of material suitable for a wraparound skirt – across the entrance. Men are expected to wash in the local stream.

You can cook for yourself on village facilities, and borrow some pots and pans, or ask someone to do it for you. If you do not bring your own food, expect to pay around Le2,000 for rice and Le1,000 for soup. If an elder turns up at dinner you should offer him some of your food. Fruit is plentiful, and often offered. Someone (normally a young child) will fetch water if you need it – tip them Le100.

You can ask for a tour of local farms, or ask whether you might be able to go out with the hunters and check their traps. Go through the chief for guides.

Bring your own loo paper, iodine for purifying water, a mosquito net, sleeping-bag liner, and your own spoon for mealtimes. Offer sugar, soap, tea and a small amount of cash (as a guide about Le10,000–20,000) as a token of respect once you have announced your presence in the village. If you hear the phrase 'Show me' at any point beforehand, that is the time to pay your respects.

is easy to pop your bike up with the goats and other produce on the roof of a poda poda for a small fee.

ACCOMMODATION

In general, accommodation in Sierra Leone is not as good as it should be. It is undoubtedly improving, as electricity flows more regularly and those with an eye for what a visitor appreciates take a firmer hold of the design reins. As it stands, the pricier joints are business-angled breeze-block hotels proud of their fridges and television aerials, devoid of soul. Guesthouses can be filthy and more expensive than you might hope. However, there are the occasional gems, which are marked throughout the text with the author's choice symbol.

In most upcountry hotels and guesthouses a single room is, confusingly, fine for a couple. It just means the bed isn't quite as large as in a double room (double beds tend to be wider than they are long – a luxury that comes with the cheapest of stays). As for pricing, some rates are per room, others per person, so check first. Tax, which stood at 15% at the time of writing, is sometimes included in the price, sometimes added at check out.

In many spots, it's worth negotiating over price, especially if you plan on staying more than one night. Only the top hotels in Freetown accept credit cards, so come flush with cash. Many hotels will not allow same-sex couples to share, even if they pose as, or really just are, friends. Others don't give two hoots.

While there's nothing in the way of luxury camping (though Bafa Resort on the Banana Islands comes close), endless opportunities beckon for a night in the wilderness – camping in ready-prepared tents in wildlife parks; bringing your own; or, better still, bedding down under a mosquito net hung from a palm tree on an island oasis.

EATING AND DRINKING

STAPLE DISHES You may hear the phrase that a Sierra Leonean has not eaten unless he's had rice. Pile on the salad, protein or sweets, but a Salone man will still walk away hungry unless he's had a plate of the stuff. There are more than 20 different Mende words to describe rice in its variant forms, from 'sweet rice' to 'pounded rice' to 'the rice that sticks to the bottom of a pot upon cooking'. Relying on white imported rice from India, Pakistan and Thailand, world price rises have hit the country hard, although 'country rice' – the brown chubby version – is also popular upcountry among subsistence farmers.

The classic dish of the nation is rice and *plassas* (also called *palaver* sauce), a word to describe any of the various green leafy sauces, drowned in fatty, lip-staining orange palm oil (also known as *pamine*), which can leave a scratchy taste in the back of the throat. Among the most popular options are cassava leaf sauce, potato leaf sauce (both a bit like spinach) and slimy *crain crain,* made from the leaves of the jute plant (*Corchorus olitorius*), and also known as Mulukhiyah, Jew's Mallow, bush okra or West African sorrel, depending on where you are in the world. It's been described by one smiling detractor as 'reminiscent of the middle of a cockroach'. (If crain crain is served with a rich pamine sauce, it's known as *obiatta*.) Whatever the main ingredient, the sauce is usually cooked with onions, fresh chillis and stock cubes. An unusual taste at first, it doesn't take long for the homely, filling nature of rice and plassas to take on a comfort of its own. Palm oil can give everything a bitter or overly fatty taste, and some prefer to use coconut oil or groundnut oil. If ever you're asked if you'd like your plassas 'white', it means having a clear oil – taken from the nuts inside the kernels rather than the soft pulp surrounding them – instead of the usual red palm oil.

If you're vegetarian, watch out. Just because a sauce is described by the relevant type of leaf that doesn't mean you won't find meat in there – chicken, beef, goat, grasscutter, duiker or monkey (depending on how rural and remote you are) and smoked fish are all favourites.

A sweeter alternative is the Salone version of satay – a groundnut sauce (often called a soup or stew) and made from peanuts, with whatever animal is to hand thrown in. The thicker the sauce, the better.

All these dishes are usually riddled with chilli pepper, so be sure to speak up if you're not a fan of having your head blown off, although as dishes are often served from giant pots there's not much the cook can do to tone things down. Another popular rice dish is *jollof* rice, cooked with tomatoes and onions, spices and stock. A much subtler flavour, it's sweet, moreish and often cooked on special occasions.

Instead of rice The other key carbohydrate is cassava. Chunks of flaky cassava with black-eyed beans (pronounced 'binch') are hard to beat. *Gari* – grated cassava – is popular in the second city, Bo. Strong on texture, it's less bland than *foofoo*, also made of cassava, which is ground up, mixed with a little water, pushed through a sieve, cooked over a slow fire into a thick paste, and then rolled into balls. Foofoo tends to be eaten with palm-oil stew, or *ebu*, as an alternative to rice. Roast cassava is heated over hot coals. The roadside traders of Waterloo, just outside Freetown, have a fine reputation for thin discs of cassava bread with a hot fish sauce. Sweet potato, pasta (from packets) and chips are found on most Freetown menus. If you still feel there aren't enough carbs in your diet, do not miss the chance to try the street-sold Fula bread known as *tapalapa*, which is rich, fluffy and almost baguette-like. For Le1,000–4,000 a stick, from wooden boxes carried high on vendors' heads, you can't go wrong. Much of the bread sold in shops is grim, and imitation croissants are mostly an embarrassment (with a few exceptions).

Side dishes Other local accompaniments include fried plantain (sometimes roasted or boiled) and bitter okra sauces with rice. Beans and plantain is a dish in itself, fatty, filling and delicious. African salad can sound marvellously exotic, but in place of passion fruit and unknown fresh-picked leaves, it generally translates as 'straight out of a tin'. The base is often luncheon meat, ketchup and mayonnaise, with some tasteless tinned vegetables and possibly a boiled egg and some tuna thrown in.

ATLANTIC TREATS Not much beats the best of the day's catch, washed down with a cold beer on the shoreline for less than the price of a hamburger back home. Among the most frequently available fish is barracuda (often called *coota*), served as delicious, moist steaks when done well. Also widely found are grouper, tilapia, the bone-laden snapper, bonita and jack – the latter grey and not as tasty as might be hoped. They tend to come grilled, fried or as kebabs. Occasionally you can find tuna. As for seafood, the real boon is 'lobster' (though it's more often crayfish – not that anyone calls it that); there are also plenty of skewered shrimp, crab and oysters plucked fresh from their rocks. Carpaccio of local fish and even sushi (flown-in) is available at some spots. Upcountry, for those who don't have a way to keep things cold, smoked fish – known as *bongo* – is a protein staple.

RESTAURANT PRICE CODES

The food and restaurant price codes used through this book are as follows:

$$$$$	Le135,000+	£14+	US$18+
$$$$	Le90,000–135,000	£9.50–14	US$12–18
$$$	Le45,000–90,000	£4.50–9.50	US$6–12
$$	Le15,000–45,000	£1.50–4.50	US$2–6
$	<Le15,000	<£1.50	<US$2

STREET FOOD All towns have a road or two lined with wooden food stands. Favourites include fried and breaded chicken; grilled meat (skewered beef, chunks of liver and heart, and goat are popular); chunks of grilled snail with raw onions and groundnut sauce; cutting grass, or grasscutter (greater cane rat), fried yams, sweet potato and plantain; eggs, whether boiled, fried or even scotch; and *attieke*, a medley dish of the ubiquitous cassava (this time fermented, crushed and steamed to resemble couscous), chicken or meat if available, chopped-up spaghetti and whatever else might be to hand, such as onion or tomato and hot pepper. Everything comes with lashings of mayonnaise and ketchup. *Fry fry* refers to any of the contents you might end up putting in your bread, such as beans. Upcountry, look out for entire grilled bush 'fowl', a small local chicken, and porcupine soup. The more remote you go, the more likely you are to come across bushmeat. At transport stops there are fairly regular offerings of grasscutter sandwich, as well as dead monkeys hung up on wood-stick tripods at roadsides and the odd deer leg and porcupine sold at market.

In shacks, bread with condensed milk is popular, and many people pour the milk straight from the can on to the bread for breakfast, adding an egg in some form if any are available. Others dip their bread into seriously sweetened tea, coffee or cocoa.

Cookeries – often no more than wooden shacks offering a bit of shade from the sun – serve up rice and sauce. In the most humble of them, you can request a plate size according to price (usually Le2,000 or Le4,000 per plate), other grander affairs charge set fees that do not usually exceed Le6,000. For the same meal in a restaurant, expect to pay Le25,000 or more.

SNACKS Don't miss pounded corn, a sugary yellow paste wrapped in kola leaf sold for Le200 a bundle. It's a shot of energy for the afternoon post-rice lull. Popcorn and roasted corn on the cob are also popular.

Morko makes for a sweet breakfast – a deep-fried mixture of ground rice with banana. Or try various *akaras*: beans or rice ground up, made into a ball and boiled or fried. Likewise fish balls, also for Le200 each, are a quick energy burst.

Biscuits include *benni* cake, made from a bitter plant and sugar and shaped into a diamond; coconut cake; bulgar cake, made from wheat; *kebbe*, rolled into a ball; and brittle groundnut cake.

Less a snack and more a social tool, the kola nut figures heavily in local shows of custom and respect. It's a ceremonial lynchpin, time-passer, dye and mini high all in one. 'He who gives kola nut gives life,' goes the saying, and this bright purple, smooth nut from the kola tree is a perfect offering for chiefs and elders. Breaking one in two or biting off a small piece and then sharing it around are established ways of building trust and unity, but take your lead from your company. While many foreign visitors sometimes mistakenly come laden with kolas as gifts for the local chief, by tradition they are in fact given from the host to strangers. Otherwise it's a bit like bringing coal to Newcastle, and will be seen as a bit cheap too, quite frankly.

INTERNATIONAL MENUS Lebanese food is widely available throughout Freetown and several spots upcountry. Expect not only hummus and *moutabal* (made from aubergine), but also *tabouleh* (parsley-based salad), *kibbeh* (minced meat in a ball), juicy *kofta* sausages, *labneh* yoghurt, *shawarmas* (strips of beef, chicken or even prawn wrapped in pitta with vegetables and a variety of extras such as hummus, mint and more depending on where you go), falafel, *shish taouk* (chicken kebab), sweet *za'atar* thyme-bread, and various sweet pastries. Burgers and **fast food** are readily available, and a couple of Freetown spots offer steak in case you get a craving. **Chinese, Indian** and **Korean** cuisine is found in the capital, a little bit of French, as well as **pizza, pasta** and even **sushi**. You can also find **ice cream**.

As far as restaurants of all colours go, from street shacks upwards, you can fairly assume, a bit like New York, that everywhere's open, pretty much all the time – where somewhere is closed on a particular day of a week we say so: otherwise we tend not to specify. Keep in mind that the government exacts a 10% tax on all restaurant sales; this is usually, though certainly not always, included in the price listed on your menu. If you're not sure, just ask.

FRUIT AND VEGETABLES Tomatoes, onions (known in Krio as *yabbas*), avocado (*pia*), aubergine, spring onions, chilli peppers, sweet peppers and cucumber are widely available. Cabbage is much more common than lettuce leaf, and you can also find pumpkins, potatoes, carrots, parsley, coriander and mint. In season, mango, orange, papaya, pineapple, banana, star fruit, lemon, lime, and watermelon are all available. Mangoes and pineapples are particularly good.

DRINKS
Hard stuff Booze is a mainstay of village life, with homemade moonshines the norm. Best known is *poyo*, or palm-tree wine (see box, page 106). Distil poyo and you have the clear spirit *omele*, so hard it also goes by the name of 'bush kerosene'; not only will it make your eyes water, they may feel like they are about to pop out of their sockets.

Manpikin (man-child) is the name of the rather less appealing local rum; be warned, it doesn't give you the bulging biceps of the hastily drawn figure in the promotional pictures – you're more likely to be turned into a dribbling fool, as the name suggests. Shot-sized clear plastic tubes, called Pegapak, contain neat gin and sell for Le1,000. Look down and you'll see the ground of some villages strewn with the discarded packets. More appealing is Beeta Kola, a dark, 15% ABV herbal bitter sold in colourful 200ml plastic bottles and surprisingly tasty (though very bitter indeed) over ice; it's also commonly believed to increase sexual potency.

Beer is widely available. The local brew, Star, comes in large and small green bottles and occasionally chubby cans. They can go for as little as Le4,000, depending on where you're buying, but more often Le6,000–8,000. If you want a big bottle, just ask for 'more time' (a reference to not only the prolonged drinking time, but also an allusion to President Koroma's brief flirtation with a term extension in early 2016). Mützig is another popular locally brewed beer (though the brand is licensed from Heineken), and is typically regarded as a bit more flavourful than Star. The newest beer on the market, Salone Beer, hit shelves at the end of 2016 and is notable for being brewed from 100% locally grown sorghum rather than imported barley. Most beers are served with a paper napkin, so you can wipe down the recycled bottle rim. Imported beers – Heineken, Carlsberg and Beck's – are also widely available (in Freetown, at least), and usually sell for at least twice the price, making them the brands of choice for well-to-do Sierra Leoneans. Guinness also enjoys affection, based mostly on the memory of the now-banned adverts suggesting it offers 'strength' (often interpreted as sexual potency).

Soft stuff Bottled Coca-Cola, Fanta and Sprite are all present; there's also sticky-sweet purple Vimto and energy drinks – Red Bull, Battery, 3X – to keep Freetowners going into the early hours. Malt drinks are also popular. Locally produced equivalent colas tend to be slightly sweeter and cheaper; some bars stock a range of imported

It's one of the most common sights on country roads outside Freetown: men hobbling along, shoulders hunched painfully as they balance two heaving yellow jerry cans dangling from either end of a bowing stick. They are not carrying water though: it's palm wine, the lubricant of village life. Such is its social significance that, local folklore goes, should the stick ever break, it's taken as incontrovertible evidence that your wife is cheating on you.

Drink palm wine from Freetown and you will be disdained as a fool. Known as poyo in Mende, the really good stuff comes from upcountry, the more remote the better, where the groundwater is sweet and the liquid stays undliluted by impurities.

Its other name – from God to Man – comes from its beautifully natural accessibility. Tappers shin up gently angled trunks, aided with a wide rubber rope to brace the weight of their bodies against the tree. Somewhere near the top, they make a lightning incision with a machete and collect the liquid sap that flows out. Then all they have to do is come back down and drink it. Only mildly alcoholic, the fresh stuff really tastes like some sort of sweet, sappy elixir. After midday it takes on greater strength, fermenting in the baking day-heat. By late afternoon it's best avoided altogether – ripening to the taste of rotten eggs, smelly socks or a mixture of the two.

If you're keen to take some away, come with an empty bottle, since most of the hooch is drunk on site at a poyo shack; an always-reliable talking-shop and the centre of gossip and local intrigue. Expect to pay about Le4,000 for a 1.5-litre bottle, or Le1,000 for a generous glass.

---

juices. Sadly there's not yet a large-scale outlet for the country's exotic fruits, but some bars do sell delicious freshly squeezed juice, whether mango, pineapple, banana or in one rather extraordinary case, avocado (head for Bliss Patisserie in Freetown to sample that one). Oasis Café in Freetown sells an innovative range of juices and icy brews. Try the gingered iced tea or the mint-laced watermelon juice for a refreshing quaff.

While thick, strong Turkish-style coffee is a favourite among the Lebanese community, green tea is the brew of choice in the provinces. Known as *ataya*, it is served in small short glasses with a healthy dose of froth on top, often from wooden stands that, like poyo shacks, serve as popular meeting points – look for the sign Ataya Base. In the bush, ataya is often shared, and the more froth you're offered the greater the honour.

Tap water isn't safe enough to drink – never mind the quality of the water treatment, the pipe network is filthy and often exposed. If cooking, boil first for at least a minute and add purifying tablets if you have them.

Bottled water is sold in all supermarkets, with a range of French and Lebanese imports. To support the local stuff, buy Blue Spring, Grafton, Luvian or Magram, bottled fresh from the local springs. A six-pack of 1.5-litre bottles costs from Le18,000. You can also buy plastic sachets of water all over the country – bar the villages that rely on well water (often cleaner than tap water) or (less reliably) the nearest stream. They sell for Le500 each. Some street-sellers offer much cheaper cold water in unmarked plastic bags – this is chilled untreated water and should be avoided.

SERVICE The concept of approaching a customer, smiling, writing down a food order, having what's on the menu, bringing dishes promptly, or even opening up the kitchen

– is coming slowly to Sierra Leone. While enthusiasm is occasionally in evidence, by and large you can expect standards of service that would make Basil Fawlty blush.

There are of course exceptions to this rule, but the colossal disinterest of most Sierra Leonean waiting staff becomes somehow familiar if you allow it, and almost strangely cosy after a while. You can also resort to your own personal game of trying to tease out a smile.

Check the bill: calculators are few and far between and it's not unheard of for large groups to be overcharged, even by more than 100%.

TIPPING A funny one this. Not many people do it, and those that do rarely hit 10%. Perhaps to compensate, some waiting staff tend to abscond with the change when you pay for your meal – assuming that you aren't bothered about a few thousand leones. Some staff go further: 'Where is my Christmas?' said one waitress as soon as her guests turned up for breakfast on the morning of 25 December, before they could so much as bite into a croissant.

Tips here really count, however, and given service standards are generally so low, rewarding any nice behaviour with a hearty tip is a healthy incentive for encouraging a little bit of pride and raising the bar.

PUBLIC HOLIDAYS AND FESTIVALS

While shops shut down for Muslim and Christian celebrations, the streets most definitely do not. At Easter, traditional dancing devils take to the streets; the national stadium fills for a 40,000-strong morning of prayer come Ramadan; and Independence Day features a night-time lantern parade. All Muslim festivals are lunar-based, so dates below are guidelines for the years to come.

1 January	New Year's Day
March/April	Good Friday and Easter Monday
27 April	Independence Day
May/June	Eid al-Fitr (End of Ramadan)
1 May	May Day
July/August	Eid al-Adha (Feast of the Sacrifice)
15 August	Assumption
October/November	Maulid-un-Nabi (Birth of the Prophet)
1 November	All Saints' Day
25 December	Christmas Day
26 December	Boxing Day

SHOPPING

HANDICRAFTS Many of Sierra Leone's craftsmen seem to have disappeared since the outbreak of the war. Large-scale population movements and the retention of youth in Freetown have ruptured the passing down of skills from one generation to another. While the dearth of artisanal activity compared with the likes of Burkina Faso or Mali is noticeable, the scene is far from non-existent; it's a question of knowing where to look.

Basket-weaving, coarse pottery, matted raffia panels and room divides, furniture made from palm wood and woven leaves are all on offer, as well as wood carvings, necklaces, leather shoes, and deeply desirable hammocks, bedspreads and outfits. Authentic masks are also highly collectable items. When shopping for them it's preferable to purchase a legitimate 'remake' of a ceremonial mask, rather than removing a genuine article, likely to be of irreplaceable cultural value.

CLOTH African prints have expanded beyond a range of wax-printed bright colours on thin cotton weaves to encompass even the most perfunctory of objects in their patterns and render them somehow tantalisingly attractive – the odd Anglepoise lamp, or an arresting eyeball and optic nerve duet, are emblazoned in bold repetitive images. A huge range is available in downtown Freetown. Complementary sets of materials – for a matching top and bottom – are sold in packets known as 'Mr and Mrs'; the Mrs goes on top.

Any tailor can make a *lappa* (length of material equivalent to that needed for a wraparound skirt) or two of cloth into a showy item worthy of a wedding or formal event – known as *ashoebi* outfits when many women wear the same thing. Bring your own clothes, and you can have Western styles and cuts copied in African materials. As for homemade cloth, there are two main types. **Gara cloth**, whose name is derived from the Mandingo word for indigo, is a form of tie-dye. No longer limited to deep purple, its multi-coloured hues now appear on bedspreads and curtains as well as outfits (shirts, skirts, dresses, vests) throughout the country. The fast-disappearing art of making **country cloth**, a thicker weave with more subtle colours stitched together in strips, is best observed in the far east and north, in the likes of Segbwema and beyond Kabala, where experts set up long wooden looms. It's easy to buy the end result in Freetown, in the form of utterly sumptuous bedspreads, rugs and hammocks. Some rugged country cloth is dyed with natural colouring and turned into large shirts, known as *hu ronko* (page 319).

HAIR To even begin to understand the life of a Sierra Leonean woman, you need to immerse yourself in the world of hair. Here the excuse, 'Not tonight, I'm washing my hair' really does mean something. Colouring, lengthening, braiding and all sorts of other fancy scalp work can put a day's plans out of whack, and women with jobs – or with boyfriends with jobs – can spend Le250,000 on a new weave without blinking. Extensions, wigs and complicated plaited patterns are among the options. Braiding costs about Le25,000 for the simplest style, depending on where you are, and a pack of extra hair usually goes for about Le20,000–25,000.

MARKETS AND SHOPS In local markets and shops expect to barter, and potentially banter too, depending on how lively you're feeling. A good rule of thumb is that some shopkeepers and traders double their asking price for foreigners. Some even give you a hint, by offering a 'first price'. Most imported goods, however, have a fairly fixed (high) price, so don't automatically take umbrage if the price isn't moving at all. The best way to get a feel is to experiment, and watch what others are charged. Since tourists are few and far between, in more remote areas the first price you are quoted is usually the right price, and you don't want to haggle people into losing out.

SUPERMARKETS Leave your special pot of Marmite at home. Freetown's supermarkets, largely run by the Lebanese community, are well stocked, with goods as niche as soya milk, sugar-coated almonds, hundreds-and-thousands, frozen spinach, Vidal Sassoon hair products, ceramic bowls and plates, and gel ink pens. Many have fresh meat and dairy counters with the likes of cheddar and chorizo (although fresh milk is an obvious absentee). Monoprix has a dizzying array of breakfast cereals; Freetown Supermarket has caviar. You'll pay through the nose for it though. Most of

Vera Viditz-Ward has spent more than 30 years taking photographs in West Africa. The trip she describes below took place in 1987, in preparation for an exhibition of 50 portraits for the bicentennial celebration of the birth of Sierra Leone. They are now installed at the National Museum and the US embassy in Freetown. One encounter was particularly memorable.

The chiefs, clothed in elaborate gowns and frequently accompanied by musicians and dancers, always commanded attention. Fascinated by the drama and pageantry, I decided to photograph paramount chiefs during such formal occasions whenever I had the opportunity. Together with American anthropologist and lecturer at the University of Sierra Leone Joseph Opala, who had studied the history and cultural significance of chiefly attire for years, we decided to embark on a nationwide portrait session of paramount chiefs.

We used a single motorcycle for all our travels. On each trip, we packed photographic equipment and supplies, clothes, food, drinking water, two gallons of gasoline, and tools to repair the motorcycle. With no dependable way to contact a chief before we arrived, we were not always sure he or she would be available.

Sometimes portrait sessions could be planned and completed in as little as 1 hour. Others required several days of organisation because of elaborate rituals surrounding some chiefly attire. For instance, before a Temne chief's supernaturally powerful gown can be removed from its sacred storage place, the *kapr mam*, a ceremonial official, needs at least one day to conduct secret ritual preparations.

On one occasion, I experienced firsthand the potency of a seldom-worn type of war gown owned by the chiefs among the Kisi, Mende, and other peoples in the south and east. Most chiefs refused to wear it for photographs, explaining that the medicines boiled into the cloth would make their hearts grow 'warm', or warlike. One Kisi chief – Chief Jabba – did decide to wear the gown after much encouragement from his advisors. While the chief was inside his house putting on the war gown, Opala and I, along with a growing crowd of curious townspeople, waited in the courtyard. Suddenly, Chief Jabba charged out of the house shouting war cries and brandishing a great iron sword. He drove everyone, including me, to the far corner of the compound. 'Snap me now!' he commanded. Under the circumstances, I photographed him from a considerable distance. Following this brief, startling portrait session, Chief Jabba changed back to his usual attire and resumed his placid demeanour. 'So,' he said matter-of-factly, 'now you've seen our special war clothes.'

the larger stores have vegetable stalls outside, and the local women quite sensibly hike their prices for supermarket shoppers. Fresh produce is much cheaper downtown, and upcountry – a Le200 orange in Kabala, for example, costs Le2,000 in Freetown.

SPORT

FOOTBALL Such is the beautiful game's pulling power that when a DJ is losing his audience's interest on a dancefloor, he'll merely shout out 'Manchester United' or 'Arsenal' to get the crowd going again. While that might not say much for the country's deck-spinning abilities, it sums up a love of football that pervades homes, streets, taxi slogans and beyond. Children play on dusty pitches in baking heat from an early age; when they don't have balls they kick around rolled-up socks or a tightly packed sphere of plastic bags tied together. Although in 2008 FIFA briefly banned international games at Freetown's national stadium because the pitch was in such an appalling state, it's well worth watching a local match with 40,000 others cheering on the action.

Unlike the amputee football team (see box, opposite) the national team, the Leone Stars, has a poor record, and struggled to get anywhere near qualification for the Africa Cup of Nations in Equatorial Guinea in 2015 (originally to be played in Morocco but relocated due to Ebola fears) or in Gabon in 2017. The national team practises at the northern tip of Lumley Beach every Sunday morning as the rest of the city's youths line up along the shoreline for keenly fought kickabouts of their own.

Local club football is closely followed, with local team Kallon FC taking part in the West African club championship. Another local club, FC Johansen, is made up of teenage boys orphaned during the war, and their 2008 trip to Sweden for the Mittnorden Cup (in which they came second) marked the first time since 2006 that Salone players were allowed to play internationally. Too often, athletes have taken the chance to abscond during meets, such as when several went AWOL at the 2000 Sydney Olympics, a further 21 disappeared at the 2002 Commonwealth Games in Manchester and another 11 at the 2006 Commonwealth Games in Melbourne. Athletes also disappeared after the 2014 London Marathon and Commonwealth Games in Glasgow.

Most Sierra Leoneans are fairly clued up about the twists and turns at the top of the English Premier League: Manchester United and Arsenal are generally the most popular teams. When ex-England captain David Beckham visited in 2008 – at one point stripping off his shirt to play with kids on the roadside dirt – fans went mad.

Sierra Leone's most famous footballing son is Mohamed Kallon, former captain of the Leone Stars national team, who played for Inter Milan and AS Monaco before announcing his retirement in 2016. A Salone sporting legend, he is feted in his homeland for both his business acumen (he owns a sports shop in downtown Freetown, a swanky nightclub near the presidential lodge, a record label, a newspaper and a radio station), and his passionate devotion to putting his wealth to good use: 'I want to give opportunities to the young talent. We also have to educate the kids about football – to get them in the right mentality,' he says. 'When you are young it's somewhat difficult to know your value, and there are a lot of things you have to watch out for if you're playing in Europe. I love my people and I have to come back. I have to pay back to my country.'

In the UK, Nigel Reo-Coker, who has played for West Ham and Aston Villa, has a Sierra Leonean father but has never played for the Lions before, while Al Bangura became a minor celebrity when playing for Watford after he was allowed to stay at the club rather than return to Sierra Leone where he claimed his life would be in danger from a secret society, something strenuously denied in Sierra Leone.

Prospects for homegrown young hopefuls will hopefully improve with Kallon's intention to set up a football academy, but were lamentably dashed when former Liverpool and Wales striker Craig Bellamy's £1.4-million, 10ha academy in the fishing village of Tombo shut down abruptly in September 2016, amid a flurry of financial mismanagement claims. Before the closure, students here received five years of academic and football training free of charge, and the Craig Bellamy

AMPUTEE CHAMPIONS

Head towards the northern end of Lumley Beach on a Saturday morning, and you are bound to see beach football played with a passion. Among the different games, one in particular is likely to stand out – the weekly practice session for Sierra Leone's Single Leg Amputee Sports Club. Formed in the amputee camp at Aberdeen, many players lost their limbs during the war, and behind their footballing skills lie heroic stories of survival. Today a nationwide network of teams exists in Bo, Kenema and Makeni, and there are plans to start up a women's team.

Watching the speed, strength and skill on show, you forget all about disability or limitations, and see an entirely new sport unfolding. Six players per team move at speed, kicking the ball while supporting themselves on crutches; the one-armed goalie dives for saves with unrestrained valour. Several spent their own money on lightweight metal crutches, in preference to the painful, heavy wooden ones they were given years ago at the amputee centre.

'All the trauma that's been a part of me is lost. Being part of this football club has totally changed my life,' says Musa Mansaray, who has been with the team since the start. 'I just feel normal.'

The team has travelled all over the world, representing the country in Brazil, Russia, Turkey and the UK – playing on the hallowed turf of Manchester United's Old Trafford and Liverpool's Anfield. Sierra Leone also hosted Africa's first amputee championships in 2007. The groundbreaking event was sponsored by FIFA, and went some way to raising the profile of the sport, bringing together teams from Liberia and Ghana. The Nigerian team made a superhuman effort, travelling overland, and arriving three days late after all their money was stolen in Ivory Coast; the Angolan team never turned up at all.

Still the event was a success, although Sierra Leonean hearts were broken when their team, pre-tournament favourites, did not make it to the final. In 2008, Sierra Leone's team was pipped to the post once again by the Liberians, when they reached the finals of the 2008 championship on Liberian home turf, following a tense penalty shootout in the earlier rounds. There was further heartbreak on the cards for Sierra Leone when they placed sixth at the fourth Cup of African Nations Amputee Football (CANAF) tournament, held in Nairobi at the end of 2013.

Anyone willing to help the team can contact them at the **Single Leg Amputee Sports Club (SLASC)** (33 Regent St, Freetown; m *076 680 481, 076 680 681, 088 680 481, 088 680 681, 077 742 151;* e *amputeesoccer@yahoo.com;* f *SingleLegAmputeeSportsClub*).

Foundation organised 2,400 youth players in some 70 clubs across the country. It remains unclear what future, if any, the academy has.

OTHER SPORTS Sierra Leone has a national cricket team, and a local rugby team has started up. There are also plenty of tennis and basketball courts, and several gyms. The president's sport of choice (he is 2008 national champion to boot) – squash – is also on offer in Freetown, while watersports have long been the pleasure of the Lebanese fast set, with speedboats and jet skis aplenty, all moored at the Aqua Club in western Freetown. At the weekends, as thoughts turn to the villas along the Peninsula, it's not uncommon to hear the question 'Shall we take the car or the

in its 2006 annual report. That law of seditious libel remains on the books and has, in recent years (particularly during the state of emergency declared over the Ebola crisis), seen several journalists arrested, including one – Paul Kamara of *For di People* newspaper – who spent 14 months behind bars in 2004–05. More recently, two others, Jonathan Leigh and Bai Bai Sesay of the *Independent Observer*, were dragged up on 26 counts of seditious libel, spent nearly three weeks in jail awaiting trial, and were forced to appear in court more than ten times before they accepted a plea deal in March 2014. Kenema-based journalist Sam Lahai was arrested and held for two nights over a social media post critical of a minister in July 2016.

Human rights groups and the Sierra Leone Journalists Association (SLAJ) have been campaigning for years for the repeal of the 1965 Public Order Act, which provides for such long jail terms for defamation. After the opposition won September's 2007 presidential election, the new information minister, former SLAJ president Ibrahim Ben Kargbo, pledged to repeal or amend it. But just two years later, Sierra Leone's Supreme Court ruled against the SLAJ when the group requested that the law be amended so that journalists who published material that was truthful (though libellous) could not be thrown in jail. As the law now stands, anyone – journalist or otherwise – who publishes libel, whether or not based in fact, risks being put behind bars. Even so, government interference and censorship is limited compared with many countries.

RADIO Given such a high rate of illiteracy, radio is the news mainstay (see box below). Listeners can enjoy lively station debates, some high-calibre reporting and up-to-the-minute news.

The Sierra Leone Broadcasting Corporation (99.9FM in Freetown; 95.0FM in Bo; and 93.5FM in Kenema), the government's official (yet politically independent) radio station, is among the most popular frequencies on the airwaves in Freetown and across the country. SLBC grew out of UN Radio, which was set up by the UN peace-building office following the war. SLBC's official launch in June 2010 was a big deal – so much so that United Nations Secretary-General Ban Ki-Moon even flew in to Freetown to mark the occasion. The station now broadcasts 24 hours a day; programme highlights include listener favourites like *Teabreak* every morning at 09.00, and *Nightline with DJ Bass*, a Krio-language show that airs nightly at 23.00.

TURN UP THE NEWS

In Sierra Leone, where less than half the population is able to read, radio is king. So much so that porters have been known to carry their radios up the steep slopes of remote Mount Bintumani, just to make sure they can catch their daily dose of evening news by the campfire.

And they're not alone. A March 2010 survey found that 82% of Sierra Leoneans listened to radio on a regular basis, up from 77% two years before. Three-quarters of the 2,000 adults who were polled around the country had radios at home – compared with 9% who had television sets and 56% who had a mobile phone. Just over half listened to programming every day; the most popular programming language was Krio, by a stretch. In contrast, only 1% of the adults surveyed had read a newspaper within the last day, and only 3% regularly used the internet. Less than a quarter could read English.

But still, radio isn't available to everyone. The biggest barrier to listening, the survey found, is the high cost of the batteries needed to run the device. Assuming you can afford a radio, that is.

As with its predecessor UN Radio, much of SLBC's material is supplied by Cotton Tree News (CTN), an NGO-funded agency with a good news edge and plenty of listener interaction. CTN also supplies Fourah Bay College's Mount Aureol station (107.3FM) and ten community radio stations across the country. BBC World Service (94.3FM in Freetown; 94.5FM in Bo; and 95.3FM in Kenema) is respected and enjoyed, and its daily afternoon *Focus on Africa* programme rebounds from taxis, street corners and households at every airing, as does the breakfast round-up *Network Africa*. Its regular news bulletins are also taken by regional radio stations throughout the country through a series of partnership agreements. The French equivalent, RFI, broadcasts on 89.1FM. In Freetown, Radio Democracy (98.1FM) broadcasts in Krio and focuses on issues of the day, running a series of lively panel talks with caller contributions. Voice of America also has a presence in Freetown, on 102.4FM, broadcasting news, chat, sports and music 24 hours a day.

Political parties also have their own stations – the APC has We Yone (88.8FM); the SLPP has Unity Radio (94.9FM). The Independent Media Commission (IMC) issued several warnings during the 2007 elections as stations affiliated to political parties accused each other of amassing machetes ahead of the vote – claims that were never borne out.

For entertainment, private stations with a heavy music focus include Skyy FM (106.6FM) and Free (95.7FM), which broadcast many more Sierra Leonean tunes than Western ones. Beyond Freetown is a range of local commercial and community stations that form the Independent Radio Network (IRN). Among them are Kiss FM (104FM) and Radio New Song (97.5FM) in Bo; Eastern Radio (101.9FM) in Kenema; Radio Mankneh (92.1FM) in Makeni; Bintumani (93.5FM) in Kabala; Radio Modcar (93.4FM) in Moyamba; Radio Moa (105.5FM) in Kailahun; Radio Kolenten (92.4FM) in Kambia; and Radio Bontico (96.4FM) in Bonthe.

NEWSPAPERS An astonishing 50-plus newspapers are registered in Sierra Leone. But diversity is no blind for quality. Only about half that number is actually published, almost all in Freetown, and many are partisan rags full of one-eyed pieces of politicking, ego massage and copyright infringement.

While the bigger titles come out daily, many others go to press when they have enough material, when the printers have enough generator fuel, or when they can afford to. Few manage a circulation outside Freetown. Record-beating numbers would break 3,000 copies a day; popular titles average 2,500.

Many journalists – painfully poorly paid – rely on 'brown envelope' handouts from groups and institutions keen to get their points across in the papers. International donors and political organisations alike offer generous food and 'transport' money to induce coverage. Frequently press releases are published word for word, including contact telephone numbers at the end. Often pieces are 'culled from the internet', be it from the BBC or other agency outlets.

Some local journalists undertake sterling investigative work to find true scoops, only to go to the person at the centre of an as-yet unpublished scandal and be requested/bribed not to publish. By no means all of the country's journalists follow this path, but it's a tempting one for many, and measured, well-supported exposés of the murkiness and injustice of much of Sierra Leonean life are fewer than would be hoped.

Screaming stories Even so, given Sierra Leone's insatiable appetite for intrigue, its newspapers rarely disappoint with a highly developed tabloid sense of scandal. Each morning brings a raft of outrageous claims, bearing only a passing acquaintance with grammar and fact, and a penchant for what one local editor describes as 'screaming headlines and no story'.

'Armed Rubbers Raid Stationary Store' and 'Kabbah: I'll be Precedent' are among the typographical corkers, while 'Lumley Man Arrested With Witch Gun Becomes Snake, Escapes', and 'Sierra Leone Launches Operation Wash Lunatics' are worthy of the *National Enquirer*.

Spats hit the headlines Long-running personal feuds often replace real news with media-industry score-settling. In 2007, Sylvia Blyden's paper *Awareness Times* published a photograph on its front cover of rival *Standard Times* managing editor Philip Neville with the headline, 'Reckless fool'. His paper retaliated with a photomontage of his rival's face attached to a naked body and accusations that Blyden was a RUF whore. 'Foday Sankoh's parlour wife?' ran the headline, as Sankoh's eyes fixed on her lower abdomen – Neville was arrested as a result.

'The Independent Media Commission views with dismay the decline in the professional standards and moral ethics of certain recent publications,' wrote the country's media watchdog back in January 2007 following the undignified spat.

The UN even said its officials became targets, as they were attacked and feared for their lives after a series of articles published in *Awareness Times* alleged the UN was handpicking the results of the 2007 presidential elections in an attempt to oust the incumbent SLPP and its hopeful candidate Solomon Berewa. Blyden was also invited for questioning by police after her paper published an image of President Koroma with two horns attached to his head.

Many believe the government does not crack down on coverage because so few Sierra Leoneans can read, and as a result newspapers are largely for circulation among the Freetown elite.

While there is no state newspaper, journals are attached to the three main political parties with varying degrees of sympathy. *We Yone* is the official APC mouthpiece, *Unity* is the SLPP's paper, and *New Vision* and *Executive* tend to toe the SLPP line. In another move showing how closely linked the worlds of media and politics are, one-time editor of *New Citizen* and head of the Sierra Leone Association of Journalists, Ibrahim Ben Kargbo, was made Minister of Information and Communications under the new APC administration in 2007.

Ones to watch The long-standing *Awoko* (**w** awoko.org) newspaper, started by the dogged, level-headed Kelvin Lewis, was the country's first colour paper, emblazoned with an image of Burkina Faso's one-time revolutionary president Thomas Sankara, a Che Guevara figure for Africa. It claims to have the largest circulation, at 2,700 copies or so a day, and manages to get a batch of them to Bo before lunchtime, as well as initiate its own investigations.

Sierra Express Media (**w** sierraexpressmedia.com), founded in 2007, is the newest kid on the block, and one of the few news outlets that wears its political independence on its sleeve. The outfit started off as a web-only news source, but within a couple of months of starting up it began printing hard copies as well. With correspondents in Europe, Canada and the UK, its focus is more global than any of the other papers.

The satirical magazine *Peep!* (**f** peepsierraleone), always eagerly awaited, is Salone's *Private Eye*. Editor Olu Awoonor Gordon is always ready to pounce on the latest political intrigue with a ready dose of wit. Another paper that carries hard-hitting stories when it can is *Concord Times* (**w** slconcordtimes.com).

Where to buy papers The best spot to pick up a paper is amid the morning traffic of downtown Freetown. Vendors display as many front-page headlines as they can and wander throughout the gridlock, selling through car windows. Most supermarkets stock a range of periodicals and magazines from the rest of Africa, Europe and North America, including *Time, Newsweek, Jeune Afrique*, and the odd UK newspaper or *International Herald Tribune*. Settle in at a beach bar in Freetown and you might even find yourself picking from publications including *The Economist* and the *Daily Telegraph* from hawkers. Another good spot is outside Crown Bakery in downtown Freetown.

TELEVISION The country has two TV stations. The older, Sierra Leone Broadcasting Corporation (SLBC; w *slbc.sl*), is run by the state. Election observers criticised it for pro-government bias, and management corruption scandals have kept onlookers in a permanent combined state of horror and amusement. Efforts to transform are, as ever, underway. If you're keen to catch a recording of the president giving a speech, or the official business of the day, this is the station for you. The only independent TV station, ABC, has had a bumpy ride starting up, but has some dedicated journalists and hunts down good stories.

Anyone with a television at home is likely to have satellite channels. South African broadcaster DSTV is among the most popular, although locals joke that it may as well stand for Dry Season Television, for all the coverage that gets through during the rains. GTV, a newcomer, has bagged the rights to show the English Premiership, which has got many people clamouring after it. The Egyptian NileSat service carries a Middle Eastern bouquet of channels, including Al-Jazeera English, Chinese state TV in English, and US films and TV shows in English.

INTERNET Sierra Leone has a huge and diverse diaspora that devours news about its homeland, and internet sources spread quicker than you can shout 'Read all about it'. *Awareness Times* (w *news.sl*) has a remarkable internet presence given its much smaller local readership, but the real online highlight is *Cocorioko Newspaper* (w *cocorioko.net*), produced in the US. Beyond that, blogging is common in Salone. Many foreign development workers and expats chart their times with varying degrees of sensitivity, interest and enjoyment, but it would be great to see more Sierra Leonean voices.

COMMUNICATIONS

MOBILE PHONES Africa is the first continent in which the number of mobile phones exceeded landlines, and Sierra Leone is no exception. For a country recently rated the least developed in the world, the fact that many people often carry at least two – sometimes three – phones may come as something of a surprise.

Competition is fierce between the main providers, via cunning tariffs, alluring prize draws, sponsorship of *Pop Idol*-style talent contests, giving away cars, and 'brand recognition', plastering not only billboards, but water towers, bars, nightclubs and houses with their slogans. Airtel and Africell are by far the dominant providers, but Smart Mobile and the state-owned Sierratel are present as well.

How to connect If you are bringing a handset from home, buy a SIM card and credit as soon as you touch down at the airport. Make sure your phone has been 'unlocked' (so it can accept other phone companies' SIM cards) before you go. The most basic handsets in Sierra Leone start at around Le180,000, but getting a snazzy smartphone is definitely a better deal at home. Buy a lower-end handset and you'll likely as not hear it called 'a PRSP phone', a quip on the government's Poverty Reduction Strategy Paper (PRSP).

SIM cards are cheap at about Le10,000 (which usually includes a small burst of credit). Most street-side stores, and any hotel, will be able to sort out a SIM card for your chosen network. While calls on the same network are relatively cheap, tariffs between networks are pricier. For this reason (and variations in coverage upcountry), many people maintain two or even three different phones, each on a different network, to keep running costs to a minimum. The newest rage is phones that accept more than one SIM card, although of course that means you can't show off your numerous handsets anymore.

Airtel (with prefixes 076, 078, 079) generally has the best coverage – in terms of reach and reliability – throughout the country, but also the most expensive tariffs, particularly when compared with other networks. **Africell** (077, 088, 030, 080, 099) is nearly as popular and tends to be cheaper than most for making international calls. If someone gives you their number by saying the network name first, that means that you should punch in the network code prefix before the main number, or, if you share the same network, you don't need to punch in the network code at all. You may also encounter numbers from **Smart Mobile** (044) and **Sierratel** (025).

While monthly contracts are available, most phones are pay as you go, with scratch cards from just a couple of hundred leones to Le10,000 or more available

SPLASH OUT

Wander down a busy street in Freetown and within minutes you're likely to come across a white-and-blue poster or T-shirt declaring 'Nor flash me, Splash me!' or a decal of a suave, red-suited stack of Leones cheesing for the camera. Confused? Don't be. You've just encountered evidence of one of Africa's most popular tech trends: mobile money.

Sierra Leone jumped on the bandwagon in 2009 with Splash Mobile Money (w *splash-cash.com*), and Airtel Money (w *africa.airtel.com/wps/wcm/connect/africarevamp/Sierra/AirtelMoney*) followed shortly after. These services allow Sierra Leone's mobile-phone users to send money to a friend upcountry, pay a bill at a restaurant, buy groceries at the supermarket, or even purchase an airline ticket – using just a mobile phone. You can even pay your electricity bill, with the money going straight from your phone to the National Power Authority.

It's not only made urban-dwellers' lives more convenient by reducing the need to carry around a rucksack full of leones, but has proven an even greater boon for rural Sierra Leoneans for whom the nearest bank can often be days away. The service also played a critical role during the Ebola crisis, when international NGOs and the National Ebola Response Centre (NERC) used it to ensure the more than 20,000 frontline health workers, many of them scattered throughout some of the most remote regions of the country, received their payments on time.

If you're planning on staying in-country for a while, or travelling in some of Salone's further reaches, it might make sense to sign up for an account and add some money to it as an insurance policy should you have difficulty getting cash upcountry. Signing up for mobile money is a separate process from activating your SIM card; just bring your ID to an agent on the street or an Airtel office and they'll get you sorted.

at every street corner. They offer units of talk-time; for example, it's nine units a minute for Airtel-to-Airtel calls, or 15 units a minute for calls from Airtel to another provider. Make sure the plastic wrappers they come in are still sealed, and that the foil on the back that conceals the number is still there. Some mobile-phone stands can send the credit direct to your phone if you give them your number, and you usually get a 10% unit bonus thrown in.

Mobiles are often stolen, so if you're bringing your own phone keep a record of all your numbers somewhere safe. If you have a smartphone that you can't bear to lose, buy a cheapie handset just for the trip in your departure country.

LANDLINES Much of the existing landline infrastructure was ruined by the war, and little has been done to rehabilitate it. Government, multilateral and NGO buildings have landline phones that sometimes work in Freetown. Even so, landline numbers sometimes inexplicably fail, or worse, connect to somewhere else entirely. Throughout this book we have tried to list mobile numbers where possible, as for most businesses this is their primary mode of communication.

A NOTE ON NUMBERS IN THIS BOOK Since landline numbers tend not to work, and mobile numbers are by their nature more transitory – more often attached to a worker (who might leave or lose their number), than a fixed desk or proprietor, it makes citing reliable contact numbers a little tricky. Plus mobiles often run out of charge or go out of reception area. We've tried our best, and as a result deluge you with up to four numbers per entry, but it's still a bit of a lottery.

INTERNET Today nearly all upmarket hotels and many nicer restaurants (in Freetown, at least) now offer Wi-Fi, so going for a nice meal and using the internet is a pleasant way to get online should you have your own device – see w onlime. com/sl/limezone/locations for a list of free Wi-Fi hotspots in Freetown.

Otherwise, the rapid expansion of mobile data means there are fewer internet cafés than there used to be, but you'll still find them dotted around Freetown, and at least a couple each in major towns like Bo, Makeni and Kenema. Outside these centres – in Kabala, for instance – many towns' only connections are courtesy of donor organisations keen to have comms in the field, and not accessible to the general public (although in a crisis you could try asking). Browsing at an internet café is usually around Le6,000–9,000 an hour.

All cellular providers now offer mobile data (whether on your phone or through a wireless modem you can purchase), and you can get a 3G connection in all major towns. Data is expensive by regional standards, with 1GB going for around Le100,000 (nearly double what you'll pay in neighbouring Guinea), but it's still the easiest way of getting online. Airtel's data pricing structure is available here: w africa.airtel.com/wps/wcm/connect/africarevamp/sierra/3g/home/tariff.

For home internet solutions, including Wi-Fi and portable modems, try **Onlime** (m 076 888 885, 030 888 885; w onlime.com/sl).

Connection speeds are unsurprisingly best in Freetown, but at the time of writing efforts were being made to spread the love out to the provinces. October 2011 saw President Koroma preside over Sierra Leone's first connection to a fibre-optic cable, dragged out of the sea and right on to Lumley Beach, which was finally brought online in February 2013, to the delight of Skype callers everywhere. In 2017, a US$28 million project was underway to lay more than 660km of domestic fibre-optic cable, connecting Freetown to cities upcountry. Once complete, connection speeds upcountry should end up a bit closer to those of their city cousins, and data prices nationwide should see a welcome drop as well.

BUSINESS AND INVESTMENT

Long gone are the days when business visitors were seen as bad news for the nation, extracting everything they could and getting on the first plane out. Since the war, government, donors and the odd investor too have been working hard to make the phrase 'Open for business' a reality, mindful of high unemployment rates, huge potential in a number of sectors, a stable post-war environment and strengthened fiscal and regulatory guidelines that might just mean money gets to where it should. The Ministry of Trade and Industry (w *trade.gov.sl*) has the latest details on progress, initiatives, statistics and surveys.

While mining still tops the agenda for foreign direct investors – whether British, Israeli, South African, Australian or from elsewhere – others are trying to forge ahead with three untapped sectors – agriculture, fisheries and tourism – that have presidential backing for expansion.

Investing in Sierra Leone even has support from the likes of Lord Stevenson, Chairman of HBOS bank, who is among those advising the Sierra Investment Fund, managed by private equity fund manager ManoCap (w *manocap.com*). ManoCap, established with the support of the UK's Department for International Development, promotes investment in Sierra Leone by channelling private funds from outside the country into those sectors that are usually ignored by foreign investors.

'Investors traditionally focus on mining, ignoring the opportunities that exist in other parts of the economy,' says Tom Cairnes, a manager at ManoCap. 'We believe that by looking outside the extractive industries we can find attractive investment opportunities, and in doing so demonstrate to others that Sierra Leone isn't the basket case that it is commonly perceived to be.'

For all the potential, colossal stumbling blocks (which consultants paid to smooth the way like to call 'challenges') still exist. Finance options for businesses are available at annual interest rates of between 25% and 30% from local banks. This extortionate rate is primarily driven by the government's requirement to raise short-term finance for its own expenditure requirements. The government borrows from banks and other financing institutions in the form of Treasury bills, at rates of between 20% and 28%. Faced with a choice, banks will always lend to the less risky government borrower before the private sector, and when they do, they charge a generous premium over the T-bill rate.

The government is, however, taking action to increase competition in the financial sector by issuing several new banking licences, mainly to Nigerian banks with large balance sheets and an appetite for risk. This will most likely lead to improved financing terms and access to finance for the private sector in the medium term.

Like several other African countries, Sierra Leone is working towards a smoother business environment so registration, permits, licences, taxes and other paperwork can be streamlined. Business registration used to take 12 administrative steps, taking 24 days (in practice it was often much more), costing US$1,580 (not accounting for bribes). That has been slashed to three administrative steps, with same-day turnaround reportedly now possible (see the Office of the Administrator & Registrar General [OARG] for details: w *oarg. gov.sl*). The Sierra Leone Investment and Export Promotion Agency (SLIEPA; w *sliepa.org*), which opened up in 2009, offers assistance to investors on start-up processes. In an effort to improve the environment for foreigners, work and residence permits have now merged, and run for five years. So if you get permission to work, you automatically get permission to live in Sierra Leone, sparing a double payment fee and the hassle of annual renewals.

Land rights and ownership, borrowing rates and dealing with bureaucracy are all thorny issues. A survey conducted by the World Bank in 2009 showed that of 150 formal firms surveyed in the country, the most frequently cited 'severe' obstacle to business was the government's tax rates (17%). Others included the access to finance (15%), electricity supply (14%), and corruption (9%). The Anti-Corruption Commission (ACC; w *anticorruption.gov.sl*) has to its great credit made dozens of arrests since 2008, including customs officials at the port – notorious for its backlog of work and ability to extort money on the side in exchange for lower bills – as well as the country's former ombudsman charged on 168 counts of misappropriating public funds. The ACC has set up a fraud-busting telephone hotline (m *077 985 985, 076 394 111*), and a website, Pay No Bribe (w *pnb.gov.sl*), where you can anonymously report corrupt officials online. Convictions have tended to avoid the big fish, however, and it remains to be seen whether the ACC can make a significant dent on pervasive graft.

In the long term, the factor that will have the biggest impact on the economic vibrancy of Sierra Leone is probably its potential to attract its large diaspora population, on the back of its rising economic fortunes. While the remittance monies being sent back play a crucial part in livelihoods at present, the real potential lies in thousands of well-trained and experienced Sierra Leoneans returning to take part in the recovery.

The Sierra Leone Investment and Trade Portal (w *sldits.com;* f *sltradeportal*) provides news of projects, investment information and jobs to induce people back home. Schemes range from commercial ginger-growing to the privatisation of 44 state enterprises. In recognition of the enormous economic impact returnees could have on the country, in 2007 the government dropped the 30-year-old law that prevented Sierra Leoneans from holding dual citizenship, which had forced many in the diaspora to give up their country of birth in favour of passports for the country in which they settled.

'I've encouraged a lot of people to come back but it's very, very hard … You have to have a passion for the country and want to see a difference,' says Kofie Macauley, who left behind a property career in the UK to start up his transport firm, which he named CamServ Salone – meaning 'come serve Sierra Leone' in Krio. 'I have come back to show others that it is possible,' he says. 'Sierra Leone is definitely a place where you can make a lot of money. Government needs to encourage people like us to come back and settle.'

BUYING PROPERTY

It's not exactly a flourishing international retail market, but the building boom of (frequently ghastly) column-clad houses on the hillsides above Freetown is here to stay. The first mortgages have arrived, and older diaspora members are being tempted home for retirement by the fantastic climate, ancestral links and low cost of living. **Regimanuel Gray** (*38 Freetown Rd, Wilberforce, Freetown;* \022 236 046; m *076 603 954;* e *info@regimanuelgraysl.com;* w *regimanuelgray.com*), a real estate developer, is committed to building more than 1,000 medium- and high-end houses, including 200 recently completed villas in the Seaview Estate gated compound beside the sea in Goderich. Each one costs a startling US$247,800 to US$334,500.

Andy McFarlane, author of the blog Home Salone: Expat family (mis)fortunes in Freetown, Sierra Leone (**w** expatfamilyfortunes.com)

Living in Sierra Leone as an expat presents nothing if not a challenge: rutted roads, power cuts, rainy-season mould and failing water supplies – usually when you've a head full of shampoo – are part and parcel of life even in Freetown's better-developed suburbs. Nothing seems quite as simple as it ought to be, and the first weeks are an emotional rollercoaster. Finding a home is a minefield, particularly if your employer isn't paying as you'll have to fork out a year's rent (up to US$30,000) up front. Check whether you'll have a direct water supply or deliveries to a tank, how much daily 'light' (state-supplied electricity) you can expect, and whether a generator's operating hours are limited. A fridge-freezer that maintains temperature during blackouts is invaluable. Apartment complexes probably have security but renting an individual home might mean hiring a watchman – if only to open your gate. No matter how swanky a place looks, you'll almost certainly discover broken cupboard hinges, wobbly toilet pedestals and rickety furniture. Good luck getting your landlord to fix them once he's pocketed your rent. A lack of skilled tradesmen, tools and materials mean you get used to 'making do'.

Brace yourself for a high cost of living. You can trawl markets for secondhand crockery, cutlery and bedding, or buy new from supermarkets. But it'll be time consuming when you're trying to adjust to a strange environment. Ship over possessions and you'll find Freetown customs officers a law unto themselves. Tales abound of people sweating it out at the port to retrieve belongings held hostage, only to then be charged for 'storage'. Some couriers ship directly to your new place; Mount Aureol is recommended. Perhaps the simplest way is to pay your airline for extra baggage. Friends of ours arrived with 13 suitcases.

When it comes to shopping, lean from your car window at the right junction and fluffy bread rolls, fruit and veg, snacks, cleaning products – even pet puppies – are available from hawkers. Markets are great for staples while local shops can be a saviour, stocking biscuits and batteries, sweets and superglue, crackers and credit (for your mobile). To stock up, most expats use Lebanese-run 'supermarkets' (think convenience stores), where you'll pay £1.20 for own-brand digestives or a dollar for a tin of beans; other luxuries – breakfast cereal or dairy products – are even more expensive. Prices vary wildly: a store with the cheapest baby wipes in town might charge twice the going rate for tinned tuna. And it

CULTURAL ETIQUETTE

GREETINGS These are a big deal, so be sure to smile, shake hands and ask after anyone you meet. Touching your left hand to your right elbow and bowing slightly when you meet someone important is a sign of respect. Sometimes, among the younger generation, a handshake is followed by touching your right hand to your chest, about where your heart is, as a sign of meaningful respect. People also go in for cheek-kissing: a total of three, usually starting with the right, is considered fond, warm and polite.

HISSING So there you are in a restaurant, bar or snack joint, and all you want is the bill, or a Coke, or even the menu. But no-one's looking. You give a persistent, snake-

might not stock jam at all. Cooking involves large gas bottles, available from petrol stations. Our first lasted four months before running out when we had dinner guests on the way.

Getting hold of cash isn't easy. Find one of Freetown's few ATMs, which dole out Le400,000 at a time, and chances are it'll be out of service. Some employers offer advances, otherwise transfer services such as Western Union or MoneyGram work for large sums. But it's slow going at banks, where a clamour for transaction forms and laborious ID process precedes a nervous dash to the car carrying a brick-sized wad of banknotes in a black plastic bag.

Some foreign postings come with a driver and a vehicle; otherwise you'll need a car. Japanese 4x4s are favoured. My 'new' (ie: freshly imported) 11-year-old Rav4 cost me US$8,500 and arrived from the US with dodgy brake pads, a punctured spare and an interior full of dog hair. Departing expats often sell cars via Freetown Announcements Yahoo group or the Freetowners Facebook group. Registration, road safety certificates, transfer fees and basic insurance cost US$100–200. You can drive for three months on a foreign licence but a Sierra Leonean permit helps avoid police attention. By law, you must carry a jack, warning triangle – available at the roadside for six quid – and stick reflectors on your bumpers (many vehicles lack functioning lights).

Taking kids… are you crazy? Well, our daughter was 16 months old when we arrived. If both parents are working, Western-style daycare comes recommended at YAS Learning Center, off Spur Road, Kidzone at Bottom Mango (page 165) and Freetown Montessori, Hill Station. For older children, the American School, for three to 14-year-olds, off Hill Cot Road, has an excellent reputation but isn't cheap (US$15,000–US$22,000 a year). Freetown's few playgrounds – at places like Family Kingdom or the YSC – have entry fees and ageing equipment… beware rusty hinges, protruding screws and hard concrete. So thank goodness for beaches, where our little one would plunge repeatedly into the sea and play with lovely local kids. Watch out for dangerous currents and steep increases in depth. There are pools at the Aqua Sports Club (seawater) and Family Kingdom (Le60,000 per entry), while hotels such as the Country Lodge offer day passes for upwards of Le50,000 a day.

You'll never quite escape life's frustrations – not when your foot goes through that flimsy shower tray *again* – but you'll become more adept at dealing with them. That's when you start to feel at home in this fun, friendly, fascinating land.

like hiss and someone comes over immediately. While Westerners may be horrified at the hiss, it has been mastered by all Sierra Leoneans, and gets attention where a raised hand or polite look goes unheeded. If it still feels too far beyond the pale, or you can't get the required volume, try a bit of teeth-sucking instead, with a head tilt in the direction of your waiter/waitress.

WHICH HAND? The left hand is associated not just with defecation, but also lovemaking and witchcraft. The right hand is associated with positive public actions such as greeting, eating, working and sacrificing. So, when accepting change, paying people, passing food, gifts or any other action involving your hands, try to remember to go with your right. If someone offers you their wrist, it means their hand is dirty or hurt, so shake their wrist instead.

ROMANCE While there are no rules, it's interesting to hear time and again the phrase *kep tik byon dor* ('keep a stick behind the door') – meaning 'always have another boyfriend/girlfriend on the go'. Men and women with four and more 'girlfriends' or 'boyfriends' are common. (Many women, famed as market traders and small-time entrepreneurs, tend to say the reason men are no good at running their own businesses is because they have too many girlfriends to look after and please with money-laden offerings.) Despite promiscuity, requests to use condoms are often met with disdain and tend to fall on deaf ears, with accusations of failing to trust a loved one, however many loved ones there might be.

It's common to be told 'I love you' within seconds of meeting someone ('I like you' is proxy for pretty much the same thing), and offers to be your 'friend' may well come with more than you bargained for. Should you have a telephone number and give it out, expect a barrage of calls, even to international numbers.

Nightclubs and bars tend to be filled with prostitutes, known also as *kolonkos* and *raray* girls, and many operate according to a series of different classes and fees. Some can be abrasive and hectoring to the extent that lone men feel awkward and exposed in bars; others wait to be approached. Though much less common, male prostitutes also exist.

MOBILE PHONES Be prepared for an onslaught of people who 'flash' you regularly: phoning and then hanging up before you answer so that a missed call registers. It means your pal has no intention of paying for a call, but wants you to know they are trying to get hold of you, and that you are expected to call back. Whether you do or not, of course, is up to you.

If anyone persistently or aggressively calls you, the advice from the phone companies – and the street – is to answer and let any pesterer's phone credit run down. They'll soon stop ringing you once they're out of beans.

Etiquette-wise, while some people still vaguely cling to the idea that you shouldn't slavishly answer your mobile – whether out of respect for any real live company you may be with, or simply to prove to yourself that you're not controlled by a flashing little box of technology – this view is certainly not in vogue in Sierra Leone. Hear your companion's phone pipe up – often with the latest hit about town – and it will get answered, whether you're in the middle of an emotional outpouring or the funniest joke the world has yet to hear. Think nothing of doing the same.

VISITORS If you are white-skinned – or even if you don't consider yourself white-skinned but you're not African – you are likely to be hailed as 'white man' in Krio, *oporto* in Temne and *pumoi* in Mende. It's up to you how you handle it. Some people hate it, offering up their own name immediately. While 'white man' is no way to address anyone you respect, it's not necessarily meant as an outright insult. More respectful epithets include 'auntie', 'ma', 'mammy' or 'sista' for a woman and 'brodha' (brother), 'pa' or 'sahr' (sir) for a man, as well as 'friend' or 'paddy'. In fact, many women are called 'sahr' too, since Krio tends not to distinguish between genders – quite a peculiar experience the first few times. Some people equate any foreigner with the foreigners they are most familiar with – plenty of white European travellers have been called Chinese, for example.

Often you may find yourself being asked, and expected, to help with people's problems – usually financially. This is not surprising, considering the amount of international aid that has been dispensed in Sierra Leone since the end of the war. Sierra Leoneans also regularly give out money, whether to friends, family or strangers. Particularly in the bush, many rural communities only associate foreign visitors with

UN agencies and international NGOs, and the idea of a tourist who simply wants to pay his or her way, observe and interact occasionally is a novel development. Requests may range considerably in scale: one conservation student was asked to provide diamond-mining equipment, machinery and expertise to a village.

IN THE BUSH Avoid whistling after dark (it is believed to attract spirits), or chewing in front of elders, which shows a lack of respect. Showing consideration also means making sure you always douse a fire at night when you go to bed – embers picked up by the wind could burn people's houses down. Wetting anything under a communal pump, like a head wrap to keep cool for example, not only holds up other people who have walked miles to fill up their water cans, it is seen as an indecently wasteful frippery. At all costs avoid straying into the community or sacred bush – usually easily identified as a clump of trees just outside a village. Do not approach it under any circumstances.

Finally, resist any temptation to ask endlessly about the war (or to a lesser extent, Ebola). Most people are trying to move on with their lives, and many have suffered directly and lost family and friends in horrific ways. Your questions could be painful to people who have already answered to legions of NGO workers and journalists, but many are too polite to say anything. It may be that people bring it up unprompted.

PERSONAL SPACE Few people go in for queuing, and barging your way through crowds – as with traffic – is often the preferred option. Touching people – on the shoulder, the thigh, the elbow; and men holding hands – is totally acceptable. While it may seem uncommonly forward, it is unlikely to be anything more than friendly unless it comes with obvious sexual intent. In villages, be prepared too for intense, prolonged staring if you look very different: privacy is not valued, and overt curiosity is considered the most natural thing in the world. Most of the time, you are treated as an honoured oddity – keep up your end of the bargain with as much warmth and friendship as is being shown to you.

FORMAL OCCASIONS Any event, even a night of music and dancing, might well start with speeches and prayers, for both Muslims and Christians. Such a night is also almost guaranteed to start 4 hours later than advertised, and resistance to boredom is a healthy character trait to nourish. Tickets for extravaganzas at the national stadium, for example, might say 20.00, but the first of the main acts is unlikely to appear any time before 01.00 and even if you leave your seat at 05.00 you'll be seen as a bit of a lightweight, quite frankly.

Weddings It's not just the bride and bridegroom who have to be into commitment. If you're lucky enough to be invited to a wedding, you really need to sign up to everything: prepare for the marriage (count on being late, everybody else will be), the reception immediately after, and the party later on that night. Most people go home, change and have a little rest before the latter stage of the evening. While dowries are still occasionally handed over in a calabash, perhaps with a little gold, thread and cloth, much more common these days is a wad of cash. Your gift should be cash in an envelope too.

Funerals Rather than black, the colour for funerals is white, and when a crowd of people fill the streets behind a vehicle with a coffin, all dressed in white, it is both uplifting and mesmeric. Funerals normally consist of a period of three or four

2

days of mourning, with numerous calls on the bereaved family, but often involve an element of celebration and farewell rather than uninterrupted grief. A further ceremony is usually held after 40 days.

LANGUAGE

Many people can give Krio lessons (see pages 344–9 for some rudimentary words and phrases); Teteh (m *077 864 563*) is a teacher who comes recommended. A course usually consists of six 1-hour lessons, which provide the basics of pronunciation, a few phrases and an understanding of the grammar. See also pages 349–55 for words and phrases from the two principal indigenous languages – Mende, spoken predominantly in the east and south, and Temne, spoken mainly in the north and west.

TRAVELLING POSITIVELY

Sierra Leone has so few tourists, and the tourism sector is full of such unrealised promise, that even turning up is a boon for the image-beaten country. Go there, have a good time, and spread the word back home that it is safe, stable and stunning, and you will do more for the country's prospects than any single handout is ever likely to.

Without the giant hotel complexes of some of the more developed West African tourist destinations, it is impossible to shut out the overwhelming poverty in a country that sits near the bottom of the UN's human development index. On too many scales, Sierra Leone comes last; in too many real lives, day-to-day existence is unimaginably tough.

Devoid of a welfare system, many Sierra Leoneans give money to beggars. Collection day tends to be on Fridays, but there's never any lack of mendicants who will approach. Some Sierra Leoneans in equally dire straits are ashamed to beg, and of course for every person who asks there are many more who don't. Giving money to beggars is an uneven way of doling out cash, is unlikely to make a shred of difference in the long term, and – if anything – encourages the idea of dependency that can ultimately drain a nation's psyche.

However, simply doing what you might do on a 'normal' visit: behaving well, taking an interest, spending your money locally and wisely, and rewarding good service somehow doesn't seem enough in a country as manifestly impoverished as Sierra Leone.

What more you might do is up to you. Although they have a chequered past in the country, supporting a charity that has a good record of co-ordinated, long-term support makes sense. All the usual suspects are here – UNICEF, Save the Children, Oxfam, Plan, Care, World Vision, Red Cross, MSF and dozens more. More direct support is another option, particularly if you find yourself becoming part of a local community. Many people will be very grateful for any support you can give, but bear in mind a few considerations. If you're keen to give money, it's crucial to look at what might work – what's needed and what's wanted – not just what you might like to do. This requires a lot of groundwork, and listening: what the women of a community might want – such as clean water nearer by – might not be what the men want – such as a generator for the chief's house.

Education is one good area – paying for new skills or training beyond the financial reach of many Sierra Leoneans can vastly improve their job prospects and earning power, for example. Likewise health: the UK charity Welbodi Partnership (w *welbodipartnership.org*) supports paediatric care in Sierra Leone, and is developing the Sierra Leone Institute for Child Health, a centre of excellence in paediatric care located at Olu During Hospital in East Freetown, the city's government-run paediatric referral and teaching hospital.

Most important, try to set up something with long-term prospects – a link between schools or a community partnership. Too often grand schemes collapse moments after the cash is handed over, because there's no-one to monitor or care about what happens next. If money is involved make it regular – a transfer to a bank account every six months is far better than a few haphazard windfalls. That way the people you are helping on the ground have the chance to make longer-term spending decisions rather than having to ask for cash at random. At every stage work closely with Sierra Leonean counterparts, and make sure they are involved all along the way. Be upfront about what is expected of you and them and make sure they do the same. It's a fine line between showing willing and promising a world you can't deliver.

On a much more immediate basis, Sierra Leone friends may well ask you for financial help in a one-off crisis. Understand that your sense of commitment can snowball. For example, if you give someone money for medicine they may well expect you to then drive them to the hospital if they get worse, pay doctors' fees, and feed them in hospital. If you work out the parameters of what you can and can't do first it will make life much easier for everyone. The mantra is not necessarily 'don't do it', but be aware what you might be committing to, and be aware of how damaging it can be to pull out halfway through. You might also relish the chance to do something hands-on and volunteer. This might well prove more a life-changing experience for the volunteer than for the supposed beneficiaries. However, the UK's Voluntary Service Overseas (w *vso.org.uk*) and US Peace Corps (w *peacecorps.gov*) are good places to start looking. Others keen to be involved at grassroots level have discovered numerous local non-governmental organisations whose work they deeply respect and have offered their own expertise – often in the realms of management, fund-raising, research or publicity. Bearing in mind the considerations above, if you develop a passion and see a place you can make a difference, go for it.

SEND US YOUR SNAPS!

We'd love to follow your adventures using our *Sierra Leone* guide – why not send us your photos and stories via Twitter (@BradtGuides) and Instagram (@bradtguides) using the hashtag #sierraleone. Alternatively, you can upload your photos directly to the gallery on the Sierra Leone destination page via our website (w *bradtguides.com/sleone*).

Part Two

THE GUIDE

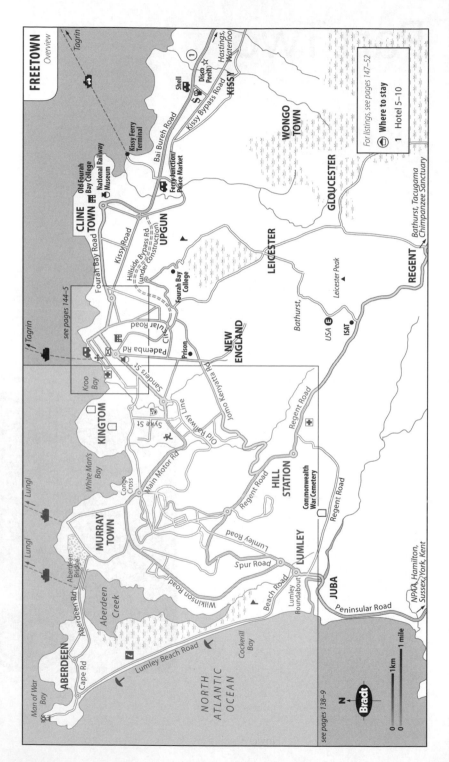

FREETOWN Overview

Tagrin

Tagrin

NORTH
ATLANTIC
OCEAN

Man of War
Bay

ABERDEEN

Cape Rd

Aberdeen Rd

Aberdeen Bridge

Aberdeen Creek

MURRAY
TOWN

White Man's
Bay

Lungi

Lungi

Lungi

Cockerill
Bay

Lumley Beach Road

Wilkinson Road

Spur Road

Beach Road

Congo
Cross

Main Motor Rd

Old Railway Line

Jomo Kenyatta Rd

LUMLEY

Lumley
Roundabout

JUBA

Peninsular Road

NPAA, Hamilton,
Sussex, York, Kent

Lumley Road

HILL
STATION

Commonwealth
War Cemetery

Regent Road

Regent Road

Regent Road

KINGTOM

Kroo
Bay

Syke St

Sanders St

Pademba Rd

Prison

NEW
ENGLAND

Circular Road

Fourah Bay College

USA

ISAT

Bathurst,

LEICESTER

Leicester Peak

REGENT

Bathurst, Tacugama
Chimpanzee Sanctuary

GLOUCESTER

WONGO
TOWN

UPGUN

Hillside Bypass Rd
(under construction)

Kissy Road

Fourah Bay Road

CLINE TOWN

Old Fourah
Bay College

National Railway
Museum

Ferry Junction/
Peace Market

Kissy Ferry
Terminal

Bai Bureh Road

Kissy Bypass Road

Shell

Disco
Porch

KISSY

Hastings,
Waterloo

see pages 144–5

see pages 138–9

0   1km
0   1 mile

Bradt

N

For listings, see pages 147–52

⊕ Where to stay
1 Hotel 5–10

3

Freetown

Set amid jungled mountains and a sweep of beach, Freetown has among the most improbable layouts of capital cities, all tangled roads snaking back and forth, keeping pace with the hills and wandering ramshackle around the coast. Brightly painted wood-slatted houses are draped over gorgeous green hills, sneaking down to a sea lined with beaches perfect for family outings, a kickaround, a swim or a cold beer. On a clear day, the picture is stunning.

While there are a few 'sights', the real draw of the capital is its atmosphere – sometimes almost suffocating in its hectic pace and dazzling in its brightness. But beneath the surface, history is everywhere, charting the birth of a home for freed slaves.

Freetown today is a city of small districts, which can take up just a handful of streets, each with a distinct character and a name borne of the communities that marked them as their own: Kissy for the Kissi farmers of the east; Congo Cross after the freed slaves of that country who were delivered here; Cline Town from liberated Hausa slave Emmanuel Cline, who in 1839 wanted to start a religious colony back in Nigeria; Kroo Town for the Kru fishermen of Liberia; and PZ after the Scottish-Greek trading partnership, Paterson Zochonis, that set up shop at the now-famous downtown intersection. Amid this patchwork of neighbourhoods is a larger rivalry between the poorer east and richer west sides of the city, which can take on epic proportions; with fashion shows, hiphop battles and beach parties all devoted to the difference.

For a town with freedom built into its name, hardship, struggle and the sort of poverty that can almost seem to render freedom meaningless are part of daily life. The city can sometimes seem hedonistic without reaching optimistic; people party to forget, sometimes they go out just to be seen. But what a party. Street parades, album launches, packed night-time beach bars and grinding dancefloors with floor-to-ceiling mirrors form partners in vanity. Most places don't really shape up until way after midnight, and staying out until first light is common. And there's always the warm embrace of a hammock on a beach to play out what's left of the next day.

The city lives by contrasts – the traditional devils that dance on one side of town while a Jesus march takes place on the other; the jobless boys who cross-train with such discipline on the beach every morning; the downtown market trading women who move like princesses with eight baskets of charcoal stacked on their heads; the students who throw themselves into politics with as much fury as they whoop at the beauty pageants that lift their spirits; the fast-paced shouting matches that halt traffic but somehow never descend into violence; the fishermen heading out to sea in the dead of night as clubs still heave with enthusiastic bodies; the mangoes and bright Africana cloth next to shocking pink pigs' trotters and secondhand bicycle parts; the ice cream melting in tiny plastic bags; and the young man selling face towels just as the beads of sweat start rolling.

And Freetown goes on; improving little by little, accompanied by grumbles but rarely rage, and largely safe. However, progress is slower than many would like.

Supply of water, roads, light, energy, healthcare and education will be shaky for a long time yet. The gridded basin of the Central Business District is enclosed by achingly poor slums, threaded with tens of thousands of plastic bags, household rubbish and abandoned machinery that collect below sea level alongside the pigs swilling in the dirt. Meanwhile faux-Doric columns go up on the well-to-do hillsides of Hill Station. The city doesn't make sense, but you can't help trying to fathom it.

HISTORY

Were it not for the discovery of an outsized beetle said to be from Sierra Leone, Freetown might not exist today. Back in 1786, when London's moral elite was busy looking for a home for freed slaves and the capital's 'black poor', several destinations were touted.

Those 380 freed black Britons who the next year sailed for a promised land, armed with £14 each, 400 guns, stationery and eight months' worth of stores, might have ended up in New Brunswick, Nova Scotia, The Gambia or the Bahamas had it not been for 29-year-old Henry Smeathman's fascination with botany.

Lured by professional envy, four collectors sent this amateur naturalist off to Sierra Leone to bring home specimens yet more exotic than the elusive Goliath beetle, first discovered in 1770, for the glass cabinets of Kew Gardens. Spending four years on the Banana Islands, 'Mr Termite' came back with plenty of ants, and the sure conviction that he had passed the happiest years of his life in that 'terrestrial Elysium' – perhaps that also had something to do with having taken two African wives.

By 1786, Smeathman, a self-confessed 'poor misfortunate flycatcher', was also deeply in debt, and quickly fixed on the idea of escorting – for a fee – former slaves from Britain to the place he labelled 'one of the most pleasant and feasible countries in the known world'. That dovetailed rather well with the lofty intentions of the nascent abolitionist movement in London, which hoped to stop slavery in its tracks and deliver freedom, land and self-government to American slaves who had fought for Britain in the War of Independence and wound up poor and homeless on the streets of London.

Somehow the pigtailed fantasist overlooked not only the fact that Sierra Leone was itself a slave-trading bastion, but that the place he praised for 'mildness and fertility' alongside 'vernal beauty, a tropical luxuriance' was also home to humidity, torrential rains and vicious sickness that were to put paid to 122 of the arrivals within the first four months of their May landing at Romarong, the Temne name for the site that was to become Freetown. The word meant – and here was a clue that went unheeded at the time – 'the place of wailers'. The hungry new settlers couldn't get anything to grow, arriving at the height of the rains with the wrong kinds of seeds, and fell back on dwindling ship provisions. These ran out when the first governor of the disastrous colony took off with the stores; in an effort to make do, some sold their clothes to survive; others, such as the once-abducted Harry de Mane (who had said he would choose 'rather to die than be carried into slavery' at the time he won his freedom), started working for slave ships – two of the settlers were even sold.

'I do not think there will be one of us left at the end of 12 month …There is not a thing put into the ground, will grow more than a foot out of it,' wrote disheartened arrival Abraham Elliott Griffith back to Granville Sharpe, the London abolitionist and architect of the whole venture.

To compound the first settlers' misery, the new turf never even belonged to them. The first treaty was concluded with the headman-but-one, King Tom, a local Temne ruler, who put his thumb print on a piece of paper he couldn't read in exchange for eight muskets, a barrel of gunpowder, iron bars, scarlet cloth, 24 laced hats and a puncheon of rum. But when another boat of 20 settlers arrived in 1788 to relieve the bewildered first batch, King Tom's overlord, King Naimbana, was having none of it. He demanded a new deal, chiefly consisting of booze in return for land. That was no guarantee of safety for the settlers, however, and after King Tom died his successor King Jemmy – no doubt angered by the fact that the captain of a passing British naval ship set fire to one of his villages – burnt Granville Town, as the settlement was first known (after Granville Sharpe), to a crisp. That marked the sorry end of the first chapter in the history of the Province of Freedom.

A new batch sailed in 1792, this time from Nova Scotia – 1,190 American slaves freed as a result of fighting for the British who had settled in Canada, but had not been given access to the land and better conditions they'd been promised in return for offering their lives. Already well integrated, with a strong sense of their own identity, and a rugged, can-do approach to the frontier lifestyle, they were made of sterner stuff than the first group of settlers, bolstered by the unflagging courage and spirit of their leader Thomas Peters. An American plantation slave who served as a British Army sergeant, Peters managed to get to Britain to complain about broken promises six years after he'd received precisely nothing for his war efforts. He then went back to Nova Scotia to deliver the news, round up his pals, and finally – with British financial support – they set sail for Sierra Leone and founded Freetown as a city of their own.

However, after the disaster of the first attempt, much of the idealism had been watered down on the British side. The new settlement lost sight of self-government and was instead set up at the behest of the well-meaning but British-run Sierra Leone Company, which would finance the undertaking but require citizens to contribute to an overseas for profit venture, trading in anything but slaves, to help make a go of the new territory. That meant it was a promised land run from London, with European-appointed officials who extracted rent from the people it was set up to serve, and, more importantly, who had been promised full independence.

Feeling let down from the start, the Nova Scotians found the going hard. Thomas Peters died with the onset of rains, as did more than a hundred others. It got worse. The French – pursuing their Napoleonic Wars wherever they could find enemy turf – attacked the settlement in 1794, letting rip with cannon from seven boats disguised with the English flag. They then landed; plundering, killing livestock and either burning or throwing what they didn't want into the river. Those who fled the charred town were rescued by canoes sent by none other than the slave traders they despised. Bit by bit, the mission's grand plans diluted. 'We wance did call it Free Town but since your absence we have a reason to call it a Town of Slavery,' wrote Moses Wilkinson, one of the early Nova Scotian leaders, to his beloved ex-governor John Clarkson.

People began to eke out a way of life. Some of those who found themselves on the Sierra Leone shore had come home to the very spots where they had first been captured, and managed to find their families once again. Vegetables eventually grew, plots of land were allotted, wood-framed buildings went up, roads were hacked into the undergrowth and rudimentary schools and medical facilities were offered; there were all-black juries, regular fishing catches and daily church services were filled with voices full of thanksgiving.

In 1795, 550 former Jamaican slaves, known as Maroons, who had fought the British for their independence and been deported to Nova Scotia, also joined Freetown. Tensions grew between settlers, their British backers, and indigenous people. An armed revolt in 1800 over land and taxes saw one man hanged and several more banished. Some Maroons even had such a rotten time they pleaded to go back to Jamaica. The expense of protecting the land from local rulers who demanded rent according to their customs took its toll on the finances of the Sierra

'WHITE MAN'S GRAVE' OR EXOTIC PLAYPEN?

As in so many other aspects, Freetown leads a double life when it comes to comfort. In the early days, the enthusiastic sentiments of the abolition campaigners took a knock from the reality of life on the ground. Sierra Leone quickly won itself a reputation as a fetid pit of sickness for foreigners, particularly in the rainy season. 'It is quite customary of a morning to ask "how many died last night?"', wrote an aghast Anna Maria Falconbridge in 1794. But many more black men and women died than white, and there were environments far less hospitable than Sierra Leone. In fact, after the damp and the squalor and the failures of those first ill-planned landings, the white man (and his wife) had rather a pleasant time.

'I had every comfort I wanted,' wrote Adam Afzelius, a Swedish botanist who by 1794 had packed his Freetown garden with rare birds, scarce plants, butterflies, giant bats and the 'most beautiful and odoriferous flowers', believing he could never wish for a better situation.

Mrs Melville, wife of a British civil servant, wrote in her diary many years later in 1841: 'I have really been very idle today, doing nothing except wandering from one window to another to gaze on the beautiful prospect of both land and sea which lies spread out before me.'

Even the man who coined the 'white man's grave' moniker, F H Rankin, said in 1836 that the place was full of 'active horsemen, bustling merchants, gay officials, [who] move on all sides with a cheerfulness ... enjoying the easy hours, released from the cares of the week; riding on the racecourse, sailing on the bright estuary.'

And when the expats got scared off by the high death rates, and began to learn that malaria emanated not from fumes but from the bites of mosquitoes that bred in damp stagnant places, they vanished from sweaty downtown. In 1904 they built themselves a new idyll, Hill Station, situated towards the mountain rainforest of the Peninsula. From the beginning it was an exclusively European residential quarter of wooden houses built on steel stilts, with its own railway. 'They had planted their seedy civilisation and then escaped from it as far as they could,' wrote Graham Greene in his 1936 *Journey without Maps*. 'Everything ugly in Freetown was European.'

The lowest, sickest part of town was left for the people the colonialists had purported to want to free. Today Hill Station is just as well-to-do, the province not only of Western diplomats – including the British High Commissioner – and expatriate workers, but ministers, the country's elite and the president.

Leone Company, which could no longer afford to bankroll a venture that had not yet turned a profit. The town of the free, by now home to 2,000 people, passed into the hands of the British government. By 1808, a year after the slave trade was abolished in Britain, the settlement become Britain's first Crown Colony in tropical Africa. The Union Jack was hoisted over the Province of Freedom. By 1821, it was capital of all the British West African colonies.

Having ended its own slave trade, Britain was somewhat stymied by the continuation of it by rivals. Soon enough, the British navy started to intervene to release slave cargoes. Whether they started out in Angola or Senegal or anywhere in between, if these 'recaptives' weren't needed as soldiers they ended up in the new colony. About 6,000 joined by 1815, too many for Freetown to accommodate, and they headed up to a series of villages presided over by missionaries in the hills of the Western Peninsula (pages 183–221). About 50,000 receptives – 200 languages among them – kept coming until 1864, when the final slave ship was intercepted. Throughout this time their children, known as *creoles*, and those of the other settlers, came to form the group most associated with Freetown – the Krios (pages 49–50). As the Krios strove for new educational and cultural heights, Freetown won plaudits as the 'Athens of West Africa'. Still small – in 1954 the city was home to 65,000 – it swelled far beyond its 300,000 capacity as people fled the provinces during the civil war, and the 2015 census counted 1,050,301 residents in the city.

GETTING THERE AND AWAY

Sited at the northern tip of the Freetown Peninsula, facing the Atlantic, getting into the capital can be a mission. For details on airport transfer options, see pages 74–5. By road, the rest of the country is reached by a traffic-choked stretch of tarmac running east from the edge of town, or on a newly surfaced road from western Freetown through the hills at the centre of the Peninsula (see pages 141–2 for details).

BY CAR It's easy, but nevertheless expensive, to rent a car and driver in Freetown. Travel within the capital and Peninsula tends to cost US$80–140 a day for a 4x4 vehicle, including driver but usually excluding fuel (Le6,000 per litre at the time of writing), while travel upcountry can run to US$150–300 a day, depending on how bad the roads are. Negotiate hard, especially if you're hiring a vehicle for a few days or more. Check the driver's licence, road tax and vehicle insurance papers, and ask what happens in the event of breakdown. Both **Flash Vehicles** and **IPC Travel**, for example, guarantee another car will come and pick you up (hence a more expensive service). Some firms end up arguing over who pays for repairs, so always agree this first, and get a receipt in the event of roadside maintenance. Also ask what provisions are made for the driver overnight if your trip involves several days away. The companies and private individuals below all offer car rental. Not all are tried and tested, but we have personal and thoroughly good experience of renting vehicles from **Flash Vehicles**, **CamServ Salone** and **Visit Sierra Leone**, while **IPC** and **KTI** are also considered stalwarts. It's always worth shopping around on price and service, particularly since some individuals may give you a better deal.

🚗 **CamServ Salone** 2 Lightfoot Boston St; m 076 778 119

🚗 **Cerra Automotive** [138 D4] 69 Wilkinson Rd; m 088 999 999, 076 760 000; e info@cerraautomotive-sl.com; w cerraautomotive-sl.com

🚗 **Chernor Barrie** [138 D3] 1 Cockle Bay Rd, Murray Town; m 076 602 374

🚗 **City Car** [139 F3] 24 Main Motor Rd, Congo Cross; 022 234 467

🚗 **Conteh Bangura** [138 B2] Bintumani Hotel, 11 Man of War Bay, Aberdeen Hill; m 030 200 447

🚗 **Dad's Car Hire** [138 D7] Freetown Rd, Lumley; 022 237 525

🚗 **Europcar** [144 D4] 21/23 Siaka Stevens St (also at Radisson Blu); m 077 444 466, 077 444 477, 077 444 488; e reservations@europcar-sierraleone.com; w europcar-sierraleone.com; see ad, 3rd colour section

🚗 **Flash Vehicles** [139 E4] 7 Spur Rd, Wilberforce; m 076 535 274; e info@flashvehicles. com; w flashvehicles.com

🚗 **Hotel Bintumani** [138 B2] Aberdeen; m 030 821 111, 030 826 666; e bintumanihotel@ yahoo.com

🚗 **IPC Travel** [144 E3] 22 Siaka Stevens St; m 030 541 231, 077 444 453; e info@ipctravel. com; w ipctravel.com

🚗 **KTI Travel & Tours** [144 E2] Santano Hse, 10 Howe St; 📞022 221 344/5; m 076 879 148, 076 610 633; e ktifna@yahoo.com

🚗 **Melian Tours & Car Rental Services** 44 Pademba Rd; 📞022 228 068, 022 228 976; m 076 713 761

🚗 **Mohamed Barrie** [144 C4] 28 Liverpool St, Wilberforce; m 076 601 801

🚗 **Moliba Car Rentals** [139 H5] 5 Bailey St; m 076 882 488, 099 347 575, 078 904 060; e moliba2007@yahoo.com

🚗 **Motor Care** 58c Lightfoot Boston St; m 076 638 434; e info@sl.motorcare.com; w sl. motorcare.com

🚗 **Sierra Leone Car Hire** 📞01489 893784 (UK); m 077 461 316, 076 345 687; e sales@ sierraleonecarhire.com; w sierraleonecarhire.com

🚗 **Visit Sierra Leone** [139 F4] 28 Main Motor Rd, Congo Cross; m 025 200 978, 076 258 258, 079 258 258; e info@vsltravel.com; w visitsierraleone. org; see ad, 3rd colour section

BY GOVERNMENT BUS If you don't have your own vehicle, this is the best option for long-distance trips. The big white-and-blue buses have a strict one-seat one-passenger policy and tend to leave on time and make fewer stops than other public transport options; they're also cheaper and tend to be safer.

The main terminus is at Wallace Johnson Street in town [145 E2], with a second stop for some destinations at Kissy Terminal off Bai Bureh Road near Kissy Ferry Wharf, where you may have to change bus (for example, for travel to Kono), which adds hours to the journey.

Buses leave daily at 07.00, but you should turn up earlier to buy your ticket and load your bags. Watch your pockets throughout. All the prices are chalked up on a blackboard, and there are daily departures to Bo (Le20,000), Makeni (Le15,000), Kono (via Makeni; Le40,000), Kenema (Le25,000), Kabala (Le30,000) and Kambia (Le18,000). Buses also go three-times weekly to Pendembu (for Kailahun; Le50,000, Mon, Wed& Fri) and Pujehun (Le27,000; Tue, Thu & Sat). An express bus runs every Monday and Thursday to Conakry (Le50,000) in Guinea, with minimal stopping. There's also a government-run airport shuttle that departs from here for Le75,000 and goes to Lungi via Port Loko.

Every so often a rumour will go round, spread by commercial vehicles that compete for custom, that the government bus isn't running that day and you'd best travel with them. Check, as it's nearly always not true: try calling the information officer of the Sierra Leone Roads Authority (m *076 200 507*), or the government bus customer service line (m *078 888 811, 078 888 822*).

BY TAXI, PODA PODA AND PRIVATE BUS The private **Melian Tours** (m *076 713 761*) runs coaches to a handful of destinations (ie: Makeni, Kabala) from near the government bus station and on a similar schedule as the government bus. For most other public transport options out of the capital – particularly if you miss the 07.00 government bus – the best bet is to head for the spot named 'Shell' in the east end, opposite 53 Bai Bureh Road. It was originally named after the filling station on the right, which – helpfully – isn't even a Shell anymore; it's now a rather dilapidated Safecon. Still, everybody knows this glorified lay-by, where you can pick up a **taxi** or **poda poda** to pretty much anywhere in the country. Poda podas also depart from the Ferry Junction/Peace Market lorry park just off Bai Bureh Road, near Kissy Ferry Terminal.

Let people know your destination and wait to be shoved into the appropriate vehicle; it won't leave until it's full. When you think it's full, it's not. Long-distance taxis tend to put two on the front seat (squeezing you half out the window or half on the gear stick depending which spot you get) and four in the back. It's not comfy, but the chat and the music generally has potential. If having the edge of a seat rammed into your back for hours on end doesn't appeal, pay double for a seat to yourself. It might seem a bit snobby, but if you're going far it can be worth it, and you can keep your bags within sight at your feet or on your lap.

Fares are likely to rise and fall in line with fuel prices, but at the time of writing shared taxis cost Le20,000 to Lunsar, Le35,000 to Bo, Le25,000 to Makeni, Le35,000 to Kabala, Le35,000 to Kenema, and Le45,000 to Kono. You can pick up transport to other smaller towns from any of these points.

To reach Waterloo, for onward travel to the beaches of the southern Peninsula, there are two ways: from the west end, pick up a mountain road taxi or poda poda at Bottom Mango (Le4,500 in a shared taxi) or Lumley roundabout (Le6,000 in a shared taxi) towards Jui junction. You'll probably have to change vehicles here for Waterloo (another Le1,500), though some cars go all the way through. If you're in the east, pick up a Waterloo-bound poda poda from near the clock tower at the Eastern Police Station, for Le5,000.

Ali Abess Transport (m *076 636 686*) is a private coach company running minibuses, which tends to set off in the early hours before dawn, from Water Street near Congo Town Cemetery in the west.

BY SEA For the moment, the world's third-largest natural harbour is underutilised as far as passenger traffic goes. Apart from the ferry to Tagrin (page 75) that goes from Kissi, cargo and passenger ships dock at Queen Elizabeth II Quay in the east of Freetown, and some cargo and passenger options, including the new Sovereign Ferries (page 76) and private vessels, dock at Government Wharf in the centre of town by Wallace Johnson Street. Most connect up to Conakry, Banjul in The Gambia, or Dakar in Senegal. For more information, contact **Sea and Land Services** (*QE II Quay, Cline Town;* \ *022 223 453;* e *sala@slsa.com.sl*) or head down to the wharf. At the time of writing, rumours of a restarted sea link to Conakry had so far proven to be unfounded.

BY AIR Most airlines with scheduled services to Lungi have their own offices in Freetown (page 74), but you can also book tickets at travel agents (pages 70–1) in town. There's also an airstrip 20km south of town in Hastings, from where **Versatile Air Services** (m *079 478 483;* e *info@versatileairservices.com;* w *versatileairservices. com*) runs occasional charter flights. Contact the **Sierra Leone Civil Aviation Authority (SLCAA)** (m *076 645 138;* e *info@slcaa.net;* w *slcaa.net*) for general aviation enquiries.

ORIENTATION

The best way to think of the capital is in three distinct sections – the hilly west, grid-like town centre and traffic-choked east. Within each of those are individual neighbourhoods, such as Aberdeen, Lumley, Bottom Mango, Wilberforce, Murray Town, Congo Cross, Tengbeh Town, Ascension Town and King Tom in the west; Brookfields, New England, Kroo Town, St John, PZ, and simply 'town' in the central area; Eastern Police Clock Tower, Kossa Town, Fourah Bay, Cline Town, Kissy Town and Calaba Town, out towards Wellington, Hastings and eventually Waterloo in the east.

Only in the central business district in historic **downtown**, the oldest part of the city, can you rely on well laid-out streets: Wallace Johnson Street, Lightfoot Boston Street, Siaka Stevens Street and Garrison Street run parallel to the seafront on a northeasterly grid; many smaller streets cross them at right angles. Midway is the iconic Cotton Tree, an old, bat-filled landmark at a roundabout joining Walpole

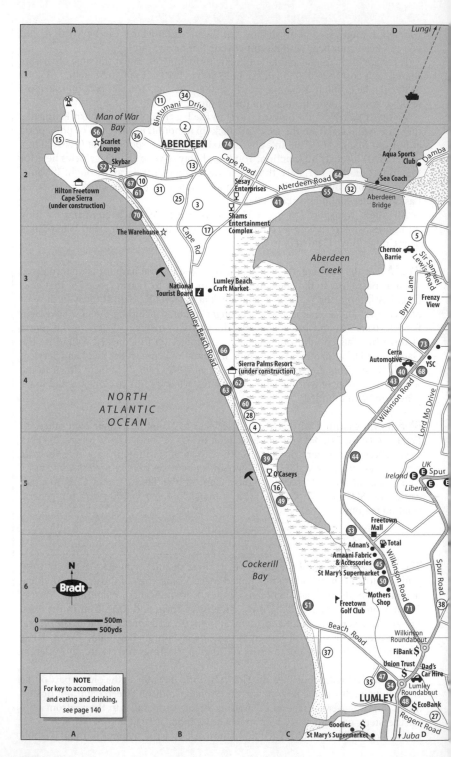

Man of War
Bay

A B C D *Lungi*

1

11 34
Bintumani Drive
36 2
56
15 **ABERDEEN** 74
☆ **Scarlet
Lounge** 13 Cape Road
☆ **Skybar** Aberdeen Road 64 **Aqua Sports
Club** Damba
52 67 10
61 Sesay **Sea Coach**
**Hilton Freetown
Cape Sierra
(under construction)** 31 25 Enterprises 55 32 **Aberdeen
Bridge**
3 41
70
17 **Shams
Entertainment
Complex** 5
☆ **The Warehouse** Cape Rd **Chernor
Barrie** Sir Samdel Lewis Road

3

**National
Tourist Board** ℹ **Lumley Beach
Craft Market** *Aberdeen
Creek* Byrne Lane **Frenzy
View**

73
**Cerra
Automotive** ● **YSC**
66 40 68
**Sierra Palms Resort
(under construction)** 43
62 Wilkinson Road Lord Mo Drive

4

63
*NORTH
ATLANTIC
OCEAN* 60
28
4

39
UK
☿ **O'Caseys** 44 **Spur**
16 *Ireland* Ⓔ Ⓔ
49 *Liberia* Ⓔ Ⓔ

5

53 **Freetown
Mall** 🛒 **Total**
Adnan's
**Amaani Fabric
& Accessories** ● 45
St Mary's Supermarket ● 50
N **Mothers
Shop**
Bradt 71 38
51 ► **Freetown
Golf Club** Spur Road
0 ————— 500m *Cockerill
Bay*
0 ————— 500yds Beach Road **Wilkinson
Roundabout**

6

FiBank $
Union Trust **Dad's
Car Hire**
$
37 47 $
NOTE 35 54 **Lumley
Roundabout**
For key to accommodation **LUMLEY** 48 $ **EcoBank**
and eating and drinking, 27
see page 140 **Goodies** $ *Regent Road*
St Mary's Supermarket ● ↓ *Juba* D

7

A B C

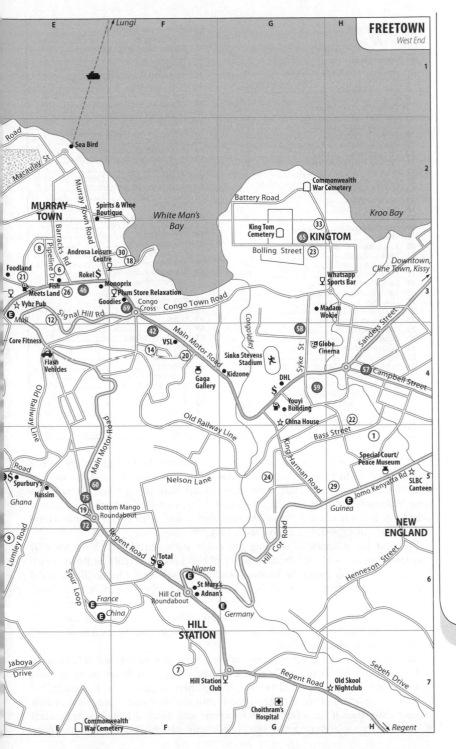

Lungi

Sea Bird

Macaulay St.

MURRAY TOWN

Murray Town Road

White Man's Bay

Spirits & Wine Boutique

Battery Road

Commonwealth War Cemetery

Kroo Bay

King Tom Cemetery

33

65 KINGTOM

Bolling Street 23

Downtown, Cline Town, Kissy

Barracks Rd

Pipeline Dr

8

6

Androsa Leisure Centre 30

18

Foodland

21

Rokel $

Fish Meets Land 26 46

Monoprix

Goodies

Plum Store Relaxation

Congo Cross

69

Congo Town Road

Whatsapp Sports Bar

Vybz Pub

Mali

12

Signal Hill Rd

Congo Valley

Madam Wokie

58

Sanders Street

Core Fitness

Flash Vehicles

42

VSL

14

20

Main Motor Road

Siaka Stevens Stadium

Kidzone

Gaga Gallery

Globe Cinema

Syke St

DHL

59

Youyi Building

China House

22

57 Campbell Street

Old Railway Line

King Harman Road

Bass Street

1

Old Railway Line

Road

Spurbury's

Nassim

Ghana

60

Nelson Lane

24

Special Court/ Peace Museum

SLBC Canteen

Jomo Kenyatta Rd

5

9

Lumley Road

19

72

Bottom Mango Roundabout

Regent Road

Total

29

Guinea

E

NEW ENGLAND

Spur Loop

France

China

Nigeria

St Mary's

Adnan's

Hill Cot Roundabout

Germany

Hill Cot Road

Henneson Street

6

Jaboya Drive

HILL STATION

7

Hill Station Club

Regent Road

Old Skool Nightclub

Sebeh Drive

7

Choithram's Hospital

Commonwealth War Cemetery

Regent

Freetown ORIENTATION

3

Street, Siaka Stevens Street (on either side), Pademba Road and Independence Avenue (leading to State House up the small hill to the east). Kroo Bay, a slum of more than 6,000 whose waters were once so clear that in 1669 French trader Le Sieur Villault found it 'better than the most delicious wines' (utterly unthinkable today), sits just northeast. Mabella, the next-door slum to the east, was once a busy natural harbour exporting charcoal to fuel French trains.

The **west** has a series of winding hill roads with stunning and occasionally disorientating views of the city, such as Signal Hill Road and Hill Cot Road, which gives a great view down to the national stadium. At sea level, Lumley Beach Road is a 5km Atlantic stretch of beach bars, breeze and speedbumps. Wilkinson Road, named after the blind, lame Methodist preacher Moses Wilkinson, curves south–north, picking up various neighbourhoods and traffic on the way, from Lumley to Congo Cross. Linking two sides of the west at its most northerly tip, Aberdeen and Murray Town, is Aberdeen Bridge.

People living in the generally more affluent west talk of the **east** side of town as if it's an expletive. Poor, highly populated, sprawling, and ill-served by any sort of infrastructure, you once had to pass through here to get off the Peninsula, but with the completion of the mountain road from the west end, many now eschew the east altogether. It has a reputation for crime and, swelled by tens of thousands of displaced people during the war, conditions can be grim and unsanitary.

But it's an underexplored, fascinating part of town, filled with trade on every scale, from solitary saleswomen hawking the smallest packet of fake hair and a few pharmacy pills out of the back of a wheelbarrow to wholesale production of fizzy drinks, cement, clay ovens and foam mattresses. Beyond PZ, Goderich Street leads to Eastern Police Clock Tower. From there Kissy Road runs past the Up Gun roundabout (named after one of three old city boundary guns from the start of the 19th century), becoming the dual-carriageway Bai Bureh Highway, passing Kissy dockyard and the ferry terminal, out to the 'Shell' transport stop, which marks the beginning of the end of Freetown proper.

MAPS Freetown maps are not easy to get hold of and are much in demand; there is talk of downtown hawkers who have tried to charge as much as US$50 for a wallchart. The booksellers downtown may be able to source you a decent map for less than this.

The 2007 ITMB map has a good fold-out city map on the flipside, while the UN-backed Sierra Leone Information Society (SLIS) has a great selection of maps, including high-quality satellite photos of Freetown (pages 92–3).

The National Tourist Board [138 B3] (*Lumley Beach Rd*; m *076 634 949;* e *ntbslinfo@yahoo.com;* w *welcometosierraleone.sl*) has also produced a series of handy fold-out town maps. These should be available at the NTB office, although they tend to run out of stock quickly; best to call ahead before stopping by. You can also try to find the maps at one of Freetown's higher-end hotels or from a street hawker.

Online, Open Street Maps' (w *openstreetmaps.org*) coverage of Freetown is impressively detailed and generally quite accurate.

GETTING AROUND

To paraphrase Jimi Hendrix: 'Freetown traffic, so hard to get through to you … Freetown traffic, all you do is slow me down.' A 20-minute car ride across town just before daybreak can take 3 hours or more during the day. It's partly down to a road network inadequate for the explosion in population and cars since the war. But ask a taxi driver, and they will likely as not tell you it has more to do with zealous traffic cops slowing everyone down with meticulous checks for paperwork and roadworthiness, requiring time-consuming payment of on-the-spot 'fines' for the privilege of carrying on regardless. Some roads downtown are one-way in the mornings, and then reverse direction or allow two-way traffic after the rush. Of course, there's nothing so helpful as a sign indicating this: you just have to know. Among the key arteries are Pademba Road (which runs alongside the high but nevertheless regularly permeable walls of the prison) and Siaka Stevens Street, both of which converge at the Cotton Tree. The lower section of Pademba Road is also blocked to traffic from the evening until 07.00 the next morning. Regent Road is one-way on the stretch going from Goderich Street to PZ until 10.00, when the direction switches. Savage Street is one-way from Brookfields to Sanders Street until 10.00 during weekdays, and the rest of the time the direction of one-way traffic comes from Sanders Street in town.

Traffic tends to be particularly bad on Siaka Stevens Street, Pademba Road and Congo Cross at rush hour, Goderich Street on the way to Eastern Police Clock Tower, and anywhere near the east's Up Gun and Bai Bureh Road. If you charter a taxi, you can plead with your driver to dodge the traffic and end up taking a series of tiny cross-cutting paths, including, towards the east, Mountain Cut, which runs parallel to Kissy Road past shacks, houses and backstreet life, as well as any number of routes through backstreet markets to get to any given part of downtown.

The first traffic lights since the war went up on Main Motor Road in mid 2016, and a recent glut of road building has seen several once-shambolic trunk roads across Freetown turned into smooth, wide boulevards, including Wilkinson, Spur, Signal Hill and Regent roads, with new tarmac on the last leading up past Hill Station and all the way through the mountains to Jui on the Bai Bureh Highway to Waterloo. Even with all this progress, the teams of construction workers toiling away in the heat won't be leaving anytime soon: surfacing works are still planned for Hill Cot Road, between Hill Cot junction (next to St Mary's Supermarket and the Nigerian High Commission) and Jomo Kenyatta Road in New England, and an entirely new route, Hillside Bypass Road, is to be built between the junction of Pademba and Jomo Kenyatta roads (next to Pademba Road Prison) and Blackhall Road, near Up Gun roundabout and the Bai Bureh Highway. They were as far as Mountain Cut in 2017, with about 2.5km to go; once complete, this will be the most direct route between the east and west sides of town.

BY PODA PODA Ragged poda poda minibuses (page 96) with their stickers and broken doors, swerve the streets on regular routes, stopping at the merest hint of a passenger. Listen for destinations cried out in loud but sometimes seemingly hard-to-catch tones that might have your drop-off point *en route*. '*Bafors bafors*' is the cry for vans headed towards Wilberforce, for example, up the hill. 'Tong' is town – meaning you'll be dropped somewhere within spitting distance of the Cotton Tree or PZ, although many poda podas head for Circular Road, a back route that's good for getting to the British Council. Lumley, Aberdeen, Congo Cross, Brookfields, St John's, Kissy (although Kissy Road itself is barred to poda poda traffic), Shell and Waterloo are among other significant stopping points. There are also 'zonal routing boards' listing regular routes throughout town.

BY TAXI Flag one down wherever you are, or try any of various pre-set ranks. For example, the chain of cars parked alongside Lumley roundabout wait to fill up to head down the Beach Road to Aberdeen. At the NP filling station facing the junction of Sir Samuel Lewis and Wilkinson roads (opposite the former Comium HQ), taxis wait to fill up before heading down Aberdeen Road. Downtown, taxis tend to queue for custom at the junction of Ecowas and Siaka Stevens streets; and at the Charlotte Street junction with Victoria Park (generally headed up towards Wilberforce in the west, and good for reaching all the way to Lumley from town). At the time of writing, the fee for a 'one-way' fare was Le1,500, although this tends to fluctuate with the price of fuel. Bear in mind that while taxis are a great place to meet people and get chatting, they are also prime pickpocketing spots.

Charter taxis If you don't want to share a cab with anyone else, you can charter a taxi just for yourself (just say '*cha cha*' and expect to pay Le30,000–40,000 an hour). More luxurious than the vagaries of chartering is to find a regular taxi you can call up whenever you like. Having the numbers of a few reliable taxi drivers can be super useful around town, so that you can be picked up from wherever you are rather than go out on the prowl for a vehicle that might already be full or headed elsewhere, particularly after dark. Some taxi drivers are used to regular charter work, are brilliant, considerate, timely and good fun. Others are over-anxious to find a foreign wife, overcharge, and drink or smoke on the job, particularly at night.

Prince among men is Osman Bah (m *077 233 584, 078 516 301*), who is based in Lumley, speaks good English and has his own private vehicle. Others with regular taxis based in the west of town include Barrie (**m** *078 729 555*) and Musa (**m** *078 828 257*), both of whom speak excellent English. John Conteh (**m** *076 944 262*), based downtown, speaks impeccable English and is used to working with foreigners.

A few others to try include Foday (**m** *076 480 280*), Osman (**m** *078 516 301*), Kevin (**m** *030 280 240*), and John (**m** *077 290 551*).

BY MOTORBIKE AND *TUKTUK* Motorbike taxis, better known as ocadas, took off in provincial towns before reaching the capital, but Freetown is full of them now – so full, in fact, that they were banned from the Central Business District and 19 major thoroughfares around town in May 2016 for the supposed traffic chaos they cause. There are still plenty of them around, mind, and the ban is unevenly enforced, but what this means is that you can expect to take some unexpected side roads and unusual routes through town to circumvent the proscribed roads. Rides cost a bit less than chartering a taxi (Le30,000 an hour) and are less safe, although your driver should provide you with a helmet. Ban or no ban, you shouldn't have much trouble flagging one down on the side of any road outside the CBD.

Three-wheeled tuktuks, locally known as *kekes*, also arrived in Freetown quite recently, and their numbers are growing quickly, thanks in large part to the fact they're not subject to the ocada ban and can roam the roads at will. They're similarly priced, however, and thus make a good compromise if you're not keen on motorcycles, but still want to save a few coins as compared with a charter taxi fare – plus you can bring two friends on the bench in back (some kekes have even started running fixed routes, as a sort of mini shared taxi).

BY BICYCLE Cycling around Freetown deserves special mention for two reasons: it's a traffic-beating way to get around town, and you often get a much better view than from the back of a crammed poda poda. It can, however, be dangerous: heavy traffic tends to make drivers both aggressive and careless, so it is advisable to have experience of city cycling if you are planning to use your bike around Freetown, and always wear a helmet.

TOURIST INFORMATION AND CULTURAL CENTRES

British Council [145 F5] A J Momoh St, Tower Hill; ℡ 022 220 775–7; **m** 076 290 111; **e** enquiry@sl.britishcouncil.org; **w** britishcouncil. sl or ◼ BritishCouncilSierraLeone; ⊕ 08.30–16.30 Mon–Thu, 08.30–14.00 Fri. Its stunning location overlooks the east end of Freetown; the canteen also does a mean shawarma. The well-stocked library is not so much the place to learn about Sierra Leone as to learn about the rest of the world, although it does contain full transcripts from the Truth & Reconciliation Commission hearings. It regularly puts on interesting cultural exhibitions, whether photographs, dance performances or theatre.

Immigration Department [145 E3] 14 Gloucester St; **m** 076 553 750; **e** info@immigrationservices.gov. sl or slid@sierratel.sl; **w** immigrationservices.gov.sl. If you're staying longer than a month, this is where to

extend your 1-month entry stamp. In 2017, renewals were charged at the same rate as a new visa – around US$100.

Ministry of Foreign Affairs and International Co-operation OAU Drive, Tower Hill; ℡ 022 229 710, 022 224 377 (Director-General); **m** 079 242 276; **e** info@foreignaffairs.gov.sl; **w** foreignaffairs. gov.sl

Ministry of Tourism and Culture 28B King Harman Rd, Brookfields; ℡ 022 242 170; **e** tourism_culturesl@yahoo.com; ◼ tourism. culture.sierraleone

Monuments & Relics Commission 23 Pultney St (PO Box 908); ℡ 022 223 555; **w** mrcsl.org or ◼ monumentsandrelics. Volunteer group that promotes the preservation of old buildings & sites of historic interest throughout the country.

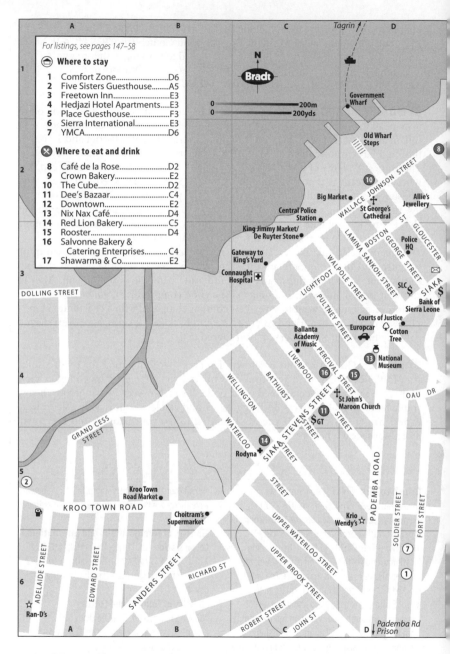

For listings, see pages 147–58

Where to stay
1 Comfort Zone..........................D6
2 Five Sisters Guesthouse..........A5
3 Freetown Inn............................E3
4 Hedjazi Hotel Apartments.....E3
5 Place Guesthouse....................F3
6 Sierra International.................E3
7 YMCA...D6

Where to eat and drink
8   Café de la Rose........................D2
9   Crown Bakery...........................E2
10 The Cube...................................D2
11 Dee's Bazaar.............................C4
12 Downtown.................................E2
13 Nix Nax Café.............................D4
14 Red Lion Bakery.......................C5
15 Rooster......................................D4
16 Salvonne Bakery &
      Catering Enterprises............C4
17 Shawarma & Co........................E2

National Protected Area Authority (NPAA)
6 Jenjen Dr, opp Regimanuel Gray Homes, Seaview Estate, Goderich; m 025 264 372, 079 983 093, 076 627 320; f NPAASL
National Tourist Board [138 B3]
Lumley Beach Rd, Aberdeen, PO Box 1435

(Yassin Kargbo, general manager); m 076 634 949, 088 867 663; e ntbslinfo@yahoo. com or info@welcometosierraleone.sl; w welcometosierraleone.org; ⏰ 09.00–17.00 Mon–Fri. Located just next to the construction site of the new Hilton Hotel, the National Tourist

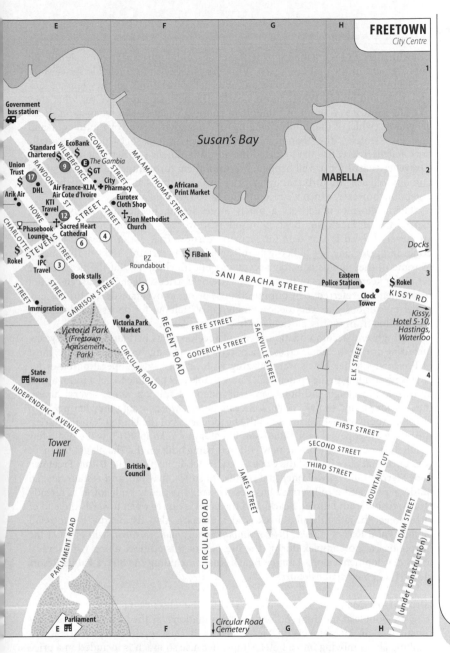

Susan's Bay

MABELLA

Government
bus station

Standard
Chartered

EcoBank

The Gambia

Union
Trust

GT

Arik Air

DHL

City
Pharmacy

Air France-KLM,
Air Cote d'Ivoire

KTI
Travel

Eurotex
Cloth Shop

Africana
Print Market

Phasebook
Lounge

Sacred Heart
Cathedral

Zion Methodist
Church

Rokel

IPC
Travel

FiBank

PZ
Roundabout

SANI ABACHA STREET

Eastern
Police Station

Docks

Rokel

Book stalls

Clock
Tower

KISSY RD

Immigration

GARRISON STREET

Victoria Park
Market

FREE STREET

*Kissy,
Hotel 5-10,
Hastings,
Waterloo*

*Victoria Park
(Freetown
Amusement
Park)*

CIRCULAR ROAD

REGENT ROAD

GODERICH STREET

SACKVILLE STREET

ELK STREET

State
House

INDEPENDENCE AVENUE

FIRST STREET

SECOND STREET

*Tower
Hill*

THIRD STREET

MOUNTAIN CUT

British
Council

JAMES STREET

ADAM STREET

PARLIAMENT ROAD

CIRCULAR ROAD

(under construction)

Parliament

*Circular Road
Cemetery*

ECOWAS STREET

WILBERFORCE STREET

RAWDON ST

HOWE STREET

CHARLOTTE STREET

STEVENS STREET

MALAMA THOMAS STREET

Board has brochures information about hotels, tour operators & airlines. Helpful staff are there to answer questions.

Sierra Leone Ports Authority Queen Elizabeth 11 Quay, Cline Town; 022 220 018/9, 022 220 537, 022 226 480; m 044 927 678; e customerservice@slpa.sl; w slpa.sl. Officially, this is the place to ask about the ferry timetable, but usually it's best to ask your Freetown travel agent as they follow the co-ordination with ferry & flights closely. In any case, turn up early, as often the ferry won't keep to schedule.

Unfortunately, this is not the happiest of sections, although it's seen some significant improvement in the past few years. While it's possible to find reliable spots as far as 24-hour water supply, electricity and internet connections go, they tend to lack soul, style and polish. What's more, nearly all hotels are expensive for what they provide, mostly as a result of prohibitive running costs due to reliance on diesel generators (which is thankfully changing) and a market skewed by multilateral and business clientele rather than more budget-conscious tourists (which is decidedly not). Furthermore, few have created the sort of ambience or design environment a traveller yearns for. It will happen, but until then, forbearance, and a little good humour will see you through. Every price range contains at least one enchanting exception, however, which we recommend to you with gusto.

Staying **downtown** delivers a much more urgent, hectic, and likely louder, experience of Freetown. Bear in mind that workers for international NGOs are never allowed to stay here for security reasons. That doesn't mean it can't be done, and prices are less ludicrously inflated, but it is certainly riskier. The quality in some of these joints is barely acceptable, but it's cheap and at the heart of the action for keen travellers or those on an extremely strict budget. The **east end** is not recommended, referred to by one guesthouse owner as overcrowded, criminal and, rather mysteriously, as 'very delicate material'. Watch out for doors that don't lock and stealing from rooms, particularly in cheaper places.

The high-end accommodation scene in Freetown has had an active few years, including during the Ebola crisis, when, rather than being devoid of clientele, most of Freetown's better hotels were buzzing with activity as the operating bases for NGOs responding to the epidemic. It's now thankfully possible to get a room again, and while most high-end hotels are still independently operated, several luxury international brands now have a presence in the city. Most notably, the Mammy Yoko Hotel in Aberdeen, which served as the headquarters of the United Nations during the war, was reopened as the **Radisson Blu Mammy Yoko** in 2015, while just a few hundred metres away, a brand-new Hilton is being built on the 7ha plot at the tip of Aberdeen that once housed the Cape Sierra Hotel. In its place, the **Hilton Freetown Cape Sierra** [138 A2] will offer 200 rooms, 20 suites, five bars and restaurants, an outdoor pool and a full-service business centre. The newly built tower is already clearly visible from Lumley Beach, and the hotel is due to open towards the end of 2018; to get the latest details, check w idea-uk.com. Also just nearby, the top-end **Mamba Point Resort** [138 A2] (**f** *mambapointlagoondafreetown*) will open at the Lagoonda casino complex during the lifespan of this edition, along with several other developments along Lumley Beach Road, including the **Sierra Palms Resort** [138 B4] (**f** *SierraPalmsResort*).

LONG STAYS Many of Freetown's hotels, in the absence of much short-term tourism, double as medium- or long-stay destinations for the host of international consultants on attachments in Sierra Leone. If this applies to you, it's worth thinking about moving into a hotel, simply because so much is included in a price that compares fairly competitively with the residential rental market. Hotels have put work into capturing this kind of customer, and many offer long-stay discounts and/or self-catering chalets aimed at long-term visitors. **Country Lodge**, **New Brookfields**, **Medrie International** and **Sierra Light House Hotel**, among others, offer discounts for long-term residents. Prices generally start at US$900 per month and go up quickly from there.

Most long-stay apartments are rented by the year or the half-year. Visit Sierra Leone (w *visitsierraleone.org/category/sierra-leone-real-estate-property*) has listings for relatively high-end locations, but there's nothing like the word on the street to help find a place, usually via local agents who take a cut of the rent. They're easy to track down once you arrive. If you're having trouble, drop into a supermarket and have a look at their noticeboards, or ask the owners if they know of any agents or landlords who have rooms going. Homestays are a good option for something shorter, and immerse you in the warmth of communal living.

EXPENSIVE

Bintumani Hotel [138 B2] (166 rooms, 50 apts & suites) 11 Man of War Bay, Aberdeen Hill, Aberdeen; m 030 821 111/826 666, 099 325 206, 076 748 407; e bintumanihotel@yahoo.com. When the Sierra Leonean government contracted a Chinese company to do up the beleaguered 1970s state hotel & then couldn't afford to pay, the company took over its running. Ahmad Tejan Kabbah cut the ribbon in 2003, but the whole place underwent another round of remodelling recently, & President Koroma was the man with the scissors for the re-reopening in 2016. It claims 5-star status, which it is not, but nevertheless its sweeping entrance hall, adequate rooms, Chinese restaurant (**$$$$**), swimming pool & tennis court make it a decent choice for a business guest. Beyond the rubbish filling the foreground, it overlooks Lumley Beach. B&B. **$$$$$**

✳ **Country Lodge** [139 F7] (55 rooms) HS 51 Hill Station; m 077 692 000, 077 611 611, 076 691 000; e reservations@countrylodgesl.com; w countrylodgesl.com. The most glamorous & expensive option in the country, with the best of the night-time views (& cool breezes!) over the city. By day, the draw of this one-time Lebanese residence is the decidedly upmarket poolside lounging area. Service is good, rooms well equipped & a 50-room extension underway means you stand a chance of finding a spot to lay your head amid all the foreign consultants who tend to rush to make this their long-term home. Equipped with a fine gym, pool (with pool bar) & tennis court, free Wi-Fi & satellite TV. Even if you're not staying, don't miss a meal at the balcony Eden Restaurant (**$$$$$–$$$$**), with the twinkling lights of Freetown for company. B&B. **$$$$$**

Golden Tulip Essential Kimbima [138 B1] (81 rooms) Man of War Bay, Aberdeen; m 079 582 465, 030 269 534;

w goldentulipessentialkimbimafreetown.com. Newly renovated & perched appealingly over the seafront, this slick business hotel became part of the Golden Tulip group in 2016 & looks appropriately sharp as a result. There's a swimming pool, fitness centre & cavernous terrace restaurant (**$$$$**) overlooking the sea, while all rooms come with satellite TV, AC & Wi-Fi. There's a buffet dinner & live band most Fri nights. **$$$$$**

Home Suites [138 B2] (29 rooms) 78A Cape Rd, Bintumani Drive, Aberdeen; m 030 222 227/8; e info@homesuiteshotelsl.com; w homesuiteshotelsl.com. Centrally located at the main Aberdeen roundabout, this super-stylish place is an excellent new option in this range. The individually decorated rooms come in a variety of sizes & shapes, & all are thoroughly modern & comfortable, with big flatscreen TVs & all the usual upmarket accoutrements. Some of the suites have kitchens, & the on-site restaurant, The Swan (**$$$$**), does continental & Italian-inspired meals. There's a well-equipped fitness centre, but no swimming pool. **$$$$$**

The Hub [139 E5] (28 rooms) 6 Regent Rd, Bottom Mango, Wilberforce; m 088 112 120/1; e info@thehub-hotel.com; w thehub-hotel.com. Formerly known as Mamba Point, this sleek & stylish hotel has fine, modern rooms with AC, satellite TV & Wi-Fi, along with a fitness centre, swimming pool & a great bar area, with pool table, shisha pipes & huge TVs. The shaded terrace restaurant is known for its sushi & fabulous views over town (**$$$$**); it's a favourite with the expat crowd. Guests get free transfers to & from the ferry. B&B. **$$$$$**

Lion Inn [139 E3] (11 rooms) 16 Wilkinson Rd; m 099 111 444; e thelion.inn.sl@gmail.com. Sharp, businesslike & often fully booked, this is a fine new option near Congo Cross. Rooms are well equipped, though a bit sparse & lacking some of the finer decorative touches compared with competitors in this range. There's a restaurant, but no pool or fitness facilities. **$$$$$**

🏠 **New Brookfields Hotel** [139 H5] (32 rooms, 50 under construction) Jomo Kenyatta Rd; m 030 000 120–2; e reservations@ newbrookfieldshotel.com; w newbrookfieldshotel.com; see ad, 3rd colour section. Opened in 2014, the tiled rooms at this centrally located business hotel are bright, breezy & comfortable, & many come with balconies & bathtubs. The on-site restaurant does good seafood grills & Indian-inspired mains, & there's a Fri afternoon happy hour on the shaded terrace. Long-stay discounts are available & a number of serviced apartments are under construction. There's also a swimming pool on the way, & it's possible the property will join a branded international chain during the lifespan of this edition. **$$$$$**

🏠 **Radisson Blu Mammy Yoko** [138 B2] (171 rooms) 17 Lumley Beach Rd; m 079 454 000; e info. freetown@radissonblu.com; w radissonblu.com/ hotel-freetown; see ad, inside front cover & 3rd colour section. The Mammy Yoko's 2-decade tenure as Freetown's finest hotel was cut short by the civil war, & the hotel itself saw fighting in 1997 before it became the UN headquarters in Sierra Leone. Walking into the lobby today, those days seem like a distant nightmare, as intensive renovations were completed in 2014 & the hotel finally reopened in its most glamorous incarnation yet as a Radisson Blu. Amenities on offer include 2 tennis courts, swimming pool, fitness centre, indoor/outdoor restaurant with daily themed buffets, & a swanky lounge bar offering select whiskys & fine cigars. Add to this the expected features like business & conferencing facilities & handsomely appointed guestrooms, & the Mammy Yoko is looking very phoenix-like indeed. **$$$$$**

🏠 **Sierra Light House Hotel** [138 B2] (46 rooms) 6 Man of War Bay, Aberdeen, PO Box 434; m 076 706 036, 076 818 888; e info@ sierralighthouse.com; w sierralighthouse.com. Despite its rather stodgy, block-like exterior, the rooms here are top-notch & all come with their own separate seating section & stellar views out over the bay. The restaurant (**$$$$**) sits above the water and is also highly appealing. Despite the lack of swimming pool, it's still a good bet to escape the business vibe, & they've now got a fitness centre as well. Wi-Fi, AC. B&B. **$$$$$**

🏠 **Swiss Spirit** [138 D6] (25 rooms) 38 Spur Rd; m 030 399 399, 077 399 399; e reception.freetown@swissspirithotels.com;

w swissspirithotels.com. With designer chic rooms spread over 3 floors, a recommended restaurant & an outdoor garden lounge, this new option just up from the Wilkinson Rd roundabout has more of a boutique feeling than many others in the range. The stylish rooms are all done up with a bit of colour & artistic flair, while the amenities are as smart as you would expect, though there's no fitness centre or pool. **$$$$$**

UPMARKET

🏠 **China Town Guesthouse** [138 C4] (12 rooms) Lumley Beach; m 076 652 377, 099 306 456; e fouadlanlan@yahoo.co.uk. Behind the unmissable Chinese façade halfway along Lumley Beach is a series of clean & modern AC rooms, decently equipped & providing an unexpectedly good, mosquito-free spot across the road from the sea. Discounts can be negotiated for longer stays. There are 2 restaurants on site (page 154) & a small supermarket attached. Wi-Fi. B&B. **$$$$**

🏠 **The Family Kingdom Resort** [138 B2] (50 rooms, 4 apts, 6 villas) PO Box 94, Lumley Beach Rd, Aberdeen; m 030 202 770, 076 777 949, 077 850 466; e fkingdomresort@yahoo.com; w familykingdom-resort.com. An extraordinary treasure trove of grounds right next to Lumley Beach, this resort has a children's playground, a well-equipped gym (free for guests), duikers & monkeys roaming free, a roof terrace for guests & plenty of faux-leather furniture in the decidedly 1970s-style rooms. There's something alluring about its eccentricity, & you can't fault the warmth of general manager S A Jaward. Plenty of spots for Lebanese cuisine too, either streetside or inside the compound. Wi-Fi, restaurant (**$$$$**), free laundry & ironing service. B&B. **$$$$**

🏠 **Hill Valley Hotel** [139 E3] (75 rooms) 34 Signal Hill Rd, off Congo Cross; m 076 610 439, 076 166 944; e hillvalleymgmt@gmail. com; w hillvalleyhotel.com. Simple & functional, although a little out of the way, this is a firm favourite with NGO-types. Renovations a few years back nearly doubled the number of rooms, although reliable sources say the walls are still a bit thin. Wi-Fi, AC, restaurant (**$$$$**) & bar. **$$$$**

🏠 **Hotel Africanus** [139 F4] (12 rooms) 1 Frazer Davies Dr, off King St, Congo Cross; m 077 700 020, 044 700 020; e nasserayoub@ hotmail.com or reservation@hotelafricanus.com;

w hotelafricanus.com. This little hotel hidden down a quiet side street offers good value in a fairly central location – thus it tends to stay full. All rooms are self-contained & come with AC, TV, fridge, Wi-Fi & hot-water showers. The restaurant ($$$$–$$$) serves up chicken & chips, grilled fish, pizza & other staples. B&B. **$$$$**

⌂ **Hotel Barmoi** [138 A2] (35 rooms) 75C Cape Rd, Aberdeen; m 030 960 016, 076 918 771; e enquiries@hotelbarmoi.com; w hotelbarmoi.com. Formerly the Cape Guesthouse, this is the most intimate of the business-hotel bunch, perching 1 of its 2 guest-only swimming pools right over the sea, with a couple of restaurants ($$$$) offering good views & a bit of breeze. Named after the owner's village in Port Loko district, its wood-panelled reception, business centre & style combine to put it among the best hotel spots in Aberdeen. Free Wi-Fi. B&B. **$$$$**

⌂ **Hotel de la Joie** [138 C5] (11 rooms) Lumley Beach Rd; m 088 068 170, 078 869 828; e hoteldelajoie@hotmail.com; f hoteldelajoiesl. Painted up in a very Santorini-feeling blue & white, this new family-run lodge has a handful of neat ground-floor rooms with fridge, nets, AC & Wi-Fi, & it makes for a good-value beachfront pick, with pleasantly switched-on staff. Several rooms also have their own kitchenettes, or there's a seafood restaurant on site. **$$$$**

⌂ **Hotobah Lodge** [138 F3] (12 rooms) 5 Boyle Ln, Murray Town; m 030 241 212, 076 241 212, 076 810 707; e info@thehotobahlodge.net; w thehotobahlodge.net. Clean & quiet, with a terrace overlooking White Man's Bay, this homely option has newish en-suite rooms with AC, fridge & hot water, with a living room/TV lounge at the entrance. Food & drink can be arranged, or otherwise you're just around the corner from Oasis and Congo Cross. B&B. **$$$$**

⌂ **Jam Lodge** [139 F4] (10 rooms) 18B, off Main Motor Rd; m 099 311311; e info@jamlodge.com; w jamlodge.com. Set in a converted old home, the vibe here still feels familial, but the colourful, good-value rooms are modern & comfortable, with fridge, nets, AC & satellite TV. There's a wraparound veranda upstairs & covered terrace bar with pool table, cold beers, & simple meals at the bottom. It's a favoured stop for overlanders passing through Freetown. **$$$$**

☀ ⌂ **Lacs Villa Guesthouse** [139 G5] (11 rooms) 3A Cantonment Rd, off King Harman Rd; m 078 215 668, 030 776 241, 025 200 595; e lacsvilla@yahoo.com; w lacsvilla.com. An utter find, with real home-from-home appeal, although it tends to fill up quickly. Split levels accommodate relics of old colonial style amid 1ha of rolling land, & an attractive balcony restaurant ($$$) overlooks a view of the Congo Valley waterfall. There's a badminton court on site if you're feeling energetic. Wi-Fi, 24hr power & hot water. **$$$$**

⌂ **Medrie International Hotel** [138 C4] (40 rooms) 36 Lumley Beach Rd; m 025 340 683, 077 841 911; 044 633 695; e abdulbundu@gmail.com; w medrieinternationalhotel.com. Though this newly constructed block facing Lumley Beach may not exactly be long on character, the facilities are good & the rates reasonable. All rooms come with AC, hot water, flatscreen TV & fridge, plus balconies for the seafront rooms. There's an attached casino, & guests also get access to the Edge Fitness branch downstairs. **$$$$**

☀ ⌂ **Oasis Guesthouse** [139 F3] (9 rooms) 33 Murray Town Rd; m 076 605 222, 077 080 250; e oasisjuicebar@gmail.com; f OasisFreetown. Set at the end of a long driveway in a grassy garden overlooking the water, this hidden gem of a place fully lives up to its name with comfortable, colourful rooms & a fabulous attached café (page 155). All rooms come with TV, AC & Wi-Fi. It's often fully booked, & justifiably so. **$$$$**

⌂ **Seaside Suites & Hotel** [138 B1] (15 rooms) 3A, off Bintumani Drive, Aberdeen; m 025 649 039, 076 224 459, 077 073 818; e info@seasidehotelsl.com; w seasidehotelsl.com. The rooms here are decently equipped, if a little crowded & overpriced, but the wide & windswept restaurant terrace hanging over the rocky shoreline is as fine a perch as any in Aberdeen. All rooms come with AC, fridge & hot water. **$$$$**

MID-RANGE

⌂ **Hotel Mariam** [138 B3] (48 rooms) 5a Off Beach Rd, Aberdeen; m 025 413 726, 025 226 545, 076 886 046, 076 629 156; e sesaymohamedlamin@yahoo.co.uk; w hotelmariamsl.com. Extraordinary hotel hidden in the backstreets of Aberdeen, where the décor resembles a patterned 1970s sofa. Favoured by diamond traders, it can get loud & brash at times. Overpriced; it does, however, have all the essentials – AC, en suites, fridge, Wi-Fi, hot-water showers, flatscreen TVs & 24hr power. It's also popular for conferences. $$$$

🏠 **Leisure Lodge** [138 B2] (18 rooms) 30 Off Cape Rd, Aberdeen; m 076 417 402, 088 321 272; e info@leisurelodgehotelsl.com; w leisurelodgehotelsl.com. Though the 'slice of heaven on earth' their brochure describes is probably stretching things just a wee bit, rooms here are nonetheless decent value & all come with AC, TV, hot water & Wi-Fi. Staff are friendly & you can even pay with a Visa card. There's also a conference hall on site. B&B. $$$$

🏠 **Raza Guesthouse** [138 D2] (12 rooms) 62 Sir Samuel Lewis Rd, Aberdeen; m 076 956 389, 030 236 385, 088 217 981; e razaguesthouse2005@yahoo.com. Downright peculiar-looking from the outside, but venture beyond the unattractive Fort Knox-style stone façade with barbed-wire trim & you find a solid choice. Rooms are clean & functional, some with balconies, & the restaurant menu ($$$$) serves up African dishes for lunch. Wi-Fi, B&B. $$$$

🏠 **Hotel 5–10** [map, page 130] (33 rooms) Teachers Av, off Bai Bureh Rd, Quarry-Kissy Low Cost Step, east end; m 079 004 662, 077 222 103, 076 685 805, 076 697 523; e hotel510@sierratel.sl or hotel510@yahoo.com. The only lodging that comes halfway recommended if you want to stay in the east end is this reasonable complex from the Sierra Leone Teachers' Union. Not particularly cheap, it's nevertheless secure & comfortable, with AC, self-contained rooms with hot water & even the option of suites. B&B. $$$$–$$$

🏠 **Charms Beach Hotel** [138 B2] 29 off Cape Rd, Aberdeen; m 088 140 316, 079 685 911, 077 754 608, 030 312 779. Though charming would certainly be the wrong word for the spartan rooms on offer here, they're nonetheless large, clean & high ceilinged, along with being more-or-less the cheapest in this part of town. Rooms come with fan or AC. B&B, no food otherwise. $$$

🏠 **Diana Guesthouse I** [139 E3] (7 rooms) 19 Mudge Farm Rd, off Aberdeen Rd; m 076 671 345, 076 716 964. A decent deal in west Freetown, the rooms here are a bit dingy, but there's a lovely spot for b/fast on a balcony overlooking the leafy compound. All rooms are self-contained, some have AC. B&B. $$$

🏠 **Diana Guesthouse II** [139 E6] (6 rooms) 26C Spur Rd, Wilberforce; m 076 671 345, 076 636 113, 078 070 211. A sister to Diana

I in Aberdeen, you can find this homely little guesthouse down a side road off Spur Rd. A little worn round the edges, it has a pretty garden filled with coconut & mango trees, all topped off with an enormous child-like portrait of Princess Diana on the garage-like front door. All rooms are self-contained, with AC, nets & hot water, & there's an upstairs sitting room & balcony. Manager Muhammad Lamin Deen is helpful. AC, satellite TV, Wi-Fi. B&B. $$$

🏠 **Jay's Guesthouse** [139 E3] (14 rooms) 1E Sir Samuel Lewis Rd, Aberdeen; m 079 640 113, 099 659 202. Noisy at night, with a blue-&-white balcony overlooking the traffic at the busy filling station & nearby bar, it's a good central spot in the west side of town. All rooms are self-contained; those at the back are quieter. The management won't allow same-sex guests to share. Hot water. AC & fan in rooms. $$$

🏠 **JC Guesthouse** [139 H4] (9 rooms) 26 Bailey St, Brookfields; m 076 687 426; e brunswickshipping@gmail.com; w brunswickshipping.com/jc-guest-house. Associated with a shipping firm that runs cargo to & from New Jersey, this is a centrally located & good-value guesthouse with homely AC rooms, a veranda overlooking the neighbourhood, & meals available on request. All rooms come with Wi-Fi, TV, hot water, & fridge. $$$

🏠 **Malama Inn Guesthouse** [138 D7] (8 rooms) 144 Regent Rd, Lumley; m 076 906 834. All double rooms are self-contained in this decent place near the Lumley roundabout; single rooms share a toilet. Ask for a room with AC. $$$

🏠 **Sweet Mother's Guesthouse** [138 C7] (13 rooms, 5 bungalows) 32 Beach Rd, Lumley; m 079 193 747, 099 920 758; e sweetmothersguesthouse@gmail.com. Painted in bright colours, this is a quirky basic find, close to the beach, with a studio kitchen for each of the bungalows, en-suite showers, proper loos & nets. Look for the section of wall painted like a zoo, with animal carvings too. Ellen's Bar, named after the owner, has a TV. All rooms are self-contained with either fans or AC. Always try negotiating on price, especially for long-term rentals. $$$

🏠 **Comfort Zone** [144 D6] (31 rooms) 1 Pipeline Dr & 47 Fort St; m 078 882 400, 077 854 396; e sigies_toksvel@yahoo.co.uk. Behind a signless brown-walled compound just off of Wilkinson Rd, proprietress Marvel Bloomer runs a tight ship, maintaining 2 buildings of well-kept AC rooms popular with long-stay visitors. There's a rooftop terrace with views over the neighbourhood & home-cooked meals on request. Their 2nd location in the city centre on Fort St is a better budget bet, with lower standard but equally neat rooms from US$20 to US$40. $$$–$$

🏠 **Sierra International Hotel** [145 E3] (36 rooms) 27 Rawdon St; m 076 780 408, 076 604 499, 077 594 749; e sierrainterntionalhotel@ yahoo.com. You can't wind up much more on top of the city centre than in this decent multistorey hotel, with a big dose of activity right outside the door. Well kept, with wood-clad walls, big beds, slightly musty rooms & efficient management. There's an appealing little restaurant ($$$) & a bar. AC, TV. B&B. $$$–$$

BUDGET
🏠 **Cockle Bay Guesthouse** [138 D3] (7 rooms) 36 Sir Samuel Lewis Rd; m 076 218 872, 030 660 935. Nice garden at the front opens on to a series of basic self-contained rooms. No hot water; bucket showers & fans; only some rooms have mosquito nets. B&B. $$

🏠 **Freetown Inn** [145 E3] (35 rooms) 18 Howe St; ☎ 022 220 915; m 076 214 344; e assad. rwatta@yahoo.com. The sympathetically priced rooms here are all self-contained & come with AC & TV, & while it's about as noisy as anywhere else downtown, the new managers seem clued up & ready to be of service. There's a restaurant (under different management) on the top floor. $$

🏠 **Hedjazi Hotel Apartments** [145 E3] (25 rooms) 32/34 Rawdon St; m 076 601 094, 076 790 750 (Musa Bangura, manager); e ihedjazi@ hotmail.com. Smartish place, opposite the Sierra International Hotel, that has a busy communal area beside the 1st-floor reception with magazines, TV & an intimate café (*), serving up daily African dishes. Rooms off this area can be a bit noisy, but their bathrooms are better than most. Choice of fan or AC room; all are self-contained. B&B. $$

✳️🏠 **Kingtom Guesthouse** [139 G3] (15 rooms) 8 Bolling St, Kingtom; m 077 430 087, 079 840 404, 078 836 738. If Sierra Leone attracted backpackers, this 3-storey block would be a perfect refuge for them. Although a little out of the way, it's well placed for easy access both to town & the more upmarket west side; & since it's right by the

power station you can nearly always guarantee light. Friendly staff, decent ply-panelled rooms & communal areas make the stilted décor somehow homely. The ground-floor bar & restaurant ($$) is great for cheap food & the odd bit of ambience. All rooms are self-contained with fans or AC, TV, fridge, & cold running water. B&B. $$

🏠 **YMCA** [144 D6] (11 rooms) 32 Fort St, near Pademba Rd, Tower Hill; ☎ 022 223 608; m 078 952 818; e ymcasl@yahoo.co.uk; w sierraleoneymca.org. A great option for facilities in the city, there's a neat little bar-restaurant ($$) serving African dishes night & day, & a good flow of guests. The agreeably priced rooms have standing fans only, & 2 rooms are self-contained. Wi-Fi is planned. B&B. $$

SHOESTRING
🏠 **Agie's Guesthouse** [139 H5] (12 rooms) 27 Willoughby Lane, Brookfields; m 076 605 071 (owner, Dr Harold Hedd), 077 853 118. This dive is included really only to make the point that plenty of 'guesthouses' are really knocking shops; not so much brothels as places couples use for some by-the-hour loving. Rooms are charged by the hour, although you can rent them overnight as well. Any guesthouse classified '4' by the tourist board ('1' is best) may well be in this category, & the atmosphere can be unsavoury & certainly unsuitable for lone women. Fans, no nets, some rooms self-contained. $

🏠 **Five Sisters Guesthouse** [144 A5] (10 rooms) 76 Kroo Town Rd; m 076 786 846, 030 393 721. It might be in the bottom-dollar section, but this old hospital is a find for the price. Dr Frank Davies constructed this 7-storey building in the heart of busy Krootown (there's a view over the slum & the sea from the back windows) in the 1960s & later converted it; he sold basic food & booze in the ground-floor shop until his death a few years back. Rooms are rudimentary but with the odd twist – look out for red leather Art Deco sofas & other oddities scattered about. A lovely 1st-floor restaurant terrace gives a view over the heaving street below, but there was no food in sight when we dropped by in 2017 (plenty of beer, though). The frontage is on the road that leads downtown, so not only are you right in the middle of the noisy ambience, you are also privy to the many funeral processions that make their way to Kingtom

Cemetery nearby. Fans only, 3 rooms share a bathroom. No nets, ceiling fans. **$**

🏠 **Place Guesthouse** [145 F3] (23 rooms) 42 Rawdon St; m 076 662 358, 076 619 884, 076 552 428, 030 267 653. Good shoestring option in the town centre, it's the cheapest of the bunch on Rawdon St. Spick-&-span, the full-on tiling – not only of floors, but walls & stairways too – keeps the place clean but looks a little odd. The little balcony over the busy trading street below provides hours of people-watching. Rooms upstairs are better, although none have AC, but it's worth paying a little extra for a larger one. TV, fans. **$**

🏠 **Sierra Leone Agricultural Research Institute (SLARI) Guesthouse** [138 D7] (4 rooms) off Lumley Beach Rd; m 077 738 225, 025 323 104; w slari.gov.sl. With provincially priced rooms barely 1km from Lumley Beach & none of the shenanigans often associated with guesthouses in this range, this SLARI-associated guesthouse is a find. Signposted some 250m off Lumley Beach

Rd, the basic rooms here all come with fans, nets & little else, but they're neatly kept & the amenable manager can rustle up meals with enough advance notice. They've only got 4 rooms, so ring ahead if you want to be sure to snag one. **$**

🏠 **St Edward's Pre-School Training Center** [139 G3] (19 rooms) St Edward's Secondary School grounds, Kingtom; m 077 870 205, 076 617 941 (Mariama, caretaker); e preschoolcenter@yahoo.com. Among the garden's hedgerows & flowers is a reliable set of rooms opening on to a courtyard near the church. Rundown but clean, you can easily forget you're in Freetown amid the quiet greenery. The communal restaurant (**$$**) is often packed with delegates from the workshops & seminaries held here; there's also plenty of light because it's near the power station, & the downtown area is close by. Each set of 2 rooms shares a bathroom. Ask if you'd like a double bed rather than twins; hot water, ceiling fans only. **$**

✖ WHERE TO EAT AND DRINK

Whether it's rice and black-eyed beans for breakfast or Indian take-away at three in the morning, Freetown can probably accommodate you. Having said that, fresh grilled fish beside the beach, Lebanese snacks, and fast food tend to predominate in the restaurants, while African dishes are cheap and ubiquitous, served up in large vats at cookeries or at a glut of glorious street food stands. Usually these don't have set opening and closing hours – they start up mid morning and keep serving until they run out of grub, often late into the night. Wherever you are you can nearly always find cold bottled water or a cold beer. Spirits, outlandish cocktails, cappuccino and delectable smoothies with fresh ingredients also have their place, but you need to know where to go. On the other hand, if you can't be bothered to go anywhere at all, the people at **Go Food SL** (m *088 100 600, 079 100 700;* w *gofood.sl;* 🛐 *gofoodsl*) arrange deliveries from a variety of restaurants around the city – see their website or smartphone app for details. The restaurant scene was picking up plenty of steam in 2017, and **Foodies Salone** (🛐 *FoodiesSalone*) is the place to find out about the newest hotspots.

Usually open all day, most kitchens start winding down at 22.30–23.00. On weekends bars stay open as long as there are revellers. Not all of the following places have food, but those that do tend to charge between Le50,000 and Le80,000 for the catch of the day – most often barracuda steak or snapper – grilled with hot chilli, with chips on the side. The northern end of the beach also has plenty of roving 'groundnut girls' who sell peanuts for Le1,000 a scoop.

Lumley Beach's 5km drag is dotted with wooden shacks, cement blocks and about half-a-dozen large glass-and-concrete construction projects, many of them Chinese-owned, in various stages of completion. Any day of the week is good for a sundowner and a bite, but Sundays after dark sees not only the beach but also the road crammed with preening youths keen to strut their stuff on the sand and at the noisier bars.

above left   Much of life takes place right on the beach in Sierra Leone — Freetown's Lumley Beach hums with activity day and night (SC) page 152

above right   Brightly coloured and creatively named, Plantain Island fishing boats prepare to unload their catch — visitors to this outpost are few and far between, so expect a warm welcome (KM) pages 229–31

below   Surf's up in Bureh, where palm-fringed shores are well-established with surfers in search of the perfect wave (NTBSL) pages 212–13

above   Travelling to Tiwai Island by dugout canoe: a visit to this tropical rainforest island is undoubtedly one of Sierra Leone's wildlife highlights (JK) pages 252–8

left   Take the 'Scenic Route' and find rural Sierra Leone at its peaceful, unhurried best. Thatch-roof mud-brick huts are still the mainstay of village life (r/S) pages 320–3

below   Getting around rural Sierra Leone is an adventure in itself: a log bridge offers passage on a road upcountry (KM)

above left Palm wine tapper in Bonthe — the sweet liquor is best savoured straight from its source (JK) page 106

above right Diamond mining in Koidu. Artisanal mining in muddy rivers and streams remains a popular way to try and earn an income (KM) pages 275–81

right Visit Bumbuna Falls, a joyous spray of water that, if timed right, form rainbows in the air, curving colourfully into the water (KM) page 311

above left The emerald starling (*Coccycolius iris*) is one of the smallest starling species and endemic to this region (MF/S) page 307

above right Even the urban jungle of Freetown will delight birdwatchers. Hear the prolific common bulbul (*Pycnonotus barbatus*) singing its sweet notes downtown (LN/S) page 177

middle Look out for the beautifully chequered pied kingfisher (*Ceryle rudis*) perching close to rivers (MM/S) page 177

left Classified as Vulnerable, the white-necked picathartes (*Picathartes gymnocephalus*) is a top sight for birding enthusiasts (fc/S) page 274

above   Aerial view of inland Sierra Leone: the country's wide-ranging habitats support a rich diversity of species (KM) page 4

right   Guinea baboons (*Papio papio*). In Krio, *babu* means any kind of monkey or chimp (IY/FLPA) page 8

below   Smaller and lighter than common hippos, the endangered and highly elusive pygmy hippo (*Hexaprotodon liberiensis*) is best sought on Tiwai Island (VW/S) page 10

above left   While many craftsmen have disappeared in recent years, it's still possible to find artisanal products like baskets, pottery and wood carvings at stalls along the roadside (r/S) pages 107–8

above right   Woman making a fishing net in Sokurala — an off-the-beaten-track village in the Northern Province (KM) page 330

left   Weaving in Kabala — the skill is slowly dying out due to a lack of interest from younger generations (KM) pages 316–17

below   Tombo, Sierra Leone's busiest fishing town: observe the fishermen as they expertly mend their nets on the wharf, or catch a glimpse of the vibrant fish market (KM) pages 220–1

above   At Easter celebrations, traditional 'dancing devils' take to the streets accompanied by a menagerie of dancers and musicians – parades both lively and intensely spiritual (KM) page 107

right   Watch the women of Sierra Leone who walk impressively for hours with baskets of bananas or rice on their heads and babies on their backs (r/S)

below   Amputee football practice on Lumley Beach – most of the players lost their limbs during the war. Their competitions have attracted international attention (KM) page 111

A virtually undeveloped archipelago composed of eight
tiny islands, the Turtle Islands are the ideal retreat:
pristine waters, perfect for swimming, and even a
hammock or two (KM) pages 240–3

In 2008, the Ministry of Tourism and Culture sent in the army, riot police and youths armed with machetes, sledgehammers, crowbars and axes to destroy all the local bars on the beach side of the strip, due to what they said were worries over environmental degradation and the 'unsightly' nature of the bar shacks. The small business bar owners campaigned hard against this, arguing Le10.4 billion (US$3.6 million, at the time) a year and 394 livelihoods would be lost. They also said they picked up the rubbish and helped maintain security on the beach. Structures started popping up again in the intervening years, and the whole exercise was repeated again in 2015. The tourism ministry said it smashed down the beach bars to make way for improvements like lighting & tree planting; these have been slow to arrive, but 2013 saw the beach road lined with solar street lamps for the first time, and a surfaced promenade running the length of the beach arrived shortly after. Today the beach path is wildly popular with joggers and strollers alike, and like mushrooms, several plucky beach bars have once again sprouted on the sand side of the road, where they seem to be tacitly accepted for the time being, so long as no permanent structures are built. Of the bars that remain on the other side of Lumley Beach Road, some are good social spots, but there are many more ugly concrete hotels-in-the-making with fake columns, flashy reflective glass and none of the charm or care of the beach bars. The tourist board's forthcoming set of building requirements for future businesses on the beach side of the road unfortunately seems likely to exacerbate this trend.

If you're keen to buy your own freshly caught fish, shrimp or oysters, head down to the **Wanpole Fisherman's Base** (midway down the beach side of the road) or the fish market near the northern end of Lumley Beach, sometime after 17.00.

Elsewhere, **Downtown** is a hive of street-food spots serving roasted corn on the cob, bubbling deep-fat-fried cakes, long plantain chips bagged up with salt, groundnuts scooped into newspaper cones, juicy fried chicken and even tasty *shawarmas*. Stay away from the street-sold ice cream, as it will be made from tap water and is a risk for many a foreign stomach. Bananas, mangoes, skilfully peeled oranges and other fruit and vegetables are widely available, alongside grilled meat, attieke and rice and sauce stands. Plenty of makeshift shacks offer take-away or quick seating, as well as a few more permanent structures to duck into when the downtown buzz becomes too much – nearly all these places close once the last office worker has gone home, so – with a couple of exceptions – come here for daytime refuelling and socialising rather than romantic late-night intimacy.

WEST END

✗ 232 Complex [138 C5] m 030 715 412; ⓕ 232complex; ⊕ (restaurant) noon–midnight daily. The newest addition to the Lumley Beach scene, this high-class hangout starts with a blast of ice-cold AC in the downstairs restaurant & opens up on to a 1st-floor balcony lounge & 'VVIP' area overlooking the beach with drinks & shisha pipes. The long menu stretches from lobster to Lebanese, plus burgers, chicken & other pub grub. The nightclub kicks off around midnight (page 160) & there's also an associated beach bar & stage directly across the street. $$$$$–$$$$

✗ Papaya [138 B2] Lumley Beach Rd; m 030 666 666, 099 215 299. This open-sided, wood-framed restaurant & bar at the north end of Lumley Beach is so popular it's almost the default meeting place on this side of town. The menu is long (though not particularly cheap), with hummus, pizza, seafood, & *shish* kebab skewers all making an appearance. There's no shortage of cold beer & cocktails going around most evenings, & usually live music on Fri nights. In case you need to do any last-minute shopping, there's almost always a souvenir seller with woodcarvings & the like out front. $$$$–$$$

✗ Roy Restaurant & Beach Bar [138 B4] 54 Lumley Beach Rd; m 079 655 677, 078 405 060; w royhotel-sl.com. Named after the Lebanese owner's favourite boy's name, the much-loved &

covered flat bread) pies, a range of dips (including moutabal) & fantastic wraps – beef, garlic chicken & even prawn shawarmas – plus falafel & a chicken rotisserie out front. Dine in the long hall with strip lighting, loud satellite TV & plenty of people eating on the hoof. A must for lunch on the go. For the evening, there's no booze served, but you can bring your own if you ask nicely. The eponymous pastry shop next door makes excellent Lebanese sweets & speciality cakes to order. $$$–$$

✗ Senegalese Restaurant [138 D4] 68 Wilkinson Rd; m 077 860 123, 078 215 595; ⏰ 12.30–midnight daily. Delicious West African eaterie with tender *brochettes* (beef skewers), attieke & spicy, stewed *jollof* rice, as well as hugely generous fish & cracking chicken. Takes so long it's almost worth getting a snack across the road at Basha's first, so settle in to your beers. The place is bare & strip-lit but somehow the atmosphere works, perhaps because it has a good local following. $$$–$$

✗ Shawarma & Co [145 F3] 2A Murray Town Rd, Congo Cross; m 088 628 441. It doesn't look like much from the outside, but this hole-in-the-wall attached to Goodies Supermarket wraps up some of the best shawarma in town, served with sour pickles & fiery hot sauce. It's pretty much take-away only, but you can grab a seat (& a beer) at Plum Store Relaxation (page 159) just up the road. There's also a branch on Lightfoot Boston St [145 E2]. $$

⊡ Gina's Frozen Yogurt & Coffee [138 D6] 125 Wilkinson Rd; m 079 919 999, 077 919 999; 🆕 GinasFroYo; ⏰ 09.00–22.00 Mon & Wed–Sat, 11.00–22.00 Sun. With free Wi-Fi, AC & a long menu of crepes, coffees, waffles, salads, sandwiches, ice creams, smoothies & shakes, it's not hard to see why this bright & cheerful café is a certified Freetown favourite. Hole up in the lofted seating area for a bit of quietude, or watch the world go by from the roadside terrace. $$$

Aberdeen

✗ Lagoonda [138 A2] 55 Cape Rd; m 099 100 100; 🖼 @mambapointlagoondafreetown. The Japanese seafood & sushi menu at this stylish waterfront restaurant underneath the eponymous casino boasts over 150 varieties of top-notch sashimi, nigiri, maki & tempura, & the indulgent selection of Lebanese meze is no less impressive. It's been a go-to for Freetown's elite for years now, with very good reason. $$$$$

✗ Toma [138 B2] 58 Cape Rd; m 099 150 319; ⏰ noon–16.00 & from 18.00 daily. Mythologised not only for its excellent food, but perhaps even more for its often-mysterious business hours, the recently reopened Toma is renowned for its short rotating menu of continentally inspired & seasonally sourced gastronomic delights. The restaurant itself is a wood-&-bamboo work of art, & there's occasional live music in the high-ceilinged bar area. Call ahead. $$$$$

✗ Indochine [138 C2] 64 Sir Samuel Lewis Rd; m 088 661 768, 076 661 768. Serving up Vietnamese, Chinese & 'Thailandese Foods', this popular spot boasts whip-smart décor, all black-&-red lacquer panels, golden gongs, lanterns, elegant lights & unobtrusive, efficient service. Expensive food by usual standards, but an evening's dining here is worth indulging in, with favourites such as special Thai chicken satay, crab with vermicelli, & beef with cumin. Authentic drinks include sake, lemongrass & jasmine tea. $$$$$–$$$$

✗ Arirang [138 C2] 82D Sir Samuel Lewis Rd; m 030 691 136, 076 691 136. Perhaps taking the prize for Freetown's most unlikely restaurant, this Aberdeen mainstay does delightful Korean barbecue, with grills right at your table for preparing meaty favourites like *galbi* short ribs & spicy beef *bulgogi*. The proprietress plays the role of resident grandma, helping you cook & even sometimes feeding you directly. $$$$–$$$

⚹✗ Grand Leone Casino Chinese Restaurant [138 A2] Cape Rd; m 088 088 088, 088 000 151. Much like the casino it's attached to, this place is aimed squarely at a predominantly Chinese clientele, & as such serves some of the most authentic Chinese (particularly northern Chinese) dishes in town. Just in case you're overwhelmed by the pages-long menu, you also get an iPad, pre-loaded with pictures of all the dishes, to scroll through & make your order. They're not always available, but the hand-pulled noodles come highly recommended. $$$$–$$$

✗ Quincy's [138 C2] 63 Sir Samuel Lewis Rd; m 076 651 655, 076 300 589. The legendary Quincy's never sleeps – & nor do their grills. They do a range of brochettes & flame-grilled meats at all hours, and while it's rare for people to eat once the nightclub gets going (page 160), in the early evening tables set out on the open-air balcony are usually quiet enough. $$$

New England

Lacs Villa Guesthouse [139 G5] 3A & 9 Cantonment Rd, off Kingharman Rd; m 078 215 668, 030 776 241, 025 200 595; w lacsvilla.com. The Fri buffet of African dishes is the highlight here, lasting from 11.00 to 16.00, for Le50,000 a head, in full view of the Congo Valley Falls. The rest of the week this lovingly tended, old-school B&B serves reliable staples from its full menu. $$$

Hill Station & Wilberforce

Eden Restaurant (Country Lodge) [139 F7] HS 51, Hill Station; m 077 692 000, 077 611 611, 076 691 000. The elegant seating combines perfectly with excellent food – try the fish carpaccio, or the rich steak stuffed with mozzarella – making this an outing to remember. Quality service too. Stop by for live music on Thu nights. $$$$$

The Hub Restaurant [139 E5] 6 Regent Rd, Bottom Mango, Wilberforce; m 088 112 120/1. An extensive menu of Italian, Lebanese, Chinese & Indian dishes – what's more they usually have everything they say they do. Poolside eating on the breezy terrace is by far the nicest option, although snacks at the smoky bar stools thronged with chatty expats can be atmospheric. The sushi bar has all the swank (& cost) you'd expect from freshly flown-in raw fish, crafted by Asian chefs, & some of the best loos in Freetown. $$$$$–$$$$

Tulip Hotel & Restaurant [139 E5] 2A Main Motor Rd, Wilberforce; m 077 075 501, 030 744 220. There's no risk of confusing this slightly shambolic place with the Golden Tulip (the upstairs rooms are decently equipped but rather grubby for the US$70 asking price) but the ground-floor restaurant is a convenient lunch or dinner spot, serving dishes like crain crain, chicken fried rice and grilled snapper; see what's chalked up on the board out front when you pass. $$$–$$

Temo Snack & Restaurant [139 E5] 2 Regent Rd (Bottom Mango), Wilberforce; m 078 897 000, 044 899 000, 099 899 000. If the above options are a bit rich for your blood, this is a pleasant hole-in-the wall doing mostly take-away at the Bottom Mango roundabout. They've also got a few tables should you want to hang around, & serve the usual Salone staples (including a good jollof rice), along with fast-food options like shawarma & pizzas. $$

CITY CENTRE

Lovetta's Kitchen [139 H4] Campbell St at Heddle St; m 076 790 336. Friendly, locally run spot with Premier League regalia all over the walls, the usual Salone suspects on the menu, full bar, AC &, of course, a flatscreen for the football. $$

Marian Ella Restaurant [139 G4] 25 Kinsella St, by Syke St; m 077 526 605; ⊕ 11.00–20.30 Tue–Sat, 18.00–20.30 Sun. Lovely little spot serving African food near the national stadium. $$

Mix Flavour [139 G4] Hannah Benka-Coker St; m 077 842 424. Small wooden shack serving cauldrons of rice & sauce daily for lunch, with simple appetising lunchstop appeal. $$

DOWNTOWN

Café de la Rose [144 D2] 2 Howe St; m 076 602 640, 076 772 919. Another pretty upstairs corner café, this has a good reputation for fish as well as all the usual African dishes. A little pricey, it's popular with local business people & good for chats. $$$

The Cube [144 D2] Maritime Hse, Government Wharf; m 025 200 915, 078 512 166, 088 138 514, ⓕ thecuberestaurantsl; ⊕ 08.00–20.00 Mon–Fri, 10.00–18.00 Sat. The 1st-floor veranda overlooking the wharf at this unexpectedly sharp restaurant inside Maritime House makes a fine place to duck in & catch your breath after a hot, hectic day on the streets of the city centre. They serve a range of West African mainstays, including fried plantains, plassas & foofoo. It's a favourite for holiday celebrations, & every Fri from noon to 17.00 they put on the delightfully named 'BuffAzz' – that is, a buffet with live jazz accompaniment. $$$

Crown Bakery [145 E2] 5 Wilberforce St; ☎ 022 223 411; m 076 254 523, 076 768 769, 030 160 081; ⊕ 08.00–16.30 Mon–Fri, 09.00–15.30 Sat. Resembling a teahouse, elegant in simple black & white, the best treats at this superb downtown institution are served until noon, including eggs Benedict & huge b/fasts; mid morning it's a good place for quiet contemplation over coffee & the best croissants in town; by 13.00 the place is packed with senior civil servants, military personnel & lunching ladies, with a sense that deals are being struck over delicious portions of Lebanese food. It's all presided over by Fadi Kesserwani, one of the doyennes of the Freetown social scene. $$$–$$

✗ **Dee's Bazaar** 38 Siaka Stevens St [144 C4] & 10 Wilkinson Rd [139 E3]; m 076 999 993, 077 248 759. Good lunch spot on the 2nd floor, you have to pass through the inside of the building (ask directions inside). Local food only (try the beans); tastes best on the tiny balcony. The pavement patio is one of the few nightspots downtown, good for a drink & snacks. They've now got a 2nd location on Wilkinson Rd. **$$**

✗ **Downtown Restaurant** [145 E2] 15 Siaka Stevens St; m 077 852 536, 076 644 655; ⏰ 08.00–17.00 Mon–Fri, 08.00–15.00 Sat. Clean Lebanese offering, specialising in sandwiches (steak, chicken, vegetarian & even *sojok* subs – sausage baps), as well as bean stews like *musabaha* & *ful medames*. Interesting daily specialities include chicken with cinnamon rice & yoghurt (Tue). Friendly management, too. **$$**

✗ **Nix Nax Café** [144 D4] 32b Siaka Stevens St, near Pultney St; m 077 171 481 (Aunty Isa); ⏰ 10.00–18.30 Mon–Sat. A cosy, petite local affair, nicely decorated with greenery on the outside, it has a different African dish each day, as well as some sturdy meat & fish regulars, all offered up to a musical backdrop of distorted reggae radio tunes. **$$**

✗ **Rooster Restaurant** [144 D4] Electricity Hse, Siaka Stevens St; m 076 706 424; ⏰ 11.00–18.30 Mon–Sat. Refusing to say goodbye to the 1970s, the dingy décor sets off the excellent selection of chicken & fast food in an unlikely fashion. Popular at lunchtimes, burgers are offered in ever-increasing size – single, 'engaged', king & 'big-time'. Seconds from the Cotton Tree, it's cheap & somehow mesmerising. **$$**

◻ **Red Lion Bakery** 65 Siaka Stevens St [144 C5] & 13 Bolling St [139 G2]; m 044 001 944, 077 001 944; w redlionbakery.com; ⏰ 07.30–18.00 Mon–Sat. Nothing fancy, but good for a decent loaf if you're passing. Their main bakery is on Bolling St in King Tom. **$**

◻ **Salvonne Bakery & Catering Enterprises** [144 C4] 28 Percival St; m 076 713 427, 088 430 247; ◼ SalvonneBakery. Serving the best baked goods in town (except perhaps the croissants at Crown Bakery) from a tiny counter – try the banana bread & rock buns. Brown bread, even though it's a long way from the dark wholegrains of home, is still a nice change from the relentless monotony of bleached white loaves. The ladies who run it (grumpy on the outside, sweet on the inside) have furnished a couple of picnic tables on the pavement out front. **$**

ENTERTAINMENT AND NIGHTLIFE

Sit up, pay attention, squeeze yourself into something tight and spangly, or slouch into something low-slung and cool; it's time to go out in Freetown. The party vibe is all about being seen, and hopping between numerous venues in one night is *de rigueur*. A small in-crowd circulates according to the place of the moment, which changes like the tide. Here's where it currently washes up.

DRINKING DENS Like Saloneans, you should cultivate a sniffiness at the quality of *poyo* (palm wine) on offer in the capital – it's diluted, bitty and often overfermented. Best to try it only when you can see a pock-marked palm tree trunk in front of you, outside Freetown. That means you can ignore the local hooch in favour of lager swilling and the odd spot of cocktail sipping. It's difficult to beat the beach strip from Lumley to Aberdeen (listings on pages 154–6) for a perfect dusk moment to start the evening, as the sun dives into the Atlantic before your eyes.

Swanky

♀ **2 Guys Restaurant & Lounge** [138 D4] 71 Wilkinson Rd; m 077 523 001; ◼ 2guysrestaurantlounge; ⏰ 16.00–02.00 Tue–Sun. Newly opened in 2017, this cool new place has a promising nightly events calendar, with salsa on Wed, club on Fri, ladies' night on Sat & Sun-night jam sessions. Happy hour is on Wed & Sat from 19.00 to 20.30, & their burgers & bar food are a surprisingly good deal.

Casual

♀ **Hill Station Club** [139 G7] Off Regent Rd; m 078 110 281, 078 398 253; ◼ HillStationClub.

A sleepy, wood-panelled throwback to colonial times, the Hill Station Club is technically members-only except for Fri, but with the right attitude you can likely talk your way in on other days. Whenever you come, it's a pleasantly time-warped way to spend an evening, & the views to Sugar Loaf Mountain can't be beaten.

♀O'Casey's [138 C5] Lumley Beach Rd; m 078 216 302; ⨍ OcaseysSalone. A bit like *Cheers!*, this expat hangout of choice is a place where everyone knows your name. Its busy, often raucous bar keeps punters entertained with live music (Fri) & an open mic night (Sat), plus there's always free table football & pool.

♀Phasebook Lounge [145 E3] 21 Charlotte St; m 078 88 6600, 076 613 948, 079 361 935, 079 074 599. One of a small handful of nightspots in the city centre, Phasebook is comfortable without being ostentatious, & boasts a full bar, white pleather booths & wood-panelled walls adorned with portraits of Salone independence heroes.

♀Plan B Wine Bar [138 C4] Lumley Beach Rd; m 076 619 650, 079 340 604. A smaller, quieter spot, popular with a local elite, more conducive to late-night chats.

☀♀Plum Store Relaxation [139 F3] 4 Murray Town Rd, Congo Cross; m 076 621 402. On first glance, this appropriately laid-back place doesn't seem much different from any of the dozens of plastic-chair saloons that dot the city (& their prices are just as welcoming), but the greatness of Plum Store lies in the details: specifically the soundtrack of retro & rarely heard Congolese & Afrobeat gems, all played at a volume immensely more agreeable than the distortion fests so common at other drinking holes.

♀Q Bar [138 B4] Lumley Beach Rd, opposite Plan B; m 078 222 444; ⨍ QAndTBarAndGrill. The simple clutch of tables & grills in the sand here

is the perfect spot for a beachside sundowner to kick off the weekend. Stop by for live music on Sun nights. There's also free billiards.

♀Whatsapp Sports Bar [139 G3] 12 Ascension Town Rd; m 078 880 232, 076 994 002, 077 782 624, 030 900 905. This unpretentious & unexpectedly agreeable bar in Congo Town is a relaxed place to duck in for a drink & catch some footie during the day, or get in a bit of partying when the speakers & the grills both crackle to life in the evenings.

Spit & sawdust

♀Androsa Leisure Centre [139 E3] Murray Town Rd; no phone. If you're after some football, foofoo or photocopies, this triple threat of a hangout near Congo Cross has got you fully covered. Beer too, naturally.

♀Frenzy View Enterprise Snacks Bar [139 E3] 33 Wilkinson Rd, near the Aberdeen Rd junction; m 077 400 149. More beer shack than food joint, with a sound system in thoroughly good working order, plus the occasional loud football match, while you sip cold lager at wooden tables. Better for aimlessly staring into space with the rest of the guests rather than fighting the din to try to make conversation. Ask at the bar for the odd chicken wing, fishball & meat stick too.

♀Sesay Enterprises [138 C2] Sir Samuel Lewis Rd, Aberdeen; no phone. Opposite Shams, this is basically just a friendly bottle shop with tables out front, ideal for a roadside beer.

♀Shams Entertainment Complex [138 B2] 86 Sir Samuel Lewis Rd, Aberdeen; m 078 101 909; ⊕ 11.00–late daily. A little more down & dirty, brightly painted in Star-brand yellow & blue, this roadside haunt really gets going late at night for a variety of themed evenings ('white & black', 'east v west', etc). It also has billiards & a few basic African dishes to mop up the booze.

WHINE AND GRIND While live-music venues are few and far between, you can shake your *tumba* (behind) in a raft of nightspots, which usually only get going sometime after midnight. Women keen to get the 'whining' (twisting your body as you wind down towards the floor with thigh-busting strength) right can do no better than make friends with other women on the dancefloor and they'll likely as not take pleasure in trying to teach you the moves. Random men can be keen to dance with you, but pawing is rare and it's generally easy to extract yourself. Most bars have plenty of *kolonkos* (prostitutes) and single, or even attached, men who aren't interested can often feel unremittingly and aggressively pursued. The solution is to hang out with a group of friends that includes women, and decline advances from the start. Buying someone a drink is not a nice friendly gesture, it's a come on – so choose your rounds carefully.

For drinking and dancing, you can't beat:

☆ **232 Complex** [138 C5] m 030 715 412; f 232complex; ⏱ 23.00–05.00 daily; entry Le50,000. Freetown's newest nightclub is also taking a credible stab at being its swankiest, so leave the flip flops & tank tops at home. Weds are for Afrobeat & reggae, while the weekends see a rotating cast of themed parties like tequila Fri & fresh Sat. The beach bar & live stage on the sand across the road is considerably more relaxed.

☆ **China House** [139 G4] Back of the Youyi Bldg, Old Railway Line; entry Le10,000. Don't miss Fri nights when local bands keep the house in thrall with reggae & renditions of local chart hits doing the rounds in poda podas all over the city. During the dry season bands set up in the open area for dancing; in the rains it's a sweaty session indoors. Even the car park gets vibing on busy nights. There's food on offer (occasionally a heaving buffet) to keep energy levels up throughout the night. Watch out for pickpockets, & keep your phone under wraps near the entrance.

☆ **Disco Porsh** [map, page 130] 87 Bai Bureh Rd, Kissy Lowcost Step; m 076 767 903. Found in the down-&-dirty east, this is a 2-storey nightclub where sweaty dancers strut & admire themselves in floor-to-ceiling wall mirrors to reggae beats (Thu), Africana (Fri) & the big Sat crescendo with 'Porsh night'. Sun is more mellow; Wed is ladies' night.

☆ **Grand Leone Casino Skybar** [138 A2] Cape Rd; m 088 000 130; ⏱ 18.00–02.00 daily; entry Le10,000. Seedy as a pomegranate, Skybar (previously known as Aces, and before that Buggy's) often consists of no more than a few women lamely moving about a bit in the dancepit hoping to snag a big spender. Still, the view over Man of War Bay from the large outdoor balcony is fantastic, there's pool & ping-pong, & on the occasions when it's genuinely popular, rather than a desultory hooker-fest, the vibe takes off, especially on Thu when they hold regular live reggae nights – at which the Sierra Leone Refugee All Stars have been known to play. Fun touches include a car (the 'buggy' of the bar's old name) suspended over the entrance, as well as half a motorbike coming out of the wall inside. Where all other clubs the world over have Wed as ladies night, Skybar bills it as the 'tumba dance' (hip-shaking, bottom firmly out) night.

☆ **Krio Wendy's** [144 D5] 25 Pademba Rd, junction with Bathurst St; m 030 237 182, 076 543 963. In town, this institution has a hectic inner-city feel when it fills up on Wed, Fri or Sat nights. By day it's called Regca Enterprises, with crates of beer stacked up on the pavement; by night the sound system takes over as DJs Tombo Wala, Native Sylman & Flesh send down the tunes. There's barely a place to sit in the minute bar, so the fun spills out into the road, lit by car headlamps. There are occasional street fights & plenty of pickpockets.

☆ **Old Skool Nightclub** [139 H7] Hill Station; m 076 264 224, 076 609 625; ⏱ 22.00–late Fri & Sat; entry Le20,000. Despite garish pink & yellow walls this classy place has AC, VIP lounge, disco lights & multiple bars. On Fri nights it can really take off, when it plays hiphop to Salone bratpackers & the odd student. Dress up.

☆ **Quincy's** [138 C2] 63 Sir Samuel Lewis Rd m 076 651 655, 076 300 589; ⏱ 24hrs daily; entry Le10,000 or more on 'show' nights. Formerly (& still commonly) known as Paddy's, this legendary bar was set up by an Irishman who was awarded an OBE for his efforts (& in a pleasing twist, 'paddy' also means friend in Krio). It's sadly no longer the centre of hedonism & intrigue that it was during the war – in the film *Blood Diamond*, the bar setting that forms the backdrop to the meeting between hot-headed journalist (Jennifer Connelly) & dodgy Zimbabwean mercenary (Leonardo DiCaprio) is undoubtedly based on Quincy's. Half outdoors, there's a fan-blown dancefloor to keep temperatures manageable & everything is arranged around a suitably large bar with service on all four sides. Added to that, the table football & the pool are free.

☆ **Ran-D's Nightclub, Bar & Restaurant** [144 A6] 50 Adelaide St; m 030 219 034, 076 605 339 (owner Gifty Davies); disco ⏱ from 21.00 Wed, Fri &Sat; free entry. A cheery, basic place downtown. Daily canteen chop is available morning to night, best taken in covered outdoor seating. The vaguely sketchy indoor disco has a mirrored dancefloor, DJ booth, spirits & beer bar.

☆ **Scarlet Lounge** [138 A2] 55 Cape Rd, Aberdeen; m 077 012 345; f lagoonda;

⏱ 23.00–dawn Wed–Sun; entry at least Le50,000. At the top end of the spectrum, Lagoonda's basement nightclub is aimed at Freetown's elite & has a couple of bars, VIP area & small tables for watching the moves. There's also, inexplicably, a life-size white porcelain dog in a cage on a raised platform. Thu is Latin night; you will be turned away if you're in shorts.

☆ **SLBC Canteen** [139 H5] Off Jomo Kenyatta St, opposite Special Court, New England; m 076 260 197, 033 132 195; ⏱ 09.00–22.00 Mon–Thu, 09.00–midnight Fri & Sat. Also pumps out live music & features local bands on Fri. Fenced by greenery & cane, it's usually a chilled hangout, but can burst its seams when it gets going. After the live band, sometime beyond 01.00, look out for performers to put the London Variety Show to shame: dancers in grass skirts, women clad in painted-on jeans shaking their behinds, quiz shows with condoms

for prizes, plus a crowd that loves to have fun. It also offers chunks of pepper chicken, roast meat & fish to revellers. Wed is ladies' night.

☆ **Vybz Pub** [139 E3] 38 Wilkinson Rd; m 078 080 853, 099 379 999; f vybzpub. A reliable bet for disco lights, DJs & the occasional live band, the crowd at this popular Wilkinson Rd hangout skews younger & you're guaranteed to hear the latest international hiphop & dancehall smashes. Keep an eye on your phone.

☆ **The Warehouse** [138 B3] 7 Lumley Beach Rd; m 030 181 118; f thewarehouseevoque. One of the most upmarket spots in town, this expat-popular place is incongruously housed inside a shabby, mostly empty strip-mall near the top of Lumley Beach, but the insides are all class. It seems to have its own centre of gravity – most nights wind up here if you're out late enough.

CASINOS Freetown betting tends to bring gamblers out in packs. All the casinos are free to enter, and you can drink at the bar without betting if you prefer. Try:

☆ **Lagoonda Casino** [138 A2] Lagoonda, 55 Cape Rd, Aberdeen; m 088 998 888, 076 672 238, 099 100 100; f mambapointlagoondafreetown; ⏱ 21.30–03.00 Fri, 21.30–04.00 Sat; order food from the restaurant downstairs. The least intimidating, most comfortable casino for newcomers. This flashy affair is located on the top floor of the complex, & done up in green felt, with a British-run management team prowling the tables. Min bets start at Le2,000, so even a wimp feels welcome.

☆ **New Grand Casino Leone** [138 A2] 72a Cape Rd, Aberdeen; m 088 088 888; e leonecasino@gmail.com; ⏱ 19.00–04.00 daily. A neon-signed Chinese affair by the beach, all garish lights & fake red trees. Try your hand at the slot machines, poker, blackjack & roulette. They run a small private room for high rollers. The restaurant serves authentic Chinese cuisine (page 156).

BEAUTY CONTESTS Forget feminism: beauty contests drive the capital wild. Politically correct they might not be, but they are guaranteed fun, and guaranteed to keep you up all night – it's rare that winners are announced before 02.00, and 06.00 is not uncommon: a bit like watching the Oscars in Europe, but without the time difference.

Categories tend to be taken seriously – beach wear and casual wear rounds are marked on criteria such as clothes, attitude, walk and looks – there's also the executive outfit and Africana category (pens behind the ear for the former, and outrageously skimpy concoctions of twigs and leaves for the latter). The obligatory speech-making section is mostly an inaudible mumble. Judging is tense, and accusations of fixing are regular.

The annual treat is the super-elite **Miss University** contest, which pits young students against each other. The 2015 event was held at Family Kingdom in December; **Quincy's** also occasionally hosts events. There's no end to the variety of contests held at a neighbourhood level – Lakka hosted the 'Inter Area Dwharf Beauty Contest' in May 2017 – so just look out for the big vinyl banners strung up around town and show up.

The male equivalent of all this pageantry would have to be the **Salone Strongest Man** competition, where shockingly musclebound men take turns deadlifting, pulling giant lorries, and flipping monster construction tyres down the track in Siaka Stevens Stadium in the hope of taking home the Le100,000,000 cash prize. It's been held each April since 2016.

CULTURAL PERFORMANCES Two cultural groups regularly put on traditional dance performances at hotels, cultural celebrations and other events. The award-winning **National Dance Troupe** (m *076 775 541*), with fire-eaters, magicians, stilt-walkers, percussionists and dancers can conjure a real spectacle (pages 176–7). **Ballanta Academy of Music** [144 C4] (*27 Liverpool St;* m *077 748 376;* e *ballanta1996@yahoo. co.uk;* f *ballanta1996*) is renowned for its expert traditional dancing, led by the charming Suleiman, a policeman who dreamt of becoming a dancer, along with its drummers and various singing and musical ensembles. You can even join in, attending a series of stretching Saturday afternoon dance lessons held at Ballanta, or enquire about drumming lessons by appointment. Performances also sometimes take place at the **British Council** [145 F5] (*A J Momoh St, Tower Hill;* \ *022 220 775–7;* m *076 290 111;* w *britishcouncil.sl*), so look out for posters. Likewise, large business hotels and the Miatta Conference Centre [139 G4] (*Youyi Bldg, Brookfields*) sometimes host cultural events. Any significant event at the national stadium might have dancers as warm-up acts too.

The **Freetong Players** theatre group (*29 Dundas St;* m *076 721 252, 077 520 100, 077 604 965;* e *freeplayint@yahoo.com;* f *freetongplayersinternational*), founded in 1985 by Charlie and Fattie Haffner, puts on the annual Tangains Festival and develops traditional folksongs, dance and storytelling for the stage. Prized Salone storyteller **Usifu Jalloh** (w *usifujalloh.com*) organised the first annual Festival For Storytelling and Games at the British Council in December 2016; he also leads the Maambena Fest up north in Kamakwie (page 306).

Also look out for a troupe of cross-dressing men who don pink wigs and bras, stuff their crotches underneath bright tights or skirts, and gyrate to music in support of the latest government communication campaign, and other cultural and educational events. Audiences tend to love it.

FILM Date night in Freetown got a whole lot more interesting in 2011 with the opening of **Lagoonda Cinebox**, a movie theatre housed inside the Lagoonda Complex in Aberdeen [138 A2] (*55 Cape Rd;* m *088 700 700;* f *cineboxlagoondacomplex*). Complete with cushy seats, air conditioning, and even freshly popped popcorn, Cinebox is the place to go to beat the heat and indulge in a little old-fashioned Hollywood escapism. The cinema shows (fairly) new releases as well as the occasional old classic. Tickets to evening showings cost Le50,000, while the kiddie-friendly matinees will set you back Le30,000. Open Friday to Sunday; check the website for film listings.

Otherwise, there's the **Globe Cinema** [139 G4] (*30 Syke St; showings at about noon, 18.00 & 20.00; entry Le1,000–3,000*), with a big screen and regular screenings of high-profile football matches, as well as films from Hollywood, Bollywood, Nollywood – the glut of low-quality films produced in Nigeria – and Hong Kong. The Freetown Secret Film Society (f *SierraLeoneCountryclub*) occasionally puts on special events here as well, including a screening of *Pulp Fiction* in January 2017. Back-street boutiques often show DVDs, usually pirated. For Le1,000, settle on hard wooden benches and share with young and old alike a surfeit of violence, sex and appalling acting, mostly in a variety of kitchen-sink soaps from Nigeria.

Pick your way through the motorbike taxis and stray dogs on Rawdon Street. Walk past the women hawking flip-flops and little plastic baggies of plantain chips. Step over an open gutter and through a low, unmarked doorway. Round a few unlit corners, then walk up a narrow set of stairs – and you've arrived.

Welcome to Hollywood, Sierra Leone style. The country may have only one Western-style cinema, but since August 2011 it has been home to its very own film school. From his humble offices amid the hustle of Freetown, the school's director aims to train young Sierra Leoneans to create their own films. In the long run, he hopes the country's homegrown movie industry might transform Sierra Leone's battered image overseas.

'Sierra Leoneans have a lot of stories to tell,' says Ahmed Mansaray, the school's founding director. But today, 'most of the stories are being told [through] the binoculars of the white man.'

If there's an African Hollywood type, Mansaray fits it to a tee: he wears a black suit, a gold-colored shirt and a dapper hat tipped high on the back of his head. He has a quick smile and an easy manner – the air of a man who could make a killer elevator pitch. He doesn't have a degree in film studies or movie production, but he's taken courses in France and Nigeria, and he's worked on movie sets in Sierra Leone since 2003. He admits that his experience is limited, but thinks he still has something to contribute.

Mansaray weaves his way through the film school's cluttered office, squeezing hands and slapping backs as he gives a visitor a tour of the premises. It only takes a few minutes; there isn't a whole lot to see. Housed inside the local Institut de Français, the film school consists of one classroom equipped with tables, chairs and a whiteboard; a small office for Mansaray; and a production room that has two computers – only one of which is working.

Despite its limited resources, Sierra Leone's first film school has drawn a huge response from locals, Mansaray says. In its first session, the school enrolled 32 students, most of them in their twenties and thirties. For a fee of Le2 million (US$450), students are taught the nuts and bolts of video production, the delicacies of movie make-up and the fine art of finalising a script.

'We want to be a very big industry that will provide quality films to the rest of the world,' he says. 'We want to see ourselves winning competitions in America and Europe.'

The IDF Film School is located inside the Insitut de Français, 29 Rawdon St. A version of this story was first published by The Christian Science Monitor.

Legendary Sierra Leone music producer Jimmy B has branched into film of late, releasing a handful of movies filmed on location in the capital including *Eagle Eyes*, *Genesis, For the Love of Money* and *Aminata 1 & 2*. Premieres tend to take place with lots of fanfare at the Miatta Conference Centre under the multistorey Youyi government building in Brookfields.

A glut of street hawkers also palm off pirated Western DVDs, with dozens of films to a disc, often in the wrong language with horrendously translated film synopses on the back covers. Police occasionally try to crack down on piracy, but when genuine discs are prohibitively expensive (Le100,000 or more), many find it hard to resist the asking price of Le10,000–15,000.

CATCH A MATCH When the national football team play, known locally as the Leone Stars, the capital gets to know about it, and with a capacity of 36,000 people the national stadium is often crammed full. Embarrassed by FIFA's admonishment of pitch quality at the stadium in 2008 ahead of World Cup qualifiers, the country has pulled up its football socks and now everything is done in style. All seats are numbered – even spots on long concrete pews – helping to reduce overcrowding. Tickets are available ahead of time in the morning, via local police stations or certain shops. Listen to local radio stations and the word on the street for details. Internationals usually cost Le20,000 for one of the stands directly in the sun (bring water, hat, suncream); Le50,000 for one of the two covered stands (11 and 14; the best option for atmosphere and protection from the elements) and a whopping Le175,000 for a seat in the presidential stand (12 and 13), where you get an actual plastic seat to yourself.

The atmosphere tends to be good natured, with patriotic fervour, flag-waving and brass band encouragement tempered by a brutal recognition of the team's limitations, which is still never quite enough to stop the expression of utter disappointment on fans' faces as Salone loses again.

If you do go, it makes sense to leave your seat a couple of minutes before a match ends to secure a smooth getaway – the rush at the gates can be unpleasant and it's easy to be crushed or squashed. It's also open season for pickpockets, so bring only the minimum and keep your hands inside the pockets where your things are in big crowds. Anyone bumping into you too forcefully probably isn't doing it by accident, so stay wary. Avoid the impromptu water feature that forms around the edge of the stadium as you enter – people tend to pee over the back of the stands and shower unsuspecting latecomers. For really packed events, they lob plastic bags of urine over the top. Nice.

GONE FISHING Freetown has plenty of spots for inshore fishing to troll for big toothy fish, such as barracuda, using artificial lures, as well as bottom fishing for snapper and grouper. Yellowjack and mackerel are also common, as well as marlin, African pompano and bonita (cobia). For livebait, the best place to go is Goderich fishing village, about 10 minutes down the coast.

It's best to avoid the rains and head out from October to March, when the water is calmest. Pack your boat with drinking water, ice, your favourite tipple or three and sandwiches, plus suncream and a hat. You can even sit back and let an electronic fish finder do all the work for you.

The **Aqua Sports Club** [138 D2] (*Cockle Bay, Murray Town;* m *076 699 023, 076 413 046;* e *aqua.fasc@gmail.com*), started in 1966, is something of a colonial-style relic, and the country's watersports centre, located just north of Aberdeen Bridge on the seaward side. Although it's members only, guests can pay a Le50,000 one-day fee to enter. If you ask extremely nicely, some boat owners – most of them Lebanese – might let you hire their boat with a skipper on an informal basis to go fishing, for about US$20 an hour, plus fuel. As well as daily fishing trips, members also go waterskiing, jet skiing, sailing and beach hopping along the Peninsula. The club also has badminton, squash and tennis courts, a mini gym and small swimming pool, as well as an outdoor café. Fishing trips can be arranged by **Toufic Haroun** (m *076 593 555*) or **Martin Bamin** (m *076 733 444;* e *martinbamin@yahoo.com*), who are both well-equipped and safety conscious and can organise packed lunches and drinks on request. Sometimes pricey, **Cape Shilling** (m *076 814 646 for Smokey*) also has speedboats for hire, at about US$100 each for a day's fishing. Anders Hansen at **Classdiving Co Ltd** (*64A Cape Rd;* m *076 373 723*) also has quality boats for hire, although his tend to be the most expensive of the lot. If you want something a little more authentic, you can ask a local skipper at any of the fishing spots along the beaches, or Man of War Bay, to take you out, but bear in mind that safety is not a prime consideration. If you do go out, take plenty of water, and a phone in case of trouble. In all cases, tip your skipper.

MUSIC CONCERTS The odd album launch, filled with noise and showmanship (including plenty of furious lip-synching), takes place at Quincy's, Family Kingdom, YSC on Wilkinson Road, and elsewhere – look out for posters around town. If a gig is at the national stadium, the main act is unlikely to appear until 01.00, and fans have been known to last until 11.00 the next day. These events often take place on a Sunday, making a meal of Mondays at the office. A series of popular concerts tend to take place around holidays times at Christmas, New Year and Easter.

Since 2016, however, the hottest ticket in town has without question been the **Freetown Music Festival** (w *freetownmusicfestival.com*). Established in 2016 and held over two nights on the north end of Lumley Beach in March/April, the festival seeks to celebrate local talent and showcases a long list of up-and-coming Salone musicians, all backed by live licks from the Freetown Uncut band (**f** *freetownuncut*). A two-day wristband costs Le100,000.

FOR THE KIDS If you're looking for some help with childcare – or if you just want the little tykes to burn off some energy at a playground – try stopping by **Kidzone** [139 G4] (*4 Main Motor Rd, Wilberforce;* m *078 277 745, 030 888 061;* e *thekidzonesl@ gmail.com;* w *thekidzonesl.com*), a 'day-care, preschool, and edutainment centre' that sits a stone's throw from the Bottom Mango roundabout. Karate classes are also on offer. Or if you're keen to do some entertaining at home, you can buy kids' toys and games from the friendly staff at **Mothers Shop** [138 D6] (*137 Wilkinson Rd;* m *077 777 706*), located just next door to Freetown Supermarket on Wilkinson Road.

Set to open in November 2017, the new **Freetown Amusement Park** [145 E4] (*Victoria Park, Tower Hill*) will be the country's largest (rather only) dedicated children's park, with a wading pool, waterslides, and variety of jungle gym-type equipment suited for all manner of climbing and clambering. Further ideas on what to do with the little ones in Freetown can be found on Andy McFarlane's excellent *Home Salone* blog (w *expatfamilyfortunes.com/expat-life-in-sierra-leone/freetown-with-kids*).

FESTIVALS

INDEPENDENCE DAY Come 27 April, make for downtown anytime after 22.00 for a lantern parade. It's great fun to make and take your own – but you're much more likely to find huge cardboard helicopters, travelling floats and masks than petite ornamental lanterns among the supportive, ever-more-tipsy crowd.

EASTER Easter Monday is an eclectic celebration of all things spiritual, family and fun, but not exclusively Christian. Religious bands that behave more like football fans than church mice chant their way loudly with pride through the streets, while downtown a series of 'devils' come out in each neighbourhood, accompanied by a coterie of musicians and dancing admirers. Giant head-to-toe masks of lions, snakes, antelopes and monkeys appear, stuck with feathers, shells, wood, hessian and raffia. On no account take a photo without permission – however much poyo is being knocked back this is still an intensely spiritual event with its own strict set of rules.

Lumley Beach is crammed as families and friends come to play football, canoe, share picnics, bathe, flirt and fly kites. Made from coloured paper, bamboo sticks and string, with long strips of cotton for tails, they take perfectly on the spring breeze. If the tail is too short, the kite is said to 'turn *foofoo*' – swirling round and round and failing to fly properly. Overhead cables in town snag some for good.

MA DENGN FESTIVAL A raucous celebration of Sierra Leonean music and culture, this mega beach party, which debuted in 2009, has quickly become a mainstay in the Freetown festival scene. Usually held in December, Ma Dengn attracts a spirited crowd with its live music, catwalk fashion shows, basket-weaving classes and tasty Sierra Leonean dishes. There's even a bouncy castle for the kids (and whoever else). For details, see 🄵 madengn.

SHOPPING

Freetown holds plenty of shopping opportunities, whether you're looking for a brand-new motorbike, a pair of diamond earrings, tailor-made clothes to dazzle or a spare bit of inner tubing.

Lumley Beach and street corners **downtown** are well serviced by street hawkers, flush with trinkets, wood carvings, leather shoes, cloth, batiks and pirate DVDs. Often their wares are simply a taster for many of the general stores located nearby: the pavements of **Siaka Stevens Street** are besieged by vendors piling up imported Chinese toothpaste beside plastic sandals, make-up, pots, pans, pants, suitcases, old magazines, packs of biscuits, school books, footballs, traditional medicine stands (tree bark to boil up for antimalaria tea, for example) and more. The main market for shoes is around **Regent Road** and, a little closer to PZ, **Free Street**, where the bonnet of any parked car quickly doubles as a makeshift trainer display shelf. Towards Eastern Police Clock Tower, **Goderich Street** has walls plastered with jeans, belts and more, perfect for window shopping from your traffic-packed taxi. Among the throng weave men and women 'toting' improbable numbers of stacked baskets filled with charcoal, bananas or bread. Even if you don't need to buy anything, these cramped streets are jaw-dropping in their ferocious intensity, colour and noise.

THE MAN IN THE BRIDGE

In Freetown, artistic endeavour can be found in the most unlikely of places. Mohamed Bangura, who lives in the hollow of Aberdeen Bridge in Freetown (yes that's *in*, not under), has created art for his home, painting the concrete buttress with a vision of how he would like the riverside area, which is strewn with excrement and rubbish, to look one day. Painted in bright poster colours, he has titled it 'Real African Society Towards Awareness'. 'I tell the people about reggae and peace,' says Bangura. 'I am the caretaker of the bridge and I take great care as a citizen. I have a vision.' Reggae-loving Bangura has painted a sign welcoming guests to the inside of his bridge '*bonka*' (bunker) alongside images of helicopters, drums, animals and black and white living in harmony, with the slogans 'together as one' and 'righteousness' daubed on the walls. 'It's a window on the world, to bring a big impact on this country. The war bring me up here so now we only talk of peace. We cry for peace.'

ARTS & CRAFTS

Occasionally on Sun street artists gather at the roundabout at the Aberdeen end of Freetown's beach road to show their wares, although attendance tends to be patchy.

Big Market [144 D2] Wallace Johnson St; ⏲ 10.00–18.00 Mon–Sat, closed holidays. This is a mixed bag as far as souvenir hunting goes. The ground floor mingles outright tat with palm-frond woven baskets, xylophones, shakers, drums & straw hats, & even some bathroom fixings at the far end. Upstairs, half the area is dedicated to stalls presided over by men selling wooden & beaded jewellery & wooden statues that aren't terribly good; the other half is the domain of women & their material, & a real treasure trove. Lightweight tie-dye *gara* cotton from Salone vies with imported Africana prints of wax super cotton; batiks compete with African costumes for most colour; but the real prize is the homespun, thick-woven country cloth made up in the provinces that proves excellent for bedspreads, wall hangings and rugs.

A word of warning. The atmosphere is lovely so long as you are polite & firm: dilly-dally or show a mite of vulnerability & you're easy prey to the stallholders. Have an idea of what you're looking for & be clear about that from the start (for example, a certain colour, price or style). Take time to pay your respects to each & every stall without getting too hung up on any particular item: there's nothing like professional jealousy to spark a fight between vendors. Having said all that, Big Market is still calm as a windless sea compared with markets in North Africa.

Bartering comes with the territory, & it's quite usual for market women to open negotiations with 'This is my first price'. Bargain hard, but be aware that they will let you walk away if you are too inflexible. Try & avoid suggesting the starting price yourself, which quickly hems you into a corner. Starting prices for country cloth depend on the quality of the weave: about Le175,000 for coarse weave; Le250,000–350,000 for something much smoother; and Le525,000-plus for the utterly tasteful blankets of plain stripes in a natural style. Any of the stalls can help, but if you want to ring ahead (though this may tie you in to a purchase out of politeness), try Alice Sankoh, specialist in *gara* materials, batik & Africana costumes (m *076 739 898*) or Isatu Bangay (m *076 735 256*), who has a good selection of country cloth.

Lumley Beach Craft Market [138 B3] ⏲ 07.00–19.00 Mon–Sat. Much smaller than the aptly named Big Market, but convenient if you're in the west end & don't have time to get to the city centre. It sits directly behind the National Tourist Board on Lumley Beach Rd & the dozen or so stalls here sell a decent array of carvings, jewellery, textiles, bags, baubles & more.

Balmaya Arts Gallery [139 F4] 32 Main Motor Rd, Congo Cross; m 076 601 209; ⏲ 10.00–17.00 Mon–Sat. This market has expensive furniture, leather, silver, paintings & cloth from the entire West African sub-region on show. Next to the restaurant of the same name (page 155), many of the collections were painstakingly collected by the recently passed owner Joy Samake. This is probably the most reliable destination for picking up pieces to take home, but don't expect any budging on the prices, which are all marked.

Gaga Gallery [139 F4] 1 College Rd, Main Motor Rd, Congo Cross, by Methodist Girls' High School junction; m 076 668 445; ⏲ 10.00–15.00 Mon, Wed & Fri, 10.00–14.00 Tue, Thu & Sat. Gaga is one of only a couple of places in the country that promote various contemporary artists' work, set up by the artist, painter, designer & art educator Louise Metzer. Browse paintings on wood, stone, bone, horn, ceramics & pottery.

King Jimmy Market [144 C3] Wallace Johnson St, south of junction with Walpole St; ⏲ Tue & Thu. This notorious haunt for 'Belgium' goods – the local slang for ill-gotten gains – is peddled right behind the Sierra Leone police headquarters. The ramshackle market is also the main fish, fruit & vegetable market for the capital.

Victoria Park Market [145 F3] East of Victoria Park, bounded by Circular Rd, Garrison St & Rawdon St. Undoubtedly the best place to buy gara & Africana cloth. It also has stall after stall of rice & fresh produce. Hemmed in by the streets, stalls & the park, the atmosphere can be hectic, & it is prime pickpocketing territory.

BOOKS

There's depressingly little in the way of official commercial outlets.

Balmaya [139 F4] (*32B Main Motor Rd, Congo Cross*; m *076 601 209*) has a selection by Sierra Leonean authors for sale. The **book stalls** along Garrison St [145 E4] between Rawdon & Howe streets in the city centre have a limited range, but also keep an eye out for the serendipity of impromptu, pavement-side butu bookshops, so-called because you have to crouch ('butu') to examine the wares. Others string up books like clothes on a washing line. You can negotiate on price, & useful & treasured finds include Sierra Leone history, poetry and first-person accounts, as well as Krio-language guides and the Krio Bible. Many of these spots also sell fold-out maps of town, although they often ask extortionate prices.

CLOTHES, BAGS & SHOES
There are tailors on every street in Freetown, & if you're staying in Sierra Leone for any length of time it's a great idea to have something made-to-measure from an African print. Buy some cloth & take it to any shop you like – many have a range of templates for African outfits, or magazines you can flick through for inspiration. In the **Ecowas Street** market [145 E2] downtown (past the secondhand clothes piled up on the roadsides), or, more hectic still, in **Victoria Park Market** [145 F3], you can pick up plenty of Africana print cotton, as well as the templates for a 'Mr & Mrs' outfit.

Eurotex [145 F2] 22 Wilberforce St, junction with Siaka Stevens St; m 076 634 500; ⊕ 09.00–18.00 Mon–Fri, 09.00–17.00 Sat. Offers roll after roll of international fabrics, whether red-sequinned for the club, pinstriped for work, tartan for a *ceilidh*, or floaty numbers for the summer. It also stocks good material for making up bags – find a template for a tailor to copy. Cloth is sold by a length known as the *lappa* (the length necessary for a wraparound skirt, about 1m).
Amaani Fabric & Accessories [138 D6] 118 Wilkinson Rd; m 078 088 337. Specialising in African prints, this is another good bet, with a wide selection of cloths to suit both men's and women's tastes.
De Original X-perteez tailoring fashion [138 A2] Aberdeen roundabout, Aberdeen; m 076 733 473, 030 733 473, 077 733 473. Among tailors who come recommended is this outfit run by Abraham Tucker, who rather ingeniously goes by the name of Tommy Hillfinger & sews Marks & Spencer labels into everything he makes. He has a good eye for how to get the best out of any pattern in the cut. It can take a while to get items back,

so check his availability, agree a date, & let him know when you're leaving.
Two Brothers Tailor [139 H4] 14 Williams St; m 076 778 948. This outfit is very good at reproductions, & has a large team so can have shorter collection times.
The Bags Man m 088 471 335. A favourite among many expats, a young man named Abraham – or 'The Bags Man', as he prefers to be called – sells pretty handmade bags & purses, as well as the occasional piece of jewellery, an impressive feat given that he lost both of his hands during the war. He tends to hang out at expat haunts like Bliss Patisserie, Freetown Supermarket & the Sea Coach Express terminal under Aberdeen Bridge, but he can meet you elsewhere if you give him a call.
Swank Couture 4 Carlton Carew Rd; m 033 400 226, 076 663 743; ⊕ 09.30–17.30 Mon–Sat. Browse the wares of couture fashion designer Jenneh Amara-Bangali, who designs for DJs & other Freetown luminaries. She came back to Sierra Leone a few years after the war ended to take up her favourite hobby, & her tailor-made clothes merge African & Western fabrics with fun plays on Western styles.
Vivid Emporium 99 Sir Samuel Lewis Rd, Aberdeen; m 078 113 538; ⊕ 11.00–21.00 Mon–Sat. Run by local fashion phenomenon Kadiatu Kamara, here you can find handmade, ready-to-wear outfits for men & women alike, as well as shoes, bags & accessories – all infused with a hip African vibe. Kamara can also custom design outfits if you're looking for a one-of-a-kind dress to wear for a big night out.
Shepor 16 Decker Land, Babadorie; m 076 603 702, 076 603 602, 033 353 774, 088 688 919; e shepordesigns@gmail.com. Run by radio DJ & entrepreneur Hannah Foullah, this company creates gorgeous accessories; mostly handbags & slipper-sandals (both Le60,000–80,000) from the recycled hessian sacking for rice & potatoes. Funky bags with outsize circular wooden handles come in a series of different colours – all utterly desirable, modern & African; great for presents. She also has smaller purses, clutch bags and notebooks with dyed hessian covers.

JEWELLERY
Street stands sell inferior, but cheaper, costume jewellery all over downtown.
Allie's Jewellery Ltd [145 E2] 13 Howe St, PO Box 705; ☎ 022 229 417; m 076 601 166;

e mohamed_sl@hotmail.com. This is the best spot in the country for handmade jewellery, often cast with diamonds mined in Sierra Leone under the Kimberley certification process, cut & polished in Europe & sent back for setting in Freetown. All this is done under the artistic eye of manager Mohamed Hassan, who trained in Manchester. Diamond earrings, rings, necklaces, with any design you care to think up or copy, are made at competitive prices. You can take in existing jewellery for repairs, as well as commission work with other stones such as rubies, emeralds & sapphires that Hassan can order in from abroad. The workshop is out back & it's fascinating to see your favoured prize crafted in front of you by skilled workers.

PLANTS

Awuna Florist 11 Signal Hill Rd, Congo Cross end; m 076 613 167. Containing what must be among Sierra Leone's few open gardens, Awuna was set up by master florist & landscaper Ore Renner & has bouquet after bouquet of bright petals for sale, or a stunning manicured grotto view to enjoy as spectator. It's best to call ahead to make an appointment before stopping by.
Eskarnn Flowers & Landscape Design Abraham Dr, Juba Hill; m 076 660 212. Another good option, where you can pick up potted plants for your garden as well as cut flowers for your dining room table. The company can also do deliveries.

SUPERMARKETS

Often Lebanese-run, they have plenty of choice (pages 108–9), although none seems ever to quite have everything you want. So it's a question of finding the best fit, or dropping into 2 or 3. Many are somewhere along Wilkinson Rd. If you're looking for fresh produce, however, the supermarket shelves won't be much help; you're better off stopping by one of the fruit and veg stalls that tend to spring up in the parking lots just outside. All should be happy to change US dollar notes for Leones with a purchase. For fish, try the **Wanpole Fisherman's Base** on Lumley Beach Rd (page 153), or the delightfully named **Fish Meets**

Land [139 E3] (*19 Wilkinson Rd; m 078 737 487, 088 446 481*), which also has frozen options, near the Aberdeen Rd junction.

Congo Cross

Goodies [139 F3] 2 Murray Town Rd, Congo Cross; m 078 857 857; ⊕ 09.00–21.00 daily
Monoprix Supermarket [139 E3] 4C Wilkinson Rd, across from Rokel Bank; m 076 617 428

Downtown

Choitram's Supermarket [145 B5] 1–3 Kroo Town Rd, downtown; m 076 669 165; ⊕ 08.30–20.00 Mon–Sat

Hill Cot

Adnan's Supermarket [139 F6] Regent Rd; m 076 616 727, 077 616 727
St Mary's Supermarket [139 F6] Regent Rd; m 088 731 818; ⊕ 09.00–21.00 daily

Juba

Goodies [138 D7] Peninsula Rd; m 078 857 857; ⊕ 09.00–21.00 daily
St Mary's Supermarket [138 D7] 2A Peninsula Rd; m 078 731 818; ⊕ 09.00–21.00 daily

Murray Town

Foodland Supermarket [139 E3] 9 Sir Samuel Lewis Rd; m 025 919 100
Spirits & Wine Boutique [139 E2] 39A Murray Town Rd; m 078 196 866; 🗲 spiritsandwineboutique

Wilkinson Road

Adnan's Supermarket [138 D6] Wilkinson Rd, next to Crown Xpress; m 076 616 727, 077 616 727
Freetown Supermarket [138 D5] Freetown Mall, Wilkinson Rd; m 077 887 788
Spurbury's Supermarket [139 E5] 39 Spur Rd; m 088 711 051
St Mary's Supermarket [138 D6] 16 Wilkinson Rd; m 099 111 111; ⊕ 09.00–21.00 daily

OTHER PRACTICALITIES

BEAUTY

For a simple grade shave, & even beard trim, men can go to any shack for a few thousand leones. For

women, hair extensions are extremely popular, as a form of socialising as much as for the final look, & you will constantly see pairs of friends & family members by the side of the road locked in conversation & laughter while braiding each other's hair. A pack of hair costs Le25,000 & a whole new hairdo can cost Le230,000. For Caucasian women, a shampoo & haircut should cost something in the range of Le70,000. Just pull up a stool & ask.

Na-Li Spa 129C Wilkinson Rd; m 088 887 777; e na-lispa@hotmail.com. Among the most favoured expat hairdressers and nail salons is this salon for men & women alike. They also do an impressive array of scrubs & massages starting at US$45/hr.
Nancy Koroma m 076 651 952. For another fun outing, get your nails done by Nancy who can bring her lip-lining, manicuring and pedicuring services straight to your door. The fake acrylic nail extensions involve a surfeit of colour, & even feature jewellery stuck through tiny holes. Get ready to make the choice of a daytime: square-tipped or round?

Becky Smith m 076 652 696; Le90,000 for a full-leg. For waxing services, Becky does home/hotel visits with her own mixture of sugar & lime, favoured by the Lebanese.
Leone Casino Massage and Beauty Salon [138 A2] 72a Cape Rd, next door to the New Grand Casino Leone; m 078 988 988, 030 688 688. This Chinese-run outfit offers manicures, pedicures & waxing, as well as acupuncture & massages for the tense & weary. The massages are good, but not cheap (by Salone standards, at least); an hour-long back rub will set you back US$40, while a 90-min full-body massage costs US$60.
Song m 076 919 927, 077 469 614. For a more affordable rubdown, try Edward Bangura, a former boxing champion who often sets up a massage table at the bottom of Lumley Beach. He charges Le50,000 for an hour-long session.

INTERNET With the proliferation of mobile internet, there aren't as many internet cafés as there used to be, but there are still a few speckled around most parts of the city, particularly as you get towards the centre. Keep in mind, though, that you don't need to go to an internet café to get online. If you have a laptop or mobile device, there's free Wi-Fi at a few-dozen places throughout the city, including most hotel restaurants and popular cafés like Crown Xpress, Gina's, Gigibonta and others. A more comprehensive list of hotspots is available here: w onlime.com/sl/limezone/locations. All upmarket hotels and an increasing number of mid-range and budget options now also provide free Wi-Fi to guests.

MEDICAL See page 86, for information on medical testing centres, hospital and doctors in Freetown.

City Pharmacy [145 E2] 18 Wilberforce St; m 076 608 351, 077 608 351. There are plenty of pharmacies all over town, but one that comes recommended is run by the friendly Emad Khoury, in the heart of town just by the corner of Siaka Stevens St (formerly Emad's Pharmacy).

Marz Chemicals Ltd [144 C4] 44 Bathurst St; ☏ 022 223 506; m 076 223 506; e marzchem@yahoo.com. This is another good bet where you can pick up well-stocked first-aid kits in addition to the standard drugs & soaps.

Emergencies There is no real emergency response service that you can rely on. However, ☏ 019 and ☏ 999 are listed as the emergency response numbers for fire & ambulance respectively. To reach the police, dial ☏ 900. The general emergency numbers are ☏ 000 or ☏ 911.

Veterinary services If you've brought your cat or dog with you to Freetown, or if you acquire one here (as many people do), be sure that your little furball gets all of the necessary treatment – from de-worming tablets to rabies jabs to the all-important neutering. There are currently two options for vets in Freetown, and if you need help with training, contact Christine at e dogtrainingfreetown@gmail.com.

With thanks to David Oades of Overlanding West Africa

As of mid 2017, one-month, single-entry visas for Liberia were available in Freetown for US$100–135 (payable in US dollars or Leones, price depending on your nationality). To buy one, stop by the **Embassy of the Republic of Liberia** [138 D5] (*2 Spur Rd, opposite the British High Commission, Wilberforce;* m *076 728 647;* e *geraldinelibemb2014@gmail.com;* ⊕ *for submissions 09.00–noon Mon–Fri & for collection in the afternoon 13.00–17.00*). Visas are usually ready in 24 hours.

The recently relocated **Guinean embassy** [139 H5] (*111 Jomo Kenyatta Rd, New England Ville;* m *077 834 154, 077 421 218;* e *ambagui_sl@yahoo.fr*) charges a usurious US$200 for a three-month, single-entry visa, which can be picked up on the same day if your form and two passport photos are dropped off in the morning.

The Sierra Leone Animal Welfare Society (SLAWS) 26A Main Motor Rd, near Congo Cross; m 076 237 228, 076 231 126, 076 601 845; w slaws.org or ◼ sierraleoneanimalwelfare. This is the cheaper of the two, offering all of the regular services at variable prices that rarely go north of Le100,000.

Special Animal Services (SAS) 48 Loop Rd, opposite the Chinese Embassy; m 076 951 800, 079 200 031; w sasaccra.com/contact.php. This Dutch-owned operation also has a small shop on site if you need to stock up on cat food or dog toys.

MONEY The ATM network in Freetown has been revolutionised in just a few short years, and while it's still common for machines to go out of service or run out of money, there are just about enough of them around town that you can generally find a working one should you need it – albeit perhaps with a bit of effort. Rokel Commercial, GT Bank, EcoBank, Standard Chartered, UBA, Union Trust Bank & others all have ATMs accepting international Visa cards in the city centre, and you'll find at least one or two ATMs at most of the city's main roundabouts, including Wilkinson, Lumley, Congo Cross and Aberdeen, as well as outside Adnan's and St Mary's supermarkets. Access Bank and EcoBank both have ATMs outside the Family Kingdom Resort at the north end of Lumley Beach, and several top-end hotels have ATMs in their lobbies, including the Radisson Blu and The Hub.

If the ATMs do end up failing you, you can draw out money against your credit card at branches of Rokel Commercial Bank, and there are plenty of licensed forex booths too, some of which are listed on pages 172–3. Along Siaka Stevens Street, there are also plenty of (illegal) 'dollar boys' who'll ask you if you need to change money, with the constant cry of 'change, change, change'. Many shops, supermarkets, hotels and restaurants can usually change money if you have bought something there too. Western Union or MoneyGram offer international money transfers.

Visa cash advances Drawing money against a credit or debit card at the downtown branch of **Rokel Commercial Bank Ltd** [145 E3] (*25/27 Siaka Stevens St;* ✎ *022 222 501;* w *rokelbank.sl*) tends to be quicker and more straightforward than the branch in the west of town [139 E3] (*1 Wilkinson Rd, Congo Cross;* m *076 605 943*). Head left at the entrance and approach one of the desk assistants with your card and passport. Then an almighty paper trail, and wait, begins, before you get your receipt, take it to the forex cashier in the main hall next door and queue up for bricks of leones. In Congo Cross you need to go upstairs & hope someone sitting behind one of the desks will turn their attention to you at some point.

Foreign exchange bureaux Among the more reliable downtown outlets are:

$ Blue Circle Foreign Exchange Bureau Ltd
18 Siaka Stevens St; ☎ 022 227 064; ⊕ 09.00–17.30 Mon–Fri, 09.00–13.00 Sat. Accepts large bills only (no US$20 or £5 notes) & checks them with a UV light.

$ Manans Foreign Exchange Bureau
17 Regent Rd; m 076 686 314; ⊕ 09.00–17.00 Mon–Sat

Wire transfer agents Below we list a few outlets (from most westerly to most easterly across Freetown), but there are many more. Any branch of Union Trust Bank, FiBank (First International) and EcoBank should offer Western Union services, while MoneyGram services are available at Afro International Ltd, GT Bank (Guaranty Trust) and Sierra Leone Commerical Bank.

Western Union
$ EcoBank [145 E2] 7 Lightfoot Boston St; ☎ 022

290 438; w ecobank.com; ⊕ 08.30–15.30 Mon–Thu, 08.30–16.00 Fri

---

WHAT'S IN A NAME?: HISTORICAL TOUR OF FREETOWN

Names and places in the capital call up triumphant moments of freedom and sorrowful passings, testament to the men who made them happen, and the places that fostered them. The gridded street layout of central downtown is the same as that of 1794, rebuilt after the French had burnt everything down – a legacy of the Napoleonic war effort that extended to West Africa as well as Waterloo. When this central area was first created, under the Nova Scotian efforts of 1792, 12 streets were cut from the bush – nine perpendicular to the waterfront and three crossing them at right angles, parallel to the shore – and each named after a company director of the Sierra Leone Company, which had paid for their passage.

The land beneath **State House** [145 E4] was home to the even earlier first group of settlers from Britain, who disembarked in May 1787 and cut their way through the bush to plant their flag at the top of this hill and called their new settlement Granville Town. **King Tom**, the Temne chief who agreed to let them land, has a neighbourhood named after him in the northern tip of the capital, now home to a football ground and one of the city's two huge smouldering rubbish dumps (known as a 'bomeh' in Krio). King Jemmy, who burnt the original Province of Freedom down, is the inspiration for **King Jimmy Market** [144 C3], a ramshackle affair of food and random electrical goods, much of it stolen – testament to the man's opportunistic side.

Known unfathomably as the **Portuguese Steps**, well-liked governor Charles MacCarthy, sent from England, erected the stone stairs that led down to the Old Wharf, which he also expanded as part of a £150,000 building spree between 1816 and 1824. **Race Course Road** commemorates one of his more outlandish ideas – regular horse racing –at Fourah Bay in the east. The walls of the central **St George's Cathedral** [144 D2], built in 1817, commemorate 'disconsolate mothers' whose sons were lost at sea and is a lovely church to visit.

Susan's Bay, now part of the sprawling seaside slum melded with Mabella, was named by Freetown governor John Clarkson after the fiancée he left behind in Britain to take up the post, and who eventually drew him back home. Before it became

$ FiBank [145 F3] 50 Ecowas St, by Sani Abacha St; 022 220 493; **w** fibsl.biz; 09.00–16.00 Mon–Fri, 09.00–14.00 Sat
$ FiBank [138 D7] 34A Freetown Rd; 022 232 994; 09.00–16.00 Mon–Fri, 09.00–14.00 Sat
$ Standard Chartered Bank [145 E2] Lightfoot Boston St; 022 440 466; **w** sc.com/sl; 09.00–15.30 Mon–Fri
$ Union Trust [138 D7] 9 Freetown Rd, Lumley; 022 226 954; **m** 033 515 105; **w** utb.sl; 08.00–18.00 Mon–Fri, 09.30–15.00 Sat
$ Union Trust [144 E2] Lightfoot Boston St; 022 226 954; **m** 077 713 539; 08.00–16.00 Mon–Fri, 10.00–15.00 Sat

$ Union Trust 48 Bai Bureh Rd, Kissy; **m** 033 522 806; 08.30–18.00 Mon–Fri, 09.30–15.00 Sat

MoneyGram
$ Afro International [145 E2] 21/bx 16 Rawdon St; 2nd Flr; 022 228 818; 08.00–19.00 Mon–Sat
$ GT Bank [145 E2] Wilberforce St; 022 228 493; **w** gtb.sl; 08.30–16.00 Mon–Fri
$ Sierra Leone Commercial Bank [144 D3] 29–31 Siaka Stevens St; 022 225 264; 09.00–15.30 Mon–Fri, 08.00–17.00 Sat

POLICE Police stations are dotted throughout the capital. They include Lumley Police Station, at the junction with Wilkinson Road; Congo Cross Police at the far end of Wilkinson Road; Aberdeen Police by the Aberdeen roundabout; Central

known as Kroo Bay, the waters to the north of the city were known as Frenchman's Bay and then promptly switched to St George's Bay in a fit of patriotic fervour by Captain Thompson, who sailed in with the Province of Freedom's first residents.

The majestic bowers of the **Cotton Tree** [144 D4] that mark the start of downtown have seen a great deal. Now the tree oversees honking traffic inching round its trunk and hundreds of bats clinging to its boughs. This was the beacon around which the first Nova Scotians cleared land on arriving in 1792, and to which the devoutly Christian settlers later walked, slow-singing hymns in tribute to the long struggle they had endured, after 65 of their party had died on the winter journey from Halifax. 'The day of Jubilee is come,' they sang. The service they held beneath the tree marked one of thanksgiving, and the moment that Freetown was christened.

It was under this tree too, as the sun was setting one day later that year, that John Clarkson – the British superintendent of the colony – told Thomas Peters, the hero of the Nova Scotians who was now furious that the colony was being ruled by a council of eight Englishmen, that 'one or other of us would be hanged upon that Tree' before they settled their differences. It wasn't long before Peters died, and Clarkson returned to England.

Wilberforce village in the hilly west of town, and **Wilberforce Street** in the centre of town, are named after the British abolitionist member of parliament William Wilberforce, who was horrified that London's black poor went unfed by the Poor Law officers, who said they had no responsibility to feed those whose origin was elsewhere. His 1876 Society for Effecting the Abolition of the Slave Trade, formed with Granville Sharp, Thomas Clarkson (John's brother) and Henry Thornton, finally bore fruit in 1807. Wilberforce was also a vice president of the Church Missionary Society, which Governor MacCarthy directed to help settle recaptives in one of eight parishes, including Wilberforce. Also in town, **Sir Samuel Lewis Road** is named after the country's first lawyer, the city's first mayor (of 1895) and the accomplished man who became the first African to be knighted, in 1896.

Freetown OTHER PRACTICALITIES

3

Police on Wallace Johnson Street in town; and Eastern Police at the clock tower at the start of Kissy Road. The **police headquarters** [144 D3] (*George St;* ✆ *022 223 001, 022 223 033;* m *088 208 933;* e *igp@police.gov.sl;* w *police.gov.sl*) is downtown. The police information line is ✆ 999.

POSTAL SERVICES   For anything substantial, valuable or timely, turn to an international courier such as **DHL** [139 G4] (*30 Main Motor Rd, Brookfields;* ✆ *022 225 902;* ⊕ *08.00–18.00 Mon–Fri, 09.00–17.00 Sat*) or **UPS** (*Redcoat Express Ltd, 82 Sanders St;* m *079 888 300, 076 230 169;* e *mskredcoatups@gmail.com;* ⊕ *08.30–17.30 Mon–Fri, 09.30–13.00 Sat*).

Sierra Leone Postal Service (SALPOST) [144 D3] 27 Siaka Stevens St; ✆ 022 225 621; e kmohamedkabba@gmail.com; w salpost. sl; ⊕ 08.00–16.00 Mon–Fri, 08.00–13.00 Sat. Freetown's post office is not what it once was. Service is somewhat unreliable, but you can always take out your own PO Box, & mail should get there, so long as there's nothing precious inside it. Likewise, you can send mail internationally from the post office, & postcards seem to make it to Europe within a week.

SPORT   The members-only **Young Sportsmen Club** [138 D4] (*YSC; 80 Wilkinson Rd;* ✆ *022 231 912*) has facilities for tennis, squash, football, basketball, volleyball, snooker and a popular café, Munchies (f *MunchiesAtYSC*). Annual memberships are available for individuals and couples; stop by to get the latest rates.

Golf

Freetown Golf Club [138 C6] Lumley Beach, PO Box 237; m 078 761 903, 076 652 445, 077 652 445. Home to the first game of golf in West Africa, Freetown has a permanent 18-hole course here. It's a private club – with an outdated dress code – but non-members are welcome for a one-off fee. Otherwise, joining costs Le2,160,000, with an annual fee of Le2,475,000 (a couple pays Le3,630,000); Le1,485,000 for a half-year. Guest use of the squash & tennis courts goes for Le120,000 an hour, while a visitor's day pass to play golf will cost you Le150,000/300,000 for 9/18 holes. The caddies' fee is Le30,000 for 18 holes, plus Le60,000 to rent clubs. Golf lessons, with any of 17 golf instructors, cost Le90,000 an hour.

Gym

Gym   Several hotels also have good fitness facilities, including up the hill at **Country Lodge**, where a scarily fit man known as Reflex teaches 'boot camp' fitness classes every Tuesday and Thursday evenings at 18.30; expect to work up a good sweat. Home Suites, Golden Tulip, The Hub, Radisson Blu, Family Kingdom and Sierra Lighthouse all have fitness centres as well. A one-month membership at Core Fitness goes for Le600,000 including classes; all of the others will charge somewhere south of that.

Core Fitness [138 D4] 80 Wilkinson Rd; m 099 959 595, 078 959 595; f corefirtnesssl. A handful of new fitness centres had just opened up in Freetown at the time of writing, of which this was regarded to be the best. They've got all new equipment, plus spinning, yoga, martial arts, boxing & pilates classes on offer – you may even catch the 2017 Salone Strongest Man champion, Amin Hudroge, training here.
Edge Fitness [138 C4] Lumley Beach Rd; m 088 800 006. A new, well-equipped gym in the same building as the Medrie International Hotel.

Physio-Fitness 36 King Harman Rd; m 077 409 040, 078 409 040; e bconton@gmail.com. This doubles as both fitness studio & physical therapy clinic.
Song m 076 919 927, 077 469 614. If you're looking for some professional one-on-one fitness help, try Edward Bangura, a former national boxing champion who now works as a personal trainer. He charges Le50,000/hr & can design a fitness regime to help you meet your goals. He's happy to come to you.

Running Though Sierra Leone made international news with a ban on jogging in July 2017, ostensibly to prevent runners who had been 'jogging in large numbers along the streets with a hint of menace, raining insults, obstructing traffic, pounding on vehicles, playing loud music, and snatching property', Freetown's fantastic scenery nonetheless makes it a rewarding, and challenging, place to jog, and it (hopefully!) seems unlikely the ban, which many see as politically motivated (and doesn't, in any case, apply to the beaches), will stand for long. Seemingly endless uphill stretches such as the climbs up Spur Road or Hill Cot Road are highly demanding, and are best done at dawn or dusk. The long, flat sand of Lumley Beach, beside the invigorating sea breeze, is also ideal for an early morning or evening run. For a real taste of youthful determination and vanity combined, check out Lumley Beach between 06.00 and 07.30. Likely as not, you'll see well-formed arms glistening with effort in the early sunlight, as young men with dreams of sporting glory pound the empty pavements, stopping only for press-up sessions. The local chapter of the famed **Hash House Harriers** (🄵 *facebook.com/groups/18700931427*) – an international drinking and non-competitive running club that gets up to no end of antics in its chase after a human 'hare' – covers many unchartered backstreets and meets every Monday evening at various locations around town. The group also organises a longer run on the final Sunday of every month, heading somewhere out on the Peninsula for a sweaty slog through the sun and sand, followed by booze and swimming on the beach. Newcomers are welcome as much for their drinking as their running prowess. Check the Facebook group to see where they'll be meeting next.

Squash President Koroma's favourite sport (he said he used to cool down after a hard day's campaigning with a game of squash, and then went on to bag the national championship in 2008), there are decent courts at the YSC [138 D4], the Aqua Club [138 D2] and the Golf Club [138 C6] (Le120,000/hr). The Hub has a free squash court 15.00–18.00.

Swimming If you fancy a break from the Atlantic, you can swim at several hotel pools, including **Bintumani** (circular & well within view of guests' rooms; Le50,000pp) and **Country Lodge** (a posing spot with sunloungers & constant attention; Le60,000pp for a day's gym membership, with access to tennis courts too). Other hotels, such as **Hotel Barmoi**, only allow guests to swim. For a seaside plunge in the capital, bear in mind that a lot of waste – human, medical, animal & industrial – ends up in the northern bays and washes round the corner towards Lumley Beach. While some wouldn't dream of heading into such water, others find that the northern tip at Aberdeen is OK, since it's protected by the cape that juts out just beside it, rather than the unshielded southern end where more detritus washes up.

Table tennis There's a ping pong club with four tables at the national stadium (*Room 155 for the action; register for Le15,000 in the office at Room 152, plus a monthly Le10,000 contribution to take care of the gym, buy balls & other administration*). National coach **John Bobson Taylor** (m *077 250 395*) is usually on hand for a speedy lesson, or contact the Sierra Leone Table Tennis Association's (SLTTA) public relations officer, **Abraham Cobba Sesay** (🄵 *abrahamcobba.sesay*). You may well meet **George Wyndham** while you're at the stadium – he's the country's most decorated table tennis player and a para athlete, no less. He took bronze at the 2013 and 2015 Para Table Tennis African Championships, and was Sierra Leone's only representative at the 2016 Summer Paralympics in Rio.

Tennis You can play tennis at both the **YSC** and the **Golf Club** (Le120,000/hr), as well as at **Country Lodge** and the **Radisson Blu Mammy Yoko**. **Amidu** (m *076 783 190*), the tennis coach at Country Lodge, offers individual and group lessons either at the hotel where he works or at the excellent Hill Station tennis courts, just around the corner. Expect to pay about Le70,000–90,000 for an hour-long one-on-one session.

WHAT TO SEE AND DO

While there are not many bona fide 'sights' in Freetown – few would consider a trip to the Courts of Justice a fun day out, for example – it is possible for a visitor to really get under the skin of the city. The locations listed below lack the slickness of tourist attractions, but they offer their own passage into the fabric of history – to walk up Freedom Steps, for example, is to touch soles with every freed slave who ever set foot in the city; while the sight of Bai Bureh's war drum in the National Museum evokes a powerful link with the past. At other times, heritage stands just off the shoulder of contemporary life, as with the well-attended Maroon Church or the hubbub of King Jimmy Market, home to the famous De Ruyter Stone.

COTTON TREE [144 D3] (*Siaka Stevens St*) Today the branches of this huge old tree rise from one of the busiest intersections in the capital, showering a flood of green over the entrance to the commercial and political quarter of town. It used to tower over the dealings of the slave trade (see box, pages 172–3). Look out for bats, which can be seen dangling from the branches by the hundreds in dry season.

COURTS OF JUSTICE [144 D3] (*Siaka Stevens St;* ⊕ *Mon–Fri; free entry*) The refurbished Courts of Justice, just opposite the Cotton Tree, is arguably the grandest building in Freetown, its Neoclassical arches redolent of colonial ideas of order and power. As with most courts, there is a public gallery that is free to enter. In stark contrast to the procedural formality and self-righteousness of the UN Special Court, a seat in the gallery gives a chance to see how justice is dispensed for most Sierra Leoneans. Some view it as grim comedy: don't be surprised to see a magistrate take a mobile-phone call while handing down a sentence.

CULTURAL VILLAGE (m *076 775 541, Saidu Kamara*) Evicted from their Aberdeen home of several decades in 2016, the cultural village, once home to some of the country's most talented musicians and dancers, was sadly in a state of flux at the time of writing, and it remains unclear if and when they'll be either allocated a new space or returned to a redeveloped plot in Aberdeen. Founded in 1963 by John Joseph Akar, himself best known as the composer of the melody for the Salone national anthem, the National Dance troupe has won prizes at competitions all over Africa, and toured destinations as exotic as Iran and Belgium. They are often wheeled out by the Ministry of Culture for almost any visiting dignitary, but it is possible to book a performance directly (only by phone for the time being), making for a superb night's entertainment. The choreography offers a contemporary twist on traditional and sacred dances from across the ethnic spectrum, featuring the appearance of some non-sacred masks. The highlight is the Temne witch-bird dance, where a giant bird struts its feathers before laying a magical egg. The physical stamina of the dancers, to drumming that never for a second lets up, all in the eerie glow of torches and kerosene-lit lamps, transports you a long way from the capital to somewhere much more primal. Whether you book your own performance or catch them at another engagement, it is customary to tip the dancers. Artists are also

Such is the capital's lush life that even the least twitchy of travellers can spot head-turning birds with only a smattering of effort. In a city whose habitat varies from marsh to montane rainforest in the space of a swoop, there are plenty of urban winged wonders.

Part-time birdman Juan Luis López Frechilla surveys the skies

Even the greyest parts of the downtown urban jungle boast some surprises: black kites (*Milvus migrans*), soar overhead, while the silhouette of the sinister hooded vulture looms over busy traders. Even more prolific, and much smaller, is the common bulbul (*Pycnonotus barbatus*), singing its sweet notes whether downtown or up in the hills, and the tinier grey-headed sparrow (*Passer griseus*). A larger city-dweller is the pied crow (*Corvus albidus*), often seen on lampposts and roadside billboards. Locals call it 'minista bird' after its religious garb – an all-black suit and a white 'shirt'.

Along the coast and in the city marshlands – never quite plucking up the courage to venture inland – is the migratory osprey (*Pandion haliaetus*), which appears during the later months of the year. This bird of prey has long angular wings and a black, grey and white underside. Look out for its smash-and-grab plunge-diving in search of supper. Flirting with the land, the usually water-bound palm nut vulture (*Gypohierax angolensis*), is a fairly easy spot along the shore and near the city's creeks. Look for contrasting black-and-white plumage and its stocky shape in flight. The beautifully chequered pied kingfisher (*Ceryle rudis*), perches closer to rivers, while Lumley's sands see the elegant slate-black western reef heron (*Egretta gularis*), enjoying a walk as much as the next beach-lover. Not to be confused with seagulls, black-hatted terns flap their pointy wings above the ocean spray.

In grassy patches throughout town, the white cattle egret (*Bulbuclus ibis*), is known to locals as 'cow's angel' for its seemingly protective presence beside cattle, although this spirited bird is really just after insects dislodged by plodding hooves. Up in the trees, the peculiarly yellow-faced African harrier hawk (*Polyboroides typus*), can wreak havoc on Freetown hair-dos in dive-bombing attacks to guard nesting offspring. As you duck, any trace of a barred grey-and-white underside, broad black trailing along the wing's edges, plus a white bar on its black tail, will help identify your aggressor. Plantains might be a local dish of choice, but the western grey plantain eater (*Crinifer piscator*), prefers to peck at other fruits with its submarine yellow bill. Its 'kow-kow-kow' cry is easily recognised across the city.

Even taking the ferry from the east end's Kissy Terminal to the airport offers the chance to spot the huge pink-backed pelican (*Pelecanus rufescens*), picking its way over shipwrecks that poke up from the shallows. All over town, look out for several species of pigeons and doves, including the laughing dove (*Streptopelia senegalensis*), whose hurried notes resemble a gentle chuckle, and the anchor-shaped swift, referred to locally as the 'crazy bird' for its insane flight paths, and you can put a Freetown feather in your cap.

prepared to offer tuition in dancing, drumming, balafon and other instruments. A 1-hour, one-off session costs a startling US$70, but you can wangle much better deals for a series of lessons.

DE RUYTER STONE [144 C3] (*King Jimmy Market;* ☉ *dawn–dusk daily; free entry*) It is an irony typical of Sierra Leone that its oldest monument is actually buried 2m underground, and only gets seen, a bit like an eclipse, or a census, once every ten years. In 1664, Holland and Britain were at war and the Dutch admiral De Ruyter sailed to West Africa to take out British settlements. On what sounds like a pretty successful campaign of destruction and pillage, he recaptured Goree, in present-day Senegal, and totalled slave forts on Bunce and Tasso islands. At King Jimmy Water (later known as Peter's Brook), a favoured watering hole of the west Atlantic coast due to the purity of its spring waters, he couldn't resist a spot of graffiti, carving 'M.A. Ruyter. I.C. Mellon, Vice Admiralen, West Fries, Vant A.D. 1664' into a stone to commemorate his campaign. His picture – and a replica of the stone – now sits in the **National Museum** [144 D4], where he looks ever so smug. The stone was rediscovered in 1923 when the King Jimmy Market was under construction – it had been silted up and now lies just above the high water mark, but because of its location beneath a busy market it is considered safer to keep it hidden rather than on public display. Wander down to **King Jimmy Market** [144 C3] (just behind the Connaught Hospital) on one of its off-days (Monday, Wednesday, Friday or Sunday) if you want a more peaceful visit – the market is the centre of Freetown's fish and vegetable trade and not for the faint of nose.

FOURAH BAY COLLEGE BOTANICAL GARDENS [map, page 130] (*Fourah Bay College, Mount Aureol;* ☉ *dawn–dusk daily; free entry*) If you are in search of green space, the best flora (not to mention views) in the city are on the campus of Fourah Bay College, which resides at the top of Mount Aureol in acres of rolling wood and parkland. The gardens are also home to **Heddle's Farm**, the ruins of one of Freetown's top addresses that has in the past served as a family home to Charles Heddle, merchant and groundnut pioneer, a convalescent home, the governor's country residence, home to the Comptroller of Forestry, and the place where Mrs Melville wrote *A Residence at Sierra Leone*. The walk up to the gardens is exhausting, and takes about 30 minutes. The climb starts just off Circular Road (off Pademba Road). Taxis congregate at the base of the hill, and will transport you for about Le10,000 if you want to go immediately. Sharing a cab costs Le2,000.

GATEWAY TO KING'S YARD [144 C3] (*Connaught Hospital, Lightfoot Boston St;* ☉ *daily*) This archway was the entrance to King's Yard, a holding pen for the 'liberated Africans', through which all ancestors of Sierra Leone's present-day Creoles passed, where they were held in temporary quarantine to check for signs of ill-health before being released into Freetown. The 1819 inscription reads, 'Royal Asylum and Hospital for Africans rescued from slavery by British Valour and Philanthropy'. There's no doubting the grit of some of its residents: boys who passed through include Samuel Adjai Crowther, the first black Anglican bishop, and John Ezzidio, future mayor of Freetown and the first African elected to Sierra Leone's Legislative Council. The gate now arches over the entrance to Freetown's only public hospital, the recently refurbished but still sparsely equipped Connaught Hospital.

KING TOM CEMETERIES The two cemeteries in the King Tom neighbourhood are entirely unrelated, and indeed could scarcely be more different. Quiet, contemplative and green, the waterfront **Commonwealth War Cemetery** [139 G2] is unexpectedly hidden away (but well signposted) behind a vehicle repair yard for the Freetown police, and home to 248 Commonwealth burials from World War I and World War II. Among the dead are dozens of (western) victims of the Spanish flu pandemic, which arrived in the region with the ailing crews of the HMS *Mantua* and HMS *Africa* in August 1918. Despite the fact the ships were supposedly under 'strict quarantine', Sierra Leonean labourers were nonetheless sent on board to supply the ships with coal. The disease quickly jumped ashore with the returning labourers, and it's estimated that a full two-thirds of Sierra Leoneans contracted the flu, and 3% of the population had died of it before the close of September that year. (There's another Commonwealth cemetery across town near Lumley roundabout, which contains the graves of 74 West African troops killed in World War II.) The friendly caretaker will show you around and ask you to sign the guestbook; a tip probably isn't necessary but would surely be appreciated.

Just a few blocks away, the **King Tom Cemetery** [139 G3] is another matter entirely. Behind a concrete wall and backing up on to Freetown's largest *bomeh*, or dumpsite, the cemetery was known as a shambles even before the Ebola epidemic struck. In an effort to bring the crisis under control, all deaths in the Western Area, whether Ebola-related or not, were directed to King Tom for burial, until the space available was quickly overwhelmed and a new cemetery had to be established in Waterloo (page 193). All told, 6,395 people were buried at King Tom over 2014–15, counting more than 80 burials per day at the height of the crisis, and marked with identical headstones, many of which simply read 'known unto God'. It's a shockingly dystopian place, and the long rows of graves stretching to a horizon of burning trash are enough to shake even the hardest of hearts. Beware, the mood here can be more edgy than contemplative – come early in the day so the squatters and/or caretakers aren't drunk; someone will undoubtedly join you on your visit, and you should tip them Le10,000 when you leave. If you've got the time, the cemetery in Waterloo is a much more reflective experience.

NATIONAL ARCHIVES [map, page 130] (*Fourah Bay College, Mount Aureol;* \ *022 227 509, 022 229 471;* ⏰ *09.30–16.00 Mon–Fri; entry by appointment only*) It may not strike you as a conventional attraction, but any interest in colonial history should be pricked by the chance to visit Sierra Leone's archives, which contain 'documents of global significance', according to the former head of the British Council. These include the original copy of the treaty that sold the Freetown Area to the British, and the hand-written journals of John Clarkson, the British navy lieutenant who brought 1,190 men from Nova Scotia to Freetown in 1792–93. Looking down the long vista of history is never easy: in this case made particularly hard by the gruelling ascent of Mount Aureol required to reach the source material. Visits are best arranged through the National Museum (see below). If you're keen for research assistance, Abou Koroma (at the archives) and Albert Moore (m *030 205 365;* e *bert_moore90@hotmail.com*) are very able.

NATIONAL MUSEUM [144 D4] (*Pademba Rd, PO Box 908;* \ *022 223 555;* m *076 688 695;* w *sierraleoneheritage.org/museum;* ⏰ *09.30–16.30 Mon–Fri; expected contribution of Le10,000*) Partially housed in what was originally Freetown's Victorian-era railway station, the collection of the National Museum is interesting, if a little forlorn. The highlight is the set of life-size '**devils**' decked out in raffia, seashells and colourful cloth that dominate the newly renovated main exhibition room. The museum is now also home to 20 display panels, produced by Joseph Opala, on Bunce Island and the slave castle's links to the US. You can also have a look at a **war drum** that supposedly belonged to the army of Temne guerrilla hero Bai Bureh. An impressive collection of ceremonial masks, costumes and musical instruments is crammed into the other of the museum's two rooms, with brave attempts at explanation. Oddities include a piece of lunar rock presented to the country by Richard Nixon after one of the Apollo moon missions, and some replica diamonds. Acting curator, Josephine Kargbo, who can be found at the entrance on most days, is a great source of local knowledge, and can arrange visits to the National Archives (page 179).

NATIONAL RAILWAY MUSEUM [map, page 130] (*National Railway Workshops, Cline Town;* m *077 423 575, 076 468 880;* e *foslnrm@outlook.com;* w *sierraleonerailwaymuseum.com;* ⊕ *08.00–16.30 Mon–Fri, w/ends by appointment; free entry but offer a contribution as you leave*) Talk about a labour of love: Colonel Steve Davies turned up with the British army in Sierra Leone to train soldiers, and ended up founding a railway museum in his spare time, with the help of the young, unemployed Sierra Leoneans he took on – some of whom are still with the museum and working as knowledgeable, enthusiastic guides. They managed to transform a dilapidated engine shed into the country's second national museum, which charts the history of Sierra Leone's railway, first constructed in 1895. At its peak, in 1908, the railway ran 365km, from Water Street in Freetown to Pendembu in the east. At Bauya the line branched to run a further 119km to Makeni. Sometimes the narrow-gauge train couldn't climb the gradient at East Street and had to reverse down the hill, belching steam and soot, to make another attempt with more speed, and smoke. The railway lapsed into disrepair in the 1970s, but a new 200km minerals-only line opened in 2011 to transport iron ore from the mine at Tonkolili. The museum itself includes heavily restored surviving rolling stock, mostly brought in from UK railways, some dating back to 1915. The highlight is a coach built for a visit by Queen Elizabeth II in 1961 to mark the country's independence.

OLD FOURAH BAY COLLEGE [map, page 130] (*College Rd, Cline Town; free entry*) The site of the first university in sub-Saharan Africa that won the country its 'Athens of West Africa' reputation is barely an echo of its former glory, having suffered extensive damage during the war. Constructed between 1845 and 1848, the distinctive four-storey, elegantly dressed laterite exterior is still standing, along with twisting ironwork stairs, but the floors have fallen through and for safety reasons it is not possible to walk among the hulk of the building. Surrounded by poyo shacks, 'ghetto' boys and women stringing out clothes to dry from its crumbling sides, it's something of a ghost. Head for Cline Town, in the area around the east-end docks. If you are taking a taxi, ask for 'Water Quay', or try and pick a vehicle up from PZ or Shell Station. It should cost Le3,000.

OLD WHARF STEPS [144 D2] (*Wallace Johnson St; ⏲ daily*) Often called the Portuguese Steps, these were built by Governor MacCarthy in 1818, and popularly referred to as 'Freedom Steps', as they were where newly liberated slaves would first set foot on Freetown soil. This is also the location where then-deputy UK prime minister John Prescott stood in 2007 to commemorate the 200th anniversary of the abolition of slavery.

PEACE MUSEUM [139 H5] (*Special Court, Jomo Kenyatta Rd;* m *076 819 242;* e *slpeacemuseum@gmail.com;* w *slpeacemuseum.org; expected contribution of Le10,000*) Set in the former security building of the Special Court for Sierra Leone, this museum was opened in tandem with the court's closure at the end of 2013 and contains exhibits on the war and its aftermath, a memorial garden and an archive of all the court's public documentation. The first exhibits were put together in partnership with an American museum designer and provide a short history of the war and reconciliation efforts, with multiple artefacts on display, including weapons, personal effects, spiritual clothing and protective amulets. Large paintings, posters and photos decorate the walls. The museum continues to gather war artefacts from around the country, but most of these have yet to be developed in to exhibits due to lack of funding to catalogue and display them. The small memorial garden at the back contains a stylised bamboo tent frame intended to represent the refugee tents that so many Sierra Leoneans called home for so long, and the high concrete walls around the garden are supposed to one day carry the names of all the war's victims. Researchers should enquire in person for access to the SCSL and Truth and Reconciliation Commission archives. Overall, it's an admirable effort at commemorating a trauma many would prefer left in the past, though as with so many things in Sierra Leone, these efforts are hobbled by a lack of adequate resources allocated to support them. The knowledgeable director, Joseph Dumbuya, can lead personalised tours with a bit of advance notice.

ST JOHN'S MAROON CHURCH [144 C4] (*Siaka Stevens St; ⏲ dawn–dusk daily; free entry but contributions welcome*) The Maroon Church is not the oldest church in Freetown – that honour belongs to the 1809 St Charles Church in Regent – but it is arguably the most celebrated. Built about 1820, its whitewashed walls and modest size give the feel of a pretty parish church, totally out of keeping with the noisy streets and high-rise buildings that encircle it. History is literally built into the walls; the timbers for the roof, and two surviving pews, come from the ships that brought the first group of Maroons from their mountain hideouts in Jamaica to Sierra Leone. Choir practice takes place on Tuesdays and Thursdays at 18.30, and the church is a perfect place to escape the grind of central Freetown for some quiet contemplation. Services are throughout the day on Sunday and occasionally on Wednesday evenings, and newcomers are warmly welcomed.

VICTORIA PARK [145 E4] (*Bounded by Charlotte St, Garrison St, Rokel St & Circular Rd;* ⏰ *dawn–dusk daily; free entry*) Founded with great fanfare in 1887 to celebrate Queen Victoria's birthday and mark the centenary of Freetown's existence, Victoria Park is just about the last bit of green space in central Freetown, and after a morning spent negotiating the streets and moneychange boys, you might be extremely grateful for it. It was being redeveloped into the Freetown Amusement Park (page 165) in 2017, and will be home to a children's playground, wading pool and possibly even a café and bar by the time you read this.

4

Western Area

The Western Peninsula is like Sierra Leone in miniature – the holiday happiness of the ocean breeze, glorious rays, pristine beaches and cosy camp fires; rainforest reserves revealing chimps, rare birds and picnic-perfect waterfalls; the legacy of the coastal West African slave trade; and some of the best-preserved examples of the country's Krio and Sherbro heritage.

On the wooded slopes of the Peninsula interior you can bathe in mountain pools, observe endangered primates close enough for them to biff you on the nose, and hike around the Western Area's threatened forests. As for the coastline, all you have to do is indulge. For 40km. It provokes a little twitch of envy across the whole of West Africa, and visitors have been known to mutter about being in 'tenth heaven' as they set eyes on beach after beach, and dip toes in bathtub-warm water. Once the setting for a *Bounty* advert, these shores really do have a taste of paradise about them: bone-white sands stretching so far it feels like you could wander them forever; wooden boats bobbing on placid waters beneath forest-covered mountains disappearing into the mist; hammocks slung between trees on islands off the coast, perfect for lazy snoozing with only the birds for company; beachside villagers practising fishing and football. Give yourself some time, an appetite for fresh fish, lobster and oysters, and get out there.

THE INTERIOR

The rainforest-clad mountains of the Peninsula rise with unlikely, wild grandeur just moments from a busy capital. Thrown up by a gurgling volcano, the slopes are a unique oddity along West Africa's north Atlantic coastline, and home to part of the Upper Guinea Forest, an acknowledged hive of biodiversity and the only remaining patch of tropical forest in the west of the country. Stretched across a narrow 37km chain of hills, 14km wide, the **Western Area Peninsula Non-Hunting Forest Reserve** is a fast-shrinking treasure, however. Logging, bush burning, charcoal collection, hunting and new housing are all putting this 17,928ha patch of wildlife in peril, and the newly surfaced mountain road (page 185) and soon-to-be-completed Peninsula highway have only accelerated this process. The bare slopes on the edge of Freetown put the capital at increased risk of flooding, as rainwater, unclogged by leaf canopy, roots and undergrowth, barrels down the hillsides into the capital and deluges the low-lying slums at the water's edge. More hopefully, the reserve was proclaimed a national park in 2013, but the declaration was still awaiting parliamentary ratification at the time of writing in 2017.

What forest is still standing is well worth exploring, criss-crossed with paths linking up the hillside villages (pages 186–7), picking their way through small settlements amid the waterfalls. Literal high points include **Picket Hill** (888m) in the south and the fairytale-turned-furious **Sugar Loaf Mountain** (760m), site of the

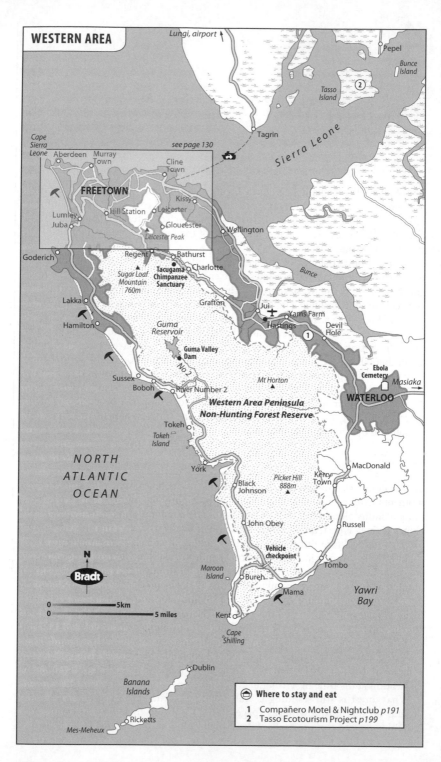

WESTERN AREA

Lungi, airport

Pepel

Bunce Island

②

Tasso Island

Tagrin

Sierra Leone

Cape Sierra Leone

Aberdeen Murray Town

Cline Town

see page 130

FREETOWN

Kissy

Lumley Juba

Hill Station

Leicester

Gloucester

Leicester Peak

Wellington

Bunce

Goderich

Regent

Bathurst

Charlotte

Tacugama Chimpanzee Sanctuary

Sugar Loaf Mountain 760m

Grafton

Jui

Yams Farm

Devil Hole

Lakka

Hamilton

Guma Reservoir

Hastings

①

Guma Valley Dam

No 2

Mt Horton

Western Area Peninsula Non-Hunting Forest Reserve

Ebola Cemetery

Masiaka

WATERLOO

Sussex

Boboh

River Number 2

Tokeh

Tokeh Island

York

NORTH ATLANTIC OCEAN

Black Johnson

Picket Hill 888m

Kerry Town

MacDonald

John Obey

Russell

N

Bradt

Vehicle checkpoint

Tombo

Maroon Island

Bureh

Mama

Yawri Bay

0   5km

0   5 miles

Kent

Cape Shilling

Dublin

Banana Islands

Ricketts

Mes-Meheux

⊖ Where to stay and eat

1 Compañero Motel & Nightclub p191
2 Tasso Ecotourism Project p199

184

catastrophic August 2017 landslide (page 42), in the north. Look out for more than 300 bird species, including the vulnerable white-necked picathartes (*Picathartes gymnocephalus*); the near-endemic Turati's boubou (*Laniarius turatii*); and a large number of other species of the Guinea–Congo forest biome, such as the red-thighed sparrowhawk (*Accipiter erythropus*); ahanta francolin (*Francolinus ahatensis*); green turaco (*Tauraco persus*); naked-faced barbet (*Gymnobucco calvus*); brown-eared woodpecker (*Campethera caroli*); Vieillot's black weaver (*Ploceus nigerrimus*); and red-headed malimbe (*Malimbus rubricollis*). Take plenty of water, a hat, a bit of food and suncream.

THE MOUNTAIN ROAD If you are in the west of Freetown and don't want to have to brave the congestion of the east end, by far the quickest way off the Peninsula to the rest of the country is via the newly surfaced road from Hill Cot roundabout to the main Peninsula road at Jui. It's a breathtaking drive through the swollen green of the Western Area Peninsula Forest, among old Krio wooden-board houses and people 'brooking' (washing) their clothes in rivers bordered by lush vegetable patches. It's now very much the preferred route for heading to and from Freetown's west end.

Getting there and away From the Hill Cot Road junction in the west end of Freetown, the 17km route takes perhaps 30 to 40 minutes in any vehicle, depending on traffic. A tarmac road heads up towards Hill Station; bear left here and continue on to Regent, where the spiffy new tarmac is interrupted by a rather inexplicable stretch of dilapidated one-way roads which reliably slows down your trip, but also offers a good look at some traditional Krio board houses and the diminutive colonial police station wedged between the two roads. The one-way system ends after about 500m and you're then back on tarmac all the way to the main road at Jui, passing the right-hand turn-off for Tacugama Chimpanzee Sanctuary after 1.7km and the new mini hydro-electric dam at Charlotte on the left 1km further on. The road continues through Grafton and eventually arrives at Jui, from where it's a right turn to Waterloo and upcountry, or left to go back into the east end.

There's plenty of poda poda and taxi transport on this route; the easiest place to pick up a vehicle is at Bottom Mango (Le4,500 in a shared taxi), but you should be able to get one from Lumley roundabout as well (Le6,000 in a shared taxi). You'll probably have to change for Waterloo at Jui junction, but occasionally vehicles continue all the way through.

LEICESTER PEAK Bristling with radio antennae, the hill nevertheless manages a certain majesty. A spate of lavish and unfinished building work blights the land around, however. Many houses are built in a start–stop manner with little in the way of planning to regulate their size, location or taste – look out for roofless Neoclassical columns stuck randomly on to porches, swathes of bare concrete, and dire efforts at showiness. This den for the new rich, both local and expat, sounds the death knell for the forest.

Leading the charge is the imposing US embassy, sat on one side of Leicester Peak. With acres of marble, super-cool air-conditioning and a stern façade, this is still apparently the 'small' size template for US embassy design. The British-led International Military and Training Team (IMATT) base is next door, protected by speed bumps, concrete and serious gates. This is a good jumping-off point for hill scrambling, and numerous back paths link to old Krio villages.

KRIO VILLAGES With names like Regent, Gloucester, Leicester, Wellington, Newton and Bathurst, this is the cradle of anglophile Christian Krios who settled as receptives among the hills, housed by missionaries keen to make the ideology of Freetown work amid the hardships of starting up in so foreign and often unforgiving an environment. This area is home to Africa's oldest stone church, **St Charles**, at **Regent**, built in 1809 just after Sierra Leone became a Crown Colony, and named after Charles MacCarthy, who became governor in 1816 and supported educational and Christianising efforts. Described by Canon Williams in the 1930s as 'the Mount Zion of Sierra Leone' the church still stands proud on top of a hill, finally finished in 1816 and renovated several times since, including after the civil war. It marked the completion of the first flurry of missionary spirit – under Reverend Johnson, the first English missionary from the Church Missionary Society (CMS) to inhabit the mountain villages, its congregation grew from nine into the hundreds. By 1825, 1,079 of 2,000 villagers were receiving religious instruction.

Villages tended to contain certain ethnic groups (Regent, for example, was at first home to Ibo, Bulom and Susu peoples). The returnees were given clothes and enough rations for half a year. But creating the hilltop villages from scratch, hidden in the dense forest, exhausted many. Freedom it might have been, but conditions were tough in the heat, amid illness and the pouring rains. Even erstwhile missionaries were disheartened. The CMS sent out 70 adult Europeans from 1804 onwards; by 1824, 38 had died and the bill had come to £70,000.

The bucolic idyll was shattered on reaching the village of **Leicester**, the first village for receptives, mostly Wolof and Bambara: 'On my coming there, my heart was almost broke,' recorded Reverend Henry During, who was appalled by the illness and suffering he found. In the end, conditions were so tough that it proved too difficult to recruit European missionaries, and the CMS went for Africans instead.

From Regent you can walk through more Krio villages to reach **Charlotte Falls** (now home to a small hydro-electric dam) or climb **Sugar Loaf Mountain**, among the highest points on the Peninsula and site of the devastating August 2017 mudslide (page 42). When During got to **Gloucester Town** in 1816 with the CMS, it was a far cry from the home he left behind in Hannover. 'I had to cut my way through in many places before I arrived on the spot fixed upon,' he wrote in his journal. What he found was 107 people who had been rescued from the chains of the slave trader, only to be sent into the forest with a European who left just as soon as he could on During's arrival. Everything leaked, so During put up a second mini roof above his bed, since the real roof did little to stop the rain.

Yet by 1817, Gloucester had a rice store, more ground had been cleared, and the village had its first masons, all labouring for God's glory due to During's evangelic influence. The result – **St Andrew's Church**, still here today – was begun in 1818 and opened in 1820, a huge undertaking given its site and scale, its two galleries stretching the length of the building, enough to fit 1,500 people. The settlement quickly became an early centre of Krio development and education: one of Gloucester's high-achieving sons was James Africanus Beale Horton, the first African graduate of Edinburgh University and a founder of African nationalism, born to an Ibo receptive family who settled in the village.

Most receptives in the colony were Yoruba, enslaved after the Owu war of 1821 and known as 'Aku', derived from their word for greeting. They quickly gained a reputation. 'From their frugal and industrious habits, the Akoos are called the African Jews,' wrote Robert Clarke, a doctor's assistant and colonial surgeon, in 1843. 'They club together their money to purchase European commodities, which they most perseveringly hawk about the streets of Freetown and in the villages.'

An old highway runs between Gloucester and Regent, a nice easy walk with good views, passing Gloucester Orphanage on the right, and vegetable patches as the route slopes further southwards towards Regent itself.

TACUGAMA CHIMPANZEE SANCTUARY Often cruelly or ignorantly kept as pets, sometimes hunted for their meat, and once upon a time exported in droves for medical testing in Europe and elsewhere, Sierra Leone's chimpanzees have dwindled to alarmingly low levels. In the early 1970s the country was home to an estimated 20,000 wild chimps; a countrywide survey that was concluded in 2010 suggested there were roughly 5,500 left, and the next census is scheduled for 2018.

It is illegal to possess, capture, kill or keep chimps as pets, but the sorry tales on offer at Tacugama Chimpanzee Sanctuary, named after an anglicised version of *tacuama* – Mende for a small local fish found nearby – show the rules are regularly ignored. One resident of the sanctuary, Christo, was kept by a welder and made to labour in his workshop; another, Solo, was forced to perform with a dance troupe as a tourist attraction. Others, kept as pets when small and sweet, were later chained and drugged with Valium as they grew strong and uncontrollable. Even the ex-president's son kept one, Jido, until he was persuaded to deliver the chimp to the sanctuary.

Today about 80 primates find safe haven at Tacugama, swinging from branches, hooting with happiness, throwing things at passers-by with the petulance of children, nuzzling each other with the tenderness of mothers attending to newborns, and picking bugs out of each other's fur with the attention of Madonna's manicurist. Even the least animal-friendly of visitors gets sucked into the magic within moments.

There are plenty of other living things on offer should further diversion be required – more than 125 bird species have been identified in and around the Tacugama Forest Reserve, and guided birding tours taking in the surrounding forests and the nearby Congo Dam are now available to visitors.

Playpen moments Chimps share 98.6% of their DNA with *Homo sapiens*, and spending time with them it is almost impossible not to recognise echoes of human emotions and feelings. Much of their behaviour appears readily understandable, particularly their calls and expressions, which are explained by a signboard at the camp entrance, so you can experiment talking chimp.

Each resident has his or her own character. Joke is particularly fond of lobbing stones at onlookers; Augusta proved almost impossible to get on with; one-year-old Chica cried in despair until she became more familiar with the place and started hanging out in her hammock. But that 1.4% difference in DNA counts for an enormous amount. 'Make no mistake: these are wild animals,' says guide Willie Tucker, which is why adult chimps are only glimpsed from behind sturdy, electrically fenced enclosures.

Each new arrival is first quarantined for three months, then later painstakingly introduced to peers until finally it joins one of the groups thought most suitable for its temperament and those of existing other members. Beside one of the biggest group enclosures is a great viewing platform perched up a tree.

Arranging a visit The sanctuary is reached by a right-hand turn-off 1.7km beyond Regent, after which it's a further 1.5km uphill from the mountain road; all but the last 100m are rough but suitable for any vehicle. Scheduled tours take place twice daily at 10.30 and 16.00, lasting about 90 minutes (m *044 625 107, 044 625 113, 076 611 211;* e *info@tacugama.com;* w *tacugama.com; adult US$15, child*

BRUNO AND BALA

The Tacugama Sanctuary story started in 1988, when husband and wife Bala and Sharmila Amarasekaran found a tiny, scared bundle of hair and big eyes for sale on a roadside 240km north of Freetown. Hearts melted by the sight of the weak baby chimp, they bought him for US$30 and, knowing that Frank Bruno was due to box Mike Tyson that night, named the furry little mite Bruno. It might have seemed a misnomer back then; years later as a 65kg alpha male, five-times stronger than a grown human, Bruno was nothing if not heavyweight.

Their interest piqued by their new charge, throughout the course of the next year the couple discovered a further 55 pet chimps in Freetown alone, and grew increasingly aware of the trade in baby chimpanzees all over the country. Expatriates seduced by their initial cuteness would soon realise that young chimps quickly grow up (about 90% of the chimps are confiscated from expats), and the Amarasekarans's second animal, Julie – who became a life-long friend for Bruno – was rescued from a Scottish woman who didn't know what to do with her.

News soon spread that there was a couple in Freetown helping chimps. By 1993, they had seven in cages in their compound, so they started thinking about creating a more permanent home for them. After rounds of meeting the Department of Forestry allocated 40ha of prime rainforest for a sanctuary, intended originally as a halfway house for chimps rescued from human mistreatment to ready themselves for a return to the wild (although none has yet been released); the EU office released the initial funding to set up the sanctuary, which opened in 1995.

Amarasekaran swapped the suit and tie of his 15-year accountancy job for the khaki shorts of a full-time naturalist, as he took over running the sanctuary. A sizeable portion of his local IT business profits still goes to help fund the cash-strapped venture, which permanently suffers from a funding shortfall.

'You would do the same, once you've spent some time with these guys,' he says. After years of interacting and observing their behaviour he can mimic chimp calls and gestures precisely, and seems to have an instinctive understanding of their moods and body language.

WARTIME During the war, the sanctuary was overrun twice, each time looted from top to bottom. The workers and the chimps were left alive, mainly, Amarasekaran thinks, because the 'sobels' – soldiers-turned-rebels – in the area knew something of the sanctuary's mission and work, and managed to convince the rebels to spare them. Still, the lack of medicines – stolen during looting – meant that five primates died of illness. Things became so desperate that Amarasekaran turned looter himself, breaking into a pharmacy in Freetown to get hold of essential drugs to treat the deteriorating chimps. The war took its psychological toll too: one resident, Little

US$5; Sierra Leonean nationals: adult Le30,000, child Le10,000). Your guide is likely to be either Moses Kapia or supervisor Willie Tucker, both chimp-lovers and good talkers with an expert knowledge; ask every question you can think of. The '**birds and breakfast**' tours require advance booking; they set out at dawn and cost US$30 per person, or US$10 if you're staying over at the lodge. They also now put on a monthly **yoga retreat** – see their website for dates and details.

Where to stay and eat Six simple but elegant lodges offer accommodation for the night amid the green forest canopy and calls of the chimps all around. All lodges

Boy, was so traumatised he starting pulling out his fur, chewing up his own fingers, and rocking back and forth in his enclosure. He died not long afterwards.

BREAKOUT In 2006, a group of 31 chimpanzees managed to escape from their enclosure, including alpha male Bruno.

Western chimpanzees are the only non-human primates that make and use tools: true to form, the chimps had worked out how to wedge open a trapdoor with sticks that separated their outdoor enclosure from their sleeping quarters. The timing was perfect: they sprung the connecting door while their cages were being mucked out, surprising a cleaner who fled without closing the main door, giving them access to the outside world.

The escape ended in tragedy when, later the same morning, a local taxi driver, on the roads near the sanctuary, stumbled into their midst and was killed by the agitated chimps, who had become unsettled by their unfamiliar surroundings following the breakout. A taxi passenger lost a finger and two more escaped back down the hill.

Although about half of the escapees came back of their own accord after a fortnight, lured by food left out around the sanctuary, others ventured further afield and have proved more difficult to track down. One, Philip, was recaptured with sedation darts in Kent at the bottom of the Peninsula, more than 30km away.

Bruno has never come back, and for a long time Amarasekeran couldn't see the point of carrying on without the sanctuary's first chimpanzee.

'I always say Bruno is the founder of this place,' he says. 'I just didn't think we would ever open again.'

Eventually, mindful of the welfare of the other chimps, he set about a revamp. The park has tightened up its safety measures: a two-door 'airlock' now separates their outdoor roaming area and sleeping quarters and there are four security posts equipped with radios located in the sanctuary that visitors can flee to in case of another escape.

In his continued absence, Bruno has become a cult figure on the Peninsula. Some claim to have his telephone number; others to have 'met' him. There was even a running joke among political cynics that the then vice president Solomon Berewa, who contested presidential elections in 2007, would call on Bruno as his running mate in the absence of any other convincing candidate.

Amarasekaran says he hears Bruno calling from the wild from time to time, and knows he's OK. With or without its most famous resident, the work of the sanctuary will go on. More of Bruno and Bala's story has now been charmingly commemorated in an illustrated children's novel, *King Bruno*, available at the Tacugama Sanctuary or w kingbruno.com.

come equipped with linens and mosquito nets and include toilets and showers en suite. Generous meals are available with advance arrangement at US$15 per person, or you can self-cater using the shared kitchen; beer, wine, water and soft drinks are also available for purchase. Lit by solar lamps and candles at night, the lodges combine atmosphere with comfort to rank among the country's most special and secluded stays.

The two original lodges – thatch huts named Julie and Bruno after a couple of the sanctuary's earliest residents – are the first you'll encounter on the short path from the parking area. There's a double bed within each hut's warm yellow walls, plus a sweet little private eating/lounging area outdoors. Further down the trail, you'll come to Christo, a two-bedroom, two-storey structure whose balcony offers a view into the forest canopy. An indoor dining area and a small but nicely equipped kitchen make for easy cooking. Nearby, Augusta is a roomy one-bedroom tree house that also has indoor cooking and dining facilities. Two new houses opened in 2017: Lucy and Phillip; both have loft bedrooms sleeping two and lounge/kitchen areas downstairs, with balconies overlooking the canopy. All use solar lights.

A night in either Julie or Bruno costs US$90; the charge for Augusta is US$140; it's US$150 for Lucy or Phillip, and for Christo it's US$180. All prices include breakfast and a chimp tour, either on the afternoon of your arrival or the following morning, and a 20% discount is offered during rainy season.

What to buy A gift store sells several fascinating books and documentaries in which Tacugama stars, including a rather pulpy account of the breakout, *Rogue Predators* and Paul Glynn's illustrated children's novel *King Bruno* (see box, pages 188–9), as well as the BBC's thoughtful documentary *Wildlife in a Warzone*, which assesses the impact of the war on wildlife in the country, and *Chimps under Fire*, about how the sanctuary kept going during the war. *National Geographic* was filming a new documentary here in 2017. Also on offer are cold drinks and crisps, as well as batiks, T-shirts, jewellery, wooden masks, postcards and other memorabilia, the profits of which go to sustain the work of the sanctuary. If you get really hooked, you can sponsor a chimp, from US$80 a year; the sanctuary will be grateful. And if you get *really* hooked, a variety of two–three-month volunteer positions at the sanctuary are also available.

Walks A series of walks set off from Tacugama into surrounding hills and villages, kindly marked up by a walking enthusiast. Minutes away, and a good start, is the Congo reservoir and dam set amid the forest. A small map of the nearby trails is available for purchase in the gift shop for Le5,000.

CHARLOTTE FALLS One of the Peninsula's most popular day-trip getaways, perfect for a picnic lunch and a dip when you've had enough of the beach, is Charlotte Falls. The falls drop suitably furious water into a primary pool, flanked by thick vegetation, which links to another lower pool that is deep enough to swim in. For the daredevil, the rainy season turns the smooth, moss-covered rocks that link these two pools into a perfect natural water slide. Drastic changes are afoot, however, as a 2.2MW mini hydro-electric dam, set to provide power to Regent, Grafton and other communities along the mountain road, is scheduled to come online here in 2018. Thus, the visiting practicalities below may well have changed drastically by the time you read this.

Other mountain village waterfalls nearby include **Bathurst Falls** in Bathurst village, and **Baptist Falls**.

Getting there and away Look out for the first signboard to your left after you've passed the turning for the Tacugama Chimpanzee Sanctuary on your right: it isn't signed to the falls, but nevertheless take this left fork in the road that winds down to the village of Charlotte, set amid the forest trees. A brightly painted house at the start of the village, on the left, with an unusually eclectic garden, is the spot to pay Sarah Wilson or her son, the head man, your Le10,000 entry fee for the falls and find a guide; follow your guide through the undergrowth, cross a small river that comes up to ankle level, and you're beside the deep pool at the bottom of the falls. Tip your guide more than the entry fee. Again, with the completion of the micro-hydro dam, visiting practicalities and even water levels here may be entirely changed, but it's a scenic spot nonetheless. Let us know how your visit went at **w** bradtupdates.com/sierraleone.

GRAFTON Just as the Peninsula became a haven for freed slaves in the early 19th century, the war and post-war years saw it turn into a refuge for those desperate to flee the fighting. The Western Area saw a huge influx of terrified villagers; 163,077 internally displaced people in August 1999 swelled to 331,987 two months later. Grafton was home to one of 12 hastily constructed official camps for them on the Peninsula. Even today a handful of homes made from the instantly recognisable regulation blue UN tarpaulins are still visible from the road, along with a series of more permanent concrete homes built to rehouse people long-term, a camp for amputees and war-wounded, and perhaps most surprising of all, a planned gated community to be built by upmarket Ghanaian developers Regimanuel Gray. All of the post-war dwellings are filled with people to this day. Roads bear names such as Reconciliation Drive, but in the Grafton Amputee and War-Wounded Camp, the indignities not only of the past but also of the present still persist. The deputy chairwoman, whose legs were cut off in an attack in a Freetown street, says politicians have long forgotten the amputees' plight, leaving most of them with the only option of going into town to beg on Fridays, hoping to make the most of local generosity on the holiest day of the Muslim week.

HASTINGS The first town you encounter south of Jui junction, where the mountain and Peninsula roads meet, Hastings begins just after the China–Sierra Leone Friendship Hospital, and is mostly of note for its airstrip, which was an important base for UNAMSIL forces during the war. Today it's occasionally used for charter flights by Versatile Air Services (**m** *079 478 483;* **e** *info@versatileairservices.com;* **w** *versatileairservices.com*); contact the Sierra Leone Civil Aviation Authority (SLCAA) (**m** *076 645 138;* **e** *info@slcaa.net;* **w** *slcaa.net*) for general aviation enquiries. Hastings was also a stop on the Sierra Leone Railway, and the ruined former station is visible on your right as you head towards Waterloo. At the time of writing in mid 2017, the dual carriageway expansion of the Freetown–Masiaka road had reached as far as Yams Farm, 3km beyond Hastings.

 **Where to stay and eat** *Map, page 184*

Compañero Motel & Nightclub (29 rooms) 1 David St, Rokel; **m** 076 879 367, 076 836 964, 077 590 467; **e** efsesay@gmail.com, companeromotel@hotmail.co.uk. If you're in need of a place to stay on your way to or from the capital, keep an eye out for a yellow building on the main road between Hastings & Waterloo (it will be on your right as you head away from Freetown). The place may feel a bit soulless, but with its AC rooms & 24hr electricity, Compañero offers a level of comfort that's unmatched in this part of the Peninsula. A nightclub next door attracts a mixed crowd. B/fast is included with a night's stay; you can also pay by the hour. **$$$$**

WATERLOO From the heart of Freetown's east end at Kissy, a new and perpetually busy tarmac dual-carriageway leads towards Waterloo, a suburb of the city and the first point at which you feel safely assured of leaving the big smoke behind. The dual carriageway is slated to stretch all the way to Masiaka by 2020, with tolls to be collected at three points along the way. Waterloo's streets remain a throng of roadside crates of vegetables, crates of beer piled improbably high, honking poda podas and careering trucks, plastic goods toppling over each other and, at night, trading lit by mobile-phone torches and solar lamps.

The 60,000-strong town owes its name to the 1812 Battle of Waterloo, because of the West India Regiment soldiers from Jamaica and Barbados who fought in it and later ended up, through various twists of fate, just outside Sierra Leone's capital and assimilated into the Krio community that grew up here. The villages of Wellington and Hastings also owe their names to black soldiers who fought for the British in the long slog against the French between 1793 and 1815, and who were pensioned off following the peace to find a home to the east of Freetown. After 1816, Governor MacCarthy negotiated land rights with local chiefs for all these villages.

When, in 1843, a riot between Aku and Ibo receptives from Nigeria caused havoc, it was resolved by joining together what became known as the Seventeen Nations of the receptives, which went on to supervise affairs and disputes and try to find a link among their varying ethnic and cultural backgrounds.

Nowadays, the real joy of any pit stop here on your way out to the provinces is a chance to sample the surprising delights of **cassava bread**. Beyond the police post and the petrol station, street traders with covered bowls sell these small, flat and grainy discs, peppered with a tongue-lashing spicy paste, in batches of ten for Le2,000. Add a portion of smoked fish (anything up to Le10,000 a fish, depending on size and season) to complete a rather extraordinary taste explosion and put your stomach in the right kind of mood for the journey ahead.

Getting there and away From Freetown's west end, pick up a taxi or poda poda at Bottom Mango (Le4,500 in a shared taxi) or Lumley roundabout (Le6,000 in a shared taxi). These take the mountain road to Jui junction, where you'll likely have to change vehicles for Waterloo (another Le1,500), though some go all the way through. From the east side, poda podas crawl to Waterloo through Freetown's traffic-drenched streets from Bombay Street near the Eastern Police Clock Tower for Le3,000. On the way, you pass the Coca-Cola signboards that proudly lay claim to every village and town here, among them the delectably named **Devil Hole** (a too-good-to-miss photo opportunity). From Waterloo, you can follow the soon-to-be dual-carriageway tarmac out east towards Masiaka and the provinces (passing the proposed new airport site at Mamamah), or branch right on another good tarmac road towards the beaches. The junction is 200m after you pass FiBank, directly before the main strip of town takes over.

🏠 **Where to stay and eat** *Map, page 193*
Aside from Waterloo's famous cassava bread and the delicious meals served at Ategbeh Garden, your options are more or less limited to street stalls and a handful of basic eating-houses along the main highway, of which **Whatsapp Restaurant**, just opposite the EcoBank, comes recommended.

❋ 🏠 **Ategbeh Garden** (2 rooms) Campbell Town Rd; m 078 870119, (+44) 7974 829285 (UK); w ategbehgarden.co.uk; ⊕ Oct–May. Run by a musical British–Sierra Leonean couple, this happy village homestead makes an entirely unexpected & thoroughly welcome getaway in Waterloo. With 2 breezy standalone cottages in the green gardens backing up on to neighbouring farm fields, it's an impressively rural-feeling idyll so close to the chaos of central Waterloo. Rooms are en suite, with wood floors, hammocks, private terraces & generator power in the evenings. Good local meals (with veg options) are available at Le60,000 a pop, & all manner of music & drumming lessons can be arranged, alongside cultural tours of the surrounding villages & beyond. **$$$**

Other practicalities There's an **Ecobank** with ATM on the road towards Masiaka, 600m beyond the main junction, or a **FiBank** offering Western Union transfers 200m before the main junction as you enter town.

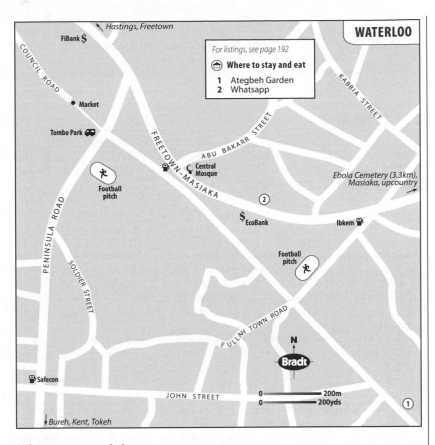

For listings, see page 192

🍴 **Where to stay and eat**
1   Ategbeh Garden
2   Whatsapp

Hastings, Freetown

FiBank $

COUNCIL ROAD

• Market

Tombo Park 🚌

Football pitch 🏃

PENINSULA ROAD

SOLDIER STREET

FREETOWN–MASIAKA

🕌 (Central Mosque

ABU BAKARR STREET

KABBIA STREET

Ebola Cemetery (3.3km), Masiaka, upcountry →

②

$ EcoBank

Ibkem 🛒

Football pitch 🏃

FULLAH TOWN ROAD

N

Bradt

🛒 Safecon

JOHN STREET

0 ————— 200m
0 ————— 200yds

①

↓ Bureh, Kent, Tokeh

What to see and do Waterloo's Paloko Road Cemetery, best known simply as the **Ebola Cemetery** (✛ *8.348187, -13.054150*), stretches over 3.5ha on the outskirts of town and holds more than 10,000 graves. It was opened in 2014 as Freetown's King Tom Cemetery (page 179) and quickly became overwhelmed by the numbers of dead requiring burial – sometimes many dozens per day – at the height of the crisis. As a precautionary measure, all burials, whether Ebola-related or not, were directed to these cemeteries during the epidemic, and 9,718 people were buried here between October 2014 and 2015 alone. The burial dates on each headstone and numerous graves marked simply 'known unto God' attest to the shocking scale and speed of the tragedy, and the silent, identical markers stretching out in all directions are a difficult and moving monument to a profoundly sad and frightening time.

While the vast majority of the graves are identical, many families have upgraded and decorated the graves of their loved ones with portraits and paeans dedicated to the deceased. One inscription notes not only the date, but the day of the week and time of day at which a widower lost his wife. The monumental anguish and epochal sense of loss felt here can be overwhelming, so allow yourself plenty of time to take it all in. The graves are set along an attractive hillside, and the mood is appropriately quiet and contemplative. The cemetery was cruelly and unexpectedly pressed in to service once again after the Sugar Loaf Mountain mudslide (page 42), and more than 300 victims were buried here over two days in August 2017.

To get here, turn left on to an unsurfaced road towards Bolima Primary School, 2.2km east of the junction with the Peninsula Road, and continue straight for just over 2km. The cemetery is just beyond the Jopor Farm and Koroma Community School. There's officially no charge, but it would be appropriate to tip the welcoming caretakers Le10,000.

BUNCE ISLAND

Vines clutch at the decaying stone bricks of the ruined fort, crevices widen, time passes. But while the plants inexorably reclaim the brickwork, Bunce Island's past – which makes it arguably the single most important former slave site for African Americans today – is going nowhere.

In 140-odd years of operation, from 1668 until 1807, British slave traders purchased, imprisoned, and loaded up an estimated 50,000 slaves at this fort, located in the Sierra Leone River. Stolen from their villages, branded on the chest with red-hot irons, slaves from Bunce Island were primarily packed off to the fast-growing rice plantations of the New World. An estimated 15% died on the transatlantic crossing – sharks followed the boats throughout the passage to America, hopeful for their share of a wretched human cargo. One English traveller who boarded a Sierra Leone slave ship in the 1770s spoke of 'two or three slaves thrown overboard every day dying of fever flux, measles, worms all together'.

Those who made it would be parcelled up and delivered as chattals – 'a choice cargo of about 250 fine health negroes,' proclaimed one 1760 South Carolina slave auction advert of a new catch from 'Bance-Island'. Other slave ship destinations included Georgia, New York, Connecticut, Rhode Island and Massachusetts.

AFRICAN AMERICAN ROOTS Ghana's Elmina Fort, along with the 40 or so others that line the coast of West Africa from Mauritania to Benin might be better known, but most of these slave castles provided labour for central and southern America. Bunce had a particularly close, and highly localised, relationship with North America, as a key supplier of rice planters to South Carolina and Georgia. The ancestors of those slaves form the backbone of the homogenous and close-knit Gullah community, which lives along the tropical coastline of those two US states, on the edge of creeks and mangrove swamps that resemble Sierra Leone. The community's language, also called Gullah, is very similar to Krio and includes a sprinkling of words from several Sierra Leonean languages, namely Mende and Vai (see box, opposite). One Salone minister called Bunce 'a little piece of Africa that was destroyed to build America.'

Visit Bunce today and it is sorely in need of preservation, with nothing in the way of explanation, but the powerful history of the island is hard to ignore. For many, the experience of stepping among its crumbling walls amid an eerie silence, having to imagine how it might have been, is harrowing enough to stay with them forever.

'I am an American … But today, I am something more … I am an African too … I feel my roots here in this continent,' said former US Secretary of State Colin Powell, after visiting in 1992.

Because of the almost exclusive role it played in supplying slaves to the US, for any American looking for a family link back to Africa there is a chance that Bunce Island and its awful past may well figure.

'Bunce is arguably the most important historic site in Africa for the United States. There are probably tens of thousands of African Americans trying to trace

'The African American populace … have been robbed of their identity,' says Amadu Massally, a US-based Sierra Leonean who is setting up a company called Fambul Tik Tours (w *fambultik.com*; f *heritagetourists*) to start slave-history and legacy trips to Bunce Island and other heritage sites in Africa and the Caribbean. 'Unlike native-born Africans, slavery is the essence of the African American. Linking to their ancestry will bring that sense of belonging.'

So far there have been three celebrated 'homecomings' in Sierra Leone, where Americans have returned to the country of their ancestors, in 1989, 1997 and 2005.

Aware of the Gullah connection, then-president Joseph Momoh visited the community in 1988, ate their food, saw their fanner baskets and heard their stories. The return trip the next year caused a media sensation as 14 Gullah people from South Carolina came on the official 'Gullah Homecoming', mirroring the journey made by the Amistad recaptives (see box, pages 218–19). The film *Family Across The Sea* depicts their moving journey (streaming at w folkstreams.net/film,166).

Then, in 1990, historian Joseph Opala found Mary Moran, an elderly Gullah woman whose family had preserved an ancient five-line funeral hymn in the Mende language of Sierra Leone. Moran's own homecoming took place in 1997; she visited the Mende village where the song her grandmother taught her is still sung, and made a tearful journey to Bunce Island.

In May 2005, a 250-year-old paper trail of well-preserved slave records led Thomalind Polite, a 32-year-old teacher from South Carolina, to track down her seventh-generation grandmother, Priscilla, to a ship that left Bunce Island in 1756. Priscilla was ten years old at the time.

'I felt like I was coming home,' said Polite, after she made the trip to Priscilla's village. 'I stepped off the plane and saw people who looked just like me.'

Another stunning ancestral link was similarly discovered when Australian academic Emma Christopher spent two years playing songs sung in a then-unknown language by Cuba's Gangá-Longobá people in villages around southern Sierra Leone, eventually discovering their source and language (Banta) in the village of Mokpanguma in a remote corner of Moyamba District. The subsequent Cuban-Salonean reunion in Mokpanguma is the subject of the 2014 film, *They Are We* (w theyarewe.com).

Extraordinarily, the reunions keep coming. On the Caribbean island of Carriacou, a group of islanders have long identified themselves as Temne, and they preserve several traditional songs and ceremonies with roots in Sierra Leone, performing them as part of the island's 'big drum' dance tradition. In 2016, a Sierra Leonean government delegation visited the Grenadian island to cement this connection, and John Angus Martin, Joseph Opala and Cynthia Schmidt published a history, *The Temne Nation of Carriacou*, in the same year. Carriacou's Temne plan to visit Sierra Leone soon (w africonnections.com).

their roots to Sierra Leone right now,' says American historian Joseph Opala, who has worked for 45 years on the links between American descendants of slaves and their West African origins. 'Sierra Leone is the most frequent result for DNA tests in the US.'

HISTORY The island was named after Captain John Bence, a wealthy London merchant and slave castle investor. Since then it slowly morphed – from Bence to Bense to (presumably in a fit of kingly devotion) George's Island, then Bance Island, and finally, today's Bunce Island.

Four London-based companies masterminded the operation in human cargo at different points – Gambia Adventures (1670–78) and the Royal African Company of England (1678–1728), both state backed; and later the more commercially minded Grant, Oswald & Sargent (1748–84) and the Company of John & Alexander Anderson (1784–1807), under whom the volume of slave trading increased.

Bunce became one of the most lucrative slave-trading operations on the West African coast: while most castles relied on government subsidies, Bunce proved profitable as a private concern.

Local tribes were complicit in the trade too. British traders leased the island from an African king on the north side of the harbour, Bai Sama, paying rent and taxes on their human export. In the late 1700s, the operation involved more than 600 African workers. African traders – generally the Fula, Mandingo and Susu – sold men, women and children into bondage in return for guns, gunpowder, cloth, swords, axes, knives, rum, wine, brandy, cider, beer, trinkets and clay tobacco pipes, taking hours to haggle over every item, and sealing each deal with a bonus (*boonyar*) of rum or glass beads. Gold, ivory, beeswax, cowhides, camwood and African sandalwood also changed hands at the fort.

French naval forces attacked the island four times, in 1695, 1704, 1779 and 1794, while pirates looted twice, in 1719 and 1720 (see box, opposite). Frequently plundered and burnt to the ground, Bunce always rose from the ashes to carry on its trade.

Etchings from the time give it an almost elegant sort of air (an original watercolour of the castle by Joseph Corry, painted in 1805, hangs in Britain's National Maritime Museum). But while the slave traders played golf assisted by caddies in woollen tartan loincloths, the slaves fought among each other for grains of rice. 'Involuntarily I strolled to one of the windows a little before dinner, without the smallest suspicion of what I was to see – Judge then what my astonishment and feelings were, at the sight of between two and three hundred wretched victims, chained and [parcelled] out in circles, just satisfying the cravings of nature from a trough of rice placed in the centre of each circle,' wrote Anna Maria Falconbridge, who dined on the island in 1791.

A British Union Jack swayed in the breeze over the crenellations, generous trees bloomed. The handsome two-storey Georgian house with its false fireplace hosted lavish upstairs dinner parties before guests repaired to an elegant formal garden. Behind the garden walls, men, women and children lived and died in their own waste, crammed like animals into an open-air slave prison.

The merchants who ran Bunce petitioned parliament not to abolish the slave trade, a battle they finally lost in 1807. In order to continue making money, they tried unsuccessfully to sell the island to the Crown Colony, and failed to establish a cotton plantation there. In 1809, the now-unemployed African workforce rioted, stopped only by troops sent in by boat from Freetown. Bunce later became a sawmill, to no commercial success, before being abandoned in 1840.

CONSERVATION EFFORTS More than 100 years later Bunce was made an officially protected historic site – Sierra Leone's first – in 1948. While nature dilapidates the ruins, a model replica sits in the National Museum, made by Sierra Leone historian Dr M C F Easmon in the 1940s.

Bunce Island was never guarded well enough to escape attack from pirates, who came in 1719 and again in 1720, during 'the Golden Age of Piracy'. Bartholomew Roberts, known as Black Bart, launched the 1720 attack. The most notorious pirate of his time, his own boat's ensign had him standing on top of two human skulls.

So when Bart descended on Bunce and hailed the chief agent from his ship to tell him he would stay away if the castle handed over its gold dust, cannonballs and gunpowder, he was more than surprised to be greeted with a resolute 'no'. In return for such insolence, he ordered a few cannonballs of his own into the castle walls. Black Bart's men managed to get to shore and capture the agent, who was still busily returning fire to men who were no longer within his sights. Furious, Black Bart, his pride wounded, wanted to decapitate him, but the agent had other ideas. He swore back at the pirate so colourfully and violently that the pirate crew intervened on his behalf, saying anyone who could out-curse Black Bart deserved to keep breathing. Royal Africa Company records corroborate that Bunce Island's chief agent indeed saved his life by 'mere dint of swearing and damning'.

Decades later, when US actor Isaiah Washington (famous for his long-running role in the medical soap *Grey's Anatomy*) stepped on to the island, one look at the decrepit architecture made him realise the island needed to be recreated. His gift of US$25,000 is helping historian Joseph Opala and interior designer Gary Chatelain engineer a 3D computer version of how the fort looked, and what conditions were like in 1805, drawing on archaeological studies and historical documents.

'Unlike the Jewish Holocaust and other terrible crimes of the modern era, the Atlantic slave trade took place before the advent of photography, and thus we can only imagine its horrors,' says Opala. 'Our computer animation will allow us to go beyond the imagination and actually see how the Atlantic slave trade was carried out.'

The animation work was intended to be just one part of a multi-year, US$5 million effort – funded by an anonymous donor – to preserve what's left on the island and to educate visitors about Bunce's grisly past. Unfortunately, irreconcilable differences on how best to protect the site meant the relationship with the donor collapsed long before anything close to US$5 million was spent. The donation did, however, allow several studies on the stabilisation and preservation of the island and its structures to go forward. Today, priority one is to stabilise the existing ruins against erosion, as for years these have been slowly but steadily crumbling in to the lazy waters of the Sierra Leone River – a trend that seems to have accelerated in recent years. Both 2012 and 2013 saw major building collapses, and some suspect the recent dredging and increased ship traffic to the iron ore port at Pepel may be having a negative effect.

Encouragingly, the island was listed as a tentative UNESCO World Heritage Site in 2012, though the ongoing lack of funding means little has been done to act on the recommendations contained in the recently completed studies. A comprehensive management plan was drawn up in 2016, and in addition to the critical need for a protective seawall and stabilisation of the ruins, further goals include building a museum in Freetown that will explore Bunce's role in the transatlantic slave trade and opening an international research centre on Tasso Island. At the time of writing, it was unclear how and when much of this work might progress. Visit the Sierra Leone-Gullah Heritage Association (w *www.slgha.org, bunce-island.org*) or the Monuments and Relics Commission (w *sierraleoneheritage.org*) for more information.

GETTING THERE AND AWAY Tucked a few miles up the Sierra Leone River, at the limit of navigation for the deep-draft ocean-going ships of days past, a trip to Bunce is a rough, windswept excursion from Freetown. Speedboat is the quickest, simplest and therefore most expensive option. **Visit Sierra Leone** (m *076 258 258;* w *visitsierraleone.org*) charges US$200 per boat, leaving from Kissi/Government Wharf, for up to ten passengers. It should take about 45 minutes, and it's emphatically worth hiring a guide to accompany you for an additional Le250,000. For less money but more hassle, head down to Kissy Ferry Terminal in the east end and charter a **motorised wooden boat** with a local captain, who can deliver you to Pepel, on the bank of the northern shores, to pick up one of the island's guardians, who can take you across in a leaky dugout canoe, or can join you in your boat. You'll need to make sure the boat will wait for you and take you back, or else you'll be in a bit of a fix. The cheapest charter is a long wooden transport boat – the sort that usually ferries about 80 people a go across towards Lungi – for about US$100. A faster, smaller wooden motor boat might cost US$200–220.

Because costs tend to be high unless you can put a group together, visiting Bunce Island as a solo traveller can be a bit of a challenge, but there are still a few possibilities for a budget-friendly visit to the island, and it's just about possible as a day trip from Freetown with an early enough start. Step one is to catch the **government ferry** (departures at 08.00, 11.00, 14.00, 17.30, 20.00 daily; passengers Le4,000) from Kissi Wharf across to Tagrin, or if you miss the early departure, one of the **small wooden motorboats** that carry people across between ferry trips. These generally carry ten–12 passengers, all with life jackets, for Le15,000 per head; look out for the guys shouting 'speedboat' at the entrance to the government terminal and follow them around the side – with no dock here, prepare to be loaded into the boat atop someone's shoulders! Once across the water in Tagrin, you should be able to find a poda poda or **shared taxi** for the 58km to Pepel (Le20,000). If not, there's a tarmac road all the way to Port Loko (75km; Le30,000), and any vehicle heading there can drop you at the turn-off, after which you'll have to either wait for passing traffic or hire an ocada for the last unsurfaced 14km, following the iron ore train tracks into Pepel. Once in Pepel, you can find a boatman to punt you across, but it's a much better bet to call one of the Bunce Island **caretakers** to arrange a pickup (before you arrive in Pepel, ideally). Spider (m *077 701 091*) or MK (m *077 662 187*) will come to pick you up; expect to pay Le60,000–100,000 for a Pepel–Bunce round trip, factoring in a few litres of fuel and a tip. Once back at Pepel, you can head back the way you came or carry on in a shared taxi to Port Loko (45km; Le25,000) and make your way upcountry. It's also now possible (and affordable) to sleep on nearby Tasso Island (see box, opposite), barely 2km from Bunce, and arrange your visit from here.

WHAT TO SEE AND DO You can't miss the **old building**, now crumbling away, which measures 30m by 9m across two floors. In front were eight **cannons**, marked with the royal emblem of King George III (GR3). Dating back to the end of the 18th century, some lay along the fortification wall and others, still visible, on the beach below. While ships keen to dock would first fire seven guns on arrival, Bunce Island's cannons soon stopped returning the salute after they set fire to the thatch on the island.

The open-air **slave yard** behind the house had one area for men, and a smaller one for women and children connected by a door. There was also a **blacksmith's shop**, **cook house** and an **underground store** for gunpowder magazines, as well as a three-tiered formal garden at the back, the **Orange Walk**, and a village for African workers called **Adam's Town** to the south end. *Bai* (king) Adam was a faithful helper to the slave traders, managing all the freed black slaves. A chief on the mainland who holds his title to this day makes an annual sacrifice in the original Adam's honour. There are also **two cemeteries**, with separate burial grounds for blacks and whites. For the traders, God's love and mercy was all well and good, as long as in heaven the races didn't have to mix.

At the other end of the island, **Devil's Rocks** is still thought by locals to house a powerful spirit. Once a year, Sammo, King of the Bulloms, would make an annual sacrifice to appease the nymph. The Bullom king would hop across in his canoe to receive his rent from Messrs Anderson, but never land ashore, because legend had it that the island would sink should he set foot on it.

THE BEACHES

Trying to do justice to the coast is like quoting an Elizabeth Barrett Browning sonnet: 'How do I love thee? Let me count the ways.'

Pick from yellow beauty; empty beauty; wild beauty: each beach has a character and style of its own, from the colour of its sand to the quality of its waves, keeping even the most easily bored beachgoer striving for a new stretch of sunny, sultry, swim-friendly perfection.

Of course, nobody in Sierra Leone knows what a boutique tourist is yet. One day they will, and the boutique tourists will know the beaches too. But for now, devoid of mass tourism, what unites the beaches is a wild, spacious feel gloriously at odds with the rabid development that usually ruins most stretches of prime ocean real estate, from Indonesia to the Algarve.

Among the more decadent games you can play is to worry over which beach is your favourite – River Number Two is pretty much the official picture-postcard choice of the nation, but there's plenty else to turn your head depending on your taste. Tokeh, full of fishing life, has the whitest sands; Bureh Town is a golden sweep of wonder; while neighbouring John Obey Beach is its hidden twin that we almost didn't want to tell you about. (We've still kept a couple secret – much more fun if you discover those on your own. Keep your eyes peeled on the coast road for unlikely bush-fringed turnings that lead towards the sea, and see where you end up.) Lakka is close to Freetown, convenient and lively; Boboh is a functioning fishing village; Mama Beach has a perfect crescent moon of sand; often-overlooked Kent has a generous sunny charm all of its own.

Most are also home to a string of Sherbro, Krio and Mende villages. At some beaches you can sleep in a hotel bed, others below some spindly twigs and thatch, at others still you can camp out under a mosquito net. While you can't argue with nature's *feng shui*, there are still some ghastly design decisions (how can you put a concrete jungle of bad beach shacks on to a beach as impressive as River Number Two, for example?), but even these never quite overpower the majesty of the surroundings.

Beach by beach, starting at the northern tip nearest the city and heading south along the coast, we give you the lowdown to hanging out on the Peninsula.

GETTING THERE AND AWAY As of mid 2017, the Peninsula road was entirely tarmac, with the sole exception of a 7.5km gap between River Number Two and Tokeh. March of that year saw a US$17 million agreement signed with Kuwait financing the completion of the remaining stretch of road and bridge over River Number Two. Until that's done, however, the northern strip of beaches (Juba, Goderich, Lakka, Hamilton, Sussex, Boboh, and River Number Two) and the southern strip (Tokeh, York, Black Johnson, Bureh, Kent, Mama Beach, and the Banana Islands) are best approached from two different directions.

Coming from the north, you're on dual-carriageway tarmac skirting the oceanfront as far as River Number Two (19km from Lumley roundabout), but after that it's a detour inland on 7.5km of rough dirt road before you're back on the bitumen at Tokeh. Poda podas regularly ply the road between Lumley roundabout and Lakka, with some continuing down to the end of the tarmac at River Number Two. If you want to do a bit of beach hopping, it's easy to find an ocada for hire anywhere along this stretch of road. If there's more than one of you, make sure the riders don't start trying to race each other to get there first, and get friendly with the term 'small small' (meaning keep the speed super low).

Until the road between River Number Two and Tokeh is complete, it's easiest to access the southern beaches from the south via Waterloo. On public transport, you can pick up a mountain-road poda poda towards Jui/Hastings at Bottom Mango or Lumley roundabouts (assuming you're coming from the west end), change there for Waterloo, and hop on a shared taxi at Waterloo's Tombo Park towards either Kent and Bureh or John Obey, Black Johnson and Tokeh. Once the last stretch of road is complete (maybe even by the time you read this!), there will presumably be taxis and poda podas running directly between Lumley roundabout or thereabouts and Waterloo, passing all the Peninsula beach drop-off points *en route*.

For better or for worse, improved accessibility has turbo-boosted development on this side of the mountains, and areas that once felt quite distant from the city are taking on a more suburban character, with luxurious, faux-luxurious, and not-so-luxurious homes springing up at a furious pace on either side of the road as far as Sussex and even River Number Two – Tokeh looks to be next in line after the bridge is complete. The views nonetheless remain spectacular, winding between lanky, long-haired palm trees, glittering sea vistas and green-covered mountains, where young men strain under huge jerry cans of palm wine, and wooden stalls line the road selling forest-fresh fruit.

If you're ready to leave roads behind altogether, you can also hire a **speedboat** from Cape Shilling (**m** *076 814 646; Smokey*), which offers a one-day Peninsula Tour for US$125 each (minimum four passengers), or try Martin Bamin, who hires out a speedboat for up to five people from the Aqua Club in Freetown (**m** *076 733 444;* **e** *martinbamin@yahoo.com*). Heading out from Aberdeen in the west of Freetown to the Banana Islands for some snorkelling by a rocky outcrop known as Mes Mieux, look out for dolphins and the odd whale if the season's right, and then stop off for a picnic on the way back at the secluded Black Johnson, Whale River or John Obey beaches. You can even squeeze in an early-evening swim at River Number Two before landing back in Freetown. Cape Shilling can provide snorkelling and fishing gear on request. It makes for a glorious, but nevertheless long, day, so don't attempt it danced-out and hungover from the night before. Tip the skipper if you're happy at the end. Visit Sierra Leone (page 71) or either Daltons or Bafa on the Banana Islands (page 216) are equally good contacts for aquatic excursions up and down the Peninsula.

Child-run checkpoints Every so often on the coast road, particularly at weekends, you may come across impromptu 'checkpoints' manned by boys. Children as young as five or six and the odd strapping teenager from nearby villages take advantage of the road's poor state of repair to erect makeshift barricades at points where vehicles have to slow down, and then demand money from passing drivers; they will claim it is a charge to mend the pot-holes. Barriers vary from bits of grass to fairly heavy branches. Their frustration at a lack of improvement in their villages since the end of the war, juxtaposed with much richer people visiting their beaches in cars that don't deign to stop or appreciate the people who live nearby, is understandable, but the practice is eerily reminiscent of checkpoints manned by children during the war. Even giving sweets, let alone money, only encourages the practice, and does nothing to create a good atmosphere for a prospering tourism industry.

Don't lose your cool, but don't slow to a halt either. Better to put some money back into these areas by stopping to buy mountains of fruit or vegetables from the side of the road from the numerous vendors along the way: that at least is trade, rather than alms.

JUBA Moments from Lumley in the west of Freetown, the urban spill-over at Juba is packed with dust, new builds and a nice stretch of sand. It's not madly favoured as a beach spot, but it's hard to beat the image of children in bright, eclectic and be-hatted uniforms on their way to class along the shore – about the best school run going.

 **Where to stay and eat**

🔺 **Elly's Guesthouse** (15 rooms) 4 Newton Dr, Juba, look out for the white signboard announcing the turn-off from the beach road; **m** 076 344 918, 088 952 320; **e** michael2005samura@yahoo. com. Not exactly a beachfront stay, this place nevertheless offers a good level of comfort within striking distance of the sea. Rooms are basic & clean, & all are self-contained. A ramshackle garden adds some charm. You can even pay a bit extra to get a room with a balcony. A restaurant serves up roast fish, chicken & chips. AC, TV, B&B. **$$$**

GODERICH A busy little fishing village just a few kilometres outside Freetown, reached by a right fork from the main road. Down in the bay wooden fishing boats are hauled in and out all day long, with grouper, snapper and barracuda changing hands on the shore. Captains and assistants chill out under the trees, eyeing the seas as they puff away on cigarettes and contemplate. Goderich also hosts a five-day cultural fair over the Easter weekend, put on by playwright and cultural champion Charlie Haffner, proud of the event's '*no usai yu komot*' (know where you have come from) motto. Known as **Tangains Cultural Festival**, it takes place in Funkia village at Goderich. Expect to see the Freetong Players (f *freetongplayersinternational*), a drama group going strong since 1994, as well as live bands, masked displays and traditional dancing, alongside canoe races, kite flying, football and fashion. Crafts, food and drink are on sale.

The general area, to the right and left of the main road, is also home to some big-wig houses, including the massive Sea View Estate development as well as the president's house, from where his entourage emerges daily in a cloud of dust and sirens on the daily commute to State House.

There was a charming artistic retreat set in Goderich until a few years ago, but today your sleeping options are thinner; ring the basic Alnax Service Guesthouse (*Gbendembu Rd;* m *076 608 511, 088 449 574;* $$) if you want to spend the night here.

LAKKA Some beaches manage aloof and exclusive, others stunning yet populist. This is a very democratic sort of offering – close to town, with a good range of eating and sleeping spots. Lakka is not blindingly beautiful by Peninsula standards but it is well established, with a reassuringly predictable tranquillity: a trusted best friend rather than a lover who steals your heart. Ideal if you don't have much time or your own transport, but want to set your eyes on a healthy swathe of sun, sea and sand. The best swimming is towards the southern end, away from fishermen, rocks and diesel spills, and nearer to St Michael's Lodge, once a fancy arched hotel that has long said goodbye to its touristic ways, and now schools former combatants and local children. Entry to the beach costs Le5,000, though this seems to be unevenly enforced.

Getting there and away The turn-off for Lakka Beach is just shy of 8km from Lumley roundabout, a Le2,000 poda poda ride from the junction with Regent Road, some 150m south of the roundabout. Beyond Goderich, the road takes you past Adonkia village (sounds like 'I don't care'), Angola Town, alongside the Sierrablock Concrete factory, and finally Ogoo Farm and the junction with Lakka Beach Road. It's a 650m walk on a flat, unsurfaced road from here to the water, or you'll surely find a **motorbike** rider who'll be happy to take you for Le2,000 or so.

🏠 **Where to stay, eat and drink**

🏠 **Palm Beach Club** (3 rooms) m 076 332 000; e peter@lakkabeach.club; w lakkabeach. club. Probably Lakka's most upmarket option, this German-owned hangout boasts a swish & stylish terrace restaurant-bar perched above the sand serving a rotating selection of fish & seafood mains. A few steps away, they've got 2 comfortable whitewashed rooms with fans & nets, as well as a self-catering apt sleeping 4. **$$$$**

🏠 **Lakka Beach Resort** (6 rooms) 1 Douglas Lane, look out for signs on the dirt track running to Lakka & take the (earlier) right fork; m 077 253 762, 088 478 721. Easy to become very fond of this rocky outcrop. Once the loo spot for the local village, it's now a lovely perch for a restaurant-cum-guesthouse on dark volcanic rock at the cusp of 2 sweeps of beach. Cut off from the shore at high tide, it has a suitably desert-island feel & the fish, chicken & lobster grilled up beside you is served with a lip-smacking, oily onion & tomato sauce. Oysters with lime & chilli sauce go down a treat if there's a catch on offer. Blue-themed, tidy rooms, with small verandas, are a touch musty but undeniably picturesque, with flushing en-suite toilets. Good hammocks too. Fishing trips to the Banana Islands cost US$100pp. Electricity 19.00–02.00, restaurant ($$$). B&B. **$$$**

🏠 **Paul's Restaurant & Guesthouse** (6 rooms) m 076 727 377, 088 811 323; e paulshinenose@yahoo.com. Tiled-floor rooms in blue & white sit on the beach facing the sea. Depending whether or not they are let out on long-term rent, there are also 3 more, slightly hidden away with a roomy shared bathroom & a flowering garden replacing the view of the open sea. A generous b/fast of omelette, fresh fruit, bread, coffee & tea is included in the price. Owner Paul Bangura, from Tombo fishing village, cooks the catch of the day, served right on the beach. Excursions include fishing (US$100 for a day trip with gear), or visiting the Banana (US$50pp) or Bunce islands (US$60pp). Fans & en suites, restaurant ($$$). **$$$**

🏠 **Tommy's Paradise** (2 rooms) m 078 438 383, 088 361 259. Run by a local fisherman & his family, this little place is perfectly simple, but no less paradisiacal for it. There are only 2 rooms, both of which come with fans, nets & running water in the en-suite bathrooms. There's a lovely shaded deck facing the beach & meals are made to order, including by some accounts the best fish & chips on the peninsula. Generator power is used 19.00–07.00. **$$$**

🏠 **Thomas' Shack** (2 rooms) m 077 292 358, 076 866 913; e Thomas_shack@gmail.com. With rooms in a newly built board house & tables in the sand out front, this appealingly rootsy spot makes for a comfortable & unpretentious address on the beach. The 2 rooms are both en suite & clean, though the walls are on the thin side. The restaurant-bar does a good array of seafood & the like, & can arrange snorkel hire, boat trips, beach shelters & more. Generator power is used 19.00–07.00. **$$$**

🏠 **Princess Beach Bar** (2 rooms) m 099 931 451. Formerly known as Cosmos & Club Mediterranean, this clean little place offers 2 large, simple, self-contained rooms just down from the Palm Beach Club. The restaurant does good meals & can arrange hiking trips & boat excursions. **$$**

✘ **Route 66** m 088 215 807. Next door to Paul's, this isn't as slick an operation as some of the neighbours, but the big elevated terrace gives great views over the beach & they've got Jacob the Cocktail Man serving the most innovative drinks on the beach at his Sweet Mot Cocktail Bar inside. **$$$**

✘ **Summer Time Restaurant & Bar** m 030 441 096. Dauda Bangura offers fish & chips for Le50,000 a plate, or lobster if it's available starting at Le120,000, at 4 or 5 bare tables just by the watchtower to the south of Route 66. **$$$**

What to see and do Lakka is one of the best places along the Peninsula to arrange a Salone-style **fishing trip** in a dugout canoe. Ask around for Sule or Nelson to see whether they can take you out – they know the fishing grounds well. It's also best to bring your own tackle, and any supplies you might need. Keep a phone with you in case you get into any difficulties.

HAMILTON The dark horse of the Peninsula pack, 5 minutes past the Lakka turning, Hamilton is emptier, with a similar clean sweep of sand, at the other end of a crescent-shaped bay. The water gets deep quickly and waves can be huge. Accommodation options are more limited than nearby Lakka and Sussex, but it's a nice place to hide out, and favoured by in-the-know Salone families wanting to avoid expats at the weekend.

Entry to the beach is via a thin rickety bridge, and there are more loiterers here than at other beaches. The wooden parasols at the near end of the beach do not belong to Samso's, the nearby beach bar, so you'll have to pay a separate fee to sit under them.

🏠 **Where to stay and eat**

🏠 **Samso's Resort** (7 rooms) m 078 764 734, 088 354 493; e samsoresort@gmail.com. Spartan but secluded, there are 5 slightly haphazard rooms

on the beach & 2 Greek-island-style whitewashed villas, each with a small veranda & twin or smallish double beds. Samso (the very friendly chap in charge, hence the name) also has use of a large, comfortable & well-equipped 2-bed, 2-bath villa, with large open-plan kitchen & living room, which can sleep up to 6 people, for US$80 a night. Note that the villa is set back a bit from the sea; if the water is high, you have to cross a rather rickety bridge to reach it. The quiet wooden beach bar does meals of fish, lobster, shrimp, chicken, chips & sauce ($$$). It pays to call ahead. $$$–$$

GUMA VALLEY DAM The 100ha reservoir, built in the mid 1960s, that supplies Freetown with water, is a beauty. You can wander over the bridge pathway that tops the dam into the jungle on the other side, and follow the winding paths to your heart's content. One of them even comes out a short walk from River Number Two Beach. Take the usual precautions – water, hat, suncream – as the effects of heat exhaustion can creep up on you before you know it. Look out for empty cartridges on the ground too – the army's jungle warfare training school is just nearby, and every so often they go on exercise, camping out for days in the wilderness and surviving on whatever they catch for meat.

Getting there and away The process for securing **permission** to visit the dam comes straight out of a Kafka novel. If you bank on a laid-back approach from officials, and don't bother applying in advance, a chap at the gates will send you back to Freetown. Smiling gets you nowhere, and it would be a thorough waste of a journey were it not for the stunning views and succulent lobster dishes 4 minutes away by car at Sussex.

First you must head downtown to the Guma Valley Water Company building in Freetown (*Lamina Sankoh St;* m *076 533 807*) to ask for your piece of paper. The public relations officer is on the seventh floor; there is a lift but don't count on it working. You may well be directed back downstairs to the chief engineer, on the fourth floor. In any case, you need to come equipped with a letter addressed to the general manager requesting permission to visit – note down the proposed date, number of people and vehicle registration if you're taking wheels. It was never quite clear what the official price list is for a person on foot, but it's Le50,000 for a vehicle. Personnel are more used to development workers with well-known international organisations and headed notepaper, so if you're a bona fide tourist the request may come as something of a surprise. Otherwise, a mere tourist may be asked to pay 'a small fine' to gain the permit.

The route to the dam is off the Peninsula road about 5 minutes after Hamilton, with a sign on the left announcing the Guma Dam and Treatment Works. Shortly afterwards you hit a gate and guard post where you show your permit, and then it's about 5km of weaving tarmac up past the treatment works and on to the dam, where you can park by the walkway bridge across the top. The gates are open 09.00–18.00 daily.

SUSSEX With a long, empty golden shoreline stretching in either direction, Sussex is a much-loved favourite. To reach the sea, you have to wade through a thick goo of sand, mud and sucking oil, part of an inlet that rises briskly with the tide (so much so that wading through might easily become swimming). On the other bank is a stretch of steep sand that drops away quickly under the water.

The beach is best enjoyed at sundown or first thing in the morning, although the tiny children and yapping dogs can be quite persistent followers, so more fun to join in with their tricks and laughter than to try and ignore them. Just before dinner, as the sun sets out above the ocean, it's one of the most romantic places in the country.

Beware strong tides at the meeting point of inlet and ocean; head away from it up the beach if you're nervous. Waves pound this whole stretch with much greater force than elsewhere – sometimes delivering you up on the shore with more than your fair dose of sand-burn, and rip tides are vicious, so don't stray too far.

Sussex is also home to the headquarters of the **Environmental Foundation for Africa** (*16 Main Peninsula Rd*; m *076 611 410*; w *efasl.org*), which has a good resource centre if you're interested in learning more about local wildlife and conservation issues.

Where to stay and eat

✳ 🏠 **Florence's Resort** (7 rooms) 20 Michael St; m 076 744 406 (Florence), 076 642 003 (Franco), 076 502 997; e info@florencesresort. com; w florencesresort.com. Bringing a touch of Mediterranean glamour to the Peninsula, this is among the best stays in the country – all elegant white plaster arches & dark wood. It was ransacked twice during the war but you'd never know it now, & the large, white high-ceilinged rooms come equipped with TV, AC & good bathrooms with hot water, along with a fridge stocked with cool wine & beer. Our favourites are Rooms 1 (top floor) & 5 (ground floor), which both have stunning views out to the sea, with wood-slatted windows you can fling open over the ocean: the sea breeze substitutes perfectly for AC through latticed wooden windows.

The restaurant ($$$$–$$$) alone is worth making your way here for, with a justly deserved reputation for fantastic seafood, which you can take on the sand by the water's edge. Lobster portions are large & nearly always available, the fish carpaccio a light piece of caper-accented joy, while the Wayne's Special of creamy seafood pasta is a hearty favourite. Some house specials, such as the Crab Venus (crab & penne in a herb white-wine sauce), need to be ordered in advance.

In case you're confused, most people call this place Franco's, although the sign on the side of the road has it as Florence's Hotel & Restaurant. That's because the place is owned by husband-&-wife team Franco, an Italian, & Florence, from Sierra Leone. It's a straight shot 400m off the main road & clearly signposted. If the hotel car park is full, some children will turn up to watch your car nearby for a fee. B&B. $$$$

🏠 **King's Lodge** (1 house with 7 bedrooms) Sussex Beach; m 076 541 236; e kingslodgesl@ gmail.com; f kingslodgesl. If you're looking to get a big group together for a weekend at the beach, this spot is a very good bet. A sprawling house that can sleep up to 17 people, King's Lodge comes with a fully equipped kitchen, a breezy terrace with lovely sea & jungle views, & an outdoor barbecue area that's perfect for cooking up the day's catch. All bedrooms have a private bathroom, & 4 have ocean views. Catering can be provided on request. Individual rooms range from US$70 to US$100/night; discounts are available if you book out the whole house. $$$$

What to see and do

Boat trips The staff at Florence's can help you arrange boat trips to the Banana Islands, or fishing trips with local guides, with a choice of either line or spear fishing. Trips to old shipwrecks and hidden beaches are also a possibility. Snorkelling gear (US$5 each, or free with boat trips) of mask, snorkel, flippers and optional weight belt is also available.

BOBOH This little-frequented beach, also known as Baw-Baw, used to host a thriving tourist trade, even whipping up its very own cocktail – the 'Pa Gbana' – a mix of fermented local grasses, coconut and lime, named after the village's oldest resident. There might not be much demand for it now, but the settlement, with its crumbling mud huts right on the beach, is smaller, quieter and considerably less hassle than larger fishing communities, such as Tokeh. Unlike other spots, here the beach is at the heart of village life: look out for the best of the brightly painted boat names – *Patient Woman*, *Beautiful Woman*, and, good advice for the brave man keen on either of the former, *Go Try*. Local fisherman Gibrilla Kanu and harbour master Jonathan Kongchaman are both one-time tourist guides who today spend most of their time hauling huge green nets (Kongchaman's own boat is named *I hope to God*). They are both great people to take you about, fix a meal or an excursion, and can help you set up camp should you wish to overnight. Further north, there are a series of deserted beach bays all known as Boboh.

Getting there and away The 'Welcome to Boboh Beach' sign seems to have welcomed its last, so look out for an unmarked right-hand turn-off 1.2km south of the turning for Florence's in Sussex; the beach is 300m along this rocky road.

Where to stay and eat Camping is probably the only bet (expect to pay around Le70,000 for the privilege of a spot (or Le100,000 to hire a tent), and you might get 'security' and a bonfire thrown in). Among prime pitches is a little private beach with appealing chill-out spots of small palm huts with cane chairs and tables. Signed the **Africana Baw-Baw Bar and Restaurant**, follow the 'Yumkella Drive' turning from the Peninsula road, head down to a car-parking area and then continue on foot down a steep rocky path. Seldom used, you'll most likely find this spot deserted, so call in at the village first, or try Jibrila (m *077 609 290*), the local head man. He charges a negotiable Le100,000 per person per night for camping, dinner and breakfast (more if you want lobster for dinner) – call ahead if you'd like to book a tent and/or meals.

Anyone locally can cook up a plate of fish and rice for Le50,000 depending on your hunger and your negotiating skills. Ask if fresh oysters and lime might be available: a treat of a beach starter. Also try asking Jonathan Kongchaman about two local houses that can occasionally be made ready for overnighters at Le150,000 per person.

What to see and do Jonathan Kongchaman (m *088 631 704*) can organise boat trips to the Banana Islands, including a lunch of lobster, fish or crab cooked up on the beach, from US$300 for six people; or a daytime swim and a picnic at the glorious John Obey Beach, for US$200 for two. He can also guide a trek via Guma Dam for (a rather steep) US$50 each, or a full-day's journey down to River Number Two, including a boat ride among crocodiles, monkeys, birds and a waterfall for lunch, for US$100 per person, or US$150 for two. Fishing excursions, with life jacket and fishing pole in a rowing boat, are also possible, for about US$50, with a quick hop to the gathering of rocks known as 'Jail Rock'.

RIVER NUMBER TWO Shallow, crystal-clear waters give this beach the hypnotic, inviting turquoise hues we have come to expect of paradise. Here the sea is swim-perfect, with not even a hint of rock; a slow, steady drop-off and, close to the shore, gentle waves. The location is difficult to top: flush against the hills, a seasonal river (known as No 2) meets the sea, creating a lagoon dotted with paint-peeling wooden boats. Behind the beach, the river runs up through the undergrowth, past crocodiles, monkeys at the water's edge and a host of rare birds – including nesting grounds for the white-necked picathartes – to a small waterfall spot perfect for lunch.

On the beach, red wooden chairs strike a bold note against the bone-white sands and blue seas behind. At weekends it is the populist *pièce de résistance*, with every seat taken, mainly by day tripping expats and Lebanese families. The main beach hosts all the games you can imagine – volleyball, football, cricket, frisbee and more. The water is the perfect temperature for a dip, but best not to snorkel or stray too far from shore: there are often strong offshore riptides here, which can be dangerous – even for strong swimmers.

During the week you can virtually have the place to yourself. Across the slim lagoon (swim across or pay a small fee to a boatman), a large strip of more secluded sand heads south towards Tokeh, great for frolicking about in the sea and jogging on.

Where to stay and eat Unlike many spots along the Peninsula, here at River Number Two the local community has come together to offer food and lodging to tourists and share the proceeds with the nearby village (*B&B* $$$; *restaurant* $$$). Staffed and run by dedicated locals who take pride in their offering, the **No 2 Development Association** (w *rivernumbertwo.com;* f *RiverNumber2*) and its 145 workers has set up a series of concrete huts on the beach for food and drink, a block with flushing loos and showers, security to ward off 'beach boys' (who are instead paid to keep the beach clean), a car park, and even a watchtower for lifeguards to keep an eye on bathers.

The association first started in 1995, in the midst of the war. When rebels retreated off the Peninsula a few years later, destroying or stealing whatever they found in their path, association members buried outboard engines, crates of drinks, signboards and generators in the sand and fled – hiding in boats far out to sea or deep in the bush. They later crept back to start up again and serve whoever made it out there at weekends. Today it's an extraordinary tribute to the ideals of the best of local co-operatives – they have a general executive, management team and elect their president by secret ballot. As a result of the money they take, all the children in the village go to school, new houses are built with free labour and the group also foots the bill for marriage and funeral ceremonies. It's the only place like it in the country. 'We have worked hard to be self-dependent,' says original president Suad Koroma, now chief advisor to the group. 'But we are also very lucky because we live in the best place in the world.'

In return, visitors pay a small entry fee (Le5,000; Le10,000 on holidays) for use of the beach; no hardship when the results of the charges are so evident. Even if you're just going for a drink you pay Le40,000 a day for the privilege of sitting at a beach hut, or Le30,000 for a set of four red wood chairs and table. Inside the restaurant, you only pay for what you consume.

A lunch of fish, shrimp or chicken is a treat (Le50,000), with lobster highly recommended (Le80,000–150,000 depending on size). Overnight options range from camping under a beach hut to staying in a concrete painted bungalow. All 15 bungalows are self-contained and include fans; some have double beds, others singles, and extra mattresses are on offer for groups, so book ahead if it matters. The best hut has a wonderful, secluded view out to sea (ask for Room 1). There's solar power and a generator through the night, but no hot water. Breakfast is an omelette plus fresh-baked bread with jam and tea on the beach. For more information, or to book, call Francis, the guesthouse manager (m *076 347 314*), Victor, president of the association (m *088 330 597, 078 349 941*), or Ibray, the vice-president (m *076 806 066, 076 464 526*).

There's also an independently operated guesthouse in town, the magnificently located **Cockle Point** ✳ (*6 rooms;* m *076 687 823, 077 073 998, 078 717 871;* e *nathancocklepoint@hotmail.com;* w *cocklepoint.com;* $$$$–$$$), set along the inlet between the mangroves and the beach. It's only some 700m from the community guesthouse as the crow flies, but accessed from a different turn-off. From the road, don't take the first turn-off into River Number Two Village, but bear right at the turning 250m further along and follow the track for 900m.

Rooms here are in either en-suite roundhouses or two-storey board houses with bed and balcony upstairs and bath downstairs. It's a delightfully secluded and laid-back kind of place with solar power, plenty of hammocks, and kayaks for guests, plus a restaurant serving a magnificent Thai red curry. Breakfast is extra and camping is available at US$10 per person.

What to see and do For a boat trip upriver to the **waterfall**, expect to pay a negotiable Le250,000 for the stealthy row-boat, which carries up to four passengers and takes 35 minutes. Expect to negotiate hard to get lower than those figures. To book in advance, call guides Patrick (m *099 872 783*) or Sheku (m *077 226 719*). Cockle Point can also arrange the trip, starting at Le50,000 per person. Climbing the falls for 'the secret view' takes an hour each way; to save time you can walk there and then have a boat bring you back. On your way you will see monkeys fishing with their tails for crabs in the river when the tide is down (as well in the morning and evening), crocodiles (if you're lucky) baking on the rocks snapping at flies, and plenty of birds.

A day trip to the **Banana Islands** costs US$250 for up to six people. For an additional Le50,000–150,000 per person (depending on the dish), you can also be treated to a picnic of fresh fish, crab or lobster, with two drinks per passenger included. Make sure you are provided with life jackets. You can stop off at other beaches, as well as smaller islands such as Tokeh Island (also known as Barracuda Island). Again, call Patrick or Sheku.

Fishing trips with live bait are also on offer, for US$150 a boat (maximum of four people). If the tide co-operates, this is an expensive, albeit satisfying way to source dinner. Look out in particular for *bonito*, and yellow jack – more fun for the catch than its disappointing grey meat. Some **surfers** have also occasionally managed to catch some decent waves at this spot.

It's a good 3km stroll south through sand and surf to **Tokeh Beach** (beating the 8km drive by road). The more sedentary visitor can settle for some beachside boutique-ing at the handful of wooden shacks selling fabric, carvings, jewellery, and even bikinis and swimming trunks, in case you left yours at home.

GUMA VALLEY NATURE TRAIL Three minutes south of River Number Two by road is the signboard for the 'Guma-No 2 River Nature Trail', heading away from the beach up a rugged dirt track into the forested mountains. The road quickly degrades, so it's better to park near the sign than struggle up it.

The towering canopy quickly closes in, and in the quiet of the forest it is possible to pick out a cacophony of birdsong, along with a host of bright insect life.

Beyond a rather unlikely sign to a toilet on the left (which turns out to be a huge unsheltered rectangular pit), there's a crossroads – turn left to head parallel to the coast or right to keep going up along a path regularly interrupted by fallen trees. It's all a little uncared for, but keep going and you can find yourself in the midst of adventure. The path up the hill eventually dwindles to a footpath that runs out of steam at a rocky river crossing after about an hour's leisurely walk. You can turn back or, if you are fit and like scrambling, follow the river down the ravine to where it rejoins the Peninsula road (at a bridge) in a no-man's-land of scrub between the River Number Two and Tokeh turnings. It's an 'off-piste' choice – with some hair-raising moments leaping between slippery rocks and over gorges and gushing waterfalls. For more information, contact the **Conservation Society of Sierra Leone** (*CSSL; 14A King St, Freetown;* m *030 522 579, 076 633 824;* e *cssl_03@yahoo.com;* w *conservationsocietysl.org*), who can also advise on how to track down the nests of picathartes making their breeding sites on the rocks. The guides from River Number Two (pages 206–8) can take you up here as well.

TOKEH Home to the whitest sands on the Peninsula, Tokeh (also spelled Tokey) was once the playground of French tourists at the now-derelict Africana resort, where visitors would chopper in direct from the airport. An old landing pad hides among the long grass at the beach's north end, and fishermen and small children on the beach still hark back to the old times now and again with cries of 'Bonjour' and 'Ça va'.

There are long-standing plans to reincarnate Tokeh's glory days as a tourist hub, but most of these were at least temporarily dashed by the Ebola crisis, and the village today remains a hodgepodge of humble homes, fishermen's shacks, and half-finished hotels spread out along several kilometres of utterly stunning sand. Developers are nonetheless salivating in the wings – Tokeh is already home to the Peninsula's newest and swishest resort – and the completion of the northern road to River Number Two and Freetown seems sure to open the floodgates of change.

Until then, and likely still for years to come, Tokeh remains among the busiest fishing beaches on the Peninsula, with dozens of brightly painted boats lining the shore, and a calm cove perfect for swimming. Head for the more secluded southerly end of the beach to enjoy the water and soak up the spectacular view back north to River Number Two, with its trademark mountain jungle hunched behind.

Getting there and away Though River Number Two and Tokeh are only 3.5km apart along the water, they're currently separated by 7.5km of rough dirt road, hooking inland between the two villages. There's no public transport along this road, but it's possible to hire an ocada to take you, or better still, just walk between the two along the beach, with a quick dugout transfer across the inlet at River Number Two. The government secured US$17 million in Kuwaiti financing to bridge this gap in 2017, and works were underway at the time of writing – there will hopefully be poda poda transport along this route during the lifespan of this edition. Until then, the easiest way to get here is with a shared taxi from Waterloo (Le7,000).

At the turn-off into Tokeh, expect a police checkpoint along the road to the beach – The Place is signed just off this road, while Tokeh Beach Resort is 650m away to the right. Follow the road straight until the tarmac ends, and you're in the heart of the village. Turn right, then left, and there's a wall on your right, which you can follow before parking up at the end. Someone will doubtless volunteer themselves to watch your vehicle, so tip them something small when you leave.

Where to stay, eat and drink

✳ 🏠 **The Place** (50 rooms) m 099 604 002; e welcome@stayattheplace.com; w stayattheplace.com. Quite possibly the nicest place to stay in the whole country, this new beachfront resort marks a spiritual return to Tokeh's tourism heyday, & the standalone luxury bungalows here would be impressive no matter the locale. They each come kitted out with fine European fixtures, high-vaulted ceilings & cool minimalist décor (including clever calabash chandeliers), along with individual terraces out front & perhaps the only central AC systems in Sierra Leone. The restaurant is divided in to 2 parts, with fine dining upstairs & more casual fare below, but the seafood & Indian-inspired dishes are divine either way. There's a waterfront swimming pool & volleyball net, & needless to say it faces out on to an utterly fabulous stretch of beach –a Tokeh constant. Massages, guided hikes & boat trips can all be arranged. **$$$$$**

🏠 **Big Bamboo Inn** (5 rooms) m 099 991 111, 099 000 050. Reached from a signposted turning 2.6km south of the main turnoff for Tokeh, this place sits on a hillside facing the south end of Tokeh Beach where River Number One spills in to the ocean. There's a huge balcony terrace (occasionally used for yoga & directly over the water at high tide) with fabulous views of the estuary, & several spic-&-span tiled rooms with AC & en-suite ablutions. It's a touch expensive for what you get, but a homey setup overall & good meals are available at request. Note that after the turnoff, it's 600m further on down a track only suitable for 4x4s. **$$$$$**

 Tokeh Beach Resort (18 rooms, 27 under construction) m 078 911 111 (Issa Basma, owner); e info@tokehbeach.com; w tokehbeach.com. One of the most popular stays on the Peninsula, Tokeh Beach Resort functions as 2 separate halves: Tokeh Palms, a new complex of multi-bedroom villas plus restaurant & swimming pool set to open in 2018, & Tokeh Sands, which offers 13 rooms, 3 bungalows & 2 cabins, all of which are simple & neatly kept, if a bit pricey. The managers run the electricity all night, & you can pay extra to get a room with AC, although the sea breeze might

be all you need. Even if you don't want to spend the night, it's worth trekking down here for lunch (**$$$$**) on the resort's beachside wooden terrace & sunbathing on its white sandy beach. Daytime excursions for snorkelling, fishing & island hopping can also be arranged. But be sure to phone ahead – especially if you'd like to reserve a room – as this place tends to fill quickly at weekends. B&B. *Fan rooms with shared bath* **$$$**, *en-suite rooms with AC* **$$$$$**–**$$$$**

✕ Africa Point m 077 238 547. Facing the mouth of River Number Two but on the Tokeh side of the water, this spectacularly located beach shack restaurant is little more than a few shady, marooned-feeling huts in the sand serving fish, lobster & the like for Le40,000–70,000. There's also 1 very basic room for rent at Le200,000. They cook all day on Sat & Sun, but it'd be wise to ring ahead & order during the week. Makes a good place to break up the walk between Tokeh & River Number Two. **$$$**–**$$**

What to see and do Snorkelling is good around the small islands off the beach. It's easy enough to fin out from the shore, and there are no strong currents. The wide selection of fish and starfish is not quite matched by coral, but there's nevertheless plenty down there. Stay away from the eels, as they can be quite inquisitive.

YORK Most visitors to the Peninsula beaches are struck by the variation in colour of the sands, from china white to copper red. York goes one step further, covered with a carbon-rich dusting of extremely fine grey. The sheltered bay is quiet enough for you not to get laughed at for covering yourself in the pencil-lead grains as part of an unlikely beauty treatment. Towards sundown, impromptu games of football start up – look out for the girls' game played with just as much needle and gusto as the boys' – which you will be welcome to join.

York Beach is actually two tiny beaches divided by a sharp rocky promontory, and the fishing boats pull up at the more southerly side. A little further round the corner is a trawler wreck – testament to the difficult currents and treacherous sandbars of this stretch of coast. York village is at the end of a short stretch of dirt off the main tarmac road – park your vehicle and then wander down through the trees to the water's edge. Visitors are few and far between, and as a busy fishing village most locals have more pressing concerns than bothering tourists, making it a particularly relaxed place to visit.

Where to stay and eat

York Guesthouse (10 rooms) m 088 775 061, 078 134 309, 077 045 160; e yorkguesthouse@yahoo.com. The big rooms at this simple guesthouse all come with nets & fans, while a handful also have AC. There's a small terrace overlooking the water, but don't expect any views from the rooms. Meals are available at request & the whole place turns in to the town nightclub on Sun nights with a massive party facing the outdoor stage – note that it all moves inside if it rains! **$$**

BLACK JOHNSON Beyond signs for Big Water and Whale River Bridge, reaching any of the various rock-fringed bays of Black Johnson is a trek-and-a-half, making it as good a spot for a secret dip as you can hope for. Take the signposted turning south of the village, passing Mama Bonaza Bar (m *077 941 748*) just after the junction, and continue about 1km down a clutch of muddy, rocky, 4x4-only tracks that will spit you out at the sea near one of the two lodges.

Where to stay and eat There are now two places to stay in Black Johnson, both on the beach about 200m apart, and reachable by 'road' along two forks of the same turnoff.

Bahamut Eco-Lodge (7 rooms) m 078/030 911 677; e martinrekab@gmail. com. Often known simply as Martin's after the owner, this agreeably offbeat outpost is set on its own little cove of Black Johnson Beach. Opened in 2013, it offers a hodgepodge of basic but comfortable mud-walled rooms with either wood or concrete floors & compost or water loos; all are equipped with mozzie nets. Martin is known for his talents as a chef, & exceptional seafood meals go for around Le80,000/plate. Boat trips & hikes are all available, including use of a catamaran for guided trips or hire to experienced sailors. **$$$**

Tito's Paradise Eco-Lodge (4 rooms, 2 under construction) m 076 621 017, 076 452 063; w jaysbar.net. Run by Jane, an expat Englishwoman, & her Sierra Leonean husband, Jay, this alluringly named locale was for many years the only option on Black Johnson Beach. Their 4 wooden huts, set just a stone's throw from the water, make for an idyllic – if basic – place to spend the night, or they also have a couple of tents if you prefer. They do both B&B & FB options for guests, but whether you're coming for a lazy lunch (**$$$**) or an overnight stay, it's essential to phone. A couple of new huts were in the process of being built in 2017. **$$**

JOHN OBEY One of the most stunning of the bunch, this sleepy little beach became a minor media sensation in the late noughties, scoring features on CNN, the BBC and a host of other major media outlets thanks to an ambitious ecotourism scheme known as Tribewanted. Alas, the people behind the project have upped stakes and moved on, but the beach they've left behind – despite ongoing issues with sand mining – remains the charmer it's always been.

The name 'John Obey' is something of a mystery – some asserting that it's down to a piece of signboard mayhem that misrendered Jono Bay. To the north, an impressive mountain backdrop descends to a river that runs behind the beach, effectively turning it into a permanent sandbar; this is where the former Tribewanted venture still stands. Like Sussex, the beach here is steep but without such violent swells and currents, and the burnished brown sand here is coarser than York. The turning is well signed from the tarmac – turn right, following the Tribewanted sign. Head left and the road forks in two – the fork to the left leads to an empty stretch of beach (dubbed 'Obama beach' by the locals), the near corner of which is favoured by 'sand farmers' to collect building materials. The fork to the right heads down to another shaded bay good for camping, with generous tree branches and a stick-made dining hut.

Getting there and away Shared taxis and poda podas from Waterloo will drop you off at the main road for less than Le7,000, from where it's a 1km walk into the village. Transport options from the north will improve with the completion of the River Number Two bridge.

Where to stay and eat On the beach of course. You can **camp** out, or string a mosquito net from a few stick-and-thatch umbrellas that locals have set up. Even to camp, you should pay something for security and a bonfire.

Estuary Resort (7 rooms) m 077 353 694, 077 732 871, 099 305 242; e estuaryresortsl@gmail. com; f theEstuaryResort. Reached from a well-signposted turn-off 700m to the north of John Obey village, this beautiful new lodge on the inland side of the lagoon takes its inspiration from traditional Krio board houses, offering accommodation in finely constructed en-suite wooden bungalows with TV & fans, all of them overlooking the river. It's a couple of hundred metres across the inlet to reach the beach itself, but they've got a fleet of pedal boats & stand-up paddleboards available for just such a purpose, & an appealing sandy riverwalk of their own just next to the open-sided bar & restaurant ($$$). B&B. **$$$$**

Tribewanted m 077 946 111, 078 626 293. With the departure of Tribewanted's international backers, the lodge here was handed over to the local community earlier than planned, & its future remained in flux at the time of writing. As of mid 2017, the John Obey community was administering the site (& seeking partners to assist with this), but a lack of organisation & investment means that standards have dropped, & the property is a far cry from its heyday a few years back. There's still nothing to fault about the location, though, & this remains one of the prettiest corners of the Peninsula. Rooms are set in the original beach shacks & otherworldly-looking mud domes, & seafood meals are available on request. **$$**

BUREH Surf's up. Among the few spots along the Peninsula where you can enjoy a good burst of waves, this is a well-established favourite. It's still fairly empty bar Sundays, which are popular with picnicking Lebanese families.

Named after the King of Boure, who controlled the watering place and extracted tributes from visiting trading ships, it's a stunning stretch of sand worthy of a monarch. Mountain-backed, the sea retreats a long way at low tide, exposing a broad stretch of deep ochre sand fringed by palm trees. The sand flats aren't only popular with human day trippers: flocks of terns take advantage of the rich insect pickings on offer, take flight en masse from time to time and fill the sky with a flurry of white. At high and low tide the water runs in and out swiftly, so don't get too distracted.

Many have been beguiled by the **surfing**, and a couple of local boys know the breaks well. While good waves aren't guaranteed, the occasional triumph of hope over expectation makes it a magical spot.

'I think of Bureh as an unpredictable love that changes like the wind but keeps you coming back for more,' says Neil Tobin, a long-term surf-loving visitor who used to drive down every weekend. 'Just when you think you've had enough, that you're tired of putting in the hours for no return, you get a great day's surf and the love affair starts all over again.'

It's a left-handed beach break, which can get up to 2m in the face of the wave but usually averages about 1m. The rainy season is the best time for surf, but of course that means getting repeatedly wet. It's fairly safe, with few currents or rips if any at all, and there are no hidden rocks or wrecks. The only annoyance is jellyfish, which can arrive in the hundreds.

The main beach stretches north, but hidden behind trees around a rocky outcrop easy enough to scamper over at high tide is a southern stretch. It's a three-mile walk north to John Obey, but with several river crossings be prepared to swim at least part of your way. There is a small car park just above the beach.

Getting there and away Take the Kent turning on the Peninsula road, turn right at the sign to Bureh, and then right again after a primary school. Entry to the beach costs Le5,000. Shared taxis and poda podas pass Bureh on their way between Waterloo and Kent for about Le7,000 (possibly requiring a change of vehicle in Tombo).

Where to stay, eat and drink You can **camp** on the beach or string up a mosquito net near the restaurant. There are also just a handful of rudimentary

open-sided shelters scattered around the beach – these are mostly run by the local community and go for Le50,000 a day; fees can be paid to the harbour master, Joshua Tucker.

🏠 **Lumthubul Gardens** (4 rooms) m 077 853 828, 077 661 959; e lumthubul@gmail. com; f lumthubul. Set right on the beach atop a little outcrop of boulders, the bungalows here are a touch sturdier than at the neighbours', with tile floors, en-suite bathrooms & little terraces opening on to the beach. There's a restaurant next door & the generator is on from 19.00 to midnight. **$$$**

🏠 **Rakis Beachfront Resort** (10 rooms, 10 under construction) m 088 881 458, 030 752 251. Just a stone's throw from the beach (yet perplexingly built facing the opposite direction), the original 10 rooms in this incongruous concrete block are looking & feeling rather neglected, but there are 10 more under construction that should be considerably more comfortable, if not characterful. Old rooms are fan only while the new ones will have AC; all are en suite. Meals on request. **$$$**

✳🏠 **Australeone** (5 rooms) m 077 424 902, 099 486 111, 088 889 957, 088 118 793; w australeone.com; f austra.leone.1. Headed up by the active & sociable team of Prince, Ibrahim & Moses, this beachfront board house is an expat favourite for weekends away from Freetown. The rooms are basic & rather close to the bar, but the vibes are good & so is the food. The guys can arrange all sorts of trips in the area. Generator from 18.00 to midnight. **$$$–$$**

🏠 **Maroon View Guesthouse** (4 rooms) m 088 538 759, 030 130 035, 078 832437; e maroonislandview.guesthouse@yahoo.com or maroonview@yahoo.com; w burehtown-guesthouse.tumblr.com. These basic beachside bungalows come equipped with comfortable beds, mosquito nets & either en-suite or shared ablutions. Levi, the dreadlocked proprietor, runs

the generator from 19.00 to 23.00, powering lights but no fans, although the sea breeze should keep you nice & cool. Food (**$$$**) is available for b/fast, lunch & dinner; it's best to order well in advance. They've also got space for camping & a few tents for hire (Le40,000/80,000 your/their tent). Boat trips can be arranged to Maroon Island, just 10mins away, or the Banana Islands further afield. **$$$–$$**

🏠 **Bureh Beach Surf Club** (6 rooms) m 088 644 273, 088 751 566, 030 258 597, 030 085 732; e johnsmallsurfer.194@gmail.com; f john. small.3975. Inspired by the example of River Number Two, this club, now officially merged with The Bureh Town Beach Boys Organisation, offers great food & basic accommodation alongside surf lessons. They recently set up a few rustic beach bungalows with mozzie nets, solar lights & little else, & toilets & showers in a separate block, or they can provide a spot for you to spend the night camping, spark up a bonfire on the beach & make sure you're safe (tents Le70,000–100,000). A restaurant area with cane chairs, tables & hammocks faces the sea, which serves up lunch & dinner of grilled, garlic-heavy fish of the day, lobster, crab, oysters (with lime, Tabasco & vinegar) & grilled chips (**$$$**), as well as omelettes for b/ fast.. Call in advance for food, & manager John Small or any of the gang can also tell you how busy the beach is before you decide to turn up. As for surfing, the club's cheery motto is '*Di waves dem go mak you feel fine*', and for a fee of Le80,000, you can get an hour-long lesson and the use of a board for the day. Or if you already know how to surf, you can rent one of the club's 15 surfboards for Le60,000/ hr or Le100,000/day. To book a lesson or get more details, contact John Small (m *088 644 273*) or Daniel Douglas (m *088 751 566*). Rooms inc b/fast for 1. **$$$**

MAROON ISLAND Tiny Maroon Island sits a 10-minute boat ride offshore. The local development organisation can organise an outing, complete with *rampala*, a fishing wire wound round a wooden stick so you can trawl for fish off the back of the boat on the way over. A return trip costs Le30,000 per person and you can take rations for the day or even overnight. Hire fishing equipment (line, bites, hook) and you can try and catch your supper, and come back to shore once you fail. Arrange visits with your guesthouse.

KENT A broad sweep of flat sand, facing the Banana Islands, bordered by gentle surf and lush forest, this is another five-star beach, with plenty of places to eat and drink. It's less private, however, since several restaurant viewing points look down over the beach.

Like many other places in Sierra Leone, Kent's beauty is stained by slavery. 'From such an idyllic setting, such a horrific trade,' said ex-UK deputy prime minister John Prescott when he visited in 2007 to commemorate the 200th anniversary of its abolition.

As you descend to the beach, look out for a two-storey building on your left, now used as a local primary school. Pass through the tiny opening on the ground floor into a darkened holding cell, without even enough room to stand. That space, little bigger than the average living room, was used to store up to 400 slaves captured from the interior before they were loaded on to ships bound for Bunce Island or another slaving centre and then on to the New World. Spending even a few seconds inside provides a chilling sense of what these human cargoes had to endure.

Getting there and away At the tip of the Peninsula, Kent is about 20 minutes from Waterloo – take the beach road, passing Benguema Barracks, then through Samuel Town, Middle Town, Macdonald, Kerry Town (where the remains of an Ebola treatment centre can be seen on the right), During Town, Russel, Tombo and Mama Beach, all on good tarmac. The trip costs about Le12,000 by shared transport from Freetown: Le4,500 to Waterloo, and another Le7,000 to Kent.

Where to stay, eat and drink Local fixer Ayna (m *088 960 325*) can arrange tents, barbecues and bonfires on the beach in Kent, with an overnight starting around Le60,000–90,000 per person. The long-serving Sengbeh Pieh Holiday Resort was shuttered when we visited in 2017, meaning that both of Kent's operational hotels are now a couple of minutes up the road from town, with neither of them especially suited to travellers on a budget.

Kent Beach Resort (Chodie's) (12 rooms) m 076 716 964, 076 370 838, 088 387 108, 030 033 208; e kentbresort@gmail.com. Reached from a right-hand turn-off 1.5km before Kent village itself, the tiled rooms here are neat enough & come with AC, TV & mozzie nets, but don't take superb advantage of the beachfront location & are expensive for what you get. There's a pretty garden area with shaded tables in the sand facing the water & meals available on request. Generator from 20.00 to 07.00. **$$$$**

Nova Afrika (11 rooms) m 099 271 389, 079 538 216, 088 799 080; e enquiries@novaafrika. com; w novaafrika.com. Reached from the same signposted turn-off as Kent Beach Resort (above), this new lodge opened in 2016 & is a much nicer option than its neighbour, though it's also a bit more expensive. Set in a sizeable beachfront compound, the whole complex is wheelchair-accessible & centred on a big round restaurant & bar (**$$$$**) decorated with some impressively intricate carvings.

Rooms are set in large black-&-white bungalows that the fastidious British-Sierra Leonean proprietress ensures are spotless, & all come with AC, hot water, mosquito nets & high ceilings. The generator is on all night. B&B. **$$$$**

Ralph's Hut m 076 762 330. Among the few spots strung out along the beach rather than crammed in at one end, Ralph can cook up fish, rice & chips in his restaurant shack. **$$$–$$**

Porsh Garden m 088 322 087. Rasta man Caesar, also owner of Disco Porsh in the east end, has set up shop here in a slightly ruinous bar with no small amount of attitude. A one-time rubbish collector in the UK, he has now devoted himself to Klin Salone (Clean Sierra Leone) & sticks to his mantra of 'You can't do tourism when the country is not clean'. It was all a bit haphazard-feeling on our last visit, but Caesar aims to please, & you can still swill a beer in a cane chair on a terrace overlooking the beach, which is surely what really matters in this equation.

BANANA ISLANDS Sitting opposite Kent Beach, this is Sierra Leone's answer to Robinson Crusoe, with just enough half-buried cannons and intrigue to add a touch of *Treasure Island*. It's perfect getaway territory, a place for moon-gazing, storytelling and general mooching.

In fact it's three islands in a long row – **Dublin**, the 'capital'; **Ricketts** to the west, joined by a makeshift bridge of rocks over a spit of sand; and tiny **Mes-Meheux** (also spelled Mesmui) at the outer edge, cut off by the sea but with surrounding waters perfect for snorkelling. The 800 or so people who live here are forced to survive on very little spring water.

History Once the domain of the powerful Caulker family – Thomas Corker arrived in Sierra Leone from England in 1684 – the Banana Islands was a bastion for slave trading, and quickly became a well-to-do spot for colonials and Krio families alike.

'We amuse ourselves for an hour or two in the cool of the afternoon in playing at Goff [golf], a game only played in some particular parts of Scotland and at Blackheath,' wrote Henry Smeathman, an English amateur botanist who lived on the Banana Islands from 1771 to 1775 gathering specimens for collectors back home, describing in his May 1773 journal one of the first golf courses in Africa. 'Our evenings we spent before supper at whist or backgammon, after supper with the bottle and pipe very cheerfully.'

Another onlooker, Mary Perth, writing in 1792, thought the island 'a wonderfully productive, healthful spot, throngly inhabited by clean, tidy, sociable, and obliging people. They have a town much larger and more regularly built than any other native town I have yet seen.'

In later years, James Cleveland, Krio grandson of another English slave trader and prominent Devonshire landowning family, controlled much of the island, later marrying into a prominent Sherbro ruling family (see box, pages 234–5). Even for a year after he died his servants continued to make up his bed and place fresh water for him in the airy court house, thinking he carried on invisibly.

In the 19th century, Governor MacCarthy persuaded the Caulkers to vacate the land in return for an annual rent. In their stead, recaptives settled the islands that were formerly a bastion of the slave trade, and British ships sent to intercept slavers based themselves here. Telltale signs of the islands' past remain: the British navy cannon labelled 1813, the wrought-iron lampposts left behind by the visiting Portuguese of the 17th century and the sunken galleon of 1628.

Getting there and away Local fishermen on any of the coast's beaches will offer to take you for around Le200,000–250,000 depending on how far away you are. Chartering a speedboat for the day from Aberdeen will cost about US$600 – try **Cape Shilling** (m *076 814 646, Smokey*).

The cheapest method is to charter a boat from Kent, the nearest village on the Peninsula, which should cost Le120,000 for up to eight people and takes about 20 minutes. You can land right on the former Banana Island Guesthouse Beach, or arrive at Banana Island Wharf, then walk up to any of the guesthouses around Dublin. Bafa Resort was also building a jetty; it will likely be ready by the time you read this. As you cross from Kent to Banana, bear in mind the sea battles that have passed before you. In 1798, Whites Lord North, an African slaver who worked for the Cleveland family, fought a bitter war at Cape Shilling – a tiny poke of land above the sea just off Kent – with the Caulkers, eventually relinquishing Cape Shilling and escaping in as high speed a chase as possible by canoe to Banana, but not before 200–300 of his people were taken captive.

Bafa Resort has its own motorised launch for transfers, with life jackets provided; the transfer is free for overnight guests or Le300,000 for day visitors. It's the smoothest way to arrive: book it in advance and it should be waiting for you when you arrive at Kent.

If you have your own wheels, either drop your vehicle at the police station (ask nicely) or by the primary school; you should pay Le10,000 per car on your return. From Freetown via the mountain road and Waterloo the trip takes about an hour, depending on traffic. You can **rent a vehicle** for the day, and arrange a pickup a few days later (pages 135–6), or find your way to Kent by public transport – not a hugely popular route so it might require some waiting about. A place in a **taxi** or **poda poda** from Bottom Mango or Lumley roundabouts to Jui and Waterloo costs Le4,500–7,500, plus a further Le7,000 or so to Kent if you can find transport going, otherwise you'll have to charter and negotiate on price.

Where to stay and eat The long-serving Banana Island Guesthouse shut down in 2016 after community disagreements with the proprietor; the village hopes to find another operator, but it's unclear if and when this might happen. See **w** bradtupdates.com/sierraleone for updates.

✻ 🏠 **Bafa Resort** (12 rooms) **m** 099 140 140; **e** info@bafaresort.com; 🄵 bafaresort; see ad, 3rd colour section. When the Sierra Leonean–American couple behind this enticing new resort on Banana Island set to work on their beachfront patch of land, they literally cleared their own stretch of beach, rock by rock (or rather boulder by boulder!), until they had uncovered perhaps the island's most enticing stretch of sand, now sheltered from the surf by all those hand-relocated rocks. Opened at the tail end of 2016, accommodation now consists mostly of standing tents fetchingly arranged around a rocky promontory, with comfortable mattresses inside & hammocks out front. They've also got big plans for a series of luxury chalets around the property, each facing their own private cove. They serve excellent seafood meals in the palm-shaded central gardens, & you can belly up to the open-air bar perched atop an upturned dugout canoe. Boat transfers are free for overnight guests & it's a great address for aquatic endeavours: snorkelling, spearfishing, deep-sea fishing (in season, Nov–Mar) & kayaking can all be easily arranged, in addition to hikes around the island. You can pitch your own tent for Le150,000. **$$$$**

🏠 **Big Sand Beach Guesthouse** (4 rooms, 4 under construction) Dublin; **m** 076 631 939, 077 220 822; **e** bigsandbeach@gmail.com. Set on a stunning curve of sandy beach just a stone's throw from Dublin village, the breezy board-built rooms at this Latvian-run lodge are basic, but you can't beat the setting. A generator runs lights from 19.00 to 23.00, or later if you're willing to pay a bit extra. Freshly caught fish (**$$**) is available for lunch & dinner daily. Harry, the proprietor, can organise beach volleyball, jungle walks or boat & fishing trips around the island. B&B. **$$$**

🏠 **Daltons Banana Guesthouse** (8 rooms in 3 bungalows) Southern side of the island; **m** 076 278 120; **e** gd065@hotmail.com; **w** daltonsbananaguesthouse.com; see ad, 3rd colour section. Cheap, fun & basic, Dalton's has 2 large, round solar-powered bungalows that are each divided into 2 or 3 rooms (all en suite, except budget rooms have a separate toilet block). The real pull is the restaurant (**$$$–$$**) on the beach – tree trunks shooting straight through gaps in the delightful upstairs loft & specially crafted thatch roof – with reasonable prices & an attractive beachside view. If Greg the Greek is around, you can arrange a discover scuba lesson for US$120pp or dives at US$50pp for those already certified, alongside fishing, snorkelling & boat tours around the island. Call ahead to check availability. Rooms come in 3 categories: budget (**$**), standard (**$$**) & deluxe (**$$$**), & beds in the 4-berth dorm are Le50,000 a pop.

What to see and do

Wander about A cannon dated 1813 sits within the grounds of the former Banana Island Guesthouse, while there's the odd Portuguese street lamp dotted about too. Dublin Cemetery is home to the oldest surviving Sierra Leone tombstone. Inscribed 1712, it commemorates a Captain Reid of the Royal Navy. Another, dated 1817, is for Lieutenant John Wale Robert, of the sloop *Siren*, who died of coast fever aged 32. These and other graves are testament to the Royal Navy presence at Banana Islands, sent to stop slaving activity after the trade was abolished in Britain in 1807. Tours also generally take in the big old bell hanging from a tree branch outside a dilapidated church. The rickety wooden houses dotted around are among the best examples of typical Krio housing, though even here they are beginning to be replaced with concrete structures. Those that still stand today have their old slats protected under zinc roofing.

Amid the crumbling buildings, the lush islands are full of fruits – guava, lime, kola nuts, papaya, bitter oranges, star fruit, pineapple, avocado, figs and 'sour sharp'.

Island tour Reaching Ricketts on foot from Dublin is a hard task, through hours of forest paths rarely cut back. If jungle adventure takes your fancy, take a guide who you know knows the route, and plenty of water and sun protection.

Most people, since they are fishermen, go by boat instead, and it's easy to arrange a trip encircling the islands. Look out for monkeys and crocodiles. A spooky dusk excursion takes in a trip to a cave of bats, which usually emerge as the sun goes down, while on the north side of the island there is a spot for collecting oysters from the rocks opposite Big Sand Beach. The coastal nesting areas in the undergrowth are bursting with water fowl.

Bafa Resort, Daltons Banana Guesthouse, or Big Sand Beach can all arrange a wide variety of boat trips and aquatic activities, as well as hikes around the islands.

In Ricketts, the old village is up the slave steps past more Portuguese lamps and an old cotton tree, home to a stunning red church. The island's headman, Diro, lives in a house decorated with an extraordinary mural of Jesus pressing a doorbell, as if he too is eager to enter.

Beaches There are five main beaches and a handful of coves: among them Old Brook Beach and Banjoko Beach (a short walk from Bafa Resort, though they've now cleared their own beach as well). Big Sand Beach is by far the best, but beyond Dublin, reachable by boat or on foot with a guide. It's a nice spot to visit with a picnic hamper (better known as a *coolman* in Krio), or you might be able to arrange lunch at the guesthouse there if you phone ahead (page 216).

Snorkel The strip of water between Ricketts and Mes Mieux is among the best in Sierra Leone for snorkelling. That's not to say it's anything to write home about by international standards, but it makes for a lovely, bright swim in calm water with relatively good visibility. You can hire equipment at Bafa or Daltons, or, if you're on a day trip with a speedboat you can bring kit with you from Freetown.

MAMA BEACH Until a few years ago, this pretty stretch of beach at the bottom of the Peninsula was little visited by leisure-seekers, but all of that changed with the opening of the French-owned Eden Park Resort in 2010. Mama Beach has since earned a reputation as a destination for aid agency retreats and weekend getaways for the NGO crowd, but plenty of the local atmosphere remains. The village itself is largely Sherbro, unusual for the Krio-heavy coast of the Western Area. Down a dirt track through the village appears a lagoon, fishing boats flying the Salone flag, plenty of *bolo bolo* (green algae) on the rocks, a good crescent of sand and the odd washed-up jellyfish.

It's not hard to see why the events of the *Amistad* case were dramatised by Steven Spielberg in his 1997 film of the same name. It unfolds with the kind of dramatic turns and reversals of fortune that normally only Hollywood can conjure, and yet it captures an integral moment in both Sierra Leonean and American history. For the remarkable story of Sengbeh Pieh and his fellow Africans is a tale not only of triumph over adversity but of race, identity and rights.

It begins in Gallinas country, in the far southeastern corner of Sierra Leone, where a number of slaves captured from their nearby villages by raiding parties were deposited at the slave-trading centre, Dombokoro, at the mouth of the Kerefe River on what is now Turner's Peninsula, a few miles north of the modern-day village of Dibia. They passed into the hands of two Spanish agents, Laigo and Luiz, and were taken on board the ship *Tecora* in the spring of 1839 and shipped to Havana, Cuba.

Despite a treaty with Britain to suppress the slave trade, in Spanish colonies the practice of falsifying papers was widespread, so that newly arrived captives appeared to have been resident since before 1820, when the treaty came into force. Under this veneer of legality, the slaves went on the market in Havana, where they were bought by two Spaniards, Pedro Montes and Jose Ruiz, who boarded a new ship, the schooner La Amistad, bound for Puerto Principe, now Camaguey in modern-day Cuba.

Taunted by the ship's cook that they were to be executed and cannibalised, the slaves resolved to act. One man had emerged as a leader on the transatlantic crossing: a Mende, Sengbeh Pieh, referred to in accounts of the time as Joseph Cingue or Cinque. Fellow captives looked to him for their lead, and his plan was clear – survive, and return home. 'We may as well die trying to be free, as to be killed and eaten,' he told them.

On their third night at sea, Pieh broke free of his neck irons and released the other slaves. They quickly located weapons and took over the ship, killing the captain, Ferrer, and his cook, and losing two of their number in the process. While they controlled the ship, the Africans, no sailors themselves, had to turn to their Spanish captives for help navigating the ship back to Africa. But while they sailed east during the day, at night Montes steered the ship towards America. After 30 days of aimless zig-zagging, without supplies left, the Amistad (which, of all things, means 'friendship' in Spanish) finally landed near Montauk, New York.

With the Spaniards alleging mutiny to the US authorities, the slaves were again taken into captivity. Attracted by the case, prominent abolitionists flocked to their cause, including New York businessman Lewis Tappen, who paid their legal costs. In the meantime, Spanish diplomacy mobilised to lobby for the return of its 'property' – the slaves – in keeping with the 1795 Pickney Treaty between the two countries.

At the resulting trial in Connecticut, what started to emerge, to an enthralled American audience that had not seen anything like it before, was the humanity and bravery of the slaves, particularly Pieh's graphic testimony of the horrors of the Atlantic crossing, and an awakening understanding of their motivation. The defence successfully convinced Justice Andrew Judson that the Africans were not slaves but free men, on the basis that they had been illegally taken from Sierra Leone. An appeal was immediately filed and the case went to the Supreme Court.

At this stage the abolitionists, mindful of the pro-slavery, pro-southern leanings of the Supreme Court, realised they needed a big-hitter to fight in the Africans' corner, and managed to convince John Quincy Adams, sixth (and former) president of the United States who by now was 74, to take on the case in the Supreme Court.

Kali, one of the slave children who had learned English while awaiting trial, wrote personally to Adams to try and convince him: 'Dear Friend, Mr Adams, you have children, you have friends, you love them, you feel sorry if Mendi people come and carry them all to Africa … All we want is make us free.'

Adams's brilliant rhetoric used the Africans' plight as a metaphor for America itself, which he portrayed as being in thrall to powerful external interests if it simply returned them to Spain. In a landmark ruling, and much to the chagrin of President Martin von Buren, who had become personally involved in the case on the Spanish behalf, the Supreme Court upheld the original ruling that the slaves were free men.

The case played a part in challenging how blacks were thought of in America, and added credibility to the abolitionist movement; quickening a discourse that was to break into civil war 20 years later.

The story often stops there, but for the Africans, making legal history was only a means to an end: returning home. After a lengthy wait, with only 35 of the original 53 captives still alive, the 'Amistads' set sail aboard the Gentleman back to Africa, accompanied by five missionaries from the American Missionary Association.

The troubled return reveals the gap between what the returnees wanted for themselves, and the pressures they were put under by the abolitionist movement. While its work in America had undoubtedly saved their lives, and financed the longed-for return to Africa, the abolitionist movement saw the captives as foot soldiers in its conversion strategy for the continent, carrying the Lord's Word to their countrymen.

Understandably, as the recaptives returned to their homeland, and discovered news of families and relatives, many drifted away from the mission and its work, leading to tensions.

Never anything other than his own man, Pieh, who had increasingly clashed with the missionaries, received news that his village of Mani, in Mendeland, had been destroyed and the whereabouts of his wife and three children were unknown. Despite all he and his comrades had overcome, the slave trade was still destroying lives in his homeland. Pieh eventually left the mission, periodically returning between long stints upcountry.

The missionaries suffered too, and eventually only one remained, finally negotiating a deal to lease land for the mission at Komende from Henry Tucker. The Mendi Mission, as it became known, survived to have a benefit beyond the *Amistad* Africans. As it grew more established, the head of the mission, George Thompson, played a key role in helping negotiate a peace settlement in the troubled region, which hastened an end to the slave raids and tribal wars. Magru, another of the *Amistad* children who had been educated in captivity, went on to study in the United States before becoming head of the mission school in Komende, and then leading the mission branch at Manya Station. The mission went on to found churches, and two notable schools – the Albert Academy for boys in Freetown, and the Harford School for girls, at Moyamba. Presidents Milton Margai and Siaka Stevens were both products of American Missionary Association primary schools, and therefore both owe their early education to the *Amistad* revolt.

Although his final fate is unknown, Sengbeh Pieh now features on the Le5,000 note, and is rightfully acknowledged as a national hero.

Getting there and away Mama is on the southernmost stretch of the Peninsula, between the Kent and Waterloo intersection, beyond Tombo, During Town, Kerry Town and Macdonald Bridge. A turning signposts the main village and beach. A second dirt turning off the Peninsula road, less well signposted, takes you straight to the resort.

 Where to stay and eat

⌂ **Eden Park Resort** (21 rooms) m 088 777 333, 079 990 990; e edenparkresort@live.fr. Peaceful, well kept, & a bit overpriced, this fully renovated, French-owned resort is a world away from the hustle of Freetown. Stay in one of the 13 salmon-pink bungalows scattered among the trees – each of which has its own toilet, shower, mini fridge & plasma TV – or you can opt for one of 8 box-like hotel rooms, which are cheaper but not nearly as nice. The restaurant (**$$$$**), whose kitchen is run by a French chef, serves up some of the best meals on the Peninsula, though service can sometimes be a bit spotty. There's also a pool, tennis courts, & children's play area. Wi-Fi. **$$$$$**

TOMBO The busiest fishing town in the country, Tombo's wharf is also the setting-off point for plenty of transport vessels that slowly ply the sea route south towards Bonthe Island. Be warned that this sort of travel is dangerous and tough – hours out at sea in the sun, no life jackets, plenty of breakdowns or groundings on sandbanks. 'I too have got stranded,' warns Abdul Koroma, Secretary General of the Sierra Leone Artisanal Fishermen's Union, who once spent three weeks trying to get back from Bonthe at the mercy of local fishing boats. Most people now go by road to link up to Kent or Freetown, but Wednesday and Saturday mornings are the big days if you want to catch a ride south (see below), and see the lively fish market at its best.

Getting there and away From Waterloo, take the right fork towards the beaches, passing the turning to Benguema Barracks, then through Samuel Town, Middle Town, Macdonald, Kerry Town, During Town, Russel and finally Tombo, on your left, all on good tarmac. A **poda poda** costs Le3,500 to Kent, at the lower tip of the Peninsula.

By sea, **transport vessels** leave Tombo on Wednesday and Saturday mornings for Plantain Island (Le25,000) and Shenge (Le30,000) – both about 3 hours away – also stopping at Tisana Wharf, Mosam, Baoma and finally Bumpetoke. They aim to leave around midday, tide depending. On Fridays, a boat heads from Tombo to Shenge, then on to Gbangbatok (Le40,000), the jumping-off point to Sherbro Island (pages 231–8), via the string of Turtle Islands – Mutti, Yele, Chepo, Nyangai, Timpima, Delken and Mobkie. Several boats leave at the same time from Tombo, so check which is which. The return trip from Gbankbatok back to Tombo leaves on Wednesdays (Le40,000). Bear in mind that reaching Gbangbatok takes a minimum of 6 hours; it's a thoroughly unrecommended means of transport. Don't even think about the boats that occasionally head from Tombo to Guinea or Liberia, which even the fishermen avoid.

For more information, or to arrange a tour of the portside, contact senior harbour master Samuel Bangura (m *078 053 713, 088 716 059*) or secretary Noah Sesay (m *078 628 813*).

 Where to stay and eat There is a rudimentary guesthouse in town, but a much better option is the **Leonor Guesthouse & Entertainment Centre** (*8 rooms with big shared bathroom, 2 self-contained;* m *076 657 593, 076 610 122, 088 452 770, 077 610 122; no fans, but a cinema attached!;* **$**) in Kissi Town, signposted left off the main road a few minutes north up the coast road towards Freetown by vehicle. The residence is at the back of the village amid the undergrowth, with a precarious path down to what is pretty much a deserted beach, and a great view of the brightly painted boats as they leave Tombo laden with goods and passengers.

What to see and do To find the busy wharf, turn off the main tarmac road down Findley Street, then right after the small orange mosque and down Wharf Road towards the sea, where you should turn right to hit the port area proper, near one of two large white mosques with four minarets. Every morning the catch comes in, with men gutting fish on the shore and handing them over to women who pile them up in baskets ready for smoking at the plant in town. Fishermen sit by the sea mending their nets, gnarled hands and keen eyes toying with sharp implements, obligatory lip-gripped cigarettes dangling, the sound of the *muezzin* hanging in the warm air above them. Industrious, bright and resolutely commercial, Tombo is action-packed and memorable. If real-life drama isn't hitting the spot, **The Lesonda Cinema** (*19 Wharf Rd*) has showings twice daily (08.30 and 21.30, featuring Nollywood hits). Ring Abdualai Bangura for details (m *077 231 592*).

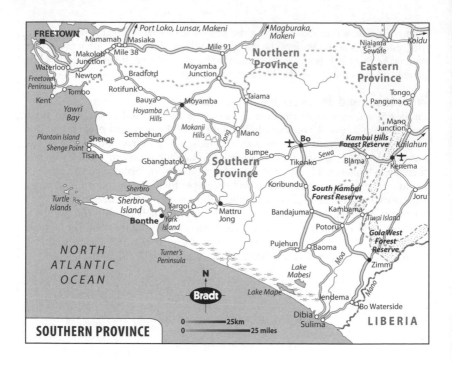

SOUTHERN PROVINCE

5

Southern Province

Jungle islands, endangered monkeys and pygmy hippos hidden in the middle of a rainforest-clad river at Tiwai; sandy beaches skimming the Atlantic for miles along the coast at Turner's Peninsula; fearsome surf and Liberian flavours down at Sulima; sun-drenched, palm-fringed idylls far out to sea at Turtle Islands; mangrove swamps teeming with birds, colonial vestiges and world-class fishing in Sherbroland; the witch hunters of Shenge; non-stop nightlife in the provincial capital Bo – the Mende heartlands of the Southern Province envelop you with their greenery, gentle good-time spirit and the chance for adventure.

The road network tends to sprawl throughout the south, with no clear way to take in all the destinations in one loop, and very little in the way of decent routes. For that reason, we've divided the region into two sections – southwest of the Bo road covering the predominantly coastal area around Moyamba, Shenge and Sherbro Island; and the Bo road and beyond, including the provincial capital, Tiwai Island and Sulima to the south and east.

SOUTHWEST OF THE BO ROAD

MOYAMBA This small, sleepy jungle town is capital of the district (of the same name) and the province's second city. It doesn't look like much now, but it was once an industrial powerhouse of the region, and a highly regarded government school turned the town into a remarkable production line for some of Sierra Leone's most important politicians, including three heads of state (the country's first prime minister Sir Milton Margai, his brother Albert Margai, and President Siaka Stevens) and Madam Ella Koblo Gulama (see box, page 226), paramount chief, Sierra Leone's first woman MP and a cabinet minister.

The district was also home to Madam Yoko, a slender sande dancer, who in the 1880s took on the mantle of her dead husband Gbanya, a powerful Mende war chief, sidled up to the colonial powers and built herself the largest chiefdom in the country, with Moyamba her capital. Described as shrewd and thoughtful, she had 20 ladies-in-waiting, plenty of slaves, and even sided with the government during the Hut Tax War. By 1906, with the ravages of age beckoning, she decided to bow out on a high. 'At the height of her authority she deliberately committed suicide because, as she told her attendants just after drinking poison, she has enjoyed to the full all that life had to give – power and love – and, now that old age had approached, found it had nothing farther to offer her,' wrote colonial administrator Sir Harry Luke shortly after her death.

Plenty of different peoples populate the largely agricultural area, in particular Sherbros and Limbas, but its importance to the Mende remains clear. Even the town name is derived from a Mende word, meaning 'send for us'.

Nowadays there's not a huge amount to do in Moyamba, other than sample fresh poyo – among the best in the country – and its lethal, distilled moonshine cousin,

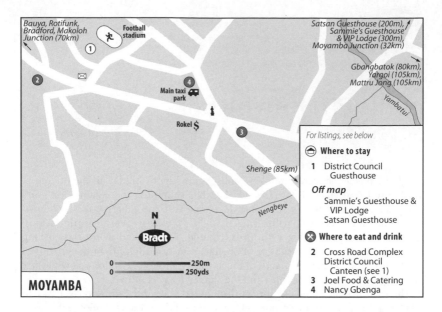

For listings, see below

Where to stay
1 District Council
   Guesthouse
Off map
   Sammie's Guesthouse &
   VIP Lodge
   Satsan Guesthouse

Where to eat and drink
2 Cross Road Complex
   District Council
   Canteen (see 1)
3 Joel Food & Catering
4 Nancy Gbenga

MOYAMBA

omele, but it can be a useful spot to spend the night on the way to the coast at Shenge or Bonthe. In fact, if you're wed to public transport, stopping overnight might well become a necessity.

Moyamba was attacked by the AFRC military junta in 1997, and, like many towns throughout the country, has yet to recover fully.

Getting there and away From Freetown, head 160km towards Bo (via Masiaka) until you reach the aptly named Moyamba junction. It's another 32km from here to Moyamba proper, on a decent earth road that was in the process of being surfaced in 2017. There is also a lesser-used (and even less maintained) unsurfaced route that branches from the Waterloo–Masiaka Highway at Makoloh junction (✪ *8.38892,–12.94805*), bumping 70km southeast through Bradford, Rotifunk, Bauya and finally on to Moyamba.

By private vehicle the trip should take around 3 hours. Public transport can take longer – factoring in breakdowns and stop-offs – and should cost about Le35,000 from the Shell stop in eastern Freetown or, slightly easier, from the Dan Street junction with Kissy Road. From Bo, a seat in a shared taxi should cost around Le30,000.

 Where to stay *Map, above*
Power is fed by the national grid and generally works at least three times a week. Most guesthouses run their power from 19.00 until 23.00 or midnight. You can always pay for extra fuel to keep the electricity running.

Sammie's Guesthouse & VIP Lodge
(12 rooms) m 076 608 939, 077 354 617.
Ostensibly the most upmarket digs in town, the large tiled rooms here have a rather split personality, with many boasting AC on one hand & bucket baths on the other. The company in charge

of roadworks to Moyamba junction had most of the rooms booked out during 2017. B&B. **$$**
District Council Guesthouse (7 rooms)
Football stadium, Coronation St; m 076 554 179, 088 211 505. If you're a football fan, you can't beat the location of this community-run

guesthouse, which is set on the 1st floor of the local (mini) stadium. Rooms are self-contained & pleasant enough, & all come with fans & nets & there's running water from 19.00 to midnight. African dishes are available at the canteen on site. B&B. **$**

🏠 **Satsan Guesthouse** (5 rooms) 6 Cole St; m 088 923 713. The premier budget option in town, it's the nicest looking, with best conditions & – get ready to melt – the name is a compound of husband-&-wife team San & Sata. The self-contained rooms all come with fans & nets. **$**

✗ Where to eat and drink *Map, opposite*

Options are limited but the **District Council Canteen** (m *076 554 179*; **$**) at the local football stadium should do the trick, serving up African rice and plassas, plantain, chicken, or groundnut stew. **Joel Food & Catering** (m *076 941 039*) near the central roundabout does a similar array of dishes, or you could also try **Nancy Gbenga** (m *078 689 181*) in the central taxi park. The **Cross Road Complex** (m *076 949 913*) has altogether too many adverts around town given what little they sell, but it's still a good spot for a roadside beer. Among the town's cookeries, fish is of the smoked variety, except during the rainy season, when people create wooden traps and stick them deep into the fast-flowing rivers to take out a catch. Make the most of the plentiful mango trees in season.

Other practicalities
There are no ATMs in town, so a transfer through **Rokel Commercial Bank** (*Siaka Stevens St*) is more or less your only option for getting cash. There was no public internet when we visited in 2017, but there's a fine mobile data connection with either Airtel or Africell; fuel and general goods are readily available.

The local radio station is Radio Modcar (93.4FM): roving reporters regularly look for fresh blood to interview, so don't be surprised as a visitor to be asked for your 5 minutes of Moyamba fame.

What to see and do
Moyamba tends to reward those who are lucky enough to be staying for a while and really get to be trusted by the town. On the surface of things, life here is pretty slow so wander the streets and see what everyone else is doing – washing, cooking, chatting. It's easy to get involved, and people are generally happy to stop and talk to you. It's worth asking around in the centre of town to see whether you can find a guide to take you on a picturesque lake walk out of the town, down an ancient trail to a secret pool deep in the jungle. While you're asking after your guide, don't neglect to check out the utterly unique **monument** in the central roundabout, replete with singers, drummers, horn-blowers, lions, and a triumphant-looking angel perched on top – a delightful contrast to the painfully drab clock towers going up in roundabouts across the country!

No visit to Moyamba is complete without going to the **Mustard Seed Foundation** (*ask for directions at 1 Swanneh St; w www.sierraleoneaid.org.uk/page/what-we-do*). This home for war orphans, many of whom have severe disabilities, has been set up by the remarkable Deborah Freeman and her daughter, Roselyn, who, without any kind of external assistance, have dedicated their lives to providing a ray of hope to, even by Sierra Leone's standards, some of society's most marginalised. The happiness and spirit of the centre is truly inspirational. Donations are welcome.

If you're feeling super dedicated, you could also set about trying to track down the **Cleveland Tombstone**. One of the greatest snatch and grabs in Sierra Leonean history, the tombstone of James Cleveland, a prominent merchant of mixed Sierra Leone–English origins, was swiped from the Banana Islands in 1798, following a long-running feud between Cleveland's son and his rival Thomas Caulker (see pages 234–5 for a fuller account). Caulker placed the stone on his own father's grave in the ancestral burial ground in Tassoh, near Moyamba in Kagboro chiefdom. The tombstone enjoyed a brief period on public display in Shenge, but was soon removed again to the bush after townsfolk complained of strange apparitions around it at night. As with some of Sierra Leone's other attractions, its location in a sacred burial ground makes it fiercely inaccessible to the occasional visitor: you will most likely need to join the poro to gain access. The inscription on the now-cracked headstone reads: 'Sacred to the memory of Mr. James Cleveland, late Proprietor of this Island who departed this life March 24, 1791 in his 37th year of his age. His surviving relative, William Cleveland, has caused this stone to be placed over his grave as tribute to the memory of a worthy man.'

SHENGE Strong in magic and Sherbro heritage, Shenge is a pretty beachside town, jutting out from the southern tip of Yawri Bay, a large expanse of intertidal mudflat that stretches south from the bottom of the Freetown Peninsula, taking in three creeks. Rich in birdlife (Yawri Bay was declared an Important Bird Area in 2013), and bordered mostly by mangrove swamps, it's a lovely, forgotten place to hole up in for a bit, sample village life at a canter and wander from one tiny, picturesque beach to the next. It's also the best jumping-off post for Plantain Island, a remarkable fishing community that sits just off the coast.

Shenge, along with Tombo, supplies the bulk of Freetown's fish. Once it was the site of a large ice factory and fresh-fish plant that kept catches fresh for export in a huge warehouse. Near the church, its tattered, forlorn remains stand as a sad monument to past industry. Today's fishermen sell to local women who, without

SIERRA LEONE'S FIRST FEMALE MP

Born in Moyamba, the daughter of the paramount chief, this 'troublesome', strong-willed child spent much of her life fighting. It took a two-year tussle for Ella Koblo Gulama (1921–2006) to gain her hold on the paramount chieftancy – her case even going all the way to Britain's House of Commons – after local elders decreed only members of the male-only wunde secret society were eligible. When she finally won election in 1953 she was promptly carried hammock-high into her husband's home town, Lunsar. She considered herself someone who got things done – she promised more schools, electricity and water for Moyamba. She got them all.

Ardent about the Sierra Leone People's Party (SLPP), a largely Mende group with its heartlands in the south of the country, she entered parliament in 1957 as one of the 12 paramount chiefs, 'to show my people that women can take their places side by side with the men folk'. By 1963, Milton Margai had made her West Africa's first female cabinet minister. Following the 1968 coup, President Siaka Stevens had her arrested for conspiracy to overthrow the government, and, charged with treason, she swapped her ceremonial staff of office for a corner of Pademba Road Prison; no mattress, no change of clothes, no bath.

A trial never came, but in the meantime her family lands were taken from her, she was deposed as paramount chief and suffered a stroke. Not to be deterred, after 17 years away from the job, on her release she stood again for election, choosing as her symbol a harmony-hopeful umbrella. Her opponent picked a cutlass. She won with 98% of the vote, and got another one of her hammock tours, this time around Freetown's Victoria Park. By 2001, she'd amassed an OBE from the UK and Sierra Leone's highest honour, the Order of the Rokel.

any means of keeping it fresh to send up the coast, smoke the catch immediately. The local industry also faces competition from the huge deep-water trawlers from China, Korea and Russia; not only do they frequently encroach into Sierra Leone's waters without the proper licences to steal fish, their propellers slice through the nets of artisanal fishermen (see box, page 242).

History   For a sleepy town, Shenge has seen a lot of action. More than a century ago, competing Sherbro families vied for coastal domination (see box, pages 234–5). It all started when Thomas Stephen Caulker, a former slave trader from England, founded the town at a useful spot opposite Plantain Island, which had already become a thriving slaving post. Town life was bolstered by the arrival of the missionaries – Americans of the United Brethren in Christ in 1855, who made their home at Shenge with Caulker's permission. Their present in return was to convert him, thanks to the efforts of Shenge-based African American preacher Reverend Joseph Gomer, who made sure Caulker died a Christian in 1871, after reigning for 40 years.

Getting there and away   Although as the crow flies Shenge is only about 75km from Freetown, the journey **by road** is the best part of a day, following beaten-up roads from Moyamba south to Sembehun and then west on smaller tracks all the way to the coast. There is no petrol station in Shenge (although you can find five-gallon yellow jerry cans – known as 'rubbers' – for higher-than-market rates with who knows what else mixed in), so stock up on fuel if you need to in Moyamba.

If you fancy trying the nautical option, wooden motorised **ferry** boats leave from the fishing village of Tombo at the southern end of the western Peninsula (page 220), every Wednesday and Saturday sometime around midday, tide-depending. A one-way berth costs Le30,000 and the return trip leaves Shenge on Mondays and Thursdays. The trip takes about 3 hours: it's crowded, exposed to the elements and without life jackets. To travel the seas in style, hire a **speedboat** from Freetown (pages 164–5); the voyage takes about 3 hours.

Orientation   Shenge consists of the main village, and another smaller village a few kilometres up the road, where the welcoming Paramount Chief Caulker lives. He is keen on tourists, and an affable and knowledgeable guide.

⌂ **Where to stay and eat**   There is one simple, perfectly adequate **guesthouse** in the town, or, if you ask the paramount chief nicely, it may be possible to stay in an abandoned, fading **summer house**, once frequented by senior politicians, including Harry Williams, a former vice president under Siaka Stevens. Much-dilapidated, without running water or electricity, you still can't beat the vista the veranda gives on to the beach, framed by swaying palms – ripe for a cold beer, a gentle breeze and the languid onset of early evening. Leave a generous thank you to the chief on departure. The guesthouse or the chief may be able to prepare food for you. At the seaside pier where day boats leave for Plantain Island, the brightly painted **Mobetty Beach Bar** can rustle up cold Star beer and soft drinks, and, remarkably, satellite TV for football lovers. Chief Caulker's neighbourhood is also home to a tiny but fun **bar**, with Star beers in steady supply. If you promise to return the empties, you may be able to take bottles back to your tent or residence.

What to see and do
Beaches   Shenge is blessed with some lovely beaches, different in character from the Freetown Peninsula. The fine sand is mainly light grey, and along this part of

'I will call in the police for the law's sake. But if I want to know what really happened, I will call the witch hunters,' is the sober, rational assessment of one educated Moyamba resident. He's not alone. For farmers who have lost their tools or had a goat stolen, families who have lost a child unexpectedly, city dwellers shorn of their mobiles, government ministers seeking re-election, a troupe of paranormal investigators is always at the ready.

Sherbroland is the place to come for magic. Home to many of the Kamajor hunting militias that formed resistance to the rebels during the war, part of their fearsome reputation came from the supposed efficacy of their magic, going into battle covered in charms and amulets that they fervently relied on to evade bullets, command mortars where to drop, turn into wild animals, and become invisible.

Akin to a travelling circus (or the A-Team), Shenge's witch hunters wander the Southern Province and beyond, bringing their special powers to bear on case after case. For a bunch of detectives, they certainly have a great sense of theatre. Grass-skirted, face-painted, wearing women's wigs and bells around their ankles; instead of a press conference, they announce their presence with an initial performance of their skills. These generally take place at night, under the light of flaming torches, a dizzying whiff of kerosene and a backdrop of furious, unabated drumming.

By the time a demonstration of their powers is ready to begin, the entire town is in attendance, rows of wide-eyed faces stretching back into the black, utterly transfixed. Most of the shows take a similar format, starting with several minutes of acrobatic feats, sweat-drenched rhythms and saucer-like eyes. In between come interludes of 'magic' that build in daring and complexity. Fire-eating and breathing, smashing a beer bottle and chewing the broken glass, perforating various body parts with skewers and lying on top of shards of glass and nails are all part of the uncomfortable mix. Performers sometimes stand up with blood running down their backs. The culmination of the show, involving a white sheet and gasps from the audience, is a physical disappearance of Houdini-esque audacity.

It's unlikely a foreigner will be able to watch the real work of the witch hunters, so these spectacles have to stand in, and can, of course, be organised for visitors for a fee – Le40,000–90,000 depending on the size of the troupe (plus kerosene for lamps).

When actually trying to divine a villain or investigate a crime scene, the witch hunters will hang out in a house until they get to the bottom of what has happened, questioning family members, summoning the spirits, mixing potions, waiting for a confession. Often they form a circle of those involved and announce a future date for the real witch hunt. Several people have been known to be so scared merely by this initial meeting that they come forward, confessing all, at once – anything to avoid the subsequent curse, humiliation and visitation of juju, which can involve various levels of pain up to and including death. In other ceremonies, bits of liver and blood are planted as a means to scout out the witch, who, in one case, was found cowering (invisibly) under a rock.

To see a performance in action, watch Greg Crompton's documentary on YouTube (w *youtube.com/watch?v=WU9nhVW8zDk*).

the coast the water is shallow for a long way. The bottom is very muddy, however; expect to sink ankle deep if you wade out.

Just north of the village, **Mission Beach** and **Church Beach** are two beauties hidden at the bottom of steep rocky inclines. Church Beach, just below a pretty little church that still holds services, faces the tiny Monkey Island, which is an easy swim away. Exploring the cemetery above is a slightly morbid if educational way of discovering the genealogy of various Caulkers, one of West Africa's oldest Afro-European dynasties. However, in delightful illustration to Sierra Leone's pagan tendencies, the most important family members are nowhere near the consecrated ground but hidden deep in the sacred bush, where no uninitiated Western eyes will ever see them. Arguably even more picturesque is the hidden Mission Beach by the UMC School, reached by another steep path.

Local justice Chief Caulker is a paramount chief with a strong sense of civic duty. If your Krio is up to the task, the local court is a good place to come to watch local justice in action.

Islands The most rewarding day trip from Shenge is to Plantain Island (see the following section for more details), but you can also explore the much smaller, uninhabited Birds Island and Monkey Island.

PLANTAIN ISLAND Listen to anyone on the mainland and they will tell you that Plantain is sinking, so get there fast. The island's residents, a clatter of 2,000 people on a penny drop in the ocean, aren't so keen to shift, however. Village life in 'pan body' (corrugated zinc) houses and huts is hectic and busy. Fishermen land their brightly painted boats, and cart around big cans of diesel to keep them going at sea. Look out for some modern takes on boat names – *Ruff Neck, D World Today* and *Black '4' Conscious* rub bows with the likes of invocations to a different sort of life force – *God Power, Friends and Family, Awareness* – and crudely painted US and UK flags adorn the wood as the green, white and blue of the Salone standard flaps in the wind above. Dark smokeries belch out oily fumes as baskets of fish are transferred to their grills.

Foreign visitors are few and far between, so you are likely to attract a fan of fascinated children spread out behind you for the length of your stay. The real treasure of a visit is getting out to the forested far side of the island, when a postcard-perfect moment on an empty sand beach is yours for the tropical taking.

History You could be forgiven for thinking the island owes its name to Sierra Leone's favourite starchy accompaniment, but it is in fact named after Captain John Plantain, a notorious pirate who operated from the island from 1720.

John Newton, founder of the Wesleyan movement and writer of the hymn *Amazing Grace*, found himself imprisoned on the island in 1746, after falling foul of the mistress of his slave-dealing employer. His dealings in the trade drew him back to the island at least twice, finally as captain of the slave ship *Duke of Argyle*, despite him converting to Christianity during the terror of a transatlantic storm in 1748.

As a slaving alternative to the islands and beaches of the Peninsula, Plantain quickly grew rich and powerful. However, as timber grew in economic stature once slavery was outlawed, Plantain lost much of its significance to Europeans. Trees grew taller and stronger on the mainland, at Bendu, not on the big salty island, and exploitative interests in Plantain waned.

They might sound like screeching banshee cries of the underworld, but the gnashing of metal barges loaded with huge cargoes of earth offer hope to a nation.

This part of Sierra Leone, near Nitti port, sits on what was once the world's largest deposit of rutile in the world, and such is the power and influence of the titanium-rich black soil, whose derivatives form crucial parts of artificial knees, suntan lotion, toothpaste, and any halfway decent pot of paint, that the entire area to the south of Gbangbatok and northwest of Mattru is known simply as Rutile.

The actual mine at Mogbwema, where a 400-ton dredge scoops out bucket after bucket of titanium ore, was once the country's largest employer, foreign-revenue earner and tax-payer. That changed in January 1995, when rebels invaded and took locals, Brits and other expats hostage, wrecking the mine and destroying infrastructure. Those who escaped fled into creeks on barges, and spent weeks in the bush.

Not until 2004 did the mine start up once again, with the help of some adventurous investors and a €25 million grant from the EU. Today the edgiest it gets is a worker patrolling in yellow hard hat, sunglasses and a tank top with the word 'Rebel' emblazoned across the front.

The company that runs the mine, Iluka Resources, hopes the mine will one day contribute 30% of the world's natural rutile production, of which it brought out 126,000 tonnes in 2015.

'A lot of workers saw it destroyed,' says John Sisay, Sierra Rutile's Executive Director until 2017. 'They were determined to see it come back again. It's symbolic of recovering Sierra Leone – of our having an economy again and putting lives together again.'

That hope was boosted in 2007 when President Ernest Bai Koroma, fresh from his first inauguration in front of a crowd of tens of thousands, made a flying visit to the site. He commissioned a second dredge, naming it Solondo after a local 19th-century warrior. In July 2008, the new dredge capsized with 50 workers on board at the time, two of whom were never recovered. The mine fights on.

Getting there and away Motorised **passenger boats** ferry people the 25-minute ride to and from Shenge throughout the day for less than Le10,000 each way. You can also take off for Tombo, on the Western Peninsula, for Le30,000, with boats leaving on Mondays and Thursdays. The journey takes about 3 hours, tide-depending. On Saturdays you can get to Gbangbatok for Le50,000; it's a tortuous 8-hour journey.

Where to stay and eat There's nowhere official to stay on the island, but you can ask permission to camp on any of the beaches, or to stay in a hut. Offer in the region of Le20,000–40,000 for a night. People can prepare fish and rice for you without too much bother if you bring your own food or pay for some. Tip them well for their service.

What to see and do
Beaches With names such as Governor Mango Beach and Amara Wharf Beach (all marked on a crude, hand-drawn wall map in the village dispensary), a trip to Plantain can feel a bit Treasure Island. In the morning, the breeze on **Boatman**

Beach, which faces Birds Island on the Tombo/Shenge side of Yawri Bay, comes from the mainland; in the afternoon it comes from the sea, making it the beach of choice at that time. **Main Beach**, facing out to sea, is the quietest and most picturesque beach, with glorious white sand. But don't expect any of the seclusion of Banana Islands; you may well be sharing the beach with a riotous game of football, and what feels like the island's entire population of children. In the water, there are a few sharp rocks underfoot, so be careful; there are also more tiny islands to swim out to if you really want some privacy.

Plantain Island is criss-crossed by tracks linking the beaches, but it's almost inconceivable that you will be able to go about incognito.

Slave pens The most important surviving historical feature of Plantain Island is the remains of its slave pens. They appear to be separated from the island, but actually top a narrow spit of land that is submerged at high tide. At low tide an eerie, treacherous walkway leads to the shattered stone walls of the cramped cubicles, now overgrown with bushes and tree branches. John Newton also had a house here after a Portuguese slave trader, Clow, transferred him from Banana Islands, and they became the first white men to live on the island. Slave-trading Newton didn't much like it himself – feeling imprisoned by Clow and his African wife, he quickly changed allegiance when another white man set up shop on the island.

SHERBRO ISLAND If parts of Sierra Leone seem isolated, Sherbro Island is the land that time forgot. No vehicles, hardly any noise, little but the birds to keep you company. Peculiar vestiges of a bygone age – defunct wrought-iron water hydrants, an old red telephone box, a smattering of tumbledown, long-abandoned shopfronts along the shoreline – only serve to reinforce how worn down and out of the way the island has become. Even Sierra Leoneans don't want to live there: when a hopeful charity set up an amputee camp on the island following the end of the hostilities, the country's war-wounded turned their noses up and refused to relocate.

Yet the island has a slow, easy charm borne of being about for donkey's years, with no pretence. A world away from Freetown, it is a wonderful place to spend a couple of lazy hassle-free days, exploring by bicycle, and by boat.

The real secret of the place, at least for the visitor, is not so much the island itself as the waters around it. You haven't captured the spirit of Sherbro until you have cruised, perused, and meandered its waterways. These rivers, estuaries and the nearby Atlantic are its link to the rest of the world, supporting creaking wooden boats laden with commuters, tangled mangrove swamps and raffia trees, riverside rice plantations, and birds aplenty. Maribou storks and colonies of pelicans nest on the local shores, seabirds drop in, and kingfishers and tropical birds can be seen on inland sorties.

With that in mind, this is the place to get your kit out, rather than off: while there are spots of bright yellow sand, Sherbro isn't really about beaches; it's about twitching, and fishing. World records are set here, for the likes of barracuda and the sport fisherman's favoured prize, the tarpon (see box, page 238). And even if you don't manage to land a whopper, take heart in the old maxim that a bad day of fishing is better than a good day of work.

History Piassava might not carry in the way of caché today ('pia-what?' we hear you cry), but export of the raffia palm fibre made the island, or at least the foreigners that traded it, rich while it lasted. By the 1930s Sherbro was a world centre for bristles, brushes and any of the other harder materials fashioned from the piassava that grows

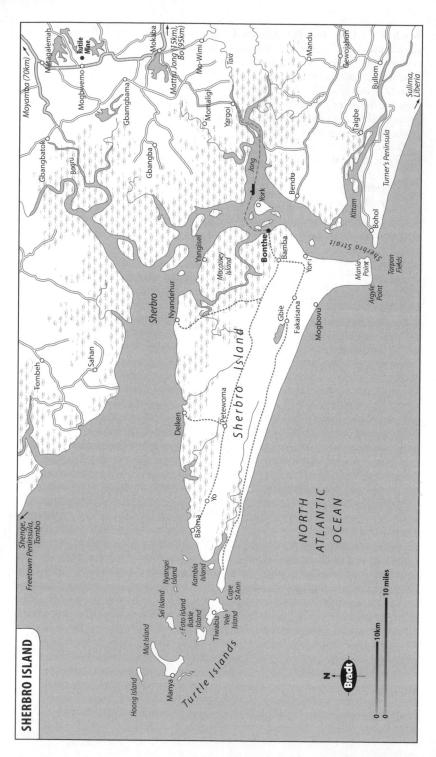

SHERBRO ISLAND

Moyamba (70km)

Matagallemah

Rutile Mine

Mokaba

Mattru Jong (15km); Bo (95km)

Mandu

Gbewojahun

Mogbwemo

Ma-Wimi

Taia

Bullom

Gbangbatok

Bagru

Gbamgbama

Mo-malgi

Momaligi

Yargoi

Sulima, Liberia

Gbangba

Jong

Bendu

Taigbe

Sherbro

York

Kittam

Turner's Peninsula

Yangisel

Bonthe

Bamba

Bohol

Nyandehur

Mocawey Island

Yoni

Mania Point

Sherbro Strait

Tarpon Fields

Sherbro Island

Gbie

Argyle Point

Fakaisana

Tombeh

Petewoma

Mogbovu

Sahan

Delken

Yo

Freetown Peninsula, Tombo

Baoma

Shenge,

NORTH ATLANTIC OCEAN

Hoong Island

Mut Island

Sei Island

Nyangei Island

Foto Island

Kambia Island

Bakie Island

Cape St Ann

Manya

Tiwabu

Yele Island

Turtle Islands

N

Bradt

0 10km

0 10 miles

232

throughout the island. European ships first started calling to buy camwood and ivory, then known as elephant teeth, in the early 17th century, later establishing trading posts. Palm produce made the island rich in the 19th century, as representatives from Germany, France and Britain fought for a commercial advantage.

The Sherbro people came into their own with their trading prowess, making the most of colonial expansion to settle land rights to trading posts. Not only was it the place where many 'tired of the dronish life of this metropolis [Freetown] … found less competition, and consequently better trade and better profits', but *The Sierra Leone Church Times* deemed it, in 1885, 'a sort of commercial Eldorado to the mercantile world'.

Dynasties still famous today – such as the Caulkers, Clevelands, Tuckers and Neales – were among the first to bridge the gap between local royalty and European partners, as well as Creole traders, who all paid rent to Sherbro kings. A Sherbro king ceded the country to the British in 1825, and in 1861 the British made Bonthe a Crown Colony, imposing English law.

Yet the Sherbro were no pushover. The last Kong Kuba (King of Sherbro), Kpana Lewis, is regarded as a local hero for organising resistance to the hut tax imposed by Governor Cardew in 1897, even though it did not apply to the island itself. His tactics, including mobilising the secret poro network against the colonialists, and banning all trade with European and Krio traders, were so successful he was eventually exiled to the Gold Coast (modern-day Ghana) for his efforts, where he died in 1912. The British, so scared of the impact of secret societies as underground resistance networks, even passed a law forbidding the use of the poro as a weapon against trade.

During the war the island was spared incursions by the RUF, but clashes between ex-government soldiers and traditional hunters – both of whom were supposed to protect the land but instead went hell for leather after it – tore the island apart. It became artificially divided into a pro-AFRC army camp and navy base in Bonthe, surrounded by pro-Kamajor camps in the outlying bush. Anyone found hopping between the two areas – even to source food from the lush rural areas, to creep in or out with goods, or to visit relatives – was treated as an enemy spy and likely to be tortured and killed by one side or another.

Getting there and away
Sherbro is not easy to get to, even though it's only 145km from Freetown. Even with a car you will have to take to the water at some point, and there's no option that combines price with ease.

By road, it's a bumpy, lengthy ride to Gbangbatok (⊕ *7.80555,–12.38301*) – down to Moyamba first and then south on dirt tracks. About 5–8 hours should do it, depending on your vehicle and the condition of the roads. You can overnight here at the **Cefra Guesthouse** (*Cemetery Rd;* m *076 760 223;* $). Mattru Jong (sometimes just called Mattru) is even further south, beyond Gbangbatok, near Yargoi (the pickup point for the boat to Bonthe Holiday Village). There are daily vehicles from Bo to Mattru Jong (Le30,000) and Gbangbatok (Le35,000).

Public transport consists of two rickety wooden **boat** services. The shorter ride is from Yargoi (⊕ *7.5728,–12.3373*), a tricky-to-find village hidden beyond a swathe of rutile and bauxite mining sites and rough dirt tracks: it's super cheap at Le10,000 one-way, with one or more boats leaving each Friday, Saturday and Sunday, tide-depending. Most people instead take the packed commute from Mattru. Known as the 'Paddy Express', the ferry leaves at 08.00 Monday to Saturday, tide-depending, for Le30,000 one-way. It often arrives in the evening. You can also charter the whole thing to yourself, for Le550,000. The boats are covered, so offer shelter from the sun, leaving you to enjoy the smell of fish on board. ⊕

Powerful families dominated life on this part of the coast. Many were formed after ambitious colonial officers and merchants married into local royalty, creating clans that could marshal their mixed European and African heritage to great effect. While tapping into the worlds of tribal loyalty and tradition, alongside Western education and influence, they managed not to be restrained by the ties of either.

The Rogers family of Vai country were born from a European and a Massaquoi (the ruling family), while Henry Tucker, from Bullom–European descent, was the most powerful slave trader in the mid 18th century, entertaining John Newton on silver platters.

One name had enough intrigue to make the Borgias blush. The Caulker dynasty, which still rules Shenge, is descended from Thomas Corker, a young Englishman who arrived at Sherbro from London in 1684 in the employ of the Royal African Company. He rose to the post of chief agent in 1692 and married a princess of the Ya Kumba family, which ruled the shores of Yawri Bay further north. The family was headquartered at Plantain Island.

In the 18th century, the marriage of a Caulker daughter with William Cleveland, an English trader from Banana Islands, seemed to consolidate the position of both houses, giving the Caulkers a foothold on the Peninsula. Their son James (Cleveland) was an extraordinary mix, exposed to the shady secret workings both of the poro society and the no less devilish rules and protocols of English public school. 'With a White Man he is a White Man, with a Black Man he is a Black Man,' John Matthews, another former slave trader, commented in 1789.

Ambition also made him ruthless. In 1785, he sent an army to Plantain Island. They cut off the head of the local ruler, Chief Charles Caulker, and with that James stuck out his own neck as the most powerful ruler along the coast.

James was succeeded on his death in 1791 by his nephew William, who lacked his steel. When the Caulkers put aside their own internal rivalries and got around to retaliating in 1798, William fled on a slave ship, and the Banana Islands came back under new chief Stephen Caulker's control. In an act of revenge, Caulker removed James's tombstone from the island and it ended up as the doorstep to his own family burial ground near Shenge.

English-influenced rulers managed yet more fiendish work under George Caulker, son of Stephen, who succeeded him on his death in 1810. Making the

To reach Mattru (⊕ *7.60564,-12.17947*), head south from Moyamba to Gbangbatok and then down through the Imperri Hills, branching east for Mattru (and west for Yargoi). From Bo, head southwest via Tikonko and Bumpe. It's well worth having a **4x4** for the bumpy ride, but a chartered **poda poda** (about Le800,000 from Freetown) should be able to make it too. (Negotiate with the driver to wait in Mattru to take you back to Freetown from Bonthe too.) The last stretch of road, after the rutile-mining area, requires a quick river crossing by 'ferry' to Mattru on the far bank. In Mattru, you can put up for the night at either **Penny Penny Guesthouse** (*Mission Rd;* m *076 784 862*) or **Madam Jeneba Guesthouse** (*Gbangama Rd;* m *076 647 634, 076 608 106*). Western Union money transfer is also available from the **Mattru Community Bank** (m *076 867 185*).

A speedboat pickup by **Bonthe Holiday Village** (even if you're not staying there) costs US$200 (for the boat) from Yargoi, and takes just over half an hour, offering

most of his education in England, George challenged traditional law when he said property should pass not to the eldest brother but to the eldest son, obviously benefitting him. He managed to win back Plantain Island for himself, while his father's brother Thomas got Banana Islands and the mainland. This branching of succession laid the foundations for a nasty and long-running conflict.

By 1832, Thomas Stephen Caulker, George's brother, was eyeing the roaring timber trade on the mainland with envy from his position on Plantain (which he ruled until his death in 1871). The slave trade was dwindling and he wanted a foothold. So he started up a vicious war against his cousin Canrebah Caulker, Thomas's son on the mainland. Both sides prepared for about a year, 'mustering war boys from all parts of the countries' and drawing in mercenaries and various factions from that region. Thomas Stephen's nephew, Thomas Kugba, even defected to lead Canrebah's troops. The conflict escalated – 'the creeks and rivulets were filled with dead bodies which became a feast for fishes and alligators,' says one record, noting skulls were strung up from thorny trees – and in 1849 Thomas Stephen's men killed a notable trader. Thomas Stephen went to Freetown to apologise and in a subsequent peace deal the kingdom north of the Cockboro Creek was awarded to Canrebah; the south was given to Thomas Stephen with an agreement the kingdom would be reunited under a descendant of George's, thus giving the Plantain Caulkers control of the mainland.

Trouble flared a third time in the 1880s, with another succession row. On George Stephen II's death in 1881 the Freetown government recognised his half-brother Thomas Neale Caulker as successor, although his slave mother made him an unpopular choice in his own kingdom. In 1887, William, a grandson of George Stephen and an old adversary of Thomas Neale's, hired Mende mercenaries to settle a host of scores, and went on a campaign through the district destroying or enslaving almost everything in his path. The British finally intervened, and William and others were arrested. The following year, after a high-profile trial that had electrified Freetown, mainly because of sympathies for William's leniency towards the Krio during his campaign, William, the old campaigner Thomas Kugba and one of their followers were hanged in Shenge in 1888, while the rest of his supporters were exiled to The Gambia.

much higher levels of comfort, speed and safety. Carving through the creeks and swamps is a stunning introduction to the island and its surrounds, although it's easy to get stuck in the shallows on dark nights.

If you don't fancy a lengthy drive down to the coast by private car or public transport, you can opt for a marathon journey by **local boat**, picking up a ride from Tombo fishing village along the Peninsula. Join one of the regular passenger vessels – which usually depart on Friday or Saturday and arrive at Gbangbatok the next day – or charter one for yourself (page 220). The Holiday Village can also arrange a 4- or 5-hour **speedboat** ride from Freetown's Aqua Club, but consult for prices. Other destinations from Bonthe include remote corners of Sherbro and the Turtle Islands, for US$600 return. Half a day's boat hire is US$200 for a skiff or US$350 for the bigger 'whaler' boat; a full day is US$350 for a skiff and US$500 for a whaler. Excursions to spot birds, crocodiles, or dolphins can also be arranged.

5

The 50km-long island is named after Sierra Leone's first inhabitants – the Bullom-speaking coastal Sherbro people. They had a rough time at the start – devoured by the Mane warriors of the 16th century, said to be devilish cannibals who invaded the island and destroyed it, and who later part-morphed into the northern Temne. The name has had them smarting ever since too – Sherbro comes from Sherabonla, one of the Mane overlords who ruled the southern Bullom people at the end of the 16th century. His legacy has done rather well – today's Sherbroland extends far beyond its namesake island, for miles into the mainland, almost as far as Moyamba to the north and Pujehun to the south. Their homelands occupy most of the low-lying southwestern coast of Sierra Leone, from the Ribi to Bum rivers, including Turtle, Sherbro and Plantain islands, and extending inland for 25–50km.

Sherbro's 'big men' were born of Henry Tucker in the middle of the 18th century, part-Bullom, part-European. Another set of Sherbro stalwarts were the Caulkers (see box, pages 234–5) – Englishman Thomas Corker (later spelt Caulker), set sail from London in 1684 and became chief agent at nearby York Island.

When US ethnographer Henry Usher Hall stayed with the Sherbro people up and down a 145km stretch of coast for seven months in the late 1930s, he considered the island one of two places he believed 'the old Sherbro culture is best preserved' (the other was at Shenge). At the time, Sierra Leone's Sherbro population numbered 140,000, with 15,000 of them on the island. Today the island is home to more like 30,000 people, a mix of Sherbro, Mende and Krio. Many of today's inhabitants speak Mende rather than Sherbro and beautiful examples of large, wood-slatted Krio houses pop up throughout the island.

Hall's black-and-white photographic images, now part of a collection at the University of Pennsylvania Museum, show a life much the same in the 1930s as it is today – men twirling fishing nets out to sea; weavers stretching out warp between tree trunks; elderly chiefs chewing the cud outside their mud huts. Two other distinctive features of political life here are secret societies and women paramount chiefs, such as Queen Yamacouba of Bonthe – who in 1785 was a signatory to an important agreement between her people and the British to use coastal land as settlement for returnees freed from slavery. Hall also captured many of these aspects of Sherbro society in his photographs. Local legend has it that the poro, the most significant secret society in the land, even started out at Yoni, the village where Hall lived on the island, and from there it spread to the mainland.

To see examples of his photographs, visit w africa.upenn.edu/sherbro/sierraleone.html.

Getting around When Henry Usher Hall was checking the place out in 1936, island transportation was via a combination of hammock and rowboat 'gig'; these days your feet are your friends if you prefer land to waterway. A speedier alternative is to hire a **mountain bike** from the Holiday Village, or ask at your guesthouse. Motor engine progress has arrived in the shape of a handful of **motorbike taxis**. If you see one, flag it down and jump on the back, paying Le1,000 for a one-way ride; it will probably already be full with three other people sharing the one spare seat.

It is also possible to catch **ferries** to other fishing villages around the coast of the island and beyond. A speedboat trip to Turtle Islands, for example, takes about 2 hours 40 minutes, with the safest seas from January to June.

Other practicalities After years without mobile-phone reception on the island, both Airtel and Africell now have service in Bonthe. There are no banking facilities on the island, so bring plenty of cash; you may want to set up an account with Airtel mobile money if you plan to stay awhile. There is a **government hospital** on Medina Street.

What to see and do

Tour the waters Taking a boat out on the waterways around Bonthe and the surrounding islands is like a trip through the Florida Everglades. The vessel guns along quietly, furrowing through millpond-still waters. At times the tangle of mangroves is so thick and close they block out the sun; elsewhere the swamps flatten out and sacred ibis wade sniffily on the banks, while rice-planters work behind them. As the estuary widens on its way to the sea at the southwest tip of the island, the sea starts to froth alarmingly as the Atlantic shelf drops away steeply.

If you hire a speedboat or charter a local fishing vessel, take binoculars. It won't take too long before you are nose to beak with birds up and down the swamp-sided rivers; you may see monkeys in trees over the river (look out for wooden-stick box traps suspended in trees made by villagers), and some very big crocodiles flat-bellied by the side of the water. You can also drop anchor at any of the villages you come across to pick up fresh seafood. Fishing huts – crude shelters called *shimbeks* – dot the banks, while tiny dugout canoes made from a single trunk are propelled by the bright chaos of sails made from scraps of plastic sheeting and bags stitched together. Women tend to fish too, mostly in rivers and shallow water, with scoop nets so big they need two people to handle them. Others rely on weirs and traps.

For a beach tour, head south from Bonthe to Mania (pronounced *maniya*) Point, where **Big Beach** skirts the coast. It's a great lunchtime picnic spot, beside a once-wonderful holiday resort now sadly dilapidated.

York Island With only four or five houses, this small village about 15 minutes from Bonthe hides its past well. Now the ground is strewn with discarded Pegapak gin shooters, but once it was a heavily fortified trading post. English traders settled on the small estuary island in the 17th century, paying a local Bullom king rent, and quickly established a settlement protected by thick stone walls and cannons, to guard against raids from rival European powers. The headquarters of the local Royal Africa Company in the 18th century, exporting camwood, ivory and slaves, it later became the headquarters of Greek trader Patterson Zochonis. While little of this past remains, the jaunt makes for a nice boat trip. The water here is crystal clear and its most promising strip of beach is near Mania, to the south.

Gone fishing Sports anglers from all over the world come to fish this part of Sierra Leone. In 2006, 12 world records in various line classes were caught in the area, weighing from 166kg to 283kg. The season lasts from October to May, and the biggest pull is a shoulder-crunching encounter with the elusive tarpon, which breed in the Sherbro and Kittam estuaries and like to hang out at the mouth to the Atlantic (see box, page 238), where the river mouth turns to bubbling surf.

Never fear if one evades you; there are plenty of other fish on offer: barracuda, bunga, red and yellow jack, grouper and giant mackerel. The possibility of fishing

The tiger of the game-fishing world, the tarpon is the most powerful, hardest-fighting fish. It's not the largest – although 2.4m is nothing to smirk at – but it's their sheer flirtiness that seduces fishing fans. They just won't give up the fight – dancing through the water; glowing silver as they leap out of it, flashing the hypnotic power of their large, dark eyes; flicking a forked tail as they cavort about. Once hooked, so too is the rod-holder. A bite can take 5 hours to land, as the giant-scaled silver king shimmies and ducks. And that's if you're lucky: tarpon are notoriously easy to lose due to snapped lines, while their jaws are designed to make them notoriously light biters. Tarpon hunting requires patience and concentration, since the slightest error will lose you your *Megalops atlanticus* ('king of the ocean').

Happy in oxygen-light water, tarpon can manage in very salty or almost fresh conditions, and tend to favour warm sandy estuary flats along the Atlantic – in North and South America, the Gulf of Mexico and Caribbean, and the length of tropical Africa, with perfect conditions at Sherbro, where everything costs a fraction of Florida prices. There's the added benefit of far less angling competition, and giant fish. A world-record tarpon was caught on fly by Yvon Victor Sebag from these waters in April 1991, weighing 128kg.

for marlin on the nearby continental shelf and bonefish on the other side of the island is also being explored.

Whether you are staying there or not, we heartily recommend splashing out on a day or half-day trip with the **Bonthe Holiday Village** (US$600 for a day's fishing; US$350 for birdwatching). Boat trips to spot crocodiles, birds or dolphins can also be arranged for similar fees. Good boats, equipment and highly knowledgeable local guides guarantee a satisfying and genuinely fun trip whatever your level of angling experience, which will live up to the observation of 19th-century American philosopher Henry Thoreau that 'many men go fishing all of their lives without knowing that it is not fish they are after'. Much cheaper, but still fun, you can also negotiate with a local fisherman to take you out in his boat.

If you do get lucky, you may want to make an offering to Kasilah, the legendary sea spirit held in awe by people on the island that controls the seas in the area, and believed responsible for any accidents and drownings. He is seen as a series of lights offshore at night, which quickly disappear and reappear elsewhere, when there is no boat to be seen or heard. Villagers tend to push out a boat laden with food; if it returns empty Kasilah has had his fill.

Tour the island Whether by bike or on foot, a wander around the island is hugely rewarding. It's hot too – so cover up and take suncream and water. The backstreets of the town, between shady mango trees and banana leaves, make for a pleasant walk, all the more remarkable for the fact that each tiny dirt pathway is proudly labelled with an official street sign. If you'd like a guided walking tour, Bonthe Holiday Village can arrange one for a fee.

Bonthe Bonthe is a port town with many wealthy sons, but few have come back. The seafront is a forlorn echo of its former affluence. The once-busy commercial street of Heddle Road is named after Charles Heddle, a trader of Scottish–African descent who pioneered the groundnut trade and was the first to export palm kernels from the area from his premises here (rival German trader Otto also has a street to his name). The abandoned shell of the one-time general store of Patterson Zochonis crumbles at the water's edge. Freeze-framed in time, the small town of about 10,000 people wears its affluent history at street corners: rusting wrought-iron lampposts, decaying water hydrants, even an enormous water tower mounted above the treeline.

Where to stay and eat If you're coming to the area to do some research, The **Environmental Justice Foundation** (see box, page 242), which has an office in Bonthe, might be able to provide you with accommodation or other logistical support. For more information, send an email to e info@ejfoundation.org.

Bonthe Holiday Village (6 ronadavels & 1 bungalow, each with 3 dbl rooms sharing a living room) Heddle Rd; m 076 532 544 (Bonthe), 076 686 299 (Freetown); e marmar@dircon.co.uk; w bontheholidayvillage.info; see ad, 3rd colour section. It's pricey by Sierra Leone standards, but when, as the owner says, 'you have to fly out every tomato', the premium begins to make sense. Besides, the sheer chutzpah of the whole undertaking is worth experiencing. Set up primarily as a game-fishing lodge, décor is spick & span rather than charming: even so, rooms are simple, homely & set in a flowering garden with a spacious restaurant & pleasant veranda. There's also a pool & a conference centre if you're looking to host a meeting. The real pull is the range of services: more speedboats than you can shake a bit of bait at (a fleet of 9 of varying sizes), birdwatching & island tours, sea transfers from anywhere up to Freetown, expert guides, & a good Beninois chef. Outside the high season for tarpon fishing (see box, opposite), which runs Jan–end May, rates come down so always ask if there's a deal going, & specify if you'd like a room with 2 single beds or a double. Boat rental costs US$600 a day for fishing & US$350 for birdwatching or dolphin-spotting. Restaurant ($$$$). Bookings can also be made through Balmaya Restaurant in Freetown (page 155). FB & B&B packages available. $$$$$

Mama's Guesthouse (5 rooms) Victoria Rd; m 076 712 662. Run by the very friendly Madame Twila, this basic but comfortable little guesthouse is an excellent budget option, with 1 large self-contained room & 4 singles with shared loos. Twila, a retiree who was born in this very compound, runs a little restaurant ($$) on-site, serving mainly barbecue chicken & fish. B/fast is available for an extra fee. 1 room has AC, the rest have fans; running water & electricity all night. $$$–$$

Council Guesthouse (10 rooms) Near Bonthe Holiday Village, Heddle Rd; m 076 994 166, 076 672 416. Funded by the local council & run by a lady named Christiana, this guesthouse is fairly basic, but you can't beat the location right on the coast. All rooms are self-contained & the generator runs from 19.30 to 23.00 (or later, if you're willing to pay a bit more for fuel). You can get b/fast for an extra fee. African dishes ($$) are available for lunch & dinner. $$

Seaside Spot Bar & Guesthouse (7 rooms) Heddle Rd; m 076 974 989, 076 648 542. If you want to forgo the expense of the Holiday Village, this is another decent option. Once a Catholic mission (& still largely referred to as such), it has slightly down-at-heel rooms, some with large porcelain sinks, set around an internal courtyard, & a wide veranda overlooking the estuary & street below. Don't expect much in the way of running water, electricity or food, but you can still find drinks & snacks at the bar. You can always have a blow-out meal at the Holiday Village & rest easy for the night here. $

What to see and do Four large churches are still active in the town, although it's hard to grasp that St Matthew's Church on Corn Street, built in the 1860s, was once home to a robed choir and big-hearted pipe organ.

The school of St Patrick's Roman Catholic Church is said to have been built from the red bricks used as ballast coming from Europe, while the United Methodist Church stands on the site originally set up as a tribute to Sengbeh Pieh, Sierra Leone hero and captive who in 1839 led a mutiny against slave traders while at sea off the coast of Cuba (pages 218–19). After an explosive court case the captives returned to Africa as free men, and an American missionary, Reverend Raymond, went with them to set up the Good Hope Mission on the island in 1850. Some say Sengbeh Pieh is buried on Bonthe, although there is no evidence to support this.

A stroll along Heddle Road, the main seaport road, takes you past wooden boats docking at the rickety pier, and oyster shells piled high on the streets before the bridge. Further to the north is a sacred poro bush. Towards the end of the road is the prison where Foday Sankoh was kept while awaiting trial for war crimes at the UN Special Court. He was incarcerated there because it was thought keeping him in Freetown was too dangerous, but he died in 2003 without ever coming to trial.

The Clock Tower, painted in the bright tricolour of the Sierra Leone flag, is an attempt to spruce the place up a little. A nearby plaque commemorates Sherbro daughter Patricia Kabbah, late wife of the ex-president, who died in 1998. From there, take a left down on to Medina Street, where you'll find the ruined remains of Bonthe Bank and a wreck of a Methodist church with stunning stained-glass windows that still catch the light in glorious fashion. Behind the town, near the airport football field, men shimmy up palm trees, tapping them for poyo, or collecting kernels. Nearby, an enormous silver balloon of a water tower rises high above the treeline. You can climb its rickety ladder and pop your head inside the empty dome, which once pumped enough from a local well to supply the whole town.

If you are in the market for great souvenirs that you don't have to put back into the water, the islanders specialise in making furniture. In a style unique to the area, boxy stools, chairs, sofas and tables are fashioned from bamboo shoots and palm trunks. They make for funky garden furniture, and cost from Le10,000 – much cheaper than Freetown prices. There's also a busy daily market offering basic foodstuffs and clothes and imported goods.

Beyond Bonthe The more ambitious traveller might appreciate a trek across the island from Bonthe to its westernmost point, beyond Baoma, just by the delectable Turtle Islands. If you plan on doing this, the middle of the island is a giant swamp, so you'll be wading through sludge, carrying your bags – and camera equipment, as one enterprising documentary-maker managed – above your head. The hike takes two days, and requires a night's camping in the bush.

Almost all the trails are inland, since the north and eastern coasts are mostly mangrove. For beach, you need to get to the west and southern peninsula. Closer than Baoma but still a hugely rewarding trek, the area that fills the southern shore nearest the mainland is a magical but strenuous 5-hour walk away through forest, marsh, river, mangrove, and even the odd spot of desert-style savannah. Head for Gbie, on a lake, and camp out on the coast. Villages on the way include Fakaisana, a little inland, and, right on the southern coast, Mogbovu. You can camp *en route* on an array of sweeping, empty beaches battered by Atlantic surf, and buy fish locally.

Ask your guesthouse to organise a guide (about Le30,000 a day). If walking the whole way in the heat doesn't appeal, hire a canoe to take you part way. A 2-hour ride between Yoni, midway down the eastern coast, and Bonthe, for example, should cost Le45,000 per person at most.

TURTLE ISLANDS The stuff castaway movies are made of: eight tiny islands – Bakie, Bumpetuk, Chepo, Hoong, Mut, Nyangei, Sei and Yele – form the Turtle Islands, an undeveloped archipelago thrown across the Atlantic just off the western shore of Sherbro Island. Each one is a slice of pure, bright sand sat amid breathtaking azure, framed by sighing palms silhouetted against a hazy blue sky.

Still inhabited, the islands have their fair share of folklore. While the local paramount chief makes his home on Chepo Island, Hoong Island is strictly for initiated men. Women passing by in boats have been known to cover their heads in towels for fear of offending the spirits there, and they certainly never cast eyes on the island. Close to the western shore of Sherbro villages such as Tombe and Moyema, the islands have been described by one old-time resident as a place where the Sherbros 'spend their evenings in groups, drinking and singing traditional songs of bravery and romance'.

Getting there and away For such a grand prize, the islands are appropriately hard to reach, more than 3 hours by **speedboat** from Freetown (100km away), and a couple of hours by speedboat from Bonthe. If you're keen to do a trip from Freetown, try asking around at the **Aqua Sports Club** (page 164) to see whether anyone is planning a trip. Another option is the **Sea Coach Express** (*Aberdeen Bridge, off Sir Samuel Lewis Rd;* m *076 551 155, 077 551 155;* w *seacoachferry.com*), which hires out boats with drivers at a daily rate that varies with the size of the boat; expect to pay something north of US$900 per day.

Perhaps the most popular way to get to the Turtle Islands, however, starts on the Banana Islands with **Daltons Banana Guesthouse** (page 216). They've got a shallow-draft boat that allows much freer navigation between the islands, coasting over and around the myriad flats and sandbanks on which larger boats would run hopelessly aground. Their standard three-day trip departs from the Banana Islands with two nights' camping on Bakie and includes all transport, tents, food and fees for US$850 per boat, with a maximum of four passengers. These tours take a deep dive into the islands' unique maritime culture; surfing and other tours can also be arranged.

From Bonthe, you round the north of Macauley Island, going past Jamaica Point between the mainland and the bulk of the island, until you reach its most northwesterly point. Nyangei is the first island you pass, before heading past Chepo and on towards Yele and Mut, further out. Tide-depending, there are plenty of sandbanks that can slow or halt your progress, so go with a skipper who knows the archipelago well, though even then you may get caught. A speedboat transfer from **Bonthe Holiday Village** (m *076 532 544/686 299;* e *marmar@dircon.co.uk;* w *bontheholidayvillage.info*) costs US$400 for a return trip in the smallest boat. You can also try to negotiate locally with **fishermen**.

Taking a **public boat** to the Turtle Islands is committing to hours at sea in a leaking wooden vessel under the glare of the sun, with little to no recourse in an emergency. That said, one leaves from the mainland at Gbangbatok more or less every Wednesday (and sometimes Thursday), stopping at Turtle on its way to Tombo on the Peninsula near Kent. It can take the whole day and costs Le50,000. The return trip is on a Wednesday. Boats tend to leave early in the morning, tide-depending.

🏠 **Where to stay and eat** Only two of the islands have ever catered officially to tourists, and at the time of writing there were no functional tourist facilities on any of the islands. Bakie is near the larger Yele, which floats somewhere in the middle of the spread. Henri Pelissier, a Frenchman who lived in Sierra Leone on and off for more than 20 years and is now the adopted father of the chief's son, built a small guesthouse on Bakie, but this was destroyed in a storm several years back. Plans exist to refurbish it, but it's unclear when this might happen. Isagah Sesay (m *076 440 230, 099 582 657;* e *isagahsesay@gmail.com*) is the very capable man from the village who managed the guesthouse, so check with him about progress, or visit

5

Sierra Leone is flush with natural resources – iron ore, diamonds, gold, bauxite and rutile can be found in rich seams beneath the ground, while thousands of hectares of forestland and fertile soils lie above it. But of all the riches at the country's disposal, one is being illegally exploited right under the government's nose: its well-stocked seas, which are being plundered by foreign fishing ships, robbing the country of an estimated US$29 million in revenue every year; an estimated 42,000 tonnes of fish were illegally harvested in 2015 alone.

Illegal fishing comes in many forms, from trawling in the in-shore exclusion zone – reserved for local boats – to fishing with forbidden equipment. Ships – mainly Korean, Chinese, and Russian vessels – have long been fishing illegally off Sierra Leone's coast, taking advantage of the fact that the government in Freetown has little ability to police its fish-heavy waters. The activity is having a devastating impact on Sierra Leone's 30,000 artisanal fishermen: their precious nets are often ripped apart by the passing trawlers, and – with stocks dwindling – the fishermen are finding it harder than ever to pull in a decent catch. That's bad news for Sierra Leoneans: 80% of the animal protein they consume comes from fish.

As far back as 2010, the government was drafting a new Fisheries and Aquaculture Bill meant to tighten up enforcement and generally overhaul the management of the sector, which constitutes close to one-tenth of GDP. That being said, despite the bill having long since been completed, it was still awaiting enactment by parliament when this book went to print in late 2017.

Assuming it does go in to effect at some point, much of the updated legislation will focus on making changes in the upper levels of government, but local fishing communities are also crucial to the fight. On that front, a British charity called the Environmental Justice Foundation (EJF) is leading the charge. EJF, which maintains a base in Bonthe, uses a surveillance boat in partnership with the fishing communities along the Sherbro River to patrol for trawlers operating illegally offshore. EJF staff are also teaching local fishermen how to use smartphones to snap incriminating, GPS-tagged photographs of foreign vessels when they encounter them at sea.

Back in Freetown, the government has also started to flex its muscles. In April 2017, Greenpeace and the Ministry of Fisheries and Marine Resources conducted a joint surveillance operation and uncovered four different vessels operating illegally off Sierra Leone's coast in as many days. Their crews were arrested and forced to dock in Freetown, and fines likely to be upwards of US$100,000 are in the works.

But there's still a long way to go – and government officials might not always be on the right side of the fight. In early 2012, the Arabic news network Al-Jazeera aired a two-part documentary that showed just how persistent illegal fishing seems to be off Sierra Leone's coast. The film also offered evidence that senior members of both the Ministry of Fisheries and the Navy were being bribed to look the other way. You can watch the Al-Jazeera documentary online at w aljazeera.com/programmes/peopleandpower/2012/01/201212554311540797.html.

For more information on EJF's work in Sierra Leone, visit the organisation's website (w ejfoundation.org).

w turtleislands.co.uk for updates. There isn't regular phone coverage on the island, but every day he paddles out to a spot where there is to check his messages. Send him a text at the number listed on page 241; he will call you back when he gets it. He checks his email on occasional trips to the mainland. Isagah can also arrange all sorts of island activities, including boat transfers from the mainland, soon in a boat of his own.

Setting up a **tent** on the beach on Bakie – or even just a mosquito net strung up between a couple of palm trees – is of course another option. You'll still be expected to make an offering to the village chief. The people of the island can point you to a suitable **camping** spot. You can also ask around about arranging a canoeing or fishing trip; one of the local fishermen should be able to accommodate you. If you're keen for a local meal, fishermen can supply dinner – fresh catch of the day, including lobster if you ask in time – while the local women can cook up a storm. Pay for your fish as you go, and give something to the chief and anyone else who helps out with the stay. Keep in mind that fresh water is hard to come by on the island, and there isn't any for sale; it's best to bring along a big load of water packets with you from the mainland.

The other option is at Sei, where tourism and speedboat supremo Alan Duncan (**m** *076 879 016, 078 773 585, 076 614 646 for Smokey*) of **Cape Shilling** has an ongoing arrangement with the islanders. Tents, sheets, pillows and even outdoor showers are provided, and you can pitch on the island's ivory-white bay, or doze under a net in one of eight hammocks hanging from coconut trees. A cook will accompany you from Freetown, bringing supplies of eggs and fresh fruit and you can eat from a large net-sided eating hut with carved table for communal dining. You might even be able to go out with a fishing boat and catch your supper ready for barbecuing later that night. Prices for sleeping, eating and transfers from Freetown and back cost around US$400–450 per person for two nights, depending on numbers (minimum six people); this is negotiable.

Alternatively you could also always brave it and turn up at an island (not Hoong) and see if the chief will put you up for the night. Take a tent, water, and all supplies you could potentially need.

What to see and do

Not much, lucky you. Swimming at Turtle is a dreamy experience: the waters are usually clear and flat, like a pleasantly warm bath, slowly ebbing away from the sandy shores into shallow waters. Just pick a side where the artisanal fishing industry doesn't leave its muck. You can also try surfing, although the water can be very rough.

You can chat to fishermen, arrange to go out in a boat, collect coconuts and buy your own fish if you fail to catch it. Of course, look out for sea turtles too. A couple of centuries back, the Sierra Leone Company's coasting cutters sailed from here with provisions, listing 21 turtles from the island.

By day huddle up with a book, go looking for dolphins or don your snorkel. Come night-time, bed down around a campfire with tall tales. Whatever you do, have no doubt that blissful indolence is your friend.

TURNER'S PENINSULA

Almost impossible to get to (we never managed more than a glimpse of it), this ramrod-straight stretch of beach is named after the country's 1825–26 administrator, Major-General Governor Charles Turner, who tried to stamp out the slave trade by extending British rule along the coast. The peninsula proper runs for about 30km, cut away from the mainland by the Kittam River, but the whole stretch of coastline hugs the mainland for 110km in a southeasterly direction from Sherbro to Sulima. Few have caught sight of it, save fishermen heading down the coast to Liberia, but by all accounts it is a beautiful sandy wilderness, bounded by marshy flats. The sluggish rivers behind have formed a mesh of spongy reed-covered islands, making it a likely home for rich mineral deposits.

History It might be a wilderness today, but in 1849 the slave factories along the Gallinas coast were attacked by the British navy, keen to stamp out the slave trade following its 1807 abolition in Britain. 'Dangerous bar and extreme isolation makes it fitted for the haunt of the outlaw and slaver,' wrote Gustav Reinhold Nylander, an early 19th-century missionary to Sierra Leone.

Some daring slavers, such as the Italian Theodore Canot managed to escape under cover of fog along this uncertain coastline, relying on their oars until they could get out to sea and put up their masts. A naval blockade the next year finally forced the hand of the traders, who'd long stopped growing rice in favour of the more lucrative slave trade, and so relied on food supplies via waterways from the Sherbro. Finally the Massaquois and Rogers renounced the trade for good, and released 300 slaves ready for export into the bargain.

Getting there and away Options for getting on to Turner's include rounding Mania Point at the southern tip of the Sherbro Strait by Bonthe. The weather and the water can be ferocious, which means even a hardy speedboat may have to abort. It's even harder to get to from the mainland, cut off by miles of swamp. A local **boat** ferries people once a week from south of Pujehun across Lake Mabesi, beyond which is the remoter-still Lake Mape and dozens of profoundly isolated pinprick villages dotting the peninsula. The safest bet may be getting to Sulima **by road** (itself no picnic), and then crossing the estuary of the river Moa on to the eastern end of the coast (no longer officially called Turner's Peninsula; see page 243). The trek up to Sherbro would be a huge escapade, likely to take five or six days of walking and camping.

TAIAMA The only real sight of note in this sleepy little pit stop 50km shy of Bo is the grand **Taiama Lodge** (*Taiama, Freetown–Bo Highway*; m *076 800 300, 076 324 000, 076 383 2020;* **$$$$$–$$$$**), an impressively ambitious, multi-building hotel that opened in 2011. The brainchild of Wilfred Sam-King, a Sierra Leonean businessman who grew up near Taiama, the lodge – by upcountry standards – is in a class of its own. Its 26 rooms (including one opulent presidential suite) come equipped with air-conditioning, satellite TV, hot water, and safes; some even have bathtubs, mini fridges and electric kettles. There's a swimming pool on-site, as well as a restaurant serving a limited range of Western fare. In the extremely unlikely event that a shoot-out should occur while you're staying in quiet little Taiama, you can rest easy: the hotel's walls and doors are bulletproof.

Although there's little to explore in Taiama itself, the lodge could be a good place for a stopover if you're on your way to Bo or Kenema, or if you have business at the main campus of Njala University, 20 minutes away. Look out for the hotel on the left-hand side of the road as you head east on the Freetown–Bo Highway; you can't miss the sprawling, cream-coloured compound.

BO

Sierra Leone's second city, and capital of the province, is known as the country's party town – Manchester to Freetown's London. That's partly because it's a student hive, and partly due to the high number of diamond dealerships here. It's lost some of its razzle-

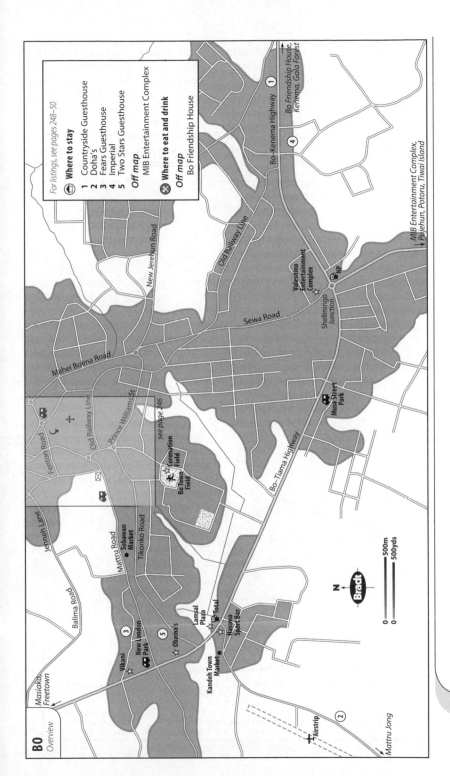

BO
Overview

Masiaka
Freetown

For listings, see pages 248–50

Where to stay
1 Countryside Guesthouse
2 Doha's
3 Fears Guesthouse
4 Imperial
5 Two Stars Guesthouse

Off map
MIB Entertainment Complex

✕ **Where to eat and drink**

Off map
Bo Friendship House

Balima Road

Jenneh Lane

Fenton Road

Old Railway Line

Mattru Road

Vikani

New London Park

3

Obama's

5

Tikonko Road

Sobawan Market

Prince William's St

see page 246

Bo Town Field

Coronation Field

Mahei Boima Road

New Jerehun Road

Old Railway Line

Sewa Road

Lamsal Plaza

Total

Kandeh Town Market

Havona Sport-Bar

Bo–Tiama Highway

Valentino Entertainment Complex

Shellmingo Junction

NP

Musa Street Park

Bo–Kenema Highway

1

4

Bo Friendship House,
Kenema, Gola Forest

MIB Entertainment Complex,
Pujehun, Potoru, Tiwai Island

N

Bradt

0   500m
0   500yds

Mattru Jong

Airstrip

2

dazzle, but once upon a time fun-lovers (and would-be lovers in general) would head here for the weekends, Freetown's cliquey social circles left far behind. Home to Njala University's Bo campus, it's full of radical, enthused young people who are determined to make the most of their studies. It's also the country's gari capital. While the casual visitor might be nonplussed by this fact, it's well worth knowing much of the rest of the country goes mad for it; making a beeline for the women who sell plastic bags of flaky, off-white grated cassava on rickety wooden stalls by the side of the Freetown–Bo Highway, and coming home with as many sacks as they can carry. Wide, flat streets contrast with the capital, making Bo a less traffic-heavy place to get around.

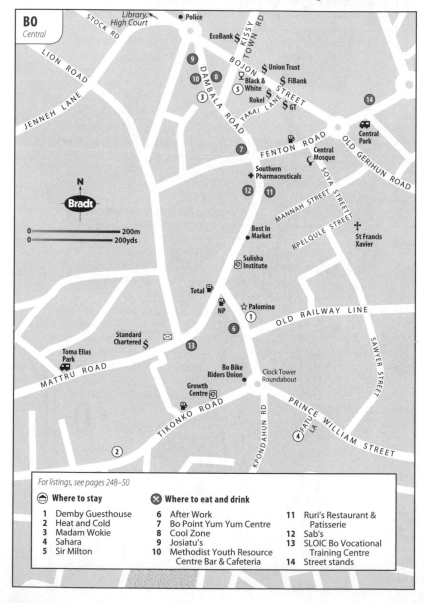

BO
Central

For listings, see pages 248–50

Where to stay
1 Demby Guesthouse
2 Heat and Cold
3 Madam Wokie
4 Sahara
5 Sir Milton

Where to eat and drink
6 After Work
7 Bo Point Yum Yum Centre
8 Cool Zone
9 Josiatu's
10 Methodist Youth Resource Centre Bar & Cafeteria
11 Ruri's Restaurant & Patisserie
12 Sab's
13 SLOIC Bo Vocational Training Centre
14 Street stands

GETTING THERE AND AWAY Bo is 3½ or 4 hours from Freetown, on a road that's perfectly smooth apart from the speed bumps that slow you down as you go through villages. The highway is busy, plied by all manner of vehicles piled high with improbable levels of goods.

From Masiaka, it's 150km to Bo: Moyamba junction is the lunch stop for almost all public vehicles, 36km out of Masiaka. Bus passengers start to salivate well in advance, keen for a hot potato leaf or groundnut soup and rice dished out from a vast cauldron at the main restaurant (which has loos) on the car park. You can also pick up soft drinks, grilled meat, biscuits and fruit from the vendors who fill the area.

As always, the **government bus** is the most reliable option, leaving Freetown at 07.00, for Le20,000. If you miss that, you can pick up **poda poda** and shared taxi transport from the Shell station in the east end, but it's a much less pleasant and much longer ride. Or hire a **taxi**, which is much pricier.

Once in Bo, transport options for onward destinations are almost endless, with a befuddling series of different pickup spots. The basic idea is that if you head in the direction you're going, you'll find transport nearby.

For traffic headed to and from Freetown, go to the transit lorry park at New London on the Bo–Freetown Highway, to the west of town. The government bus passes through Bo daily at 06.00 and sometimes 17.00 too, although taking the later connection means you'll be travelling in the dark, which is not recommended. **Abes**, a fast private minibus company, leaves before dawn, at about 04.00 or 05.00. Poda podas and occasional taxis tend to come through all day until about midnight, charging Le30,000–35,000), and stopping at Mile 91 and Masiaka *en route*. As per usual, taxis pack two passengers in the front and four in the back.

From Toma Elias Park you can pick up local transport to Mattru Jong (Le30,000), Rutile (Le30,000) and Gbangbatok (Le35,000), or to the Liberian border at Jendema (Le90,000). A ride to Zimmi, in the far south, should cost Le50,000; and to Pamelap, at the Guinean border in the north, Le60,000. There are also rides to all the nearby towns, such as Moyamba (Le30,000), Tikonko (Le10,000) and Bumpe (Le15,000). Inside the park there are a few food spots serving cheap rice and plassas or soup for Le2,000–5,000 a plate.

For onward travel to Kenema, an hour east on a good tarmac road, head for Musa Street Park along the Bo–Kenema Highway to the west of Sewa Road. It costs Le18,000 for a seat in a shared taxi; slightly less in a poda poda. Vehicles stop at places on the way – Gerihun and Blama, for example. Cars to Pujehun (Le25,000) also depart from here.

For travel south towards Potoru or Pujehun, most vehicles go from either the Central Park on Fenton Road or the so-called 'Pujehun Park', which is really just roadside parking at the Pujehun Road junction. A seat in a shared taxi to either destination costs Le25,000–30,000. If you're headed to Sulima, it's best to first aim for Zimmi or Jendema and change vehicles there.

ORIENTATION Bo Town is cupped by the Freetown–Kenema Highway, nestling to the north of it. Feeder roads connect north to the town centre, which is framed by a tall isosceles triangle of tarmac. The main roads to look out for include Main Sewa Road, which leads out of town to the Freetown–Kenema Highway; Mahei Boima Road, which joins up with Main Sewa Road; Fenton Road, containing all the auto shops and the market, and Bojon Street, which joins with Kissy Town Road at Black and White's Restaurant.

GETTING AROUND Bo is an ocada-tastic town, with **motorbike taxis** whizzing by. It's easy to flag them down, for Le2,000 per ride 'one-way'.

🔺 **WHERE TO STAY** *Map, page 245, unless otherwise stated*
Mains power in Bo was reasonably reliable when we visited in 2017, but most hotels will switch on a backup generator in case of outages overnight, with the cheaper options typically on from 19.00 to midnight, and the nicer hotels through the night until about 07.00.

🔺 **Countryside Guesthouse** (22 rooms) 2 entry points: 70 Bo–Kenema Highway & 114 New Gerihun Rd; m 076 639 851 (owner Pius George), 076 883 527 (Emo, manager), 076 990 202 (Mrs George); e piusbgeorge@yahoo.com. A bit outside the centre along the road to Kenema, the slightly musty rooms do a good job covering the basics: hot water, bed nets, fridge, satellite TV, AC & en-suite bathrooms (without a door). The high point is the pleasant garden, containing a pretty eating area ($$$), hammocks by the pool & decrepit tennis courts. Non-guests pay Le15,000 for a dip. Lights are on from 19.00 to 07.00 & discounts are available for longer stays. B&B. $$$

🔺 **Doha's Hotel** (40 rooms) 103 Towama Rd; m 079 944 444, 099 944 444; e reservations@ dohashotel.net; w dohashotel.net. Just over 1km south of the Total garage junction, at the centre of Bo's bar scene, this is the newest, nicest address in Bo. The modern rooms, each named for a different African country, come in 5 different categories & all start with AC, satellite TV & hot water. The poolside restaurant does good Lebanese & Sierra Leonean dishes, & the VIP bar upstairs is open late. There's also Wi-Fi & a small fitness centre. $$$

🔺 **Imperial** (11 rooms) 9 Pessima St; m 076 499 636, 078 419 842. A touch out of the way, the hotel's rather extraordinary pebbledash exterior masks a favourite haunt of local dignitaries. Simple rooms are suitably equipped with hot water, TV & fridge. A good restaurant ($$$) includes b/fast, as well as African lunch dishes & a regular buffet. The hotel taxi does expensive trips into town, or hop on the back of a Honda for Le2,000. B&B. $$$

🔺 **MIB Entertainment Complex** (30 rooms) 485 Bo–Koribondo Highway; m 078 410 814, 078 762 880, 030 746 721, 088 704 263; e mibinvestment2016@gmail.com. Set 3km south of Shellmingo junction on the Zimmi Road, this new place is a bit removed from the action, but becomes a hive of its own at weekends, when (noisy) weddings, graduations & other celebrations take over the compound. The rooms are neat, & all come with AC, TV & en-suite ablutions. There's also a swimming pool, bar & rather indifferent restaurant. $$$

🔺 **Fears Guesthouse** (8 rooms) m 076 640 351, 076 606 375. There's nothing to be afraid of at this family-run guesthouse in the backstreets behind the New London transport park. (The unusual name is actually just a combination of family members' names.) Rooms are homely & trim, with AC, TV, mozzie nets & en-suite facilities. B&B. $$

🔺 **Madam Wokie Hotel** [map, page 246] (34 rooms) 25 Dambala Rd; m 076 977 631, 076 921 774, 076 600 868. The sister act to the Sir Milton (below) just over the road, prices & standards match up. Fine basic rooms are a little more institutional in feel than the attractive chaos next door. This one has a car park but no (functioning) restaurant. B&B. $$

🔺 **Sahara Hotel** [map, page 246] (53 rooms, 30 under construction) 4 Fatu Lane, off Prince William St; m 079 776 293, 088 322 604. Nice, continually expanding modern block with reasonable starting prices for basic rooms & a canteen-style restaurant ($$). TV & AC are available in some rooms; all but the cheapest single rooms are self-contained. B&B. $$

🔺 **Sir Milton Hotel** [map, page 246] (28 rooms) 6 Kissy Town Rd; m 076 600 868, 076 531 154 (Jelani Kamara, manager). A stalwart (it's named after the country's first president) in a good central location, this is probably the best option for a cheap stay. Basic but difficult to fault for the price, rooms comprise en suites, hot water, bed nets & b/fast. Pay extra for TV or AC. Try & get a smile from the restaurant ($$) staff & you should qualify for some kind of discount. Meals are European & take a while – generally chicken or fish with chips or couscous. B&B. $$

🔺 **Heat and Cold** [map, page 246] (31 rooms) 42 Tikonko Rd; m 076 706 175, 088 142 546, 078 208 344. Every room has a surprisingly pleasant veranda at this otherwise characterless multistorey block in the centre of town, & the fact it's the tallest thing around means you get a generous helping of breeze included in the price of a room. For the heat enthusiast, fan rooms start at Le100,000, while connoisseurs of cold will prefer some AC for Le200,000; all come with TV & hot

Visit Gola Rainforest National Park,

a world renowned biodiversity hotspot and Sierra Leone's "Green Diamond". Walk in the footprints of elephants, watch primates and hear the calls of chimpanzees. Visit cocoa farmers, cultural shows, stay in Eco-lodges, experiencing village life. This pristine rainforest is home to over 600 butterfly and 300 bird species, including the vulnerable Picathartes.

Conservation Society of Sierra Leone

14a King St. (off Congo Cross) Freetown, Sierra Leone
E: ecotourism.cssl@gmail.com
M: (+232)(0)79 443 420

Bonthe Holiday Village

Luxury big game fishing camp
15 self-contained rooms

Fine French cuisine
Boats for fishing and pick-up

Bonthe Holiday Village, Heddle Rd, Bonthe. Book via Balmaya Restaurant, Freetown +232 76627799
www.bontheholidayvillage.com, info@bontheholidayvillage.com, marmar@dircon.co.uk

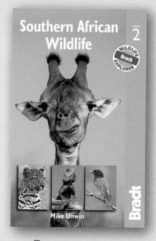

 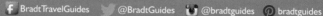

MOST TRUSTED AND **RELIABLE TOUR**
OPERATOR IN SIERRA LEONE

TOURS

VISAS

VEHICLE HIRE

AIRPORT TRANSFERS

HOTEL RESERVATIONS

FLIGHT TICKETING

CRUISE SHIP HANDLING

"Thank you to VSL for helping me with visa, flight, water taxi, vehicle, currency exchange, and accommodation needs! It made for a very easy and friendly first business trip to Sierra Leone. Looking forward to working with you again!" - Jennifer Cramer

As tour operators since 2004, we put visitors at the forefront of everything we do, because we always want you to leave with the desire to return.

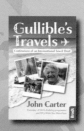

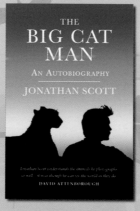

water. There are a few budget single rooms using shared facilities out back. No food. **$$–$**

🔺 **Demby Guesthouse** [map, page 246] (11 rooms) 3 Tikonko Rd; m 078 301 198. Just across the street from After Work, this rather rundown establishment offers very basic rooms off a pretty open breezeway. 2 rooms are self-contained; all have fans & mozzie nets. The popular Palomino nightclub is located downstairs, so steer clear if you're looking for peace & quiet. B&B. **$**

BO'S BIKE RIDERS

Mustapha Sesay was abducted by the Revolutionary United Front (RUF) from his village when he was 12 and given a wooden stick to practise shooting. One day it was replaced with the real thing, a general-purpose machine gun. 'We would ambush trucks on the highway when we wanted to get food,' says the 22 year old. 'We were trying to liberate this country, this land.'

More than ten years later, he rides a motorbike in Bo, zooming passengers who pay 20 pence to cling on behind him around the town's busy streets. Sesay is a member of the Bo Bike Riders' Association, an extraordinary product of the post-war years. The town is home to nearly 5,000 motorcycle taxi drivers, of whom more than 80% are ex-fighters drawn from conflicting factions.

More than 70,000 fighters were disarmed at the end of the war, mainly by the UN, each given Le300,000 (US$100 at the time) in exchange for their weapon. Many drifted into riding motorcycle taxis after skills-training schemes funded by international donors closed down or ran out of money. The ex-fighters still find life tough, and political parties occasionally try to recruit them as bodyguards. Just as taxi drivers tend to pay their sponsor Le10,000–50,000 a day to hire their car, so the bike riders have no access to credit to buy their own vehicles and pay a daily rental fee to bike owners. Often three drivers share one bike, as there are not enough to go around. They make between Le40,000 and Le150,000 (US$10–33) a month, from rides in and around the city centre, which their organisers say is not enough.

'We work together as a means of creating revenue for unemployed youth so they don't go back to the bush, but they are very poor. Sometimes they come here to sleep on wooden benches in the open,' says the association's legal advisor Solomon Rogers. 'Unemployment led to the war: an idle man is a devil's workshop. The bike riders can be very volatile.'

Sesay was fed drugs on the frontline to stay high. Having lived through that, he is determined not to go back to war: 'It pains us to imagine our past, I don't like to reflect on it. We don't get money now but nothing can make me fight again.'

A casual pit stop at the bikers' Bo headquarters reveals an unlikely repartee between former enemies. Sesay's 40-year-old colleague, Femi Rashid, joined the traditional Kamajor hunters to defend the country against Sesay and the rest of the rebels. His entire body is scarred with small gashes from a series of magical spells intended to make him impermeable to bullets. He says he also made himself disappear when rebels attacked. One-time adversaries, today Sesay and Rashid work side by side, helping the bike riders get by, meeting youth groups and urging peace and conciliation.

'Once they were fighting and now they are working together. It's amazing,' says David Ngombu from international aid organisation Conciliation Resources. 'They are all from the same Sierra Leonean family, and they have got back together.'

5

🏠 **Two Stars Guesthouse** (19 rooms, 4 sharing a bathroom) 14 Sillah St; m 076 643 679. Sweet enough & super-simple, with rooms named after Champions League footballers. Rooms here range from a single bed with no fan & no net, to a double with fan, net, & TV as well. The generator is on from 19.00 to midnight & they can cook for you with advance notice. $

✖ WHERE TO EAT AND DRINK *Map, page 246, unless otherwise stated*

✖ **Bo Friendship House** [map, page 245] Bo–Kenema Highway; m 076 602 861. A sizeable place by the main road, keener on serving up booze, football & slow dances than food, but can still manage the likes of chicken fried rice, couscous & salad, so long as you order in advance. $$$

✖ **Sab's Restaurant** 25 Dambala Rd; m 076 311 313; ⏱ 08.00–18.00 Tue–Sun. Though it was closed for renovation (& expansion) in early 2017, this fiercely AC'ed spot should be open again by the time you read this & is good for a decent falafel or shawarma. You can also order pizzas, burgers, & other Western dishes from its long-ish menu. A couple of TVs perched on the wall tend to show Hollywood movies. $$$–$$

✖ **Cool Zone** 46b Dambala Rd; m 076 678020/658924; ⏱ 08.00–23.30. Like a musty café from an old-English time-warp, the fake flowers wrapped around grey columns & crackling old plastic tablecloths do the trick. Serving homely African dishes, chicken, couscous, salads & shawarmas, this place scores high on choice & old-school atmosphere. In the rainy season, it's likely to have enough (hydro-powered) electricity to power the ice cream & popcorn maker – a treat. $$

✖ **Josiatu's** 53 Dambala Rd; m 076 400 111, 078 126 535. Its billing as a wine bar is not exactly accurate, but they do Salone staple dishes during the day & there's beer & music in the shaded courtyard by night, with a live band on Fri. They've got some rather tired-looking fan & AC rooms as well ($$–$). $$

✖ **Ruri's Restaurant & Patisserie** 28 Dambala Rd; m 077 737 373, 079 600 600. This 1st-floor joint does fast-food favourites like shawarmas, pizzas, burgers & the like, alongside more traditional Sierra Leone dishes & a selection of cakes & pastries. $$

✖ **Bo Point Yum Yum Centre** Fenton Rd. This bright blue *pan body* (corrugated zinc) shack is a conveniently central spot for a quick omelette sandwich & a sugary tea or Nescafé. $

✖ **Methodist Youth Resource Centre Bar & Cafeteria** Dambala Rd, opposite Cool Zone; m 078 577 510 (Bob Momoh, manager), 078 504 600; ⏱ 08.00–18.00. Make your way past the brightly painted HIV awareness signs on the walls & you have a great choice of freshly prepared, classic African dishes served from vats in the canteen by a team of women. It's a friendly place, with some pleasant spots in a central compound to munch away in. Beer too. $

✖ **SLOIC Bo Vocational Training Centre** 1 Mattru Rd; m 078 861 006, 077 031 921. Run as part of the capacity-building programming at the Sierra Leone Opportunities Industrialisation Centre (SLOIC), this is a good canteen for lunch, particularly if you're waiting around at Toma Elias Park. $

✖ **Street stands** Fenton Rd. Great nosh to be had here, with plenty of grilled meat, fry fry stands with beans & bread, gari stands, cookeries serving rice & sauce from a big cauldron, & attieke women. $

🍷 **After Work** 1 Tikonko Rd; ⏱ 09.00–late daily. Popular with development workers & locals alike, beer in this almost-garden setting tastes good. There's occasional finger food like pepper chicken & roast meat, but the point is to kick back, relax outdoors and enjoy a well-earned drink. $$

ENTERTAINMENT AND NIGHTLIFE Be warned that every nightclub in town closes during the month of Ramadan, except Black and White's.

🍷 **Black & White Bar** m 078 720 596. Next to the Sir Milton Hotel & something of a landmark in central Bo, this place has been around for ages – it was the town's first racially integrated drinking hole – & even gets a mention in Richard Dowden's *Africa: Altered States, Ordinary Miracles*. With open sides & a 1st-floor perch overlooking the busy streets below, it's a good spot to catch a bit of breeze & boozy banter, along with the football, of course.

☆ **Coronation Field** Bo Town Field. When it's not hosting football matches, this is the town's main concert venue for visiting musicians & acts. Gigs tend to start late & finish early the following morning.

☆ **Havana Sport Bar** Bo–Kenema Highway & Towama Rd; ⏱ until 03.00 daily. Directly opposite the eponymic Total station at the same junction as Lamsal Plaza, this mostly outdoor bar is probably a shade nicer than its sibling across the street & has plenty of loud music, terrace seating & big outdoor grills piled with fish & meat.

☆ **Lamsal Plaza** Bo–Kenema Highway & Towama Rd; ◑ until late daily. Directly next to a Total filling station & almost universally referred to by that name, the cluster of bars at this junction represents the epicentre of Bo's nightlife scene, & it's a rare night you won't find something (boozy) or other going on here. At Lamsal Plaza itself, there's terrace seating out front, billiards inside, cold beer & snacky food.

☆ **Obama's Bar & Restaurant** Bo–Kenema Highway; ◑ 08.00–midnight daily. A few hundred metres removed from party central at the Total garage, this presidentially inspired pub is another reliable address for cold beers in the evening, with a nice open-sided bar area perched a few metres above street level & football on the flatscreens.

☆ **Palomino Restaurant & Nightclub** 3 Tikonko St; m 076 726 251. Once flashy, but now looking a bit trashy; head here if you're in After Work across the road & fancy making a night of it.

☆ **Valentino Entertainment Complex** Sewa Rd, Shellmingo junction; m 078 688 777; ◼ valentinoentertainment; ◑ until late daily. If the scene at the Total garage gets a bit too raucous for you, this welcoming courtyard nightspot makes a fine antidote. The crowd varies depending on the night, but it generally skews a bit older than the occasionally adolescent competition. Live bands play once or twice every weekend (usually Fri & Sun), & other nights there's often a DJ or other event.

☆ **Vikani Nightclub** New London, Bo–Freetown Highway; m 076 875 971; ◑ 20.00–05.00 Wed–Sun. Once the high-class establishment in town, it's been outdone by the newcomers & feels a little worn by comparison, but it was undergoing renovations in 2017 & still manages to attract a loyal, well-to-do crowd.

OTHER PRACTICALITIES

Banks Bo is now home to a healthy complement of ATM-equipped banks, and makes a good place to stock up on cash for excursions around the south. Most banks are on or near Bojon Street, including **GT Bank** (*14 Bojon St*), **Union Trust Bank** (*7 Bojon St*), **Rokel Commercial Bank** (*20 Bojon St*), **FiBank** (*11 Bojon St*), **EcoBank** (*5 Kissy Town Rd*), and **Standard Chartered Bank** (*4 Mattru Rd*).

Internet At the time of writing, internet connections in Bo were about as good as in Freetown – which is to say not especially fast, but decently reliable. If you've got your own device, the most pleasant way to get online is probably to use the Wi-Fi at the restaurant at Doha's Hotel (and maybe go for a swim while you're at it). Otherwise, there are a couple of centrally located internet cafés including the **Sulisha Institute** (*2 Dambala Rd; m 076 535 534*) and **Growth Centre** (*14 Tikonko Rd; m 078 873 333*), the latter of which also has a canteen attached.

Medical Southern Pharmaceuticals (*27 Dambala Rd; m 076 633 443; ◑ 08.30–18.00 Mon–Fri, 08.30–14.00 Sat*) offers Bo's biggest range of medicines and toiletries. There are plenty of other pharmacies to choose from, including **Mama Hawa** (*13A Bojon St*) and **Kakua Pharmacy** (*31a Fenton Rd; m 076 301 537*).

Shopping If you're looking to stock up on food, the Lebanese-owned **Best In Market** (*10 Dambala Rd; w bestinmarketsl.com; ◑ 09.00–21.00 Mon–Sat*) is the biggest in town, with a wide variety of canned goods, toiletries, snacks and the like. Otherwise, there's **Bo Mini Market** (*6 Dambala Rd; ◑ 09.00–14.00 & 15.00–21.00 Mon–Sat*), which is small but well stocked and you can pay in, or change, US dollars. It also makes juicy burgers and shawarmas to take away.

AROUND BO

South of Bo on the Pujehun Road, the bridge over the Sewa River is a good spot for a picture and a pitcher of poyo. It's only 10 minutes out of town, easily reached by motorbike taxi. A little further on from the bridge, a sign on the right reads 'Gondama beach 300m', pointing off to a beach. Stretching away in both directions from the busy area for 'brooking' clothes are good patches of yellow sand among the black rocks at the side of the river.

Further south on the same road, look for the sign saying 'Globe', which also leads off to the right to a more secluded river beach, manned by members of the local community 'social club' – trying to improve themselves and make a buck in the process. Locals might know it better as Magbwema Beach, the village just after the signboard.

POTORU A small and quiet town, Potoru is the last main stop on the way to Tiwai Island. The wider area is home to the country's largest rubber plantations, the product of most of which is currently taken out – often smuggled – through Liberia.

The wood-roofed market has limited supplies, but prices are cheap. There's usually smoked fish, tins of tomato purée, kola nuts (Le200 for five), chives (Le100 a bunch), red and green chillis (Le200 for a handful), sesame snap biscuits and more. Further down the road, there's a tiny cookery in front of an abandoned building serving a hearty lunch. A delicious dish of cassava balls and black-eyed beans goes for an improbably low Le1,000, while there is also the usual rice and plassas, and fish soup with rice.

The **Environmental Foundation for Africa (EFA)** (m *076 611 410;* w *efasl.org;* $), an NGO based just outside of Freetown, has three basic rooms in need of renovation with pit latrine and bucket showers, if you need to stay the night. It's easy to get transport here from Bo for around Le30,000.

TIWAI ISLAND A visit to this tropical rainforest island is undoubtedly one of Sierra Leone's wildlife highlights. Encircled by the slow-flowing waters of the Moa River, you are immersed in the sights and sounds of one of the world's densest and most diverse chimpanzee and monkey populations and more than 700 species of plant life, not to mention the pygmy hippo, a squat little nocturnal beast found only in Liberia, Ivory Coast, Guinea and Sierra Leone.

It's a pleasing adventure unmatched by anything else in the country – far from Freetown and, accessible only by motor launch, you camp in unusually good conditions. The name Tiwai might mean 'big' in Mende, but at 12km² (measuring 6km by 3km at its longest and widest points), it's easy to make the island your own, and a rare chance to hole up in a corner of the Upper Guinea forest region of West Africa (one of 25 'biodiversity hotspots' in the world), with the highest mammalian diversity of any tropical forest.

History Split between two chiefdoms (legend has it that half of the island was given as a dowry to the family of one chief's daughter's husband), there has been past competition for its verdant bounty, resulting in slash-and-burn farming, animal hunting and timber logging. But the committed, honest work of the Environmental Foundation for Africa (EFA) has encouraged local communities to see the long-term benefits that research and tourist visitors can bring, ensuring that poaching is now virtually non-existent on the island.

Declared a game reserve in 1987, it was first identified as a valuable ecological site in the late 1970s, when Professor John Oates, an anthropologist from Hunter College of the City University of New York, conducted surveys on the island. He has since written extensively on its ecosystems – from conservation strategies and the ratio of protein to fibre in leaves, to why the olive colobus monkey mixes with the Diana monkey. After Oates's unearthing, the island became a prime spot for primate research (see box, page 259).

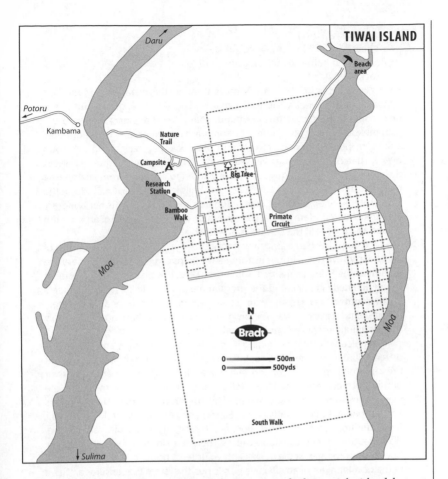

TIWAI ISLAND

Daru

Beach area

Potoru

Kambama

Nature Trail

Campsite

Big Tree

Research Station

Bamboo Walk

Primate Circuit

Moa

Moa

N

Bradt

0 — 500m
0 — 500yds

South Walk

Sulima

The war destroyed not only the research and tourism facilities on the island, but put wildlife populations at risk. Guides fled for their lives, targeted because rebels presumed they had wads of cash and, as government employees, saw them as the enemy.

'We were working when I heard the gunshots,' said one guide. 'We left the island by boat but I heard the rebels were asking for me; because I was working with payments they thought I had money. I took to my heels, took a different route and stayed there. I was in the bush for 18 days. They were searching for me.'

When they got to the island, the rebels took everything – generators, motorbikes, outboard engines, camera materials, tents; even the campsite's freezer.

'They poached the animals,' said the guide, of both the rebels and the government soldiers later stationed on the island. 'They nearly killed all the monkeys.'

Chimps largely escaped with their lives because for most Sierra Leoneans, particularly Muslims, their meat is close enough to human flesh to be considered taboo.

It was not until 2003 that research restarted on the island, with the aim of creating a protected area suitable for biodiversity research, conservation and ecotourism. Now Tiwai Island is a wildlife sanctuary under Sierra Leonean law, and hunting on the island is prohibited. Getting the island ship-shape once again has meant convincing local communities not to farm, hunt or log, and the only way to do that is to show that the interest and deep pockets of researchers and tourists would eventually count for more, as long as proceeds from the sanctuary are fairly distributed. EFA tries to attract higher education and research institutions to pay for fieldwork on the island for months at a time; in 2007, the first researchers since the war arrived to study monkey calls and behaviour. A Fulbright scholar from the University of Georgia in the United States arrived soon after, looking for the shy pygmy hippo, and the island's research station continues to host visiting scholars from institutions across the globe.

Getting there and away Tiwai is about a 5- or 6-hour **drive** from Freetown, so depending on how you're travelling you can get there in one long-ish day or break up the journey with an overnight stay, most likely at Bo, 90km away. From Bo, take the tarred road south through Koribundo towards Pujehun. After about 48km there is a left turning towards Potoru signposted for Zimmi and the Moa River. Roadworks destined for Zimmi and the Liberian border had just reached Potoru at the time of writing in mid 2017. Follow this new tarmac for about 25km until you hit Potoru, where at a small roundabout you should take the left fork. Take the clearly marked right-hand turning after about 3km and continue 13km through secondary forest to the village of Kambama, opposite the island on the west bank of the Moa River. Kambama (✪ *7.55639,-11.36468*) is where you should leave your vehicle; the island's **boat** can transport you to the island's jetty – a short walk from the campsite – in 10 minutes. The cost of the boat ride is included in the entry fee – Le50,000/100,000 Sierra Leonean/foreigner for a day visit. Alternatively, you can plump for a local canoe if you've not yet had enough adventure getting there, but you'll still be liable for the visitor's fee.

If you don't have your own vehicle, take **public transport** south from Bo to Potoru, which takes about 2 hours and costs around Le30,000. The one daily trip leaves from the Central/Pujehun Park on Fenton Road at about 13.00–14.00. From Potoru, hop on the back of a motorbike taxi for Le15,000 to Kambama. The road is a dirt track after Potoru, though it's not too bad by Sierra Leonean standards and a saloon car should be able to get through without much trouble in the dry season.

If you're extremely lucky on timings, your trip to Tiwai may coincide with EFA staff travelling from Bo, or at least Potoru. Call the head office (m *076 611 410*), located 15 minutes outside Freetown, to check.

🏠 **Where to stay and eat** The island has a basic, comfortable **campsite**, with tents and hammocks, dining and washing facilities. Domed tents are permanently set up on five forest platforms, under open-sided wooden roofs. If you need more tents just ask – there are usually a few spare. The bigger ones are roomy enough to sleep up to four people comfortably, with plenty of space for gear, and a fair share of holes gives accommodation to the odd ant or spider from the forest too; two-person tents are also available. All tents come equipped with mattresses, which are nice and soft if a bit musty. The shower water smells reassuringly, and pungently, of disinfectant, and there's a block with flushing loos. If you'd prefer something a bit sturdier, the **research station** is a short walk away and has six double rooms for hire with beds, mosquito nets, solar lighting, and running showers in shared bathrooms.

You'll probably spend time lounging in the central dining-cum-relaxing area, set in an extremely atmospheric, grass-carpeted forest clearing. It was destroyed by a storm in 2015, but has since been rebuilt and is once again looking sharp. If you prefer to do your own cooking, the staff can set you up with a stove and cooking utensils, or simply an open fire. But if you feel like being pampered, they can provide you with a hearty local meal finished off with sweet fresh pineapple. (Note, however, that any meals should be ordered well in advance – ideally at least a day or two ahead – in order to allow the cook ample time to source the necessary provisions, unless you come with your own ingredients.) A simple but filling breakfast of bread and Laughing Cow cheese is also on offer.

Tent accommodation costs Le215,000/115,000 per foreigner/Sierra Leonean per night, including forest entry, or Le260,000/145,000 at the research station. It's Le100,000/50,000 per foreign/Sierra Leonean day visitor. You can book via the headquarters of the EFA (m *076 755 146, 076 611 410*; e *info@tiwaiisland.org*; w *tiwaiisland.org or* w *efasl.org*) to arrange a guide, who will organise transport across the river, walks and provisions, or contact the park directly by SMS: Alusine (m *079 286 038*), Ibrahim (m *076 297 071*), or Dolly (m *078 152 560*) can all handle booking enquiries.

Visitors should bring enough cash to pay for food, drinks, transport and loo paper. You can buy bottled water, sodas and Star beer on the island; shockingly, there are no marshmallows, however, so if drinking round the fire and toasting sweets is your late-night idea of camping, come well equipped.

Other practicalities The closest mobile-phone coverage is at Potoru, 15km away, but there's a sweet spot near Kambama where staff can pick up and reply to SMS enquiries.

What to see and do There are long-standing plans to add to the guided walking circuits currently offered, but as of now there are only a handful of routes typically used. Don't let that stop you from coming up with your own ideas about what you want to see, however, and asking to go and visit whatever occurs. Most important on Tiwai, don't try to rush your stay: most visitors stay only for one full day, arriving late at night and leaving first thing after a second night, which seems an over-hasty waste of two full days' travelling from Freetown. Better to stay two full days at least, and arrive with willingness to potter, ponder and wander on your own. Bring that book you want to finish, and a head ready for daydreaming.

Guides Currently Tiwai is the only site in Sierra Leone that offers such a well-established ecotourism facility, boasting a near-guarantee of observing some of the rarest wildlife in the world. This is only made possible by the dedication and expertise of excellent guides. A branch high up in the canopy you've not even noticed often turns out to be a primate limb or bird wing. Not only are they mean spotters, the guides' mastery of different animal calls is a show on its own, as they can mimic birds and monkeys with ample skill. Many have survived the war and come back to the island they fell in love with, living and working in exceptionally difficult circumstances. It's always nice to tip them.

Wander with the wildlife Exploring the island's dense forest is a *Lost World*-like incursion, beneath 30m giant redwood trees, thick vines and *lianas*. Most otherworldly of all are the outsize, cathedral-like splays of giant bamboo shoots to slip between.

As well as hippos, monkeys and birds (see below), the island is home to a variety of mongoose – Liberian, slender, marsh and Gambian – otters, rats and squirrels, including the African giant squirrel, and shrews.

Researchers have created a strict grid system of tracks in the northwestern part of the forest. Each track has a letter or a number, so if you pay attention you can get yourself round the grid and home on your own. Setting out on these tracks offers the best chance of finding monkeys, because the primates are used to humans wandering below them on surveys, and the guides know their bearings exactly. In total you have 50km of walking paths to explore.

Mimic the monkeys Tiwai has a high density of primate life, including the globally threatened Diana monkey, olive colobus monkey and western chimpanzee; plus the red and black-and-white colobus, the sooty mangabey, Campbell's monkey and lesser spot-nosed monkey.

Early morning is the best time for spotting, and the earlier you can get up the better. Tracking these animals in their natural habitat, with none of the gimmickry or tricks employed by more game-rich countries catering for a more sedentary tourist market, is genuinely exciting.

The first sensing of colour and noise high above your head is an unmissable thrill. If you glimpse what looks like an orange hair-dye attempt gone badly wrong, you've probably just stumbled on the red colobus, all brash and burnt, while a lithe, angular jumper is most likely the black-and-white colobus.

The primates are highly sensitive to what's going on below, easily spooked, and tend to stay almost exclusively in the upper canopy of the trees, which means they are usually at least 90m away; keep your neck craned and a pair of binoculars nearby.

Pursue the pygmies When intrepid BBC documentary makers turned up to spend weeks trying to catch sight of the cheeky little nocturnal things on film, the best they got was a dark blur. So, while it's super unlikely you'll get to see a pygmy hippo anywhere other than at a zoo, the point is they are here on Tiwai.

And that's really saying something. In 1993, a survey estimated as few as 2,000 of the *Choeropsis liberiensis* remained, found elsewhere only in the Gola rainforest in Sierra Leone and in parts of Liberia, Guinea and Ivory Coast. Now Sierra Leone is thought to be home to 80 to 100 hippos.

Endangered and threatened, the pygmy hippo is a solitary nocturnal animal, eating swampy vegetation on land and in the river. While they're not particularly territorial, they do like their own space and make that pretty clear to everything around them by wagging their tails vigorously when they defecate, so the faeces scatter everywhere around.

With a lineage going back 60 million years, the pygmy hippo is the relation of both the more recognisable common hippo (*Hippopotamus amphibius*) and the whale family. An adult weighs about 160–270kg, and is 1.5m long, standing 1m or so high, with a 20cm tail. Where the common hippo has webbed feet, the pygmy has separated toes with sharp nails, and its incisors and canines are tusk-like and grow rapidly. It spends most of the day in the cool of swamps, hollows or rivers, emerging to feed on vegetation during the late afternoon and at night, travelling on a network of regular paths that tunnel through thick vegetation.

If you're feeling lucky, suffer from insomnia, and can avoid snapping too many twigs, head to the cove near the island's research station where pygmy hippos have been seen before. Go late, late into the night, with a guide. And when you fail to spot anything, you can ask the guides to tell you over an early breakfast about the times when they have had more success than you. If you seek reassurance that this isn't all a massive wind-up there is plenty of evidence of footmarks and spoor on the muddy shallows around the island.

Get twitching With more than 135 different bird species on the island, including eight types of hornbills and the white-breasted guineafowl, have your binoculars, your tick-list and your sweet cooing calls at the ready.

Travel the river You can take a trip around the island in a canoe or motorboat, watching birds fly overhead or river turtles surface. Night tours can search for the pygmy hippopotamus by boat too. At the time of writing, ambitious plans to buy kayaks for the island and offer longer river tours had long been discussed, but seemed more or less on hold as of 2017. Should they get off the ground (or on to the water, as it were), one possibility would be an expedition downstream to the surf-heavy Sulima on the coast near Liberia, where the Moa River flushes out into the Atlantic after its journey from Guinea. With a night or two camping in the bush along the way, and miles of jungle banks and wildlife to explore, this, if it starts, would be one of the country's must-do activities. Also on the Moa, Tacugama Chimpanzee Sanctuary (page 187) has plans for a research centre and visitor accommodation on Jaibui Island, just a few kilometres downstream from Tiwai – call or check their website for updates.

Beach moment Just in case you pine for the sandy joys of the western Peninsula, the island even has its own secluded beach, off its northwest tip. It's easy to get lost on the trails to and from this hidden stretch of sand, so it's best to ask a guide to escort you. Access is seasonal, since during the rains the beach is hidden underwater, and admittedly the sand is a bit coarser, but you can enjoy a cooling swim in clean, fast-flowing fresh water. Look out for river otter paw prints, as they sometimes like to play on the sand. If you're lucky (or unlucky, depending on your mood), you might see a crocodile.

ZIMMI

Zimmi lives and breathes its border-town status with anxious gusto – there is plenty of last-ditch buying, refuelling and contraband passing through. Something of a mini diamond and gold rush has brought prospectors flocking to areas that haven't been overmined to the same extent as Kono. They head deep into the nearby forests, but Zimmi is their base for all the diamond lust. Tourism is not a word with which many are familiar down here, and most locals will automatically think you are involved with the diamond trade in some way. So be careful where you point a camera, and it's best to check in at the police post if you plan to stay a night or two.

Getting there and away The highway from Bo to Liberia should be complete within the lifespan of this edition, making access to Zimmi and beyond easier than ever. A few shared taxis head this way daily from Bo's Toma Elias Park for Le50,000. Despite being geographically closer, access from Kenema (pages 263–9) is somewhat trickier, and requires a roughly 3-hour ocada trip (Le150,000) on a road in variable condition, or catching a more-or-less daily poda poda.

It's 43km from Zimmi to the Liberian border post at Jendema/Bo Waterside, passing two turn-offs to Sulima after 34km and 40km; using either route it's another 25km on bad roads to Sulima. Transport from Zimmi to Jendema will be smooth sailing once the new road is complete, but there are no immediate plans to upgrade the route to Sulima. An ocada for the 58km from Zimmi to Sulima should run you about Le90,000 and around half that for the 27km from Sulima to Jendema.

If arriving from Potoru in your own vehicle, you will have to take the **ferry** – a wooden raft connected to steel cables that is pulled from one side of the river to the other – just before Zimmi. Officially it's a 'government' ferry with salaried boatmen, but they look as though the last time they were paid may have been when Sierra Leone still exported rice, so a tip of around Le10,000 per vehicle is appropriate. This will soon be replaced with a bridge as part of the ongoing roadworks. Zimmi is the last place you can be sure of filling up with petrol or diesel before the border.

🏠 **Where to stay and eat** If you're headed to or from Liberia, there's actually a wider selection of accommodation at the border in Jendema. Here you'll find a handful of basic guesthouses, including **Vision** (m 076 190 133), **Coco International** (m 076 795 419) and **Home Pride** (m 088 815 351, 076 553 688).

🏠 **Sileti Guesthouse** (2 rooms) m 078 356 061, 076 420 218, 076 899 440, 076 967 320; e info@ golarainforest.org. About 5km outside Zimmi, this little guesthouse inside the Gola Rainforest National Park (pages 269–75) is worth a bit of a detour if you're looking to spend the night in the area. Both of the rooms are self-contained & come with mosquito nets & clean linen. Solar power keeps the lights on until around 23.00. You are welcome to use the basic little kitchen to cook your own meals. **$$**

'On 18 December 1982 at approximately 16.05 while following a group of *Cercopithecus diana* monkeys on Tiwai Island, I heard loud, repeated hammering or chopping noises which sounded similar to a human chopping wood,' wrote biologist George Whitesides of the University of Miami. Despite the scholarly tone, the breathy excitement of the discovery shines through.

'I investigated these noises, and upon approaching to within about 50m from the source, deafly detected chimpanzee vocalizations ... Intermittent bursts of hammering continued until about 16.30 at which time the vocalizations and vegetation disturbance ceased. Upon close investigation of the location at which the chimps were first detected, I found numerous freshly opened pods of *Detarium senegalense* (Caesalpiniaceae) scattered in an area about 10m in diameter ... I could open pods only with the aid of a hammer ... The most likely method for cracking *Detarium* nuts seems stick *use* ... Several sticks that could have been used for this purpose were found at the site.'

And so it was that scientists first stumbled across evidence that chimpanzees were capable of using tools. In February 1985, Tiwai specialist John Oates found two stones lying near each other at the southern end of the island, pitted with the apparent effort of cracking nuts, whose open shells lay nearby. Then, the breakthrough. Two days later, Robert Kluberoanz watched an adult male chimpanzee break open a nut with a large stone, with seven other chimps nearby. There were 13 of these cracking anvils, each surrounded by broken nuts.

Community Guesthouse (4 rooms) Located behind the community hall, Zimmi. There's no running water or electricity at this basic, village-run guesthouse, but it's a convenien place to spend the night if you're on your way to the Liberian border. The loo is out back. **$**

Where to eat and drink Huddled around the police post, as you come in on the road from Potoru, are a clutch of good **chop stands** (**$**) serving dishes such as pepper chicken and fresh cassava leaf sauce.

SULIMA Sulima really is the end of the road. It has the air of a place forsaken by Sierra Leone – market traders quote prices in Liberian dollars rather than leones, the local brews hail from across the border, and everyone speaks with a vaguely American twang to their pidgin. Without doubt, there are more Liberians than Sierra Leoneans in Sulima, many left over from the (Liberian) civil war, attracted by the fertile but dangerous fishing waters, and the relative stability and familiarity of a village that is physically and spiritually closer to Monrovia than Freetown, but with a few more years' head start in the recovery stakes than their own shattered homeland.

The town has had to develop its own ad hoc traditions to cope with the influx of foreigners. Every Liberian resident is assigned a Sierra Leonean 'stranger father', a local elder to whom they are responsible, and who will vouch for them.

Geographically, this exposed, wild stretch of coastline is a different country from the misty mountains and bathwater-warm seas of the Freetown Peninsula – here is only thunderous surf that only the foolhardy would want to swim in. Even 100m from the sea, behind the sandbank that protects the town, you can hear the roar of titanic waves battering the steep shoreline. It's a spellbinding place nevertheless, with the best surfing in the country.

History Sulima has always been a sought-after trading post. In 1872, the British used it as their customs station, and they had to fight to keep control of it. Gangs set about diverting trade away from Sulima by making the most of domestic river routes inland along the Kittam River. A British captain eventually, against orders, took 50 policemen, marched inland and destroyed the trading posts, to the delight of his superiors back home, and Sulima regained its status. Jewish trader John Myer Harris, who was among the first Europeans to join the poro, also lived in Sulima. In later years, the village was a favoured retreat of President Siaka Stevens, as the burnt-out ruins of his summer palace testify.

Getting there and away If you have a 4x4 vehicle you can rely on, and the willpower to leave Freetown at dawn, it is possible to reach Sulima at the end of one very long and trying day, but once the ongoing Bo to Jendema roadworks are complete all but the last 25km of your journey will be on tarmac. Being just shy of halfway time-wise, Bo makes a good place to break up the journey, and it's simple to get onward transport to Zimmi (Le50,000) or Jendema (Le90,000) the next day, from where you can connect to Sulima. Alternatively, you can approach from Kenema on rough roads via Joru and Zimmi (roughly Le150,000 for a Kenema–Zimmi ocada). Sulima sits a further 58km from Zimmi (about Le90,000 on an ocada) and 27km from Jendema.

You may also hear of offers to go by sea to Sulima from the Freetown Peninsula. It is not clear that this is safe, as once round Mania Point, off Sherbro, the continental shelf drops away dramatically, totally changing the nature of the waters. Any approach by boat, particularly after June, when the rainy season hits full swing, should be considered extremely dangerous.

There are rather amorphous plans to introduce canoes to Tiwai Island (pages 252–8), which could be used to get downriver to Sulima in two or three days.

Where to stay and eat It's a small town, with a slightly sceptical curiosity about unannounced visitors that borders on downright suspicion, so new arrivals might consider popping in to the police post to greet the local constabulary, and definitely pay a visit to the chief, Siaka Massaquoi, and offer him some provisions such as oil, eggs, tea or sugar.

Riverview Guesthouse (9 rooms) m 078 323 932. Sulima's long-serving Mamie Sombo Guesthouse stopped accepting guests in 2016, but the newer Riverview has stepped ably in to the breach. Rooms have either shared or en-suite ablutions & all come with fans. There's generator power in the evenings & home-cooked meals on request. **$**

What to see and do The crocodiles in the swamp behind the beach are worth a look. Ask for a local escort and head down at sunset to see them coming out of the water. Walk to the *barmoi*, the long sandbar that cuts into the river Moa, to see the surf on one side and Turner's Peninsula on the other. In the other direction lies the Mano River, which bisects Liberia and Sierra Leone.

The real heart-in-mouth show in Sulima is watching dugout fishing canoes negotiate the treacherous approach back to shore. Their craft sluggish beneath a mountain of fish, men who have been up all night hauling nets have to find the strength and mental awareness to scan the horizon, predict the passage of the waves, spot their opportunity and then paddle like madmen. One mistake and the entire catch ends up on the ocean floor. Watching safe from shore, alongside a crowd of local women with sweaty bundles of Liberian dollars stuffed into their hands and bras, it's impossible not to start hollering into the wind at the boats to make it home safe. And somehow, the fish you buy afterwards tastes that much sweeter.

In moments of leisure (and there will be a few of them in Sulima), kick back with football and a beer or three. It's a recurring feature of Sierra Leone, and perhaps a natural consequence of globalisation, that even in the most basic of fishing villages goggle-eyed children who have never learnt to read or write can watch the buttock-waving of Beyoncé and the goal-scoring of Yaya Touré thanks to satellite TV. And while it seems likely Beyoncé may never make it down here personally, Sulima does count among its residents at least one American, in this case Woodie Butler, better known as American Woodie (m *079 999 922;* e *americanwoodie@gmail.com*). Woodie has big plans for his adopted village, including an upmarket 'diamond safari' lodge and even a reality TV series following his adventures diamond mining, with hopes to show off Salone in a positive light.

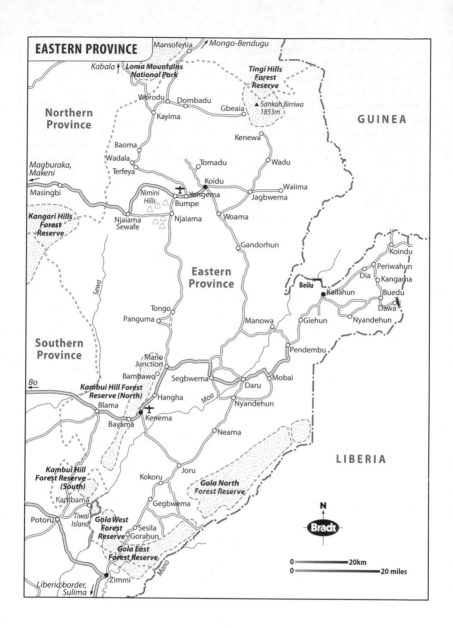

EASTERN PROVINCE

Mansofenia   Mongo-Bendugu

Kabala   *Loma Mountains National Park*   *Tingi Hills Forest Reserve*

Northern Province

Worodu   Dombadu   Gbeaia   ▲ *Sankan Birriwa 1853m*

Kayima

GUINEA

Kenewa

Baoma

Wadala   Tomadu   Wadu

Magburaka, Makeni   Terfeya

Koidu   Waiima

Masingbi   *Nimini Hills*   Yengema   Jagbwema

Bumpe

Kangari Hills Forest Reserve   Njaiama Sewafe   Njaiama   Woama

Gandorhun

Koindu

Periwahun

Eastern Province   Dia   Kangama

Beilu   Kailahun   Buedu

Dawa

Tongo   Manowa   Giehun   Nyandehun

Panguma

Southern Province

Pendembu

Mano Junction

Bo   Bambawo   Segbwema   Daru   Mobai

Kambui Hill Forest Reserve (North)   Hangha   *Moa*   Nyandehun

Blama   Kenema

Bayama

Neama

LIBERIA

Kambui Hill Forest Reserve (South)   Kokoru   Joru

Kambama   *Gola North Forest Reserve*

Potoru   *Tiwai Island*   Gegbwema

Gola West Forest Reserve   Sesila Gorahun

Gola East Forest Reserve

N

Bradt

Liberia border, Sulima   Zimmi   *Mano*

0 ——— 20km
0 ——— 20 miles

6

Eastern Province

The east is diamond country, home to the gem that has made Sierra Leone infamous. The effect of the trade on the physical landscape is impossible to miss, muddy pits pockmarking the spent earth like moon craters. But the land has been ravaged by more than spades and diggers; this was the epicentre of the conflict for many years, and while it waxed and waned elsewhere in the country, lawlessness and combat around the diamond fields became endemic.

It's also a place of unrelenting beauty, home to rich biodiversity in the country's first rainforest national park, jungle-covered hills, and a glut of rare birds, ancient trees, chimps and the odd pygmy hippo (you should be so lucky). It's a mission to get there, however, and infrastructure is still rudimentary. Even if you don't make it to Gola, hiking in hills that surround the main towns and wading on hidden river beaches and under waterfalls is easily within reach.

If you're lured by the thrill of seeking out a stone, or immersing yourself in the seedy underbelly of the business, you should head for Kenema, the diamond-buying capital, with a surreal buzz born of judging carats and clinching deals. Head to the mining town of Koidu and you'll see the hard graft that goes into hunting down the mythical big find, usually without success. Both are fascinating, urgent, and occasionally nasty places, bumping along the poverty line; home to sweat and greed and cowboy dashes at once-in-a-lifetime riches.

KENEMA

Among Sierra Leone's prettier towns, beautifully situated among the Kambui Hills, Kenema is where two worlds collide: as far east as most of the diamond dealers are prepared to go, and as far west as most of the diamond miners dare stray from their concessions.

This makes it stone central. Almost every neat single-storey bungalow on the main street has a garish sign outside advertising diamond-dealing services: this is where the dealers, often in the employ of one of the big Freetown-based exporters, buy rough stones from local miners.

Now Sierra Leone's second-largest town, Kenema may rue the day that, in 1931, two large diamonds were found in its environs. Everything else stopped, virtually overnight, including farming, and a thriving carpentry and timber industry. By the 1950s the town was bursting with new arrivals, all desperate for a taste of the action, bewitched, certainly in those early days, by the twinkling passport out of poverty that might be buried at the bottom of the garden. As a result, Kenema has shaken off the sleepy pall of other countryside towns. It's a frothy carousel of activity, where everyone knows a man who knows a man who can cut you a deal. Huge amounts of money move around the town every day, but as the rutted (though improving) streets, tumbledown buildings and street

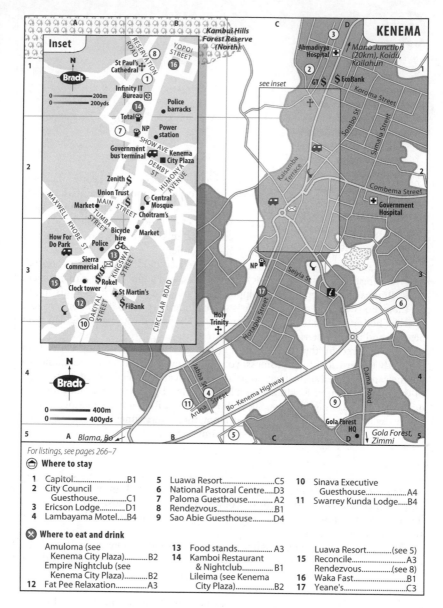

KENEMA

Kambui Hills Forest Reserve (North)

Inset

Ahmadiyya Hospital

Mano Junction (20km), Koidu, Kailahun

St Paul's Cathedral

YOPOI STREET

EcoBank

GT

Korama Street

Infinity IT Bureau

0 ——— 200m
0 ——— 200yds

Police barracks

Total

Power station

NP

Sombo St

Sumala Street

Government bus terminal

Kenema City Plaza

Kaisamba Terrace

Combema Street

Zenith

DEMBY ST

HUMONYA AVENUE

Government Hospital

Union Trust

Central Mosque

Market

MAIN STREET

TUMBA ST

Choitram's

Bicycle hire

Market

Seivia St

How For Do Park

MAXWELL KHOBE ST

Police

KINGSWAY STREET

NP

Sierra Commercial

Rokel

Clock tower

DAKIYAL STREET

St Martin's

FiBank

CIRCULAR ROAD

Holy Trinity

Horahua Street

Dama Road

N

Bradt

0 ——— 400m
0 ——— 400yds

Jabba St

Aruna Street

Bo-Kenema Highway

Gola Forest HQ

Gola Forest, Zimmi

A   B   C   D

Blama, Bo

For listings, see pages 266–7

Where to stay

1	Capitol............B1	5	Luawa Resort............C5	10	Sinava Executive
2	City Council	6	National Pastoral Centre....D3		Guesthouse............A4
	Guesthouse.........C1	7	Paloma Guesthouse............A2	11	Swarrey Kunda Lodge.....B4
3	Ericson Lodge.........D1	8	Rendezvous............B1		
4	Lambayama Motel.....B4	9	Sao Abie Guesthouse..........D4		

Where to eat and drink

	Amuloma (see	13	Food stands............A3		Luawa Resort............(see 5)
	Kenema City Plaza)............B2	14	Kamboi Restaurant	15	Reconcile............A3
	Empire Nightclub (see		& Nightclub............B1		Rendezvous............(see 8)
	Kenema City Plaza)............B2		Lileima (see Kenema	16	Waka Fast............B1
12	Fat Pee Relaxation............A3		City Plaza)............B2	17	Yeane's............C3

scamps show, most of it stays locked away in small, strong safes and securely wrist-handcuffed suitcases.

The town nevertheless manages a family feel, warm and welcoming, while sucking you into its captivating, compulsive world. Many NGOs make it their base in the east, while the student campus provides a young educated presence in search of fun.

As a regional base it offers good walking nearby, it is an ideal springboard into Gola, the country's first national park rainforest, and also has a small handful of fine accommodation choices and easily loved nightspots. The weather is cooler than in

Freetown, the town is in reasonably good shape, and it's easy to get around. Settle in enough and you can start to ignore the diamonds.

GETTING THERE AND AWAY Transport to Kenema is easy to pick up from Freetown, 309km away, or from the capital of the Southern Province, Bo, about an hour away on a good tarmac road. The **government bus** from Freetown charges Le25,000 and takes between 4 and 5 hours, while the short 67km hop from Bo costs Le18,000 by **shared taxi** (a bit less by **poda poda**) and takes about an hour. Most vehicles arrive and depart from the 'How For Do' Park [264 A3] behind the clock tower roundabout, while the government bus has its own terminal [264 B2] 750m north on Hangha Road.

Heading towards Koidu, there's a good tarmac road as far as Mano junction, from where the road deteriorates into a rocky 4x4 track, cutting through rolling hills and forest until you emerge at Bumpe on the Makeni–Koidu road, about 80km and 3–4 hours later. Towards Kailahun, it's new tarmac all the way to Pendembu (also via Mano junction), and roadworks were just beginning on the remaining 30km in April 2017. There are generally at least one or two vehicles headed in each direction every morning for Le40,000–50,000. For Gola, the tarmac road runs out just a few kilometres after the town finishes.

A glut of battered Mazda and Honda bikes also regularly leave Kenema for the provinces, and if you don't have a private vehicle this may be the cheapest way to get around. You can hire them to take you as far as Gola North along the eastern frontier, with prices starting around Le50,000 for a ride to Joru. There are many police checkpoints on these roads. To get to Potoru, in the south near Tiwai Island, take a poda poda, taxi or Honda to Blama, some 20km east on the Bo road, and then change.

ORIENTATION Kenema's centre is essentially one long main drag, Hangha Road, running southwest–northeast, bordered by the string of Kambui Hills to the east, which rise higher in the north, and the Moa River to the west, which runs the length of the country south to the coast at Sulima. The easily spotted clock tower at the southern end of town (don't miss a chance to go up to the top for the view), which looks like a weird space rocket about to take off, was built by the Pakistani battalion of UN peacekeepers stationed with the UNAMSIL mission. Here the Freetown road joins the Zimmi road, and acts as a convenient reference point. Most of the social activity takes place along Hangha Road, although if you have time it's worth exploring the criss-crossing matrix of backstreets, which take you past countless little homes and boutiques, bushmeat markets and other oddities. There's a market south of Choitram's supermarket, and even an airstrip to the northeast of the centre.

GETTING AROUND Even if you have your own vehicle, leave it in your compound and opt instead for **motorbike taxi** to nip around town. They buzz around like flies and are easily hailed from the side of the road. A one-way ride to any destination in the centre costs Le2,000, or you can hire a bike for the day for about Le110,000. Most riders carry spare helmets for the passenger, but these often lack chinstraps, making them more window dressing than safety feature. There is a **bicycle-rntal stand** [264 A3] (m *076 359 231 for Kebbie Kamara*) on the spot opposite Rodyna's Pharmacy.

WHERE TO STAY As of 2017, government electricity in Kenema was reasonably reliable, but most of the hotels below will fire up a generator overnight should service be interrupted.

🛏 **Capitol Hotel** [264 B1] (43 rooms) 51 Hangha Rd; m 078 322 223, 088 322 223; e info@capitol-tc.com; w capitol-tc.com/capitolhotel.html. This is where the president stays when he comes to town, so you know it has to be pretty flash. Rooms are clean & fairly spacious & all come equipped with AC & Wi-Fi, although those facing Hangha Rd get a bit of street noise. There's a new swimming pool & open-sided 1st-floor restaurant. B&B. **$$$**

🛏 **Ericson Lodge** [264 D1] (13 rooms) 48 Swarray St; m 076 410 722, 079 832 578; e ericsonlodge15@gmail.com; ⨍ ericsonguesthouse. Proprietor Louisa Musa has turned this cosy guesthouse into the most comfortable stay in Kenema. Spotless rooms have AC & fans; all are self-contained. The restaurant is a nice spot to grab some chicken & chips, although food is slow to arrive. B&B. **$$$**

🛏 **Luawa Resort Hotel** [264 C5] (11 rooms, 12 under construction) Wahma Abu Rd, Deima Area; m 078 000 888, 078 201 282, 077 276 416; e luawareservations@gmail.com or luawaresortkenema@gmail.com. In a pleasant green compound a bit removed from the centre, this newly remodelled place has a variety of well-kept tiled rooms with AC, hot water & mini fridge. The swimming pool & outdoor bar are quite popular, & the whole place is often booked out for weddings & such at weekends. **$$$**

🛏 **Paloma Guesthouse** [264 A2] (15 rooms) 10 Sahara St; m 076 889 999, 077 889 999; e palomaguesthouse@mail.com; w palomahotel.net. This concrete-heavy construction wouldn't win any beauty contests, but the rooms are undeniably smart & central, with Wi-Fi, AC & hot water. There's a breezy restaurant on an upstairs terrace. **$$$**

🛏 **Rendezvous** [264 B1] (18 rooms) 2 Reservation Rd, opposite St Paul's Cathedral; m 076 311 088, 076 226 749, 078 440 445; e constantthomas36@gmail.com or vkpandemoi@gmail.com. Much loved for its fun vibe (there's a popular restaurant attached (**$$**), secure, clean & decently kept. All rooms are self-contained; AC & carpet in some rooms, fans in all. Watch out for the wonky staircase. **$$$**

🛏 **Sao Abie Guesthouse** [264 D4] (5 rooms) 2 Torkponbu Rd; m 030 277 016, 076 715 213, 076 589 259. This spot has a pretty breakfasting area, with great views of the town, although the rooms disappoint. Located near the Pastoral Centre,

about 10–15mins' walk from the centre of town, signs from the main road & beyond are still easily missed. All rooms have fans, a few have AC, & there's a large communal living room. Friendly staff can do food on request. B&B. **$$**

🛏 **Lambayama Motel** [264 B4] (16 rooms) 2 Aruna St; m 076 639 140, 078 681 852. Huge rabbit warren of a place that sprawls, Tardis-like, over a much larger area than seems physically possible. Again, most rooms are a touch dingy, although running water is reliable. All open on to a very pleasant courtyard in a quiet area. If you fancy splashing out, the wood-lined Room 11, a standalone hut, is by far the best option. All rooms have standing fans. Food on request. B&B (1 per room). **$$**

🛏 **Swarrey Kunda Lodge** [264 B4] (8 rooms: 7 dbl, 1 sgl) 14 Swarrey Kunda St; m 078 186 400, 076 702 984, 088 933 142. All rooms self-contained (3 with AC); friendly welcome; b/fast, lunch & dinner on request but order well in advance. TV room with chairs; generally a bit dingy; hot water on request. About 2km from the centre of town in a quiet residential neighbourhood – turn left off the main road to Freetown at a sign for the reproductive health centre. **$$**

🛏 **National Pastoral Centre** [264 D3] (31 rooms) At the end of Dawa Rd; m 076 951 081, 079 474 651; e bstarken@eircom.net or aberewa@yahoo.com. Set amid acres of palm & mango trees, with the odd trailing jacaranda & the noise of town wafting up from below, this is a calm & lovely hideout & its air of quiet contemplation is unlike anywhere else in the country. It's a seminary for trainee Catholic priests, which explains the tranquil, reflective mood. The viewing platform is perfect for drinking in the magnificent view of the surrounding Kambui Hills along with the odd beer or 2. In contrast, the Centre's 14 self-contained rooms are unsurprisingly cell-like & soon warm up under naked corrugated-iron roofs. Evening meals are available upon request. B&B. **$$–$**

🛏 **City Council Guesthouse** [264 C1] (8 rooms) Reservation Rd; m 078 478 955, 030 348 823. In a walled compound on the right a couple of hundred metres beyond Rendezvous, this unmarked government guesthouse has clean en-suite rooms with fans & nets & a backup generator until midnight. No food, but still the pick in this range. **$**

🛏 **Sinava Executive Guesthouse** [264 A4] (8 rooms) 7 Blama Rd; m 088 495 410. Don't be fooled by the 'executive guesthouse' appellation: this long-neglected stalwart offers only dingy (albeit high-ceilinged) rooms with fan, & oesn't

seem to have a functioning backup generator. Still, it's undeniably cheap & central. **$**

✕ WHERE TO EAT, DRINK AND DANCE

✕ **Fat Pee Relaxation** [264 A3] 3 Blama Rd; m 076 667 120. A stone's throw from the central roundabout, this is a good lunchtime filling station & will have expanded into a larger restaurant & bar by the time you read this. **$$**

✕ **Kamboi Restaurant & Nightclub** [264 B1] Hangha Rd & Show Field Rd; m 076 640 300. This cavernous place behind the Total station on Hangha Rd is a reliable bet for African dishes or fried chicken & fish at around Le25,000, plus beer, football & movies on a handful of flatscreen TVs. **$$**

✕ **Luawa Resort Hotel** [264 C5] Wahma Abu Rd, Deima Area; m 078 000 888, 078 201 282, 077 276 416. A little way out of town, this family-run place makes a good respite from city-centre chaos, unless there's a wedding on, in which case you'd have a quieter time in the central market. The kitchen serves up tasty African dishes, & there's a swimming pool plus open-air bar & billiards under a shaded terrace nearby. **$$**

✕ **Rendezvous** [264 B1] 2 Reservation Rd, near the junction with Hangha Rd. Covered in coloured disco lights, this perennially fun & popular restaurant hosts the odd night-time talent show & even *tambola* (bingo). Grilled fish is good & the pepper soup even better. **$$**

☀✕ **Waka Fast** [264 B1] 34 Hangha Rd; m 079 331 111; ⊕ 08.00–midnight daily. This modern restaurant & snack bar (with superb murals on the exterior) does good & affordable Lebanese food alongside pizzas, sandwiches & ice cream, with AC, Wi-Fi, & even shisha pipes to sweeten the deal. There's no booze, but they're

open late & have a shaded terrace out front. Delivery too. **$$**

✕ **Yeane's** [264 C3] 49 Blama Rd; m 079 651 478. This growing national chain is a comfortable spot to fill up at any time of day, with a menu stretching from the usual rice & plassas to the more esoteric 'lobster in love' & grilled jumbo shrimp. **$$**

✕ **Amuloma** [264 B2] Kenema City Plaza; m 078 430 490. Though the 'open 24 hours' printed on their sign should perhaps be taken with a pinch of salt, this ground-floor eatery nonetheless keeps long hours serving up basic meals & drinks. **$$–$**

✕ **Lileima** [264 B2] Kenema City Plaza; m 076 640 295, 076 611 872. This upstairs chop shop at the Kenema City Plaza serves a rotating menu of Salone favourites, chalked up daily on a board at the base of the steps. **$$–$**

✕ **Food stands** [264 A3] Right opposite the police station on the main drag, these stands serve beef or steak in bread with *kankankan* (hot spice) seasoning & mayonnaise for a pittance. **$**

♀ **Reconcile** [264 A3] 1 Blama Rd; m 076 660 935. Once known for its steaks, today the kitchen operates haphazardly if at all, but the bar nonetheless remains a reliable address to sit outside & watch the world go by. **$**

☆ **Empire Nightclub** [264 B2] Kenema City Plaza; ◧ empirekenem. If it's disco lights & Nigerian pop you're after, look no further than this AC club at Kenema City Plaza. There's a Le20,000 cover charge & Wed is ladies' night.

OTHER PRACTICALITIES If you're in need of a **tailor**, head for Maxwell Khobe Street [264 A2–3]. For a taste of a vibrant religious service with plenty of dancing, visit **Holy Trinity Church** [264 B4] on Blama Road.

Banks Opposite one another at the north end of Hangha Road, **EcoBank** and **GT Bank** [264 C1] both have ATMs accepting Visa, as does **Rokel Commercial Bank** near the clock tower. **Sierra Commercial Bank** [264 A3] also changes currency, while wire transfers are available at **Afro International** (*1st Fl, 27a Hangha Rd;* m *076 833* 330) or **Union Trust Bank** [264 B2].

Internet Infinity IT Bureau [264 B1] (*51 Hangha Rd;* ⊕ *09.00–22.00 daily*) is the town's busiest internet café, right in the middle of town. An hour of reasonably quick surfing (by Sierra Leonean standards) costs Le7,000. Not far away, **Ieyebee Ent** [264 B2] (*Kenema City Plaza*) is another decent option for getting online (or just use the Wi-Fi at Waka Fast).

Medical Rodyna Pharmacy (*9 Hangha Rd;* m *076 437 143, 078 117 167*) has a sparkling interior, well-stocked shelves and helpful staff. Look for it near the police station. **Choitram's** [264 B2] (m *076 678 444*), an Indian-run supermarket at the lower end of town, sells imported goods, and can change large-denomination dollar notes with a purchase.

Tourist information The small **tourist office** [264 D3] (*45 Dama Rd;* m *076 384 448*) is on the way to the Pastoral Centre, on the right of the road from town. This is a good place to enquire about excursions into the Kambui Hills. To arrange a trip to Gola Rainforest National Park, contact the **Gola Forest Programme** on Dama Rd (page 271), or **Kenema's Forestry Division** [264 D5] (*Gola Forestry Division, Maxwell Khobe St*). The Forestry Division also has a greenhouse and an interesting plant nursery to help increase yields via traditional farming methods, both of which you can visit.

WHAT TO SEE AND DO

Go diamond (window) shopping You may have longingly pressed nose to glass on a Tiffany & Co display case, but there'll be nothing between you and a diamond in Kenema, except perhaps a few thousand bucks. A visit to a diamond dealership is a giddying opportunity to see a lot of dollar-per-square-inch, as well as half-wonder what all the fuss is about. Most outfits double as something else – be it a bicycle-repair shop, a store selling garden tools and auto parts, even the odd fabric salesman. Whatever trade it might be, the chap behind the counter will likely have a stone or two in a little bag buried in his safe.

Don't let excitement and/or avarice draw you into too-good-to-be-true con tricks. While the diamonds may gleam (some fine rough stones come out of the ground in such good shape they almost look like they've already been cut), the shine of unscrupulous capitalism is even more blinding. Not only do you run the risk of being scammed – like the American who shelled out thousands of dollars for what turned out to be bits of glass – but it's also illegal to take a stone out of Sierra Leone without the proper documentation and export certification.

To buy a diamond legitimately, you first need to purchase a one-off tourist licence from the **Ministry of Mineral Resources** (*5th Fl, Youyi Bldg, Brookfields, Freetown;* \ *022 240 059;* m *076 641 445 for Mining Officer Ibrahim Barrie in Kenema;* w *slminerals.org*). Once you have your stone – which may have a value of no more than US$2,000 – you need to take it to be valued at the **National Minerals Agency (NMA)** in Freetown (*NMA Compound, New England Ville;* m *079 250 702, 079 252 446;* e *info@nma.gov.sl* or *iskamara@nma.gov.sl;* w *nma.gov.sl*) for tax purposes, even though you have already paid for it. You pay a 3% tax on the GDO-decided value of the stone and receive your very own Kimberley Certificate, wax stamps, brown paper, string and all.

Hill walking The walking around Kenema's nearby hills is a good way of escaping the town's occasionally claustrophobic atmosphere. Set out early with plenty of water and a picnic lunch. Make sure you ask for a guide from your guesthouse though, as there are paths through the thick vegetation that it helps to know about.

The **Kambui Hills Forest Reserve** lies 5km west of Kenema on the road to Blama, and its northern and southern sectors are bisected by the highway to Bo.

It is primarily demarcated a regulated logging area for the timber industry, to provide incomes to local communities, but it is also rich in wildlife, and home to the highest peak in the east, which stands at 645m.

Birdlife runs to 200 species, including the **long-tailed hawk** (*Urotriorchis macrourus*), **black bee-eater** (*Merops gularis*), **Ansorge's greenbul** (*Andropadus ansorgei*) and **Fraser's sunbird** (*Deleornis fraseri*); the reserve is also home to a number of primate species, including the western chimpanzee, red colobus monkey, black-and-white colobus monkey, sooty mangabey, and Diana monkey; and some of the rarer duiker species.

Bayama, the last police checkpoint before the turn-off to Kenema on the Bo–Kenema Highway, is the gateway to **Kambui Hills South**. While you might want a guide for bigger treks, there is an easy-to-find waterfall nearby: park at the police checkpoint and follow the path straight back for about 2km along a fairly flat road; the waterfall is at the end. It's small, but there's enough of a pool for a swim and it's a nice spot for a picnic or an undisturbed run. (Birders should also check out David Karr's 2014 trip report from Kambui South: w cloudbirders.com/tripreport/repository/KARR_SL_TiwaiKambui_11_2014.pdf.)

Closer to town, strike out along the Nyandeyama road, which eventually feeds into a footpath that leads to the hills.

For something further afield, ask at your guesthouse (or the Forestry Division) for advice on finding a guide to take you into the forest. In the other direction, **Bambawo** village (reached by a left-hand turning at Ngelehun, 1.7km before you reach Mano junction) is the jumping-off point for **Kambui Hills North**.

If you don't have time for the hills, head to the pretty grounds of the **National Pastoral Centre** in town for a peaceful walk.

GOLA

Parliament's 2011 legislation that created the 71,000ha Gola Rainforest National Park came as a relief to conservation groups that had for years been calling for action to try to safeguard Sierra Leone's last truly untouched patch of tropical evergreen rainforest.

Ravaged by rebel groups during the war, logged extensively between the 1960s and mid 1980s, and exploited in pursuit of the lucrative and well-established bushmeat trade with Liberia (see box, page 272), the forest has finally earned the protected status that it has so long and so sorely needed.

Among the last pristine rainforest in West Africa, the forest was given a clean bill of health during a 2008 flyover by wildlife-lovers, when a helicopter set off from British ship HMS *Endurance*, which was surveying the state of conservation along the coast. This is a boon for a country with fast-disappearing forests. Once upon a time, up to 70% of Sierra Leone was covered in forest; at the time of independence in 1961, it was 40%, while today only 5% of this original cover remains. A further 33% of the country is covered in secondary growth forests, and 11% of the total land area is now under some form of protection.

Gola was last logged in 1986. However, until just a decade ago the jungle still faced threats from mining companies keen to get at reserves of gold estimated to lie beneath its canopy, as well as gem-grade diamonds. Despite legal protection dating back to 1926, at least two mining companies were granted licences between 2005 and 2007. However, those licences were later cancelled, and in February 2011 parliament created the legislation that made Gola a national park – the country's second, after Outamba-Kilimi. The president officially opened the park at a

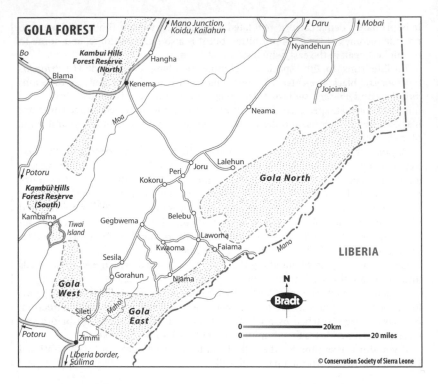

GOLA FOREST

Bo
Blama
Kambui Hills Forest Reserve (North)
Hangha
Kenema
Mano Junction, Koidu, Kailahun
Nyandehun
Daru
Mobai
Jojoima
Moa
Neama
Potoru
Kambui Hills Forest Reserve (South)
Kambama
Tiwai Island
Gegbwema
Kokoru
Peri
Joru
Lalehun
Gola North
Belebu
Lawoma
Kwaoma
Faiama
Mano
LIBERIA
Sesila
Gorahun
Njama
Gola West
Sileti
Maho
Gola East
N
Bradt
0 ———— 20km
0 ———— 20 miles
Potoru
Zimmi
Liberia border, Sulima

© Conservation Society of Sierra Leone

ceremony in Lalehun in December of that year. Encouragingly, Liberia's parliament has now done the same, declaring a new, 88,000ha national park in September 2016, more than doubling the area of forest protected as part of the now trans-boundary park. On either side of the border, Gola's protected status makes it illegal for anyone to harvest the forest's timber, dig up its minerals, or poach its wildlife.

Such restrictions make winning over communities who live alongside the forest, and hunt its ever-dwindling stock of animals, even more important. The Gola Forest Programme, a partnership between the government, the Royal Society for the Protection of Birds (RSPB) and CSSL, financed by the EU and FFEM, a French environmental fund, among others, has developed mechanisms to improve the livelihoods of highly impoverished communities. The European Commission and French government have both contributed around £3 million towards the project, which includes the recruitment and training of more than a hundred national park staff, including forest guards and research technicians to patrol Gola's boundaries and monitor wildlife. The RSPB and US-based group Conservation International paid approximately £1 million each into a £6 million trust fund to cover the park's running costs and deliver community benefits to more than 100,000 local people every year in perpetuity. The hope is that responsible tourism, along with fees directed at the community, can help persuade people of the value of keeping the forest intact. Therefore, as a visitor, making the effort to visit this wilderness proves to local people that there are tangible tourism benefits to preserving their natural habitat.

EXPLORING GOLA Even by Sierra Leone standards a trip into Gola and back is a tall order. The three fragmented parts of the park – North, East and West – are situated between the large Moa and Mano rivers, extending almost 750km². To experience the majesty of the place, you can't explore it in a few hours – you need to take your time, and camp. From north to south, at a speed of about 3–4km/h (which is a rush, requiring fitness and no stopping) through dense vegetation, you might walk the whole thing in 15 days. Alternatively, you can cross sections of Gola from west to east in two days. A good two-day trip involves getting to Joru, equipping yourself with camping gear, heading off to Belebu, Lalehun or Sileti and then penetrating into the heart of the forest.

Below the canopy, the air is close but cool, and little light penetrates. Guides can show you restful spots in the forest, such as waterfalls and cascades into natural swimming pools. The odd basolith (an exposed hill empty of trees), sometimes three days' hiking into the wild, gives fantastic views of the surrounding treetops.

GETTING THERE AND AWAY, AND WHERE TO STAY The **Gola Forest Programme** (*164 Dama Rd, Kenema;* m *078 356 061, 076 420 218, 076 899 440, 076 967 320;* e *info@ golarainforest.org;* w *golarainforest.org*) has set up some basic accommodation at the forest's edge, and can also equip you with basic camping gear to head off deep into the forest.

Entry fees cost US$18 per person per visit (day or overnight), plus a US$18 community fee, also per person per visit. Visitors are strongly encouraged to stop by the Gola Forest Programme's office in Kenema to alert them to your visit and pick up a free **permit** before heading into the park. There is also a series of guiding fees – US$15 for a Gola guide (per guide, per day, for up to six people); US$5 per person per day for a porter; US$5 for a camp assistant (per assistant, per day, for up to six people); US$5 for a community cook (per cook, per day, for up to six people) if you bring your own ingredients. If you let the park handle your food needs, it's US$10 per person per day including all meals. Camping equipment costs US$10 per person per night. Prices for Sierra Leone nationals and students are discounted.

Currently there are several basic accommodation sites at a number of villages on the forest's edge. At **Belebu**, in Tunkia chiefdom in Gola North, a guesthouse with eight rooms, resplendent in green and blue paint, offers mattress foam on the floor in box-like cells, and, impressively, a proper loo and shower in a tiled bathroom. Accommodation costs a standardised US$10 per person per night at Belebu or any of the other sites listed below. It's a 45-minute, 29km ride to Joru, then a further rocky 11km to Belebu, costing about Le70,000 each way with a **motorbike** and taking roughly 2 hours. A **4x4** can make the trip, but not a normal vehicle.

Sileti, the southern headquarters of the programme, has two double beds, water supply and generator electricity in the evenings. From Sileti you can also take a 45-minute walk down to a campsite beside the Mahoi River.

Another option, in Gola North, is **Lalehun**, 15km east of Joru, an important picathartes site for avid twitchers, where you might also see the Gola malimbe. There, you can stay at the 'presidential lodge,' which hosted President Koroma and Liberian President Ellen Johnson Sirleaf when they came to declare the border-hugging forest 'a peace park' in 2009 – a vision more fully realised in 2016 when the Liberian side became a national park in 2016. The two rooms are basic but comfortable, with generator power available. Lalehun is also the site of the national park's official visitors' and research centre, which has recently built guest rooms and staff quarters for 20, complete with solar-powered lights and flushing loos. In the very far north of Gola North, in Malema chiefdom, there's another spot at **Jojoima** village (a Le100,000 ocada ride from Kenema, or also accessible from Daru, 20km away on the surfaced road to Kailahun).

Such has been the impact of demand for bushmeat from neighbouring Liberia that when the border was temporarily closed in the 1980s, one Sierra Leonean newspaper ran the headline: 'Monkeys were saved'.

While the market stalls of most towns and villages in Sierra Leone feature bushmeat stands, the country's large Muslim population, which views primate flesh in particular with disdain, has ensured the trade never flourished to the same extent as in Sierra Leone's predominantly Christian neighbour.

The fact that the Liberian authorities have traditionally done a better job of safeguarding wildlife (at least until the 1991–2003 war), and set aside 1,300km² of forest for Sapo National Park, only ensured that Sierra Leone's own hunters and foreign foragers became de facto suppliers to the still-thriving industry.

Primate bloodlust started much earlier. Widespread monkey culls in the 1940s and 1950s in Sierra Leone included a bounty paid on the head of each dead animal. Local farmers, already hostile to a wildlife population seen as a threat to crops, granted Liberian gangs free rein to operate in Sierra Leone's forests, exporting the meat in return for leaving heads and tails for the farmers to claim their reward. The policy eventually stopped, but by then the precedent for allowing the organised mass slaughter of monkeys was established. By the 1980s, an estimated 300 tons of bushmeat left Sierra Leone each month.

Today, most bushmeat hunting is still done with guns, even though they have been banned since the end of the war. Many small antelope, including duikers, are lured into the sights of a shotgun through false calls from a whistle. Around the edges of the forest, traps are frequently set, and these can also catch animals such as pygmy hippos that tend to stick to the same clearly established paths.

If you are out and about in Gola, or other forested areas, you might occasionally see spent shotgun cartridges on the ground. Other telltale signs of poaching activity include discarded nickel-cadmium batteries, which are used to power spotlights when hunting at night. In the past, Gola's rangers have found their lives under threat from hunting gangs. Part of the Gola rehabilitation programme involves a large grant to pay their salaries, and there are encouraging signs that many communities are beginning to tire of the incursions by gangs from Liberia to hunt on their land.

The best way to reach Gola East is also via Joru, heading south to Faiama or Njama, or southwest towards Zimmi, 85km away, and stopping off at the staff quarters at **Sileti**. This will also give you access to Gola West. Tiwai Island Wildlife Sanctuary, 10km west of Gola West, is also a good branching-off point, via Potoru (pages 252–8).

The Gola Forest Programme has 4x4 vehicles for hire, charging either US$100 a day or US$100 for a round-trip pickup and drop-off out of Kenema if you'll be hiking (without vehicle) in the park for more than a day.

In addition to the Gola Forest Programme office, you can also try visiting the **National Tourist Board** office in Kenema or call in and ask at **Kenema's Forestry Division** (*Gola Forestry Division, Maxwell Khobe St*) for advice on arranging a trip. In Freetown try the **Conservation Society of Sierra Leone** (CSSL; *14A King St, Freetown;* m *030 522 579, 076 633 824;* e *cssl_03@yahoo.com;* w *conservationsocietysl.org; see ad, 3rd colour section*) for more details. The Gola Forest Programme office can source guides locally, many of whom are old-time hunters-turned-rangers. In Belebu, ex-hunters Amara Fobay and Moussa Koroma (known as 'Redman') come highly recommended.

WILDLIFE Across its 750km², Gola has one of the most diverse wildlife populations in the country. The most recent surveys available show the presence of 50 mammal species, 2,000 different plants – including 77 orchids – and a staggering 333 species of birds.

Gola North has the more rugged terrain, rising to 475m, while Gola West and the southern part of Gola East contain lower-lying land. The marshy swampland around Mogbai (35km²) in Gola North, and Wemago (23km²) in Gola East on the side of Bagra Hill, contain the best wildlife; their remoteness means they have been exposed to less intensive hunting than Gola West in particular.

Gola East used to contain a healthy population of about 60 **elephants**, and the more remote Gola North, 50; but virtually no research has been carried out since the war, and only a small handful are thought to remain today. A number of primates can be found in the park; in addition to **chimpanzees**, the forest's 11 species include two endangered monkey species; the Diana monkey and the western red colobus, both most often found in Gola North.

MAYBE MONEY DOES GROW ON TREES

Scientists estimate that nearly one fifth of global greenhouse gas emissions, which are driving up temperatures and wreaking havoc on weather systems around the world, have come as the result of deforestation. As climate talks focus on new ways to get people to 'keep forest as forest', schemes hawking saleable credits for 'reduced' or 'avoided' deforestation are being developed, and the UN-backed REDD+ (Reducing Emissions from Deforestation and forest Degradation; w un-redd.org) programme, through which donor nations and organisations would be required to pay developing nations to conserve their forests as part of their efforts to mitigate climate change, is slowly gaining traction. The government of Sierra Leone is hoping the Gola rainforest can help it get in on the game.

A feasibility study sponsored by the Royal Society for the Protection of Birds (RSPB) showed that the sale of Gola's credits on the voluntary carbon market could generate about US$1 million, which would be enough to cover the park's annual operating costs. Earning the credits, however, requires enforcing the park's borders and keeping out the miners, timber harvesters, and poachers that threaten the integrity of the forest. Working with the RSPB, a 30-year REDD+ project was initiated in Gola in late 2012, and though credit sales remain voluntary and thus represent only a fraction of the park's operating budget, audits showed that conservation efforts at Gola nonetheless avoided the emission of 1.19 million tonnes of CO_2 between August 2012 and December 2014. You can even support the initiative yourself by purchasing credits (at US$10 per tonne) on the Gola Forest website (w golarainforest.org).

'Carbon financing is a win-win for the environment and for economic development,' said the president at the official opening of the national park in December 2011. 'By protecting our forest we can generate substantial income while retaining all of the natural benefits that a living, breathing forest provides.'

For more information, contact: e golareddproject@rspb.org.uk.

The swampland downstream of Mogbai and the Kwadi and Makoi rivers in Gola North is home to the **pygmy hippopotamus**. An endangered species, with only about 2,000–3,000 thought to remain worldwide, between 80 and 100 may exist throughout the whole of Sierra Leone. In the dry season, what few pygmy hippos there are may move up towards the Kwadi River, escaping the activities of fishermen. Their movements are poorly understood, but intensive surveys conducted at Gola over 2010–14 found that they seem to often reside close to major rivers and on the fringes of, rather than deep within, large tracts of forest, often outside park boundaries. Given that these habits put them at a high risk of human conflict, a programme training youth volunteers from surrounding villages to understand and advocate for hippo conservation in their communities has been in place since 2016.

The forest also has **leopard**, but don't count on seeing one. In 2008, a camera trap recorded the first confirmed sighting in years. Since then, more camera traps have been installed but there's little evidence of further confirmed sightings. Gola is also home to the elusive, elegant bongo and other **rare antelope**, the vulnerable zebra duiker, black duiker, the rare nocturnal bay duiker, and the vulnerable Jentink's duiker – all of which have suffered heavily under the hunter's shotgun. Look out too for flying squirrels, mongoose, otters and civets.

It is the **birdlife** that really sets the heart racing in Gola. Of 333 species so far recorded in the forest, 14 are of conservation concern, including the endangered **Gola malimbe** (*Malimbus ballmanni*), a black and yellow weaverbird that's been reliably spotted in a remote area near Lalehun since 2007; the **rufous fishing-owl** (*Scotopelia ussheri*), recently downlisted from endangered to vulnerable, can also now be seen regularly along the riverbanks inside the forest. The forest also holds up to 30 observed nesting sites of the **white-necked picathartes** (*Picathartes gymnocephalus*). Most of 53 nest colonies that have been discovered occur in and around Gola North, where there are plenty of overhanging rocks suitable for nesting. One of the main locations for this is Lalehun, 14km from Joru. The vulnerable **Nimba flycatcher** (*Malaenomis annamarulae*), very rare in Gola, is dependent on primary forest, with fleeting sightings in the Mogbai area. The **yellow-bearded greenbul** (*Criniger olivaceus*) and **western wattled cuckoo-shrike** (*Lobotos lobatus*), are two more vulnerable residents. An impressive range of herons, storks, ibises, ducks, hawks and eagles, guineafowl, francolins, doves, turacos, cuckoos, owls, nightjars, swifts, kingfishers, bee-eaters, hornbills, tinkerbirds, honeyguides, swallows, tits, sunbirds, starlings, weavers and parrots have also been recorded here. (For some further reading, David Karr's excellent 2015 trip report is available here: w cloudbirders.com/tripreport/repository/KARR_Sierra_Leone_04_2015.pdf.)

A two-week **butterfly** field visit in 2006 recorded 370 species, leading to predictions that there could be more than 600 varieties at large in the forest, which would make up more than 80% of all Sierra Leone's butterfly species, many of them rare and endemic. Among these is the extremely rare *Cupidesthes savatoris*, which was first collected in the 1890s in Moyamba. The number of butterflies tends to act as an indicator for the number of species of all other organisms (for every one butterfly one can usually count on 800 more species), indicating just how diverse Gola's fauna is, with perhaps half a million species present. The forest is so little explored or surveyed that, if you're really eagle-eyed, you might even find a new species that could be named after you.

Gola also has its fair share of **bees**, and the Gola Forest Programme painstakingly encourages local honey makers to farm bees rather than kill them. The dark, strong honey that hails from the forest is beloved in Sierra Leone not only for its taste but its cosmetic and medicinal properties – a cure-all for impotency, poison and other ailments. Honey makers have tended to embark on one-off raids, burning bees out of their patch, but now willing apiarists are taught to make rattan hives, baited with sugar or perfume, for colonies of 80,000-plus bees; they are also making a living off the worker bees. The best time to buy a pint of honey, which goes for around Le10,000, is during the dry season, from Melma or Zimmi chiefdoms (though honey is generally available in many of the surrounding villages).

For those interested in archaeology, excavations in Guara chiefdom, near Joru, have revealed two megalithic monuments: one of two upright stones in an 'L' shape, and another of eight stones ranged upright around a central stone.

KOIDU

Like gold-rush America, Sierra Leone's diamond-mining capital can feel just as madly exciting, and just as desolate. Known as the Wild East, it has lured in many with the promise of riches, and yet the techniques employed are not much changed in 70 years. Next to mean homes and battered infrastructure – a cruelly ironic reminder that mining rarely makes communities rich – men, and children, still scrabble around in pools of muddy, golden water with enormous pancake-like sieves, trawling the depths for a speck of something special. They can go months without finding anything.

Horribly pillaged during the war, Kono district became its shifting frontline, as factions and, later, UN troops vied for control of the lucrative diamond fields fuelling the violence. People dug up their roads, their gardens, even their floors in the hope of bagging a gem. Dusty and empty, the town feels eerily quiet on some days, exuberant on others. A babble of languages and nationalities – Australian, Russian, South African, Indian, Chinese, Israeli, Bulgarian, Korean – throng the late-night drinking dens to swap tales of success or despair, or lose themselves to the charms of the beer and local girls. The local Kono people (of the same name as the district) long ago lost their own control over the land – ethnicities from all parts of the country park themselves in Koidu in the hope of a bright spark. That gives the town some edge, particularly when politicians come touting for votes – it's one of the few potential tinderboxes in the country.

There's little shine to the town itself, however. It might be sitting on top of a big foreign-currency earner, but it's a hardscrabble and hard-edged kind of place, with few obvious charms, though if nothing else, the roads are looking much better these days. Coffee and cocoa are regularly dried out in their tons on the roadsides during the dry season, and the weather is positively sweater-worthy from December to February, with chilly nights continuing well into the morning, even after the sun is up.

HISTORY Koidu's troubled modern history is not the first time slaughter has visited the region. In 1893/94, two raiding parties acting on behalf of the Sofa chief Kemo Bilale started extending influence in the region by dirtying their hands in existing regional conflicts. This began to alarm elements of the British colonial administration, which had promised protection to the local Kuranko population.

At the town of Tekwiama, the British 'came upon a scene of horror and desolation. The town had been burnt, and heaps of dead bodies with the hands tied behind were lying all around us …The place was a veritable city of the dead'. In a chilling precursor of what was to become the civil war's calling card a century later, in 1894, a man attacked by Sofas in the east was found by the British with his right hand cut off from the wrist, and his right ear also severed.

The British eventually defeated the Sofas at Tungea, killing more than 250 and capturing 150, but not before their own troops had been mistakenly attacked in a

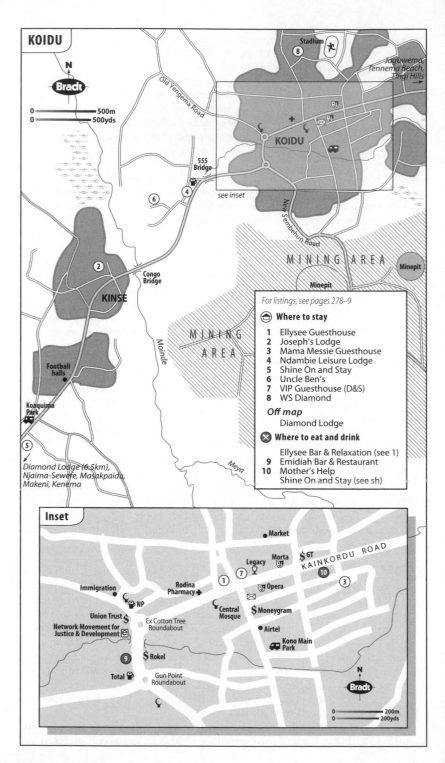

KOIDU

N

Bradt

| 0 | 500m |
| 0 | 500yds |

Old Yengema Road

Stadium

8

Jagbwema,
Tennema Beach,
Tingi Hills

KOIDU

555
Bridge

4

see inset

6

New Sembehun Road

MINING AREA

Minepit

2

Congo
Bridge

KINSE

Moinde

**MINING
AREA**

Minepit

Football
halls

Koaquima
Park

5

Meya

Diamond Lodge (6.5km),
Njaima-Sewefe, Masakpaidu,
Makeni, Kenema

For listings, see pages 278–9

🛏 Where to stay

1 Ellysee Guesthouse
2 Joseph's Lodge
3 Mama Messie Guesthouse
4 Ndambie Leisure Lodge
5 Shine On and Stay
6 Uncle Ben's
7 VIP Guesthouse (D&S)
8 WS Diamond

Off map
　 Diamond Lodge

✖ Where to eat and drink

　 Ellysee Bar & Relaxation (see 1)
9 Emidiah Bar & Restaurant
10 Mother's Help
　 Shine On and Stay (see sh)

Inset

Market

Legacy　Morta

$ GT

KAINKORDU ROAD

7　**1**

10

Immigration

NP

Rodina
Pharmacy

Opera

3

Central
Mosque

$ Moneygram

Union Trust $

Ex Cotton Tree
Roundabout

Airtel

Network Movement for
Justice & Development

Kono Main
Park

9

$ Rokel

Total

Gun Point
Roundabout

N

Bradt

| 0 | 200m |
| 0 | 200yds |

case of friendly fire by a French contingent that was also on the hunt for Samori Toure and his warriors, leading to the deaths of the young officers in charge of both expeditionary forces.

GETTING THERE AND AWAY Two main roads connect this diamond outpost to the rest of the country. From Freetown, by far the most sensible way (and the choice of all public transport from the capital) is north to Makeni (about 3 hours) and then east for 24km to Magburaka and another 13km to Matotaka (where there's a junction for an unsurfaced route to Bo), after which you'll pass north of the little-visited **Kangari Hills Non-Hunting Forest Reserve** (accessible from the Bo–Matotaka road; see David Karr's 2014 birding report here: **w** cloudbirders.com/tripreport/repository/KARR_SL-Kangari_11_2014.pdf) and onwards through Masingbi after 47km, and a final 73km stretch on to Koidu.

The road from Makeni is newly surfaced, and a private saloon car can get through without trouble in under 2½ hours. The **government bus** costs L40,000 from Freetown, and may involve changing buses in Kissy, adding to the time.

If you are already in the east, the second option is to strike north for 115km from Kenema on a rough and rocky 4x4-only road with several hilly sections. It can take nearly 4 hours in the dry season, up to 6 hours in the rains, and it's not a favourite for public transport, though there's supposed to be at least one vehicle a day (Le50,000) when it's dry.

There are two main drop-off points in Koidu. One is the poda poda stand at Koaquima, under an old filling station canopy before the centre of town (if you're arriving from the west). Pick up transport here if you've missed all the early leavers in town. The central park in Koidu, best known as Kono Main Park, is packed with taxis for charter, poda podas and the government bus, which leaves at 06.00; arrive with plenty of time to bag a seat and second-guess its moment of departure. **Melian Tours** (**m** *078 919 097, 077 902 003*) runs to Freetown at the same time. If you're a fan of doing things the hard way, there's also a weekly departure or two to Mongo-Bendugu on the back road to Kenema (pages 263–9).

ORIENTATION Koidu is a strung-out town in two parts: a kind of western suburb on the main road into town that all visitors will pass through, with most of the decent hotels and plenty of roadside nightspots; and the more built-up commercial centre of town. It's had to grow quickly – in 1927, before diamonds, there were only 100 people living there. In fact, it's two towns in one – Koidu and Sefadu (the older part) – and is regularly referred to by any of three names, Koidu, Sefadu and Kono. Unfortunately, some of the town's most iconic (and useful) landmarks disappeared during recent roadworks: entering town from the west, the first roundabout you encounter once had a derelict artillery piece at its centre, earning it the rather disconcerting moniker of 'Gun Point', while the junction 250m to the north (heading left towards the town centre) used to be home to a massive cotton tree, which was unceremoniously chopped down in 2015 (shakily justified with the claim it was occupied by irritable bees, malevolent witches, or both). Though the namesakes have disappeared, the names themselves are going nowhere fast, and navigating by 'cotton tree' or 'gun point' will be widely understood.

 WHERE TO STAY *Map, opposite*
As of mid 2017, Koidu was getting national electricity most evenings until 01.00–02.00, after which hotels generally switch on their backup generators until morning.

🏠 **Diamond Lodge Hotel** (16 rooms) Airfield Rd, Yengema; m 076 738 361; w diamondlodgehotel.com. Set 10km outside of town on the Makeni road, this newly built lodge is aimed squarely at the business & mining market, with inflated prices to match. The tiled rooms come with AC, TV, & hot water. B&B. **$$$$$–$$$$**

🏠 **Shine On and Stay** (28 rooms) 210 Masingbi Rd, Koaquima; m 030 894 697, 079 243 738; e barazakenneth323@gmail.com; w shineonandstay.com. Recently renamed & refurbished, but still better known as the (ex-) Kono Hotel, this is the priciest spot in town & also the best. A favourite with the mining crowd, their restaurant/bar (see below) is the place to come in the evening to soak up Koidu's distinctly strange atmosphere. Rooms are spacious & clean, & all are self-contained with TV, Wi-Fi, AC & hot water. Management is responsive, & there's a nice new swimming pool (open to non-guests for Le30,000/day) in the green, flowered courtyard. B&B. **$$$$–$$$**

🏠 **WS Diamond Hotel Kono** (12 rooms) 1 Moiga St; m 077 565 383, 030 686 890, 099 812 256, 079 906 060; e bobby@wsdiamondhotels.com; w wsdiamondhotelskono.com. With an on-site gold & diamond office, nightclub (Versace Mansion, opposite), BBQ restaurant & well-kept rooms ranging from US$40–90, this American-owned outpost knows its market well. It's centrally located & rooms come with AC, TV, hot water & Wi-Fi. **$$$$–$$$**

🏠 **Ndambie Leisure Lodge** (8 rooms) 48 Masingbi Rd; m 076 857 196, 079 806 882, 079 777 706; e ndambieleisurelodge@yahoo.com. Set in what feels a bit like an overgrown family house, the large ground-floor rooms here (all with fridge, AC & TV) are nothing to shout about but fine for the price range. Meals & drinks are available, & Wi-Fi is supposed to be on the way. **$$$**

🏠 **Ellysee Guesthouse** (3 rooms) 28 Kainkordu Rd; m 078 514 060, 030 120 053. A little bit chintzy, but a good choice if you want to be right in town. Rooms are clean & self-contained with AC, TV & even a fridge. There's a bar & restaurant downstairs. B&B. **$$$–$$**

☀ 🏠 **Uncle Ben's** (51 rooms) Sahr George St, 555 spot; m 077 210 976, 076 599 511; e unclebenshotel@yahoo.com. An utterly reliable guesthouse started by its eponymous owner, Uncle Ben's is quiet & pleasantly out of the way, & favoured by NGO visitors for its smooth-running ambience. The older block of accommodation is still quite comfortable (all en suite) & certainly the best-value accommodation in town, while the more expensive rooms are quite swish, with AC, hot water & TV (but no Wi-Fi). There's a nice gazebo where meals are served, though party people should be warned there's no alcohol served &, according to the signage, definitely no fornication on the premises. Heading west out of town, make a right 250m after the '555 spot bridge', where hawkers used to sell 555 brand cigarettes. B&B. **$$$–$$**

🏠 **VIP Guesthouse (D&S)** (17 rooms) 36 Kainkordu Rd; m 077 572 090, 078 467 972. Great if you want a ringside seat on the main drag; less good if you're averse to hubbub & a healthy dash of seediness. Every room is self-contained, with TV & usually a fan. The reception is a little concealed, down an alley to the right of the building. Don't hold back negotiating on the price of the room; they start at an overpriced Le150,000 a night. B&B. **$$**

🏠 **Joseph's Lodge** (20 rooms) Off Masingbi Rd, by Congo Bridge; m 076 333 401, 099 190 442. Joseph's offers clean, basic rooms with fans & bed nets on a quiet side street at the west end of town. Heading away from town, bear right at the foot of Lebanon Bridge, just after crossing Congo Bridge. There's no food available, which could be inconvenient given the location. **$**

🏠 **Mama Messie Guesthouse** (5 rooms) 32 Dabunde St; m 030 372 935, 076 613 207. Formerly the Tosby Guesthouse, this little establishment, which sits on a quiet side street a block off the main drag, has ceiling fan & en suites, making it a passable budget option. Dinner available if ordered in advance. **$**

✖ **WHERE TO EAT AND DRINK** *Map, page 264*

✖ **Shine On and Stay** 210 Masingbi Rd, Koaquima; m 030 894 697, 079 243 738; 🕗 07.00–23.00 daily. Smartest destination for food in town. Dishes may take a while to turn up, so take advantage of the free Wi-Fi or polish your mining chit-chat with an expat crowd sporting scars, attitude & accents. When the food arrives, it's thoroughly decent – pizzas, good chicken curry, steak, fish, salad & Lebanese dishes. The long bar serves imported as well as local beer. **$$$**

✕ Ellysee Bar & Relaxation 28 Kainkordu Rd; **m** 078 514 060, 030 120 053. This friendly diner-style restaurant serves up cold drinks & affordable African dishes in AC'ed surroundings. With year-round Christmas lights & a TV in one corner, it manages a certain cheer. They were searching for a new chef when we visited in 2017. **$$$–$$**

✕ Emidiah Bar & Restaurant 8 New Sembehun Rd; **m** 077 594 909, 078 688 745. This simple-as-can-be roadside haunt is much more restaurant than bar; it's got a friendly proprietress & does a variety of rice & plassas daily, plus local interpretations of shawarmas & burgers. **$$**

✕ Mother's Help Restaurant 63 Kainkordu Rd; **m** 076 301 970; ⊕ 10.00–22.00 Sat–Thu. Simple shack popular for tasty b/fasts & local dishes for next to nothing, served all day. Choose from outdoor seating set back a little from the road or the indoor canteen. As well as the usual rice & plassas & groundnut soup, look out for plantain, liver & black-eyed beans. It also has a well-stocked fridge for beer & soft drinks. **$$**

ENTERTAINMENT AND NIGHTLIFE A town of cooped-up, frequently down-on-their luck miners, Kono by night beats even the daytime's standards for seediness. Perhaps the best of the nightspots is **Versace Mansion (WS Nightclub)** (*1 Moigua St*; **m** *077 565 383*), where the pumping nightclub is packed most nights of the week, including Wednesday for ladies' night. **Legacy** (*8 Kainkordu Rd*; **m** *076 287 794*) is firmly on the spit-and-sawdust end of the spectrum, but it's worth a quick educational peek for the pool table and racy murals, and Justin the manager is a welcoming chap if you can find him. A few kilometres away on Masingbi Road in Koaquima, a handful of rough-and-ready football viewing halls top a small embankment above the road.

If you feel like escaping into fiction, **Morta Theatre** (**m** *076 818 680*), a 'cinema' in the market area of town on Kainkordu Road, mostly shows live Champions League games, and the odd martial arts or Nollywood DVD. Tickets cost Le2,000, Le2,500 or Le3,000 for a 'Presidential' seat. More popular, the **Opera Cinema** is opposite the VIP Guesthouse on Kainkordu Road, chaotic and always packed for the daily afternoon football match.

OTHER PRACTICALITIES

Banks With the thirst for gems, Koidu – an otherwise small town – is well served by **banks**, but there's still only one ATM in town, at **GT Bank** at the east end of Kainkordu Road (so have a backup plan if it's out of service!). Otherwise, the local branch of **Rokel Commercial Bank** (*2 New Sembehun Rd*; ⊕ *08.30–15.30 Mon–Fri*) does Visa encashments on the spot (as long as you have your passport with you). You can also choose to receive money via **Western Union** at the Kono branch of **Union Trust Bank** (*5 Old Yengema Rd*; **m** *077 713 516*). **EcoBank** also has a storefront on Kainkordu Road, but its opening seems to have been stalled for several years now and it wasn't functional in 2017.

Internet For internet access, the **Network Movement for Justice and Development** (**m** *077 867 499*; ⊕ *09.00–18.00 Mon–Sat*), housed in a big blue building by the ex-cotton tree roundabout, opens its doors to surfers for Le10,000 an hour, with Wi-Fi and printing also available. If you've got your own device, the most pleasant place to connect is the restaurant at Shine On and Stay (see opposite), where you can surf freely if you're eating or drinking.

Medical There are several **pharmacies** in town, including **Rodina Pharmacy** (*24 Main Rd*; **m** *076 624 624*) and **Richard's** (*38 Kainkordu Rd*).

As far as Valentine's Day presents go, this has to be the big one. On 14 February 1972, the fourth-largest diamond in the world was found in Sierra Leone's Kono district. The 'Star of Sierra Leone', as it became known, all 968.9 carats of it (one carat is 0.20 grams), weighed about half a pound in the rough. By the time the experts had finished with it, 17 cut stones emerged – 13 of them flawless. The largest, at 143.2 carats, was flawed and diamond mogul Harry Winston, who had bought the lot, decided on a recut. He went to master diamond-cutter Lazare Kaplan, who studied the stone for a year, and performed the cut live on US TV to an audience of hundreds of thousands. All the stones from that recut are now set in the Star of Sierra Leone Brooch, and the largest is a 53.96 carat, pear-shaped dazzler.

As if to belabour the point of just how rich Kono's diamond fields really are, March 2017 saw Evangelical pastor and part-time artisanal miner Emmanuel Momoh unearth Sierra Leone's biggest find in 45 years and the 13th largest in world history, a mammoth, yet-to-be-named 709-carat diamond the size of a hockey puck. (Four of the world's 20 largest diamonds have now been uncovered in Kono alone, more than anywhere but South Africa.) To the approval (and in some cases bewilderment) of Sierra Leoneans everywhere, Momoh turned over the stone to the government in the hope that proceeds from its sale would be used for the further development of the district; President Koroma has promised a transparent process and fair distribution of proceeds to Momoh and the state. The diamond remained under lock and key at the central bank in Freetown awaiting valuation and sale when this book went to print.

WHAT TO SEE AND DO Before the war Koidu used to have a bit of glitz – there were cinemas and even jet skiing on the lake in one nearby diamond enclosure. Today, although it's hard to call it an attraction, sampling the atmosphere of Kono may feel a bit seedy at times but it is also intoxicating.

As far as sights go, it's hard to miss the big mining operation on the right-hand side of the road as you head down the main drag in Koidu. That's the kimberlite pipe that's being mined by Koidu Holdings, which sells 60% of the mine's 500,000-carat annual output directly to Tiffany & Co, with production set to continue until at least 2030.

It's impossible to avoid, or ignore, the sheer venality of the diamond trade, pursued with single-minded determination that is both awesome and appalling, and dominates the local economy. Alongside the usual cooking pots, sandals and forks found in nearby markets at Yomadu, diamond shakers for sifting gravel are also on sale. When you see a man gouging out a dugout canoe from a tree on the side of the road, it's more likely so that he can go diamond hunting on a lake with a shovel than fishing with a line.

This is a million miles from the sanitised, airlocked display cases of Old Bond Street or even engaged ring fingers the world over: it's where the great diamond trade begins, and it is far from pretty. Illicit or not, conflict or not, looking for alluvial diamonds is wretched, backbreaking work, carried out by those who have abandoned their sickles and crops to sieve dirt in the desperate hope of a tiny, elusive sparkle that might pay for their children to go to school, or medicine for their families.

Good morning (singular)	*ay-ing tshend*
Good morning (plural)	*way-ing tshend*
Good afternoon (singular)	*ay-ing tayi*
Good afternoon (plural)	*way-ing tay-i*
Good evening (singular)	*ay-ing goo'a*
Good evening (plural)	*way-ing goo'a*
How are you? (singular)	*i tsh'nde?*
How are you? (plural)	*oo tsh'nde?*
What's your name?	*i twe*
Thank you (singular)	*ay-ing gwa-ee*
Thank you (plural)	*way-ing gwa-ee*
I am going	*mbay-i ta*
Come, let's go	*na mway-i ta*
my people	*mba mwe noo*
my children	*na day-in-e noo*
my child	*na day-in-e*

Still, mining is paid at Le8,000–14,000 a day, which means it counts as a decent wage, and there's always that chance you'll get lucky. But for most of the workers, toiling 12 hours a day, they won't have found a diamond in a year – many have never come across one – but still they struggle, bent double in the baking heat, sweating, filthy, unfulfilled.

For the mid-ranking companies relying on mechanisation, often financed and run by foreigners, the environment is just as economically precarious, if a little more physically comfortable. As dusk falls and the big 4x4s come racing back into town from their upcountry mining haunts, the tension is palpable. 'Did you get one?' comes the inevitable question as the first beer fades. 'A nice little 40 carats today,' comes the poker-faced reply, a tiny flicker around the eye marking relief, pride and the prospect of more luck tomorrow.

Some of the country's estimated 300,000–400,000 artisanal miners work right beside the main road in town, as well as much further out in the forests. To arrange a visit, try the regional office of the **Ministry of Tourism and Culture** (*45 Dama Rd, Kenema*), or, if they're not too busy, the local office of the **Ministry of Mineral Resources** (ask for directions). You could also visit the Kono branch of local NGO the **Network Movement for Justice and Development (NMJD)**, close to the old cotton tree roundabout in the centre of town. The organisation has been involved in lobbying government, donors and the mining industry, and is at the frontline of compiling research documents to try and keep track of both the benefits and the bedevilments of Sierra Leone diamond mining.

For a good view over the town and beyond, head to the top of any of the nearby hills. One within easy reach of town is at the end of the track off Old Yengema Road.

AROUND KOIDU

RIVER BEACHES AND WATERFALLS Sierra Leonean beach culture isn't confined to the coast, and when a town is as tough as Koidu can be, it's good to know there's somewhere to chill out nearby. East of the town, 10km along the rutted dirt road to Jagbwema, look out for a tiny turning at Meiyor, also referred to as Wondma, in Fiama

Among the Kono, children are traditionally named according to their birth order and gender. For example, in a family with two older girls and a younger boy, they would be known as Sia, Kumba, and Sahr, and the next child would be either Finda or Tamba. In families where a man has children with more than one wife, the naming order remains specific to each mother – ie: if each wife had one girl child, they would both be Sia. If a woman somehow manages to have seven boys or seven girls (or both!), the seventh of each will be known as Mani. Most Kono people have a traditional name using this system, even if they use Christian or Islamic names as well.

You'll be sure to get plenty of laughs and start more than a few conversations if you sort out your Kono name and start using it around town.

Girls:
1st: Sia
2nd:Kumba
3rd: Finda
4th: Yei
5th: Bondu
6th: Fea
7th: Mani

Boys:
1st: Sahr
2nd: Tamba
3rd: Aiah
4th: Komba
5th: Kai
6th: Sahr Fea (*second Sahr*)
7th: Mani

chiefdom. Take a left, heading north for 1km past a new sand mining operation to end up at **Tennema Beach**. A sandbar offers calm and a pleasant picnic spot on the bank of a slow river. Further on, children fish with long sticks, and women wash their clothes and themselves in the water near a tiny set of falls, though this relative idyll may be set to disappear given the ongoing demand for sand. The manmade **Ecoma Beach**, also along the river, is great for a quick swim or picnic, but you definitely need a 4x4 and local guide to find it. Much larger, the river beach at **Njaiama-Sewafe** is supremely popular at holidays such as Christmas and Easter, when stereo systems start pumping. It's 40km to the west of Koidu, on the Makeni road out of town. A motorbike taxi should cost about Le30,000, but there's plenty of public transport going that way in any case. There are also waterfalls along the Soa River about 40 minutes along the road from Masingbi; it's a nice place for a picnic or a walk, and easy to find.

MASAKPAIDU It's really just a ditch, and by no means a must-see, but nevertheless it's a historic ditch, abandoned only when the Sofas sacked the place in 1893. Now uninhabited, this village in Kono's Nimmiyama chiefdom, near Njaima-Sewafe on the route to Makeni, is a fortified settlement that dates from around 1800, in the pre-protectorate days of the hinterland, and strategically sited at the meeting point of the Bafi and Bagwe rivers. All that is left now are stumps of cotton trees, and the 8m-deep, 274m-long trench running around the defensive stockade. The village had two entrances, each with a bridge that was taken up at night.

CAPTAIN LENDY'S GRAVE Captain Lendy, the British officer who was killed by a mistaken French attack in 1893 (pages 275–6), is buried at **Waiima**, east of town in Fiama chiefdom, 5km further east from Jagbwema. Both Lendy and his French counterpart, Lieutenant Gaston Maritz, died in the blue-on-blue incident – both parties mistook each other for the Sofa warriors they were hunting – and were buried on the spot side by side along with their men, beneath a memorial cross. In 1933, a larger monument was erected.

TINGI HILLS A birding pleasure, Tingi Hills Forest Reserve is the most easterly forest in the country, 470km from Freetown and sat flush with the Guinean border. The massif is also home to Sierra Leone's second-highest spot, Sankan Birriwa, whose twin peaks are separated by a dramatic gorge. The higher is 1,853m, with the other also above 1,800m. There are much sharper inclines and craggy faces throughout this range than Loma, so its 119km^2 make for good rock climbing. Savannah and shrubland make up the lower reaches, changing to forest and grassland higher up, while streams flow down into both the Mano and Sewa rivers.

The area became a forest reserve in 1947 and a non-hunting forest reserve in 1973, and as with several of the country's outstanding wildlife areas, it's slated to become a national park, though this process seems to be moving at a rather glacial pace. The main threat to habitat comes from bush fires, which occasionally cause considerable damage to the forest cover. Another potential long-term danger is mining, which takes place along the rivers at the southern end of the reserve. There is no management plan for the area, and no immediate development plans exist.

Getting there and away There are two routes here: both require time, effort and your own transport.

From Koidu Town, head east for 70km, about an hour, on a decent unsurfaced road to Jagbwema, a pretty, sprawling town set amid jungle-sided hills, then northeast to Wadu. The road is passable but regularly descends into tough, unforgiving rutted track, and you'll need a **4x4** or a sturdy **motorbike**. At Wadu, ask locally about the condition of the roads, and whether to branch right (northeast) via Sami and Mangadu-Kissitown, or left (north–northwest) up to Kenewa, via Kamadu and Kurako, and possibly west on to Kiagbasima. You can see the peaks of Sankan Birriwa from Nekoro, a village on the southern end of the reserve.

You can also head west out of Koidu and take the stretch of road heading north towards Kurubonla from the Makeni–Koidu Highway (page 329). At Worodu, 24km south of Mansofenia, branch east, on a road that leads to the mountain. The road is passable as far as Dombadu, but no further, so then it's a 25km walk to Gbeaia, near the foot of the range.

To arrange a guided visit, get in touch with Kennth Gbenga's Fact Finding Tours (pages 70–1) or the Conservation Society (page 70) in Freetown.

Where to stay and eat You have to **camp**, but there are plenty of good spots along the hill range that lead to the main peaks. Animal tracks and unkempt paths are the easiest ways to move around, but meet with a local chief and ask for a guide in one of the villages at the bottom of the hills first. There are year-round streams and some wells in the villages, but no piped water.

Wildlife More than 200 bird species have been identified so far, including six species of global conservation concern. One of these, the **Sierra Leone prinia** (*Prinia leontica*), has a restricted distribution in the country. The beloved **white-necked picathartes** (*Picathartes gymnocephalus*) has also been recorded in the remnants of closed forest in the reserve. The Tingi Hills are also the only site where **Baumann's greenbul** (*Phyllastrephus baumanni*) has been found in the country. If you hanker after more exotic bird names, take your pick from the **red-thighed sparrowhawk** (*Accipiter erythropus*), the **dusky long-tailed cuckoo** (*Cercococcyx mechowi*) and

A CURSED RESOURCE

Diamonds from Sierra Leone have been linked with everything from bankrupting the economy to funding al-Qaeda. Not only did top-quality gems fund factions in the civil war, keeping its child soldiers topped up with drugs and weapons, there is evidence that throughout the 1990s the West African trade in illicit diamonds worked as an effective money-laundering operation for Colombian cocaine traffickers and Russian and New York Mafia. As recently as 2008, the US State Department claimed that diamond receipts from Sierra Leone were going towards Hezbollah, in south Lebanon.

Smuggling and illegal activity has long been rife. As early as the 1950s diamond rush, 20 years after the first diamond was found, there were an estimated 76,000 illicit miners in Kono district. From the start, Lebanese and Mandingo traders have loomed large in the trade as middlemen, and most of the handful of licensed exporters in Sierra Leone today are Lebanese.

An estimated 300,000–400,000 artisanal miners (many of whom are legitimate) account for 80–90% of all diamond exports. In addition to artisanal mining, two foreign mining companies are now extracting diamonds from kimberlite pipes and dykes on an industrial scale, and several foreign companies mine alluvial stones with diggers and mechanisation.

In the Siaka Stevens era, the president and his cronies left diamond affairs to Lebanese businessmen. Between 1930 and the 1970s, diamonds accounted for more than two-thirds of the nation's export earnings and a quarter of GDP. During the 1960s, diamond revenue alone accounted for almost 70% of Sierra Leone's foreign-exchange earnings. But by 1988, legitimate, declared diamond exports were down to 48,000 carats, from two million carats in 1970, robbing Sierra Leone's people of any hope of seeing a gem windfall.

During the war, Kono turf changed hands repeatedly, and civilians were forced to mine from 1994. The RUF held Koidu in 1992 and then not again until 1995,

naked-faced barbet (*Gymnobucco calvus*). Birders David Karr and Kenneth Gbenga visited here in late 2015, and you can see their trip report here: w *cloudbirders.com/tripreport/repository/KARR_SL_TingiHills_09_2015.pdf.*

Forest **elephants, buffalo,** the odd **pygmy hippo,** the **western chimpanzee, red colobus, black-and-white colobus** and **sooty mangabey** have all been spotted.

THE FAR EAST

The estranged tongue of land that pokes deep into Liberia, rich in coffee, cocoa, cassava, palm oil and known for the quality of its loom-weaving, was coveted so much by Charles Taylor that he wanted it as part of his vision of a Greater Liberia. He came pretty close too: it was from here that Foday Sankoh's bush war took root, aided by Taylor-backed Liberian fighters. The war also finished here, and such is the slow pace of rehabilitation that the devastation feels like it could have been wrought only last year. Combined with high levels of poverty, gutted buildings and poor access to education and health, **Kailahun** has a reputation as 'the forgotten district'. The eastern border was among the last bits of Sierra Leone's boundaries to be settled, and Guinean troops didn't leave the disputed village of Yenga until 2013. The hunt for minerals is keenly followed along the border area, and as a result tensions are palpable.

before being driven out by Executive Outcomes four months later. After the 1997 coup, extensive mining and smuggling increased, and in December 1998 the RUF once more launched a successful assault on Kono. Not until July 2000 did the UN embargo diamond exports, and only in 2002 did the government retain control of Koidu and Tongo fields.

Whoever controlled the diamond fields, the pattern of exploitation was usually the same. Stones would head out through the jungle into neighbouring Liberia. In Monrovia deals would be done with a host of unscrupulous buyers, often at cut-price rates. Then, with few international safeguards, the diamonds would move seamlessly into the legitimate market, which for raw stones is based in Antwerp.

The figures speak for themselves. Liberia has never produced more than 150,000 carats a year, for example, but in 1996, Belgium imported 12.3 million carats of diamonds from Sierra Leone's neighbour. Numbers likewise shot up in Ivory Coast, while Sierra Leone's official exports dwindled to US$1.5 million in 1999.

While the numbers today are much better, thanks in part to the end of the war and the impact of the (imperfect) Kimberley Process – more than US$150 million in diamond exports went out of the country in 2015 – smuggling continues and working conditions are tough. Stagnant muddy water forms in the artisanal mining pits, which breeds malaria and sometimes children drown. The industry union, which has only 6,000 grassroots diggers to its name, says people are not seeing the benefits. 'Abuse, misuse, ill treatment – these are some of the reasons that led to the war; that's why people decided to join the rebel leaders,' says Ezekiel Dyke, General Secretary of the United Mineworkers' Union, which wants workers' wages to be increased from the current going rate of about US$1.50 a day. 'But the workers are still suffering and being mistreated. We are trying to regulate the informal sector – to increase wages and make sure that working conditions are looked after.'

Worn down by being the epicentre of regional conflict for many years, Kailahun's inaccessibility means it is likely to stay poor for a long time yet. Much of what produce grows in the rich soils around the town goes straight across the border to Guinea or Liberia (whose borders meet near the town of **Koindu**). Fula traders, many from Guinea, also trade what little cattle there is, and cloth. Koindu is home to a well-attended weekly market on Sundays, drawing traders from around the region. Once a major international trading centre, its heyday, when bank branches lined the road and electricity and running water were taken for granted, is long past. Donor organisations have attempted to reinvigorate market life, but bad roads hamper its accessibility.

Home to Mende and Kisi people, the far east remains a bastion of SLPP support. Secret societies, ceremonies and traditional cultural practices are the bedrocks of life here. Masked devils parade through the streets during festivals and cultural ceremonies, and people tend to rely on traditional treatments rather than conventional medicine.

GETTING THERE AND AWAY More than 400km from Freetown, reaching this area has long been a difficult and time-consuming affair, but this has changed drastically in recent years. As of mid 2017, a good tarmac road runs all the way to Pendembu, less than 30km from Kailahun. The 73km route from Segbwema to Kailahun is a

SIERRA LEONE'S COCOA COMES BACK TO LIFE

Back in the 1980s, cocoa was a mainstay of Sierra Leone's agriculture sector. But then the war came, raging fiercely in the southeast – where cocoa trees flourish – and exports of the crop nearly disappeared. From 1991 to 1992, exports dropped by almost 80%. Today production remains well below pre-war levels, but cocoa beans are nonetheless making a resurgence, and growers of the crop in Sierra Leone's far east are tapping into the organic, fair trade corner of the market.

Ten years of little to no production meant not a drop of pesticides or other chemicals tarnished the rich, loamy soil. Over the past decade, with support from the World Bank, the UN Food and Agricultural Organisation and other donors, the government has been working to train the country's 60,000 cocoa farmers in how to grow the crop efficiently – and sustainably. The German development agency, GIZ, has been especially active in Kono and Kailahun districts since 2014, training youth farmers in cocoa-production methods and revitalising plantations that were neglected during the war. Many of Sierra Leone's cocoa plantations remain idle to this day, sometimes simply due to a lack of expertise with the crop; many children lost their parents to the war before they were taught about cocoa cultivation and now own land they simply don't know how to farm. More than 5,000 young people have now participated in these trainings, and 4,500ha of cocoa-producing land in the two districts has now been rehabilitated under the programme.

The private sector has also taken notice. In 2009, the UK's Divine Chocolate, a company that specialises in organic and fair trade confectionary, began sourcing cocoa beans from Kpeya Agricultural Enterprise, a co-operative of 1,200 cocoa farmers scattered around Kenema and Kailahun. Another British company, Willie's Delectable Cacao, followed soon after, snapping up Sierra Leonean beans to use in its 'Sierra Leone 70' bar, a hunk of 70% chocolate that's laced with ginger and lime – now hard to find in shops, but still available on Amazon.

Most recently in July 2017, the Gola Forest Programme, in partnership with the RSPB and CSSL, debuted their own 70% dark and 50% milk chocolate bars made from cocoa harvested by the Goleagorbu Cocoa Producers Organisation, a collective of some 2,000 farmers living on the fringes of the park. It's early days yet, but they intend to reach UK shops in the not-too-distant future.

Sierra Leone's production still pales in comparison to that of regional heavyweight Côte d'Ivoire, which produces about 1.4 million tons of the beans every year (40% of the global supply) and Ghana, whose growers exported some 860,000 tons over 2013–14. By 2011–12, Sierra Leone's annual crop had grown to 16,000 tons, but sales fell 25% during 2014–15 thanks to the Ebola crisis. Even with this uneven progress, exports are more than triple what they were in the dark days of the war, and, with the right training and investment, the government hopes that figure will continue to grow.

gorgeous drive through rainforest, partly following the old railway line to Pendembu – you may spot the odd remnant of track if you look closely. Nearer to Kailahun the road is bordered by coffee and cocoa plantations specked with citrus trees.

Shared taxis run between Kenema and Kailahun every morning. If you're driving, head 23km on the road that leads north to Koidu as far as Mano junction, then branch east for the 25km to Segbwema and loop round via Daru (where you cross the Moa River) for 45km to Pendembu. It's there the tarmac ends, with the final 28km to Kailahun in awful shape. Roadworks were just beginning on this section in mid 2017, so it should be complete during the lifespan of this edition. Once this happens, the 115km route between Kenema and Kailahun shouldn't take much more than 2 hours, but allow a couple more if you're heading onwards to the border, as there were no roadworks headed that way just yet.

To reach Koindu, to the northeast of Kailahun, you can go 53km via Buedu (a reasonable surface, which will likely eventually be tarred), or hug the northeast border for 33km via Dia – a shorter but more rudimentary route. South from Kailahun into the Kisi chiefdoms the route is extremely bad, with a series of poorly constructed and unreliable log bridges. A motorbike taxi between Kailahun and Koindu should be in the region of Le20,000–25,000.

From Freetown, the **government bus** runs to Pendembu (Le50,000) on Mondays, Wednesdays and Fridays, where cars and motorbikes wait to ferry you the rest of the way to Kailahun. Buses return from Pendembu on Tuesdays, Thursdays and Saturdays, and it's safe to assume the route will be extended to Kailahun once roadworks are complete.

Border crossing
Most local people move between Sierra Leone and its neighbours on informal bush routes, but there are a few large official crossings too.

Among the most regular local crossings (where there should now also be an official checkpoint) is Beilu, the old refugee crossing point, a 1-hour walk north of Kailahun, where you can get to Guinea via a tiny wooden boat across the Moa River for a few thousand leones. From Kailahun, turn right on to Manosewalu Road just before the central mosque, carry on straight for 3km, then make a left at Kpemalu village, from where it's just under 2km to the river.

Official checkpoints to Guinea and Liberia also exist just after Koindu. From Koindu, it's 7.5km to the Liberian border and 5km to the Makona (Moa) River, which forms the border with Guinea. At this Liberia crossing, there are checkpoints either side of the border and a no-man's-land in between. These crossings are rarely used by foreigners and you're likely to attract a lot of attention and requests for bribes, on both sides. Just past the army camp at the border there's a great view of the rapids.

You also reach Liberia by continuing 10km east from Buedu, to Dawa, which sits just beside the border.

KAILAHUN
Kailahun, capital of the district of the same name, means Kai's town. It was built as the great Kisi warrior Kai Lundu's capital in 1880, after he was victorious in war against his foe Ndawa. Today, despite still bearing the lingering hallmarks of wartime destruction and deprivation – one building is known as 'the slaughter house' – it is nevertheless slowly rebounding and remains surrounded by green jungle beauty and the fertile soils that made the place rich. The town is lined with once-pretty, now rundown two- (and occasionally three-) storey buildings. Look out for Paramount Chief Banya's big white house (it used to be pink) in the town centre, near the clock tower roundabout.

The town is arranged around this rather odd dual roundabout with a clock tower in one of the central islands, and divided from there into a series of small neighbourhoods (known as sections). Coming from Pendembu, the first section is Kula, after which you pass the NGO Plan's office on the left (it's revealing that NGO buildings are the best landmarks going); followed by the Belebu section (home of a new marketplace that traders have largely refused to relocate to), with a fuel station on the right, before hitting the main roundabout with the paramount chief's house. The main road, Mofindor

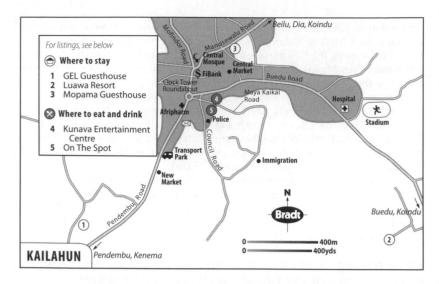

For listings, see below

🏠 **Where to stay**

1 GEL Guesthouse
2 Luawa Resort
3 Mopama Guesthouse

✕ **Where to eat and drink**

4 Kunava Entertainment
   Centre
5 On The Spot

KAILAHUN *Pendembu, Kenema*

Street, is lined with small stalls and Pa Jalloh's, at the end, calls itself a supermarket with the odd tin of sardines, soft cheese, water and soft drinks.

You can pick up a motorbike taxi from the main roundabout, for L2,000 a trip. Kailahun has mobile-phone reception for both the Airtel and Africell networks.

🏠 Where to stay *Map, above*

🏠 **Luawa Resort Hotel** (52 rooms) Buedu Rd; m 077 809 616, 077 870 165, 078 201 282, 076 603 568; e luawareservations@gmail.com. This newly opened hotel in Kailahun is by far the most comfortable option in this part of the country. With its AC rooms (generator 19.00–07.00), satellite TV & rather pricey restaurant, Luawa doesn't exactly blend into its surroundings, but it's a welcome stop for any weary traveller who's made it this far from Freetown (better still, a swimming pool is in the works). The fan-only rooms are a good budget option at Le175,000, while the pricier rooms with AC & hot water start at Le290,000 – still good value for what you're getting. **$$$–$$**

🏠 **GEL Guesthouse** (5 rooms) Off Pendembu Rd; m 099 908 112, 076 815 552, 076 758 206;

e gelsierraleone2012@gmail.com. Your best bet if the Luawa is full, located on your way into town where there are clean, emphatically cheap rooms with fans, nets & generator power (19.00– midnight) in a nice green compound next to the National Electoral Commission (NEC). Meals can be arranged with plenty of advance notice. **$**

🏠 **Mopama Guesthouse** (7 rooms) Manosewalu Rd; m 076 522 321, 076 864 344, 076 819 357, 088 485 842. Closer to the centre of town, this guesthouse has basic but acceptable self-contained rooms with fans, nets & generator power (19.00–23.00) .**$** self-contained rooms with fans, nets & generator power (19.00–23.00). **$**

✕ Where to eat and drink *Map, above*

While there's little in the way of larger shops, tins, vegetables, some fruit and dried fish can be rustled up from stalls around the centre, and Friday is market day. Kailahun used to occasionally run out of basic foodstuffs, but today it's generally only fuel that can be a problem, so top up in Kenema if you're driving. To fill your belly, your two main options are conveniently just across the street from one another: **On The Spot** (*Maya Kaikai Rd*; m *076 895 146, 088 881 460*; ⏲ *until midnight daily*), also known as Peace Garden, does a daily dish of rice or cassava and plassas, or even the likes of chicken and chips with a bit of notice, while **Kunava Entertainment Centre** (*Maya Kaikai Rd*) is a decent alternative just opposite.

Other practicalities FiBank (*Mofindor Rd*) does Western Union transfers and is your only banking option. The government **hospital** is on Buedu Road and there are several pharmacies; **Afripharm** (*Pendembu Rd;* m *078 985 454*) is convenient near the central roundabout. There is no public internet.

What to see and do For a drinking session and a bit of outdoor dancing, the bar at **On The Spot** (opposite) is lively on Wednesdays (ladies' night) and weekends (Friday is Africana night), also attracting what's left of the town's NGO workers. It has such luxuries as a generator and sound system.

On Independence Day (27 April) many people head out to 'the beach' at Beilu, complete with generator and sound system. Look out for the fast current and quicksand though, attributed locally to a devil under the water who targets those not from Kailahun.

Kailahun is set amid the beautiful, rolling hills of the Kisi chiefdoms, which give views not only of Sierra Leone but also overlook Guinea and Liberia. You can usually get to the top in a couple of hours. Bear in mind several have sacred significance and therefore ask permission from the town chief first, hiring a guide if necessary. **Kangama**, an hour (about 15km) northeast from Kailahun on the way to Koindu, is home to the **Jawie Mountain**, which makes for a fairly steep climb and has stunning views over all three countries. Avoid the midday heat. In Wala chiefdom, 45 minutes from Kailahun, **Nyandehun Mambabu** is a higher peak with qualities so magical it is said the spirits of the ancestors come out of the hill and inhabit the masked devils you may see on cultural occasions in town, so be sure to seek permission first and only attempt getting here during the dry season.

SIERRA LEONE ONLINE

For additional online content, articles, photos and more on Sierra Leone, why not visit w bradtguides.com/sleone.

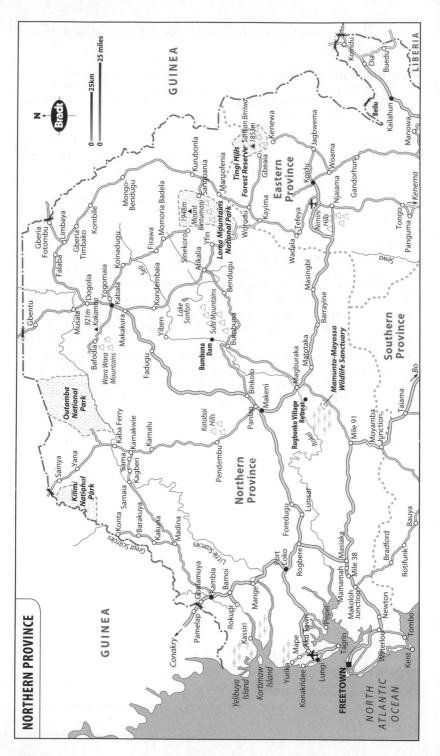

GUINEA

GUINEA

LIBERIA

N

Bradt

0   25km
0   25 miles

NORTH
ATLANTIC
OCEAN

Eastern
Province

Southern
Province

Northern
Province

Koindu
Dia
Buedu
Beilu
Kailahun
Manowa
Woama
Gandorhun
Kenewa
Jagbwema
Koidu
Njalama
Kenema
Woama
Tongo
Panguma
Kenewa
Gbeaia
Mansofenia
Sangbania
Kurubonla
Mongo-Bendugu
Kombile
Gberia Timbako
Gberia Fotombu
Falaba
Limbaya
Sewa

Tingi Hills
Forest Reserve Sankan Biriwa
▲ 1853m

Loma Mountains
National Park
Mount
Bintumani
▲ 1948m

Nimini
Hills

Kayima
Wojodu
Tefeya
Wadala
Masingbi
Barrayine
Matotaka
Magburaka
Matotaka
Bo

Mamunta-Mayosso
Wildlife Sanctuary

Rogbonko Village
Retreat
Rokel

Mile 91
Moyamba
Junction
Taiama

Yfin
Alikalia
Sinekoro
Bendugu
Kondembaia
Firawa
Sell
Koinadugu
Kabala
Yogomaia
Dogolia
Musaia
Bafodia
Wara Wara
Mountains
Makakura
Fadugu
Yiben
Lake
Sonfon
Sula Mountains
Bumbuna
Bumbuna
Dam

Katobai
Hills

Panlap
Binkolo
Makeni
Pendembu

Kamalu
Kamakwie
Kaba Ferry
Sama
Kagberi
Samaia
Barakuya
Konta
Kakuta
Madina
Great Scarcies
Little Scarcies

Outamba
National Park

Kilimi
National
Park

Sainya
Yana

Gbentu

Pamelap
Conakry
Kambia
Rokupr
Kassiri
Bamoi
Mange
Gbalamuya

Port
Loko
Rogbere
Foredugu
Lunsar
Masiaka
Mile 38
Bradford
Bauya
Rotifunk

Yurika
Mape
Konakridee
Lungi
Tagrin
Pepel
Aku Town
Makoloh
Junction
Newton
Waterloo
Kent
Tombo

FREETOWN

Yelibuya
Island
Kortimaw
Island

Mamamah

921m
▲ Kakamba

7

Northern Province

The Northern Province is probably the most scenically varied and rewarding part of Sierra Leone. Home to the highest mountain in the Upper Guinea region, the country's largest province is a giddy mix of lush rainforest, mist-capped mountains, unexplored coastline, intrepid hiking trails, and abundant plant, bird and animal life. The cooler climate and hilltop breezes act as a Siren-like distraction from the incessant noise and heat of Freetown, and much of the region is opened up by one of the best tarred roads in the provinces, which cuts the journey time from the capital to Makeni, the region's principal town, to 3 hours.

Largely Muslim and home to a majority of Temne and Limba, the north is traditionally a land of cattle breeding and agriculture, which suffered heavily during the war but has kept its spirit intact. A stronghold of the APC Party, which came back to power in 2007 after a post-war hiatus that saw politics dominated by southerners, and the ancestral home of President Koroma, northerners are looking forward to a new prosperity. Two big iron ore mines have come online in the region in the past decade, bringing a flood of investment into dusty outposts like Lunsar and Makeni (see box, page 47). Another symbol of progress is the Bumbuna Dam, which supplies power to Freetown and a few other scattered parts of the country. Delayed by several years, it finally started pumping in late 2009; set in a mesmeric natural beauty spot it also carries high hopes for the area's tourism possibilities. A second dam to be built 30km north at Yiben, dubbed Bumbuna II and also long delayed, should quadruple the country's electricity supply when it comes online in 2021.

Whether you plump for encounters with rare monkeys and hippos at Sierra Leone's first national park, visits to fishing villages and turtle watching along the northwest shore, or a weekend break tramping through the hills and bush around Kabala, you are in for a treat up north. In fact, the only tragedy is that you won't be able to do it all – there is simply too much ground to cover and not enough good road – so it's a good idea to prioritise. But make sure you leave time if you can for an ascent of Mount Bintumani, the statuesque, remote peak that inspires every traveller who has the chutzpah to try to tame it.

FROM FREETOWN TO MAKENI

The road from Freetown to Makeni is good tarmac, making it a very easy 3 hours' drive. If you're coming from Freetown, at **Brama**, the first town after the police checkpoint, are three **handicraft stalls** (m *076 960 061*) selling attractive handwoven baskets in several sizes and colours along the road. Laundry baskets made with coloured straw should cost Le45,000 (but you may have to barter a bit); there are also shopping baskets (Le25,000) and smaller shallow open baskets (Le20,000). Twenty minutes further on, after the small market town of **Masiaka** (where you'll find the turn-off for Bo), children and women make use of the speed bumps that slow the traffic at either end of the one-lane **Rogbere Bridge**, selling bagged-up fruit and vegetables through car windows to travellers keen to make the most of upcountry prices so close to the capital. The new bridge under construction here may interfere somewhat with their business model but, depending on the season, you should still be able to find limes, plums, cassava, sweet potato, bananas, guavas, coconuts, pineapples, grapefruits and cucumbers here.

LUNSAR A recently restored mining base, Lunsar is a small town with little to interest the traveller, but, like all of Sierra Leone, plenty going on beneath the sleepy surface. Home to the President of the National Council of Paramount Chiefs, Paramount Chief Bai Koblo Queen II has his home to the north of town, on the way towards Makeni. The town is clustered south of the highway, with the daily market, motorbike taxi stand and a few bars all sat close to a mini roundabout. A big yellow cathedral, **St Peter's** – complete with stained-glass windows and a cave-like shrine – towers over one end of the town. On the outskirts is the **St John of God Catholic Hospital** (Mabesseneh, left fork off the main road heading north). Supported by the Spanish order St John of God, it has both expatriate and local staff and is one of the best medical facilities in the country, with paediatric and adult medical and surgical facilities.

Lunsar is the first stop outside Freetown where you can see evidence of Sierra Leone's mining resurgence. This is the site of the Marampa iron ore mine, which you can spot off to the right as you head down the main road towards Makeni. Look for the oddly flat-topped hill looming on the horizon. The site has been known as a prime spot for iron ore since a geological survey in 1926, and the first mining operations started in 1930. But production stopped in 1975, and the mine was forgotten until, more than three decades later, it was fully refurbished, shipping out its first batch of iron ore in more than three decades at the end of 2011 (see box, page 47).

Lunsar's St Joseph Institute, run by an Italian priest, Father Mario, has been teaching technical skills and crop maximisation to the region's youth for a good number of years. He was kidnapped during the war, and much of the excellent laboratory was destroyed, but the centre goes on.

Lunsar was also the site of a large Ebola treatment centre run by the International Medical Corps; it's now disused but still visible on the right as you leave town headed towards the capital.

Getting there and around Lunsar is a 2-hour hop from the east end of Freetown, on a good tarmac road, 31km further on from Rogbere Bridge. A **shared taxi** from

---

TALKING TEMNE: PROVERBS

If I pour water on you, then wash yourself

Walking along the bank of a river is not crossing it

If one sees a nice shoe one does not know how that nice shoe is hurting the person wearing it

Don't throw stones where you keep bottles

See pages 354–5 for Temne words and phrases.

Asked to go and fetch water at the age of 12, Rugiatu Turay, her three sisters and her cousin were stolen away by family members and what is politely referred to as 'circumcised'. Rugiatu calls it torture. She was blindfolded, stripped, laid on the ground and heavy women sat on her arms, chest and legs. Her mouth was stuffed with a rag. Her clitoris was cut off with a crude knife. Despite profuse bleeding she was forced to walk, had hot pepper water poured into her eyes and was beaten.

An estimated 88% of girls undergo female genital mutilation (FGM) in Sierra Leone. A recent child rights bill dropped any mention of the subject at the last minute, politicians baulk at it and international aid organisations have until recently been too scared to tackle the issue for fear of being labelled cultural imperialists and stoking resentment rather than changing behaviour. However, in 2008 ten UN agencies came out in public and called for an end to the practice, which can cause haemorrhaging, infection (including HIV), painful menstruation and intercourse, as well as numbing feeling. FGM can also contribute to fistula, infertility and complications in childbirth, while the shock of the procedure can cause death.

November 2014 saw the practice banned for the first time in Sierra Leone (subject to a Le500,000 fine), but this was done out of fear of FGM's potential to spread Ebola, rather than due to its deleterious effects on women's health. During the epidemic, cases of FGM did indeed see a historic decline, and though the law officially remains on the books – seemingly with tacit support from the president – it goes largely unenforced and prevalence rates are returning to pre-epidemic levels.

Rugiatu is among the small coterie of anti-FGM campaigners based outside the capital Freetown, and the only one in the country to score noticeable results. She has adopted 14 children, several of whom she has taken into her care just to keep them safe from undergoing cutting. As a result of her campaigning, more than 40 'practitioners' have laid down their blades and vowed to halt their role in the traditional bundu initiation ceremony, in exchange for money and help in finding new ways to earn a living.

It's not an easy practice to stop, however. One female practitioner who said she would stop the cutting was kidnapped by members of the bundu society. Both her and her seven-month-old baby were beaten and taken to the bush for three days without food or water; the mother was raped. Their lives were saved only by Rugiatu's intervention.

By way of reward, Rugiatu has received death threats and been attacked by juju men armed with machetes. But she failed to die so many times that locals now think she has special powers. She has. She has perseverance and belief and fight, as well as grace, intelligence and fierce logic. And after so many years in this fight, her hard work may have some reward after all – Rugiatu was appointed Deputy Minister of Social Welfare, Gender and Children's Affairs in 2016.

Her organisation, the Amazonian Initiative Movement (AIM), is always in need of funding and support. You can email it at e aimsl2001@yahoo.co.uk or find them on Facebook at **f** AIM Sierra Leone.

the capital's Shell stop costs Le20,000 one-way. The main drop-off point in Lunsar is a petrol station at a crossroads; the second is known as Madigbo junction, a smaller crossroads near the multistorey building of the Amazonian Initiative Movement (AIM), a group that campaigns against female circumcision (see box, page 293).

South of the highway in the centre of town, the main **poda poda** stand is just outside the wood-strutted village market. A seat costs a minimum of Le18,000 to Freetown, and it's also easy to flag down trasport from the side of the highway. There is a motorcycle taxi stand at the main roundabout.

Where to stay, eat and drink On the Lunsar–Makeni Highway, **De Freezer Restaurant and Sports Bar** (m *078 812 394;* ⊕ *09.00–01.00 daily*) is the most promising spot, serving chicken and chips, grilled fish and imported beer. Also on the highway is a branch of **Yeane's** (m *076 705 116*), a local chain with other locations in Makeni and Bo. A little further down the road towards Makeni, there's also **Alan's Phase II Bar & Restaurant** (⊕ *07.30–midnight Mon–Fri, until dawn Sat, from 10.30 Sun*), with its two pretty thatched huts. In town, by the main roundabout and opposite the marketplace, is **David's Villa Entertainment Centre** (m *076 238 690*), a small, self-professed nightclub offering chicken and meat and televised football matches for a lively crowd. The **town hall**, a large yellow building set behind the market, also has a music night every Saturday. Several **cookeries** serve plates of rice and plassas or fish soup.

There's no real reason to spend the night in Lunsar, but should you want to, the **Bai-Suba Resort** (m *099 603 195;* **$$$–$$**) and **Jaward Hotel** (m *088 621 744, 076 111 122;* **$$$–$$**) both have decent air-conditioned rooms.

The grandly named **Hollywood Video Complex Centre** (*27 Delco Rd;* m *077 838 347*) shows football matches and the usual glut of Nigerian, American and Hong Kong kickathons, for Le700 a go. The wood-poled **Hi-Tech World Soccer Complex** (*1 Color St;* m *077 491 257*), also flickers away day and night.

Other practicalities There's now one ATM in town, at **GT Bank** on the main Makeni road. Otherwise, **Western Union** money transfer payments are available at the Marampa-Masimera Community Bank (m *078 235 926, 076 920 764;* e *mmcblunsar@yahoo.com*) by the roundabout.

North of Lunsar, at **Foredugu**, a weekly Tuesday market, known by its Temne name of *luma*, sells clay pots amid the usual plastic goods and clothes.

MAKENI

Capital of the north, Makeni was an RUF stronghold during the war when rebels entered in 1998 and stayed, sparing it from the widespread destruction felt by other towns that became targets rather than homes. It's now home to a glut of new hotel projects, several supermarkets and a shiny new clock tower in the middle of town.

The reopening of the iron ore mine at Tonkolili, about an hour's drive east of the city, has brought global capitalism to the dusty streets of the town (see box, page 47). The Bumbuna Dam now delivers a reasonable trickle of electricity to Makeni's homes and businesses, and a spate of road building has smoothed the once-bumpy journey across the city. Makeni also now counts the likes of English football hero David Beckham among those who have visited and stayed overnight. The town – long a stronghold of the All People's Congress (APC) Party, and the nearest big town to President Koroma in his youth – undeniably has a new sheen, and is tied with Koidu as the fourth-largest city nationwide.

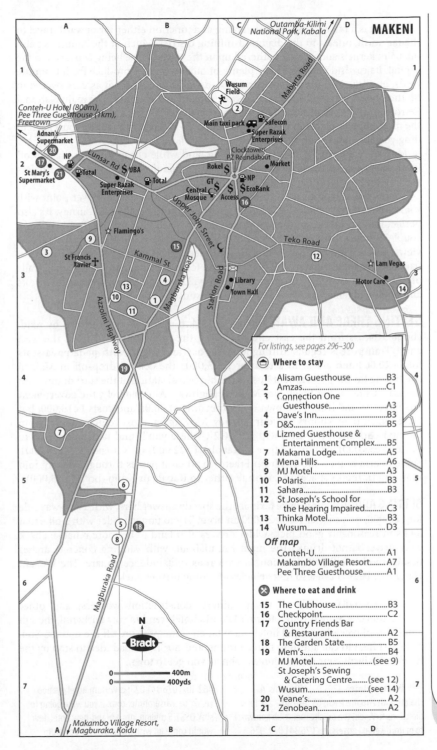

MAKENI

Outamba-Kilimi
National Park, Kabala

Wusum
Field

Main taxi park   Safecon
Super Razak
Enterprises

Clocktower;
PZ Roundabout

Conteh-U Hotel (800m),
Pee Three Guesthouse (1km),
Freetown

Adnan's
Supermarket

NP

St Mary's
Supermarket   Total

Lunsar Rd   UBA   Total

Super Razak
Enterprises

Rokel   Market
NP
GT   EcoBank
Central   Access
Mosque

Flamingo's

St Francis
Xavier

Kammal St

Teko Road

Lam Vegas
Motor Care

Library
Town Hall

Azzolini Highway

Magburaka Road

Station Road

Upper John Street

Maharta Road

N

Bradt

0   400m
0   400yds

Makambo Village Resort,
Magburaka, Koidu

For listings, see pages 296–300

Where to stay

1   Alisam Guesthouse..................B3
2   Amzas.....................................C1
3   Connection One
        Guesthouse..........................A3
4   Dave's Inn..............................B3
5   D&S.......................................B5
6   Lizmed Guesthouse &
        Entertainment Complex......B5
7   Makama Lodge.......................A5
8   Mena Hills..............................A6
9   MJ Motel................................A3
10   Polaris...................................B3
11   Sahara...................................B3
12   St Joseph's School for
        the Hearing Impaired..........C3
13   Thinka Motel.........................B3
14   Wusum..................................D3

Off map
        Conteh-U..............................A1
        Makambo Village Resort........A7
        Pee Three Guesthouse...........A1

Where to eat and drink

15   The Clubhouse.......................B3
16   Checkpoint.............................C2
17   Country Friends Bar
        & Restaurant.......................A2
18   The Garden State...................B5
19   Mem's....................................B4
        MJ Motel...........................(see 9)
        St Joseph's Sewing
        & Catering Centre..........(see 12)
        Wusum.............................(see 14)
20   Yeane's..................................A2
21   Zenobean...............................A2

Makeni is a busy transport stop, acting as a junction either for onward travel to the far north, or east to the diamond-mining district. Much of the country's palm oil, palm kernels and rice are gathered up in the town before being conveyed to the capital. Its roadside markets have plenty of quality market produce fresh from the fields, at a fraction of Freetown prices, and traffic queues form as cars swerve to fill their boots with sacks of cassava, sweet potato and plantain. The main National Petroleum (NP) petrol station on the main highway (of five in the town) – among the most popular places to refuel in the country – is busy with market touts keen to drag you away for a look at the best their stands have to offer.

Makeni is known for its gara tie-dyeing, and while cheap imports that rip off local designs have taken their toll on local handicrafts, the process nevertheless remains an important part of life for many women.

There's not a huge amount to do, but the town is a decent stopover point with some welcomingly comfortable lodging if you want to break up a journey. It's also perfect for easy hikes into the half-dozen decent-sized hills around the town. For a couple of hours' hard but satisfying hiking you will be rewarded with spectacular views. Go for a jog in the early morning and see market women carrying baskets of fruit and veg into town (and all thanking you for exercising). Any of the small trails off the sandy roads that run from the town will lead you through beautiful forests and fields with amazing views at sunrise and sunset.

GETTING THERE AND AWAY Makeni is 135km northeast of Freetown by road, about 3 hours from the east end (or using the mountain road from the west end). Transport is regular throughout the day and night, with **poda poda** seats for Le20,000 and a seat in a **taxi** for Le25,000. The central drop-off in Makeni (including for the government bus) is the big petrol station at the start of town, on the north side of the Freetown–Makeni Highway. Alternatively, the **government bus** heads to and from Freetown every morning at 06.00 and costs Le15,000, but leave longer than 3 hours for your journey. Moving on, most vehicles depart from the taxi park near Wusum Field [295 C2], where you'll find taxis going east to Kono (Le35,000), or north either to Kabala (Le22,000) or Kamakwie (Le20,000). You can also hop on the bus from Freetown when it passes through Makeni mid morning (if there's space) to continue either to Kabala or Kono (both Le15,000).

GETTING AROUND Motorbike taxis are the speedy answer here, with a one-way ride for Le2,000, or a charter for Le20,000 an hour. Try to target a rider with a bike that looks in reasonably good nick. Older drivers also tend to be more reliable; check your driver is not drunk. The main roundabout, with vaulting concrete arches beside another NP petrol station, is known as Indpendence Square. The Wusum Hotel (see below) can also rent vehicles for going further afield.

 WHERE TO STAY With so many miners, construction workers, and other contractors churning through town, Makeni's hotels tend to stay fairly full, though a number of recently opened hotels have taken some pressure off the market. Still, it doesn't hurt to call ahead to book a room, and nor is it a bad idea to stop by the hotel to confirm your reservation as soon as you get to town.

 Wusum Hotel [295 D3] (50 rooms, 4 chalets with 2 rooms each) 65 Teko Rd – ask for directions to 'Apex', the on-site nightclub known to motorbike taxi drivers; m 076 341 079, 076 462 407, 076 341 028; e wusum.hotel@yahoo. co.uk; w wusumhotel.com. If you were going to sink US$1.5 million into a brand-new hotel, few would come up with Makeni as the optimum

LIFE ON THE STREET

Poverty is a fact of life for many in Sierra Leone, a truth that is perhaps felt most acutely by the country's youth. According to the first survey of its kind in Sierra Leone, nearly 50,000 children across the country have to support themselves by working on the street – selling themselves for sex, hawking groundnuts or oranges, or simply begging passers-by for the odd coin or hand-out of food.

That survey, which was conducted in in late 2011, was sponsored by an NGO called Street Child Sierra Leone, which has been helping the country's youth move off the streets and back into family homes since it was founded by British headhunter Tom Dannatt in 2008. Working in partnership with Help a Needy Child in Sierra Leone (HANCi), a local NGO, the UK-based Street Child has opened two centres in Makeni, where staff offer needy children food, clothing and counselling. Once the children reach the centre, the organisation works to put them back in touch with their parents or other relatives; they've found safe, stable homes with extended family for thousands of children already. Since the Ebola crisis in 2014, Street Child has assisted more than 12,000 orphans and other children affected by the epidemic. They were also at the forefront of the humanitarian emergency response to the August 2017 mudslide, distributing over 25,000 packages of food and 2,500 sets of clothing in the immediate aftermath.

The organisation focuses its work in Makeni, where the number of sex workers has sadly risen in line with the influx of miners and other foreign workers into town. But Street Child has also started working in Lunsar, and it's reaching out to rural communities, building schools in remote areas under its Every Child in School initiative. If you're curious to learn more about Street Child, stop by The Clubhouse, its restaurant and bar in Makeni (page 299). All of the restaurant's proceeds directly support the NGO's work. Street Child also accepts international volunteers (page 71), and organises the Sierra Leone Marathon (m *sierraleonemarathon.com*), held in Makeni every May since 2012. For more information, visit m street-child.co.uk.

site. Until his sudden passing in 2016, such was ex-National Petroleum (NP) chairman Vincent Kanu's commitment to his hometown; he built 3 swimming pools, a gym & a conference hall; imported 27 containers' worth of fixings from Italy, France & other European design centres; designed rooms with sliding glass doors on to balconies; & sculpted a picturesque glade packed with fairy lights & deer. Kanu bet that an international-standard hotel in Makeni made sense – relieving the pressure to stay tied to cramped, overcrowded Freetown, it's much better placed for eco-trips into the upcountry wilderness. Tourism aside, the all-mod-cons approach caters for the numerous, high-paying miners & development officials who are passing through & keen for decent accommodation. The prices are steep & service is hit-and-miss, making this place worse value for money than many of the nicer hotels in Freetown – but if you're missing the comforts of home, the Wusum is a good bet. Impressive carvings in the restaurant (**$$$$**) are all made by local artists, while the nightclub is the best in town. It also has 4 2-room 'chalets', good for long-stay residents, & a new block was under construction in 2017. Non-guests pay Le35,000 to swim. Same-sex couples pay extra. Wi-Fi. **$$$$$–$$$$**

🏠 **Conteh-U Hotel** [295 A1] (75 rooms) Off Kay St; m 078 012 322, 076 605 665; e hotelcontehu@yahoo.com. In a large, mint-green compound just off the main road from Lunsar, rooms here are set in triplex chalets & all come with TV, AC, fridge & mozzie nets. There's Wi-Fi in the central building & meals on request. **$$$**

⌂ D&S Hotel [295 B5] (8 rooms) Azzolini Hwy; m 078 344 088, 088 575 100. Upstart neighbour to the Mena Hills Hotel, this new place next door offers slightly more expensive, no-nonsense tiled rooms with AC, hot water, fridge, TV & Wi-Fi (& a few come with balconies). There's a comfortable open-sided restaurant area on the 1st floor. **$$$**

⌂ Makama Lodge [295 A5] (32 rooms) 3 Konteh Dr, off Agienold St; m 099 318 280, 076 409 700. There's little to differentiate this newish place on the south end of town from any of the other hotels in this range, but the new block of rooms that was under construction when we visited in 2017 should be among the sharper options in Makeni once complete. **$$$**

⌂ Makambo Village Resort [295 A7] (28 rooms) Azzolini Highway (at the 186km mark); m 088 317 170, 088 891 611, 076 433 560. Another couple of kilometres past the Mena Hills Hotel, Makambo offers 28 clean, spacious & well-tended rooms, each with a hot-water shower, satellite TV, fridge & AC. It's a bit soulless, but you can't beat the comfort level – & it's a much better deal than the Wusum. A restaurant serves European & African dishes (**$$$**). B&B. **$$$**

⌂ Mena Hills Hotel [295 A6] (13 rooms) 155 Azzolini Highway (at the 184km mark); m 077 219 461, 077 357 307, 079 765 650; e hotelmenahills@ gmail.com. Located a couple of kilometres down the road that heads towards Magburaka, this place feels a bit like your great-aunt's house: cosy & comfy, if a bit heavy on the chintz. All rooms have AC, fridge, TV & hot-water showers. There's a full-service restaurant. B/fast inc. **$$$**

⌂ MJ Motel [295 A3] (20 rooms) 14 Azzolini Highway (at the Makeni/Mena junction – hence MJ – on the Freetown Highway headed east to Kono); m 076 947 944, 088 852 485; e mjmotelmakeni@ mjmotelsl.com; w mjmotelsl.com. Conceived as a transit stop in 1996, the brainchild of retired PE teacher E B Kamara is hands-down the best of the mid-range options, with restaurant (**$$$–$$**), en-suite bathrooms, hot water, satellite TV, mosquito nets, standing fans, AC, Wi-Fi & nice enough service. Vandalised & heavily looted during the war, it was a slow journey back to full fitness, with a late-2005 reopening. A low-key outdoor bar is a fine spot for a pricey meal or a beer. You can now even request the 'Beckham suite', the MJ being the place where the footballer stopped over on his whirlwind 2008 tour. B&B. **$$$–$$**

⌂ Amzas Hotel [295 C1] (45 rooms) 7 Field Rd; m 076 464 981, 076 707 260, 077 154 441. This stadium-side high-rise serves up decent, if slightly grungy, rooms within its soulless concrete confines, a variety of (slightly overpriced) categories with the option of AC or standing fans. The best thing about Amzas is the location – near the centre of town & the market, with good transport options at night. No mosquito nets, but the showers have decent water pressure & staff are happy to bring a bucket of hot water for washing. If you're feeling up to the noise levels, ask for a room overlooking the town football stadium for the perfect match view, or box seats when touring musicians shimmy their dance shows long into the night. B&B. **$$**

⌂ Connection One Guesthouse [295 A3] (9 rooms) 29 Albert St; m 078 482 108, 088 727 760. A clean & pleasant little guesthouse located down a quiet street about 500m off the main highway, this is a good budget option. Rooms are basic, but most have AC & private toilets. B&B. **$$**

⌂ Dave's Inn [295 B3] (11 rooms) 2 Electricity Rd; m 076 460 865, 077 472 118; ◻ davesinnhotelmakeni. Though it was full when we visited, long-time Makeni residents recommend this as a reliable budget pick; rooms come with nets, fridge & AC. B/fast inc. **$$**

⌂ Sahara Hotel [295 B3] (62 rooms) m 076 577 649. Under the same management as the Sahara in Bo, this grey multistorey affair isn't the prettiest set-up in town, but the AC rooms are decent & there's a resto-bar on the ground floor where you can catch the football. Some rooms have balconies, but they've crammed the 2 buildings so close together that the only view from these is of your neighbour's wall. **$$**

✳ ⌂ St Joseph's School for the Hearing Impaired [295 C3] (10 rooms) m 076 507 368, 076 705 433; e stjosephshis@gmail.com. In a converted classroom building on the grounds of this church-run school, this is a relaxed & welcoming option, with spic-&-span 1st-floor rooms with ceiling fans, mozzie nets & either en-suite or shared ablutions. A few rooms also have AC. There's a kitchen for guests, honesty bar stocked with beer & soft drinks, & a small library with plenty of novels. There's also plenty of opportunity to get in on a game of footie with the kids, or just see what they're up to at the Sewing & Catering Centre (page 300) out front. **$$**

🏠 **Alisam Guesthouse** [295 B3] (6 rooms) 68 Magburaka Rd; m 076 617 960, 078 831 987, 077 720 790; e calimamydixon@yahoo.com. With a familial vibe, central location & clean self-contained rooms with nets & AC or fan, this is a solid budget option. B&B, plus meals on request. **$$–$**

🏠 **Pee Three Guesthouse** [295 A1] (6 rooms) Off Kay St; m 079 721 529, 088 358 920. In a cute green compound on a quiet backstreet near the Conteh-U, the en-suite rooms here come with either fan or AC (all have nets) & are small & simple, but well kept & good value for the price. Meals require advance notice, but cold drinks are readily available & there's a summer hut to enjoy them under. **$$–$**

🏠 **Polaris** [295 B3] (7 rooms) 23 Loyah St, opposite the Thinka Motel; m 088 058 249, 088 272 911, 076 843 734. Sweet owners who treat guests warmly, & can provide plenty of home-cooked food & tips on things to do in town. All the basic but well-cared-for rooms are self-contained & come with bed nets & either fan (Le80,000)

or AC (Le180,000). Recommended by a former volunteer who lived there for months & felt like she had been adopted by a Sierra Leonean family. B&B. **$$–$**

🏠 **Lizmed Guesthouse & Entertainment Complex** [295 B5] (20 rooms) 112 Azzolini Highway; m 076 894 565. Cheap as chips & just as cheery, husband-&-wife team Elizabeth & Mohamed (hence the Lizmed) breathe cleanliness into the most basic, stuffy rooms going. Bright tie-dyed gara cloth adorns the beds, while the attached bar & video club runs regular Nigerian TV nights. Running showers, fans, mosquito nets. Big renovations were afoot in 2017: expect sharper new rooms, potentially with AC. B&B. **$**

🏠 **Thinka Motel** [295 B3] (12 rooms) 24 Loyah St; m 076 805 542, 077 475 337. If only this basic guesthouse matched its high-profile marketing, which manages almost as many roadside adverts as the place has rooms. The pot of gold at the end of this rainbow, however, is little ore than a dilapidated dive, & you'd be infinitely better off across the street at Polaris. **$**

✕ **WHERE TO EAT AND DRINK** Makeni's dining scene has come a long way in the past few years, thanks in large part to the influx of foreign capital – and foreign workers. Today you can find decent pizzas, hamburgers, and other Western fare, in addition to wine and imported beer. A number of **food stalls** (**$**) nestle on Station Road, including **Checkpoint** (**$**), which has the best jollof rice going, hamburgers and the odd cold beer, from lunchtime until late. Street food is also in fine supply around the market area, and, by night, in the street that links the Rogbaneh Road roundabout to Amzas Hotel at the NP junction, with meat sticks and liver sandwiches. There's bush fowl on the street known as 'Ladies' Mile' at night, outside Flamingo's Nightclub. Finally, don't be surprised to be offered a local delicacy on the street – whole roasted monkey.

Apart from the market (page 302), the best place for fruit and veg is along the side of the main Freetown road, just across the street from St Mary's Supermarket. In the dry season you can find mangoes, pineapple, grapefruits, sweet potatoes and bananas.

✕ **Wusum Hotel** [295 D3] 65 Teko Rd; m 076 341 079. The restaurant inside Makeni's most expensive hotel is popular with miners, ministers & paramount chiefs, although it can turn into a bit of a hooker-fest in the evenings. Staff serve wine & imported beer alongside Western-friendly dishes like barbecue chicken, grilled cheese, & even steak. The service tends to be less than friendly, even by Salone standards. **$$$$**

✕ **The Clubhouse** [295 B3] 40 Magburaka Rd; m 076 339 611, 078 207 770; ⊕ 10.00–late daily. With its big-screen TV & pleasant, umbrella-

shaded outdoor seating, this is a favourite with the local expat crowd. Come for a little taste of home, or at least something different from standard Makeni fare. You can order chicken *cordon bleu*, a bacon cheeseburger, veggie pizza, or simply a heaped plate of nachos – & they'll even deliver. It's a bit pricey for Makeni, but all proceeds go to support Street Child (see box, page 297), a local NGO, so you can feel good about indulging. The managers put on regular quiz nights & other evening events, to the delight of the Makeni expat crowd. **$$$–$$**

✗ MJ Motel [295 A3] 14 Azzolini Highway (at the Makeni/Mena junction on the Freetown Highway headed east to Kono); m 076 947 944, 088 852 485. This popular hotel does good African dishes & a smattering of European ones, but order well in advance. Try the meat stew with jollof rice, chicken burger, or tasty fried chicken & chips. **$$$–$$**

✗ Yeane's Restaurant [295 A2] Opposite St Claire Bldg, Azzolini Highway; m 078 594 932; ⊕ 07.00–late daily. This popular 1st-floor spot located opposite St Mary's Supermarket tends to stay full on weekend evenings & for big football matches. Try the tasty chicken & chips, shawarmas or fried rice. **$$$–$$**

✗ Country Friends Bar & Restaurant [295 A2] St Claire Bldg, Azzolini Highway; m 077 719 746, 076 243 915; ⊕ 08.00–23.00 daily. Between the 2 main supermarkets, this is a good place for a spot of groundnut, jollof or the usual leafy plassas over rice. There's a covered terrace out front, football on the TV, & even supposedly live music on occasion. **$$**

✗ St Joseph's Sewing & Catering Centre [295 C3] m 076 507 368, 076 705 433. Right out front of the school for the hearing impaired, this student-run workshop serves unpretentious local meals during the week & sells African-style clothing as well, including hand-dyed gara cloth (page 298). **$$**

♀ The Garden State [295 B5] Azzolini Highway; m 076 666 962; ⊕ until late daily; Le5,000 entry. Painted up in impossible-to-miss American colours (there's even a Statue of Liberty), the name of this large & popular outdoor nightclub is a reference to New Jersey, where the amiable owner spent many years before returning to Sierra Leone. It's busy from more or less Wed (ladies' night) through the weekend, with reggae every Thu. **$$**

♀ Mem's [295 B4] Azzolini Highway, on the right as you head out of town towards Magburaka; ⊕ in the evenings daily. By day, this place is the drinks distributor for the northern district; by night, it's the cheapest bar in Makeni, entertaining lively crowds on its wide terrace. Nice atmosphere with not-too-loud music. African dishes are sometimes on offer. **$**

♀ Zenobean [295 A2] 6 Azzolini Highway; m 078 542 442, 030 287 070; ⊕ 07.00–midnight daily. The kitchen didn't seem to be operating very regularly here in 2017, but it's still a fine bolthole for a cheap bottle of Star on the main drag. **$**

ENTERTAINMENT AND NIGHTLIFE The town's premier nightspot is **Apex disco** [295 D3] (*65 Teko Rd; entry Le10,000*), within the Wusum Hotel complex, which started off as a bar but such is the toe-tapping desire of locals it's now evolved into a club. The busiest nights are Wednesday (ladies' night), Friday (Africana night) and Saturday for happy hour. Just down the street from Apex, the neon-lit, eccentrically painted **Lam Vegas** [295 D3] (*m 077 316 728*) pumps out tunes for a sizeable, dance-ready crowd. **Flamingo's** [295 A3] (*Ladies' Mile; m 076 751 325, 076 705 479; entry Le5,000 Wed, Fri & Sat, other nights free*), opposite Buya's Motel, is a pumping venue that some prefer to call 'Flaming Ho's' – since it's heavy on the kolonkos. Friday is African night, and Wednesday is ladies' night. It also shows football and films for Le1,000. A large Star beer costs Le7,000. A better bet is **Dauzy** [295 A2] (*Azzolini Hwy*), or **Mbalu's** [295 A2] (*Azzolini Hwy, between MJ Motel & the Fatima Institute College*).

The best place to get chatting to locals is in one of Makeni's numerous poyo bars – Le1,000 will buy you a glass. Ask for it 'sweet' – local slang for freshly made.

Wusum Field is the site of the **stadium** [295 C1], named after the large hill that lies behind it. Football by day, and music extravaganzas by night, keep the patch of dust that stands in for a pitch and its rickety surrounding stands well attended, making it worth a look if something's going on. Tickets for events usually go for Le4,000. Makeni is also home to an amputee football team and a regular club team, the Wusum All-Stars, and they play most weekends during the season.

OTHER PRACTICALITIES Befitting its growing status as the economic hub of the north, Makeni is now home to a handful of ATM-equipped banks. **Rokel Commercial**

Bank, **GT Bank**, **Access Bank** and **EcoBank** are all clustered around the main clock tower [295 C2], while **UBA** is 800m away on Lunsar Road [295 B2]; all accept Visa cards. Otherwise, **Western Union** money transfer is available at **Rayoh Enterprises** [295 D3] (*1A Rogbaneh Rd;* m *077 713 523, 076 150 054;* ⏰ *08.30–16.00 Mon–Fri)* and **Sabsco Enterprises** [295 D3] (*26 Rogbaneh Rd;* m *076 697 716;* ⏰ *08.00–18.00 daily*). To change money or load up on groceries and other sundries, head to either **St Mary's Supermarket** [295 A2] (*St Claire Bldg, 2 Azzolini Highway;* m *076 693 939;* ⏰ *09.00–21.00 Mon–Sat, 10.00–21.00 Sun*) or its neighbour **Adnan's Supermarket** [295 A2] (*Azzolini Highway;* m *088 421 820;* ⏰ *09.00–21.00 daily*), both of which are small but well stocked, with everything from Snickers to Syrah. The filling station in the centre of town, known as **PZ**, also has some snacks, including tasty scotch eggs for Le4,000 a throw. The local radio station, serving both Makeni and the rest of the northern Bombali district, is **Radio Mankneh**, on 95.1FM.

For **internet**, a good bet is **Apex** [295 D3] (m *076 341 079;* ⏰ *08.00–17.00, Mon–Sat*) at the Wusum Hotel; closer to the centre, **Super Razak Enterprises** (m *076 625 952*) has two locations, one on Lunsar Road [295 A2] and the other on Rogbaneh Road [295 C2].

In the event of any car trouble, the local branch of **Motor Care** [295 D3] (*Teko Rd, on the left-hand side as you head towards the Wusum Hotel;* m *076 638 434;* w *sl.motorcare.com*) can help set things right.

WHAT TO SEE AND DO Wusum (pronounced 'usum') **Hill**, to the west of town, is worth an early-morning or evening climb, giving a good vantage point of the surrounding countryside. Start at the waterworks on the outskirts of town and head straight up – it gets steep at times so you may have to resort to scrambling on all fours. You don't need a guide but many young children will love to escort you for a few leones. Leave about 40 minutes for a round trip, and take plenty of water. If you are feeling ambitious, you can push on down the other side of the hill for a wander through the villages. People are extremely friendly, and will guide you back to Makeni.

Makeni Town Hall [295 C3], on Station Road, was the former headquarters of the Revolutionary United Front (RUF). Once painted an unmissable pink, it's a decidedly more formal white these days, but still bears the scars of its military past. Compound Street is also home to a monument dedicated to former president Valentine Strasser. All that is left now is a forlorn pair of shoes and an inscription.

The statuesque **mosque** [295 B3], in peeling green paint with tiered minarets, is well worth a look if you're on Station Road. On the same road, between the mosque and the NP petrol station roundabout, the dilapidated colonial-style **post office** [295 C3] is also eye catching with its three arches and worn-down paint.

If you have an afternoon to while away on traditional arts and crafts, Elizabeth (m *076 894 565*), of the Lizmed Guesthouse, can run lessons on how to make **gara cloth**. You will first need to scour the market for raw materials (expect to spend about Le150,000 for a large square of cloth) and ink (Le10,000), and it's polite to give Elizabeth something for her time too. While you may go home with a single giant piece of garishly tie-dyed cloth, it's the time spent chewing the fat and talking about Makeni life while you work that makes the activity worthwhile. The St Joseph's School for the Hearing Impaired's Sewing & Catering Centre (m *076 507 368, 076 705 433*) is another good address for gara cloth dyeing, and informal lessons are easily arranged. Finally, if you are in Makeni for some time and craving a little distraction, the **library** [295 C3] (*Sierra Leone Library Board, Makeni Town Council, Station Rd;* m *077 483 303 (librarian)*) has a selection of African books and local newspapers, along with a sporadic Wi-Fi connection.

Whatever you do, don't miss a foray into the **market** [295 C2] – two large well-stocked concrete blocks populated by an array of vendors offering everything from mangoes from the nearest tree to imported cosmetics. Padlocks, mattresses and beanie caps proliferate outdoors, while food and jerry cans of liquor named 'Superman Rum' and 'Bumba Gin' bring the warehouses to rowdy life. It's at the main clock tower (also known as 'PZ') roundabout downtown and busier during the week than at weekends.

AROUND MAKENI

The road southeast from Makeni heads for the diamond fields of Kono, an easy 2½ hours away (slightly longer on public transport) on a newly surfaced road (page 185). The main town *en route* is **Magburaka**, 25km away, but the real highlight for the backpacking type is the stop at **Matotaka**, about 35km from Makeni, where all public transport loads up on food. Bubbling cauldrons of fish and meat soup, shiny fresh vegetables, coconuts cut open in front of you, and, regularly, bushmeat to make your toes curl – small monkey hands, young antelope hinds – are all on offer, snapped up as treats by city folk.

Matotaka is also one of the few gateways to Bo from the north that cuts out a return to Freetown. Poda podas head south, irregularly, on a bad 95km strip of road for Le25,000–30,000. Before **Masingbi**, 84km east out of Makeni, the small village of **Barrayine** (not signposted) sells lovely and otherwise hard-to-find crafts on the roadside. These include straw-woven palm-wood footstools and beds in the same style.

MAGBURAKA A 25km hop to the southeast of Makeni on good tarmac, this town is home to President Koroma's old school, Magburaka Government Secondary School for Boys. Once a prefect there, Koroma said in a Good Friday speech in 2008 that it was at this school that 'the foundation of what I am today was solidly laid … by a dint of hard work, dedication, and the help of the Almighty'.

Today you might be forgiven for not quite understanding how. Magburaka is a small-town centre for trade in rice, palm products, kola nuts and tomatoes, with a Chinese-owned sugarcane plantation. After several sorry years of abandonment and vandalism, the hotel scene is finally showing some signs of life and the once-grand **Riverside Guesthouse** (*24 Makeni Rd;* m *077 531 811;* w *riversidemagburaka. com;* **$$**) was rehabilitated and reopened in June 2013; the **Havana Guesthouse** (m *078 100 077;* e *barrie20115@yahoo.com;* **$**) is another option in town.

If you pass through, consider a trip to the **poyo factory**, one of the few in the country: perhaps that's among the reasons the country's top politicians are so fond of the place.

ROGBONKO VILLAGE RETREAT If you're eager to get a taste of life in an African village, but not so keen on giving up all of the comforts of home, then Rogbonko Village Retreat (m *076 877 018;* e *info@rogbonkovillage.com;* w *rogbonkovillage. com*) might just be your thing. Visitors stay in basic but comfortable mud huts that come equipped with mattress-covered beds and flushing loos. During the day, you have the chance to wander through the village and enjoy a glimpse of rural life.

The brain behind the venture is Sheka Forna, a British–Sierra Leonean businessman whose father was born in Rogbonko (and whose sister, Aminatta, is perhaps Sierra Leone's most famous author). The whole idea of 'village tourism' might sound strange, or a bit Disney-Worldish, but the retreat is small enough – and set up with enough care and input from the local village – that it works.

Getting there and away Rogbonko is pretty out of the way, so if you're lucky enough to have access to a **4x4**, that's definitely your best bet. Expect the trip to take about 60 minutes from Makeni or 4 hours from Freetown. Alternatively, you could take **public transport** to Magburaka, then try to find an ocada driver willing to take you the rest of the way. nce you make your booking, you'll be given detailed instructions of how to find the village.

Where to stay and eat The retreat consists of a handful of thatched mud huts that are set back slightly from the village itself. Each sleeping hut has two double bedrooms, a shared toilet, and a pleasant shaded porch. Sheets and mosquito nets are provided, although you might like to bring along your own towel; there's an enclosed spot for bucket showers out back. There is no electricity.

Dine on homemade traditional dishes, finished off with fresh fruit, for your evening meal. Or if you prefer to do your own cooking, you're welcome to bring along supplies and make use of the simple outdoor kitchen that's set up just next to the huts. The cost of a night's stay is US$20 per person, with additional charges for meals and tours around the village.

What to see and do Kick back, relax, and get a taste of village life. You'll be rewarded if you take it easy and allow yourself enough time to adapt to the village's gentle pace. That means taking some time to get to know the locals: stop in to pay your respects to Rogbonko's elders, chat with the women who are pounding cassava or threshing rice outside their homes, or teach some songs to the crowds of children who will likely be following you around. If you're feeling restless, go for a ride in a dugout canoe to explore the quiet little jungle streams nearby, or take off down one of the narrow wooded paths that lead out of the village, keeping your eyes peeled for birds and other wildlife along the way.

MAMUNTA-MAYOSSO WILDLIFE SANCTUARY This wetland is so sleepy that even the birdwatchers have mostly flown elsewhere. Still, for adventure in a swamp, it's not bad. Once upon a time, it had a good old number of elephants: local legend has it that Pa Bambara, a Temne from the Kamara clan who married into the local Kurankos and then lived at Mamunta, hunted elephants. According to tradition, he gave a tusk from his kills to his wife's father, Masa Kama.

The area is known for its colourful past. Even its former name, Kolifa, is derived from a word meaning 'monkey-killer' after the amount of bushmeat on offer, and the number of cunning hunters in the area.

Whatever their skills, they didn't quite catch everything; this 20km^2 nature reserve (first protected in 1972) – a series of inland lakes in the midst of savannah grassland – is today home to plenty of birds and small mammals, as well as the rare short-nosed crocodile. It is located 30km south of Makeni, on tough roads; you'll need a 4x4 or a sturdy motorbike taxi to get there. Take a tent, food, binoculars, and enjoy wildlife and solitude. **Fact Finding Tours** (*Lumley Beach Rd, Freetown;* m *076 520 122 (Kenneth Gbengba);* e *factsfinding@ yahoo.com*) can organise a visit (see David Karr and Kenneth Gbenga's 2014 birding trip report here: w cloudbirders.com/tripreport/repository/KARR_ SierraLeone_11_2014.pdf), or alternatively ask at the Conservation Society of Sierra Leone (CSSL).

North of Makeni are three likely destinations – the country's first national park, Outamba-Kilimi, to the far north via Kamakwie; the nearby waterfalls and hydro-electric dam at Bumbuna; and the much-loved, breeze-swept town of Kabala to the northeast. The latter two are both jumping-off points for a climb into the Loma Mountains and the mist-shrouded peak of Mount Bintumani.

OUTAMBA-KILIMI NATIONAL PARK If you've ever dreamt about waking up to the patter of monkey pee on your tent (flysheets do have their uses), then the country's oldest national park is for you.

In Outamba, a sighting or two of hippos, chimps and endangered monkeys is pretty much guaranteed, while the luckier may spot elephants and crocodiles, and researchers and some locals even talk of elusive leopards.

Skirting the Guinean border, it is in fact two parks for the price of one – Kilimi, with 243km² of savannah grasslands to the west, and Outamba (named after Mount Ukutamba, on the northern border of the park), more heavily wooded with 741km² to the east. There are *bolilands* too – large seasonally flooded areas – beside the Great Scarcies and Little Scarcies rivers (known locally as the Kolenten and Kaba). For the moment, unless visitors are particularly curious, exploration is generally limited to the Outamba side, where there is a basic campsite and guides. Kilimi, however, has two large lakes, and buffalo, waterbuck and bushbuck roam the savannah flatlands.

History The name might be abridged to OK, but this beautiful park is far from it. Attacked during the war, rebels invaded the park and destroyed all the facilities – blasting open a safe (you can see the bullet holes today) and breaking pretty much everything else, reducing the buildings to crumbled wrecks and burning vehicles when they weren't stealing them. They dismantled the washing block and even dug

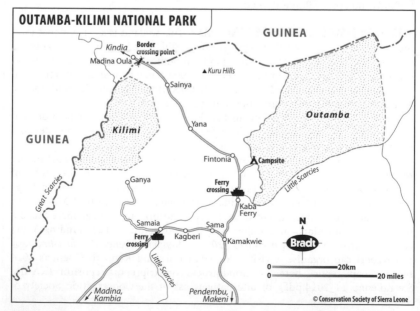

OUTAMBA-KILIMI NATIONAL PARK

© Conservation Society of Sierra Leone

up and severed water pipes deep below the ground so that the showers wouldn't work. As a result, the park desperately needs conservation, investment and tourism management, all of which will be warmly welcomed when it does come.

Environmental protection Outdated wildlife laws have made preservation tough. Even though OK was made a national park in 1995, the 1972 Wildlife Act – which the government has recently spent several years revising but has yet to change officially – has left gaping holes in conservation and management. Among them is its woefully lax rule against elephant hunting: kill one and you have to pay a hefty Le80 fine – all of £0.01 today. Chimps might be endangered, but the old law says it's fine for any man to hunt two apiece, along with two hippos, ten crocodiles and two elephants thrown in. All that will be overhauled at some stage, but until it is, unlicensed game hunting has a green light.

A series of wildlife censuses, vegetation maps and botanical, mammal and local farming techniques and land productivity surveys throughout the 1970s and 1980s helped establish how best to preserve the area, including a government resettlement scheme of 23 villages to help guard against hunting, tree felling and cultivation. However, lacking money and motivation, it has still not happened.

Despite a post-war ban on guns, poaching continues. Hunting is heaviest in Kilimi, of elephants, chimpanzees and monkeys. Many blame armed hunters who nip across the border from Guinea, but perhaps that's because no-one wants to admit that any guns exist in Sierra Leone. Local fishing methods, which employ small mesh-size nets and poisonous herbs, may pollute or degrade the aquatic systems and render the water unfit for consumption. Honey gathering takes place destructively, by cutting down and burning trees, with bushfires resulting both from this and subsistence farming. Emergency funding in the 1990s alleviated some of the logistical problems faced by the park's management and enhanced surveillance and law enforcement, but a general lack of post-war investment and suitable legal protection continue to impede progress.

When to go The best time to visit is during the dry season (November–April), especially to guarantee a sighting of hippos at their watering holes. Just before the rainy season starts, in March and April, when the savannah woodland is at its lowest, the small population of forest elephants known to cross between the park and Guinea are thirsty enough to make it to the river to drink and bathe. Bear in mind these are also the hottest months of the year (temperatures in March can reach 28°C, while in December they drop to 4°C). Nights tend to be chilly, particularly during the harmattan (November–February; page 4).

Getting there and away Nearly 300km north of Freetown, you can get to OK from the capital in one tiring 6-hour day, although trip time will vary according to vehicle and season. Better to break up the journey with an overnight stay in Makeni. From there, it's 86km to Kamakwie. Take the northern road for Kabala and fork left after a short distance at Panlap. From this turning you'll pass through Yoni, President Koroma's home village, after 3km (look out for his house on the right), and continue another bumpy 29km to Pendembu, with the Katabai Hills also to your right. Continue north 40km through Kamalu, and 13km further to the last town of Kamakwie, which sits 26km south of the park entrance. Roadworks on this route were underway in 2017, but seemed to have a long way to go. If you don't fancy pushing on from Kamakwie, **White House** (m *030 783 755, 030 169 363, 088 101 440, 076 872 020*; e *haririj@hotmail.com*; **$$**) has surprisingly trim rooms starting at Le120,000 at the entrance to town; the rudimentary **Vasco's Guesthouse** (**m** *077 307 840*; **$**) also has a room or two near the football pitch for Le50,000. If you're here during April, Usifu Jalloh's annual Maambena Fest Literacy and Cultural Festival (**m** *usifujalloh.com*) is held over Independence Day.

Beyond Kamakwie, it's 12km to the Kaba Ferry over the Little Scarcies (see box, below) and a further 6.5km to the entry turn-off; and then another 6km to the camp, through two small villages.

If you are on public transport, take a shared taxi or **poda poda** from Freetown to Makeni (Le20,000) and then on from Makeni to Kamakwie (Le25,000). From there the best option is probably to pick up a **motorcycle taxi** for the final leg. You'll have to negotiate a price, but Le50,000 one-way, including petrol, should be sufficient. If you want to cross the border, it's 52km north out of Kamakwie on red dirt roads all the way to the foot of the Kuru Hills and Sierra Leone immigration at Sainya, and a further 10km to Madina Oula on the Guinean side – it should cost Le80,000–120,000 on an ocada, which is your only transport option unless you've got your own 4x4.

For the Kilimi side of the park, take the left fork at Kamakwie, heading west past Sama and Kagberi to the Tompari Ferry at Samaia, from where it's about 20km north to the ranger station at Ganya. There's a road that can take you all the way from Kambia, 105 horrendous kilometres for roughly Le200,000 depending on the season (you pay a premium in the rains, when clearly you shouldn't be trying to take this route at all). There's no public transport here, though you may find a very) occasional 4x4 headed to Madina junction, the largest town between Kamakwie and Kambia.

 Where to stay The camp at OK is rudimentary but despite the paucity of facilities the lovely location in a shady clearing by the side of the river is exceptionally pretty at all times of day. The long-drop loos and showers are covered on three sides only by walls of palm fronds, you can forget any notion of grid electricity, and there's no tap water, which means a bucket shower (heated on request) or bathing in the river are your only options as far as hygiene goes. Eight huts with single or double beds are available for Le50,000 per person (Le15,000 for Sierra Leoneans), but their zinc roofs can get a little hot for comfort. You could also take a camp bed and rig up your

---

FERRY WITH A DIFFERENCE

Before reaching the park there's the small matter of the Kaba River (the Little Scarcies). The solution? The rather grandly named Kaba Ferry. Unlike more conventional ferries, there's no need to book; there's no official price; no official timetable; and certainly no slot machines. This ferry is more raft than vessel – some floating steel and wood with a cable pulley system to drag you and your vehicle across in a matter of minutes. Looking at it you wouldn't think it had a chance of comfortably holding a two-ton 4x4 without fuss. But so long as you turn up between 07.00 and 18.00, it's not blowing a storm, and there are a couple of attendants happy to pull you across, you should be in luck. In terms of tip, about Le10,000 is expected for a private car, although a taxi would offer much less; few foot passengers pay anything. The two old ferries (there is another, the Tompari Ferry, on the Kambia–Samaia route) occasionally go out of action, halting traffic for days, especially during the rainy season, and at that time of year the high, fast-flowing river makes the crossing much more dangerous.

own mosquito net outside (or just bring your own tent) for Le30,000. You can also pay a bit extra or bring your own generator diesel should you want (noisy) light. The trails below are priced individually, and a guide fee of Le10,000/5,000 per foreign/Sierra Leonean participant also applies to all activities. Since the arrival of Africell reception nearby in 2017, the easiest way to book is to contact the park directly, but do note that there's not reception everywhere – if your calls don't go through, just send an SMS and they'll get back to you. Contact **Mustafa Mansaray** (m *099 564 544*), **Hassan Issa Kamara** (m *088 622 682*) or **Kalie Kamara** (m *088 247 751*). Some people never manage to get in touch with the management and just turn up at the park; generally they are accommodated but it's a much nicer experience with warning. Keep in mind that there is a park entrance fee of Le30,000/10,00 per foreigner/Sierra Leonean, payable on departure alongside your food and activity fees.

✖ Where to eat and drink If you let them know when you call in your booking, camp staff will prepare two meals a day for Le65,000 per person (or Le25,000 if you bring your own ingredients), but Outamba-Kilimi is serious BYO territory for pretty much everything else. There's occasionally a drinks seller on site with bottled beer, water and soft drinks, but this can't be relied upon and thus it's imperative you bring your own water at the very least, and don't skimp on this – excursions will leave you tired and dehydrated. To cook for yourself, basic ingredients are available in Kamakwie, but stock up in Freetown or Makeni if your tastes demand more than rice and an African sauce.

What to see

Primates These include the western chimpanzee, red colobus monkey, black-and-white colobus, the sooty mangabey, Campbell's monkey, green monkey, the lesser white-nosed monkey, and the Guinea baboon.

Other mammals The top two spots are, without doubt, **leopard** and **elephant**. They are also rare. Look out for large mammals, including buffalo, bush pig, bushbuck and a range of duikers – bay, Maxwell's, black, red-flanked and yellow-backed. Clawless otter and side-striped jackal, as well as African civet, and brush-tailed porcupine are also present. Nile **crocodile** and **hippopotamus** are easily seen from the water. It is thought possible, although not confirmed, that the pygmy hippopotamus may occur.

Birds More than 256 species of birds have been recorded, and the park was officially designated an Important Bird Area (IBA) by Birdlife International in 2001. Notable species present in the park include the scarce, endemic **emerald starling** (*Coccycolius iris*) and thousands of watering birds found on the bolilands. Many can be spotted near the perennial Lake Idriss (ask for directions). The park is also home to three species of global conservation concern, one of which, the **pallid harrier** (*Circus macrourus*), is a rare migrant. Lake Idriss and the river courses seasonally support a good population of wintering plovers, sandpipers, herons and egrets: look out too for kingfishers, cormorants, hawks, eagles, geese, bustards, drones, pigeons, francolines, guineafowl, hornbills, touracos and weavers.

What to do Staff can organise a range of tours run by guides whose tracking skills and bushcraft are generally first-rate, although language is sometimes a problem. The one viewing platform, a tree house near a hippo pool, was out of service in 2017, but is well positioned to observe sedentary and migratory birdlife, should it eventually be repaired. Access to the viewpoint, however, can be difficult straight after the rains, when the undergrowth takes over and paths disappear. In fact, the lack of a network of well-marked paths is another of the park's problems, with rangers fighting a losing battle against the ferocious growth of the forest. With a fair bit of advance planning, however, it may be possible to camp out in the park as part of a multi-day walking tour to track down your animal of choice. This is seen as a good way to search out some of the monkey colonies.

Hippo canoe trip Paddling yourself down a wide, mirror-calm river, perfectly reflecting glorious green trees on all sides, to sidle up to groups of hippos snorting in the water is probably the most exciting element of any trip to Outamba. The hippos tend to have four hangouts – the wetter the season, the lower down the river and the further from camp their wallowing. The first spot is about a 15-minute paddle away, the second about 25 minutes.

Staring down Africa's most dangerous beast is both breathtaking and unnerving. As everybody is keen to remind you, they are mostly docile creatures when in the river. Only on land are they aggressive, and that's usually when a mother is concerned for her offspring.

Still, sitting in a long silver metal bathtub, knees barely above the water, staring at up to 20 one-ton hippos as their snorts, grunts and splashes echo with eerie volume in the stillness of the dusk air, one is hyper-aware of the precariousness of the situation. While sturdy, the boats can tip easily – in 2005 one capsized, and a guide was drowned. Thankfully, there are now life jackets on offer, though be ready to swim should you need to. The current is much safer in the dry season.

Nile crocodiles also stake out the banks in the early morning, so watch for them on the ride. It's best to avoid a river run in the middle of the day; towards the close of day the river is filled with biting black fly. The journey back is upstream, so double your paddling times. The trip costs Le25,000 each (Le10,000 for Sierra Leoneans), plus an additional guide fee of Le10,000/5,000 per foreign/Sierra Leonean participant.

Elephant walking safari Elephants are rarely spotted, but even if you don't come face to trunk with one, heading off into the bush makes for a great little exploration across the river from camp. Your guide will point out plenty of animals and birdlife; if you're doing particularly well you might catch sight of some pachyderm dung. Assuming it's been rebuilt and the tracks have been cleared, you can head to the tree-house viewing platform and beyond (go later into the dry season to maximise your chances). The excursion costs Le25,000 each (Le5,000 for Sierra Leoneans), again with a guide fee of Le10,000/5,000 per foreign/Sierra Leonean participant.

Fishing Camp staff can usually provide a fishing line for a river tour in a canoe, or for perching on the riverbank, but if you're intent on fishing it would be safer to bring your own. You can also collect fresh oysters from the riverbed – good for bait, or food, depending on how adventurous you're feeling.

BUMBUNA DAM One of the most beautiful spots in the country has been off-limits to tourists for years, falling instead into the lucky hands of Italian contractors working on a giant hydro-electric dam project, who have enjoyed a virtual monopoly on its magnificent views and profusion of bird and animal life.

The country's first hydro-electric dam – a piece of engineering almost sculptural in its beauty that you can now walk over the top of – was 30 years in the making. The series of intense environmental impact assessments, to ascertain the effect of flooding the Seli River, turned into one of the most in-depth studies of wildlife in Sierra Leone. In the course of their work, conservation experts discovered chimpanzees, rare orchids, butterflies, birds and more at the foot of the Sula Mountains (pages 310–11), which rise on the other side of the river as it snakes northwards to Lake Sonfon. It's a blessed place.

People have lived in the area since 2500BC – today signs of an ancient settlement comprising a hunters' camp, a blacksmithing area and a male secret society ritual area still remain. The Limba, Temne and Kuranko people who live here found refuge in the region as 'warrior-kings', such as Almamy Suluku (a Biriwa Limba) and Samori Toure (a Mandingo), expanded south. Relocation to make way for the dam took its toll – some families had to be resettled, and the twisted rope bridges to hop from one side of the river to the other are now gone forever.

Getting there and away You have two options. From the Freetown–Makeni Highway, continue north to Binkolo 10km away on the Kabala tarmac road. There, branch right on a dirt track for 32km to Bumbuna. Or head south from Makeni for 24km to Magburaka, and then northeast for 47km for Bumbuna. Via Binkolo seems to be the preferred route, but the 'correct' option can change depending on time of year and the condition of the road surface, so seek advice before setting off. You can take a seat in a local taxi or poda poda transport to Magburaka for around Le15,000, and then arrange onward travel, but it's pricey, t Le35,000 for a motorbike or Le85,000 or more for a hired car (although this is negotiable).

Where to stay and eat In theory, the site at the top of the dam where the Italian contractors lived and worked will one day be turned over to a private concern to manage for the enjoyment of visitors. All it needs is a canny operator to spot the potential here.

Once the site is made open to the public, even in the short term, tourists could stay in the well-equipped, sturdy bungalows with en-suite, fully functioning bathrooms that housed the contractors. Not stunning, but luxury of a sort. Camping in the forest around the reservoir will be an option one day too. There is already a motorboat at the jetty, ready to ferry visitors up and down the waterways. For now, it's not the sort of place you can turn up to or demand a bed, unless you know a dam worker or the tourist board is in a position to help you. You still need a permit from the **Ministry of Energy and Power** (*24 Brook St & 49 Waterloo St, Freetown – may soon relocate to Stronge Tower, 3 Pademba Rd*; m *076 362 654/369 538*; e *info@ energy.gov.sl*; w *energy.gov.sl*) to visit; expect to be turned away if you don't have one. Still, it is well worth making enquiries in Freetown – for more information on visiting, contact the **National Tourist Board** in Freetown (*Lumley Beach Rd*; m *076 634 949*; e *ntbslinfo@yahoo.com*; w *welcometosierraleone.sl*) or contact the Italian engineers directly at their offices near Congo Cross: **Studio Pietrangeli** (*2 Millicent Dr, Freetown*; \022 231 196; e *bumbuna@pietrangeli.it* w *pietrangeli.com*).

What to see and do For the moment, enjoying Bumbuna waits on concessioning the running of it to a tourism contractor, which still had not happened seven years after the completion of the dam. But it's worth checking, as this is eventually supposed to change. As before, contact the tourist board or Project Implementation Unit in Freetown, or the Bumbuna Watershed Management Authority (BWMA; m *076 600 749*), which has been set up to handle the concessioning process.

Poolside life Behind the reception centre is a perfectly sited open-air swimming pool with a stunning mountain backdrop. Lounging about on the sizeable deck area, cocktail-in-hand, thatch huts set about you, is hard to beat.

POWER TO THE PEOPLE?

By the mid 2000s, Bumbuna had become a bit of a bogeyman, a byword for unlimited potential that remained unrealised, bogged down in corruption, ruined by war: a metaphor for Sierra Leone itself.

But then, finally, the dam was finished. In early 2010, it began supplying 50MW of power, distributed throughout a series of towns headed south to the capital. In mid 2007, the whole country managed only 10MW (7MW in Freetown), so this has made a huge difference. Even so, Freetown itself has a requirement of 60MW and you can be sure that as soon as people have a taste of power, they'll want a whole lot more. The whole country needs at least 250MW, so there's still a long way to go.

When the war came the dam was almost complete, but then in 2005, after the structure had weathered the worst of the fighting, locals stole all the transmission cables from the pylons, carted them off to Freetown and melted them down for scrap. Some US$10 million of donor money later, replacement cables were rigged, scrap exports banned and police chiefs came up with a deterrent: as soon as a section of wiring is completed, turn on the power. 'Once they start dying they'll leave it alone,' said one triumphant law enforcer.

The president made energy supply his priority as soon as he got into the hot seat, and has inaugurated a series of 2.2MW mini hydro dams at Charlotte, Bankasoka and Makali to make the most of the river-rich land's 1,200MW hydro potential. Some 30km north of Bumbuna at Yiben, another major dam is already in the works. Known as Bumbuna II, it's set to dwarf its predecessor and will feed an impressive and much-needed 200MW in to the national grid once complete. It's already behind schedule – though thankfully not yet to the degree of its namesake – and will come online in 2021 at the earliest.

Dam excursions A motorboat is available for excursions on the grand lake in front of the dam, and you can walk round the whole thing in four days, following small forest paths and camping out in the bush. Nature walks through 'Rashida's Forest', birding walks, hiking routes up to lakes in the Sula Mountains, forest camping on top of 'Radio Hill', fishing and boating, are all on the cards. You can search for the elusive, nocturnal pygmy hippo in the Sandia and Kadubia areas. Chimpanzees and other primates, including Campbell's and spot-nosed monkeys, are regularly seen from the lake. A canoe is better for wildlife viewing as it's less noisy; although nearby chimpanzees tend to react with loud calls to the sound of the boat engine, as it is probably the first time they have ever heard one.

Wildlife It's not as richly endowed as it once was, but the moist evergreen forest around the Seli River still hides a wealth of wildlife within its galleries. In a series of studies in 2006, it was found to have a plant biodiversity within the top 5% of the whole Upper Guinea ecosystem. Along the Seli and Mawoloko rivers several villages have confirmed the presence of bongo antelope and pygmy hippos, after their rice farms were destroyed by them. These villages include Kadubia, Kafogu, Kamacelon, Kamabaray, Kamasindigwey and Kagborey. There are other mammals too – from the more frequently spotted Maxwell's duiker to the less common yellow-backed, black and bay duikers, bushbuck, forest buffalo, royal antelope, hyrax, porcupine and the common warthog.

As for chimps, between 33 and 58 individuals have been recorded, in four different family groups. Owing to the impact of bushmeat hunting by rebels during the war and some villagers after, it seems that the black-and-white colobus monkey is now extinct locally, but several other species are still swinging from the branches – **Campbell's monkey**, **spot-nosed monkey**, **sooty mangabey**, **green monkey** and **baboon**.

The keen eyed can look out for 444 species of **butterfly**, including just over a third of endemics recorded for the country. Among the unusual butterflies recorded is the extremely rare *Neurellipes staudingeri*, as well as the yellow-fringed *Charaxes nobilis claudei*, which can fly at up to 50km/h, as well as the brown *Euphaedra aberrans* and *Euphaedra afzelii*, two local West African endemics found on Bumbuna's 'Radio Hill'. So far 22 species of amphibians have been recorded, including the *Ptychadena oxyrhynchus*, a sharp-nosed ridged and speckled **frog**, reported only in Bumbuna, as well as 17 snakes, 20 orchids and 259 bird species. Of these, five **bird** species are of conservation concern, with suitably tongue-tantalising names: the **Sierra Leone** (or white-eyed) **prinia** (*Prinia leontica*); the **yellow-casqued hornbill** (*Ceratogymna elata*); the **rufous-winged illadopsis** (*Illadopsis rufescens*); the **black-headed** (-capped) **rufous warbler** (*Bathmocercus cerviniventris*); and the **copper-tailed glossy starling** (*Lamprotornis cupreocauda*).

AROUND BUMBUNA DAM

Bumbuna waterfalls Behind the small town of Bumbuna itself, a 15-minute drive away from the dam, are Bumbuna's waterfalls, a joyous spray of water that escapes almost at horizontal speed from the river. Children fish from below with hand-cut wooden sticks, bending in the breeze. If you time it right, rainbows form in the air, straight out of the sides of the waterfall, and curve colourfully into the water, or straight out at you. It's a great spot for a picnic, or, at the very least, a gape. Ask for directions in the town.

Lake Sonfon It's known as a mystical place of traditional worship and a customary haunt for cultural ceremonies, but if the world's gold miners have anything to do with it, Lake Sonfon might not stay peaceful for much longer. The mountainous lake, and the lush Sula Mountains that stretch beyond it to the southeast, sit on a series of well-proven gold lines and likely diamond hoards. In fact, one of the country's first foreign-run gold plants is set in this region. Artisanal gold panners have known the mountains' secrets for years of course, and still work the rivers and tributaries that flow down from Sula; a number of artisanal mining pits and camps are today visible along the lakeshore.

Several small streams feed into the lake, which is surrounded by hills, forest and grassland, and on a quiet evening filled with the sound of birdsong. Even swollen by rains, it's not as suited to an outdoor dip as one might hope, strewn with thick green algae. Still, a magical mushy-pea-green lake amid beautiful landscape is quite a sight. Some say its magical status rests on the assertion that no-one can sail a boat from one side to the other.

Getting there and away It's 350km northeast of Freetown, on patchy roads. From Bumbuna head east for 33km to Bendugu, 40km south of the lake. At this point ask locally for the tracks leading north up to Benekoro, a village 8km west of the lake. Keep asking directions as you go, and find a guide at Benekoro. You can also head to Sonfon from Kabala (pages 312–18), 45km north, on the same road that takes you to Mount Bintumani via Alikalia and Yfin, turning off the main road at Makakura and passing Kondembaia, 15km north of the lake. It takes more than an hour to drive the bad road from Kabala, even in a 4x4, though there were supposedly works planned on this route in 2017 – ask in Kabala to find out how they've progressed. To arrange a guided visit, Fact Finding Tours (pages 70–1) or the Conservation Society (page 70) would be good places to start.

What to see and do

Wildlife In 1994, experts recorded 115 species of birds at the lake and in surrounding vegetation, including the little-known **emerald starling** (*Lamprotornis iris*), which makes its home in the Upper Guinea forest region. There are also plenty of herons and egrets. Buffalo haunt the area, but lakeside sightings are rare.

KABALA Mention Kabala to anyone in Salone and a visible look of relief, and quite possibly delight, generally passes over their face. It's cold, they'll say. And quiet. While it certainly doesn't pass for Iceland, a cool breeze is pretty much guaranteed. Combine that with some fantastic walking trails amid lovely countryside and the town is a welcome respite for frazzled visitors seeking to escape the humidity and hustle of the coastal regions.

Containing Yalunka, Kuranko, Fula, Mandingo and Limba, it is really two towns in one – Kabala and Yogomaia. Local legend tells that the former got its name when in colonial times a European asked where on earth he was. He got the reply 'Ka Bala', meaning 'Go and ask Bala', who was obviously a knowledgeable sort of chap. The name made its way on to the map for good.

Kabala is not just a pretty place. The area is famed as the centre for the cattle-tending areas of the largely Muslim north, and its climate also puts it among the best sources of fresh produce in the country. The pressure for arable land and animal pasture has led to battles – both political and occasionally physical – between the

FULA PHRASES

Hello/thank you	*djarama*
How are you?	*tanala?*
I'm fine, how are you?	*tanala tong?*
How is your family?	*bangu rehmandegoy?*
Where do you live?	*kohuntor wonder?*
What's your name?	*honor ineh teda?*
My name is …	*mimi ineh teh …*
uncle	*bapa*
auntie	*yei*
brother	*cotor*
sister	*jaja*
Let's eat	*arie ymeh*
wait	*habor*
stop	*archew*
It's enough	*archereni*
I like you	*meme idoma*
It's all right	*archereneh*
Your child is all right	*borbor nor saley*
Whose business are you doing?	*business ondu wadata?*
Where did you go yesterday?	*ontor yada arkpy?*
I am going/goodbye	*meme yahee*

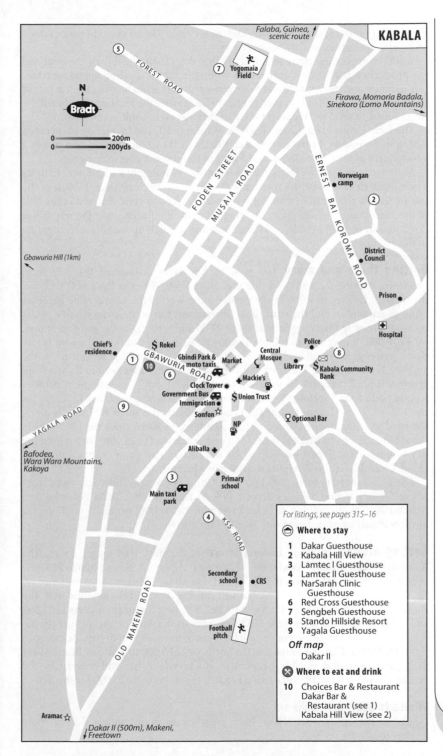

Falaba, Guinea, scenic route

KABALA

FOREST ROAD

⑦ ⑤ Yogomaia Field

Firawa, Momoria Badala, Sinekoro (Lomo Mountains)

N
Bradt

0 ___ 200m
0 ___ 200yds

Norweigan camp

FODEN STREET

MUSAIA ROAD

ERNEST BAI KOROMA ROAD

② District Council

Gbawuria Hill (1km)

Prison

Hospital

Police

Chief's residence

$ Rokel

Gbindi Park & moto taxis

Central Mosque

① ⑩

GBAWURIA ROAD

Market

Library

$ Kabala Community Bank

⑧

⑥

Mackie's

Clock Tower

Government Bus

$ Union Trust

Immigration

Sonfon

⑨

YAGALA ROAD

NP

Optional Bar

Bafodea,
Wara Wara Mountains,
Kakoya

Aliballa

③

Primary school

Main taxi park

④ KSS ROAD

For listings, see pages 315–16

⊖ **Where to stay**

1 Dakar Guesthouse
2 Kabala Hill View
3 Lamtec I Guesthouse
4 Lamtec II Guesthouse
5 NarSarah Clinic Guesthouse
6 Red Cross Guesthouse
7 Sengbeh Guesthouse
8 Stando Hillside Resort
9 Yagala Guesthouse

Off map
Dakar II

⊗ **Where to eat and drink**

10 Choices Bar & Restaurant
Dakar Bar & Restaurant (see 1)
Kabala Hill View (see 2)

Secondary school

CRS

OLD MAKENI ROAD

Football pitch

Aramac

Dakar II (500m), Makeni,
Freetown

Northern Province   THE FAR NORTH AND NORTHEAST

7

313

Fula herders and traders on one side, and the sedentary farmers on the other, whose crops are regularly ruined by hungry cows.

Another depressing irony in Kabala is that despite the quality of the land and the productivity of farmers, agricultural infrastructure is so ill-equipped for trade, refrigeration and storage that much of the booty heads straight off to the markets of Freetown where it will fetch a much better price, leaving the local markets bereft. 'At times I have to send to Freetown for cucumber,' says one cook in the town.

The local Limba chief, Chief Gbawura Mansaray III, can be met on his veranda sitting in a wooden throne with Queen Elizabeth II's initials carved into it; he's a good source of local knowledge, and happy to share some of it with visitors.

More striking than the town itself is the giant, looming black cliff next to it; it's never quite clear whether it's menacing the town or watching over it. Most of the fun in Kabala comes from striking out on long hikes to crest this and other hills of the surrounding countryside, stopping off at local villages along the way to ask directions or pick up a guide, and then returning to catch up with Kabala's nightlife in the evenings.

Getting there and away The road to Kabala is tarmac all the way from Freetown, making for a smooth ride that takes about 5 hours (in a **4x4**) to travel the 305km. It takes in some lovely views on the way as the countryside becomes more mountainous and the road rises. **Government bus** is the most reliable public transport, leaving Freetown daily at about 07.00 and arriving in the early afternoon, for Le30,000. It may stop to refill in Freetown's Kissy lorry park on the way, where Kono passengers get off and Kabala passengers pile in, which adds time to the journey. If you miss the 07.00 departure, **poda podas** and **taxis** head to Kabala from Freetown's Shell taxi park, or get a vehicle to Makeni and change there. A place in a poda poda from Freetown to Makeni costs Le20,000, then another Le20,000 for the 120km from Makeni to Kabala. Leaving Kabala, the main taxi stop is along the road to Makeni where it meets KSS Road, some 500m from the clock tower. From here, cars go to Makeni (Le22,000) and Freetown (Le35,000) throughout the day (though most depart between 07.00 and 08.00), and most other destinations (Koidu, Kambia, etc) will require a change in Makeni.

There's a secondary lorry park known as Gbindi Park near the clock tower, from where Guinea-bound vehicles depart. 4x4s to Faranah via Gberia Fotombu and Mamou via Gbentu go once or twice a week for Le100,000, generally on Thursday or thereabouts to co-ordinate with weekly lumas in the area.

Getting around In town, **motorcycle taxi** is the best way to get about. The **Koinadugu Bike Rentals Association** (*chairman is Alpha Jah Barrie,* m *076 995 491; logistics officer Ibrahim Jalloh,* m *076 589 031*) has about 75 bikes and is stationed on the main clock tower roundabout, but you can flag down a bike anytime from the roadside. A short hop around town costs Le2,000; hire for an hour costs Le25,000 and a day around town about Le70,000, plus at least a litre or two of fuel (in the region of Le6,000 per litre). For one-off trips out of town, expect to pay, for example, Le30,000 for the 23km to Musaia, to the north, or Le70,000 to Bintu or Bindi, 45km away. Less noisy, and much less expensive, is a **bicycle**. A handful areavailable for rent by the main roundabout, costing Le5,000 for an hour; Le20,000 for the day.

 Where to stay *Map, page 313*
Nearly all the options are cheap, basic guesthouses, some with a slightly more homely touch than others.

Stando Hillside Resort (22 rooms) Old Makeni Rd; m 078 644 344, 557 205. This new complex near the hospital is the ritziest spot in town, & while that may not be saying much in Kabala, it's certainly the place to be if hot water & AC are on your must-have list. The rooms are set in pastel green 2-storey bungalows in a rather vertiginous, black-&-white chequered hillside compound, & all come with fridge, net & TV in addition to the aforementioned AC & hot water. Generator all night, but meals require advance notice. **$$$–$$**

✳ **Kabala Hill View** (4 rooms) Off Agriculture Rd; m 076 222 561, 078 072 840; e kabalahillview@gmail.com; w kabalahillview. org. The prettiest of the lot, this friendly guesthouse offers 4 basic rooms that are self-contained & neatly kept. The real highlight is the veranda, which offers a sweeping view over Kabala & out to the Wara Wara Hills beyond. The friendly bar attached makes for a nice place to while away an evening & does meals (**$$**) with a bit of notice. A generator runs fans until midnight. **$$–$**

Lamtec I Guesthouse (15 rooms) 3 Kodakayaka St; m 079 055 605, 077 232 796. The 7 new rooms here are self-contained, while the thoroughly austere older rooms have wooden double beds with nets & use basic shared loos. Manager 'Lamtec' Lamine Bangura offers no restaurant, but plenty of stout. Generator runs 19.30–07.00. **$$–$**

Lamtec II Guesthouse (10 rooms) KSS Rd; tel numbers same as previous entry. The rowdy younger brother to Lamtec I, this one comes with a popular nightclub attached. Rooms are basic but reasonably clean. All come with double beds & 5 are self-contained. Generator runs all night. The restaurant (**$$**) serves up basic African dishes. B&B. **$$–$**

Sengbeh Guesthouse (30 rooms) 4 Shaw Dr, facing the Yogomaia football pitch; m 076 519 433, 076 221 360, 077 957 151. The best of the basic accommodation options in town, most rooms in this guesthouse, which opened in 2007 & was expanded in 2011, have en suites; all have fans, mosquito nets, TV, power 19.00–midnight (or later if you're willing to pay for fuel), but no hot water. Secure compound with parking available; good views over Kabala's hills & it manages to be comfortable as well as basic. Staff can prepare an evening meal (**$$**) if you order well in advance. B&B. **$$–$**

Dakar Guesthouse 23 Gbawuria Rd; m 079 587 075, 079 767 787. The rooms behind this popular restaurant & bar are none too private, but they seem reasonably kept & certainly are cheap; some are self-contained & all come with nets & fans. **Dakar II**, some 500m outside town on the road to Makeni, is under the same management & a much quieter alternative, with equally budget-friendly self-contained rooms. The Senegalese owner is an engineer with the firm responsible for roadworks throughout the district, so he's also a good contact for onward travel conditions. **$**

NarSarah Clinic Guesthouse 27 Forest Rd; m 088 622 138, 078 827 824, 076 605 331, 076 889 849; e peacemakerkargbo@gmail.com. In a quiet compound at the edge of town facing Gbawuria Hill, this sleepy guesthouse is associated with a community clinic set up by a Sierra Leonean expat in the US. It's basic but cheap & clean, & rooms come with mosquito nets & 24-hour solar power. **$**

Red Cross Guesthouse (5 rooms) Gbawuria Rd, opposite the school field; m 076 966 285, 076 656 510. Forgive the wonky walls – they were built by war-affected children from the CAR Centre (pages 317–18), this simple place not only includes tidy rooms with en suites, nets & standing fans, but also a shop selling goods from the centre's artisans, including soap, furniture, gara dresses & more. Friendly staff run the generator until midnight. It was locked up tight on our last visit, so have a backup plan. **$**

Yagala Guesthouse (8 rooms) 22 Gbawuru II St, Gbawuria I; m 076 809 696, 099 620 365. Under new management, this is a cosy & simple stay, with all the basics in place. Clean rooms have nets, & 4 are self-contained. Generator runs until midnight. No b/fast at the moment, but there are plans to build a restaurant & bar alongside some new AC rooms. **$**

✖ Where to eat and drink *Map, page 313*

For **street food**, head for the town's main roundabout, near the motorbike riders, where street stands sell groundnut and hot pepper soup, and attieke. At night the range widens to rice buns, liver and beef skewers, fish stew, fish balls, roast and pepper beef, scotch eggs, fried sweet potato, roast cassava, roast cuts of goat, peanuts, sweet tea and boiled eggs. Unless you're going to a disco, this is also the place to hang – grab a beer, join a pew at a dice-games' shack, and people-watch.

✗ **Choices Bar & Restaurant** 17 Gbawuria Rd; m 076 697 809; ⊕ 07.00–late daily. Rarely lives up to its name, generally offering African dishes, chicken & fish pastries & some stodgy, doughy cakes, but the outdoor seating area is livelier than other joints. **$$**

✗ **Dakar Bar & Restaurant** 23 Gbawuria Rd; m 079 587 075, 079 767 787; ⊕ until late daily. Despite having an owner from Dakar, this popular corner haunt doesn't serve many Senegalese dishes (but a special order might be possible). You'll get a hearty plate of the usual suspects like rice & plassas or groundnut stew, depending on the day. It's also a favourite spot to catch the football, with crowds spilling out on to the street for big matches. **$$**

✗ **Kabala Hill View** Off Agriculture Rd; m 076 222 561, 078 072 840; ⊕ 09.00–midnight daily. Proprietor Alpha Koroma is the man behind this welcome addition to Kabala's dining scene, though meals here should be ordered well in advance – call at lunchtime to arrange your dinner, as they may have to visit the market for ingredients. Sit outside & enjoy a cold Star & some tasty pepper soup as you gaze out over the Wara Wara Hills in the distance. There's even a modest library, table football, a Monopoly board, & playing cards if you're looking for some quiet evening entertainment. **$$–$**

Entertainment and nightlife

Aramac (*14 Charles St; entry Le5,000–10,000 depending on the night*) is a disco/nightclub run by Nassir Mackie, who, rather usefully, is also owner of the main pharmacy on the clock tower roundabout, so he can sell you your hangover relief the next day too. Look out for the 'New Lebanon' sign daubed on the dancefloor wall. Weekdays – Wednesday in particular – can be just as lively as weekends.

Lamtec II (*KSS Rd*) shows films or football nightly in its lively bar, and **Sonfon Nightclub** (*3 Sheki Bockarie St*) is another good option on Wednesdays and Saturdays. Strong on football during the season, it also shows Supersports at the weekend. **Dakar** (see above) is a good central spot for a beer at a picnic table, but expect blaring TV and a general din as the night wears on; **Optional Bar** is a similar, though sleepier, pick, but thankfully it's not mandatory to stick around. For music concerts, the town's **two football fields** (the town field is in Yogomaia; the other is close to Kabala Secondary School) often fill up if a big act such as K-man is in town, usually for Le5,000 a ticket. Look out for posters and listen to the word on the street.

Other practicalities

Mackie's Pharmacy (*14 Fodey Yallah St*; m *077 566 662*; ⊕ *08.00–22.00 daily*), by the roundabout, is one of two pharmacies in town. It sells cold drinks during the day and can also change foreign currency, including euros. There's no public internet in town, but if you belong to an NGO you might be able to go online at the CRS or other NGO offices.

There are still no ATMs in town, so arranging Western Union or a cash transfer from Freetown are currently your only banking options. Either can be arranged at **Kabala Community Bank** (*Old Makeni Rd*; m *077 481 276*) or **Union Trust Bank** (*Sheki Bockarie St*; m *088 580 664*). **Rokel Commercial Bank** (*Gbawuria Rd*) also has an outpost here, but it's only open on Wednesdays.

What to see and do

Cloth Kabala used to be a centre for weaving. Nowadays it's on the decline: many of the practitioners have died and young people are not interested in taking up the

A visit to Kabala at New Year pitches you into one of the rowdiest and most remarkable parties in Sierra Leone. People travel from all over the country for a two-day New Year's Day extravaganza, part-fair, part-warehouse party, on top of the huge black cliff of Gbawuria Hill, part of the Wara Wara range, which towers behind the town.

'We believe when you go there you will be cleansed, purified, like an initiation,' the local chief told us. We expected something traditional: hand-whittled flutes, ceremonial robes or traditional drumming perhaps, on a sacred site where the ancestors used to make sacrifices, and cows are still occasionally slaughtered right at the top of the precipitous rock.

We could not have been more wrong. Make it up there and you are greeted by a heady mix of booze, beats and bawdiness. People ferry enormous stereos, entire crates of beer and car batteries (to power the music) up the treacherous path to the summit, mostly on their heads. Girls climb up with backpacks, only to disappear behind a rock and emerge dressed to kill in tiny miniskirts, high heels, sparkling jewellery and enough make-up to guide in a helicopter in the dark. The lads meanwhile swagger about in skinny jeans, basketball vests, trainers and sunglasses looking every bit the West Coast rap stars they idolise.

While the streetwear and the strutting is remarkable, the views are even more spectacular from the bare slab of granite at the top – the town laid out below, surrounding hills enticing you with the thought of more climbing, kites swirling in the abyss below. And yet you share the moment with young men armed with loud-hailers, blaring out unfathomably irksome siren noises, all in the name of purgative renewal. There is even a fairground-style game at the top. The whole thing is extraordinary.

Both routes up the hill are hard going, but one is steeper than the other. They start near each other, to the left of the chief's house, and anyone can indicate the way. The climb up takes about half an hour: stop for plenty of breaks along the way, and take a generous ration of water. On the way down, trips on sprawling tree roots and slides on loose-packed earth are easy, especially the morning after the night before's celebrations. To add a further trial, revellers often light bushfires along the way, so the climb up and down can be smoky, and thronged with drunken revellers falling over as they try to pass each other. As the afternoon draws on and inebriation levels rise, tempers can fray, so it might be worth planning on an early exit if the atmosphere turns a little aggressive.

skills; very little native cloth or cotton thread is made or sold anymore, while the market is flooded with cheap Chinese synthetics or recycled hand-me-downs. Yet there is a much-higher-than-average concentration of tailors in town, a telltale sign of the rehabilitation programmes that were run in the wake of the war – elsewhere in Sierra Leone ex-combatants tend to be mechanics and taxi drivers. In Kabala it is still possible to learn about the making of three different types of cloth – gara, country cloth and hu ronko.

Gara The Red Cross-funded Child Advocacy and Rehabilitation (CAR) Centre wrapped up their operations in Kabala a few years ago, but taught gara-making as part of its post-war rehabilitation programme for many years, along with carpentry, metal works, masonry, soap-making, hairdressing and more, so despite the centre's closure, many of its graduates continue to work around Kabala. If you're interested in learning how to make gara yourself, former CAR operations co-ordinator, Oliver Mansaray (m 076 966 285) or project supervisor Kaba (m 077 467 184) should be able to put you in touch with a teacher.

Country cloth Once a rice farmer, Sarah Kamara is one of three women at the Norwegian-funded war-wounded camp on the edge of town who weaves distinctive, black-and-white-checked country cloth.

She says she is lucky to be alive, let alone weaving. Sarah still bears the scar on her chest where she was shot in an attack on her hometown of Yfin, at the foot of the Loma Mountains, during the war. A mixture of native medicine, and finally treatment in Freetown, helped her recovery, but feeding her four children is still difficult. Her husband has long since become blind so no longer works as a farmer.

She now makes country cloth on a simple, homemade loom outside her cramped compound in Kabala. The checked cloth is woven in long, thin strips that can later be stitched together to form garments. It takes her about three weeks to finish one length, for which she charges about Le110,000. If you are interested in buying some of her cloth, ask for her at the 'Norwegian camp'.

Hu ronko At another house, on Bilimaia Street, the elderly Moussa Mara works with natural cloth in the old hu ronko style (see box, opposite) that so few make today. He sells the cloth by the yard, and would charge L160,000 to make a shirt. Demand has waned, so he doesn't weave every day, but can work to commission, and will let you watch.

Walks Surrounded by hills, many visitors love getting out and about for a meander or a bracing walk, as they prefer, through the villages. The most obvious hike is up the flat-topped hill that overlooks the town (see box, page 317). It's a decent climb, and the views from the top are impressive, although less so during the harmattan between November and February. The Wara Wara Mountains spread out to the northwest of town, towards Bafodea. Kakamba peak, at 921m, is the highest, but more enchanting is the Wara Wara's Kaboia Hill, said to be inhabited by *kumba*, the guardian spirit of all Limba, who all the departed gather to in the afterlife. Ask at your guesthouse for a guide (Kabala Hill View is especially good for this; page 315), or to be pointed in the right direction.

AROUND KABALA

Cave art A rock shelter near Kakoya, a Limba town in Bafodea chiefdom, is home to Sierra Leone's only known rock paintings, recorded by DeCorse in 1988. The repeating designs are ovoid, consisting of a white outline with a series of dots inside. Their exact meaning is unclear, but it is thought they may relate to female excision rituals that are still widely practised among the Limba. There have been relatively few surveys of rock painting and cave art in Sierra Leone, and West Africa in general, compared with other parts of the continent.

Northern border crossing into Guinea In these remote reaches of the country, officials say there are 68 border crossing points throughout the northern districts of Koinadugu and Falaba, six of them official and only three of them functioning.

WHAT'S IN A LOOSE MAN'S SHIRT? THE MAGIC OF RONKO

In public everyone plays safe, calling it the 'chief's gown'. But the hu ronko's secret moniker has always been 'the witch's gown'. The garment – once prized by hunters, warriors, secret societies, chiefs, blacksmiths and even politicians – is a thing of power to be revered, a protector of people against natural and supernatural weapons of war. Who needs armour, fear, or a vague sense of self-preservation, when a magic top can repel attacks by swords, knives, arrows and bullets? The really good ones can protect you against invisible attacks too.

A knee-length, loose-fitting top, with a chest pocket often set askance (perfect for amulets and charms), hu runkos are made of five to eight coarse bands, spun from local cotton, and then sewn together in rough-hewn vertical strips.

Made and worn by the Limba, Kuranko and Yalunka, the colours come from natural dyes: mahogany tree, acacia root and kola nut extractions that vary from yellow to brown to deep russet and rust, and pack plenty of protective punch – in Limba the word for 'dye' is the same as 'medicine'.

The garment is then daubed with thick black vertical lines holding motifs in between, such as spiders, circles, stars, crosses, fences, clocks and the rising sun, the last sometimes associated with the APC, whose politicians once upon a time posed for campaign poster shots wearing their hu ronkos. Sometimes only this thick black muddy ink is infused with magical powers; sometimes the whole tunic is dipped into a herb-filled potion. First handed down among a chosen few in the early 20th century, so dangerous and important was the process that some hu ronko-makers – always men – even practised their craft in secret, deliberately working only inside their dimly lit homes so no-one could see them.

These days, you're lucky if you can find a craftsman working cloth at all. 'Native handmade hu ronko has had its birth, life and virtual death in Sierra Leone in some 60 years,' says Simon Ottenberg, Emeritus Professor of Anthropology at the University of Washington, who carried out field research in Bafodea – 50km west of Kabala and a centre of Limba hu ronko production – in the late 1970s and again 30 years later.

Until the 1950s, most wives spun thread from hand-picked cotton, while their husbands wove; but today the few hu ronko men left rely on imported fabric, and young people lack interest in the skills. You're more likely to find cheap Chinese knock-offs in the markets of Freetown than authentic garments in the villages of the north. When Ottenberg went back to Bafodea after the war had put a stop to all production for a decade, nearly all the makers he knew had died. If you find an example of anyone still practising the art, you've found a rare thing indeed.

Gberia Fotombu is the main entry point for the district and a route good enough to get a vehicle across, provided you've all the right forms and paperwork to hand. Elsewhere, the porous borders see a constant flow of people crossing unofficially back and forth, along with contraband including cigarettes, fuel, gold, general foodstuffs and motorbikes.

Getting there and away Take the 'Scenic Route' northeast from Kabala (pages 320–3), 53km to Falaba Town, keep going for 7km and then turn off at the small

Katrina spent three days bumping along the 'Scenic Route'. This piece, describing the trip, was first published by Reuters.

The chief is gesticulating wildly and I see spit flying out of his mouth. I am pretty sure I have offended him but don't understand much of the local Kuranko language, so I ask the man next to me who speaks some English. 'Oh, he's just saying he's made you his wife,' he replies. 'Nothing to worry about.' I'm still trying to come to terms with accidentally eating monkey last night. I wasn't sure what I was expecting when I took a motorbike taxi tour across 320km of Sierra Leone's northeastern back roads. But marriage and eating monkeys weren't what I had in mind.

I ride behind Ibrahim Koroma, the self-styled 'task force' of the Koinadugu Bike Riders' Association, who agreed to rev his Chinese-made machine smuggled from Guinea along village paths, with me hanging on the back. He says he will minimise the 'gallops' for me and drive like I'm his old mother. As the bones in my back clonk against each other I'm glad he doesn't see me as his younger brother.

Apart from our noisy passage, the sense of isolation from the modern world is complete. There is no phone coverage for days, tall grasses brush my crash helmet and the area is so remote that there is not even a discarded Coca-Cola bottle in sight.

When we reached Kurubonla Town, a collection of mud-built homes topped off with thatch or tin, someone was sent to beat a drum to gather everyone to see an unannounced stranger – me. Not long afterwards, I seemed to have acquired a husband. The very least I can do is say thank you and shake his hand. Oh, and ask his name. He takes off his hat and puts on special ceremonial headgear, coloured gold with burnt red patches, and we pose for marriage snaps. Possibly into his seventies, Chief Mamburu Marah looks quite fetching. Despite his public

Limbaya junction. That journey alone once took up to 6 hours in a **4x4**, but the roadworks from Kabala begun in 2017 will speed this up considerably once complete; the remaining 14km stretch until the border lies outside the project's remit, however, so add 2 or more hours for this. Passing the village of Yogobe after about 6km, you reach immigration at the Yalunka village of Gberia Fotombu, confusingly also known by a Fula name of Koindu Kura (not to be confused with any of the other various Koindus that are also helpfully near the border at other points). A **motorbike** can do the whole thing much quicker, in about 5 hours (this will again be quicker when the roadworks conclude). The border is officially open 06.00–18.00 and paperwork is fairly hassle-free, with an immigration and customs office. Beyond the Sierra Leonean side there's about 10km of no-man's-land before you reach Guinean bureaucracy in Hérémakonon. You need a visa in advance for entry into Guinea (page 72).

Visas As of 2017, the only Sierra Leonean border crossing offering visas on arrival was at Pamelap, so if you're hoping to enter the country here, you will need to arrive with your visa already taken care of, either from a Sierra Leonean embassy abroad, or Visit Sierra Leone's visa service (page 72).

TAKING THE 'SCENIC ROUTE' On the ITMB map of the country, a route skirts the Guinean border from Kabala, heading north, swooping to the east and finally

declaration of our betrothal, I was able to slip away later with a promise to come back and see him soon.

MONKEY BUSINESS The local chief of Mongo-Bendugu, another small town, was less amorous but no less obliging, finding us a place to stay for the night in the school principal's house. A local policeman was kind too, offering to share his meal. He worried local food might not be suitable, mentioning rice and potato leaf sauce. 'Nonsense,' I said, and we tucked in. I took some meat too, since it's a bit of an honour to be offered it. It was the best I've ever had – rich and tender with not a trace of gristle. As I chomped, I noticed one of the bones, flat and disc-like, and the question flew out of my mouth. 'Er, what meat is this?' 'Monkey,' came the reply.

The policeman, who couldn't stop laughing, tried to make me promise that when I wrote his name down in my notebook, I wouldn't remember him as 'the man who made me eat monkey'. He said the monkey was probably shot in neighbouring Guinea, slow-roasted and brought over the border.

Civilians are banned from having guns in Sierra Leone following its 1991–2002 civil war. This has annoyed hunters, who have lost their symbol of virility and main income-earning tool. They have become more inventive, laying bush traps for deer and other animals. But everyone agrees chimpanzees, which are protected under Sierra Leone law and can be five times as strong as a man, are far too clever to fall for such tricks.

The small West African country is home to several more rare primates, including the endangered Diana monkey and red colobus. But most locals aren't fussy when it comes to supplementing their diet. 'The type of monkey you net in the trap is the type of monkey you kill,' was how one local put it. 'It's delicious for us and very nice to eat.'

heading south, bisecting the Loma Mountains (see box, pages 326–7) and the Tingi Hills to end up in Koidu, capital of the Eastern Province. The road is marked 'Scenic Route' and has a little perky graphic of a camera, conjuring up notions of the sort of thing that might get your grandparents out for their Sunday afternoon stroll. Nothing could be further from the truth.

Note that travel conditions along this route are set to change entirely when the 160km of road between Kabala and Kurubonla is tarred – works began in Kabala in early 2017 and will likely take several years to complete.

What it's like This is rural Sierra Leone at its peaceful, unhurried, beautiful best. Monkeys may well amble across your path, villages are spotless, with rice and chilli peppers drying outside the smooth ochre walls of immaculately tended Susu huts, while calabashes and vines nestle in their thatch roofs. At the frequent river crossings women will be 'brooking' their clothes, while mist still lingers in the tall trees above them and bananas overhang the roadside; in season a profusion of flowers burst into colourful life. You might also catch sight of people making local fishing baskets – nets within a frame for scooping into rivers, as mud bricks bake in the sun and the reliable ataya shacks pour froth-filled glasses of Chinese green tea.

Bushmeat is common in this remote area, where the scarcity of beef and pork caused by dire road infrastructure means people have to look elsewhere for a source of protein. Antelope, porcupine, grasscutter (cane rat: known locally as 'cutting grass') and even monkey are all likely offerings, mixed in with the usual cassava or potato-leaf plassas.

How to do it It might be described as the 'Scenic Route', but a walk in the park it is not – impassable during the rainy season, the hungry, churned-up laterite sucks in almost anything that moves. Even in the dry season, the tracks here have so many 'gallops' (Salone politeness for bone-crunching pot-holes), it's hard to avoid a bruising.

A sturdy **4x4** is your only reliable four-wheeled option – public transport stays well away from the Kabala–Koidu loop, with one minor exception: as of mid 2017, Mongo-Bendugu was served by one, or occasionally two, public 4x4s weekly from Kabala (via Limbaya, etc) and the same from Koidu (via Kurubonla, etc), with fewer or none going during the rains. That said, transport options are likely to improve dramatically from the Kabala side as roadworks progress towards Kurubonla.

Thus, for the time being, **motorbike** remains one of the best ways of going beyond Kabala on day trips, precisely because local rural roads are so churned and narrow that two wheels can pick their way much better. Plus, you can always jump off and push through a tricky patch if need be, although sometimes it feels like you're walking more than you're motoring. The number of short river crossings also demands mastering a number of techniques: jumping between rocks, pulling yourself gingerly along trunks and branches, and taking off shoes and socks and wading.

Negotiate hard, but Le120,000 for the day plus five or six litres of fuel as a decent (and suitably generous) guide price for hiring a bike in Kabala. You should also make sure that the driver takes responsibility for all expenses such as repairs and his own food and lodging, especially if you are taking on long distances: alternatively, an all-inclusive Le250,000 a day will definitely keep everybody happy. Some destinations have pretty much set fees, such as Dogolia, 14km from Kabala, for L30,000 one-way; Musaia (19km) for Le30,000; Bindi (45km) and Bintu (51km) for Le75,000. You can do the Kabala–Koidu stretch described above in 2½ days.

Pick your driver well. While some might come with rather terrifying titles, such as 'taskforce leader' (at least denoting notions of discipline and respect), others are young speed freaks or keen to tell you they've experience of your hoped-for route where they've none. You want someone you'll get on with, as a lot of the trip will be just the two of you, talking of everything from secret societies and circumcision ('you can't sex unless you've been circumcised') to learning ('education is your farm: you grew up in a book').

A HANDFUL OF KURANKO PROVERBS

Small drops will fill a river

Even dirty water can put out a fire

If you come upon the head of a goat on the approach to a town, do not conclude that the young men of that town do not like meat

If they slap you on your bald head, you must have taken your cap off

Towns on the way From Kabala take the road heading out towards Falaba. It's about an hour (15km) to **Dogolia**, which has a weekly Sunday cattle market, and a police checkpoint at Sinkunia (40km).

From there **Falaba** (55km) is about 3 hours away by motorbike, and it's another hour to **Limbaya** (the turning-off point for the road to the Guinean border, described on pages 319–20 – 62km from Kabala), then on to Gberia Timbako (wrongly labelled Gberia Fotombu on the ITMB map; 74km from Kabala) and Kombile (87km), a wide, open town. **Mongo-Bendugu**, named after the river (*mongo* means river) is a fairly sizeable administrative town, 53km south of Limbaya and 115km from Kabala.

The Kuranko town of **Kurubonla**, 162km from Kabala and 48km south of Mongo-Bendugu, which has a fabulous view of the peak of Bintumani on a clear day, has its weekly market on Wednesday, and is the projected end of the line for the road-surfacing works from Kabala begun in 2017. **Mansofenia**, a long strip of a town 20km further south, has a weekly market on a Friday; it's likely to be the first place you can find bottled water or a canned soft drink after Falaba.

The further south you get, the closer you are to diamond country. **Worodu** is the turning point for the Tingi Hills to the east, followed by Kayima, a mountain gateway town with a weekly Monday market. Continue south through Wadala, which has a busy weekly Friday market, and finally **Tefeya** to reach the main Makeni–Koidu Highway.

Where to stay There are no guesthouses on this route, so it's a matter of rocking up in a village or town and politely requesting to see the chief (see box, pages 100–1). Ask him nicely for a place to stay and he should be able to oblige.

MOUNT BINTUMANI The highest point in West Africa (well, west of Mount Cameroon's 4,095m), Mount Bintumani isn't known as the king of the mountains ('Loma Mansa' to the Kuranko) for nothing. Even finding yourself at the foot of its 1,948m, among the range of the Loma Mountains, takes some doing, and trying to manage an ascent in the rainy season approaches madness; not that people haven't done it. Look out for Bintumani herself – the female spirit that lives on the mountain. There is more than one way to climb this mountain: you can scale the beast in a day if you're dead set on speed; or seven, if you're keener on taking your time, camping out in the wilderness, spotting herds of buffalo and trekking through rainforest that even the rebels didn't reach.

Despite years of suffering during the war, at the hands of fighters and later poachers, the mountain's rare environment within the Loma Mountains Forest Reserve went unprotected. A team of experts who visited in 2008 finally made the clear-cut case to turn the mountain into a national park and make wildlife preservation in one of the country's most diverse ecosystems a priority.

Thanks to this fantastic biological diversity and years spent lobbying the government, conservation efforts in the Loma Mountains are ever-so-slowly beginning to bear fruit: the Forestry Division drew up a management plan in 2012 and the area was finally proclaimed a national park in 2013. Implementation of the management plan has been slow, however, and the national park declaration still needs to be ratified by parliament, but it's encouraging progress nonetheless, and the unique natural, biological and cultural landscape of the Loma Mountains is more protected today than it's ever been.

Flora and fauna

Animals The Loma Mountains Non-Hunting Forest Reserve (LMNHFR), of which Mount Bintumani is a part, contains potentially the largest area of undisturbed

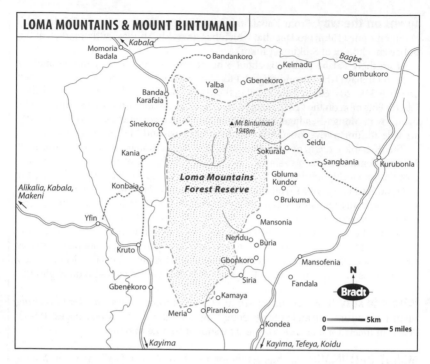

LOMA MOUNTAINS & MOUNT BINTUMANI

montane forest within the Upper Guinea region: of its 332km², approximately 75% of the original canopy survives.

Its remoteness has insulated it from serious environmental degradation, leaving it rich in mammal species, with the most diverse selection in the entire country. Research by Aaron Kortenhoven undertaken for the University of Miami has shown that the 49 species found on Loma represent greater than 70% of Sierra Leone's large mammal fauna, 31% of them do not occur outside West Africa and 14 are endemic to the Upper Guinea forest zone.

Most interestingly, the Tacugama Chimpanzee Sanctuary (page 187) conducted a chimpanzee survey here in 2010 and found an estimated chimp population of more than 1,000, giving Loma far and away the highest density of chimpanzees in the country. They can be observed regularly, in part due to their fondness for nesting in riverine gallery forest, which is prevalent in the mountain range, providing the headwaters for a number of Sierra Leone's main rivers.

Kortenhoven's 2009 research also revealed that two species at risk of extinction in Sierra Leone and endangered throughout their range – the **pygmy hippopotamus** and **bongo** – were recorded here, as were leopards, golden cats and serval cats. The Loma Mountains are also home to bay duiker, black duiker, water chevrotain, red colobus, and Diana monkey, all of which are endangered. Other primates that can be readily observed in the forests of Loma include the sooty mangabey, black-and-white colobus, red colobus and lesser spot-nosed monkeys.

If a local guide starts enthusiastically pointing out large troops of 'gorillas' and 'baboons', it's well worth knowing (before you start bragging about your trip to see Sierra Leone's best-kept secret) that in Krio 'gorillas' means baboons (the nearest place you'll find a real gorilla is in east Nigeria) and 'baboons' (*babu*) means chimps and occasionally monkey.

A bat survey of Loma in 2008 also recorded the first incidence of the rare **Hill's horseshoe bat** (*Rhinolophus hillorum*), in the country. The 41 species of amphibians also recently recorded in Loma include the endangered **Guinea screeching frog** (*Arthroleptis crusculum*), which occurs only in montane grassland, and was known previously only from the Tingi Hills and Nimba Mountains.

Birds The Loma Mountains also count as one of Sierra Leone's ten Important Bird Areas, and surveying suggests they are home to at least 332 bird species; more than half of the species recorded in the country. Of these, 11 are of global conservation concern: including the **rufous fishing owl** (*Scotopelia ussheri*), **yellow-bearded greenbul** (*Criniger olivaceus*), **Sierra Leone prinia** (*Schistolais leontica*), **yellow-headed picathartes** (*Picathartes gymnocephalus*), **yellow-casqued hornbill** (*Ceratogymna elata*), and **brown-cheeked hornbill** (*Bycanistes cylindricus*) – all classed as vulnerable; and the near-threatened **pallid harrier** (*Circus macrourus*), **black-headed rufous warbler** (*Bathmocercus cerviniventris*), **rufous-winged illadopsis** (*Illadopsis rufescens*), and **copper-tailed glossy starling** (*Hylopsar cupreocauda*). The **crowned eagle** (*Stephanoaetus coronatus*), among the largest birds of prey in Africa and also near-threatened, is also a common sight in the noon-day skies around Loma. The **lesser kestrel** (*Falco naumanni*) is a rare migrant here.

Plants Nine species of plants are also known to be endemic to the Loma Mountains. A more recent survey of the vegetation in the range found 13 species that were recorded for the first time in Sierra Leone, extending the range of these species further west of Liberia and Ivory Coast, and one species of Sterculiaceae (*Cola* spp) that has never been seen before, and is currently being studied at the University of Cocody in Ivory Coast.

Making the climb There are three main routes up the mountain, described below. Some take longer than others but in all cases reasonable fitness and an unflagging desire to keep going is needed much more than skill – there's no need for climbing equipment (unless a particular rock formation takes your fancy).

However, the going is steep most of the way, with few flat stretches, and some people don't make it right to the top. Make sure you have comfortable, worn-in walking boots and waterproofs that keep out the rain without retaining too much heat. Most important is taking a little time to organise water intake and other provisions on the ascent.

Climbing should be avoided in the rainy season – not only because of the hazards of climbing but also because the dirt routes to the mountain bases can become completely impassable.

Chiefs, guides and porters Whichever village you take as your jumping-off point, pay your respects to the local chief (offering money – Le50,000 is a good amount, although you may be asked for significantly more – and offering some other small gifts such as soap and sugar will help with bargaining).

Even if the maps were good enough (which they are not), you'd be crazy not to go with a guide who knows the mountain. Bush paths covered by tall elephant grasses, confusing forest tracks and gnarly trees that all look the same would be among the least of your concerns should you decide to attempt the trek on your own.

While it's pretty humbling to huff and puff your way up behind backpack-laden porters scampering ahead of you in plastic flip-flops, only the keenest, sturdiest and most pig-headed of visitors would carry their own kit, food and water.

MOUNTAIN LIVING

Aaron Kortenhoven, an American biologist, grew up in Sierra Leone and loved Bintumani peak and its Loma Mountains so much he ended up living on its slopes for two years as part of his graduate studies. Here he explains why it's the most beautiful place he's ever seen, and the pressing social and environmental problems affecting a tropical montane rainforest (forest that grows on mountains and above an altitude of 1,000m) idyll, home to pristine wildlife.

I have yet to meet a person, Sierra Leonean or not, who has not been moved in a profound way after seeing only a few of the wonders Loma has to offer. I don't think a traveller has experienced the best Sierra Leone has in terms of natural beauty and pure awesomeness if they stop short of Loma. Maybe you won't even need to climb Bintumani to be amazed.

My love and fascination for the Loma Mountains started in 1988. I was 14 and a family friend was going to climb Bintumani and asked if I wanted to come along. The answer was 'of course'. I grew up in Foria, a little village about 35km west of the Loma Mountains, where my parents worked as missionaries for more than 20 years. This gave me the opportunity to grow up immersed in the Kuranko culture, speaking the language, learning the traditions and understanding the Sierra Leonean bush through the eyes of a Kuranko hunter. I had seen the Loma Mountains in the distance every day for years – they were legend in my mind and the source of many late-night stories from village elders. My first trip there did not let my imagination down and led to many subsequent trips.

'NEVER THINK IT HAS NOT BEEN SEEN' In my first ventures up Loma, wildlife was abundant and easily viewed. Even at this early age, I knew that if I were ever to work with or study any sort of wildlife in Sierra Leone, it would have to be in the Loma Mountains.

I left Sierra Leone in the mid 1990s and returned in 2005 to commence research for my doctoral dissertation in biology. My research was, at the time, going to focus on forest buffalo (*Syncerus caffer nanus*) behaviour, but it proved difficult to manage hours of directly observing animals as a result of prior poaching. So over the course of my time there the focus of my research changed from behavioural to ecological: my new topic is how forest-type bushmeat hunting affected the abundance of the greater ungulate (hoofed animals) community on the Loma Mountains.

To conduct my research I built a camp near where most of you will come out on to the mountain grassland, after 4 hours of a gruelling rainforest hike. Ask your guide and they will show you where it was, if it is not still there. The camp was basic, but we did have solar-based power for charging equipment as well as ham-radio communication with the outside world. Living on the mountain was

It's easy to arrange for a porter at one of the starting points – about Le50,000 a day is the going rate, although you may initially be asked to pay twice that amount, so expect to negotiate. Plan to bring enough provisions to feed your porters a full three meals a day. (You can try asking them to bring their own food along with them, but recent experiences and reader feedback have proven that you'll likely end up feeding them anyway.) It's a good idea for everyone in the party to bring high-energy snacks. Whatever you decide, negotiate with the guides and the chief

peaceful, and truly the only place on earth where I have been that I have not heard or seen any other people, other than my assistants, for months on end.

During my research on Loma, I learned the mountain and its terrain like a well-loved poem that can be recited by heart. Every ridge, every valley and every boulder became etched in my memory, so much so that when the authors of this book sent me a picture, I not only knew where the picture was taken, I knew what was behind this picture and what was on the periphery that the lens did not capture. Yet even with such an intimate knowledge of Loma, I saw new things every day I was there.

I am sure that for you, the first time visitor, it will be the same. Never think you have seen it all, and never think it has not been seen. The first time I thought I was the first to enter a valley, I came across a hunting camp; the second time I thought this I looked down and saw a piece of metal that, after digging it out of the ground, was identified as a deeply weathered (but still recognisable) spearhead. Spears have not been used in Sierra Leone for more than a hundred years, not since before Sierra Leone was drawn on a map.

BUSHMEAT THREAT After returning to the country in 2005, searching nationwide for potential research sites and not having much luck finding buffalo elsewhere, I returned to Loma, knowing that I would at least have a decent chance in its remote ridges and valleys. I found buffalo, but I found also that the proliferation of small arms during Sierra Leone's civil war, and people's ever increasing need for alternate sources of income, had penetrated far into the Loma Mountains. Not only buffalo, but all wildlife had taken a big hit.

However, Loma was still the beautiful, serene, daunting, majestic and unbelievably unique place I remembered. It is still the most beautiful place I have seen in all my travels, and indeed a place all Sierra Leoneans should treasure as part of their heritage.

I immediately started working with local chiefs and governmental authorities to create awareness of the effects of over-hunting and highlight the potential the Loma Mountains has as a tourism destination if its wildlife and forest remain intact. The chiefs were receptive and soon began talking among themselves about how to self-police the area to block bushmeat traders. The bushmeat hunters, unlike traditional hunters, kill whatever they come across; nothing is taboo, as everything fetches money for them.

Only time will tell if the 'seeds of conservation' planted during my research will sprout and flourish. I strongly believe that all people travelling to these mountains have a role to play in Loma's protection, and this can be done by continuing to instil in the peoples surrounding these mountains the sense of what a unique and precious place they have. A much more direct way of protection is asking your guide/s not to carry a gun and telling them why you don't want this.

with extreme patience – they have their own way of doings things and are not geared up for slick customer service.

In fact, rather than porters looking after their wards, climbers frequently take on the task of looking after the porters. Many forget food, warm clothes, water and, sometimes, the route; some don't like carrying things. Check all this before you set off, and make sure that either you or they have at least a couple of meals' worth of rice or cooked food, and plenty of water and water bottles.

Peak moment Whichever way you go up, the top is the top. Stumbling on to the exposed plateau, the wind buffets, the near-sheer drops enthral and the view, on a clear day, is breathtaking.

A pile of small stones, assembled into a kind of pyramid, is your legacy. Adding to the waist-high pile with a rock of your own forms your tribute to the mountain, and your achievement in climbing it. Hidden deep between the rocks may well be a weather-beaten plastic bag with a couple of decidedly dog-eared exercise books in it. That's the official visitors' book – if you can't find any older entries, it's because some rogues inexplicably made off with the previous ones in 2014. Don't forget to take a swig of something rousing.

A little way off from the rock pile is a small rock circle, the site for the still-practised sacrifices that villagers claim will appease the mountain spirits and keep visitors and locals safe. Others pray to Mecca. To the east of the peak is a jungle-shrouded waterfall worth seeking out with a guide who knows the mountain well – you'll have to fight your way through the undergrowth. Don't go on your own.

What to take

Kit For nights, a lightweight tent is good, although many prefer a hammock strung up under a waterproof, mosquito-proof covering. Bring a lightweight sleeping bag. Bank on at least three litres of water a day per person – an absolute minimum. There's plenty of water lower down the mountain, so containers and purifiers (tablets, iodine or a filter) are essential, along with enough bottled water to get you through the first day (remember that chlorine doesn't kill giardia). Streams higher up the mountain sometimes dry up in the dry season. Guides rarely have water containers, so bring some for them too and make sure that someone in your party has a big pot to cook in.

Many people prefer back-carried bladders, such as a CamelBak or Platypus, which cut down on water-bottle stops and allow you to drink little and often. To avoid a stitch, take small sips rather than gulps, and warm the water up in your mouth before swallowing. Some people find walking sticks soften the climb – bring your own or cut one of your own.

A first-aid kit, weatherproof matches and lighter, as well as blister treatment, are all sensible. Likewise a head torch. Binoculars are a must if you hope to approach the sharp eyes of your guides when they ferret out a bird, a buffalo or a baboon in the camouflaged distance. Plenty of mosquito spray is also a necessity. There is no mobile-phone reception; if you're lucky enough to have a satellite phone, take it. If something goes wrong it's a long way down.

Clothes Walking boots and a couple of pairs of socks are the best footwear option. Wear long trousers – despite the heat, covered legs will minimise the discomfort of the biting insects and scratching leaves that easily draw blood. Similarly, threading your way through tall, razor-sharp grasses means you'll be glad of some lightweight full-length sleeves on top too. The top of Mount Bintumani is exposed to fairly strong, chilly winds, and the whole area is prone to rainfall during the wet season, so pack a waterproof or wind breaker. It's cold in December, for example.

Food A hot meal is all very well, but stuff as many sugary snacks – sweets, chocolates, energy bars – into your pockets as you can. For evening meals, your guides can readily make a fire to boil hot water for sweet tea, soup, pasta and other carbohydrates – pot noodles are easy. Spare propane/butane gas cylinders for stoves are hard to come by.

Route 1: Sokurala: climbing from the east Not only is this the shortest route – some can get to the top and back to the village in the foothills in a day – it's also the only route where you have the peak in view from the outset and for a great deal of the rest of the climb too. While you're likely to see much less in the way of wildlife, it's still worth keeping your eyes peeled for chimps and monkeys, while the ever-changing array of woodland, forest, high passes above the treeline and rock-like scrambles is stunning.

Getting there and away Sokurala (◈ *9.2124, -11.0531*), at the foot of the mountain, is a small village reachable only by foot. The nearest village is Sangbania (◈ *9.1920,-11.0138*), 6km away, and 8km west of the road running north from the Makeni–Koidu Highway to Kurubonla.

From Freetown, it's most of a day's driving in a **4x4** to get there. If you're taking **public transport**, start very early from Freetown and you may also be able to get there in a (long) day. Head north to Makeni and then east towards Koidu on the newly surfaced highway. Finding the turning to Kurubonla from the Makeni–Koidu Highway can be tricky: it's at Bambakuna junction, better known as Mambodu checkpoint (◈ *8.6483,-11.1888*) which has a petrol station on it, 130km after Makeni and about 30km before Koidu. Look out for signposts to the mining companies SLDC (Sierra Leone Diamond Corporation) and Milestone at the turning, plus a tall cellular mast on the right.

It's easiest to find the route by asking for well-known towns on the way to Kurubonla (◈ *9.19509,-10.94854*) – Wadala (◈ *8.71647,-11.22912*), a market town that comes to life on a Friday, Kayima (◈ *8.88746,-11.15920*) and Mansofenia (◈ *9.07991,-11.03609*) (the last big town before Kurubonla). From the Makeni–Koidu Highway, it's about 5 or 6 hours on the 79km stretch towards Kurubonla, with several river crossings From Mambodu checkpoint/ Bambakuna junction, head north for Bendu, 5km away, and, keeping left, on to Bongema, another 7km, and later Wadala. Follow the road as it bends right for Mboama, 6km further on, then another 7km to Bendewa and 9km further to Kayima, about 1½ hours from the Makeni–Koidu Highway. From Kayima it's a good half-hour 12km stretch to Worodu, a small town with a police checkpoint. On your way out of town, take the road bending left at the fork (the right fork heads for the Tingi Hills), past Feckiah (say that one out loud for a laugh) 7km later, then Fandaa, another 11km further on. The last main town is Mansofenia, 2km further up.

If you're coming from Koidu, the most direct route branches north from the Makeni–Koidu Highway just west of town at Motema (◈ *8.61055,-11.01872*), first passing through Yengema after 3km and reaching the Bafi River at Yomadu (◈ *8.7439,-11.1047*) after another 19km. (There's a parallel road also leading to Yomadu from Bumpe junction (◈ *8.61028,-11.07992*); the Motema road seems larger, but double-check conditions locally.) Bear right to continue north out of Yomadu, and you will join the route explained above (from Mambodu checkpoint) after another 23km, just south of Kayima.

Once you pass Mansofenia, a big market town along a long strip of main road, continue north for 13km, about 40 minutes on bad roads. If you get to Kurubonla you have gone too far, but you can ask the chief permission to stay there for the night and plan and equip your mountain climb there by sourcing some of your porters and offering money to the chief. If you go via Kurubonla, there is a 'tradition' that you pay the town chief and section chief Le20,000 each, so that they can pray for your safe return from the mountain.

Heading straight for Sangbania saves time, but is also more difficult. On the road from Mansofenia to Kurubonla take a left turn shrouded in tall grasses at the village of Kumbaforia (⊕ *9.15560,–10.96023*), just before a deep, wide river about two villages before Kurubonla, 13km north of Mansofenia. Start asking for Kumbaforia as soon as you get to Mansofenia. Follow that road for a further 9km – over a log bridge and a village – until you hit Sangbania. The dirt road is hairy at times, with several river crossings on the way, including an improbably rickety log bridge that should be able to take a 4x4, although it has previously collapsed (test it first). At Sangbania, you'll have to ditch the vehicle to set out on a speedy 1-hour hike to Sokurala, the mud-hut village at the foot of the mountain. Ask the chief if you can park your car or motorbike at Sangbania for the duration of your hike up 'the big hill'. You can also ask him if you can stay the night in your tents, or if he has a room for the night, or whether, if you're a large group, he can make the school compound available. This is also a good spot to pick up some of your porters. The trick is to share the wealth – you'll need a guide from Sokurala, but try to take porters from both Sokurala and Sangbania to avoid a diplomatic incident and keep all the villages friendly (with each other, as well as with you). If you're lucky, Sangbania might send you away with some hot, sweet coco yam to sustain you.

If you don't have your own vehicle, head for Koidu and then arrange a **motorbike** all the way up to Sangbania, or a combination of first **taxis** then a motorbike. A taxi won't make the road beyond about Wadala: this is also the last place to reliably find motorbike transport any further. Alternatively, hire a 4x4 and driver in Freetown if you don't have your own wheels, or ask around in Koidu.

Sokurala Sokurala is a small place with about 250 people, most of whom tend their fields by day, leaving the village a little ghostlike during the daylight hours. If you want to find porters or guides it's best to wait until the evening once everyone is back in town, or else send someone from Sangbania ahead to let people in Sokurala know you are coming the next morning. Such is its remoteness that it doesn't have a well or much in the way of vegetables. All water is fetched from a stream, and villagers frequently tuck into plain rice with nothing but some hot chilli for flavour. Featherless chickens patter aimlessly about, women make fishing nets and there is a tiny mosque – it's the building in the centre of town without a veranda, while the chief's house was until not so long ago the only dwelling with a tin roof, befitting his regal status. Rice goes for about a third of what you'd pay in Freetown here; chickens come cheap as well.

The town chief, Bangali Marah, who doesn't speak English or Krio really, loves the mountain like it's his own. He has sent his children to be educated elsewhere, but he's not budging for anyone. 'The most important thing in staying here is for this mountain,' he says, with great pride over his stewardship. He commissions villagers to keep the paths clear, and believes in knowing its terrain by foot. As he says: 'It's very impossible to take the vehicle on your head up the mountain.' Marah also knows that tourism might just help the area out. 'If you love this mountain please try to know our difficulties,' he says.

Occasionally he likes to guide people himself, but the youth chairman Sundu Marah, who isn't looking too youthful himself, is the more likely bet. He usually undertakes route clearing at least part of the way. There is a tradition that you pay the guide or chief as soon as you have descended from the peak, by the rocks. You can pay the porters on leaving the village to go home.

Sample itinerary
Day 1 Travel from Freetown to Sangbania, off the Koidu–Kurubonla road

Day 2 Walk to Sokurala, the village at the foot of the mountain, and get climbing; camp on the mountain

Day 3 Scale the peak in the morning and descend to Sangbania

Day 4 Back to Freetown

The route You could get up to the top and down again in one day if you are prepared to push yourself, but there's no need. Much better to take time over the flowered swamps, river crossings, tall grasses, steep earth tracks, shaded fragrant woodlands, perky petals in yellow, purple and red, as well as rock boulders reminiscent of giant stone rabbit droppings. On the flattish hike from Sangbania to Sokurala, look out for the extremely low standards of scarecrow.

There are no fixed facilities on this side of the mountain, but various resting points have earned themselves monikers as Camps One, Two, Three and Four. The first section of the hike, up to Camp One, in a wooded area, is by far the hardest part as it's steep and tends to be taken at a fast pace. Still, it only takes about an hour, and you will still have Chief Marah's words ringing in your ears: 'Whosoever can make Camp One can make the mountain.'

Camp Two is a bunch of rocks with a glorious vantage point of the peak, just as you emerge from the forest at the upper edge of the treeline, into a landscape resembling the Scottish Highlands. You can camp just after Camp Two at the edge of the treeline, or in an exposed clearing by rocks at the bottom of the final peak, known as Camp Three, about an hour away. There's no stream here, however, so fill up just after Camp Two. At Camp Three, leave all your bags at the rocks and take only sweets, water, and something a little stronger for the 45-minute early-morning scramble up to the summit, finding a navigable route through the rocks and clutching hold of clumps of grass to steady yourself as you go. Then it's back down to the village in time for lunch and on to Sangbania. From here you can either stay the night in Sangbania and get back to Freetown the next day, start the drive back and ask for a place to stay for the night at whatever village you reach on the way back to the highway (like Mansofenia), or reward yourself with a more luxurious night in Koidu or Makeni, should you get off the mountain early enough and feel so inspired.

Route 2: Sinekoro: climbing from the north
This route probably offers the best combination of some serious sub-canopy forest trekking – barely on offer if you climb from Sokurala to the east – and minimal time. Unlike the Sokurala ascent, it involves arriving from Kabala in the north. Like Yfin (pages 334–5), it also includes a night stop at Aaron Kortenhoven's old camp, which has latrines, shaded areas and a spring – all of which count as luxury on this hill. Note that the camps mentioned in these two routes are different from the camps mentioned in the east route from Sokurala.

Getting there and away From Freetown, head north to Kabala. From Kabala you really need your own vehicle, unless you're prepared to bump away on the back of a **motorbike taxi** (which is Le120,000 to Sinekoro, and more in the rains). On four wheels, you can try to pick up a **4x4** in Kabala – among others, the folks at Kabala Hill View (page 315) or Joseph Jawara (m 076 936 007) can introduce you to a driver with whom you can negotiate a price to Sinekoro.

From Kabala head out east, past Yogomaia, towards Koinadugu (⊕ 9.53702,–11.36932) on the road to Firawa (⊕ 9.3586,–11.3015). Ask for plenty of directions

PORT LOKO'S MOST FAMOUS SON

A national hero who embodies defiance of colonial mastery and bravery in battle, Bai Bureh is like Robin Hood and the Trojan prince Hector rolled into one. Born in 1840, the son of a local Loko war chief and a Temne mother, he ruled over the Kingdom of Kasse, not far from Port Loko. Not only did his status demand a wonderfully eccentric escort – his wife carried his sword on her head, accompanied by a fiddler and a palm-wine jug carrier – he could also appear as an elderly woman or an animal, walk among the people unseen, or live unscathed underwater.

Despite being known for his skills as a warrior (he was nicknamed Kebalai – 'one who never tires of war'), he was a political force too, and was among six Temne signatories who begged the British authorities to let them run their own affairs – 'both all the big palavers and all the small ones' – in December 1896. The letter, full of politeness and not a hint of a threat, got them nowhere. Instead the British went on to impose a house tax to raise funds to patrol and administer their colonial expansion to the rest of the protectorate in 1898, utterly disavowing the hopes of many local rulers. Having flirted with diplomacy, Bai Bureh got tough.

Leading the Hut Tax War of 1898 in the north, first he fought in the open, but then – outnumbered and learning fast – switched to guerrilla tactics, hiding his men in the bush that lined the sides of the roads, digging protective stockades in dips in the ground, and firing from trenches concealed with palm stems.

As Governor Cardew raised the ransom on Bureh's head from £20 to £50 and then £100 as he continued to evade capture, Bureh nimbly fought back with a reward of his own, offering £500 for Cardew's own head. But unlike the Mende of the south, who embarked on a full-scale purge of whites and Krios, he made sure he avoided attacks on missionaries or traders.

Despite significant early successes, the resistance couldn't last and after ten months, with his men surrounded and hungry, he finally gave himself up in November 1898. Considered too popular to execute, he was instead deported to Ghana, although once things had settled down he returned to his homeland – and his chieftaincy – in 1905, dying in 1908.

His legacy lives on, however, and Bai Bureh's likeness has graced the Le1,000 note since 1994, but oddly enough it's just that – his likeness. Because it was believed that Bai Bureh had never been photographed, the portrait on the bill is based not on Bureh himself, but modelled after a rather imaginative statue of Bureh made in 1963. Fifty years later in 2013, a former Peace Corps volunteer in Sierra Leone encountered, bought, and donated a previously unknown photo of Bai Bureh, which was taken after his capture in 1898. Both the photo and the statue are now on display in the National Museum in Freetown, but there's no word yet on when the Le1,000 note might sport a more faithful rendition of this hero of the north.

in town before setting off. The rough but scenic route winds through dense forest, broken by farmers' fields and villages of mud huts with thatched roofs. Be prepared to do a lot of waving. Children in particular seem to take a lot of excitement from a passing vehicle, often running after it yelling greetings.

In the dry season, from January until about the end of May, you should be able to drive all the way to Sinekoro in a 4x4. In the wet season, however, you can probably get your vehicle only as far as the village of Momoria Badela (◈ *9.32435,–11.24632*) about 4 hours from Kabala, since the Bagbe River, 2km beyond Momoria Badela, is a furious flooder during the rains. Long spanned by only a traditional 'hammock bridge' – a pedestrian crossing woven out of liana vines that's equal parts ingenious and unnerving – the Bagbe's two shores look set to be connected by a modern bridge in the next few years, thanks to the advocacy of former finance minister (and potential 2018 APC presidential candidate) Kaifala Marah and the Bridging Bintumani Community (◗f *bintumanibridge*), who have been agitating for the project for years. If crossing the Bagbe on foot, it's 8km to Banda Karafaia (◈ *9.2697,–11.1919*) and a further 5km to Sinekoro (◈ *9.23034,–11.19699*), a 3–4-hour walk in total.

Sinekoro Literally at the end of the road, Sinekoro is a picturesque village set against a backdrop of lush jungle. Hills loom in the distance and streams and rivers flow nearby. Residents are friendly and happy to host you for the night (you should compensate them for this), or you can pitch your tent somewhere out of the way. As ever, offer gifts such as tea, sugar and canned meat and potentially money to the chief. Ask him about accommodation and tell him you would like to hike Bintumani and he will assign porters and guides to help you. You will need to negotiate the price slightly. There was a rudimentary guesthouse under construction here in 2017.

Because Sinekoro is the town most used to climbers, the 'fees' here tend to be a little higher. Some groups have paid as much as Le260,000 for the privilege of scaling the mountain, apparently subsidising local landowners and the good of the Tonkolili district in general. You might even get a receipt, and at least you can't claim that the funds are lining the pockets of officials in Freetown rather than going to local people. See Andrew McFarlane's excellent 2016 trip report from Sinekoro here: w expatfamilyfortunes.com/2016/11/20/climbing-mount-bintumani.

Sample itinerary
Day 1 Travel from Freetown to Kabala, and on to Sinekoro

Day 2 Hike to Camp Two

Day 3 Scale the peak and go back down to Sinekoro

Day 4 Back to Kabala (and possibly on to Freetown if you start early)

Day 5 Back to Freetown

Note: If you park at Momoria Badela, however, add an extra day of walking.

The route Setting out from the village, the path winds through a flat, forested area broken up by various banana and palm plantations and farmers' fields. It passes through a shallow river, where you should consider halting for a quick, refreshing dip on a hot day. A small clearing by the river constitutes Camp One, which is a good spot to bed down for the night if you started off from Sinekoro late in the day. From here, the path begins to climb, reaching a gently sloping grassy area. It then plunges into thick, ancient forest and the climb begins in earnest. After 4 or 5 hours of steep, sticky ascent the forest breaks suddenly and opens up into a lush, grassy plateau. Directly across the plateau is Camp Two, Aaron Kortenhoven's old research station, and there are some stunning views: adequate recompense for a remorseless uphill yomp that sees you shift from 365m to 1,370m. The forest has had little logging or poaching penetrate its higher reaches and slashing through the dense forest with a machete can be incredibly disorienting and even the guides sometimes get lost.

At Aaron's old camp, where transect lines go up through the jungle to allow researchers to divide up and count the wildlife, fresh-tasting spring water runs down the mountain. Monkey calls and chimp chatter are likely to be your company for the evening at the location high above the treeline on the edge of a stream. Here you are high enough to miss out on the rainclouds and storms below you, giving a guaranteed, pin-sharp view of the stars above.

The next day's 600m climb to the top is a joy, with a scramble through long grass and rambles through gently rolling countryside with craggy outcrops. Look out for antelope and buffalo on the way. After 2½ hours or so, the route steepens to hit the peak.

Route 3: Yfin: climbing from the west
This route is the longest way up, although the starting point is the nearest of the three to Freetown. If you're not an enthusiastic walker the uphill stretches are seriously draining; for the keen, however, this offers a few days of contour-crossing, dense jungle walking at its relentless best. Discounting transport (a day each way), you can do the trek in 3½ days, but most prefer four or five. Certainly, whenever hikers have squeezed their trip into anything less than that, they always end up wishing they'd gone a little slower, and not found the whole thing quite so agonising.

Getting there and away From Freetown, head north for Makeni. From there, there are two ways to Yfin (✦ 9.1200,-11.2713), and road conditions can change – what worked last year may be no-go this season depending on the ferocity of the rains, so check first.

At the time of writing, the more popular route is the one that goes north out of Makeni but branches right at Makakura (8km south of Kabala; ✦ 9.52133,-11.58088). From there it's a southeasterly, mud-filled wiggle through Kondembaia (✦ 9.3831,-11.5649) and Alikalia (✦ 9.1535,-11.3874), among others, for 75km. From the turn-off at Makakura, it should take you 3½–4 hours to reach Yfin in a **4x4**. Note that as of 2017 there are plans to tar the entire Makakura–Yfin route, so ask about progress in Kabala or Makeni.

The alternate route runs from Makeni via Binkolo, 10km north towards Kabala (✦ 8.95384,-11.97777), then northeast on graded dirt to Bumbuna (75km from Yfin; ✦ 9.0439,-11.7475) and finally east on a poorly maintained route all the way past Bendugu (✦ 9.0630,-11.4894) and Alikalia, about 16km before Yfin. It's likely to take about 6 hours.

Yfin At Yfin Town, the chief – with an MBE and a proud strip of medals for his efforts in the West African Rifles back in World War II – is well used to groups of climbers tramping through, and can supply guides and porters. Bring gifts such as soap and sugar, as well as a readiness to offer money too. He can also arrange accommodation in a local hut or house if you need a place to stay before starting the climb (pay a donation). The most insightful person to speak to in town is the local school's headmaster, however, whose dedication to his hometown, along with years spent abroad, make him absorbing, inspiring company. He can round up porters and guides, as well as help with negotiating a price – any help visitors can provide with school materials in return is gratefully appreciated.

Sample itinerary
Day 1 Travel from Freetown and stay the night in Yfin

Day 2 An easy 9km walk along rolling paths through villages; stay the night in a school in Konbaia, a good place to find a guide for the summit (and proposed site for the national park HQ)

Day 3 7 to 8 hours' walking from Konbaia to Camp Two, the campsite below the summit, up a gradually ascending trail through the rainforest

Day 4 3 hours' walk to the summit then back down to Camp Two (you could push this and get right back down to Camp One, although most walkers who've done so say they would prefer not to)

Day 5 Walk from Camp Two down to Konbaia; some walk straight back to Yfin

Day 6 Walk 2 hours to Yfin and travel back to Freetown

The route One of the most exciting parts of this route comes on the first day. After passing through several villages, a hammock bridge made from intricately woven liana vines spans a narrow gorge and thrusts you into the forest that carpets the base of Mount Bintumani. Anyone with a fear of heights will find crossing it a fairly high-octane experience – just try not to think of *Indiana Jones and the Temple of Doom*. Just after the rains, the bridge is, literally, at its most ropey.

The walk ducks through lowland evergreen forest, savannah and montane forest-grasslands. If you carry on past Konbaia, the trail will take you all the way to Sinekoro – an 11km journey (20km from Yfin) that should take you about 5 hours from Yfin on foot. From Sinekoro, the route is the same as the one described on pages 331–4, in the *Sinekoro* section.

THE NORTHWEST

PORT LOKO Worn down and scattered, Port Loko is more of a place to pass through than rest up. But it wasn't always that way: it was once the site of fierce fighting between the palm oil and camwood-trading Loko people, who gave their name to the town, and Temne warriors in the 1850s. So large was the Temne army that their camp was reputed to have been bigger than Freetown, and the war lasted ten years, until a final horrific battle that lasted a night and a day saw the Lokos routed and, finally, massacred at the hands of the Temne as they fled.

Skirmishes between the Loko and Temne had endured for many years before that. In the annals of oral history, the man reputed to have 'taught people the art of war' and introduced the first guns into the country, the Temne warrior Bai Farma, had also totalled Loko trading settlements.

More practically, Port Loko is also the turn-off for getting to Lungi airport by road (fuel is available from Total), and taxis or poda podas connect from here to Lungi, Pepel and Tagrin, as well as Kambia, Makeni, and of course Freetown. Should you want to stick around, the reliable **MJ Motel** (m *078 358 962, 076 660 611;* e *mjmotelportloko@mjmotelsl.com;* w *mjmotelsl.com;* **$$$–$$**) chain has a location here with good air-conditioned rooms and a restaurant/bar.

KAMBIA This town is worth a lot more than a quick stopover on a journey to or from the Guinean border, 8km away. If you're travelling overland and it's your first taste of the country, then slow down and don't rush on to the capital. It's the perfect spot to unwind for a day or two – 'In this place you forget about all the Freetown

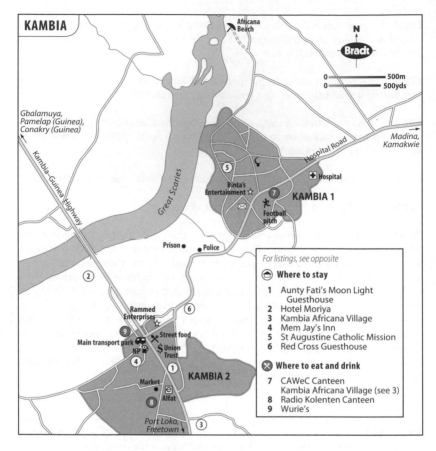

For listings, see opposite

🛏 **Where to stay**
1 Aunty Fati's Moon Light Guesthouse
2 Hotel Moriya
3 Kambia Africana Village
4 Mem Jay's Inn
5 St Augustine Catholic Mission
6 Red Cross Guesthouse

✖ **Where to eat and drink**
7 CAWeC Canteen
  Kambia Africana Village (see 3)
8 Radio Kolenten Canteen
9 Wurie's

wahala (troubles),' said one happy visitor. It's also a model of what well-organised, small-scale rural tourism could feel like in Sierra Leone.

Shiny motorbike taxis spin around the streets, and thatched roofs top many of the mud-brick homes. Charcoal, palm oil and spare parts are sold along the roadside, next to women making soap, while the sparkling new bank (still with no ATM, though) gleams opposite them.

The town itself is today split in two: the old town, set back from the Sierra Leone–Guinea Highway in a higgledy-piggledy span of streets, is now called Kambia 1, to the northeast. The 'gentrification' is happening at Kambia 2, alongside the main drag heading to the border and further west of it, as new mud-brick builds hurriedly go up. The old town is still home to many sad wrecks of houses burnt out during the war: sometimes all that remains are the once-lofty concrete columns and decorative balustrades, a sign of chiefly and trading affluence long gone. Today the newly surfaced streets are graced by worn and weary NGO and UN signboards, part of the post-war, and now post-Ebola, reconstruction effort Kambia sorely needs but in many ways remains stubbornly out of reach.

The local football team plays every evening at about 17.30 opposite the red-and-white-painted APC compound. In the rainy season, canoes fill up with fresh shrimp by the bridge, well worth a look.

Getting there and away From Freetown, Kambia is more than 170km away, a journey that takes about 2½ hours in any vehicle, thanks to a fine stretch of EU-funded tarmac beyond Masiaka. **Public transport** can take 4 or 5 hours.

At the Masiaka junction take the second exit, towards Port Loko, then after Rogbere Bridge, at Rogbere junction 20 minutes later, take the second exit signposted to Conakry. At this stage, keep an eye out for the railway/ tracks along one side of the road – that's the 200km iron ore railway, connecting the Tonkolili mine to the coast at Pepel. The Mange Bridge over the Little Scarcies River, 42km on from Rogbere junction, makes for a nice photo stop.

The road passes through the small town of Bamoi, 18km after the bridge, which has a huge *luma* (market) every Sunday. People start turning up from the Friday before, bringing kola nuts from Kailahun in the east, as well as palm oil and rice, while trucks from Guinea arrive loaded with cloth, tomatoes and groundnut oil.

The government bus connects to Kambia daily for Le18,000. (The twice-weekly Freetown–Conakry bus does not stop at Kambia.) A seat from the east of Freetown costs Le30,000 in a shared taxi. From Kambia, vehicles leave from the transport park, sat near the police checkpoint in Kambia 2 on the main drag, just behind a petrol station. There are a handful of departures every day, but people start arriving from 05.30, so turn up early if you want to be sure of a seat for the morning departure.

From Kambia to Guinea, it's Le5,000 by poda poda or **motorbike taxi** to Pamelap, just on the other side of the border. It costs Le70,000 from Kambia to Conakry, about 3 or 4 hours away; it's easier and cheaper (45,000 Guinean francs) to find Conakry-bound cars in Pamelap. Other destinations include the market at Bamoi (Le3,000 for the 10km trip); Rokupr (Le6,000 for 19km); and Madina junction (40km to the northeast for Le20,000). Changing vehicles in Madina junction, it's also possible to continue to Kamakwie (for Outamba-Kilimi National Park), 107km away on bad dirt roads, but transport is very infrequent on all stages of this route.

Getting around As well as the transport park, there are many **motorbike taxis** around town, parked opposite the police checkpoint, as well as in Kambia 1. A single ride costs Le2,000, or you can negotiate for an hourly rate – anything from Le10,000 to Le20,000 an hour is decent. AbdualiSamba Jalloh (m 076 803 532), with his fancy shoes and shiny shirts, comes tried and tested.

🏠 Where to stay   *Map, opposite*

🏠 **Hotel Moriya** (25 rooms) m 030 414 105, 076 210 113; e kebefodaymaligie@yahoo.com. Opened in 2013 & set in a green & flowery riverside compound with a few good views of the bridge, this is the newest & sharpest hotel in town. Fan rooms are a bit dark & cramped compared with those with AC, but all are tiled & businesslike, & there's an outdoor restaurant (**$$**) with a nice breezy terrace. The generator runs from 19.00 to 07.00, & Wi-Fi is supposedly on the way. **$$$**

🏠 **Kambia Africana Village** (11 chalets, 6 suites, 28 rooms) Sierra Leone–Guinea Highway, at the entry to Kambia 2 (on the right if you're coming from Freetown); m 076 654 798, 076 626 144, 030 409 990; e ibnjai2002@gmail.com. Easily the best place in town, making a few days' stay

an absolute pleasure. Started by ex-town planner, politician & eco-stove manufacturer Ibrahim Njai to make sure he'd have an income 'in my old age when I'm not able to hustle', it is full of tender loving care – rows of acacia trees, flowering plants, pretty little chalets with gara tie-dye sheets, wall hangings, ceilings made of locally produced palm-frond challa mats, & spic-&-span en-suite European bathrooms. The thatched *rogbaneh* (Temne for 'gathering place') bar is a great chill-out spot towards the back, or you can opt for either the 'beer garden' or 'the nest', with colourful umbrellas up front. The main restaurant (**$$$**) & bar area, in deep maroon & cream, has great local food (order early) & a peaceful atmosphere. 24/7 security on site, electricity guaranteed 19.00–07.00, & paid

Wi-Fi with a portable modem at Le30,000/day. Generous discount for Sierra Leone nationals. AC rooms $$$, fan rooms $$

🏠 **St Augustine Catholic Mission** (8 rooms) m 079 317 951. In a pretty compound in Kambia 1, the rooms here are clean & en suite, though they're typically only for volunteers & other church functionaries. They may well accommodate you if there's room, though, so long as you ring up & ask in advance. Generator power in the evenings. $$

🏠 **Aunty Fati's Moon Light Guesthouse** (9 rooms, 6 self-contained) Kambia–Guinea Highway, Kambia 2; m 079 220 229, 076 945 730. Set in a courtyard along the main road, the most basic of Kambia's offerings still has a touch of charm. Unlike other budget options staff can rustle up African dishes if ordered well in advance, & Aunty Fati is as friendly a host as you're likely to find anywhere. Most rooms are en suite, with nets, fans, European loos & bucket showers. Watch out for the lurid design decisions – red walls, blue lights & a roaring nightclub attached – best to avoid

this place if you want peace & quiet, especially on weekends. Generator power 20.00–late. $

🏠 **Mem Jay's Inn** (5 rooms) Yard 25, off the main highway at the road with the 'The Door Christian Fellowship Church' sign, Kambia 2; m 077 719 328. A little unmarked guesthouse named after owner Memouna Jalloh & once upon a time Kambia's best. It tries hard – look for the hopeful, wall-filling picture of a huge gracious lobby in their own tiny seating area. Set in a dusty, workaday compound, rooms here are basic, but undeniably cheap. Most are en suite with bucket showers, as well as gara sheets & mosquito nets. No food. $

🏠 **Red Cross Guesthouse** (5 rooms) m 076 839 468, 076 845 701 (Lamine), 076 818 405. Part of the Red Cross compound, you're likely as not to see babies being weighed in the complex, along with various other nursing duties. It's basic but decent enough, with nets & bucket showers; it was being fully refurbished in 2017, after which all rooms will be self-contained. Electricity 20.00–01.00. $

✖ Where to eat and drink *Map, page 336*

Kambia Africana Village is the most salubrious spot in town, but order well ahead for African dishes including rice and plassas, grilled chicken and chips or try millet 'pap' porridge with plenty of sugar for breakfast. Further on in Kambia 2, by the police checkpoint, there's **street food** – meat sticks and attieke mostly – while the **Radio Kolenten Canteen** also does daytime rice and plassas lunches. Hidden behind the taxi park (make a right at the Africell kiosk just after entering the park from the main roundabout) is a small row of chop shops and *ataya bases* (tea houses), with **Wurie's** probably the best among them, dishing up fried potato and pasta creations every evening.

In the old town, the most reliable bet is the **CAWeC Canteen** (*Hospital Rd;* m *076 472 999, 030 401 444;* ⏱ *08.00–22.00 daily;* $$) upstairs at the back of the Community Action for the Welfare of Children compound, which serves up rice and pasta basics with a variety of sauces, as well as omelettes and the like. Meals are a touch expensive for what they are, but it's for a good cause and there's cold beer and football on the flatscreens in the evenings.

Entertainment and nightlife In Kambia 1, **Binta's Entertainment** is your best bet for boozing and a bit of dancing, while down the hill the curiously named **Rammed Enterprises** serves up imported and local beer at all hours amid thumping music, just shy of the main roundabout. If settling in on a wooden bench and brushing up on your Playstation skills is up your alley, there are a few **video game shacks** on the embankment above the main roundabout that'll give you a shot at the latest FIFA instalment for pennies on the hour.

Other practicalities There's still no ATM in town, so if you're short of money – and border crossings can do that to you – **Union Trust Bank** (*Sierra Leone–Guinea Highway, Kambia 2;* m *030 236 937, 030 236 988;* ⏱ *08.30–15.30 Mon–Fri*) does

Western Union money transfers. Moneychangers hang around in the taxi park and it's easy to change dollars or Guinean francs to Leones here. You can get online at **Alfat Internet Café**, 500m down the road towards Freetown.

There is a government **hospital** on Hospital Road in the old town.

What to see and do

Head for the beach The town might be landlocked, but **Africana Beach**, created by the owner of the Kambia Africana Village, is a lovely spot on the edge of the Kolenten River (also known as the Great Scarcies River) in the Sandamorie neighbourhood to the west of the old town. It was once the main spot for passing into Guinea through the forest, and you can see a concrete slab on the opposite bank where the 'ferry' used to dock. To the right, the river wends its way north, heading into a waterfall after three-quarters of a mile. To the left, it heads back into the old town over a series of rapids that keep the crocodiles out, before broadening into an area as wide and spread out as a lake that's ideal for swimming in. A small sand beach huddles under the shade of wild mango trees and palms at the side of the water; the thatch huts and bamboo benches haven't been maintained since the Ebola crisis for a lack of clientele, but it's still a delightful spot for a picnic and cold beers in the shade. The sun sets behind the forest, casting perfect light across the water and conjuring a stunning early-evening moment; though watch out for the resilient biting black flies. There's no entry fee, and though there aren't currently any bar facilities on site, Africana Village can provide lunch and cool boxes with notice. A dugout canoe with a life jacket costs US$10 per person per hour, and one day there may be kayaks, so you can sample the rapids too. Ask someone at the Africana Village to take or direct you; the caretaker for the place is called Almamy.

Culture, crafts and artisans Woven palm frond *challa* mats, of the sort found on the ceilings of the Kambia Africana Village, are made at Masama village, not far from town. Another village, Mambolo, is also a centre for pottery. Take a motorbike or a taxi, or ask the Africana to arrange a trip for you.

Women sometimes make gara tie-dye cloth at the Red Cross complex, by the guesthouse, so ask to see if you can watch the process and buy some too.

On a tributary of the Kolenten River, north towards Madina, artisanal diamond diggers go to work in the muddy waters. With a guide and suitable delicacy, you can watch them at their alluvial mining site. It's a much less intense experience than seeing alluvial mining amid the frenzy of the eastern diamond centres (pages 263–89), and more welcome for it. Ask at the Africana or speak to a motorbike taxi driver. The Africana can also arrange for you to see dance performances by Susu and Temne groups.

Wildlife Boat- and bird-lovers can take a trip down the Great Scarcies River from Kambia towards Rokupr, near the estuary as it disgorges to the sea on the coast. The 19km ride, in a motorised boat, again organised by the Africana, costs from US$100 to US$200 per trip, including the car ride from the port at Rokupr. Don't forget your binoculars, or your camera. Give the guesthouse two weeks' notice to be sure they can have the boat ready and waiting in the right place; when you reach Rokupr a vehicle can return you to Kambia.

There is also rather apocryphal talk of a chimp colony, about 10km from town, along the road that runs north to Limba country, on the banks of the same river. Stories abound of clever chimps who, after waiting for little children to pick mangoes in the woods, come out and scare them away, leaving the primates to gorge themselves on the mountains of ready-picked booty left behind.

THE BORDER CROSSING From Kambia it's an easy 10-minute drive on a tarmac road to Gbalamuya, 8km away, on the Sierra Leonean side of the Guinean border. The crossing spot is more commonly referred to as **Pamelap**, the first town you reach on the Guinea side, about 200m away and within sight from Sierra Leone. A new EU-funded binational customs and immigration building opened here in 2012.

The offices on either side of the complex are currently open 07.00–18.00 daily. You can buy an entry visa for Sierra Leone, but not for Guinea, on the spot (page 72). Passport formalities usually go off without too much fuss. At the border you will only be given a one-month, single-entry visa, however, so it's much better to come with one in your passport already.

If you have a vehicle, you may be asked for a *laissez passer* they will say should have been issued at the embassy, but if you're travelling in your own private vehicle with a *carnet de passage* that should be sufficient, even though not everyone may be familiar with it (page 78). As with all officials, particularly those in charge of borders, patience and a smile go a long way.

LUNGI You might hope that the capital's airport would at least be in the same region as the capital, but no. Freetown's international airport is here, at Lungi, on the coast in the Northern Province. Mention of the words 'airport' and 'Lungi' in the same sentence tends to elicit huge sighs, so start practising some pre-emptive skyward eyerolls and resigned teeth sucking. Every so often people mention plans to move it, or, in a leap into fantasy, bring up plans to build a bridge across the Sierra Leone River to create a seamless link between capital and airport. Neither is likely any time soon.

The town itself is all mud-brick thatch and quiet, except for the roars overhead. On first impressions, there's very little reason to go to Lungi, unless you are going to the airport, but if you want to base yourself outside Freetown for a few days and explore the virgin coastline, islands and wildlife that stretch up towards Guinea, this place offers good high-end accommodation outside the capital.

Getting there and away See opposite.

Where to stay

Lungi Airport Hotel (44 rooms) Tulun Rd; m 077 787 777, 077 797 777, 076 660 055; e reservation.lungihotel@hotmail.com; fLungiAirportHotel. This overnight airport stop is newly spruced up & really quite swish – AC, satellite TV, swimming pools, tennis court, Wi-Fi, volleyball court, restaurant ($$$$–$$$) & shops, even a casino & tropical gardens. Plus it's only a 2min drive away from the airport (although watch out for prohibitive taxi charges of up to Le50,000). Better yet, it's only 10mins by foot from the beach & a perfect evening sundowner. Watch out for mosquitoes. It tends to fill up, so best to book well ahead if you can. B&B. $$$$$–$$$$

Harmony Hotel (19 rooms) Off Airport Ferry Rd; m 076 329 595; e harmonysierraleone@yahoo.com; w harmonyhotelsl.com. Another option, somewhat further from the airport. All rooms have AC, mosquito nets, & are self-contained. Restaurant on site. $$$$

Alisam Guesthouse (22 rooms) 46 Lungi Ferry Rd; m 078 831 987, 088 721 014; e calimamydixon@yahoo.com. This blood-orange-hued multistorey block is a firm favourite among travellers from Freetown who have to overnight in Lungi without the benefit of an expense account. Management is attentive, & the trim rooms all come with AC, fridge & en-suite facilities. B&B. $$$

Lungi Airport Lodge (3 rooms) 4a Humper St; m 079 601 085; e ghazali@tiscali.co.uk. More a part of the village than any of the above, this

British–Sierra Leonean-run guesthouse feels like a family home, with simple en-suite rooms with hot shower & either fan or AC. The owners used to manage an Afro-Caribbean restaurant in Blackpool, s good meals can definitely be arranged. Advance bookings can also be made through Airbnb. **$$$**

✗ Where to eat and drink All the **hotels** serve food, and the **airport** has a decent café with Sierra Leone's equivalent of pub grub (frankfurters, bacon and egg) downstairs. Once you're in the departure area, **The Coffee Zone** (m 088 828 282; ⨍ *coffeezonesl*) upstairs does coffee (naturally), along with rather pricey shawarmas, burgers and the like, and there's a big television to while away the hours.

Should you have some more time to kill and would rather spend it outside an airport lounge, Lungi is also awash with bars and nightclubs – **Lungi Lounge** (m 077 658 565; ⨍ *Lungi.Lounge*), **De Embassy** (m 078 360 474; ⨍ *deembassyniteclub*), **Transit** (m 076 636 106), and **Sand Bar** (m 076 623 027; ⨍ *sandbarlungi*) are all within a few blocks of the airport.

THE NORTHWEST COAST North of Lungi, the coast is utterly undeveloped and well worth an expedition.

It is home to what are thought to be Sierra Leone's earliest inhabitants – the Bullom speakers along the imaginatively named Bullom Coast, which stretches north from Freetown towards Guinea. All sorts of tales circulated about the Bullom, including a grizzly account published in the English-circulation *Sierra Leone Royal Gazette*, of just how they disposed of their leaders. Not for them the human frailty of natural death, but instead, when their kings seemed likely to pop it, they 'cut their throats, and bury them in secret – sacrificing two human victims, who are buried in the same grave!' wrote one observer in 1826.

Today the area is pretty quiet by comparison, but nonetheless an eye-opener. The wildlife-rich wetlands are a nature enthusiast's dream. Dolphins dancing through the surf are a frequent sight out on the water, endangered sea turtles mate on the empty beaches, and birds swoop in and out of the profusion of creeks and mangrove swamps.

Getting there and away By road, you can skirt round from Freetown via Port Loko, to Lungi, a 4–5-hour trip. Or you could make use of one of the airport ferries to get to Lungi and explore from there. But a **boat** ride up the coast is the best way to travel. Hire a classy launch (try the Aqua Club or Cape Shilling; page 99), or you could travel by local motorised boat, but they are heavy, overloaded and slow in relentless heat without shade for hours at a time. One heads to Freetown from Sunday to Friday, leaving at about noon but depending on the tides, for Le20,000 one-way. From Freetown's Fourah Bay Road, at Water Quay, you can catch a daily boat ride to Yelibuya for Le20,000. Big passenger vessels are not safe: in August 2007, more than 50 people drowned after a boat capsized in heavy rains near the northern border with Guinea.

The ideal compromise is to rent a small local wooden motorboat. It's a more leisurely journey than a speedboat, but you aren't paying through the nose, especially if you can find a few other people to take the trip with you, yet quicker, safer and more comfortable than public transport. The **Conservation Society of Sierra Leone** (*CSSL; 14A King St, Freetown;* m *030 522 579, 076 633 824;* e *cssl_03@ yahoo.com;* w *conservationsocietysl.org*) can recommend suitable boatmen, or you can ask around at Lumley Beach, or Kissy Boat Terminal for a fisherman who looks to have a sturdy boat and a decent price. Wear life jackets.

What to see and do Just north of Lungi, at **Konakridee** lies a fine stretch of white-sand beach. This was the proposed site for a wildly ambitious US$500 million planned city, luxury resort and golf course project (3km inland at **Mape** village), which was scheduled to be built in 2014 but failed to get off the ground. For now and what seems to be the foreseeable future, it's still all yours as far as tourism goes. White sands, a tent and fresh fish are all you need: ask the village chief if you can camp out or whether there's somewhere to stay in the village.

Just a bit further north, **Yurika** village is home to the **Sierra Paradise Resort** (m *077 989 155, 078 939 392;* e *romeoisblack@gmail.com;* w *sierra-paradise.com;* f *Sierra Paradise Resorts; B&B;* **$$$$$**), a charming French–Salonean-owned hideaway with a clutch of five brightly painted en-suite rondavels in a palm-studded compound between the beach and a meandering creek. There's a thatched beach bar, French-inspired seafood menu, and a range of activities on offer, including boating, trekking, fishing and 4x4 excursions. Though it's only 6km from Konakridee as the crow flies, there's no road connection (and a couple of inlets that you'll need a canoe to cross, should you fancy the walk). From Lungi, head 9km along the road to Port Loko and take the left-hand turning at Aku Town, continuing 12km on an earthen road through Mape village and across an old steel bridge now surfaced with logs.

Another option worthy of mention is the **Bathkerot Malambay Guesthouse** (m *076 268 409, 030 027 214*), which sits just outside Mambolo (⊕ *8.9192,-13.0363*), 26km west of the main road that connects Port Loko to Kambia. Owned by Kolleh Bangura, the director of Sierra Leone's National Protected Area Authority, who grew up in Malambay, the guesthouse was due to open in December 2017, with promises of evening electricity and as many as 20 rooms for visitors.

Also on the Little Scarcies, around 10km downstream, **Kychom** (⊕ *8.9289,-13.1425*) is home to at least one rudimentary guesthouse. It's 38km from Kambia on dirt roads, accessible from a left-hand turn-off 200m towards Guinea after the bridge over the Great Scarcies. Either here or Mambolo makes an excellent jumping-off point for tours of the nearby bird- and crocodile-filled marshlands.

Further west, at the estuary of the Kolenten (Great Scarcies) River, is **Kortimaw Island**. To the east, the creek disappears inland, past Kychom, Kassiri and Mambolo, right up to **Rokupr**, the location of a rice research station well situated among the marshy flats. Set up in 1934 to experiment with rice varieties, its became the West African Rice Research Station (WARRS) in 1953 with responsibility for other English-speaking West African countries. It now studies boosting the production not only of rice by experimenting with different grains, but also sorghum, millet, banana and plantain. Boats regularly head up the river as far as Kambia, the district headquarters, for trade, or it's an easy 15km journey on a newly surfaced road.

Travelling by boat, the coast-hugging journey demands constant negotiation with the sucking mud flats, compensated by magnificent sights of pelicans, palm-nut vultures, yellow-billed kites, egrets, reef herons and terns. Even boats used to the trip are regularly marooned, and forced to wait for rising waters to carry them off again.

Almost in Guinea, **Yelibuya Island** (⊕ *8.9510,-13.2601*) seems more like one big fishing net than an island for people who live there. The beach is crammed with action – fishermen dragging in their haul, clambering between brightly painted boats, taking in their makeshift sails, cursing the holes in their nets and then patiently tending to them.

A couple of soldiers are permanently stationed on the island, along with a rickety motor launch, on the lookout for pirates who often come down from Guinea armed with rusting AK47s and blades, and then steal back across the waters. Money to fuel the patrol boats has long been a problem when it comes to catching them, let alone the much bigger foreign boats further off the coast, breaking international maritime laws by infringing the 8km exclusion zone into which only artisanal fishermen are allowed.

The island itself needs a lot of improvements: when we visited it was proud of its rule that there should be no defecation on the beach. There's still no secondary school, but mobile reception should now finally stretch to the island. There's a small primary school and a marketplace of wooden stalls, but no fresh water, since the salt gets everywhere on this shallow stretch of land, even into deep boreholes, so residents have to buy their water at a premium from across the river.

It's not an obvious place to stay the night, but the microcosm of the fishing life that, like Plantain Island, has stayed largely unchanged for centuries is fascinating to behold. If you feel like it, you can ask Chief Bangura Adekalie, delightfully nicknamed Bearbuzzle (you can ask), for somewhere to stay for the night.

Appendix 1

LANGUAGE

KRIO It gets called pidgin English, even broken English, but anyone who thinks of Krio as a simple business is in for a shock. Many of the words are easily recognisable from their English counterparts, but equally the likes of *pikin* (from the Portuguese for child), *yabas* (from the Arabic for onion) or *waala* (from the Hausa for trouble) are a long way from Shakespeare.

The tongue started as a trading language for tens of thousands of freed slaves from all over West Africa, Europeans and other merchants. It evolved from contact with English-speaking sailors and traders in the 1700s, and the post-1787 Creole community of freed slaves who later took it as their own.

If someone is particularly kind to you, you can get away with thinking you're really quite proficient with a few dropped first consonants, a bit of an accent, an *aw di bodi* here and there and a beaming grin. But, officially written and taught in phonetic symbols, complete with diphthongs, tense markers, its own grammatical structure and vocabulary, there's no doubting Krio is a language in its own right.

'The speech of the Sierra Leone streets cannot be called a patois of English,' said the Liberian statesman and pan-Africanist Dr Edward Blyden in a Freetown lecture in 1884. 'It is not the pigeon English of China nor the unintelligible lingo of the West Indies … It is a transfusion, so to say, of numerous African idioms and phrases … the proper designation of the Sierra Leone vernacular would be – *mixture of mixtures, all is mixture* … It has acquired a sacredness of its own. It is the language of the domestic life, of courtship, of marriage, of death, of intensest joy and deepest grief.'

Usage In official settings, English is always best for an opening gambit. In fact, attempting your half-baked Krio with a besuited professional might be seen as quaint, but could also be taken as downright patronising. If you want to change money with the dollar boys, pal up with a street hawker, or chat to a farmer (and even then some will rely much more on older ethnic tongues), then Krio is first choice.

So experiment with carefree abandon, no need to be bashful. You'll get it wrong, but the more you try the more likely you are one day to get it right. For Toma Bakarr and Tom Cairnes, whose quick and easy beginner's guide is a useful first step on the road to learning Krio, the benefits of bothering are clear: 'The taxi driver who once ignored you now talks to you like a friend. The shopkeepers double rather than triple their asking price, and Sierra Leoneans will warm to you much quicker.'

Tense markers Very briefly, if you want to put an action into the past, present or future, break up the verb and stick in a tense marker. For example, *Ah bin go* means I went; *Ah don go* means I have gone; *Ah de go* means I am going; and *Ah go go* means I am going to go or

IF IN DOUBT, MAKE SOME NOISE

It's extraordinary how far a high-pitched 'eee' can get you. Wonderfully emotive, in Salone drama-laden sounds can convey more intensity and feeling than even the most floridly verbose of sentences. Inject a well-chosen note of scepticism and you can probably secure a reduction on your latest hoped-for purchase; a slightly slower, more drawn-out *eh* acts as a show of disbelief – useful whether discussing politics or taxi prices – while a powerfully empathetic *hmmmm*, combined with some head shaking at your interlocutor's tales of misfortune can win you a friend for life. *Osh* or *osh-ya* means sorry.

Another way to show disdain is with the lip-sucking that might accompany a plumber's estimate. Try tutting and breathing in sharply through clenched teeth, leaving your tongue at the roof of the mouth. Add a shake of the head and some narrowed eyes and you'll look thoroughly dissatisfied.

I will go. If you want to get fancy with the pluperfect tense (I had gone), then put the two past markers together – *Ah bin don go*. That's far from the whole story but it's a start.

Old-school English English in Sierra Leone can be deliciously formal, starchy and antiquated (just when you thought you'd never hear the phrase 'nefarious acts' spoken aloud, think again). Whereas someone English might reach for the words 'not much' to describe something they don't do very often, a Sierra Leonean might deliver 'seldom'. Likewise, archaic English makes a showing in many Krio words: *ahmbohg* (from humbug) for disturb; *veks* (from vex) for angry; *lukinglas* (from looking glass) for mirror; *yanda* (from yonder) for over there; *drohz* (from drawers) for underwear; *motoka* (from motor car) for car; *pala* (from parlour) for living room; and *soba* (from sober) for serious.

Sierra Leone's English often has some odd flavours. Do not think someone is about to start a fight with you or jump on the defensive if they come up to you asking, 'What is your problem?' for example. More often it's an attempt to offer assistance.

If you hear a phrase such as 'shweng shweng' or some vaguely oriental-sounding variant, it means people can't understand a word you say. It's a comic phrase that describes the way people in Sierra Leone think foreign languages sound, pretty much a Salone take on 'gobbledegook'.

Basic Krio phrases Spellings of Krio words below follow an attempt at making them easy to say without resorting to the phonetic language in which the language is taught. It should get you on the right track, but listen out for accent and pronunciation on the streets, and practise.

Greetings

hello	*kusheh-o*
hello everybody	*una kusheh-o*
how are you? (Literally, how is the body?)	*aw di bodi?*
how are you sir/madam?	*aw du sa/ma?*
good morning	*mohnin-o*
good morning sir/madam	*mohnin sa/ma*
good morning everybody	*una goodmonin-o*
how's the morning going?	*aw di monin dey go?*
good afternoon	*good aftanun*
good evening	*gud ivnin-o*

| how's the night? | aw dis net? |
| how is the family/wife/work? | aw di fambul den/wehf/wok? |

Responses

I'm fine (the body is fine)	di bodi fine
not bad, how are you?	di bodi nor bad, how usef?
can't complain (Literally, I tell God thank you)	ah tel god tehnki
I'm well, and you?	ah wehl, aw yu sehf?
fine (Literally, the body is in the clothes)	di bodi de na klos
I'm doing fine	well ah de do fine
the afternoon's not bad	di aftanun noh bad

Meeting someone

what's your name?	we yu nem?
my name is ...	ah nem ...
I'm glad to meet you	ah gladi foh mit yu/ah gladi foh sabi yu
I'm very glad to meet you	misehf, ah gladi tumohs foh mit yu
what do you do (for work)?	na wetin yu de du?
see you later	we go si bak

Thanking people

thank you	tenki ya
thank you everybody	una all tenki
say thanks to your people/family for me	tell yu fambul dem tenki for mi
I thank you very much	ah tell yu bohku bohku tenki

Flirting

I bought this ring for you	ah bai dis ring foh yu
that girl is as good looking as my girlfriend	da gal fein lehk me gal
I want you to be my girlfriend	ah go want mehk yu bi mi gal frehn
don't you have a wife?	yu noh get wehf?
I'm not married	ah noh mared
I am married	ah mared
I have a husband/wife	ah get osband/wef
I like/want you	ah lehk yu
I rather like him/her	mi at tek am

Dealing with hassle

please don't waste my time	du yaa noh wes me tehm
everyone has his own troubles	ohlman de pan in you waala
leave me alone	lehf mi
shut your mouth	seht yu mot
don't beg me	leh go mi
go away/get out (very strong, but not quite as rude in the same way as it is in English)	foh kohf
I'm very tired	ah taya baad
my money is finished	mi kohpoh dohn dohn
what makes you want to fight?	wetin mek yu lek foh feht?
I don't have anything	ah noh get natin
there is nothing	natin noh de
leave me alone/don't bug me	slak mi

Money and shopping

how much do you want to pay?	*ow mohs yu wan pe mi?*
how much do I have to pay?	*ohmohs ah get foh pe?*
how much for the …	*ow mohs foh di …*
won't you lower the price for me?	*yu noh go lehs mi?*
can't you give me a price reduction?	*u nor go less mi smol?*
it's too expensive	*ee tu dia*
I will reduce the price	*ah go lehs*
here's your money	*luk yu mohni*
OK it's not bad	*ok ee noh bad*
I'm just looking	*ah jehs de luk round*
can you help me?	*yu kin ehp mi?*
how much does this item cost?	*aw mus for dis tin ya?*
you have to give me change	*u for gi mi change*

Accommodation

how much is a room for the night?	*aw mohs for wan room for net?*
can you do my laundry for me?	*una kin brook for mi?*
I want room service	*ah wan room service*
do you have a taxi service here?	*una get taksi service na ya?*
do you have internet?	*una get internet?*

Eating and drinking

I'm hungry	*angri de kech mi*
it's time to eat	*ee dohn tehm foh it*
can I have the menu please?	*ah kin get di menu pliz?*
do you have everything on the menu?	*una get all wetin dae na di menu?*
what do you have and what do you not have?	*wetin una get en wetin una noh get?*
I am not ready to order yet	*ah nor ready yet for oda*
can I have some water?	*ah kin get wata?*
can you bring the bill?	*yu kin kam wit di bill?*
you can keep the change	*yu kin kip di change*
please serve us right now, we will go soon	*duya sav mi wan tehm, wi go wan foh go jisnoh*
I don't like (hot) pepper too much	*misehf, ah noh lek pehpeh plehnti*
how's the food?	*aw di chop?*
it's good	*ee gud*
too much hot pepper	*tumohs pehpeh*
the food is tasty	*di chop swit*
I like it	*ah lek am*
it's enough	*ee du so*
add more/some	*put moh/some*
how much for this meal?	*na ohomohs foh dis chop?*
can I have my bill?	*ah kin geht mi bill?*
haven't you made a mistake?	*yu noh dohn mek mistek?*
here's the money, where's my change?	*luk di mohni, we mi chenji?*
we don't have change now	*chenji noh dae yet-o*
wait a bit	*yu wet smohl*
we would like …	*wi go lek foh get …*
I am full, thanks	*ah dohn behlful, tehnki yaa*
come on let's eat, you're invited	*kam leh wi it*

I have just eaten, I'm full	na jisnoh a it, a behlful
I can't now, let's try another time	ah noh go ebul naw, leh wi wet ohda tem
I like cold beer	a lehk kol bia
let's chill at the bar	leh wi go blo na baa
can I have the water?	duya pas mi di wata?
I am drunk	ah de go chack/da poyo done chack/ poyo chack me/e don chack me
he's a bit tipsy	he juhs don begin foh chack

Getting around

driver, are you going to …?	drayva, u de go na …?
how much should I pay you?	how mohs ah for pay yu?
driver, I want to charter you	drayva, ah wan cha cha yu
driver, let me out here	drayva, drop mi naya
can you turn down the music a little driver?	u kin dol u music smol drayva?
how far	aw fa
how far are you going?	aw fa u de go?
what time are you leaving?	nohmohs o'khlok ye de lehf?
when do you go?	ustem you de go?
the tyre has a puncture	di taya dohn bohs
the road is so bad	di rod bad tumohs
it has lots of pot-holes	ee geht plenty galohp
all passengers out	meki di pasenja dehn kam dohng una kam dohn
everybody back in	mek ohlman go insai bak
we don't want to stop	wi noh wahn fo tap na rod
are we there?	wi dohn rich?
can you show me the road to …	yu kin sho mi di rod foh …
how far is it from here?	ow fa ee dae frohm ya?
where does this road go?	usai dis rod dae go?
please go slowly	tek tem/small small
can you show me the way to town?	yu kin show mi di road for go na tohng?
can you show me where the supermarket/ beach/club/shop/police station/hospital is?	yu kin show mi di supamarkit/ bich/klob/shop/polis station/ospital?
can you show me where I can get a taxi?	yu kin show mi usai for get taksi?
please show me the market	duya show mi di makit
where is the hotel/restaurant/toilet near here?	usai otel/di restorant/toilet de nay a?

Health

I have come to see the doctor	ah de cam si di docta
I am not feeling well, doctor	ah nor de fil wel docta
I have a headache	ah de fil mi ed de at
my whole body is hurting	mi bodi de at
I want to do the test	ah wan do tes
which hospital/pharmacy should I go to?	wis ospitul/famacy ah foh go?
how much should I pay?	aw mus ah foh pay?
Is this the medicine I should take?	nar dis merecine ah for take?
I get pain in my …	ah get pain na me …
hand/arm, back, stomach, head, neck, throat	an, bak, bele, ed, nek, trot

Questions

who is	*udat*	which part	*uspart*
which	*us*	what	*wetin*
which one	*uswan*	what's the time?	*wetin na di tehm?*
which kind	*uskain*	how	*aw*
which type	*us taip*	where	*usai*
what do you call this?	*aw foh kohl dis?*	when	*ustem*

Everyday nouns

bank	*bahnk*	town	*tohng*
market	*makit*	shady dealing	*yuki yuki*
home	*om*	palm tree	*bolie*
house	*os*	friend	*paddy*

Useful words and phrases

yesterday	*ehstade*
today	*tide*
tomorrow	*tumara*
day after tomorrow	*nehxt tumara*
please/I'm sorry (*ah beg* is for emphasis)	*duya (ah beg)*
I try	*ah de trai*
don't be discouraged	*noh poil yu at*
take care, be cool, take things as they come	*na foh bia*
sorry (expression of sympathy)	*osh yaa*
is that right?	*nohto so?*
that's right	*na so*
what can you do about it?	*aw foh du?*
tit for tat	*yu du mi/ah du yu*
man has to rely on his fellow man for survival	*man liv bai man*
he's stubborn	*he get strong eahrs*
don't cheek me	*dohn was mi faes*
gossip	*kongossa*
I sleep late	*I slip pasmak*
fake	*guinea guinea*
stingy	*krabbit*
do your flies up	*bloh yu nohs*
show off	*bluff*
except	*unlehs*

MENDE
Basic Mende phrases

good morning	*bua/wu wua*
good afternoon	*bia/wua na*
good evening	*buva*
goodnight	*mu kpawkaw*
goodbye	*muya hoe*
how are you	*gbaw bi gaahu*
I am well, thank you	*nya gaahu gbuangaw-e, bi sieh*
all is well	*hinda nyamu gbii na*
sir	*ndakpe*
yes	*eh*

no	*sao*
thank you	*bi se*
what is your name?	*bi le-i?*
my name is …	*nya laa a …*
where do you come from?	*bi hiyea mi law?*
I come from …	*ngi hiyea … law*
what is the news there?	*gbeh vaa na?*
I do not understand	*ngi hugo*
I did not hear	*ngi menini*
I am sorry	*gbe hoe*

Conversation

what's your news? (if arriving)	*beva bi?*
what's your news (if hosting)	*beva na?*
are you Mende?	*mendemo (lo) abie?*
do you understand Mende?	*bi Mende yiei mero/melo?*
do you understand/hear?	*bi mero?*
I understand a little	*ga mero kru kru*
do you hear/understand?	*ba mero?*
he talks Mende	*a mende yia le lo*
what does he say?	*ye gbe?*
speak slowly	*yia lele*
who is it?	*ya mia?*
who are you?	*ye lo abie?*
I am glad to see you	*nya gohuneingaw-e bi lawya*
is your father/mother there?	*bi keke/nje law na?*
are your father and mother well?	*bi kei lo na, bi njei lo na?*
they are well	*tiana*
are they there?	*tia na?*
he/she is there	*taa na*
how is he/she?	*aw ngi gaahui?*
give him/her my greetings	*nga va ngi ma*
give … my greetings	*nga ya … ma*
what is it?	*gba mia?*
what is the matter?	*gbele?*
tell me all about it	*huge ange panda*
have you finished?	*bi gboyoa?*
can you do this?	*bag u bi ji we?*
I do not know	*ngi go*
do you see it?	*bi to?*
is this it?	*ta ji?*
it is	*ta mia*
what have you come to do?	*gbaw bi waa piema?*
I have come to work	*ngi waa vengemaa*
I am going	*ngi ya-o*
I have it	*ta ni yeya*
it is mine	*nyawo mia/nyawo le*
we will see each other again	*ma law gbawma hoe*
I shall go back tomorrow	*nga yamalaw sina*
I shall come on Sunday	*migbee law ba wa mbei*

Travelling

where have you come from?	*bi hi milo?*
where are you going?	*bi lima mi law?*
where are you going?	*bi lima mi?/bi li mi?*
I am going to …	*ngi lima … law*
it is far?	*maangwango?*
where is it?	*mindo/milo?*
which direction?	*mi yaka?*
it is far?	*ta kuhama?*
where are you?	*bia mi/bia mindo?*
I have never been there	*ngi ya li na*
when will you go back there?	*migbee law ba yama na?*
I am going tomorrow	*gi lima sina-oh*
last week	*hokii na hu ge*
have you seen it?	*bi toi lo?*
I have seen it. It is fine	*gi toi lo. Nyandengo*
the road is bad	*peli nyamungo*
there is water in the road	*njei lo pelihu*
that water is deep	*njei na susungo*
do not go there	*ba li na*
do not go far	*ba li ngwango*
I go/I come	*gi ya ngi wa*
they have come	*ti wai lo*
let us go	*a mu li-oh*
he is coming	*ta wama*

In town

let's go to town	*wa mu li tei hu*
what town is this?	*tei gbe a ji?*
who is the chief of this town?	*ye law mahei le tei ji hu?*
I am stopping here	*ngi gelema mbei law*
come let us go there	*wa mu li na*
go to my house	*li nya yeepele bu*
I don't know your house	*ngii bi welei gaw*
here is a seat, sit down	*heiwulii gbe, hei*

At the market

yesterday I went to the market	*ngi liilaw gbengi njawpawwahu*
how much?	*i lole?*
how much is it?	*gbwe jongaw mia?*
how much is this fish?	*nye ji gbwe jongaw?*
how much are the eggs?	*teyalui gbwe jongaw?*
what do you want to buy?	*gbaw bi longaw by ngeya?*
let me buy some rice	*gbee ngi mbei yeya*
the cassava is finished	*tangei gbii i gbeyenga*
do you want onions?	*bi longe-ee a yabasii-e*
this meat is rotten	*huei ji lulange-ee*
they are expensive	*tia ba gbangaw*
this is expensive	*ji ba gbangaw*
they are not expensive	*ba i gbani*
can you lower the price?	*yeesawngaw-i mayei kulo?*

reduce it, or I do not buy	*maye, ge ngeya*
I accept	*gi kurua*
take it away, I am not buying	*di la, ngengeyama*
do you sell cloth?	*ba kula majia law?*
I sell it	*ga majia law*
this cloth is not good	*kuleji I nyandeni*
I don't want anything else	*ngii loni a hani weka gbi*
give me my change	*nya sinjii ve*
I want food	*nya longo a mehe*
I want water to drink	*nya longo a njei ngi bole*

Feelings, dating

I want you/like you	*nya longo a bie*
do you like me?	*bi longo ange?*
I do not want you/like you	*ngi loni a bie*
stop that!	*gele ma!*
I am going to lie down	*gi ya ngi la*
I am going to sleep	*ngi ya yima*
I am going for a walk	*gi ya jijiama*
I do not like it	*ngi loi la*
he is angry	*ngi li dewea*
that man is patient	*numui na a hinda hou li ma*
I am tired	*ngi gbaha*

Weather

it is cold	*kolengo le*
it is hot	*kpandingo le*
it is wet	*ndelingo le*
the rain is starting to fall	*njei I wa*
the rain is approaching	*njei lo wama*
what do you want?	*gbo bi longwola?*
dry season	*ngeevolei*
rainy season	*haamei*

Health

what's the matter?	*gbaw bi ma?*
where does it hurt?	*mi mia a gbale bi ma?*
when did it begin?	*migbee law I tawooni?*
what are you doing?	*gbaw bi piema?*
I am sick	*nya hegbengaw-e*
I have fever	*nya mavulango le*
I have caught cold	*kole i nya houa*
it hurts very much	*i gbalea gbotongo*
he has diarrhoea	*ngi goihu a lewe*
I want to go to the hospital	*nya longaw ngi li hawspitui hu*
is the doctor there today?	*dawkita law na ha?*
when will he come back?	*migbee law a yama?*
I am getting better	*nyaa fisama*
sickness	*hegbe-I*

Numbers

1	*yela/ita*	22	*nu yela gboyongo mahu fele*
2	*fele*	30	*nu yela gboyongo mahu pu*
3	*sawa*	31	*nu yela gboyongo mahu pu mahu yela*
4	*nani*	32	*nu yela gboyongo mahu pu mahu fele*
5	*lolu*	40	*nu fele gboyongo*
6	*woita*	50	*nu fele gboyonogo mahu pu*
7	*wofela*	60	*nu sawa gboyongo*
8	*wayakpa*	70	*nu sawa gboyongo mahu pu*
9	*tau*	80	*nu nani gboyongo*
10	*pu*	90	*nu nani gboyonogo mahu pu*
11	*pu mahu yela*	100	*hondo yela*
12	*pu mahu fele*	101	*hondo yela mahu yela*
13	*pu mahu sawa*	200	*hondo fele*
20	*nu yela gboyongo*	300	*hondo sawa*
21	*nu yela gboyongo mahu yela*	1,000	*tousin yela*

Days

Sunday	*lahadi*	Thursday	*alikamisa*
Monday	*tene*	Friday	*juma*
Tuesday	*talata*	Saturday	*simbiti*
Wednesday	*alaba*		

Months

January	*pegbaa*	July	*nanaw-i*
February	*vui*	August	*dawii*
March	*nyawawlii*	September	*saa*
April	*buwui*	October	*galoi*
May	*golei*	November	*lugbu-yalui*
June	*suejue-i*	December	*pondoi*

Commands

come here	*wa be*	I go/I come	*gi ya ngi wa*
you	*bia*	call …	*… luli I wa*
get out/go out!	*gbia!*	come and see	*wa bi to va*
go	*ali/alioh*	talk slowly	*yia lele*
wait	*mawulu*	answer me	*duma nya we*
all right	*kurungo le*	bring me water please	*neago je kone*

Other useful words

baby	*ndolaa*	money	*kpowo-i*
basket	*samba-ei*	mosquito	*undit-i*
book	*buku-i*	nose	*haama-ei*
bottle	*sani-i*	palm tree	*awkpaw-i*
box	*kani*	person	*numu-i*
child	*ndo-i*	river	*njeiya-ei*
dirt	*jawaw-i*	sister	*ndeenyaalo-i*
finger	*tokovo-i*	stone	*kawlaw-i-ei*
fire	*ngawmbu-i*	uncle	*kawpawyoi*
forest	*ngola-ei*	village	*fula-ei*
horse	*so-i*	water	*je*

TEMNE
Basic Temne phrases

hello	*seke*
good morning	*ndiraie*
good afternoon	*mpiary*
good evening	*ndirao*
how are you?	*to pe mu-a?*
I am fine	*min yenki*
what's your name?	*nges uhmu-a?*
I am …/my name is …	*mine yi …*
how old are you?	*molo tur-ren ung ba-a?*
how much does it cost?	*molo-a?*
thank you	*muhmo*
please	*mari*
excuse me/I am sorry	*kuhba'ri mi/nemthene*
help me	*mar mi/der nu*
goodbye	*owa*

Questions, answers, commands

be careful	*yoh k'thegbe*	I'd like to go to …	*i yema ko ro …*
enough	*beki*	I'll be back	*i t'kul der*
how do I …	*to me …*	leave me alone	*mi/gbepe mi*
hurry up	*busor*	maybe	*uh loko lom*
I am full	*min numruh*	stand up	*t'muh/yokane*
I am going home	*i kone ro seth*	stop	*tey*
I am going to …	*i ti/tuh kuh ro …*	take me …	*keruh mi …*
I am on my way	*i yi r'rong*	what	*ko-a/ko r'ka-a*
I don't have	*i baye*	what are you doing?	*ko muŋ yo-a?*
I know	*i turruh*	when	*uh loko-a*

Transport and time

bus	*ung boss/podapoda*	street	*ung trit*
car	*ung lorry*	taxi	*ung taksi*
gas/petrol	*ung pentrol*	walk	*koth*
junction	*ung yonkson*	today	*thonong*
outside	*ro kang*	tomorrow	*ninung*
police	*o' polis*	afternoon	*ryang*
provinces	*ro gbang*	night	*ruh foy*
roundabout	*ung t'ntebul*		

Eating, drinking and shopping

market	*ro yopowa*	orange	*ung lemre*
female trader	*o tread*	peanut	*muh kunt'r*
shop/store	*ro shop/ro s'thor*	water	*uh munt*
money	*ung kala*	soft drink	*ung sof d'rink*
bargain	*fof molo'*	bar/pub	*ung-bar*
plenty	*gbuthi*	alcohol	*mubber*
food	*da ruddi*	drunk	*kuh tis*
bread	*kuh bo*	tailor	*o thela*
snacks	*uh konye*	head tie	*ung gbasa*
biscuit/cookies	*kuh biskit*	flip-flops/slippers	*afbak*

candy/sweet	*kuh swit*	hat	*ung bonnet*
coconut	*kuh gbara*	trousers	*e yankra*
grill	*ung kolpot*	boot	*ung but*
medication	*ung tol*	shoe	*ung koftha*
onions	*kuh yaba*	sneakers/trainers	*e krep*

Other useful words

man	*wanduni*	dustbin	*ung muru*
woman	*wunibom*	ear	*ung lens*
child	*o wath*	finish	*kuh pong*
boy	*wath runi/wanth uruni*	happy	*o bonnè (mi)*
girl	*wath bera*	house	*ung seth*
friend	*o' yathki*	in the open	*gberkethe*
beard	*uh kake*	mosquito	*ung mis*
bed	*kuh f'nnt*	mouth	*kuh s'ng*
blind	*fith*	neighbour	*owe s' futuhne-e*
bold/fearless	*gbakanda*	poor	*mone*
braids	*muh roo*	power outage	*ung sum*
cholera/dysentery	*ung runt*	rich	*yola/ruh yola*
door	*kuh dareh*	rubbish	*yathri*
sand	*kuh s'nt*	tree	*uh k'nt*
shout	*ala sonko*	uniform	*e ashobi*
sit down	*sidom yiruh*	upset	*bansuh*
tap	*ung pomp*	window	*ung winda/kuh fenk*
thief	*o key*		

LANGUAGE BOOKS *Krio in a Nutshell*, by historian and former Sierra Leone Peace Corps volunteer Joseph Opala, is the most comprehensive guide to Krio going, but it is unfortunately out of print so you'll likely have to find it in a library. Two weighty A4 volumes focus first on grammar and vocabulary before progressing to a series of practice exercises. The only catch is that, quite properly, it relies on the phonetic alphabet to spell out all the words, making it devilishly hard going at times unless you are prepared to put in the effort first to understand the symbols.

Easier (and easier to find) but less comprehensive is the *Peace Corps Krio Language Manual*, a revised edition of which was produced back in 1985. It sidesteps phonetics and tries to spell everything the way it sounds (as we have done). It's available online at **w** livinglingua.com/course/peace-corps/Krio_Language_Lessons, or street hawkers and small book booths in Freetown often sell new printouts or dog-eared old copies – either are worth their weight in gold. The only bilingual dictionary available is the *Krio-English Dictionary & Phrasebook* by Hanne-Ruth Thompson and Momoh Taziff Koroma, published in 2015 and boasting 4,000 entries.

Around Freetown, various book stands have the *Le we learn Krio* series, which provides anyone with a basic grasp of the language the welcome opportunity of improving vocabulary. Written entirely in Krio, it is tough on the absolute beginner.

For a fascinating look at missionary work in action, look out for the Krio Bible and Koran, and bibles translated into other languages. Likewise, look out for Krio, Temne and Mende dictionaries if you're straining for more words.

As for Mende, there are two readers from the early 20th century: *The Mende Language* (Kegan Paul, Trench, Trübner & Co, 1908; freely available at **w** archive.org/stream/mendelanguagecon00migeuoft), by F W H Migeod, and the Reverend A T Sumner's *Handbook of the Mende Language* (Government Printing Office, Freetown, 1917). Both are products of their time, dripping with colonial arrogance, full of tips on picking up porters for forays into the interior, and requests to be handed firearms and riding boots. However, they are also both solid on the grammatical basics of Mende. Older still are the *Principles of Mende Grammar* and *Vocabulary (Mende English)* (both Mendi Mission, Sherbro, 1874; freely available at w archive.org/details/PrinciplesofMendeGrammar), published by the American Missionary Association's Mendi Mission and thought lost until 2014, when it was discovered in the collections of Cambridge University and digitised. The Peace Corps' guide is, as you might expect, considerably more modern, and available for free at w livingua.com/course/peace-corps/Mende_Language_Lessons.

For learners of Temne, there are a few equally dated resources, including another from the Reverend A T Sumner, *Handbook of the Temne Language* (Government Printing Office, Freetown, 1922) or Christian Frederick Schlenker's *Grammar of the Temne Language* (Church Missionary Society, London, 1864; freely available at w archive.org/details/grammartemnelan00schlgoog) and the more readable *A collection of Temne traditions, fables and proverbs* (Church Missionary Society, London, 1861; freely available at w archive.org/details/acollectiontemn00schlgoog). For something this side of World War II, Peace Corps also produces a Temne manual, available at w livingua.com/course/peace-corps/Temne_Language_Lessons.

The ever-busy Reverend A T Sumner also produced the *Handbook of the Sherbro Language* (Government Printing Office, Freetown, 1921), or there's John White's *Sherbro and English Book* (Mendi Mission, Sherbro, 1862; available freely at w archive.org/details/WhiteSherbroAndEnglishBook).

Appendix 2

FURTHER INFORMATION

BOOKS The legendary Sawyer's Bookshop at Water Street in Freetown may have long since closed, but storytelling is alive and well. The country punches above its weight in terms of literature and history, although much of the wealth of written material is sadly not widely available.

Sierra Leoneans have shaped thinking about Africa both inside and outside the continent. The polymath James Africanus Beale Horton, the son of slave recaptives, wrote in 1868 *West African Countries and Peoples, British and Native: And a Vindication of the African Race* (Edinburgh University Press, 1969), one of the first works of African nationalism. A well-picked collection of his medical and political writings, *Africanus Horton* (Longman, 1969), is also available. Bishop Samuel Ajayi Crowther, delivered to Freetown from a slave ship when he was just five, wrote a memoir of his early life on the Colony, *The African Slave Boy* (Wertheim & Macintosh, 1852), which once again fascinated audiences in Britain and Africa as one of the first first-person, non-white accounts of African life.

Civil war A huge amount has been written about the conflict in Sierra Leone, much of it very good and spanning a range of perspectives. For the most thorough account of the war, you can read the full report of the country's Truth and Reconciliation Commission, which is available online at **w** sierra-leone.org/TRCDocuments.html.

A Revolt of the Lumpenproletariat Published in *African Guerrillas*, James Currey, 1998. This essay makes the argument that alienated youth was key to the formation of the RUF and the war.

Ashby, Phil *Unscathed; Escape from Sierra Leone* Pan Books, 2003. The best of the boy's-own-style literature that came from the involvement of British forces in Sierra Leone, which tells the true story of Ashby's daring escape from rebels keen to eat his heart when serving as a UN Peacekeeper in 2000.

Beah, Ishmeal *A Long Way Gone; Memoirs of a Boy Soldier* Sarah Crichton Books, 2007. This account of fighting with the Sierra Leone Army is one of the most moving and disturbing accounts of the civil war. Startling vividness and extraordinary candour give words and voice to the experience not only of thousands of children in Sierra Leone, but of child soldiers around the world. Writer Sebastien Junger called it 'one of the most important war stories of our generation', although it's also been the subject of controversy: Australian journalist Peter Wilson has claimed some of the timeline makes so little sense that he doubts elements of the book's veracity.

Bergner, Daniel *Soldiers of Light* Penguin Books, 2005. The most stunning war writing comes in journalist Bergner's beautifully written, moving portrait of child soldiers, mercenaries, priests, missionaries and diplomats.

Campbell, Greg *Blood Diamonds* Westview Press, 2004. This makes heavy weather of its central premise – that love-struck American couples fail to realise the deadly origins of the stones that represent all things romantic and eternal – but nevertheless has some meaningful insights into how smuggling worked during the war.

Coulter, Chris *Bush Wives and Girl Soldiers: Women's Lives Through War and Peace in Sierra Leone* Cornell University Press, 2009. The author interviewed more than 100 women in putting together this compassionate account of women's experiences during and after the war.

Denov, Myriam *Child Soldiers: Sierra Leone's Revolutionary United Front* Cambridge University Press, 2010. Denov, a professor of social work at Montreal's McGill University, offers a thorough and haunting account of what life was like as a child soldier. She also examines how the youths have dealt with these experiences as they have made the transition to adulthood.

Ellis, Stephen *The Mask of Anarchy* New York University Press, 1999. While principally about Liberia's turbulent power struggle, this excellent account provides rock-solid background on how Sierra Leone's war was influenced by Charles Taylor and other West African and international interests.

Farah, Douglas *Blood from Stones* Broadway, 2004. The *Washington Post* investigative journalist reveals how he happened on a link between the country's gemstones and funding for al-Qaeda.

Fowler, William *Operation Barras; the SAS Rescue Mission* Cassell, 2005. For the nitty-gritty of what went wrong, and right, when 11 British soldiers were captured by the West Side Boys, a rebel splinter group, in 2000, this account charts the action relatively well, although fills the book with broader history better sourced elsewhere.

Gberie, Lansana *A Dirty War in West Africa* Hurst & Company, 2005. This taut account disputes much of the thesis of the essay, *The Revolt of the Lumpenproletariat*, and, perhaps because the author saw many of the RUF atrocities first hand, has far less time for their 'political' motives.

Keen, David *Conflict and Collusion in Sierra Leone* James Currey, 2005. This strikes a balance between differing views of the RUF and their motivation, and is well regarded.

Peters, Krijn *War and the Crisis of Youth in Sierra Leone* Cambridge University Press, 2011. In this account of the origins of the war, the author, a professor of development studies at Swansea University, focuses on the tensions that developed between landowners and unemployed rural youth.

Richards, Paul *Fighting for the Rain Forest* International African Institute, 1996. Among the more academic assessments of the war, this was the first serious attempt to understand what lay behind the RUF's brutal campaign. Heavily criticised for being too apologetic, it nevertheless gets to the heart of the rural disenfranchisement felt at the very fringes of Sierra Leone.

Smillie, Ian et al *The Heart of the Matter: Sierra Leone, diamonds & human security* Partnership Africa Canada, 2000. This account contains much of the most solid data on the diamond trade in Sierra Leone.

Voeten, Teun *How De Body?* St Martin's Press, 2000. An account of the author's time as a photojournalist documenting the war, it hits an awkward tone at times, taking a little too much glee in his various near-misses.

First-hand accounts

Burton, Richard *Wanderings in West Africa* Constable, 1991 (first published 1863). The country has an unfavourable chapter in Burton's account.

Butcher, Timothy *Chasing the Devil* Vintage Books, 2011. Following in the footsteps of Graham Greene on his *Journey Without Maps* (see opposite), Butcher travels on foot through Sierra Leone and Liberia, describing the scenes, characters, and adventures that he encounters along the way.

Falconbridge, Anna Maria *Narrative of Two Voyages to the River Sierra Leone during the years 1791–1792–1793* Liverpool University Press, 2000 (first published 1801). This book describes sickness at sea, slaves on Bunce Island and the political traumas of trying to reorganise the Freetown settlement in 1791 at the behest of the Sierra Leone Company, with her first husband, abolitionist and drunkard Alexander Falconbridge. It consists of a series of letters written to an imaginary friend.

Forna, Aminatta *The Devil That Danced on the Water* HarperCollins, 2002. The Sierra Leone-British journalist and author's debut novel is an elegiac farewell both to the idyllic Sierra Leone she knew as a child growing up and to her father, executed under the Stevens regime, as well as an attempt to piece together what exactly happened to him. Full of detail on the delights of the country, woven around the dark political backdrop that has characterised its recent history, it is essential reading.

Greene, Graham *Journey Without Maps* Heinemann, 1936. Before he started writing novels (see box, page 134), Graham Greene was a bit of an amateur explorer. In 1935, he and his cousin journeyed overland from Sierra Leone into Liberia, covering 350 miles, mainly on foot. His account offers a rare look at rural Sierra Leone in the decades leading up to the country's independence from Britain.

Huxley, Elspeth *Four Guineas; A Journey through West Africa* Chatto & Windus, 1954. Teeming with colonial arrogance and dated witticisms, devoting one chapter of four to Sierra Leone.

Jackson, Michael *In Sierra Leone* Duke University Press/Chesham, 2004. The anthropologist and poet, who has written on the Kuranko, penned this highly personal account of his time in the country.

Joy, Emily *Green Oranges on Lion Mountain* Eye Books, 2004. This is pretty much Bridget Jones for West Africa – a young doctor volunteer with an expanding waistband, huge dose of unrequited love and a growing appreciation for first-time surgery in Serabu Hospital in the south of the country. It's by no means a must-read, but if you're volunteering it's a nice taster.

Kingsley, Mary *Travels in West Africa* Phoenix, 2000 (first published 1897). The country features only briefly.

Wellesley Cole, Robert *Kossoh Town Boy* Cambridge University Press, 1960. Another autobiographical account of growing up in the country.

Health

Hofman, Michael & Au, Sokhieng (editors) *The Politics of Fear: Médecins sans Frontières and the West African Ebola Epidemic* Oxford University Press, 2017. This is a scholarly analysis of the panicked and often-calamitous global response to the disease, and the leading role taken by Médecins Sans Frontières in its eradication.

Quammen, David *Ebola: The Natural and Human History of a Deadly Virus* W W Norton & Co, 2014. Expanded and updated from the author's *Spillover: Animal Infections and the Next Human Pandemic*, this is a commendable social and scientific examination of the disease.

Richards, Paul *Ebola: How a People's Science Helped End an Epidemic* Zed Books, 2016. Part of the African Arguments book series, this is an analysis of the successes and failures of local and international responses to the disease, drawing on first-hand research in Sierra Leone.

Wilson-Howarth, Dr Jane, *Bugs, Bites & Bowels* Cadogan, 2006

Wilson-Howarth, Dr Jane, and Ellis, Dr Matthew *Your Child Abroad: A Travel Health Guide* Bradt Travel Guides, 2014

History and culture

Alie, Joe *A New History of Sierra Leone* Macmillan Education, 1990. Alie, a Fourah Bay history professor, has written this history primarily for secondary school use, which is at its best when describing the shapers of Krio thinking and society, and their clashes with British authorities.

Alldridge, T J *The Sherbro and its Hinterland* Macmillan, 1901. An introduction to the area.

Clifford, Mary Louise *From Slavery to Freetown* McFarland, 1999. Charting the tale of the Nova Scotians.

Davidson, Basil *African Slave Trade* Atlantic Monthly Press, 1961.

Davies, Muriel Emekunle *What's Cooking? Start Cooking: Traditional Sierra Leonean Recipes* (2nd ed) Rotimi E Nelson, 2017. Includes recipes for over 100 Sierra Leonean and West African dishes.

Ferme, Mariane *The Underneath of Things* University of California Press, 2001. A dense ethnography of 'violence, history, and the everyday in Sierra Leone'.

Fyfe, Christopher *History of Sierra Leone* Oxford University Press, 1962. For a long time based at Fourah Bay College, Fyfe has written this comprehensive history, which is not matched in length, breadth and depth.

Fyfe, Christopher *A Short History of Sierra Leone* Longman, 1979. Abridged from the above work is this accessible school-level guide.

Fyfe, Christopher (ed) *Sierra Leone Inheritance* Oxford University Press, 1964. A fascinating collection of primary documents running from the first recorded oral histories right up to the proclamation of independence in 1961. It provides a feast of insights into tribal wars, slave trading, European influence and growing Krio anguish.

Hochschild, Adam *Bury the Chains* Pan Books, 2006. This book is full of charm, wit and storytelling as it charts the efforts to abolish slavery, and with it, the birth of Freetown.

Lowther, Kevin G *The African American Odyssey of John Kizell: The Life and Times of a South Carolina Slave Who Returned to Fight the Slave Trade in His African Homeland* University of South Carolina Press, 2011. This is a recent biography of an ex-slave turned abolitionist who became one of Freetown's original settlers in 1792.

Martin, John Angus, Opala, Joseph & Schmidt, Cynthia *The Temne Nation of Carriacou* CreateSpace Independent Publishing Platform, 2016. This short book explores the connections between Sierra Leone and a group of people on the Grenadian island of Carriacou who identify as descendants of the Temne people.

Newton, John *The Journal of a Slave Trader* The Epworth Press, 1962. This primary material is a full account of the three voyages Newton made to the Sierra Leone coast. This volume also contains his essay *Thoughts upon the African Slave Trade*, written 30 years later; a penetrating, honest, graphic and troubled account of the horrors of the trade of which he used to be part.

Schama, Simon *Rough Crossings* BBC Books, 2005. The slave trade figures heavily in Sierra Leone's history, and while it ranges far and wide, Schama's account captures the interesting dimension played by the American War of Independence in agitating for a land and rights for former black slaves who sided with the British in the fight for their own freedom.

Sierra Leonean Heroes Privately published, 1987. A riveting bite-size account of the 'fifty great men and women who helped to build our nation', which you should be able to track down in-country.

Wyse, Akintola *The Krio of Sierra Leone: An interpretive history* Howard University Press, 1991. This book traces the history of the Krio people, from their earliest days as a collective entity all the way through to contemporary times.

Literature

Achebe, Chinua *Things Fall Apart* Heinemann, 1958. Essential reading for any visitor to West Africa, for its rendering of the devastating effects on traditional life and customs brought about by the encroachment of colonialism. Set in Nigeria, however.

Beah, Ishmael *Radiance of Tomorrow* Sarah Crichton Books, 2014. A new novel by the author of *A Long Way Gone*, this tells the story of refugees returning home after the war and attempting to rebuild their lives.

Casely-Harford, Gladys *Take Um So* 1948. Virtually impossible to find now, but look out for this book of Krio poetry published in Freetown.

Cheney-Coker, Syl *Last Harmattan of Alusine Dunbar* Heinemann International, 1990. Voted among Africa's 100 best books, this award-winning novel is a vicious satire of the descent into corruption and cronyism that blighted the post-independence era.

Conton, William *The African* Heinemann Educational Books, 1960. This book has been called Sierra Leone's *Things Fall Apart*.

Decker, Thomas Krio translations of Shakespeare plays. Little-known in English, these translations are popular and still occasionally seen in Sierra Leone; they inspired a generation of playwrights to start writing in their mother tongue.

Easmon, Raymond Sarif *Dear Parent and Ogre* Oxford University Press, 1964.

Easmon, Raymond Sarif *The New Patriots* Longmans, 1965. Modern drama.

Fishing in Rivers of Sierra Leone People's Educational Association of Sierra Leone, 1987. A lovingly compiled hotch-potch of village tales, poems and proverbs from all over the country, which you might just be lucky enough to pick up from a Freetown street stall.

Forna, Aminatta *Ancestor Stones* Bloomsbury, 2006. Forna's second book, a novel, tells the story of a woman gathering her family's history through the tales of her four aunts.

Forna, Aminatta *The Memory of Love* Atlantic Monthly Press, 2011. Set in Freetown during the closing days of the war, this novel follows three very different men as they struggle to come to terms with the violence they have witnessed. A touchingly rendered story, this novel was shortlisted for the 2011 Orange Prize for Fiction.

George, Crispin *Precious Gems Unearthed by an African* Arthur H Stockwell, 1952, and Nicol, Abioseh *The Truly Married Woman and other stories* Oxford University Press, 1965. Both these books are a good introduction to Sierra Leone oral traditions.

Glynn, Paul *King Bruno* Gola Books, 2013. An illustrated children's novel about Bruno, the alpha-male chimpanzee known for escaping the Tacugama Chimpanzee Sanctuary.

Greene, Graham *Heart of the Matter* Vintage, 2001 (first published 1948). Perhaps Sierra Leone's best-known international literary cameo. The West African home of colonial policeman Scobie is never explicitly named, but its oppressive presence is as much a part of the novel as his own inner life.

Hill, Lawrence *The Book of Negroes* Black Swan, 2010. This gripping work of historical fiction traces the life of a girl who is stolen from her West African home and sold onto a slave ship on Bunce Island. After many years as a slave in South Carolina, she wins her freedom and, eventually, returns to her home continent as one of the original Krio settlers of Freetown. The book was first published in North America in 2008, but under a different title: *Someone Knows My Name* (WW Norton & Company).

Kourouma, Ahmadou *Allah is Not Obliged* Heinemann, 2006. This fictional, darkly tragicomic story, told first-person by a child soldier, is set in the jungle of Ivory Coast and Liberia.

Sesay, Mohamed Gibril and Kainwo, Moses *Songs That Pour the Heart* New Initiatives, 2004. An affecting collection of poems. They have found writers – by day tax inspectors, chemists, engineers, businessmen and teachers – who might otherwise 'have kept their writings in cupboards because they have not got the means to publish them'. This post-war anthology – 'the dreams of the rainbow happenings that would end the deluge and restore the land' – corrects that.

Nature

Ayodele Cole, Professor N H *The Vegetation of Sierra Leone* Njala University College Press, 1968. If you can find an old copy, this book comes with a handy line-drawn field guide of what in some cases was present 40 years ago and is now sadly extinct.

Borrow, Nik and Demey, Ron *Field Guide to the Birds of Western Africa* 2nd ed Princeton Field Guides, 2004.

Checklist of Birds of Sierra Leone African Bird Club (ABC; **w** africanbirdclub.org). For more experienced birders, this guide provides a useful list of all the species present and their local status. The Conservation Society of Sierra Leone (CSSL) booklet also covers birds.

Field, G D *Birds of the Freetown Area* Fourah Bay College Bookshop, 1968. For birdspotting in the capital, you can't beat this guide.

Gledhill, David *Checklist of the Flowering Plants of Sierra Leone* Fourah Bay College, 1963. Wide-ranging but not exhaustive.

Gledhill, David *West African Trees* Longman, 1972. The most accessible guide to the flora of the region.

Kingdon, Jonathan *The Kingdon Field Guide to African Mammals* 2nd ed Princeton Field Guides, 2015. The guide of choice. *Mammals of Ghana, Sierra Leone and The Gambia* The Trendrine Press, 1998. For more specific information.

Savill, P S and Fox, J E D *Trees of Sierra Leone* Private print, 1967. For a complete run-down of Sierra Leone's tree life, if you can find it, this is the most comprehensive resource.

Sinclair, Ian, Ryan, Peter and Hockey, Phil *Birds of Africa South of the Sahara* Penguin Random House, 2010. An overview of the whole continent. Ryan contributed a box on birding to this book.

Robinson, Phillip T, Flacke, Gabriella L & Hentschel, Knut M *The Pygmy Hippo Story: West Africa's Enigma of the Rainforest* Oxford University Press, 2017. This lengthy text is the most definitive account yet published on this enigmatic and little-studied species.

Wildlife and Nature Reserves of Sierra Leone. In-country, ask at the Conservation Society of Sierra Leone (CSSL) for a copy of this 20-year-old guide, an accessible, well-researched and informative primer.

Williams Serle *Field Guide to the Birds of West Africa* HarperCollins, 1977.

Other West Africa guides
For the full list of Bradt's Africa guides, see **w** bradtguides. com/shop.

Briggs, Philip *The Gambia* Bradt Travel Guides, 2017.

Briggs, Philip *Ghana* Bradt Travel Guides, 2016.

Connolly, Sean *Senegal* Bradt Travel Guides, 2015.

Manson, Katrina and Knight, James *Burkina Faso* Bradt Travel Guides, 2012.

Sykes, Tom *Ivory Coast* Bradt Travel Guides, 2016.

Velton, Ross *Mali* Bradt Travel Guides, 2009.

FILM AND TELEVISION
Cinematically, Sierra Leone is probably best known for *Blood Diamond* (2006), directed by Edward Zwick and featuring Leonardo DiCaprio, Djimon Hounsou and Jennifer Connolly. When you mention you are going, some of the graphic depictions from this film are probably the first images that will stick in other people's (and perhaps your own) minds. While not remotely like Sierra Leone now, and whatever you think of the film's accuracy, it has all the ingredients of a watchable blockbuster, and has the intelligence to confront some of the realities behind the war. *Lord of War* (2005), starring Nicolas Cage, depicts the role the international arms trade had in fuelling the wars of Liberia and Sierra Leone.

While not set in-country, Steven Spielberg's Oscar-nominated *Amistad* (1997) tells the story of the US court case that involved Sengbeh Pieh and his fellow captives, tried for the murder of a Spanish slaving crew (see box, pages 218–19). More recently, British film *Amazing Grace* (2006) told the story of William Wilberforce's attempts to abolish slavery in Britain. The film of the book *Heart of the Matter* (1954) was actually shot in Freetown, giving a historic glimpse of the law courts, the wharf and city streets.

For a close look at the political fallout from the war, watch *War Don Don* (2010), an award-winning documentary by American filmmaker Rebecca Richman Cohen. The film centres on the Special Court for Sierra Leone, particularly the trial of Issa Sesay, a leading member of the

Revolutionary United Front. Visit the film's website (w *wardondonfilm.com*) to find out how to stream or order a copy.

Recent history and loveable fauna combine for a fruitful seam of 'wildlife in danger' stories to feed the nature documentary machine. BBC4 made the delightful *Wildlife in a War Zone*, which is periodically aired, and features Mount Bintumani, Tiwai Island and the Tacugama Chimpanzee Sanctuary.

Like so much else in Sierra Leone, its most powerful stories have been made by Africans. Sorious Samura shot to prominence for his covert filming of atrocities on the streets of Freetown, mostly perpetrated by Nigerian ECOMOG and Sierra Leone Army troops. He followed up *Cry Freetown* with the equally traumatic *Return to Freetown*, and his most recent documentary *Blood on the Stone*, for CNN, revealed the still-pitiful life of diamond diggers and the attitudes of their unscrupulous bosses.

Difficult to track down in the US or Europe, *Ezra* (2007), by the Nigerian director Newton Aduaka, was celebrated in Africa when it won the Etalon d'Or at Burkina Faso's prestigious FESPACO Film Festival for its portrait of a child soldier caught up in Sierra Leone's civil war.

Another diamond-related spin-off familiar to viewers of MTV is *Bling: A Planet Rock* (2007), which came out shortly after *Blood Diamond*, in which a group of rappers, perhaps inspired by Kanye West, go to Sierra Leone to see the results of the diamond industry.

To get a taste of what life is like for a hip, 20-something Freetowner, keep an eye out for Vickie Remoe's television show on SLBC. You can also watch episodes of her show online at w vickieremoe.com. Or, if you're already in Freetown, look out for Remoe's DVDs, which are on sale at various supermarkets and other shops around town.

MUSIC For sounds of Sierra Leone, there is little available in the West. The music of S E Rogie can be found on *Palm Wine Music* (Cooking Vinyl, 1988). The blind musician Sorie Kondi's beautiful, haunting music can be bought on CD in Freetown and online – if you know where to look. His latest album is called, heartbreakingly, *Without Money, No Family* (Luke Wasserman Audio, 2007; w cduniverse.com). Formed in a camp in Guinea, the Sierra Leone Refugee All Stars have toured their brand of reggae around the world, and recorded *Living Like a Refugee* (Anti, 2006) followed by *Rise and Shine* (2010, Cumbancha). Among Western artists, Kanye West's *Diamonds from Sierra Leone*, from the album *Late Registration* (Roc-A-Fella Records, 2005), is a searing attack on the bling culture cultivated by rap artists in either blissful or wilful ignorance of Africans dying to supply the trade. Folk-soul legend Terry Callier has also recorded *Sierra Leone*, on his fine 2002 album *Speak Your Peace* (Mr Bongo, 2002), a haunting paean for a country in flames. For modern Sierra Leone the streets of Freetown and Salone friends are your best tutor. See *Chapter 1, Background Information*, page 3.

WEBSITES
Travel information

w visitsierraleone.org If you have time to look at only one site online, this is it. Started by Bimbola Carrol, a Sierra Leonean in London who so longed to do something meaningful in his home country he moved back, it probably does more than any other platform to raise the profile of Sierra Leone internationally. The product of years of painstaking work, it's a travel guide, blog compendium, discussion forum, newsfeed, hotel guide, and language resource neatly rolled into one. 'The biggest challenge that Sierra Leone faces is tackling the negative perceptions that have been caused by years of war,' he says. 'I love telling everyone how beautiful and misunderstood Sierra Leone is.'

w welcometosierraleone.sl The official tourist board site, this is also worth a look, although its contents are often eclipsed by Carrol's site.

w sierra-leone.org Peter Anderson's website is a superb compendium devoted to the country he loves. First introduced to Sierra Leone as a Peace Corps volunteer in Kono years back, he's

A2

never left, and his decades of knowledge are lightly worn with this delightfully serendipitous collection of photos, proverbs, stories and historical documents and more. A must.

w ecosalone.org Sponsored by the German NGO Welthungerhilfe, this website offers detailed information about where to stay, what to see, and what to do on the Western Area Peninsula, from exploring Krio history in Regent to tracking down a good storyteller on Banana Islands. Check out the suggested itineraries, admire the pretty photos, and start daydreaming about a weekend at the beach.

w sierraleonetravel.com Although flogging his own services, Kevin McPhillips's website has helpful, if thin, background information, although his personal account of arriving in Freetown is highly entertaining.

w fatbirder.com Twitchers should visit Fatbirder for news on the latest bird sightings.

w fco.gov.uk Up-to-the-minute travel and safety advice from the UK's Foreign Office.

w travel.state.gov Along similar lines comes travel advice from the US State Department.

Facts

w cia.gov/library/publications/the-world-factbook/geos/sl.html Easily digestible, stat-heavy approach, across geographic, social, economic and political indices.

w statehouse.gov.sl The official government website contains information on government ministers and presidential appointments.

w ernestkoroma.org The president's own website.

w state.gov More background information, this time from a US perspective; the State Department also publishes an annual human rights report on Sierra Leone.

Current affairs, culture and news

A few diaspora websites maintain strong links to the homeland, with rousing hopes and big dreams, such as the Friends of Sierra Leone US website (w *fosalone.org*).

w allafrica.com/sierraleone Pools content from Sierra Leone news sources.

w bbc.co.uk/news/world/africa This site often carries Sierra Leone stories, as does w africa. reuters.com.

w awoko.org Among the most active and most popular local newspapers.

w cocorioko.net Reflective online newspaper published from North America.

w pen-international.org Local branch of the international literary association run by poet Mike Butscher, established 'to rekindle a lost culture of literature, writing and reading in Sierra Leone'.

w sl-writers-series.org Information about the latest home publishing.

w 40acrescanada.com This diaspora-run website aims to promote young Sierra Leonean artists, musicians, actors, models and the like.

w amistad.org A well-designed and comprehensive account of the Amistad Revolt, with full timeline and detail of the slave trade.

SIERRA LEONE ONLINE

For additional online content, articles, photos and more on Sierra Leone, why not visit w bradtguides.com/sleone.

Index

Page numbers in **bold** indicate the principal entry; those in *italics* indicate maps

INDEX OF ADVERTISERS

JAN 1 8 2019